WRITING by CHOICE

ERIC HENDERSON

CONTRIBUTING WRITER (Part Five)
CHRIS HIGGINS

OXFORD
UNIVERSITY PRESS

OXFORD

UNIVERSITY PRESS

70 Wynford Drive, Don Mills, Ontario M3C 1J9
www.oup.com/ca

Oxford University Press is a department of the University of Oxford.
It furthers the University's objective of excellence in research, scholarship,
and education by publishing worldwide in

Oxford   New York

Auckland   Cape Town   Dar es Salaam   Hong Kong   Karachi
Kuala Lumpur   Madrid   Melbourne   Mexico City   Nairobi
New Delhi   Shanghai   Taipei   Toronto

With offices in

Argentina   Austria   Brazil   Chile   Czech Republic   France   Greece
Guatemala   Hungary   Italy   Japan   Poland   Portugal   Singapore
South Korea   Switzerland   Thailand   Turkey   Ukraine   Vietnam

Oxford is a trade mark of Oxford University Press
in the UK and in certain other countries

Published in Canada
by Oxford University Press

Copyright © Oxford University Press Canada 2006

Library and Archives Canada Cataloguing in Publication

Henderson, Eric Paul
Writing by choice
contributing writer (Part Five) Chris Higgins.

Includes index.
ISBN-13: 978-0-19-542077-7   ISBN-10: 0-19-542077-2

1. Academic writing.   2 Report writing.   3. English language—Rhetoric.
I. Higgins, Chris.   II. Title.
PE1408.H39 2005   808'.042   C2005-906434-X

Cover design: Joan Dempsey
Cover image: Masterfile

1 2 3 4 – 09 08 07 06

This book is printed on permanent (acid-free) paper ∞.

Printed in Canada

Contents

Preface   xv

Acknowledgements   xvii

Part One: Developing "3-D" Skills: Thinking, Reading, and Writing   1

1. **A Choice-Based Approach**   2
2. **Thinking and Writing: The Composing Process**   2
      2.1 The Traditional Linear Model   3
      2.2 Process-Oriented Models: Discovery Drafts   3
      2.3 Process-Reflective Writing   4
3. **Thinking and Writing + Reading**   6
      3.1 Diffuse versus Focused Reading   9
      3.2 Responding Critically and Analytically through Questions   10
        3.2.1   Before Reading   10
        3.2.2   First Reading   12
        3.2.3   Second Reading   13
4. **The Writing Situation**   14
      4.1 Writing Purpose   14
      4.2 "A" is for Audience   15
        4.2.1   Knowledge and Interest   17
        4.2.2   Writer–Reader Relationship   18
        4.2.3   Audience Orientation   19
5. **Stages in Essay-Writing**   21
      5.1 Pre-writing   21
        5.1.1   Questions and Brainstorming   22
        5.1.2   Freewriting and Clustering   23
      5.2 Research   25
      5.3 Organization   26
        5.3.1   Scratch (or Sketch) Outline   26
        5.3.2   Formal Outline   26
        5.3.3   Graphic Outline   27
      5.4 Composing: First Draft   29
      5.5 Revising: Final Draft   29
        5.5.1   Overview   29
        5.5.2   Clarifying Meaning   30
        5.5.3   Underscoring Ideas   30
        5.5.4   Solidifying Structure   30
        5.5.5   Fine-Tuning   31
6. **Kinds of Essays**   31
      6.1 Expository versus Argumentative Essays   31
      6.2 Narration   32
      6.3 Description   32
      6.4 A Special Case: The Personal Essay   33
        6.4.1   Sample Student Essays   35

6.5 The In-Class or Examination Essay 36
   6.5.1 Recall 36
   6.5.2 Organization and Time Management 37
   6.5.3 Discernment and Adaptability 38
   6.5.4 Sample Student In-Class Essay 39

Part Two: Essay and Paragraph Basics 43

1. Introductions 44
  1.1 Functions of Introductions 44
    1.1.1 Reader Interest: Logical, Dramatic, Emotional 44
    1.1.2 Other Features 46
  1.2 Introduction Length 47
    1.2.1 Starting at the Very Beginning 48

2. Thesis Statements 50
  2.1 Kinds of Thesis Statements 50
    2.1.1 Simple 50
    2.1.2 Expanded 50
    2.1.3 Indirect 51
  2.2 Effective Thesis Statements 51

3. Outlines 54
  3.1 The Value of Outlines 54
  3.2 Organizing an Outline 55
  3.3 General Guidelines 55
  3.4 Developing an Outline with Thesis Statement 56

4. Paragraph Essentials 57
  4.1 Essays and Paragraphs: Topic Sentences and Wraps 57
  4.2 Unity 58
  4.3 Coherence 59
    4.3.1 Organizational Patterns 60
    4.3.2 Logical Sentence Order 60
    4.3.3 Repetition and Synonyms 60
    4.3.4 Parallel Structures 60
    4.3.5 Transitions 60
  4.4 Development 62

5. Conclusions 65
  5.1 Functions of Conclusions 65
  5.2 Two Kinds of Conclusions 66

Part Three: Essay and Paragraph Development 69

1. Developing Your Essay through Substantial Paragraphs 70
  1.1 Rhetorical Patterns 70
    1.1.1 Definition—What Is It? 71
    1.1.2 Chronology—When Did It Occur? 72
    1.1.3 Description—What Does It Look Like? 73
    1.1.4 Narration—How Can It Be Told? 73
    1.1.5 Process—How Does It Work? 74
    1.1.6 Personal—Why Should It Affect Me?/How Does or Did It Affect Me? 74
    1.1.7 Classification/Division—What Kinds Are There? 75
    1.1.8 Cause–Effect—What Is The Cause? 75

1.1.9 Question–Answer—What Is The Answer? 76

1.1.10 Example/Illustration—How Can It Be Shown? 76

1.1.11 Problem–Solution—How Can It Be (Re)Solved? 77

1.1.12 Cost–Benefit—What Are The Advantages and Disadvantages? 77

1.1.13 Analogy—How Is It Like Something Else? 78

1.1.14 Compare and Contrast—How Is It Like and/or Unlike Something Else? 78

1.2 Primary and Secondary Methods 79

2. Essays Using a Primary Method 81

2.1 Definition Essays 81

2.1.1 Sample Essay 82

2.2 Compare and Contrast Essays 83

2.2.1 Block and Point-by-Point Methods 84

2.2.2 Sample Compare and Contrast Essay 85

2.2.3 Excerpt from a Compare and Contrast Essay 86

3. The Design of the Essay: A Two-Part Model 90

3.1 Kinds of Claims: Fact, Value, Policy, and Interpretation 90

3.1.1 Claims of Fact 90

3.1.2 Claims of Value 91

3.1.3 Claims of Policy 91

3.1.4 Claims of Interpretation 91

3.2 Support: Evidence and Credibility 91

3.2.1 Organization of Evidence 92

3.2.2 Kinds of Evidence 92

3.2.3 Credibility 93

Part Four: The Argumentative Essay 97

1. Rhetoric, Argument, and Persuasion 99

1.1 Staking Your Claim 101

1.2 Arguable Claims 102

1.3 Specific, Interesting, and Manageable Claims 102

1.3.1 Specific Claim 103

1.3.2 Interesting 103

1.3.3 Manageable 104

2. Working Your Claim: Kinds of Evidence 105

2.1 Facts, Statistics 106

2.2 Authorities, Experts 107

2.3 Examples, Illustrations, Case Studies, Precedents 107

2.4 Hypotheses, Analogies, Description, Personal Experience 108

3. Working Your Claim: The Rational Basis of Argument 109

3.1 Inductive Reasoning 109

3.2 Deductive Reasoning 110

4. Refuting the Opposing View 112

4.1 Conditions for Rebuttal 112

4.1.1 Topic 112

4.1.2 Audience 112

4.1.3 Purpose 113

4.2 Two Strategies for Refutation 113

4.2.1 Strategy A: Acknowledgement 113

4.2.2 Strategy B: Point-by-Point Refutation 114

5. "Please Sign Our Petition": A Case Study   **115**

6. Categories of Faulty Reasoning   **117**
   6.1 Logical, Emotional, and Ethical Fallacies   117
   6.2 Fallacies and Slanted Language   122

7. Organizing an Outline for Argument   **124**

8. Rhetorical Function of Parts   **124**

9. Sample Outline for an Argumentative Essay   **125**

10. Sample Essays   **126**
   10.1 Sample Student Argumentative Essay #1 (APA Style)   127
   10.2 Sample Student Argumentative Essay #2 Annotated (APA Style)   129
   10.3 Sample Student Argumentative Essay #3 (MLA Style)   133
   10.4 Reading #1 (APA Style): "Cloning and Identity"   137

Part Five: The Expository Essay   **151**

1. The "Three-Part" Essay: Exposition, Research, Synthesis   **152**
   1.1 Research—Finding and Exploring   153
   1.2 Synthesis I—Assimilation   153
   1.3 Organization—Arranging   154
   1.4 Synthesis II—Integration   154
   1.5 Documenting: Following Procedures   155

2. What Is Research?   **155**

3. Who are these experts . . . and where can you find them?   **156**

4. A Note about the Internet   **157**

5. Research Proposals   **158**
   5.1 Purpose   158
   5.2 Format   158
   5.3 Sample Research Proposals   159

6. Researching Your Topic   **161**
   6.1 Exploring   161
   6.2 Research Note-Taking   162
   6.3 Organizing Research Notes   162
   6.4 Cross-Referencing   163
   6.5 Some Useful Research Strategies   163
       6.5.1 Assimilating   163
       6.5.2 Arranging   163
   6.6 Using Contradictory Evidence   164

7. Sources of Research Material   **164**
   7.1 The Range of Sources   165
       7.1.1 Primary and Secondary Sources   165
   7.2 Start Your Research by Looking at Secondary Sources   165
       7.2.1 Books   166
       7.2.2 Periodicals   166
       7.2.3 Locating Journal Articles   166
   7.3 Internet Searches   167
       7.3.1 Some Popular Databases   169
   7.4 Some Notes on Library Research   170
   7.5 Alternative Information Sources   171
       7.5.1 Interviewing   171

8. Summarizing Your Sources   **172**
   8.1 Summary   172
   8.2 Précis   172
   8.3 Abstract   172
   8.4 Annotated Bibliographies   173
   8.5 Paraphrase   173

9. Outlines for Research Essays   **173**

10. Integrating Secondary Sources   **175**
   10.1 Plagiarism   175
   10.2 Summary, Paraphrase, Direct Citation, Mixed Citation   176
      10.2.1 Summarize   176
      10.2.2 Paraphrase   177
      10.2.3 Direct Quotation   177
      10.2.4 Mixed Citation   178
   10.3 Signal Phrases, Ellipses, and Brackets   179
      10.3.1 Signal Phrases   179
      10.3.2 Ellipses   180
      10.3.3 Brackets   181

11. Documentation: Citations and References   **182**
   11.1 Choosing Your Citation Style   182
   11.2 Necessary versus Unnecessary Citations   183
   11.3 The Major Documentation Styles   184
   11.4 APA Citation Style   184
      11.4.1 APA In-Text Citations   184
      11.4.2 APA In-Text Citations by Format 186
      11.4.3 APA In-Text Citations: Internet Sources   187
      11.4.4 APA In-Text Citations: Non-Textual Sources   188
      11.4.5 APA Citations in the References Section   188
   11.5 MLA Citation Style   193
      11.5.1 MLA In-Text Citations   193
      11.5.2 MLA In-Text Citations by Format 194
      11.5.3 MLA In-Text Citations: Internet Sources   196
      11.5.4 MLA In-Text Citations: Non-Textual Sources   196
      11.5.5 MLA Citations in the Works Cited Section   196
      11.5.6 MLA Internet Citations   200
      11.5.7 MLA Citations for Non-Textual Sources   201
      11.5.8 MLA Footnotes   202
   11.6 Chicago Citation Style (Note)   202
      11.6.1 Chicago Style In-Text Citations 202
      11.6.2 Chicago Style Footnote/Endnote Citations by Format   204
      11.6.3 Chicago Style Bibliography   207

12. The Formal Précis   **212**
   12.1 Main Features of the Précis   212
   12.2 Rhetorical Stance   213
   12.3 Signal Phrases   213

13. A Method for Summarizing   **214**

14. Sample Précis   **214**

15. Sample Student Essays   **218**
  15.1 Sample Student Expository Essay #1 (APA Style)   219
  15.2 Sample Student Expository Essay #2 (MLA Style)   223
  15.3 Sample Excerpt from Student Essay (Chicago Style)   228
16. Reading #2 (APA Style): "Marketing Movies on the Internet"   **230**

Part Six: The Literary Essay   **239**

1. Common Ground   **240**
2. Literature as a Unique Encounter   **240**
3. Kinds of Literary Essays   **241**
  3.1 Response   241
  3.2 Evaluation   242
  3.3 Literary or Critical Analysis   242
4. Text-Centred and Context-Centred Approaches   **242**
5. Evaluating Student Essays   **243**
6. On the Road to the Rough Draft   **244**
  6.1 Method for Developing an Outline or Draft   245
7. When You Write about Literature   **246**
8. Theory into Practice: A Sample Poetry Analysis   **247**
9. The Literary Genres: Poetry, the Short Story, the Novel, and Drama   **251**
10. How to Approach a Poem   **252**
  10.1 Intuitive Approach   252
  10.2 Text-Centred Approach (the inside-out approach)   252
  10.3 Context-Centred Approach (the outside-in approach)   253
  10.4 Sample Student Literary Analysis   256
11. Fiction Forms   **258**
12. The Short Story   **259**
  12.1 The Single Effect   260
13. The Novel Tradition   **260**
14. How to Approach Fiction   **262**
  14.1 Plot   262
  14.2 Character   263
  14.3 Setting   263
  14.4 Narrative Point of View   264
  14.5 Orientation to Reality   264
15. How to Approach Drama   **266**
  15.1 Comedy   267
  15.2 Tragedy   268
16. The Literary Research Essay   **268**
  16.1 Primary and Secondary Sources   268
     16.1.1 How to Use Secondary Sources   269
     16.1.2 Reliability of Sources   270
     16.1.3 Currency   270
  16.2 Revising the Literary Essay   271
  16.3 Sample Student Literary Research Essay (MLA Style)   272
17. Reading #3 (MLA Style): "The Urban Working Girl . . ."   **278**
18. A Brief Glossary of Literary Terms   **294**

Part Seven: Sentence Essentials   **301**

1. Grammatical Groundwork   **302**
  1.1 Grammar and Usage   303
  1.2 A Choice-Based Grammar   304
    1.2.1 The Grammar of Reading and Writing   305

2. Introducing . . . the Parts of Speech   **306**
  2.1 The Parts of Speech at Work   306
  2.2 Substantives: Nouns and Pronouns   307
    2.2.1 Functions of Nouns and Pronouns (Substantives)   307
    2.2.2 Kinds of Pronouns   308
  2.3 Verbs   309
  2.4 Modifiers: Adjectives and Adverbs   311
  2.5 Joiners: Prepositions and Conjunctions   312

3. Introducing . . . the Sentence   **313**
  3.1 What Is a Sentence?   313
  3.2 The "Invisible Subject" Sentence   315
  3.3 Four Errors of Incompletion   316

4. Introducing . . . Phrases and Clauses   **319**
  4.1 Phrases   320
    4.1.1 Prepositional Phrases   320
    4.1.2 Noun and Verb Phrases   320
  4.2 Clauses   321
    4.2.1 Using Conjunctions to Join Clauses   321
  4.3 Errors of Combining   323
    4.3.1 The Run-On Sentence   323
    4.3.2 The Comma Splice   324

5. Punctuation   **326**
  5.1 Commas   326
    5.1.1 Use Commas to Separate Items in a Series   327
    5.1.2 Use Commas to Separate Independent Clauses   327
    5.1.3 Use Two Commas to Separate Parenthetical Information   329
    5.1.4 Miscellaneous and "Comma Sense" Uses   331
  5.2 Other Forms of Punctuation   335
  5.3 Semicolons   335
    5.3.1 Semicolon with Independent Clauses   335
    5.3.2 Serial Semicolon   337
  5.4 Colons   338
    5.4.1 Formal Uses   338
  5.5 Dashes and Parentheses   339
  5.6 Punctuation Prohibitions   344

6. Apostrophes   **345**

7. Agreement   **349**
  7.1 Subject–Verb Agreement   349
    7.1.1 Verbal Disputes   349
    7.1.2 Finding the Subject   349
    7.1.3 Mistaking the Subject   350
    7.1.4 Rules for Subject–Verb Agreement   351

8. Pronouns at Work   **354**
  8.1 Pronoun–Antecedent Agreement   354
  8.2 Problematic Pronouns: Inclusive Language   355

8.3	Pronoun Reference	358
	8.3.1 No Reference (missing antecedent)	359
	8.3.2 Remote Reference	360
	8.3.3 Ambiguous (Squinting) Reference	360
	8.3.4 Broad Reference (Vague Reference)	361
8.4	Pronoun Forms (Case)	364
	8.4.1 Personal Pronoun Forms: Case	364
	8.4.2 Possessive Pronouns	367
	8.4.3 Gerunds and Participles	367
	8.4.4 Relative Pronouns	368
	8.4.5 Interrogative Pronouns	369
8.5	Pronoun Consistency	371
9.	**Sentence Construction Errors**	**372**
9.1	Misplaced Modifiers	373
	9.1.1 Adjectival Modifiers	373
	9.1.2 Adverbial Modifiers	374
	9.1.3 Fixing Misplaced Modifiers	374
	9.1.4 One-Word Modifiers	375
	9.1.5 Dangling Modifiers	376
9.2	The Parallelism Principle	380
	9.2.1 Identifying and Fixing Parallelism Problems	381
	9.2.2 A List or Series	382
	9.2.3 Compounds	384
	9.2.4 Correlative Conjunctions	385
	9.2.5 Comparisons	386
10.	**Summary Exercises**	**390**
	Part Eight: Achieving Clarity and Depth for "3-D" Writing	**393**
1.	**Effective Style: Clarity**	**394**
1.1	Cutting for Conciseness	395
	1.1.1 Doubling Up: The Noah's Ark Syndrome	396
	1.1.2 Phony Phrases	397
	1.1.3 The Small but Not-So-Beautiful	398
	1.1.4 Those Un-Intensives	399
1.2	Writing Directly	400
	1.2.1 Passive Constructions: The Lazy Subject	400
	1.2.2 Black Hole Constructions	403
	1.2.3 Numbing Nouns	404
	1.2.4 Euphemisms	405
1.3	Working towards Precision: Wise Word Choices	408
	1.3.1 Precision and Logic	410
1.4	Working towards Specificity	411
	1.4.1 Verbs with Vitality	412
	1.4.2 Prepackaged Goods: Clichés	413

2. **Providing Depth: Variety and Emphasis**   **414**
    2.1 Sentence Variety   414
        2.1.1   Length   414
        2.1.2   Structural Variety   416
    2.2 Creating Emphasis   416
3. **Proofreading: Perfection *Is* Possible**   **418**
    3.1 Proofreading Methods   418
    3.2 Guidelines for Proofreading   419
    3.3 Common Errors   419
4. **Essay Presentation**   **420**
5. **Common Words That Confuse: Guide and Exercise**   **421**

Appendices

A. **Tense Encounters with Verbs: A Summary**   **431**
B. **The Journalistic Essay**   **435**
    Some Features of Journalistic Writing   437
C. **A Special Case: On-line Learning and Writing**   **439**
    A Sample On-line Discussion   441
D. **Peer Edit Forms**   **443**
    Formal Outline   444
    Argumentative Essay First Draft   445
    Expository Essay First Draft   447
    Literary Essay First Draft   449
Index   **451**

Preface

Writing by Choice is designed to improve writing skills and empower the student writer. While the first objective might seem modest, the second might seem somewhat over-reaching, though in most other pursuits, empowerment is an inevitable consequence of improvement. This should be the case with writing as well.

By the time students begin post-secondary study, they are familiar with the do's and don'ts of writing essays. They may expect that college writing will give them more of the same or may be surprised when instructors give them rules that contradict what they have been told. First and most frequent questions instructors face are those of limits: "Do you want the essay to have five paragraphs?" "Are we allowed to use 'I'?" "How many words does it have to be?" Such questions, and many others, imply that students have previously been taught stringent guidelines for the writing of essays. While guidelines are essential, they should not hamper thought or expression. They should not deprive writers of choices, but enhance their ability to make *informed* choices given the wide range of variables affecting different kinds of writing tasks.

At the post-secondary level, student writers are capable of and should assume responsibility for making informed choices. Only by doing so can they take up the challenges offered by their disciplinary studies and by the wide variety of workplace writing tasks that may lie ahead. In a world that increasingly values solutions to its problems, the knowledgeable, adaptable writer will always be in demand, since written forms of communication are likely to reach the widest possible readership—to be heard, considered, and acted on.

Writing by Choice provides students with a detailed, holistic, and widely applicable approach to developing writing skills at the college and university level—and beyond. Writing at university can be considered goal-centred, but in this text the goals are approached more often through questions that student writers can ask themselves than by a series of conditions or requirements that must be satisfied. The approach to many topics in *Writing by Choice* is through open-ended questions, rather than via definitive statements. Thinking and writing are treated as closely connected; reflection should inevitably precede selection.

The text's developmental approach stresses the steps involved in any writing project. It enables instructors or students to choose to omit specific steps in a process. For example, a class in intermediate or advanced composition may possess a level of knowledge that makes it redundant to focus on paragraph unity; but the instructor may focus extensively on the more complex area of paragraph and/or essay development. The same approach can be used in the grammar section, which begins by identifying the parts of speech and proceeds through to the complexities of parallel structure. On the other hand, in most introductory composition courses, a full review of the structure of English, as it is provided here, is the necessary starting point.

As the Contents pages reveal, the composition sections of *Writing by Choice* are not organized around the teaching of the traditional rhetorical modes. Detailed treatment is given to three kinds of essays: argumentative, expository, and literary—the kinds typically assigned in first-year composition and literature courses. Part One gives a briefer treatment of the personal, or "expressive," essay and provides an overview of the composing process, reading strategies, the writing situation, stages of essay writing, and other kinds of essays. Specialized writing contexts also considered in *Writing by Choice* include the in-class or examination essay, on-line writing, and journalistic writing.

A common belief, namely that students have difficulty applying the grammar rules they learn to their own writing, is countered here by an incremental approach to the acquisition of grammar skills that is designed to enable students to assimilate these crucial skills. The grammar and the composition sections stress the developmental approach of identifying, applying, and integrating. Almost all of the many examples in the text are taken from students' writing, allowing students of this text to see the relevance of its material to their own writing. Sentences and paragraphs from students' writing also are used in the exercises, which reinforce rules and concepts as they apply to realistic, everyday writing contexts—ones that have occurred and will occur to students as they write.

Some of the exercises in *Writing by Choice* narrow the focus to one learning objective while others require students to integrate several objectives. Exercises are designed to engage students on their own as well as in group or collaborative environments. Many instructors consider editing by peers an indispensable part of collaborative learning; peer edit forms are included in the Appendices. An important feature of this text, full-length student essays illustrate expressive, argumentative, expository, literary, and in-class writing as well as MLA, APA, and Chicago documentation styles. The writing by students represents a variety of disciplines, including biology, classical studies, economics, environmental studies, history, kinesiology, literature, political science, and psychology. Three longer selections from the academic, business, and professional worlds of the kind that students encounter in their research also are included as teaching/learning devices.

Writing by Choice seeks to instill the basic principles of effective writing and to give student writers the knowledge they need to make successful and empowering choices in their writing in college and university and in their future business, professional, and personal lives.

Acknowledgements

I first want to thank Madeline Sonik, who proposed and nourished the notion that an innocuous 40-page grammar text could aspire to something more. I am indebted to Jane Tilley at Oxford University Press Canada for being so receptive to the idea of this book. Many thanks to Senior Acquisitions Editor Laura Macleod for her enthusiasm and understanding at all points along the way. Thanks also to the expertise of Brad Lambertus and Marta Tomins—and especially to the diligence and attentiveness of copy editor Laurna Tallman (with a passing nod to the blackflies in Marmora, Ontario, which helped keep Laurna indoors and on task throughout the late spring). I wish to gratefully acknowledge the Director of the Writing Program at the University of Victoria, Kim Blank, for his interest in the project; Susan Huntley Elderkin generously wrote most of the text for On-line Learning and Writing; Colleen Carpenter bravely soldiered through the entire manuscript, making invaluable comments. The indefatigable energy of Chris Higgins is reflected by her substantial contributions to the section on expository writing. Madeline Sonik-Henderson was always willing to take up my sometimes strange writing challenges.

Finally, but certainly not least, I want to thank my many students over the years for providing the motivating force for this book; their commitment to writing is reflected in many of their sentences with which the book is enlivened.

PART ONE

Developing "3-D" Skills: Thinking, Reading, and Writing

1. A Choice-Based Approach
2. Thinking and Writing: The Composing Process
3. Thinking and Writing + Reading
4. The Writing Situation
5. Stages in Essay-Writing
6. Kinds of Essays

1. A Choice-Based Approach

Many student writers fear writing, believing they lack the skills to write successfully, that what they write will be imperfect, and that they may receive a poor grade due to these imperfections. Once you set words down in concrete form, they become something to be analyzed and judged—by you and, ultimately, perhaps, by someone else, such as your instructor. When writing an essay as part of a course requirement, you *know* your writing is going to be analyzed, evaluated, commented on, and graded. If your writing can be seen as a *concrete* representation of your thoughts, those thoughts, now concretized in the form of your essay, receive a *concrete* mark. A mark given for a paper, like the pin that fixes the butterfly to the display backing, suggests something permanent and possibly not to be challenged.

Making that commitment to a "public" form of discourse is difficult and often intimidating, but it need not be traumatic. Most first-year composition courses are designed to give you the information you need, much of it in the form of general rules, applicable to a wide variety of writing tasks that lie ahead; other information will be specific to individual tasks; and still other information will involve making choices. The generic and the task-relevant information will be vital to your success as a writer academically and professionally. But your ability to make choices, more than anything, will affect both your present and future writing at those times when you will not be aware of, or governed by, rules, standards, or conventions.

University-level writing has been the subject of much inquiry in the last 40 years. Writing teachers, along with writing theorists and researchers, have raised important issues and put forward valuable models designed to help explain the writing process and assist the student writer. In spite of this activity, no model has emerged as the "best" or "right" one, owing partly to the many kinds of writing tasks possible both in and out of university, to the complexity of these tasks, and to the inability to explain precisely how our internal processes work to enable us to create and communicate meaning through written texts.

One of the most common models used in teaching writing is the linear one that asks the student writer for a written "product," usually an essay or report, after clearly defining a goal (purpose), thinking about it (pre-writing), planning it (research and outlining), drafting it, and revising it. The five-paragraph essay is the most well-known example of such a written product. With an introduction containing a thesis statement, three body paragraphs with clear topic sentences, and a conclusion that restates the thesis, the five-paragraph essay has proven adaptable to many different situations.

> The ultimate goal of writing courses is to enable you to write by choice rather than by chance—to make the choices that reflect your purpose in writing, your audience, your task-specific requirements, as well as the way you think and who you are: your ideas, beliefs, and values.

2. Thinking and Writing: The Composing Process

A reader of an essay might comment that the student "put a lot of thought into it" or, conversely, that "Not much thought went into it." Such comments oversimplify the relationship between thinking and writing. Because of the complexity of many university-level writing tasks, like essay-writing, it is a good idea to consider writing as inseparable from thinking.

Essay-writing gives student writers the opportunity to exercise a variety of kinds of thinking. To come up with and develop a topic, you will probably begin with a concept or abstraction; by free association or other similar strategies, you will try to make connections in order to narrow the topic's scope and increase its manageability. Most kinds of writing activate different skills at different times. In addition to linear or associative thinking, you might utilize your abstract or your concrete perceptual capabilities and such cognitive skills as analysis (breaking down) and synthesis (putting together). The various approaches to the thinking-writing process may stress one activity over another, but they all have one aim in common: to make you more conscious of how you write in order to make your writing more successful and, hopefully, more enjoyable. Three writing models are introduced below: traditional-linear, process-oriented, and process-reflective. You may want to experiment with each to see which ones work well for you.

2.1 The Traditional Linear Model

Writing is often taught as though it were a linear, sequential process. To a large degree, it is. Even when the writer discovers, say, in the first draft that the order of points isn't logical and has to return to the outline and reorder these points, the process can still be considered linear—going backwards before going forwards again. In this approach, the activities of engaging and re-engaging with the topic are still important, but the traditional linear model recognizes that virtually all writing has a purpose and a goal that the writer is trying to achieve. Although the writer is proceeding linearly towards a goal, the means used to get there can be complex, variable, and often unpredictable.

The traditional approach to essay-writing is to divide it into several stages, beginning with what is sometimes called *inventing*, an explorative stage in which you may start with nothing more than a subject area, a topic but no thesis (a statement about the topic), or perhaps something even less defined. This is where pre-writing strategies come in: these are systematic methods to generate ideas when you are otherwise faced with "writer's block." When you have enough ideas and have made connections among some of them, you may be ready to formulate a thesis.

As you continue expanding and exploring, you will soon find yourself able to construct an outline, which will clarify the relationships among the main points. The further you move along in the process, in the traditional linear model, the less you will be *thinking about* a topic and the more you will be relying on specific methods and forms with measurable objectives. After constructing an outline, you will begin your rough draft with the objective of creating unified, coherent, and developed paragraphs; and after you have completed the draft, you will revise it by paying particular attention to grammar, punctuation, sentence structure, and such mechanics. One practical benefit of learning and using this traditional model is that it is directly applicable to a large number of university-level and workplace tasks, in which objectives are clearly defined and form is important—such as scientific experiments and business letters—and that can be adapted to a variety of specialized functions.

2.2 Process-Oriented Models: Discovery Drafts

Although most "public" forms of writing, including the essay, are goal-centred, you can arrive at this goal by different routes. In the traditional linear model, the outline is the focal point of composing: one of the goals of pre-writing is to come up with a thesis statement and enough to say so that you can construct an outline. Once constructed, outlines serve as a point of reference for drafting, ensuring you don't go far off track.

In *discovery drafts*, however, process is a major focus. The goal of the discovery draft—sometimes referred to as *directed freewriting*—is to clarify your thoughts and discover what you want to say about a topic. This kind of writing can be useful for those who feel inhibited by the traditional linear approach, which requires a clearly defined goal, expressed as a thesis, before proceeding to the outline and draft. In process-centred writing, you do not let formal matters like phrasing, sentence construction, or grammar stand in your way. You try to get your thoughts down on paper and not be too concerned with inconsistencies or even contradictions; keeping up the flow of words is vital.

The discovery draft is complete when you know what you want to say. Because what you come up with is complete, though usually far from "finished," you may now find it easier to make an outline or, allowing several hours to pass, return to the draft with a more objective perspective in order to expand on important points and work on their order. With a clearer focus and structure in mind, you then write a second draft.

This draft will look very different from the first: unimportant ideas and irrelevant details will have been discarded. Ideas and their support will still be the primary focus, rather than sentence-level concerns like word choice, grammar, and style—but it will be closer to a final draft. Typically, composing this way requires at least three drafts, each successive draft more clearly focused and more detailed than the previous. The final draft, consequently, will be the result of careful revisions at the sentence level. After completing the first or second draft, you might be asked to submit it to your instructor or to a peer editor for feedback. Getting input is often an important part of the process-oriented approach.

This form of drafting may be offered to the student writer as an appealing alternative to the traditional model where structure precedes the act of drafting. In the discovery draft, drafting is a precursor to form rather than an extension and development of it. Whereas the stress in the traditional model is on what you *need* to write, the stress in the discovery draft is on what you *want* to write and the discovery of your purpose for writing.

2.3 Process-Reflective Writing

Typically, composing involves periods of intense writing balanced by periods of reflection; the meditative periods may lead the student writer to further develop an idea, to qualify it, or perhaps to abandon it in favour of another line of thought. The writer may stop to recall, to analyze, or to reconsider. Observing the habits of students during in-class writing exercises, especially long, essay-type exams, reveals a typical pattern of writing and reflecting: students write steadily and intensively for varying lengths of time; they look up or away from their writing for shorter but distinct "breaks." A third characteristic activity is looking over what they have written. Some students find the time to outline their main points, but many don't. Because students know they are expected to include a thesis statement in their introduction, discovery drafts are a less viable option for in-class essay-writing when there is seldom time for complete rewriting.

Although it stresses process and enables the writer to sort out many, often conflicting, ideas, the discovery draft should not be written hastily. It should embody your well-considered thoughts on a topic. It should be as thorough and detailed as possible—perhaps longer than the required essay length to allow for the inevitability that much of what you say will need rethinking and reordering—and usually quite a bit of pruning back.

So, what model, if any, do students use in such cases? Often it is a variant of the model that most experienced writers use: a "process-reflective" approach in which they focus on where they are going by looking back at what they have written, keeping the original goal in mind throughout.

As you write, your thinking is affected in two related ways: writing narrows future choices and opens up new possibilities. A choice, once made, excludes choices that may have existed before, while it creates new options. In this way, what you *have written* serves to give direction to what you *will* write. By writing down your thoughts, you become conscious of them, and they become subject to your control. As a result, your thinking becomes clearer. Just as it is said that clear thinking produces clear writing, writing (especially clear writing) produces clearer and more directed thinking. In process-reflective writing, you reflect on your process in order to make your writing and your thinking clearer.

Process-reflective writing seizes on the necessary connection between writing and thinking, that variable, back-and-forth nature of the composing process that involves a continuous interchange between thinking and writing, rethinking and rewriting. Student writers undergoing timed assignments share with seasoned writers their immersion in the writing experience, and they tend to ask similar questions, albeit unconsciously, in their reflective moments: Where have I been going? Where am I going now? Is my purpose the same as it was when I started? How does what I have said determine what I need to say? What do I need to say (or do?) to get me closer to my goal?

In the process-reflective approach, you may not need a formal outline, but you should be clear on purpose and thesis before writing, perhaps through intensive pre-writing activities. As the draft proceeds, you become more conscious of structure by building on what has come before. Since you are concerned with connections between ideas, it makes sense to find appropriate transitions (word or phrase connectors, see Part Two, Section 4.3.5), since they reveal shifts in thought. As you look back, you can ask if your transitions reflect the relationships between ideas that you want to convey. In addition, rephrasing a previous point often helps writers achieve the clarity they seek. Process-reflective drafts, like discovery drafts, are often longer than final drafts, since reflection is geared towards the writer's clear thinking, and a trial-and-error approach may be needed to achieve this clarity.

Process-reflective drafts written outside of class encourage you to take an analytical approach to your writing. Since these kinds of skills develop over time and through writing and reading experiences, it may be difficult to approach your own writing objectively and critically; however, the more experience you gain as a reader, peer-critic, and writer, the easier it becomes to take this approach. Typical activities of process-reflective writing are questioning, clarifying, expanding, emphasizing, and eliminating what seems incompatible with the thesis, or qualifying it to bring it in line with your thesis. You may add words or cross them out, but (as is the case with traditional and discovery drafts) you should not focus on grammar, punctuation, word choice, spelling, or other mechanics.

The completed draft will be a more finished (though probably not a polished) product, requiring less revision than the discovery draft—of course, it will have taken longer to write. You may want to construct an outline after writing the draft, though an outline often is discovered within the draft itself. Instead of submitting outlines or rough drafts for feedback, writers following this method can submit partial drafts, consisting of at least an introduction and first body paragraph. You and your peer editors can reflect on the paragraph's potential for further development, such as what links could be used to connect it to a hypothetical following paragraph.

The chart below compares the three approaches to the composing process. Although their distinct qualities are stressed here, in reality writers often use different composing methods at different times without necessarily being conscious of using one or the other.

	Traditional Linear	Process-Oriented	Process-Reflective
Content	focused on what you need to write	focused on what you want to write	focused on what you are writing
Structure	shaped and determined by structure	finding a basis for structure	uncovering and using structure as you write
Relation of parts/points	co-ordination–subordination	relationship to a central idea; unity	coherence; transitions
Typical activities	following an outline, developing sub-points, giving detail, illustrating, completing	pursuing a topic, revealing and developing its potential, expressing fully	clarifying, evaluating, questioning, reiterating, filling gaps, connecting
Typical questions	Are my points relevant? Do my sub-points develop my main points? Are they ordered logically?	Is my topic clear to me? Is my purpose clear? Do I know what I want to write? Do I have important things to say?	How did I get here? Where am I going from here? How can I get there? What will make my thinking clearer?
Typical number of drafts required	two: a rough draft getting down ideas and a draft focused on the revision processes	at least three, with successive drafts more focused and detailed than the previous	two: a first draft focused on content and clarity and a second focused on revision and mechanics
Potential uses	typical workplace writing tasks; some academic writing: business, science; expository essays; research essays	creative, expressive, or explorative writing; personal essays	exam writing; some professional and academic writing; argumentative essays; critical/focused reading
Writing mode	progressive	transformative	integrative

3. Thinking and Writing + Reading

Most of us read for pleasure, at least sometimes. We choose what we want to read, when and where we want to read. Even when you read for pleasure, though, you are subjecting the text to a more intense analysis than may at first be apparent. On one level, of course, you are reading words for meaning. Sometimes, you read words whose *denotations* (literal meanings) are known to you; at other times, words have *connotations* (associations) that may affect your reading. You are continually determining and re-determining context as you follow the pattern of the words, their meanings, and associations as they combine with other words and larger syntactical structures to create an overarching pattern of meaning.

This kind of reading is primarily a one-way activity; reading to grasp content is essentially "passive" reading. But this one-way activity becomes two-way when you begin responding to the text. In a literary text, you may make personal associations—

recollections, emotions, desires—or experience the simple pleasure of escaping into another world that is in some way like your own. Consider, for example, the beginning of the short story "Friend of My Youth," by Alice Munro:

> I used to dream about my mother, and though the details in the dream varied, the surprise in it was always the same. . . . In the dream I would be the age I really was, living the life I was really living, and then I would discover that my mother was still alive. . . . Sometimes I would find myself in our old kitchen, where my mother would be rolling our piecrust on the table, or washing the dishes in the battered cream-colored dishpan with the red rim. But other times I would run into her on the street, in places where I would never have expected to see her.

In theory, a person could read this passage merely by focusing on the meanings of the words and trying to grasp the literal meaning of the passage. But most readers will find themselves engaged in some deeper way, forming associations that are dependent on the nature of their experience and outlook. Now, consider the beginning of another text, also about dreams, roughly the same length as the first:

> Religion was the original field of dream study. The earliest writings we have on dreams are primarily texts on their religious and spiritual significance. Long before psychoanalysts, sleep laboratory researchers, and content analysts arrived on the scene, religious specialists were exploring dreams in a variety of ways: using dreams in initiation rituals, developing techniques to incubate revelatory dreams and ward off evil nightmares, expressing numerous dream images in different artistic forms, and elaborating sophisticated interpretive systems that related dreams to beliefs about the soul, death, morality, and fate.
>
> —Wendy Doniger and Kelly Bulkley, "Why Study Dreams? A Religious Studies Perspective" in *Dreaming: Journal of the Association of Dreams* 3, 1 (1993)

The root word of *criticism* means *judge*, which does not necessarily imply a negative judgement. When you respond critically, or judge, you weigh the various factors relating to or having a bearing on something, as a judge impartially weighs the evidence before him or her to arrive at a verdict. An *inference* is a logical conclusion based on facts.

One difference between your responses to the two passages might have occurred at the first level: there might have been specific words or phrases, such as "content analysts" or "incubate revelatory dreams," in the second passage that caused you to reach for a dictionary, while in the first, it is less likely the language would have been unfamiliar.

In reading the paragraph above, you no doubt went beyond one-way reading. Though you may have formed some personal associations, you probably reacted more critically: the writers were making general statements about the use of dreams in religious societies and cultures, and you were probably beginning to consider the use of dreams in this or a similar context. If you continued to read the article, you would have proceeded to make certain inferences and draw conclusions based on the writers' statements and the way they were presented. You would have, perhaps, begun to test the claims and propositions based not only on your own experience but also on your sense of their logic and consistency: Is the claim logical? Is it valid considering the circumstances? Is it truthful? Reliable? Is it consistent with previous claims? When you engage in this process and ask these kinds of questions, you are responding *critically* to a work.

A writer may say something directly or may present evidence from which the reader can draw a conclusion. For example, Doniger and Bulkley provide factual evidence that ancient societies developed highly sophisticated methods for studying dreams—perhaps just as complex as the methods today of psychoanalysts and dream researchers. The writers don't directly say that the ancient methods were as complex, but readers could legitimately make that inference.

The main point is that while both passages above require you to react at some level beyond that of simple comprehension, the second passage calls forth a more critical response. In critical thinking, you use two-way reading to determine the validity of an author's statements, to test them by considering the logic and consistency behind them, and to determine whether the evidence presented supports the author's claims. Of course, if you were interested in creative writing, you could read the Munro text critically, also, focusing on her writing strategies and techniques.

The main difference between what we usually call "reading" (that is, "two-way reading") and what can be called "three-way reading" or *3-D* (Dimensional) *reading* is that in the latter you respond *consciously and analytically* to the text. Reading actively forges the connection between the *what* and the *how* of an essay. Being fully engaged in the reading-thinking-writing process is a valuable way to augment your writing skills, as well as your reading and thinking skills. A critical analysis of a literary work involves both a critical *and* an analytical focus: you employ the critical vocabulary applicable to literature in order to analyze the writer's theme and the strategies used to convey it. For example, as part of a critical analysis of Munro's story "Friend of My Youth," you might consider her use of the first-person ("I") point of view.

As a homework assignment, you may be asked to write a response based on a 3-D reading of an essay you've studied. As you respond in writing following this method, you complete the cycle that incorporates reading-thinking-writing: you read a text; you think about it critically; you write about those thoughts, making them conscious and thereby closing the cycle of learning that started with reading. You can then go back and begin the cycle again by rereading the piece, rethinking it, and, perhaps, responding to your more developed perceptions by writing about it again. Responding to essays and other texts and thinking about the conscious choices that the writer made will lead you to reflect on your own writing processes and enable you to make sound and *conscious* choices in your own writing.

> 3-D reading at the university level means taking a three-step approach to the acts of reading/thinking/writing where you:
> 1. focus on understanding
> 2. use critical thinking to test the validity of the statements
> 3. analyze and evaluate the work, considering the methods and strategies that the writer has employed to make it effective (or not).

Active Reading

Reading to Understand Meaning (Content) ⟶ One-Way Reading

Reading to Respond (Associative/Critical) ⟶ **Two-Way Reading**

Reading to Analyze Techniques (Analytical) ⟶ 3-D Reading

The model above is not intended to illustrate levels of successive difficulty or complexity. In a highly specialized text, for example, it may be quite difficult to grasp content; in fact, understanding the precise meaning of certain terms might be the key to analyzing such a text. What is usually true, though, is that these levels represent a "progressive" approach to reading where it is first necessary to understand content before proceeding to respond critically or analytically. Thus, active reading *at all three levels* is essential to your success in responding to the kinds of challenging texts you encounter at the university level.

3.1 Diffuse versus Focused Reading

The process just described may sound intimidating; it may appear that a lot is being asked of student readers when they are told to produce a close reading of an unfamiliar work. They may believe that in order to come up with a close reading it is necessary to pay careful attention to every word; consequently, they may assume that university-level reading is always careful, attentive, microscopic reading. Rather, there are purposes for which diffuse reading and scanning are useful just as there are purposes for which attentive and even microscopic reading are necessary. By no means should every source be read word for word. Even texts may deserve selective reading. Different sorts of reading may be needed according to subject matter: for history, attentive reading dominates; poetry requires intensive analysis at the level of letters in words; sociology, for example, in case studies, necessitates seeking particular patterns of information, often of the sort that can be outlined; mathematics and chemistry may have to be read even more closely than poetry; and so on. Thus, it is important to distinguish between reading that is *diffuse* and reading that is *selective*, such as scanning or focused reading.

Something that is diffuse is spread out; it covers a large area. By contrast, focused reading is concentrated on specific aspects or areas of the text. In this sense, focused reading is specialized reading—it asks you to become a specialist (mathematician, historian, literary critic, etc.) in your reading of the text.

The use of the word "text" should be clarified. There are primary and secondary texts in most subjects (see Part Five, Section 7.1.1 for the distinction between primary and secondary sources). Some are "text books" of the type produced for the study of math and science that may comprise most of the reading for the course, likely with the accompaniment of laboratory work and records. Some texts are books that individually convey one or more aspects of the core concepts being studied in a course. A history or language course usually will comprise many primary texts. Further reading of secondary texts doubtless will be required in most arts courses: books on similar topics or of similar kinds, and critical works that examine the primary texts. The student has to adapt different reading techniques to each of these sorts of materials.

When you set out to read with only a general purpose in mind—such as entertainment—you are practising diffuse reading. Of course, your reading may become focused at certain times, if, for example, a particular passage interests you. In conducting research for essay-writing, you need to be able to scan catalogue entries, journal indices, book contents pages and indices, reference books, and other types of sources in order to find the materials that will be useful and supportive of your essay topic. Once you have located most of your secondary sources, you will need to scan *them* to determine which are the most valuable for your purpose, so that you begin your focused reading with the most useful. It can be very frustrating to discover the most useful resource is the one you have left reading to the last.

Most active reading assignments in college or university are focused rather than diffuse—especially the primary works that you will read and reread in order to respond to them critically and analytically. Focused or selective reading is most effective when it follows a plan—you employ deliberate strategies and ask specific questions in order to get as much from the reading as possible without spending the additional time you would need if you were reading microscopically, word for word, or even letter by letter. A focused reading lays out a general plan to follow.

3.2 Responding Critically and Analytically through Questions

Focused, active reading can be triggered by asking questions about a primary text or text book. These can be asked before reading, while you read, after you've completed the first reading for content, or during later readings. Some of the questions relate to content; other questions may evoke a personal response; others require you to read critically or analytically. Active reading characteristically involves each of these different responses at different times. Of course, your response to any of the questions can change at any point in the reading process as you gather more information and can test some of the writer's early propositions.

3.2.1 Before Reading

If you wanted to go on a trip somewhere far away, you probably wouldn't just head for the nearest terminal and purchase a ticket for your destination, but would learn about that place before you risked your money. Pre-reading can give you valuable information to help you plan your reading of a text; it can give you an agenda, just as planning a trip will enable you to prepare an itinerary. When you select a book, ask yourself, "How much and what parts of it are useful to me?"

If your assignment is to write about a common theme in two Canadian novels, you must read actively the two primary works with an eye to the chosen theme. In addition, you may need to read other works by those writers. And you will need to find critical works dealing with that theme, preferably in the Canadian context, if possible relating specifically to your primary authors and the specific works you are examining. The secondary writers can be scanned and read quite selectively for what they have to contribute to an understanding of that theme.

If you are researching a topic, such as changes in subsidized housing policy during the last 50 years in Toronto, you are going to need primary documents from the City of Toronto's Archives, journal and newspaper articles, and books that may treat the subject in a wider fashion but bring Toronto policy into the discussion.

If you are researching an aspect of Aboriginal history in Saskatchewan during the 1900s, there may be no primary texts on the subject. You will need to consult a range of texts, documents, newspaper archives, journal articles, and university archives to compile primary information on your subject. Secondary sources could provide you with methods and points of view for analyzing these sorts of data. From some secondary authors, you might need little more than their research plans.

Information about the writer could alert you to his or her qualifications, for whom the book or essay was written, and possible biases of the writer. In articles in the sciences and social sciences, an "abstract," a concise summary, may precede the article, giving an overview of the writer's hypothesis, method, and results. Abstracts direct readers to those articles most relevant to their own reading or research interests (see Part Five, Section 8.3).

- **What information is given by the work's title?** Even a work's title can convey a lot of useful information about content, organization, tone, or rhetorical purpose. For example, consider the assumptions you would make about works with the following titles—both deal with the settlement of Canada's Prairies:

Buckley, Helen. *From Wooden Ploughs to Welfare: Why Indian Policy Failed in the Prairie Provinces*

Owram, Doug. *Promise of Eden: The Canadian Expansionist Movement and the Idea of the West, 1856–1900.*

Both titles contain words that inform their readers about rhetorical purpose, as well as time and place. The title of the first book suggests its author will analyze, and perhaps criticize, the causes for the failure of Indian policy. In the second title, the words "Promise of Eden" and "idea" suggest Owram will focus on perception and ideology behind the movement during the specific years indicated. As opposed to the titles of literary works, the titles of non-fiction works—including many academic books and articles—need to inform readers about content. Often, as with the two titles above, the first part of the title encapsulates the work through an appealing image or stylistic device (Buckley uses the alliteration of "*Wooden*" and "*Welfare*"), while the part following the colon gives specific information about content.

Other pre-reading questions include the following:

- **How long is the text?** Few people begin an essay without leafing through the pages to find the ending; this impulse reveals how much reading time it will require. It is best, whenever possible, to complete the reading at one time, since general impressions are important. With a book, you can follow the same procedures with relevant chapters or sections.
- **Who is the author?** Do you know anything about him/her?
- **What is his/her profession?** Nationality? Are any other important or defining characteristics apparent or notable?
- Does he/she belong to or **have affiliations** with a specific organization, group, or community?
- Does he/she seem to be **an expert** in the field? What shows you this?
- **Why was the book/essay written?**
- Is the essay/book **divided into parts**? Extra spacing between paragraphs could indicate divisions. Are there headings throughout the essay? Sub-headings? Do they inform you about content or organization? In a book, you would look for chapter titles and, perhaps, headings within individual chapters.
- **When was the essay/book written?** The date could be found in the beginning, in a footnote at the bottom of the first page, or after the essay. In a book, the publication date usually appears on the copyright page (the other side of the title page). The most recent date is not necessarily the relevant one for your purpose; for example, the book may be a reprint of a much earlier edition and you are looking for the first, or some other, edition. On the other hand, if the book is a second or revised edition, changes or updates making it more current may be most useful to you. Essays that appear in an edited collection will probably have earlier publication dates than the collection itself (though essays are sometimes commissioned for a volume and would then bear the same date).
- **To whom is the essay/book addressed?** Who was it written for? If an essay, what publication does it appear in or did it appear in, and what does this information tell you? If the publication is a journal, it could be a refereed scholarly

journal or one that is not refereed. A refereed journal is one in which the articles have been evaluated by knowledgeable peers and will be assumed to be more reliable by your instructors if you are writing a research essay.

If a book, **who is the publisher**? An academic or university press? Again, if you are writing a research essay, a scholarly publication might be a more reliable source than a trade publication since the latter are usually designed for a wide, non-specialized audience.

- What is the **level of language** used? Does it seem difficult, specialized? If the answer is "yes," you may have to do a little background reading or exploratory research—and ensure you have your dictionary handy.
- Is there **an abstract** that summarizes the entire essay? Usually, abstracts precede the essay; occasionally, they can be found after the essay. In books, the "Preface," "Introduction," or "Foreword" might give you this information, thus saving you from unneeded reading. Editors of essay collections often summarize the specific essays in introductions or forewords.

3.2.2 First Reading

It's a good idea to first read the essay/chapter for content and general impressions. Some people like to underline or highlight important passages; but ensure that you don't underline or highlight too much or it will be hard to discriminate, on the second reading, between the main ideas and the less important ones. Remember that when you read a text for the second time you can underline or highlight additional passages that strike you as important—in fact, you will be better equipped to tell what is more important and what is less important *after* you've read through the work once.

Other people prefer to make annotations, such as comments, thoughts, associations, criticisms, questions, or additions, in the margin of the text (assuming you own the text!). Still other people prefer to respond to the text on a separate piece of paper, keeping their own responses and the source text apart. If you don't know which method works best for you, experiment. Responding in some way to the text is the most natural way to make it relevant to you, even if that means you just write abbreviations or symbols, such as ?, ??, !, N.B., or ★, ★★, or ★★★, in the margin to denote levels of importance. Also see Part Five, Section 6.2, Research Note-Taking.

Your early written responses to a reading can be compared to your first explorative attempts to discover a topic or an approach to a topic during the inventing stage of writing. You may feel tentative about recording your thoughts, but simply giving them written form can be helpful; it will give you something to build on as you consider and reconsider the reading.

- What are your impressions of the first few paragraphs?
- Is there a distinct introductory section?
- What is the tone? (i.e., the writer's attitude to the subject matter—for example, familiar, objective, detached, casual, humorous, ironic, formal, informal). Tone can vary greatly from discipline to discipline or even from journal to journal, with scientific writing, typically, sounding the most detached.
- What kinds of words are used? More specifically, what is the vocabulary level? (simple, sophisticated, general, specific, specialized).
- Is jargon used? "Jargon" consists of words and expressions used among members of a designated group or in a particular discipline that its members would understand, but which people outside those groups would not necessarily understand. Jargon is a kind of specialized diction.

- What kind of essay is it? (persuasive, expository, personal, narrative, descriptive, combination of different kinds).
- What is the essay/chapter about? Do you know anything about the subject? Do you know of (have read) other works on the subject?
- What is its main point or thesis? Is it readily identifiable?
- Are the essay's/chapter's main points identifiable? In paragraph topic sentences, for example?
- Do the points seem well-supported? Is there always enough detail provided?
- Are secondary sources used? Does the writer use footnotes, endnotes, or parenthetical references?
- Is the text easy to follow? Are the points clearly expressed or is the meaning sometimes unclear? Note areas where the meaning is unclear to you. You can underline unclear passages with a different coloured pen or place question marks in the margin.
- Does the author always seem confident and certain about what he/she is saying? Does he/she ever express reservations or doubt? Does he/she ever appear to contradict himself/herself?
- Does he/she seem to change his/her position at any point?
- Does the work shift its focus—if so, is there an apparent reason for this?
- Does the work seem to build? Does it get stronger or weaker? Where?
- Is there a distinct concluding section? Is it satisfying?

Here is an excerpt from a reader's response to a first reading of an argumentative essay. Notice the use of underlining and annotation:

First of all, <u>sport of big business and big propaganda was allied to nationalism</u>. If England lost a football match against Germany the people were made to feel as if the <u>Battle of the Somme</u> had just been refought (and that maybe it would have been a better result if they'd played cricket). If England won the game of football the Union Jack was in blatant evidence, as a symbol of a national victory. It is no accident that the English say (a false claim in any case), that "the Battle of Waterloo was won on the playing fields of Eton."

topic sentence

WWI battle in which many British lives were lost

think of today when a Canadian team plays a U.S. team

<u>One might easily think that sport has taken the place of war</u>. Not at all. Sport is a means of keeping the national spirit alive during a time of so-called peace. <u>It prepares the national spirit for the eventuality of war.</u>

seems opinionated--biased?

why does he say "so-called" peace?

—Alan Sillitoe, "Sport and Nationalism," in Herbert Rosengarten and Jane Flick, eds, *The Broadview Reader*, 3rd edn (Peterborough, Ont.: Broadview Press)

3.2.3 Second Reading

In your second reading and successive readings of a work, your ability to apply critical and analytical skills is of paramount importance. With practice these skills will become active in all your reading. As well, these are the kinds of questions we will be asking in

Part Three, Essay and Paragraph Development, and other places in this text as they pertain to your own writing.

- Was the Introduction effective? What made it effective or not?
- What specific strategies did the writer use to draw you into the work? (questions, quotation, anecdote, narration, description, analogy?)
- Was the author's purpose in writing the work clear from the start?
- What audience was the work written for? Was the choice of words always appropriate for the audience it was aimed at?
- Why did the writer use the tone/voice that he/she did?
- Was the main thrust of the work argumentative (did it try to persuade you to change your mind about something?), or was the intent of the writer to explain or explore something? Or was it something different—to describe something or tell a story, for example?
- Was the main point of the work (the thesis statement) announced in the Introduction? If so, what was the thesis statement? Can you put it in your own words?
- How, specifically, were the points backed up? What kinds of evidence were used? (examples, illustrations, facts, statistics, authorities, personal experience, analogies?)
- How did the writer organize the work? Was one method used more than any other? (compare/contrast, definition, cause and effect, narration, description, division, other?)
- Did the author appear reliable? Trustworthy? Fair?
- How were the main points arranged? Was the strongest point placed near the beginning, middle, or end? Was the most effective order of points used?
- Did the work depend more on logic or on emotion?
- Did the writer appeal to a set of values or standards?
- What inferences were readers called on to make? Did there appear to be any lapses in logic? Was deductive reason used effectively? Was inductive reason used effectively?
- If the points were not always clear, what were the reasons for this lack of clarity? (specialized language, insufficient background given, poorly constructed paragraphs, faulty or ineffective writing style, inconsistencies or contradictions in the argument?)
- Was the Conclusion effective? What made it effective or not?

4. The Writing Situation

4.1 Writing Purpose

As a student writer you need to consider all the factors that could have a bearing on your writing task. You should be clear about your purpose before you begin your essay, just as you should be clear about an author's purpose before you make inferences and draw conclusions about a work you have read. Assessing purpose could involve any number of the questions below—either broad concerns or more specific ones. If you are uncertain about any of these points, you should seek clarification—either by asking your instructor or by utilizing techniques, such as pre-writing and discovery drafts, designed to clarify purpose.

- Will you be choosing your own topic or have you been given a specific topic? If the latter, will you have to narrow the topic?
- What kind of writing will you be doing? What form will it take—a response? book report? formal essay? scientific report?
- What main activity will you be involved in—explaining? arguing? narrating? describing? summarizing?
- Does the assignment stress learning objectives or does it ask you to rigorously apply concepts and practices already taught?
- What specific skills will you need to demonstrate for the assignment? How important is each in terms of the overall assignment? For example, will you have to define, summarize, synthesize, analyze, compare and contrast, classify? If the assignment includes a specifically worded question or statement, pay particular attention to verbs, such as *evaluate or assess, summarize, explore, explain, argue for or against, discuss, describe*: they all indicate a different purpose for the essay.
- Will you be using your own ideas? Will you be basing these ideas on recollection, observation, opinions, readings, class or group discussions?
- Where do your interests lie relative to the topic? How can you find out what they are and develop them further, if necessary?
- What level of knowledge does the assignment require? What level of specialization?
- Will the assignment test originality—new approaches to an old problem? inventiveness? imagination? creativity?
- Should your language be formal, like that of most academic disciplines? Will some informality be acceptable—the use of contractions and/or some informal diction? Under what circumstances?
- Will you be using other people's ideas or research? Will you get them from books and articles or other secondary sources? interviews? surveys?
- How much preliminary reading do you expect to do? What kind of reading?
- Will you be submitting work in progress, such as pre-writing assignments, an outline, plan, audience profile, or rough draft?
- Is there a specified length? Is it a word or page range? Will penalties, i.e., marks deducted, be applied if you write slightly outside the range?
- How much time will be allotted to complete the assignment? For example, an in-class exam would require a different assessment of purpose than that of an essay assigned weeks in advance.

4.2 "A" is for Audience

Almost everything is written with an audience in mind—readers with common interests, attitudes, reading habits, and expectations. There are many ways to test this generalization. For instance, pick up a children's book with one hand and the closest textbook with the other. Differences will be readily apparent. Most likely, the textbook will weigh more than the children's book; it will have more pages, and the print will be smaller. The cover of the children's book will be colourful, perhaps gaudy; the cover of the textbook will probably not attract your attention. Its primary purpose is to give basic information in an aesthetically pleasing form—no more.

Publishers have expectations about their readers: children's book publishers expect their readers will be looking for something to catch their interest. If the cover is appealing, a typical reader or parent might turn to the first page and begin reading. A typical text-book reader might read no further than the title, or might turn to the index or table of contents to get a general idea about content or to see how thoroughly a specific topic is covered. If the first few sentences of the children's book do not intrigue the reader, the book will probably be returned to the shelf; if the index of the textbook is insubstantial or does not include the expected subjects, the textbook will probably be returned to the shelf.

Part of determining the essay's purpose involves "designing" it with an audience, or typical reader, in mind. Therefore, the kinds of questions that pertain to publishers, book designers, and marketing specialists also pertain to student writers.

When physicist Stephen Hawking set out to write his popular book on cosmol-ogy, *A Brief History of Time*, audience concerns were uppermost, as is evident in his first paragraph. Italics show where readers are specifically addressed:

> Where did the universe come from? How and why did it begin? Will it come to an end, and if so, how? These are questions that are of interest to *us all*. But modern science has become so technical that only a very small number of specialists are able to master the mathematics used to describe them. Yet the basic ideas about the origin and fate of the uni-verse can be stated without mathematics in a form that *people without a scientific education* can understand.

In addition to mentioning the kind of audience he has in mind (curious people with no scientific training), other features show his awareness of audience. He begins with straightforward, general questions. His chooses direct language and simple sentence structure. If he were addressing his book to the "specialists" referred to in the fifth sen-tence, he probably would not have used the phrase "a very small number of specialists," but rather, perhaps, "cosmologists, astrophysicists, and mathematical physicists." The tone of the passage also shows his concern with audience. It is inviting and not patron-izing, implying that a non-specialist reader is capable of understanding difficult con-cepts. Clearly, Hawking wrote the way he did because he wanted to meet the expectations of his target audience.

Writers want their message—that which is communicated to a reader—to be received, and almost all want it to be accepted (one exception might be writers who simply want to get their opinion across to a hostile audience). Looking at the writer–reader relationship this way, you could consider it a kind of contractual arrange-ment with responsibilities on both sides. What responsibilities would a writer have in this relationship to make it more likely the message will be received and accepted? What responsibilities, ideally, should a reader have in this relationship? Add to the list below, assigning additional responsibilities in this contractual arrangement:

Responsibilities of Reader	**Responsibilities of Writer**
1. to read attentively and closely	1. to use appropriate language and a clear, readable style
2. to test the writer's claims for logic and consistency	2. to reason fairly, logically, and with consistency
3.	3.
4.	4.
5.	5.

Reader-based prose is focused on the reader. It makes clear communication a priority and acknowledges the active role of the reader in the communication process. Reader-based prose is geared towards the particular audience directly or indirectly invoked. *Writer-based prose*, by contrast, is much less directed towards its audience and the shared writer–reader role: private journal writing is one example of a writing activity where there is no need to acknowledge and accommodate a reader.

One of the requisites of reader-based prose is accessibility and clarity of meaning. Ensure the prose is error-free and that ideas are expressed directly and concisely (see Part Eight). In addition, there should be neither obvious gaps in logic, nor unreasonable or unwarranted assumptions concerning what the reader knows about a topic. In some cases, it may be necessary to define terms or clarify specific points. Even if the intended audience has specialized knowledge about a subject, it's safe, at a minimum, to assume *the reader knows a little less about the subject than you do.*

In the following example, the writer should have accommodated a general reader by giving more information. A reader could legitimately ask what a "deer tag" is and how it is "filled." A reader should not have to fill in gaps.

In 1998, there were more than 1 million deer tags handed out in Pennsylvania; of these only 430,000 tags were actually filled.

Most writing assumes the existence of an audience capable of discerning, evaluating, and judging. However, an audience can be characterized or profiled in a variety of ways. You should bear these in mind when you assess your essay's purpose and when you make choices about what to include or not to include, what level of language and tone to use, how to develop your ideas, how much background to provide, what kind of support to use, and other rhetorical matters.

You can characterize an audience according to four criteria:

* *knowledge*: the background, expertise, or familiarity with the subject
* *interest level*: the extent of audience interest or potential interest
* *the reader–writer relationship*: the way an audience would be expected to respond to the writer
* *orientation*: the attitudes and emotional/ethical positions that define a typical reader.

Writers need to consider the audience for whom they are writing and decide on particular techniques and strategies to appeal to this audience and meet its expectations.

Awareness of an audience's level of knowledge and interest, their relationship to the writer, and their orientation to the subject, writer, or the argument can be determined through various questions (see below page 18).

4.2.1 Knowledge and Interest

General—A general audience is one with no special defining or characteristic assumptions about, or expertise on, the topic, and whose degree of interest is variable—for example, all students at your college/university; readers of the *Globe and Mail* newspaper.

Implicit—An implicit audience is the range of groups and/or individuals to whom the communication is aimed; an implicit audience shares certain assumptions,

Meeting the expectations of an audience does not necessarily mean telling its members what they *want to hear* but, rather, doing everything you can to make it more likely they *will hear* you and understand you. For example, if you don't meet their expectations by using familiar terms or explaining unfamiliar ones, they will be less likely to "hear" you and understand you; hence, they may be less receptive to the points you make. It is more effective to write *to* your audience than *for* your audience.

knowledge, and competencies, and approaches the communication with expectations that are usually fairly broad, though not as broad as those in the first category—for example, first-year science students at your college/university; readers of the Entertainment section of the *Vancouver Sun*.

Explicit—An explicit audience is one or more groups or individuals to whom the communication is aimed; an explicit audience shares specific assumptions and approaches the communication with well-defined expectations—for example, graduate chemistry students at your college/university; the Arts and Books section of the *Montreal Gazette*. If you are writing for an *explicit* audience, you may use specialized terms and expect the average reader to understand them.

Generally, readers with some knowledge about a topic would also be interested in the topic, with an *explicit* audience being more interested than either *general* or *implicit* audiences; however, there is not always a direct correlation between knowledge and interest, and in many cases they can be considered separate areas.

Knowledge and Interest Questions

1. How much do you know about potential readers? How much do you need to know? What assumptions can you make about them? What might they value? What ambitions and goals might they possess? How could your writing appeal to their values and goals?
2. In what ways might the members differ from you? From one another? Consider such factors as where they live, their ages, gender, occupation, education, ethnic and/or cultural background, social status, politics, religion, hobbies, entertainment.
3. Is there a specific group of individuals you want to reach—other students? scientists? people your age? people of different ages?
4. If their knowledge about a subject is less than yours, what would help them better understand the topic—background information? facts and figures? examples? reference to experts?
5. If their interest in a subject is less than yours, what could help them better relate to the topic—examples? anecdotes (short narratives)? analogies (comparisons)? personal experience?

Exercise

In terms of their knowledge and interest, what general or specific assumptions could you make about readers of a trendy e-zine; a trade journal; an academic English journal; a book about recent discoveries in palaeontology; a non-scholarly book on a topical subject?

4.2.2 Writer–Reader Relationship

Many student writers assume that the only reader who *really* matters is the instructor, the one marking the essay. But if you imagine you are writing a report for your boss, rather than an essay for your teacher, it may be easier to move away from this practical but somewhat limiting mindset. Your boss may have commissioned the report and may be the one receiving it, but the report itself may be read and studied by many other people after your boss reads it. In such cases, you do not write for your superior but for an indeterminate number of people, many of whom you will not know. You would need to know the expectations of such a group of individuals, as well as those of your boss. You should consider an audience comprised of these kinds of hypothetical readers.

Of course, it's also important to acknowledge your instructor as a reader by following directions given for the assignment. For example, if you are required to include a title page with the instructor's name on it beneath the name or number of the course, not including this information would be failing to meet his or her expectations. The presentation of your essay is one area that demands your careful attention since instructors vary in their requirements; for instance, one instructor may require you to use 12-point size type while another may say that a point size between 10 and 12 is acceptable. At the very least, you will not make a favourable first impression if you use 10-point type in the former case.

Writer–Reader Relationship Questions

1. What is your relationship to the audience? Student to instructor? Student to student? Another kind of peer-based relationship, such as individual to professional associates or members of a group/community you are part of—for example, an organization of rock-climbers? Architects? Members of the union you belong to? Employee to employer? Employer to employee?

2. Do your readers expect you to conform to the conventions of a particular form or discipline? What are the specific formal requirements? (These questions are important when considering purpose as well.)

4.2.3 Audience Orientation

Audiences can be thought of as having potential *positive, neutral,* or *negative* orientations towards the subject, the writer, or the argument. Assessing audience orientation is especially vital whenever argument is involved. Many people form attitudes about matters of common interest, though they may be open to other views. Consider the subject of cloning. How might the orientation of members of a scientific community differ from those of a religious community? Would all scientific or religious communities have identical orientations? What could affect differences? What about the orientation of an audience of undergraduate philosophy students?

Orientation Questions

1. What is your audience's attitude towards your topic? What preconceived views might its members hold? What has informed these views (any of the factors mentioned above, such as education or where they live?) About what do you need to be sensitive in your audience's background?

2. If they are unsympathetic to your views, how could you make them more sympathetic? How could you bridge the gap between you and them? (See Part Four, Section 4, Refuting the Opposing View.)

The following questions could be relevant to all the above areas: What kind of writing does your audience expect or appreciate—simple and direct? complex? subtle? original? Could you use humour? Would they understand or value irony? How could your knowledge of audience affect your writing style or your tone?

Remember that you should consider not only what you know or need to know about your audience, but your own attitude to them. Is it essentially positive? neutral? negative? cautious? mistrustful? What attitudes will the audience expect you to hold? What attitudes might disturb or offend its members, making them less likely to "hear" you?

Collaborative Exercise I—Assessing the Writing Situation

Selecting one Purpose variable and one Audience variable from each category of column three (knowledge, interest, relationship, and orientation), discuss how you would approach writing an essay if you were given one of the 10 Topics from column one. How could you ensure that your message is received and accepted? How could you meet audience expectations? Try to be as specific as you can about approach and strategy. Hint: Start with Purpose, follow with Topic, and then choose Audience variables, considering assumptions about that audience and the way they would affect your writing choices. You can use the questions above under Purpose and Audience as guidelines.

Topic	Purpose	Audience
smoking in public places	formal essay	general knowledge
schizophrenia	in-class essay	implicit (moderate knowledge)
abolishing final exams	tell something that happened to you (narration)	explicit (specialized knowledge)
snowboarding	to explain (exposition)	low interest
conservation	to persuade (argument)	moderate interest
downloading music from the Internet	to summarize (put ideas in your own words)	high interest
the structure of DNA	to use research	superior–subordinate relationship
age discrimination	to explore or discover	peer–peer relationship
victim's rights	to describe	positive orientation
Weblogs ("blogs")	to define	neutral orientation
		negative orientation

Collaborative Exercise II—Formulating an Audience Profile

You can come up with an audience profile by considering the four criteria characterizing an audience. In groups of three, interview the other members of your group, asking questions that will enable you to assess your audience according to its knowledge, interest, and orientation (you can omit Writer–Reader Relationship, as it will likely be one of student-to-student). Assume your purpose is to persuade your audience. Therefore, if you follow the chart in Collaborative Exercise I, you could use the following topics: smoking in public places, abolishing final exams, downloading music from the Internet, victim's rights, or Web logs (Blogs). You can also make up a topic of your own that you feel strongly about and would like to argue for or against.

Collaborative Exercise II—Formulating an Audience Profile – *continued*

Write a four-paragraph profile based on the results of your interviews. Devote a paragraph to each of knowledge, interest, orientation, and strategies to consider in order to appeal to your specific audience. If you wish, you can pre-read about two strategies for refutation in Part Four, Sections 4.2.1, 4.2.2.

In many cases, your instructor will tell you the intended audience for your essay, perhaps a general audience or one made up of first-year students.

5. Stages in Essay-Writing

Once you have considered purpose and audience, you are ready to begin narrowing your topic. Whichever composing method works best for you, writing an essay inevitably means working steadily towards a goal. Although you may allot more time and energy to one stage or the other, you will generally write an essay in four or five stages, depending on whether you use research to help support your points.

1. **Pre-writing (Inventing)**: thinking about and coming up with a topic
2. **Research**: finding background information and supporting evidence
3. **Organization**: determining the order of points; outlining
4. **Composing: first draft**: getting down your ideas in paragraph form
5. **Revising: final draft**: revising and editing to achieve the finished version

External factors could determine the time you devote to the pre-writing stage: if you are assigned a specific topic, you won't have to spend as much time as someone who is simply told to "write on a topic of your choosing." Similarly, if you have the option of not writing a formal outline, you may spend much less time on outlining—perhaps by writing only an informal scratch outline—than someone asked to complete a formal outline.

5.1 Pre-writing

Much of what you accomplish during this stage will take place in your mind. Pre-writing strategies are designed both to clarify your thoughts about the subject and to enable you to generate useful ideas, some of which you will use in your essay; others can be discarded as you clarify your topic. Pre-writing often brings you to the point where you can write a tentative thesis statement and, in many cases, determine your main points.

Kinds of pre-writing strategies include *asking questions* about the topic; *brainstorming,* by yourself or with others; *freewriting,* in which you write continuously for a specific length of time without editing yourself; and *clustering,* or *mapping,* in which you graphically represent your associations with a subject.

All these pre-writing techniques work by association—utilizing one or more of questioning, brainstorming, freewriting, or clustering will enable you to trigger associations, to tap into subconscious ideas and feelings. These methods are process-oriented, not goal-oriented; this makes sense as, obviously, you do not have a clear goal yet. By employing these methods, you are taking a step towards achieving it. Pre-writing is an especially worthwhile activity in the traditional linear model since it may help generate the points that will bring you closer to a thesis statement and, possibly, an outline of your main points.

Although pre-writing techniques work similarly, they have unique differences and may be useful for particular kinds of essay. Questioning is often a good strategy for expository essays in the sciences and social sciences where your hypothesis can be framed as a specific question or series of questions you will try to answer. Because freewriting often makes unconscious or emotional connections, it can be useful for beginning personal essays; it can also be helpful in literary essays where you might freewrite to determine which elements of the work interest you most: setting, character, point of view, or other ones. Because clustering, unlike brainstorming, questioning, and freewriting, is spatial and enables you to visualize and schematize the interrelations among your thoughts, it is often useful for starting argumentative essays, which rely heavily on logical connections. The most important thing is that you learn to work with whatever method(s) serves you best.

5.1.1 Questions and Brainstorming

Asking questions and brainstorming are tried-and-true approaches for finding out more about a subject. Although you can pose any questions, asking the traditional journalistic questions *who*, *what*, *why*, *when*, *where*, and *how* can be helpful for almost any subject, such as "roommates":

Who: Who make the best roommates?
What: What are the qualities of an ideal roommate?
Why: Why are roommates (not) necessary?
When: When is the best time to start looking for a roommate?
Where: Where can you find a roommate? Where can you go for privacy when you have a roommate?
How: How do you go about finding a good roommate? How do you get along with a roommate?

In brainstorming, you write down your associations with a subject. You can list words, phrases, or sentences. You can then begin looking for ways to connect some of the items by asking what they have in common. How can they be categorized? You can often combine brainstorming with one or more pre-writing methods. For example, if you began by asking the journalistic questions about the subject "roommates," you could brainstorm about the qualities of an ideal roommate, using the question *what?* to generate a list. You could continue to use these two methods by then asking *why* the most important qualities you listed through brainstorming contribute to a good roommate.

Although brainstorming can produce a list that looks something like an outline, the object is to come up with as many points as possible and then to connect them in some way; you don't need logical connections to begin with between any one item and the next.

In addition to listing random associations on one subject, you could set up the brainstorming session by applying different criteria to a topic. For example, using a topic like private and public health care, you could list your associations under *pro* and *con*; you could also list similarities and differences between two related items, such as two addictive substances, two movie directors, or two racquet sports; or you could divide a general category, such as contemporary music, into sub-categories and list your associations with each. These specific kinds of lists are useful when you know that your essay will employ a primary method of organization, such as cost-benefit, compare and contrast, or division/classification.

5.1.2 Freewriting and Clustering

In *freewriting*, you write for a designated period of time without stopping, usually five to 10 minutes. You can freewrite without any topic in mind and see where your sub-conscious leads you, or you could begin with a specific subject or topic, though you may well stray from the topic and talk about something else. That's okay. You don't censor or edit yourself, or concern yourself with spelling or grammar. You are concerned with flow and process and shouldn't worry about mechanics or content. In some freewriting, you don't use any punctuation or capital letters: you just write without lifting your pencil from the page. Many people, though, prefer to use punctuation occasionally and to write mostly in sentences. The important principle is that you do not stop. If you can't think of anything to say, you write something anyway, such as "I can't think of anything to say," "what's the point in this?" or even "blah, blah, blah" until another idea or association comes to you.

If you enjoy freewriting and find it beneficial, you can follow it with a looping exercise. In *looping*, you underline potentially useful words, phrases, or sentences; then, you choose the best one to focus on as the beginning point for more freewriting. You can also take the most useful phrase, sum it up in a sentence, and begin freewriting using the sentence as a starting point. Although freewriting is a popular pre-writing strategy, you can use it at any point in the composing process—if you get stuck on a particular point or experience "writer's block" when drafting your essay.

Freewriting has several functions:

- It can free you from writer's block. A typical problem in beginning to write is feeling you have nothing to say; freewriting can "break the ice."
- It enables you to express undiscovered feelings and associations; in other words, it gives you access to an area of your thinking or belief you might not have known about.
- Included with looping, it can help you narrow down a topic and, sometimes, come up with a thesis and main points.

Two freewriting examples follow. The first, the result of 10 minutes of freewriting in which the writer chose the topic "inspiration," shows how, through a series of stops and starts, doubts and questions, the writer arrives at an insight about herself and what she values. In the second shorter example, the writer discovers a potential thesis for an essay.

How can a person get inspired? On many occasions I have found myself in front of a perfectly blank page. I stare at the ridges the fine lines that are created by the drying process the paper undergoes the fine blots of perhaps ink or some sort of goop that you constantly see in recycled paper (which I hope is just ink and try not to think about toilet paper and how it too gets recycled and put with the rest of it. Then I stop and think about the environment and say well, things could be worse). So how does a person get inspired? Will the change of pencil to ink make a difference? Does a person think about all the goals they have to accomplish then panic when their mind draws a blank? Does it happen often? I believe so my experience has taught me that my mind does not work like most minds. It is unorganized, it speaks to itself (yes I often do find myself talking when no one is around). So you can now see how hard it is to get inspired with a mind like that. Can I inspire someone else? Perhaps! Do I have a source of inspiration? Not at the moment! And here I am writing nonsense and trying to just think (this isn't worth part of my grade). I'd say that most students do just that. They probably stop and think about how much it will count in their final grade and from there they give their time a value. "Is this worth an all nighter?" So how does a person get inspired? At some point, someone must have stopped and thought about this, maybe even written a book. You see for a person like me it's not a question of time for writing. It's more of the breakthrough that inspiration gives and also the research I conduct in order to receive this inspiration. After all this ranting I have found my source of information. RESEARCH. Now I can worry about the time I've wasted just thinking about that. Trying to build a five-paragraph essay with proper grammar and spelling.–I.H.

The following is a sample of a five-minute freewriting exercise. When the time was up, the student was asked to underline anything he thought was usable. In this case, five minutes of writing yielded an interesting topic that was complete enough to serve as a thesis statement (shown by double underlining):

Bureaucracy can be very disturbing you can get parking tickets even when there is no parking left and you are forced to park by the yellow line and you think you'll be gone early enough in the morning where was the bureaucracy when you needed them to make the decision in the first place and it can also lead to you having to take english 100 over again because you didn't get the B- required for the elementary post-degree program even though you feel your writing should be at least a high B or A average and the teacher says just be more clear and some comma errors and gives you a mediocre mark who's to say that the best teachers are the ones who get the A average because I think the best teachers are the ones who know what it's like to struggle because they have learned hard work and they have also learned patience these two things are the most important things being a teacher or they are up there anyway–Y.M.

Y.M., who chose to freewrite on "bureaucracy," began with a complaint about parking, which triggered another complaint, concerning his mark in a previous English course. He continued to follow this train of thought as he complained about how the teacher had marked his writing. This led him to consider the qualities of a good teacher, which, he discovered, have nothing to do with marking or education but with the idea of having to struggle and overcome obstacles. Y.M. could then proceed to test the validity of this claim by finding evidence to support it.

Clustering, or mapping, is an associative technique that is represented graphically rather than linearly. On a blank piece of paper, you circle your subject and then think of related words or phrases, which you record and circle, connecting each with the word or phrase that gave rise to it. Using the clustering method can help you develop your main points and provide a structure for your essay. Unlike questioning, brainstorming, and freewriting, in clustering you form distinct clusters of related words and phrases, which may be developed into main points. You can often see other relationships between circles in one cluster and those in another. In the example, below, dotted lines represent other possible connections.

The following is the result of a group clustering exercise that began with the subject *vitamins*, and produced this thesis statement: *Due to media hype and the promise of good health, more people than ever are taking vitamins before they really know the risks involved.* The statement needs further work, but it is a solid start.

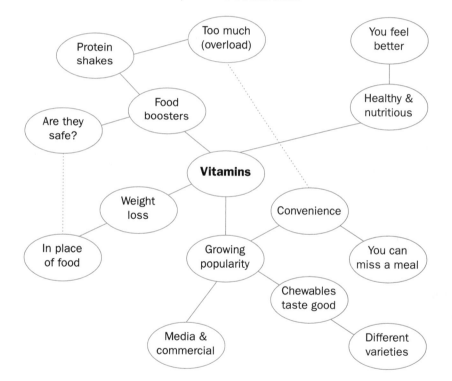

5.2 Research

If your essay is to be research-oriented, you will do most of your research in a library or in a similar environment where you have access to written and electronic material. However, not all research is library research because not all evidence is garnered from secondary sources; personal interviews and personal observation can be carried out elsewhere. Also, research may involve determining what you already know about a topic and consolidating this information or adapting it to your particular topic. Research is indispensable to university-level reading, thinking, synthesizing, and writing. For a detailed analysis of research methods, see Part Five.

5.3 Organization

Students rightly associate organization with outlines. Knowing how to construct a usable outline is a valuable skill that can save time: referring to your outline in the drafting stage can prevent you from getting off-track. As outlines give you a specific plan, they can be reassuring, instilling confidence as you draft your essay. Three kinds of outlines are discussed below: scratch, formal, and graphic outlines:

5.3.1 Scratch (or Sketch) Outline

A scratch (or sketch) outline represents only your main points, usually just by a word or phrase. Scratch outlines provide a rough guideline and give you flexibility in developing your points. They can be used for discovery drafts, where the purpose and most of the essay's substance are unknown; they may also be perfectly adequate for short essays; as well, they are helpful for planning in-class essays where limited time can make formal outlines impractical.

5.3.2 Formal Outline

The formal outline includes sub-points as well as main points, so you are able to represent more of your essay's organization. Formal outlines clearly show relatedness through their hierarchical arrangement; you can see at a glance how the parts interrelate—which is especially useful in longer essays and in those employing a complex structure, such as compare-and-contrast or research essays. Formal outlines are also a good choice for writers with underdeveloped organizational skills, or a lack of confidence in these skills, since the outline can be used to remind them of their original plan; graphic outlines may be a viable alternative for these writers as well.

Most formal outlines reveal the relationships among the different elements through the use of co-ordination and subordination. Co-ordinate (equal) and subordinate (not equal) elements are shown through the numbering system common to formal outlines:

> Generally, you need to divide every category into at least two sub-categories, so you never have only one sub-point under a main point in a formal outline.

```
I.
     A.
     B.
          1.
          2.
               a.
               b.
II.
     A., etc.
```

Points I, II, III, etc. are co-ordinate or equal, as are sub-points A, B, C; 1, 2, 3; etc. However, sub-points A, B, and C are subordinate (not equal) to main points I, II, and III, just as 1, 2, and 3 are subordinate to A, B, and C.

The first level (main) points are not indented, but each successive level is indented one or more spaces from the previous level. An outline comprised of main and sub-points is a two-level outline; one comprised of main points and two levels of sub-points is a three level-outline. It is not usually necessary to go beyond three-level outlines unless the essay is very long or one point has considerable development.

Formal outlines can be divided into **topic outlines** and **sentence outlines**. Topic outlines show paragraph topics and their development, usually through just a word or phrase. Sentence outlines show more detail and use complete sentences in parallel format. Student writers are often asked to submit formal outlines either before or when they submit the final version of their essays. Formal outlines can be compared to an engineer's blueprints, revealing how a structure is to be put together. For examples of formal outlines, see Part Two, Section 3.4 and Part Four, Section 9. An example of a two-level topic outline follows. This outline was used as the basis for a student essay, the final draft of which appears in Part Five, Section 14. Inevitably, the writer made a few changes when he drafted the essay.

Topic Outline for Creatine: An Effective Ergogenic Supplement

Tentative thesis: to evaluate recent findings concerning the use of oral creatine supplementation to improve muscular strength and power, improve speed, and decrease necessary recovery time.

I. Introduction
    A. Brief history of its use
    B. Explanation of how it works
II. Decreased Recovery Time
    A. Physiological explanation
    B. Studies supporting conclusions
III. Increased muscular strength
    A. Training effect
    B. Physiological explanation
    C. Studies supporting conclusions
IV. Increased speed
    A. Physiological explanation
    B. Studies supporting conclusions
V. Possible costs of creatine use
    A. Findings from research
    B. Anecdotal evidence
VI. Conclusion
    A. Summary of main points
    B. Recommendations for use

5.3.3 Graphic Outline

Graphic outlines show connections through spatial, rather than linear relationships. A flow chart is a kind of graphic outline used to represent complex, multi-layered plans or procedures. For example, it can show the sequence to follow in a scientific experiment or can be used to clarify the steps in a procedure in which many variables are involved, such as the steps in approving a loan or conducting a survey. Graphic outlines are especially useful for writers who work best with visual aids. One way to construct a graphic outline is to put your main points in rectangular boxes, using vertical arrows to show the order of the points; horizontal or diagonal arrows can show sub-points or support.

Graphic outlines typically look more like working outlines than formal outlines do. As needs are redefined, changes can be shown through arrows, parentheses, crossings-out, or additional boxes (or other shapes). You can think of graphic outlines as temporary road signs, aiding and guiding the traffic of your thoughts while construction is ongoing.

The example below applies a graphic outline to the topic of this section: the stages of essay-writing. Vertical arrows represent the sequence of stages (the main points), while horizontal arrows indicate sub-points: composing choices for writers. The two-pointed arrow shows the interrelationship between questioning and brainstorming discussed in Section 5.1.1. The parenthesis around "research" indicates that research may or may not be part of the composing process; finally, the vertical arrows under "final draft" show that each activity in the circle is performed in the order indicated. The arrows, then, show sequence, while the use of ovals, rather than rectangles, calls attention to the fact that "re-seeing," "editing," and "proofreading" are not to be treated as major stages like "pre-writing," "outlining," "first draft," and "final draft." Graphic outlines must be logical but, as mentioned, can be customized to reflect the writer's needs.

All outlines written before or during the first draft should be considered working outlines in the sense that they may change as your thinking changes or as you come across new evidence. Outlines should be considered organizational aids, which can be altered or adapted—not just as ends in themselves. Although formal outlines are most beneficial when followed closely, they should never impair spontaneity. Using outlines successfully is a matter of adopting a flexible attitude towards them and becoming familiar with your own unique composing processes.

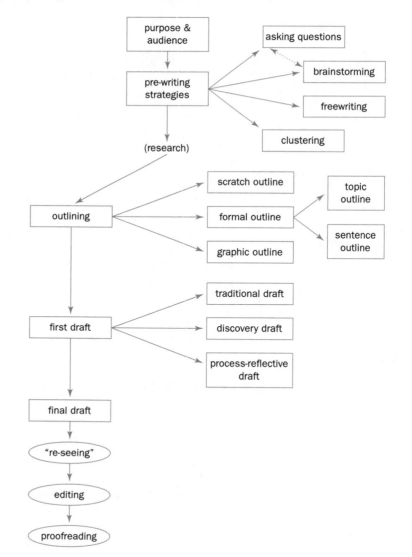

5.4 Composing: First Draft

Getting words on paper in sentence and paragraph form is the most challenging stage for most writers. The different approaches to writing the first draft have been discussed above at Section 2, The Composing Process. Your traditional rough draft is based on your outline; your discovery draft uncovers your thoughts on a topic and your purpose in writing; your process-reflective draft is really an "essay-in-progress" that develops incrementally towards a form more finished than in either the traditional or discovery draft.

In first drafts, student writers should not be overly concerned with grammar, spelling, punctuation, or citation format (if you have done research). Your focus should be on setting your ideas down. In the case of the essay-in-progress, though, you may sometimes find yourself rearranging sentences, providing transitions, or working on other "road-clearing" activities to eliminate obstacles to clear thinking. If you find it difficult to paraphrase (summarize in other words) something you've written, your thinking may not be clear about that point and you should consider revising it.

5.5 Revising: Final Draft

The final draft probably is the most frequently undervalued stage of the writing process. Many student writers think that the final draft is the place to apply the few necessary touch-ups that essays inevitably require. They may have assumed they were supposed to "get it right the first time." However, professional writers almost never do, so why should this be expected of student writers?

Remember that most first and second drafts are essentially rough efforts to put the essential components of your thinking into words. To change the rough into the smooth requires a new focus: *on the written document*. When you revise, you want to build on its strengths. This process could involve any or all of the following:

- **O**verview of purpose and audience
- **S**olidifying structure
- **U**nderscoring ideas
- **C**larifying meaning
- **F**ine-tuning

You can reorder the initial letters above to make the acronym FOCUS as an aid to memory.

5.5.1 Overview

Conduct an overview of purpose and audience, which involves looking again at your original objectives. Ask yourself honestly whether the essay fulfils the purpose for which it was designed and whether it speaks specifically to your intended audience. Reassessing your original objectives seldom leads to major changes but may necessitate a shift in focus in your introduction or minor alterations in the body of the essay. For example, you might find a point that seemed relatively unimportant in your outline turned out to be very important: you might need to rewrite a part of the

Before deleting material that doesn't seem to belong in the paragraph, see if you can move it to another part of the essay for a better fit.

introduction to be consistent with the revised emphasis. On the other hand, you might find that you have over-developed a point that is only slightly related to your thesis, so that you decide to delete a part of a body paragraph. You might also now find that your choice of words was occasionally too informal for your audience and that you need to eliminate colloquial (informal) expressions.

5.5.2 Clarifying Meaning

Try reading complicated or unclear parts of the essay aloud. Will the members of your audience understand your meaning? Potentially ambiguous passages should receive your close attention. Wherever a sentence seems awkward or just overly long, consider rephrasing and restructuring for directness and clarity.

It is hard to attain an objective perspective when you look back at what you have written, especially if you have just written it. Allotting some time between the completion of the first draft and your revision will enable you to see your essay more objectively. Also, getting someone else to read over your paper can give you valuable input, especially if he or she can point out unclear passages. Seeing the places where other people have difficulty will highlight those specific places for close attention. The problem may be as small as a word out of place or one that means something different from what you thought. Such seemingly small errors can obscure the meaning of an entire sentence and affect the impact of a paragraph. Work on these specific passages if you find they are unclear or awkward.

5.5.3 Underscoring Ideas

The body paragraphs will convince the reader of the validity of your thesis and of the soundness and thoroughness of your support; here your main ideas are introduced and developed. Reviewing your body paragraphs might mean going back to your notes, outline, or early drafts to see if you can further support an idea that now strikes you as undeveloped. Or, you might include an example, illustration, or analogy to make an abstract or general point more concrete and understandable. The question to ask is if all your points are as strong as they could be.

What if you now see that a point is underdeveloped but you don't know how to go about developing it further at this stage? Remember that pre-writing strategies can be used at any point in the process; their main purpose is to generate ideas. Try a brief freewriting session (or whichever method works best for you) to help you expand on the undeveloped point.

5.5.4 Solidifying Structure

In order to solidify your structure, return to your outline. Does your essay's structure reflect your original plans for it? Do you see any weaknesses in the outline you didn't see before? Can the structure of the essay be made any more logical or effective? If the essay's structure seems strong, look at each paragraph as an essay in miniature with a topic sentence, full and logical development of the main idea, and a concluding wrap. Not all paragraphs need to be constructed the same way, but all paragraphs do need to follow a logical sequence. Is the paragraph unified and coherent as well as adequately developed? Are paragraphs roughly the same length, or are some conspicuously short or long?

Some writers feel discouraged when they re-read what they have written. That is why it helps to think in the comparative degree rather than the superlative degree when you revise: you want to make your essay strong*er*, clear*er*, and *more* readable. When writers make changes to their drafts most often it is not because their early drafts were wrong or defective in some way but because on reflection they discover better ways to say what they wanted to say. After all, you know much more about your topic now than you did at any other stage in the composing process.

5.5.5 Fine-Tuning

While working on the final draft could involve some large-scale adjustments it will almost certainty involve some small-scale ones. In the first stage of final drafting, focus on large, "global" concerns. The second stage—editing—shifts the focus to the sentence and to individual words. This means you need to ensure that each sentence is grammatical, that your expression is clear and concise, and that appropriate transitions are provided between sentences. You can also refine your style, asking, for example, if there is enough sentence variation: can you combine sentences to produce more complex units, or can you use different sentence types to make your prose more interesting? Finally, the mechanics of presentation should be double-checked during the editing stage. The third stage is the final review—proofreading for mechanical errors and typos. For a full treatment of efficient writing and editing strategies, as well as proofreading guidelines, see Part Eight.

6. Kinds of Essays

Essays can be classified according to the traditional ways of organizing information for written or verbal communication. These are known as the **rhetorical modes of discourse**: **argument, exposition, narration,** and **description**. Because argumentative and expository essays are discussed in detail, they will be introduced here briefly. Narration and description are discussed more fully in Part Three, Section 1.1, Rhetorical Patterns, as well as briefly below.

6.1 Expository versus Argumentative Essays

Often, expository writing is contrasted with persuasive or argumentative writing. Exposition explains; argument persuades your audience to change its mind or see your point of view. Whereas argumentative essays rely partly on facts to present as strong a case as possible, expository essays may not use argument at all. An expository research essay in the sciences, typically, will not state the writer's opinions (if it does, it will be considered an argumentative essay); its conclusions will result from the use of fact-based sources of information, such as scientific studies. There may be an element of argument involved or implied, but the essay will take an objective stance towards issues of argument. An expository essay may consider different or contrary views on a controversial issue without entering into the debate and taking sides—the result will be an expository and not an argumentative essay. Once the writer takes sides, the essay becomes argumentative.

Sample topic for an expository essay:

> How the skeletal evolution of the penguin enabled it to adapt to an ocean environment.

Sample topic for an expository essay that might use some argument:

> What we can do to alleviate the impact of global warming on the Emperor Penguin habitat on Roosevelt Island.

Do you think that this topic implies an argument? How do you think argument might be involved—either directly or indirectly?

Sample topic for an argumentative essay:

> Nations must act quickly and collectively to put an end to global warming, which is destroying penguin habitats in the Antarctic sub-continent.

Verbs like *must* and *should* usually signal argument.

6.2 Narration

Narration orients the subject in time. If you recall the excerpt by Alice Munro, you will see that the writer is telling a story. That is what *narrative* does: it tells about something that has happened or is happening, relating incidents (usually, but not always, chronologically) and often revealing character. The narrative pattern is commonly used in fiction and in personal essays; it can be used selectively in fact-based essays as well. A literary essay analyzes literature, but generally aspires to the objectivity of a fact-based expository essay.

6.3 Description

Description is spatial; it orients the reader in space, giving concrete information, primarily about what is seen, but it can also make use of the other senses. If you use description in an expository essay, it's important to be as concrete as possible and avoid general, abstract words or phrases.

Narration and description are often useful to convey immediacy. The discriminating use of either in factual writing can lend drama, directness, and impact to your essay. Consider the following as sample openings of fact-based expository essays:

Narrative:

Pali is five-years-old. She lives in sub-Saharan Africa in a small hut made of straw, mud, and cow manure. She lives with her two sisters, 13 and 15, and a brother, 2. She awakes at 2 a.m. Her older sister has returned home from her occupation—selling herself as a prostitute—in order to make enough to feed Pali and her siblings. She is now caring for Pali's brother who has severe diarrhoea. He has AIDS; he was born with it. Both of their parents are dead. Their father died of AIDS two years ago; their mother was beaten to death one year ago after admitting that she, too, had AIDS. Such stories are not uncommon in sub-Saharan Africa today.

Description:

Today, Victoria's Parliament Building is the symbol of BC's government, and much of the interior is jammed with modern office equipment. However, visitors can stroll around the meticulously landscaped grounds during the daylight hours and, at night, view the building lit up with its geometric array of lights outlining one of the city's architectural wonders. Interior highlights include the giant rotunda, its walls adorned with historic murals. If you are lucky, you might discover a tiny spiral staircase that leads to the top of the main dome and end up in the stately legislative library which seems to retain the musty smell of BC's past.

—Stephanie Prizeman

6.4 A Special Case: The Personal Essay

The personal essay focuses on you, the writer. Because the goal is to *express*, rather than to argue or explain, this kind of essay is also called the *expressive essay*. In contrast to typical argumentative and expository essays, personal essays may employ narration and description. A personal essay might tell a story about what happened to you or describe the way you felt about something. Personal essays use the first-person voice (*I, me, my*), but you might occasionally include dialogue as well.

The personal essay hones in on some aspect of the writer's life; thus, it could take the form of a memory, a perception, an experience, or an incident in which the writer was involved. Most published personal essays make the connection between the writer's life or thoughts and the larger world in which both writer and reader live. Effective personal essays pass the "test of relevancy": they convince the reader through use of the first-person perspective that the personal experience recorded has an important bearing on the lives and experiences of others.

The following is from an award-winning personal essay, "First Passage," by Madeline Sonik. The "ship" referred to is *The Queen Mary*. Notice how the writer addresses the reader directly. However, while she is ostensibly talking about herself throughout the essay, she is really talking about the world she was born into; one of her purposes is to acquaint the reader with this past world and to contrast it with the present world of the reader:

First Passage

By

Madeline Sonik

Imagine me, a few splitting cells in my mother's belly, a fraction of a millimeter across, an alien life form making my way down her fallopian tube in order to leach blood from her cushioned nest. It will be six weeks before my sexual identity emerges, before the XX combination of my chromosomes unfolds, before my mother starts to question the lateness of her period, the tremendous inescapable nausea of her mornings that began on the ship and didn't end for eight months. It is 1959, three years before the structure of DNA is discovered, 21 years before recombinant DNA technology will make it possible to add moth genes to tomatoes in order to prevent them bruising. In the future, there will be controversy over the speed with which genetically manufactured crops are marketed. A modified corn crop in the U.S. will prove lethal to harmless monarch butterflies. . . . But this is a problem for the future, one which my mother will not be alive to witness.

Personal essays are often an ideal starting point for student writers as they begin to work on developing their writing skills, not because they are less difficult to write than other kinds of essays, but because the writer comprises his or her own research and is thus free to work on perspective while attempting to establish his or her own distinctive voice. Personal, or expressive, essays encourage the development of an authentic inner voice; they can also be used as tools to self-exploration.

Student writers may find it easier to come up with a topic for a personal essay than for other kinds of essays; after all, personal essays are *about* the writer. For example, the classic "first day back" question "What Did You Do on Your Summer Holidays?" can be a fruitful means for exploring the relationship between the self and nature or the self and the human world.

Still, many student writers may find the prospect of talking about themselves intimidating and may initially be unwilling to "make public" a part of their own lives and experiences. The personal essay need not be "tell all." We constantly make public our perceptions, views, and experiences to friends, family, classmates, or other groups of people. To do so satisfies the universal need to be part of a community of shared experience. Personal essays are one additional embodiment of the impulse to express oneself communally and should be written within the student's range of comfort with personal expression. Essays have the advantage over some other forms of public discourse in that the writer has more time to reflect on what he or she is saying and to reconsider and revise if something does not feel comfortable.

Thus, personal essays may be utilized as a means of introducing you to the practice of academic writing or as a means in and of itself with the goal being the development, extension, or mastery of this form.

6.4.1 Sample Student Essay

The personal essay below explores one aspect of the relationship between self, nature, and humans.

How I Spent My Summer

by

Christy James

My past summer was filled with six-in-the-morning wake-up calls and little baby trees. I planted trees all summer, up in the forgotten Northern Alberta forests, where three men equipped with three machines can cut down hectares on hectares of natural habitat in a matter of days.

Just around the corner from this, the tree planters work. We work every day, driven by the same capitalistic impulse: the loggers look at a mature tree and see dollar signs; we see "creamy" flat clear-cuts, and drool. We plant through the nastiest of situations, chanting "eight, nine, ten cents" a tree. Plant one thousand, make a hundred; plant two thousand, make two hundred. We're the semi-well-paid, exploited plantation workers of Canada. We're students, willing to sell our souls and Canadian comforts for the sake of a quick, hard-earned buck. Love and destruction live simultaneously in a paradox where the good land is the land that is dead and brown.

We are tree planters. If you were to meet one of us, we'd gnaw your ear off with endless stories about what the food was like, how horrible the land was, or the rain we had to endure. We take pride in our grueling jobs. We romanticize and forget in the off season all the environmental damage we rely on for our work. In these jobs, every day, we see animals as they wander across clear-cuts triple the size of the university campus. We see moose, deer, elk and bears on a regular basis.

I was planting in my land one day, and there she was—a black bear: the "Thing" that you are warned about. I have had many kinds of encounters with many bears. I've seen them trapped on the side of the road by tourists' cameras, watched them pick at garbage in dumps, and even heard them sniffing outside my tent. This was different; this was a real bear—in the wild.

But she just looked at me, uninterested. I sang loudly to her, so she knew I was there; and I went slowly backwards, continuing my movements so I wouldn't provoke her. She just stayed where she was, sniffing my pesticide-doused baby trees. She was aware of us, knew we weren't going to harm her. She was just checking out her raped territory. At that moment, I wondered who really belonged there: the bear or myself. As she walked along the tree line and disappeared into her shrinking forest, I knew the answer.

Questions to Consider

1. What is the writer's attitude towards her job as a tree planter? Does she try to justify or excuse the damage that is done by clear-cutting? Why or why not?
2. How does the language she uses (for example, "We're the semi–well-paid, exploited plantation workers of Canada") demonstrate her attitude to her work? Find other examples of words and phrases that express strong views. How do such word choices affect your opinion of the writer and her essay?
3. Why does the writer devote so much of the essay to a description of her job and comparatively little to her encounter with the bear?
4. Write a 300–500 word personal (expressive) essay on one of the following topics, ensuring that the incident or experience you describe is about you but that someone who is *not* you could relate to it.

   a. What you did on your (summer, winter, spring) break?
   b. A surprising discovery you made about someone you thought you knew well.
   c. The time you did something you really didn't want to do.
   d. The funniest or most embarrassing incident in which you were involved.
   e. An incident that took place in the natural world that showed you something about nature, yourself and/or the world you live in.

6.5 The In-Class Essay or Examination Essay

Inevitably, you will have to do in-class writing, at least occasionally, during your academic career. Typically, this kind of writing will be timed, and you will be evaluated on the basis of your success in accomplishing the assigned task; you will be called on to demonstrate both your knowledge of a subject and your writing skills. You may be permitted access to a text, to notes, or to a dictionary; or it may just be you, your pen, a few sheets of paper, and a writing surface—possibly a cramped one.

In some respects, this kind of situation is artificial. Where but in a college or university classroom are you compelled to sit immobile for up to three hours as you urge your reluctant pen across a piece of paper in pursuit of the "best" answer? At the end of the time allotted, your answers will be analyzed and a grade assigned—a grade which, possibly, will affect your future. This scenario is a recipe for stress.

Although in-class writing—especially exams—might be considered a necessary evil for many, they serve several practical purposes. They evince a kind of life skill, demonstrating your ability to think, read, and write under pressure. Although they usually test your recall, they also often test other less apparent but important qualities, such as organization and time management, discernment and adaptability—even, possibly, creativity and imagination.

6.5.1 Recall

Whether the discipline is English, history, anthropology, biology, or business, in-class or examination essays will require you to remember information from lectures, textbooks, and discussions; however, there are other factors that may also be crucial. Preparing to write an essay can be different from preparing to be tested on factual material as in a short-answer or multiple-choice exam. Although you may not be required to cite dates and biographical details of a writer whose work you have studied in an English class, in history, you may need to know these kinds of facts. However, being familiar with the *terminology* of your discipline is *always* vital. That doesn't mean you need to be able to write as if you had studied the field for years, but that in your answers you should be able to communicate effectively in the language of the discipline. For example, if you are writing an English literature exam, you will need to be able to understand and refer to terms used to analyze prose, poetry, and drama.

One thing that is true across the disciplines is your need to be aware of *basic principles, procedures, and methods stressed throughout the year*. If you are asked to write one or more essays, you will need to know the rudiments of essay format and structure. If you are asked to write a summary of a text, you will need to know how to summarize; if you are asked to write a critical response to an essay you have not seen before, you will need to know what critical and analytical resources to bring to bear on a reading—based on your classroom experience throughout the year.

Even if you know that memorization will be important for the exam, you will not be able to remember everything. Allowing enough time for a complete and leisurely review of your notes, the course texts (especially highlighted sections), and instructor comments on term essays and tests will help you distinguish the essential from the less-than-essential and enable you to focus on what you need to know. Although it's important to have a grasp of certain facts and details related to the course, essays more often test the *application* of a few facts than the sheer volume of your recall. Use whatever methods you're comfortable with in committing these basic facts to memory: writing out important material, reading critical points aloud, making personal associations, using verbal or visual aids, or using self-testing strategies—all can be effective methods of study and reinforcement.

Write It...Say It...
Imagine It...Experience It...
Picture It...Draw It...
Test It...Repeat It...
Understand It

6.5.2 Organization and Time Management

A simple truth is that the few minutes you spend in planning your approach to the questions are often worth much more than any equivalent amount of time supposedly saved by diving right in. The advantages are two-fold: beginning the in-class assignment with a general plan is necessary so you can ensure you will write a complete exam with all the parts apportioned according to the exam instructions; second, planning the exam will give you a sense of control over circumstances that, otherwise, have been determined by someone else.

Once you have decided how the exam will be divided up and how much time should be spent on the various parts, stick to your plan. It's common to run over the time allotment for the first question; if you find yourself doing this, it's best to jot one or two points in the margin or on another piece of paper, if you're allowed rough notes, which you can follow up on, time permitting.

Do you begin with the longest question, the shortest question, the hardest or the easiest question, the one worth the most marks or ones worth fewer marks? Opinions vary on the best starting point, but it's probably safest to begin with the question you feel most comfortable with. Writing a confident answer can make you feel at ease when responding to the other questions.

It might seem too obvious to say that you should read the general exam instructions carefully before beginning, but it's surprising how often students, in their urge to start, fail to do this. Read every word and underline key words or phrases to reinforce their importance and to keep them in mind as you write. Of course, the same applies to each question (see Discernment and Adaptability, below). Remember that writing skills are connected to reading and thinking skills. The person setting the in-class essay or exam can legitimately argue that the student who misreads a question and writes a response based on this misreading, or on a superficial reading, has not truly understood this interconnectedness. Furthermore, the student who misreads loses credibility as a writer; he or she has not demonstrated the ability to follow directions. This is especially important when the question makes a qualitative distinction of some kind: "answer three of the following five questions"; "respond to *either* question one *or* question two." Also pay attention to the verb used to introduce or frame the question or topic; *discuss*, *compare and contrast*, and *explain* give you three different instructions.

Finally, plan to allow at least five minutes per question (more if possible) to look over the exam after you've finished writing, to ensure that nothing has been omitted and that the marker will be able to follow your ideas. Final checks and careful proofreading are important at this stage—so, also, are small additions, such as those providing transitions in language and thought. A final, thorough check will likely be more beneficial than the scrambling effort to give as much information as possible before time expires. Furthermore, instructors prefer to read a thoughtfully revised and carefully proofed essay, even one that has some deletions and a couple of arrows, to one that is meticulous-looking but unclear in places. Neatness is important, but completeness and accuracy are more so.

6.5.3 Discernment and Adaptability

Once you have done the necessary preparation for writing and are focusing on the individual question(s), you need to

1. distinguish what is important from what is less important and
2. adapt the question, if necessary, so you can bring forward strong, well-chosen points and provide support for these points.

If the question is already specific, this second step may not be necessary. In the sample essay question below, the writer has underlined the important parts of the question and has already begun to shape his answer by attempting to rephrase or elaborate on the question. At this stage, he is essentially looking for clues, hints, and suggestions for writing his response.

Before he can proceed from topic to thesis statement, he has to decide on his approach to the subject. The subject of discrimination is very large, and if he does not put some thought into limiting it, he may find himself becoming too vague. One of the common weaknesses of in-class essays is the tendency to generalize, to be too broad. Therefore, first limiting the topic, finding a distinct area to make your own, will result in a more manageable essay.

When you limit or refine a general topic, you want to achieve *focus* and intensity. What do you personally know about the topic? Have you or anyone you know had experience with it? How can you relate the topic to your own knowledge base, your skills area? Finding where you are knowledgeable is the key to refining the topic in order to use your demonstrable strengths to best effect.

All essays will benefit from examples and illustrations. They not only are a form of evidence that will give you solid support for your points but also turn the general and abstract into the concrete and specific. Key, or representative, examples are particularly useful in in-class essays because you can build on them, using them to structure your essay as you expand on the representative qualities of your example.

The student who wrote the essay below was given 90 minutes, enough time to brainstorm, to develop an approach to his topic and a thesis statement, and to prepare a scratch outline. Using recall, effective time management, discernment, flexibility, and bolstering his points through many examples, he was able to write a successful paper under stressful exam conditions. Of course, you may not be given this much time to write an in-class essay; as a result, you might not be able to develop each point as thoroughly as this writer has done. For another example of an in-class essay, see Part Three, Section 2.1.1.

6.5.4 Sample Student In-Class Essay

Exam question: Although Western cultures have striven to identify and eradicate many of the more obvious faces of discrimination today, subtle and covert forms of discrimination, particularly racism and sexism, exist in our lives, which can be activated by day-to-day circumstances. Discuss this form of discrimination as you believe it exists today.

Student's Response: Although Western cultures have striven to identify and eradicate many of the more obvious faces of discrimination today, subtle and covert forms of discrimination, **(i.e., that are not acknowledged by society)** particularly racism and sexism, exist in our lives, which can be activated by day-to-day circumstances **(this makes them escape everyday notice)**. Discuss this form of discrimination **(i.e., hidden subtle forms)** as you believe it exists today **("believe" suggests that I can use opinion—as long as it is supported by facts and examples)**.

by Jon Zacks

Although racism is often not expressed overtly today, it is still very much alive. The fact that it often takes subtle forms makes it no less harmful; in fact, it could be considered more harmful. Our society has embraced a dominant ideology, which, while it accepts and tolerates "others," continues to affirm white, middle-class males as the power bloc. This is particularly obvious in the media, in politics, and in the critical standards promoted by academia.

Discrimination in the media is perhaps the most difficult form to see, and thus to attack. However, an attentive viewer will realize just how pervasive it is. Perhaps the best examples can be found in film and television culture. Dominant cinema is one of the most powerful ideology mechanisms in contemporary North America. In film, no representation is ideologically neutral. Rather, mainstream cinema is laden with the hegemony that is encoded into the images we see. Films such as the *Die Hard* trilogy and *Indiana Jones* are examples of this. In these films, the white male hero saves the world from the disorder caused by the "others." Using binary oppositions, these "others" are set up as inferior and threatening to our comfortable existence.

Of course, it is not only the fictional in media that serves to promote this dominant ideology. Contemporary news media is rife with hegemonic treatment of public events. Never has this been more evident than after the terrorist attacks in New York City in September 2001. The media immediately set the terrorism up as the work of radical religious fanatics, Arab extremists, and anti-capitalist fundamentalists. By setting the terrorists up as others, retribution is justified. As well, national security is once again promoted by showing that these others live elsewhere and will be contained. The dominant ideology was thus served by "othering" the Islamic Arabs, and glorifying the (mostly white male) heroes at home. While there have been objections to the mistreatment of minorities in the US, the media has conveyed the message that these minorities must be accepted (superficially) because they are now American. The fact that the media is so successful with this hegemony also suggests that this latent racism is present not only in the powers that be but also in society itself.

In politics in general, this hegemony is promoted. The incidents since September 11 have shown American politicians trying to accommodate minorities while essentially serving the interests of the majority. Indeed, this is typical of politics in general. We can see regular occurrences of governments making changes to the system so that minorities will feel less oppressed. However, these changes are mere concessions. What is becoming obvious is that the entire system is built on discrimination, power, and patriarchy. This system must make concessions to accommodate the oppositional voices and avoid losing power. It is not until people realize that the system is indeed built on subjection and patriarchy that true changes can be made.

A final example of discrimination can be seen in academia. Areas such as art history, history, and cultural studies provide examples of discrimination within the educational and academic worlds. For example, History in Art has long been viewed as essentially a history of Western Art. Most of us are familiar with the works of great European artists of the Renaissance, etc. Indeed, this art has become the canon of art. While almost everyone knows of the Mona Lisa, very few people are aware of any Aboriginal, African, Indian, Chinese, Japanese, Mesoamerican or Native art. Many see the Mona Lisa as the greatest painting created. By contrast, we often see Native American art as ugly or primitive. Western arts have the support of art critics, who endorse the concepts that mainstream art is beautiful, while oppositional art is just that: oppositional. Not until these marginalized art forms are viewed as equal can they stand alongside dominant art. There are many people who would argue that Native arts, for example, have been accepted in Western culture. However, they have not been *truly* accepted. Rather, it has been an egregious fetishization of marginalized culture. We buy Native arts because we see them as novel and feel good about having a Roy Henry Vickers (a Native-American hybrid) beside a Picasso or a Renoir.

Western culture continues to endorse the discriminatory hegemony that has plagued it since oppositional voices first began demanding acceptance. Our culture has heard these voices, and rather than changing the very structure upon which it has been built, it has made superficial concessions. As media and culture have shown, oppositional voices are tolerated, but they are still marginalized. It is not until we deconstruct our culture and realize that it is founded on discrimination that this discrimination can be eradicated. And, as always, the hardest thing to fight is complacency. If someone is not aware that the system is unjust, there is no reason that he or she would realize that it needs to change.

Questions to Consider:
A. 1. How did the writer limit the topic? Do you think he has an area of expertise or specialization that he was able to use to adapt the topic to capitalize on his knowledge?
   2. Identify the thesis statement and the main points (the latter take the form of topic sentences for the body paragraphs). Why do you think he used the order of points he did?
   3. Some of the writer's statements could be contested. Do you think that, within the constraints of the in-class essay form, the writer has adequately supported his points? How has he done this? Has he failed to do this anywhere?
   4. Returning to the exam question, do you think the writer directly addressed what he was asked to address? Suggest other viable ways that a student writer could respond to the question.
B. Give yourself 90 minutes to write a 500-word response to the question.

PART TWO

Essay and Paragraph Basics

1. Introductions
2. Thesis Statements
3. Outlines
4. Paragraph Essentials
5. Conclusions

1. Introductions

Almost everything you read will begin with an introduction. It may not be called the "introduction," but it will inevitably function as an introduction by giving a preview of what will follow. The reader is greatly helped by this information—whether the document is a book, an article in a scholarly journal, a class essay, a sales proposal, or a résumé.

The kinds of introductions student writers are asked to write are made up of one or more paragraphs, and should, like all paragraphs, show unity, coherence, and development; the *specific* function of the introduction, however, is to introduce the essay.

It's useful to compare the preparations for writing the essay's introduction to the care you would take when meeting someone for the first time. Just as there are people you don't notice because they don't present themselves well, or you notice them for the wrong reasons, so there are introductory paragraphs that aren't noticed or are noticed for the wrong reasons. As one of the most important parts of your essay—some would say the *single* most important part, since ineffective introductions often mean that the essay itself won't be read—it is worth spending time on writing introductions that meet the requirements below. They will draw the reader into the essay and provide necessary information, satisfying the expectations of your audience.

1.1 Functions of Introductions

1.1.1 Reader Interest: Logical, Dramatic, Emotional

Introductions create **readers' interest.** The **logical** approach is the most common and traditional way to create interest. You begin with the general and proceed to the specific where the "specific" is your thesis statement. This is also called the **inverted pyramid** structure.

general or universal statement

more specific statement

most specific (thesis) statement

Writers of expository, argumentative, and literary essays often use this model. Logical openings enable you to situate your own approach to a topic within a larger context. In this way, you can establish the topic's relevance and where it fits in as you progressively become more specific. Your thesis statement usually will be the last sentence of the introduction towards which you have built your emphasis. In the following introduction, student writer Ian Stock begins with a general claim and gradually brings the subject into sharp focus—Laos's dependence on hydroelectric power. The pyramidal development is important for the general readers who may not know much about Laos and the topic:

> Rivers have always been a central part of civilization. From the banks of the Tigris and Euphrates was born the idea of civilization, and almost all subsequent peoples have relied on rivers for trade, transportation,

irrigation, fishing, and drinking water. The Lao of Southeast Asia are one such people, living for thousands of years in villages by the many rivers of that country. They have depended on their waterways for clean drinking water, irrigation for their crops, and fishing. The heart of the Lao river system lies in the Mekong River, the longest river in Southeast Asia. Laos is a landlocked country and is therefore doubly reliant on its rivers as a source of trade. Impoverished by war and political turmoil, Laos has turned to its rivers to provide a new, modern resource: electricity.

In another kind of logical approach, you begin by mentioning something *familiar* to the reader and proceed to the *unfamiliar*. The following opening illustrates this approach:

While the intelligence quotient (IQ) has long been a useful tool to determine one's intelligence, a new development in the study of human intellectual experience has expanded to include one's emotional state. It is called Emotional Intelligence, or EQ.

—Student Writer Chin-Ju Chiang.

The **dramatic** approach can be used in various ways: you could begin with a quotation (though citing from a dictionary is *not* a good example of the dramatic approach), a question, a personal experience, an illuminating statistic, a description of a scene, or a brief narrative, such as an anecdote.

Unlike the logical approach, here you begin with something quite specific: the object is to surprise or intrigue your reader. Advertisers and marketing specialists often use this approach to catch the attention of the reader or viewer in order to sell their product. Remember, though, that the object is to gently surprise, not to shock or startle. Although it is used more often in argumentative than expository essays, it can prove effective in some expository essays as well, as the example below illustrates. In the following paragraph, the student writer creates a scenario that enables the reader to experience an unfamiliar martial art first-hand, just as she experienced it.

Imagine a circle of adults and children dressed in white pants with different coloured cords around their waists. Everybody is clapping and singing in an unfamiliar language—entranced by what is unfolding within the circle. Musicians are playing drums, tambourines, and an instrument that looks like a stringed bow with a gourd attached. There is an inescapable feeling of communal energy within the circle. Uncontrollable curiosity lures the unknowing spectator; peering into the circle exposes two people engaged in an intense physical dialogue. Kicks and movements are exchanged with precision and fluidity, which create a dance-like choreography. What is being witnessed is called a *roda* (pronounced ho-da, it means "circle" in Portuguese). A person's first encounter with this intriguing display of physicality and grace is an experience not easily forgotten. I did not forget my first *roda*, and, consequently, I later began training in this Brazilian form of martial arts—*Capoeira* (pronounced cap-where-da).

—Student Writer Kerry Hinds

In the **emotional** approach, you begin with a claim or statement designed to arouse an emotional response. Although some of the same strategies as those mentioned above might apply, the stress here is not on surprise or directness but on the presumed underlying fund of sympathy, or shared feeling, between writer and reader.

If you use this approach, you need to ensure that the typical reader will respond in the way you wish. Emotional openings need to be sufficiently broad so that most people will share your feelings about the issue (unless, of course, you are addressing an audience that feels the way you do). Emotion-based introductions are sometimes used by those who want to alert the public to an important concern—a serious health risk or the incidence of missing children. The topic in the following example is one that many college and university students have strong emotions about; for general readers, the introduction might be considered more dramatic than emotional:

> Recently, nearly 3,000 demonstrators concerned about proposed tuition hikes in BC marched in downtown Victoria protesting the government's decision to end the tuition freeze. Though their efforts did not succeed, the protest did succeed in questioning whether education should be considered a right or a privilege, as higher education fees will make it increasingly difficult for many poorer people to afford university. In essence, an increase in tuition will divide society along the lines of wealth by increasing the influence of those who can afford the kind of education that will keep them at the top of the social and economic ladders. But raising tuition fees in BC will not only contribute to the socioeconomic stratification of society but also increase the dominance of the wealthy in academia and society at large, as well as increase the burdens on students who have to work outside of school to finance their education.

1.1.2 Other Features

Of course, an introduction could use more than one method to attract interest. The writer could begin with a question and then proceed to develop the rest of the paragraph through the logical approach. The way that you choose to create interest should be relevant to your topic, your purpose in writing, and the audience you are writing for.

Introductions serve other functions:

- To announce your topic and the main point: the **thesis statement**, usually occurring near or at the end of the introduction, gives the main point of the essay and must have two parts: the topic itself plus a comment on the topic (see Thesis Statements, below, Section 2.2).
- The often-overlooked final characteristic is that introductions not only serve to introduce the *topic* but also serve to introduce the *writer*. The introduction is the place where the reader first comes to know that he or she is in competent hands. The introduction is the writer's first chance to establish his or her *credibility*. In the introduction, the writer should present himself or herself as knowledgeable about the topic as well as a reliable and a trustworthy source. One of the ways this comes across is through good writing; another way is by appearing rational, fair, and in control.

You may notice that some academic articles don't use any of the kinds of introductions referred to above. They may begin with a direct and concise statement of the problem or purpose and may even include the study's findings in the introduction. This is often the case with scientific articles designed for those with specialized knowledge of the subject area.

Introductions often—though not always—indicate in some fashion not just the *what* of the essay but also the *how*: the method that the author plans to use to develop the main points. What organizing principle will be utilized? Examples of organizational patterns include description, narration, definition (saying what something is), chronology (time order), compare and contrast, and cause/effect, along with several other patterns discussed below under Part Three: Essay and Paragraph Development.

Writers in the academic disciplines often use a slightly different approach in their introductions since their essays, typically, are much longer and more complex than those you will write as an undergraduate. They might begin by giving necessary background about their topic; this background might include an overview of the major works in the field or the various positions relative to the topic; it might include a review of specific studies. Following this background information, the writer explains his or her own approach, usually in the form of a thesis statement. For an example of such an introduction, see the first paragraph of the excerpt from "The Worlds We Live In: Gender Similarities and Differences," by Meredith M. Kimball (Part Three, Section 2.2.3, Excerpt from Compare and Contrast Essay).

1.2 Introduction Length

In the introduction you should not *develop* your main points, but that doesn't mean that skimpy is better. Some successful introductions are quite brief; others are longer. The length of the introduction will depend partly on the length of the essay itself; it may also depend on your decision whether to include the main points of your essay (expanded thesis) or background information. For example, student writer Scott Fedyshen required a lengthy introduction to set up his points. In general, an introduction should not be more than 10–15 per cent the length of the essay, but you should check with your instructor for specific guidelines.

Anyone who has experienced the death of a loved one knows the emotional pain that can follow. When bereaved, it is common and natural to go through the grieving process as part of mourning. However, each one's grief experience will be different; there is no universal concept that defines the truly individualized experience of grief. Traditional bereavement theorists have claimed that it is necessary to deal with the emotional pain caused by a death in order to resolve one's grief (Bonanno & Field, 2001). These theorists also suggest that those who do not follow the normal grieving process are likely to experience complicated grief symptoms—in particular, delayed grief in which grief symptoms will arise later in more severe forms. However, new studies suggest that avoiding grief may be an adaptive and effective form of coping with a loss. Such studies also claim that a delayed grief construct, as suggested by traditional theorists, is invalid, and that the importance of grief counseling is minimal (Stroebe, Stroebe, Schut, & Bout, 2002). New research related to bereavement and the grieving process provides important information on acceptable ways to grieve and appropriate methods of coping. These new findings allow for better understanding of the way people handle loss.

Because the writer planned to focus on "new studies" in grief theory, he felt it necessary to summarize "traditional theories" before moving on to his thesis in the final part of the introduction. Alternatively, he could have chosen to state his thesis earlier, saving a discussion of traditional theories for the second paragraph. In this case, he chose to begin with the familiar before outlining the findings of new studies; thus, he opted for a longer introduction than if he had discussed "traditional theories" in the second paragraph.

Although the introduction should never overbalance the rest of the essay, there's no reason to shy away from including your main points and expressing them fully if the introduction seems to call for this. For example, the following thesis statement needs to be longer because it doesn't clearly convey to the reader what the main points of the essay will be. In this case, the writer needs to be more detailed and precise.

> Pets are important in that they can unify, heal, and are an unavoidable part of human nature.

In general, the introduction should be as complete as it *needs* to be but no longer than it *has* to be.

Do we know what the writer means by these items? As an expanded thesis statement that includes the main points of the essay, it is inadequate because it will likely baffle readers, not inform them.

> *Revised:*
> Pets are important in bringing people together, helping them recover from an illness or depression, and enabling them to express important human values, such as love.

1.2.1 Starting at the Very Beginning

As the introduction is such an important part of the essay, its first sentence is particularly important. Ineffective openings may be too general, obvious, too abrupt, overstated (making a false universal claim), or irrelevant:

Too General or Broad:

> In the twentieth-century, many historic events have occurred around the globe, especially in Europe, Asia, and America.

The "especially" phrase does nothing to make this assertion less broad.

Obvious:

> As population continues to rise around the world, the need for transportation will also increase.

Too Abrupt:

> First Nations' self-determination and self-government must come from within.

The previous example also suggests a strongly partisan point of view that might be quite acceptable if audience members clearly supported this kind of self-government; but it could alienate members of a general or neutral audience. It might be considered overstated.

Overstated—False Universal Claim:

Everyone these days has used a computer at one time or another.

There are many people in the city where you live who have not used a computer; there are not many claims that the "everyone" claim would satisfy.

Irrelevant, or "So What?"

Few people know that sea otters can live to the age of 15 years.

This could be an effective opening if the statement really fell into the category of "believe it or not"—but it doesn't.

Collaborative Exercise

Consider the following opening statements and what makes them ineffective, whether one of the reasons above or something else. How could you revise them to make them more effective and interesting?

1. Franz Anton Mesmer discovered hypnosis in the 1770s.

2. Although email is a modern communications miracle, it is also the biggest nuisance ever invented.

3. It is said that ignorance is bliss.

4. I guess we would all like to look like Kate Moss if we could.

5. There are many issues surrounding end-of-life treatment of terminally ill individuals.

6. Leprosy is, without doubt, the most brutal disease known to humanity.

7. Why not buy the best-made sports car the world has to offer?

8. The movement of people away from the Catholic Church today is mostly due to its teachings on issues like abortion, women's equality, and homosexuality.

9. Sports are something we all watch.

10. In all American literature, no character ever gave more thought to moral decisions than Huckleberry Finn does.

11. Most people in our society today dream of growing up, marrying, and getting a good job so they can start a family.

12. Have you ever thought what it would feel like to score the winning overtime goal in a Stanley Cup game?

Collaborative Exercise – *continued*

13. The importance of education has been reiterated many times.

14. Who was Roger Bannister?

15. The imposition of school uniforms in Canada should be carefully considered if the country truly wishes to improve the quality of education.

Writing an introduction requires time and patience. You should not feel discouraged if, after having produced an outline, you cannot come up immediately with what you consider a strong introduction. It may be best to return to your introduction *after* you've written the rest of the essay. In fact, some instructors believe that the introduction should be the last part of the essay you write.

2. Thesis Statements

Nearly all essays need a thesis statement, the main point of your essay or what you will be attempting to prove. A thesis statement has two parts: the *topic* and *the comment*. It does not just state a topic. For example, *My essay will be about life in residence at the University of the South Pole* states a topic and does not comment on it. But the thesis *Life in residence at the University of the South Pole helps prepare you for life after university* also makes a comment about the topic. *Life in residence at the University of the South Pole* is the topic; *helps prepare you for life after university* is the comment. It tells the reader how you will be addressing the topic, what your focus will be.

2.1 Kinds of Thesis Statements

2.1.1 Simple

Simple thesis statements have the two components of a thesis statement. Simple thesis statements may be sufficient for some or most of your essays. However, you should at least consider writing an expanded thesis statement for essays of more than 500–750 words. Check with your instructor for specific guidelines.

2.1.2 Expanded

Expanded thesis statements give more detail, usually by including your main points. *Life in residence at the University of the South Pole helps prepare you for life after university* is a simple thesis statement. However, it can be turned into an expanded thesis statement by including the main points:

Life in residence at the University of the South Pole helps prepare you for life after university by making you independent, by reinforcing basic life skills, and by teaching you how to get along with other penguins.

2.1.3 Indirect

In an indirect thesis statement, the main point or thrust of your argument is not explicitly stated but is implied in your introduction. Writers of expository essays do not often use indirect thesis statements, though experienced writers may sometimes use them in personal or argumentative essays. One of the best-known examples of an indirect thesis statement is in Jonathan Swift's satiric essay "A Modest Proposal," published in 1729. Swift advocates the sale of one-year-old children to the wealthy, who will buy them to eat! The "modest proposal" is designed to call attention, in an absurdly callous way, to the problem of poverty in Ireland, which Swift felt was being ignored by the wealthy.

2.2 Effective Thesis Statements

Effective thesis statements should be interesting, specific, and manageable.

Interesting: the thesis is likely to attract the reader, especially the general reader, to the topic and the essay.

Specific: the thesis isn't so general, broad, or obvious that it lacks relevance; it informs the reader about what will follow.

Manageable: the thesis sounds as if it can be reasonably explored in the space of the essay.

Exercise

A. Look at the following statement of a topic:

My essay will be on aliens.

Consider the three following thesis statements and evaluate their effectiveness using the three criteria:

It is probable that aliens exist somewhere in outer space.

It is clear that aliens have infiltrated the highest levels of the Canadian government.

Everyone is curious about the possible existence of aliens.

B. If you were asked to write an essay on the way that television influences people, which of the simple thesis statements below would be the best one(s) to use? Rate each according to whether it is interesting, specific, and manageable. Be prepared to explain your decisions:

1. Television is one of the most entertaining media.

2. Television violence is affecting children these days by increasing the number of shootings in schools.

3. Television has helped change the way we live today compared to the way our grandparents lived 50 years ago.

4. Television programming today crushes our individuality by creating a dependency that is very hard to escape from once we are hooked.

5. Television is losing its influence today thanks to the increasing popularity of the Internet.

Exercise – *continued*

6. "Reality" television shows, beginning with *Survivor*, are misleadingly named as they simply offer a new form of escape under the guise of "reality."

7. Television is a great babysitter for pre-school age children.

C. Write your own thesis statement on the topic of TV's influence, using any pre-writing technique you feel comfortable with and making sure that you include the three requirements of a good thesis statement.

D. The following thesis statements are either simple or expanded. Identify the type; if they are simple thesis statements, add detail, turning them into expanded thesis statements.

1. Regular, moderate doses of stress not only are inevitable in today's world but also can be good for you.

2. As consumers, we must keep ourselves informed about the activities of the industries we support.

3. Although poor waste management has already had a significant impact on the planet, through recycling, waste reduction programs, and public education, future damage can be minimized.

4. Education is viewed as a benefit to individuals, but too much education can have negative results.

5. Many people today misunderstand the meaning of success.

Collaborative Exercise

In groups, use a pre-writing technique to formulate a thesis statement that has all three characteristics of an effective simple thesis statement. Begin with a choice of broad subject areas, such as the ones suggested below. When each group has come up with a thesis statement and written it on a piece of paper, exchange it with another group's and have that group evaluate its effectiveness according to the three criteria. One mark should be given for a thesis statement that is interesting; another mark should be awarded if it is specific; and a third mark should be given if it seems manageable (half marks are possible). When each group has completed the evaluation process, discuss the ratings and the rationale behind them.

After each group has received feedback on its thesis statement and revised it accordingly, use another pre-writing technique to come up with three main points. Then reword the simple thesis statement so that it is an expanded thesis statement. The thesis statements can again be marked.

Possible topics: aliens, books, clothes, diet, energy, fads, ghosts, history, image, justice, karma, laughter, malls, nature, opinions, pets, Quebec, residence, science, taboos, (the) unconscious, virtual reality, waste, xenophobia, youth, Zen Buddhism.

Exercise

Read the following introductory paragraphs. Then evaluate them according to the criteria: *interesting*, *specific*, *manageable*. Underline the thesis statement. Can you suggest ways to improve any of the paragraphs?

1.

Clothing has always reflected the times, and a prime example is the bathing suit. From their most cumbersome and unattractive beginnings to the array of styles we see today, bathing suits have always reflected the lives of the women who wore them and the society in which they lived. In the last hundred years, roles of the sexes, improvements in women's rights, changes in the economy, and perceptions of body image have all played a part in bathing suit design.

—Student Writer Stephanie Keenlyside

2.

What is it about the Italian Mafia that fascinates millions of people? Could part of the answer lie in Hollywood's depiction of a 5' 9", 275-pound Italian named Bruno Francessi who drives a black Cadillac, wears $3,000 silk suits, and claims to have "two" families; or is it the way the media creates celebrity status for Mafiosi people and events? The media and film industry portray a mobster's lucrative lifestyle as the result of thoughtless killings, a regimen of violence and corruption. But to fully understand the mob lifestyle, one must understand how mobsters operate—not what they appear to be on the surface, but the structure, conduct and economic realities that created their power and enable them to maintain it. As someone who lived close to this power, I know that behind the media perception lies a fundamental belief in and adherence to a system.

—Student Writer Dino Pascoli

3.

The sport of bodybuilding has evolved considerably through the ages. Starting with muscle man competitions, it has now turned into what some would call a "freak show." Bodybuilding is a sport that requires its athletes to display their best aesthetically pleasing physiques on stage; they are judged according to specific criteria. Many factors leading up to the judging itself contribute to the outcome of the competition; for example, nutrition from whole foods and supplements, and low body fat percentage from proper diet and cardiovascular training all contribute to the success of the competitors. Steroids, too, are a major factor in professional events like the International Federation of Bodybuilders (IFBB) competitions, where athletes are not tested for drug use. Anabolic steroid abuse plays a large role in bodybuilding, often resulting in adverse health effects.

—Student Writer Mike Allison

4.

Two 20-year-old Vancouver men were street racing three years ago when one of the cars, a Camaro, struck and killed Irene Thorpe as she crossed the street. The car was going so fast that Thorpe was thrown 30 metres into the air. Both men were convicted of criminal negligence causing death. They were given a two-year conditional sentence to be served at home, put on probation for three years, and had their drivers' licenses revoked for five years. Like most street-racing tragedies, this one was preventable. Though the street-racing phenomenon has been around for decades, it is growing exponentially. Recent movies have glorified this activity, enticing young, inexperienced drivers. The increase in street racing has led to an increase in the injuries to racers, spectators, and innocent bystanders. In addition, racing often results in property damage and is associated with assault, weapons offences, and drug and alcohol abuse. To help combat this growing problem, anti-racing legislation needs to be introduced and strictly enforced. Furthermore, an education program needs to be implemented and legal racing venues created.

—Student Writer Maureen Brown

5.

Why does my cell phone not work? Why do I get radiation poisoning when I travel by plane? Why is the light switch not working? These are the kinds of questions we ask ourselves when solar flares are striking the Earth. Solar flares originate from the sun. Every eleven years, the sun switches its magnetic poles, causing the magnetic fields to twist and turn in the atmosphere above sunspots, which are eruptions on the sun's surface. The magnetic field seems to snap like a rubber band stretched too tightly. When one of these fields breaks, it can create energy equal to a billion megatons of TNT exploding. The magnetic fields seem to flip and reconnect after they break. Solar flares occasionally head towards the Earth, and even though we are 1.5 million kilometres from the sun, these flares can reach us in fewer than two days. While the Earth is experiencing a solar flare, multiple problems can occur— from malfunctions of orbiting objects to disruption in power systems and radio signals. Yet, while the flares can produce these problems, they can also create the most beautiful and unusual auroras seen around the world.

—Student Writer Nicholas Fodor

3. Outlines

3.1 The Value of Outlines

Three kinds of outlines were introduced in Part One, Section 5.3. Not all kinds of writing require an outline, but, in general, the more formal the writing task, the greater the need for an outline. Even in less formal tasks they are useful: they help clarify your thoughts, enabling you to discover order out of the chaos of jumbled thoughts; they also save you time, preventing you from getting off topic or rambling.

Using outlines effectively is really a matter of timing. You would not put together an outline without having a thesis or a central idea in mind. A formal outline would be less useful if you had not thoroughly researched your topic and decided on your main points. The outline is the skeleton from which the fleshy contours of your essay will take shape. Your audience will notice these contours and will not likely stop to think about the planning and structure that went into the essay; but in any organized and coherent piece of writing, the outline will always be apparent to anyone who looks for it. In this sense, any well-written formal document will contain an *implied outline*. Summarizing (Part Five, Section 8) is one way of discovering the implied outline in the work of another writer.

3.2 Organizing an Outline

An outline is a vertical representation of ideas and their support. This pattern is shown through a *hierarchical structure*—usually one of subordination, which literally means "the act of ordering (*ordinate*) under (*sub*)." General and introductory points are like headings; under them (*subordinate* to them), you will place ideas arising from the main points (related, less important points, expansions of the main point, examples, evidence); these can be considered sub-headings. See Part Four, Section 7; Part Five, Section 9; and Part Six, Section 6 for detailed discussions of outlines for particular types of essays.

Although outlines typically proceed from the general (main) points to the specific (sub)points, another ordering principle is also involved: *emphasis*. You can order your main points and your sub-points according to the strength of the argument presented in each. Order of points is particularly important in argumentative essays. You can begin with your weakest, or least important point and proceed to the strongest, most important point: the *climax order*. You can use the *inverted climax, or dramatic order*, beginning with the strongest point and ending with the weakest. Or you can use a mixed order in which you begin with a moderately strong argument and follow through with the weakest argument, before concluding with the strongest. The number of main points and the strength of the opposing argument are factors that can help you determine which method is best for your topic and your approach to it.

3.3 General Guidelines

1. Decide on your topic and the main point you want to make about your topic; you can use brainstorming, question/answer, clustering, or freewriting to develop ideas.
2. Divide outlines into Introduction, paragraphs for development, and Conclusion.
3. Plan for a *minimum* of five paragraphs altogether unless told otherwise.
4. Ensure you have one main idea per paragraph.
5. Divide your main ideas (points) into sub-points (at least two per paragraph) that develop the main idea.
6. Represent the relationship between main ideas and their points of development (or sub-points) graphically by indenting sub-points or, more formally, use a combination of letters and numbers (see Part One, Section 5.3.2).
7. Ensure that the main points themselves are ordered logically and effectively.

3.4 Developing an Outline with Thesis Statement

Topic: using cars versus bicycles for transportation

Brainstorming List. Check marks indicate items from the brainstorming list that were used to create the outline.

Cars

cars faster and more convenient ✓
status of having a car
    –you can drive friends
    –car pooling
people who work on their cars as hobby
expensive ✓
    –gas
    –upkeep to keep running
bad on environment ✓
    –greenhouse effect
    –global warming
    –use of valuable resources
traffic jams
    –frustration (road rage)
    –rush hour delays (time)

Bicycles

takes longer to get anywhere
    –but maybe not during rush hour
    –what if you have to bike a big distance every day? ✓
nice to take a car in bad weather
    –but park far away at the university
healthy
    –healthy lifestyle ✓
    –fitness, you'll live longer ✓
    –good for heart
    –reduce stress ✓
    –helps with mental health
save money
    –gas and upkeep ✓
elderly/handicapped can't use
most cities encourage bikes
    –build bicycle lanes
    –good for the environment ✓
    –fewer vehicles

Outline

Paragraph 1: Introduction
I.   Scenario: Describe traffic at 5 p.m. leaving Toronto.
II. Concession: Cars are faster and more convenient.

III. Thesis statement: People who drive a short distance to work or school should bicycle instead. Although a car is faster and more convenient, riding a bike is cheaper, easier on the environment, and improves your health.

Paragraph 2: The expense factor
I. Bikes save $$ compared to cars (topic sentence).
    A. There are gas and routine costs.
    B. There may be expensive breakdowns.
        1. My friend recently paid $400 for a new carburetor.
        2. With the money you save, you can buy neat things for biking.

Paragraph 3: The environment factor
I. Using bikes reduces the number of cars, which is good for the environment (topic sentence).
    A. Cars contribute to greenhouse effect.
    B. We feel good because we are helping the planet.

Paragraph 4: The health factor
I. Your health will be improved by biking (topic sentence).
    A. You will experience physical health benefits.
        1. You will keep your cardiovascular system strong.
        2. You can lose weight or maintain a healthy weight.
    B. You will live not only longer but also *better* (mental).
        1. You will reduce stress.
        2. You will feel better about yourself and gain confidence.

Paragraph 5: Conclusion
I. Concession: Bikes are not going to replace cars completely.
II. Reinforce thesis: Because it's cheaper, better for the environment and for us as individuals, the number of those using bicycles is increasing; this is a healthy trend all around and should continue into the future.

4. Paragraph Essentials

4.1 Essays and Paragraphs: Topic Sentences and Wraps

Creating effective paragraphs is as important as creating an effective essay structure and writing effective sentences. Paragraphs and essays share a *macrocosmic* structure. They both have beginnings, middles, and ends: the beginning announces what is to follow, usually in the *topic sentence* of the paragraph or the *thesis statement* of the essay. The topic sentence does not need to be the first sentence of the paragraph; it could, for example, be placed at the end, and the preceding sentences could lead up to it. Without a clear topic sentence, however, the paragraph will appear unmoored, and the points will lack force; without a clear topic sentence, the paragraph will also not be unified (Section 4.3 below).

The middle of the paragraph usually develops the main point(s), while the ending provides a satisfying conclusion. The concluding sentence may act as a *wrap*: it sums succinctly the one main idea in the paragraph. In the following paragraph, student writer Jordan Van Horne successfully wraps the main idea, which is introduced in the first (topic) sentence:

> **If speed limits were abolished on highways, the necessity for law enforcement officers to patrol the highway for speeders would be curtailed**. As a result, police chiefs might have more officers to assign to special community projects, such as MADD or drug awareness projects in elementary schools. These officers could spend their time on a variety of social and community projects that would benefit a large number of youths precisely at the time when they need this guidance. In addition, more officers could be allotted to other important areas that are typically understaffed today, such as surveillance and patrol duty to prevent drug smuggling. **Surely the presence of police in the community or their dedication to large-scale projects such as drug-smuggling would be more beneficial to public safety than having them patrol the highways**.

The difference between an essay and a paragraph is, of course, that the essay ends with the conclusion. Successfully constructed paragraphs not only provide satisfying endings to paragraphs but also lead the reader into the following paragraph. This is often done through transitions, words or phrases that provide logical connections.

In addition to their *macrocosmic* structure, paragraphs and sentences share a *microcosmic* structure through the co-ordinate and subordinate relationships of their elements. That is, within each paragraph and each sentence, the various elements are interconnected through these two kinds of relationships. Co-ordinate elements are equal elements, functioning independently within the unit (the paragraph or sentence); subordinate elements are subsets of co-ordinate elements and depend on their relationship with them. Paragraphs contain one main point and at least two supporting or subordinate points. Every complete sentence will have at least one co-ordinate (independent) element and may have one or more subordinate (dependent) elements.

Below we provide a brief discussion of unity and development, and a somewhat expanded discussion of coherence. *Paragraph and Essay Development* is discussed in a separate section following *Unity* and *Coherence*.

All paragraphs in formal writing should possess unity, coherence, and development.

4.2 Unity

Each paragraph focuses on *one* central idea, usually announced in the *topic sentence*. It's usually best to place your topic sentence very near the beginning of the paragraph, though you may want to experiment with different placements. *The topic sentence anchors thought in the sentence*, so this anchoring *could* occur in the beginning, middle, or end. The topic sentence contains the central idea. In the unified paragraph, all sentences in the paragraph relate to the main idea.

Paragraphing, however, is not a mechanical process. Although the principle of one idea per paragraph is sound and logical, it may sometimes be difficult to determine where one idea ends and the next one begins. Also, it may happen that when you revise your

Although there is no "perfect" paragraph length, some instructors will give students an ideal range—such as between four and six or seven sentences—to ensure each paragraph is sufficiently developed but not so long that it becomes complicated and hard to read.

essay you see that one paragraph is substantially longer than the others. In such cases, you can determine a logical place to divide the paragraph into two smaller paragraphs. In the outline given above (Section 3.4 above), for example, there is more detail under Paragraph 4 than under any of the other paragraphs. It may be that when the first draft is written, the writer will discover that the fourth paragraph is disproportionately long and will choose to divide it into two paragraphs, the first focusing on physical health benefits and the second on mental health benefits—a logical and justifiable division.

In the case of short paragraphs, writers should consider combining them, as short paragraphs may strike a reader as underdeveloped and simplistic. When combining short paragraphs ensure that logical transitions are used between sentences (for examples of transitions, see Section 4.3.5 below).

4.3 Coherence

It is often easy to identify a paragraph that contains more than one idea and fix it by starting a new paragraph where the second idea is introduced; but identifying a paragraph of your own that lacks coherence may be more difficult.

Someone who is incoherent doesn't make sense; someone who is coherent is easy to follow. It is the same with a paragraph: one that lacks coherence may be hard to read, and the reader may not know exactly why. The paragraph may seem confusing; the ideas might be jumbled or disconnected.

Consider in the following two examples how a professional writer and a student writer achieve coherence through balanced structures. The professional writer is speaking about the plight of today's teachers; she uses repetition of words and phrases, rhythmical patterns, and figures of speech to make her point more effective. The student writer evokes the new awareness of his friend during a camping trip after the death of his friend's grandfather; coherence here is achieved largely through the use of repetition, rhythm, and balanced structures:

> [L]iterary study today is a profession simultaneously expanding intellectually and contracting economically like some Spenserian snake. So many books, so little time; so many conferences, so few jobs. The list of articles and books to master gets longer every year, and the gap between the academic star—the frequent flyer—and the academic drudge—the freeway flyer—gets wider. Those who do not have jobs feel angry; those who do feel guilty.

> —Elaine Showalter, *Teaching Literature*

> On previous trips, we had noticed the smell of nature when we woke and filled our lungs with fresh air, but this time he noticed the smell of the water and of the rain-sprinkled flowers. We had often looked at the stars on a clear night, but this time he spoke of the deep darkness of the sky; we had always seen the ground we stepped on, but this time he saw the footsteps left behind us.

> —Student Writer Walter Jordan

There are specific methods you can use to ensure your paragraphs are coherent, or easy to follow.

4.3.1. Organizational Patterns

Use organizational patterns to achieve coherence. Coherent paragraphs often follow a distinct pattern. Paragraphs can be given a spatial, chronological, cause and effect, logical (general-to-specific or specific-to-general), familiar to unfamiliar, or other pattern. Organizational or rhetorical patterns are discussed in detail in Part Three, Section 1.

4.3.2. Logical Sentence Order

Use appropriate, logical sentence order, whether working from the general to the specific or any other pattern; if one idea does not logically proceed from the previous one, then the paragraph will not be coherent. Similarly, there may be one or more gaps in a paragraph that need to be filled in, perhaps by inserting a sentence.

4.3.3. Repetition and Synonyms

By repeating key phrases you can help the reader follow the main idea in the paragraph. While repetition enables the writer to reinforce the core idea in the paragraph, it's often advisable to think of alternative words and expressions; synonyms (words that mean the same thing as, and can therefore replace, other words) can be useful. Experienced writers consider the rhythm of the sentence, often placing the repeated words, or key words, at strategic points in the paragraph. Many writers number their main points in order to make the sequence of ideas easy to follow.

4.3.4. Parallel Structures

Experienced writers also use parallel and/or balanced structures to achieve coherence. One of the reasons why so many readers can remember the beginnings and endings of Charles Dickens's novels is that Dickens often employed balanced structures: "It was the best of times; it was the worst of times" (*A Tale of Two Cities*).

4.3.5. Transitions

When you use transitional words or phrases to connect one idea to the next, be careful to punctuate correctly. In some cases, a comma may be correct, but in many other instances, you should either begin a new sentence or use a semicolon before the transitional word or phrase; see Part Seven, Section 4.2 for the grammatical rules for joining dependent and independent clauses.

Transitional words and phrases guide the reader from one sentence to the next, signalling the relationship between them. Often, just adding the right transitional word gives the paragraph the coherence that is needed. Some of the most useful transitions are listed below:

- **Transitions of Limit or Concession**: *admittedly, although, it is true that, naturally, of course, though*
- **Transitions of Cause and Effect**: *accordingly, as a result, because, consequently, for this reason, if, otherwise, since, so, then, therefore, thus*
- **Transitions of Illustration**: *after all, even, for example, for instance, indeed, in fact, in other words, of course, specifically, such as*
- **Transitions of Emphasis**: *above all, assuredly, certainly, especially, indeed, in effect, in fact, particularly, that is, then, undoubtedly*
- **Transitions of Sequence and Addition**: *after, again, also, and, as well, and then, besides, eventually, finally, first . . . second . . . third, furthermore, in addition, likewise, next, moreover, similarly, too, while*

- **Transitions of Contrast or Qualification**: *after all, although, but, by contrast, conversely, despite, even so, however, in spite of, instead, nevertheless, nonetheless, on the contrary, on the one hand…on the other hand, otherwise, rather (than), regardless, still, though, whereas, while, yet*
- **Transitions of Summary or Conclusion**: *in conclusion, in effect, in short, in sum(summary), so, that is, thus*

In spite of their helpfulness, transitional words and phrases can be overused. Too many can clutter the paragraph and the essay; in addition, try to avoid wordy transitions as they, too, produce clutter (examples include *in spite of the fact that, due to the fact that, first and foremost, finally in conclusion, in the final analysis*).

Remember, too, that a transitional word or phrase, by itself, does not provide a link in thought—it cannot be a substitute for that link; it can only assist the reader to move from one idea to the next. As mentioned above in point 2, writers need to be careful that there are no gaps in thought and that they have written with the reader in mind. The reader needs to be able to follow the writer's logic every step of the way. In the following passage, the writer has left something out, and no transitional word alone could bridge the gap:

> Society relies on an unbiased newscast in order to gain a true perspective on current events. "Front line" employees are entering the TV news field underage and under-educated, thus often producing ill-informed reporting.

The writer has quickly moved from a generalization about the need for "unbiased" reporting to an example of one of the causes of "ill-informed reporting," but has not linked the generalization and the example One logical link would be that newscasts today are sometimes biased or ill-informed. Then the writer can proceed to give examples of or solutions to this problem; as it is, the problem has not been stated clearly.

Paragraph Exercise: Coherence

The following passage also contains a gap; provide a logical link to make it coherent.

The surprise attack on Pearl Harbor forced the US to be more aggressive in world politics. This interventionist policy has recently evolved into a policy of pre-emptive strikes on those perceived as a threat to U.S. security.

Unified paragraphs, then, refer to one central idea; in coherent paragraphs, one sentence leads logically to the next sentence. Here are two diagrammatic representations of unity and coherence in which the sentences are represented by arrows:

S1 = sentence 1
S2 = sentence 2
S3 = sentence 3
S4 = sentence 4

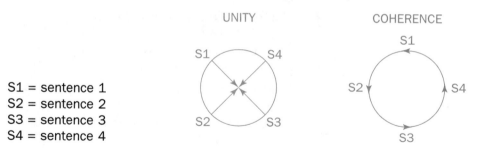

4.4 Development

Developing each paragraph ensures that the essay itself will be substantial. While the essay might use one main organizational method, it could combine different methods from paragraph to paragraph. A paragraph that utilizes one method consistently to develop its main point is likely to be coherent.

Paragraph Exercise: Unity

The long paragraph below needs to be broken up into several smaller paragraphs. Determine the natural paragraph breaks and mark where the new paragraphs should start. Remember to avoid a succession of very short paragraphs; occasionally, short paragraphs are acceptable, or even desirable, but too many of them make for choppy and disconnected writing.

In argumentative essays, defining something is often the first stage of an argument in which you go on to develop your thesis statement through means *other than* definition. On the other hand, definition essays can expand and elaborate on a subject, using a variety of organizational methods to do so. Definition often provides a necessary starting point for an argument; the success you have in getting your reader to agree with your definition will help establish your credibility as a writer and, in this way, strengthen your argument. Defining something also enables you to set the terms on which you want your argument to rest: successful definition enables you to take control of a potentially contentious, controversial, or abstract topic. Although it can be effective to use definition in argumentative essays, it can be an essential part of expository essays. Essays in the natural sciences and social sciences often begin by defining terms that the writer will employ throughout the essay; it may, in fact, be crucial for the writer to establish the sense or connotation of one or more terms that have been subject to a variety of definitions in different studies in the writer's discipline. Many academic texts—above all, introductory textbooks—include a glossary or index of common terms that is designed to make it easier to apply terms correctly. Definitions often change over time and according to place, as well as according to cultural, national, social, and other variables. For example, the way you would define privacy today would likely be different from the way it would have been defined 25 years ago, due partly to technologies that have made it easier for others to access personal information.

When you have decided on logical paragraphing, look at the way the paragraph was divided in this text (the revised paragraphs are in Part Three, Section 2.1)

Paragraph Exercises: Coherence

I.   Coherence through paragraph organization.

You can use different ways to organize paragraphs, such as from the general to the specific or the specific to the general, according to time or chronology, in spatial order (to describe a person, object, scene), by comparing and contrasting, or by the arrangement of details from the least important to most important.

Paragraph Exercises: Coherence – *continued*

A. How are the ideas developed in these paragraphs according to the methods described?

B. Besides the main organizational method(s), find other ways that the writer has achieved coherence.

They came over the land bridge connecting Asia with Alaska, those first men of the Western Hemisphere. The date was between 20,000 and 30,000 years ago. They were hunters, dressed in the skins of the animals they hunted. Their weapons were stone-tipped spears. All this was long before Homer, before the dynasties of Egypt, before Sumer and the Land of the Two Rivers, and, of course, long before the Christian Bible was written. At that time, the glaciers that covered Canada and parts of the northeastern United States during the last ice age were melting. They melted first along river valleys, which turned into great misty, fog-haunted corridors between receding walls of ice.

The hunters roamed south along those corridors, pursuing animals for food and clothing. They died eventually, as all people do, and their children came after them in the long stammering repetition of humanity everywhere. The animals they hunted were principally caribou, bear, and mammoth—the latter long since extinct in North America. Camps of those early men have been discovered recently. They are the ghostly forbears of modern Indians and Eskimos.

—Al Purdy, *Aklavik on the Mackenzie River*

C. What do you think the writer might have written about in the next paragraph?

II. Coherence through sentence order.

Combine the sentences below in the most logical order to form a coherent paragraph; one sentence is not relevant to the topic of this paragraph and should be discarded. Supply any necessary links between one sentence and the next. More than one order may be possible. Be prepared to *justify the particular order* you used to achieve coherence.

1. The disaster was caused by several safety procedures not being followed.

2. Nuclear energy power plants, although very potent and about 50 to 80 times more efficient than coal-burning plants, produce wastes that are more hazardous than those of coal-burning plants.

3. The explosion at Chernobyl not only contaminated the immediate surroundings but also contaminated areas several hundred miles away.

4. The effects of radioactive wastes are long-lasting and may affect the environment for thousands of years.

5. The disaster at the Chernobyl power plant in the Ukraine occurred in the summer of 1986.

6. A lack of respect for potential disaster led to one of the biggest human-made disasters our planet has known.

Paragraph Exercises: Coherence – *continued*

7. Nuclear energy will be able to meet the energy requirements of our society.

8. This contamination was due to the nuclear fallout.

9. Because of this disaster, a large area will no longer be habitable to human life for thousands of years.

10. Radioactive wastes are very damaging to the environment.

11. As is the case with everything on this planet, with great power comes an even greater responsibility.

III. Coherence through use of repetition, parallel structures, and transitions.

Even though a writer uses a specific organizational method and carefully orders his or her points, a paragraph may not be coherent if there are not enough appropriate transitional words and phrases to link these points. In addition, such devices as repetition and even rhythm can help achieve coherence. In the following paragraph, student writer Grace Chau uses transitional words and phrases, repetition, and balanced constructions—all of which serve to make the paragraphs more coherent. If these words and phrases were taken away, much of the paragraph would be unclear. Transitions are in boldface type, repetitions are in italic, and balanced constructions are underlined.

> **In contrast to** allopathy, in Traditional Chinese Medicine (TCM), organs are viewed as "networks"—**that is**, functional physiological and psychological domains—**rather than** discrete anatomical structures. All our organs are related; **in fact**, our body, our behavior, and the environment we are in are also interconnected. **In other words**, TCM focuses more on the *context* where the disease exists than on the disease itself. **Such emphasis** on *context* implies that the way *people* get sick and can be treated are highly personalized.
>
> *People* with different *symptoms* may have the same underlying problem, requiring similar treatments; yet *people* with the same *symptom* may need completely different remedies. While we are equally endowed with our basic *parts*, our lungs, heart, kidneys, liver, and so on, our way of co-ordinating these *parts* is individualized. **For example**, if arthritis is due to an invasion of "heat" (inflammation), it is different from the same condition with a different cause—**for example**, "cold" (reduced circulation) or "dampness" (accumulation of fluids). **In the first case**, practitioners would administer cooling herbs; **in the others**, warming or diuretic herbs would be used.

Exercise

A. Read the paragraph below to determine how the writer has used transitions and repetition to achieve coherence. Underline transitions and repetitive devices. Identify the topic sentence. One of the ways to achieve coherence is to number your points, though unnecessary numbering can add to clutter. Do you think that it was a good choice for the writer of the passage below to number his points? If so, why?

Exercise – *continued*

Critics of the World Trade Organization argue that its approach to globalization causes more harm than good because it undermines democracy. The WTO is undemocratic in several respects. First, ambassadors from member nations are appointed, not elected. Second, the coalition known as the "Quad," comprised of the European Union, the United States, Japan, and Canada, holds almost all the real power. In theory, at least, such decisions as new membership, rule changes, and rule interpretations of WTO rules should be voted for with a three-quarters majority. In practice, however, the "Quad" determines the WTO agenda. Third, WTO trade talks are held in secret to avoid public criticism and scrutiny. Furthermore, an organization that is not elected controls trade so effectively that it possesses the power to supersede the power of elected communities, states, and even nations on any issue, however ambiguous, related to trade.

—Student Writer Tao Eastham

B. Read the paragraph below to determine how the writer has used transitions and repetition to achieve coherence. Underline transitions and repetitive devices. Identify the topic sentence. This paragraph is an introductory paragraph to a chapter of a book. What topic do you think will be developed in the next paragraph? Why?

The news media's power to trivialize anything that comes to their attention is almost magical. News service advertisements talk about providing a "window on the world" or a report on "history in the making." But the nightly television newscast and the daily newspaper fall far short of these ideals. Instead, we get a fast-paced smorgasbord of unconnected and disembodied news stories where meaning and context are lost in the rapid-fire delivery of colourful prose and dramatic pictures. As a result, much of what passes for news is instead isolated, unconnected, and almost meaningless bits of information—in effect, the news is trivialized. This trivialization operates at both the structural level of news gathering and dissemination, and at the level of individual news stories. We have termed this style "the trivialization effect."

—adapted from R.A. Rutland, *The Newsmongers*.

5. Conclusions

5.1 Functions of Conclusions

Unlike the "surprise" ending of some short stories, the conclusion of an essay should have been prepared for every step of the way—both by the introduction and by the points that have been developed within the essay itself. So, if an essay contains a surprise ending, it indicates some serious structural problems in the body as well.

Conclusions should be predictable in the sense that they are prepared for, but *not* boring or merely repetitive. A conclusion that simply repeats the thesis statement may satisfy one of these requirements: it will be predictable; but it will also be redundant. It will leave the reader with the impression of a static, undeveloped argument.

In your conclusion, you need to find a way to bring the reader back to reconsider the thesis statement in light of how the thesis has been developed through your main points. So the conclusion *recalls* the thesis statement and brings it to bear on what, specifically, has been discussed in the body paragraphs.

5.2 Two Kinds of Conclusions

Introductions and conclusions are not like identical bookends with the books (body paragraphs) in between, though their primary importance is to tell and remind the reader of the thesis. Conclusions can underscore the importance of the thesis in two ways: (1) they can reiterate the thesis using different words that stress its importance, perhaps by a call to action if you are arguing for a specific policy; (2) they can suggest a specific way that the thesis could be applied, perhaps by presenting a possible scenario or asking a question that the thesis gives rise to (without necessarily answering the question). These two strategies for concluding essays suggest two fundamental patterns:

1. a *circular* conclusion: this kind of conclusion is most concerned with reminding and reinforcing;
2. a *spiral* conclusion: a spiral conclusion refers to the thesis but also leads suggestively beyond it.

A **circular conclusion** "closes the circle" by bringing the reader back to the starting point. It is particularly important if you use this kind of conclusion that you do not simply repeat the thesis statement word for word, but show how it has been proven or affirmed. A **spiral conclusion** might point to ramifications or results of the thesis or suggest follow-up research that needs to be done. Sometimes, conclusions can provide an occasion for personal reflection, such as your acknowledgement of the way that your thesis has affected you or people you know. This kind of conclusion, however, is more acceptable in personal and some argumentative essays than expository ones. If you have not used personal experience in the essay, it might be jarring to do so in the conclusion.

Conclusions often work from the specific to the general, whereas the Introduction often starts with the general and works towards the specific (the thesis statement)—the "inverted pyramid" structure.

Introduction

Conclusion

There are specific things you should avoid in your conclusion:

- restating the thesis statement word for word
- mentioning a new point; conclusions should recapitulate the old in an interesting way, not introduce something new
- giving an example or illustration to support your thesis; examples belong in your body paragraphs
- writing a conclusion that is very much longer than your introduction. Exceptions sometimes occur—especially in the sciences and social sciences where essays may end with a lengthy Discussion section.

Set your conclusion beside your introduction to check that it fulfills all the above functions of a conclusion and relates to your introduction in a satisfactory way.

Introduction / Conclusion Exercises

Consider these sets of paragraphs, which form the introduction and the conclusion for two essays. Is it clear from the introduction what the writer will be discussing? What kind of introduction did the writer use? Is it clear from the conclusion what the writer has discussed? What kind of conclusion is each writer using?

Write a brief analysis of how the two parts of the essays intersect yet, at the same time, operate independently. Consider strengths and possible weaknesses. Remember that the paragraphs should not only function as effective specialized paragraphs but also display unity, coherence, and development.

A. An expository essay; topic: a racial incident in Canada's past

Introduction:

One of Canada's most important features, which figures prominently in its self-presentation to the world, is as a peaceful nation that respects the individual and celebrates multiculturalism. The country is known for its cultural and ethnic diversity. Often, however, Canadians idealize their image and push inequality out of their presentation of their country. However, if we look carefully at the history of Canada, there have been many occasions when the clean image of national tolerance has been seriously undermined, such as in the Komagata Maru incident in Vancouver in 1914.

Conclusion:

Although much has changed for the better since the beginning of the twentieth century and Canada is justifiably proud of its diversity today, people sometimes ignore past incidents of racial discrimination. Since the Komagata Maru incident is not well-known, it is important that people hear about it so they can be aware that even in a democratic country like Canada injustice and intolerance have occurred in the past and will continue to occur unless people learn from the past and guard against such incidents.

—Student Writer Ruth Wax

Introduction / Conclusion Exercises – *continued*

B. An argumentative essay, topic: smoking and organ transplantation.

Introduction:

The atmosphere grew tense in the cramped hospital room as eight-year-old Marla looked up through frightened eyes, trying to be strong for her mother. Everyone was trying to be hopeful, but Marla instinctively knew that she would not be getting a heart transplant in time; the waitlist was long, and an organ match was unlikely. Although Marla was an otherwise healthy girl, there were others on the transplant list who were ahead of her, though not all of them had as good a prognosis. Due to the scarcity of organ donations in comparison to many in need, serious debates have arisen concerning the suitability of some potential heart and lung recipients. Some feel that everyone should have equal right to a transplant and that there should be no pre-conditions relating to what they see as lifestyle choices, such as smoking. Others advocate that smokers should be refused transplants on medical or moral considerations since smokers are more likely to experience complications after surgery. Given the current crisis of long waitlists and variable success rates, lung and heart transplant candidates should be required to quit smoking at least six months prior to surgery in order to reduce smoking-related complications and maximize transplant success.

Conclusion:

The scarcity of organ donations and the length of waitlists have placed an increasing obligation on the part of health care professionals to ensure the best outcome for their patients. Denying transplants to those who refuse to quit smoking may appear to discriminate against smokers and their lifestyle choice. However, doing so would result in better odds for post-transplant success and would involve the most efficient use of limited health care services and resources. In short, health authorities should move to institute clear guidelines on pre-surgery smoking restrictions for the benefit of both individuals and the health care system.

—Student Writer Annie Gentry

PART THREE

Essay and Paragraph Development

1. Developing Your Essay through Substantial Paragraphs
2. Essays Using a Primary Method
3. The Design of the Essay: A Two-Part Model

1. Developing Your Essay through Substantial Paragraphs

Effective paragraphs are unified, coherent, and well-developed. Unified paragraphs focus on one topic; coherent paragraphs make sense and provide logical connections for the reader to follow the author's train of thought. Well-developed paragraphs contain information supporting their main idea according to consistent patterns, thus contributing to the essay as a whole.

Well-developed paragraphs illustrate, reinforce, expand on, or in some other way support what the writer is trying to prove. Well-developed paragraphs provide the meat and the muscle of the essay. The *body* of the essay will not be complete until the spaces between the main points—the skeletal frame—are filled in. There are various ways to add "flesh," "muscle," or substance to the body paragraphs. These methods, known as *rhetorical patterns*, are discussed below.

In this section, we are concerned mainly with developing paragraphs to ensure the essay will contain well-supported points. In some essays, the writer chooses to employ one method primarily while using other methods of development in supporting roles. An essay may set out principally to examine a cause-effect relationship, for example, but may use different methods to introduce, clarify, illustrate, or expand the main points. Two such primary organizational methods, definition and compare and contrast, will be discussed in Part Three, Section 1.2 as they apply to *essay* development. But first we will consider the many ways that writers can develop their key points through *paragraph* development, through the use of rhetorical patterns.

Having a wealth of different choices at hand is one of the keys to writing a complete and interesting essay. Which ones should you use for your essay? The choices that a writer makes will depend on many variables, including the kind of essay, the purpose in writing, the topic, the audience, the essay's primary organizational method (if there is one), the main points and their order (climax, reverse climax, or some other), along with a host of other interrelated factors.

Being aware of the various rhetorical patterns can help writers who find themselves in various difficulties with their writing. Those who need discipline, a sense of order, or a system can consciously shape their ideas according to specific, useful patterns —channels into which to pour their cascading thoughts. Other writers may spend countless minutes, or even hours, thinking about a topic without generating ideas; others may simply lack confidence in their ideas. These kinds of writers can use the various methods of development to formulate specific questions, which are useful in getting the thoughts flowing.

1.1 Rhetorical Patterns

A topic may lend itself to a particular method of development; in fact, in some cases, your main organizational method is given to you by the topic itself, so from that you will know how your points should be developed. For example, for the topic "Which is more important at university: acquiring skills or getting good grades?" you might guess that the essay should be organized to compare and contrast. For the topic "Solutions to the problem of homeless people" you would know that the essay should be organized as problem-solution where you briefly describe the problem and then suggest ways to solve it. On the other hand, if the topic were "Do you believe that homeless people today are a problem?" you might develop your essay in a similar way, but the *problem* of homelessness would be much more important than the solutions, which you might not mention at all or, perhaps, only in your concluding paragraph if you chose to use a spiral conclusion.

Even if the topic determines the *main* way that the essay should be developed, there will likely be opportunities to consider different methods for developing individual paragraphs.

Analysis, meaning *to loosen* or *dissolve* as well as to *separate* or *break up*, is sometimes considered a distinct method of development. But when you analyze, you are really loosening, then separating, something in order to subject it to close scrutiny. Many organizational methods involve this process. Thus, you analyze when you divide and classify, compare and contrast, consider problems and solutions, costs and benefits, etc. Not all methods truly involve analysis—description, narration, examples, and analogies do not—but many of them do. Analysis is one of the keys to critical thinking.

One way to generate methods of development is to ask questions about the topic:

What is it? . . . . .definition
When did it occur? . . . . .chronology
What does it look like? . . . . .description
How can it be told? . . . . .narration
How do you do it? . . . . .process/"how to"
How does it work? . . . . .process/"how to"
Why should/did it affect me? . . . . .personal
What kinds are there? . . . . .division/classification
What accounts for it? . . . . .cause–effect
What is the result/effect? . . . . .cause–effect
What is the answer? . . . . .question–answer
How can it be shown? . . . . .example/illustration
How can it be (re)solved? . . . . .problem–solution
What are the advantages/disadvantages? . . . . .cost–benefit
How is it like something else? . . . . .analogy
How is it like and/or unlike something else? . . . . .compare and contrast

Each of these questions leads to a particular method for developing an essay topic or a main point. Each method is explained below and is followed by an example. Let's say your topic is "fast foods." It would be possible to use any of the methods below to develop an essay on this topic.

1.1.1 Definition—What Is It?

Define something in an essay in order to tell the reader precisely what you will be talking about. Defining a subject, such as an abstract concept, can also help you understand your topic better and, perhaps, help you organize your main points. By "fast foods," do you mean something like a "Big Mac?" Do you mean food that you can buy at a store that is quickly heated and eaten? Both could be considered "fast foods," but they are not the same. Student writer Mik Nuotio concisely defines "peer-to-peer file sharing" for his general audience and then uses the division pattern. (For "definition" as a primary method, see below, Section 2.1.)

> Peer-to-peer file-sharing (P2P) is a technology that enables users to share files among themselves without the use of a central host of the files (traditionally called the client–server model). In P2P, each client acts as a "mini server" and can both send and receive files. The information regarding the files on each client usually is distributed in one of three ways. The first involves the use of a central server to store this information and the use of a protocol for clients to update the central server with file information whenever they connect or disconnect from the network. A more modern method for distributing information about files on different hosts, "hybrid P2P," involves the use of certain hosts on the network to maintain the information and distribute it. The third approach, called "decentralized P2P," is similar to hybrid P2P, but differs because it uses each individual host on the network to store and share file information.

1.1.2 Chronology—When Did It Occur?

Developing a time line is often a good way to start the body of your essay; it can be used elsewhere—in your introduction or in your body paragraphs—too. When did fast foods begin, and when did they truly begin to affect people and society? In employing the chronological method, you do more than simply look back to a specific time: you trace the topic's *development over time*. If you looked back to a specific time and compared an aspect of the subject to that aspect today, you would be *comparing and contrasting*. Tracing the evolution of fast foods in the last 10 years might provide evidence that many fast-food restaurants have been forced to expand their choices and reduce their portion sizes to counter the perception that these foods are unhealthy. Applying this method of development, then, could also involve a cause–effect or problem–solution approach; *see below.*

> The earth shook as father and son wrestled high above the clouds; Kronos, the dreaded father who ate his children, battled his powerful son to rule the Earth. However, Zeus, whom the Fates had protected as a child from Kronos's mighty jaws, triumphed once again, becoming, in the words of Homer, "father of gods and men"; his children would honour his victory as a celebration known as Olympia. From 776 BC, the Olympic Games occurred every four years to celebrate Zeus's success. By AD 260, the Games' importance had deteriorated so much that they were held only occasionally, until the Roman Emperor Theodosius outlawed them completely in AD 394. The Olympic Games were founded on a profound religious significance, specific ideals about athletes, and strict rules that enabled the Games' long existence and prohibited the inclusion of women. As Olympia changed, the founding principles that had originally made Olympia so significant were disregarded, eventually leading to the end of the ancient Games.
>
> —Student Writer Courtenay O'Brien

1.1.3 Description—What Does It Look Like?

You can use description at any point in your essay to add concrete, physical detail, but you probably do not want to develop an essay *primarily* through description. You can often describe something by using the **spatial** method of organization, a particular kind of descriptive method. In the spatial method, you describe something in a systematic manner—for example, from left to right, or as you approach the object. You could describe a fast food burger from the sesame-seed top bun with its assorted condiments and "extras" to the plain lower bun. As with the chronological method of development, the descriptive and spatial methods are often suitable for either introductions or early body paragraphs, though they can be used at any point if the need arises.

> The Parc Guell, constructed between 1900 and 1914, was originally intended as the setting for a garden city. The park is fairy tale-like in appearance: the first building one sees on entering the site resembles a gingerbread house. The rounded corners on the brown façade and colourful decoration of the window sills give the building a magical, playful appearance. Other structures that stand out within the park include a giant fountain shaped like a lizard and a mile-long bench that winds along one path in the park. The most remarkable feature, though, is Gaudí's use of beautiful, multi-coloured tile work throughout.

—George R. Collins, *Antonio Gaudí and the Catalan Movement 1870–1930*, 15

1.1.4 Narration—How Can It Be Told?

A story can lend drama and directness to an argument and to illustrate a point. To relate a scene or incident, or even include some dialogue, can be an effective way to introduce your topic, or narration could be used sparingly in one of the body paragraphs to bring a point home to the reader. Through observation and a little imagination, a visit to a fast-food restaurant could produce interesting stories about those who eat or work there. Narration is a natural method in personal essays, but can also be used in argumentative essays, and even in expository essays, as the example below shows about the legendary origins of coffee. Because description and narration are generally considered more informal, you should ask your instructor before using them extensively in formal essays.

> Legend has it that one day, Kaldi, an Ethiopian goat-herder, noticed his goats were so frisky when they returned from grazing that they "danced." Curious about the source of their excitement, Kaldi followed them the next day and observed the animals eating the berries of a nearby tree. Kaldi grabbed some berries himself and soon experienced a slow tingle that spread throughout his body. According to the legend, Kaldi was soon "dancing" alongside his goats.

—Mark Pendergrast, *Uncommon Grounds: the History of Coffee and How It Transformed Our World*, 1999

1.1.5 Process—How Does It Work?

Although process essays are usually fact-based essays that relate the chronological, step-by-step stages of a process, this method of development can also be used in some argumentative essays. If you were writing on the pros and cons of using a particular computer program, it might be helpful to describe how the program works. (Obviously, you need to have some factual knowledge about something to describe its process.) This method can also be used for less technical subjects—for example, "How to Impress Your Boss, or Professor, in 10 Easy Steps." Remember that relating a process focuses specifically on the successive steps in a *sequence*. Since the production of fast-food burgers is often a regimented process, you could describe this process from the time a customer places an order to the time it is handed to him or her.

> The traditional method of painting icons is a long process, requiring a skilled and experienced painter. The artist takes a wooden panel, one with the least amount of resin, knots, and risk of splitting, and covers it with cheesecloth. A gesso is then made from rabbit-skin glue and calcium carbonate (chalk). It is applied to the panel seven to ten times and then polished by hand until it is mirror-like. The original is traced to perfection and then transferred onto the gessoed surface. After this, gold leaf is laid on everywhere it is required (backgrounds and halos, for example). Egg tempera paint is freshly made from powdered pigment and egg yolk and is applied from the darkest dark to the lightest light with an egg-white glaze spread on between each coat.
>
> —Student Writer Magda Smith

1.1.6 Personal—Why Should It Affect Me?/ How Does or Did It Affect Me?

Personal essays are focused on the writer—an aspect of his or her life or a relevant experience. A personal experience in an essay gives an element of immediacy and, sometimes, drama; it can also add credibility. Don't use personal experience extensively, unless you are writing a personal essay, but using it selectively can be an effective way of involving the reader. Personal experience is more applicable to argument, but it can be used judiciously in some expository essays too (check with your instructor). In successful personal paragraphs and essays, the writer is able to make personal experience seem relevant to the reader. (See also Part One, Section 6.4.)

To apply your personal experience to fast-food restaurants, you might consider your visits to such restaurants as a child when the busy and exciting atmosphere itself was more important to you than the food. Student writer Brian Gregg began his expository essay on college binge drinking by citing a recent personal experience; such an approach would be particularly appropriate if his audience were composed mostly of college students:

> Exam time is approaching at my university, and stress levels are at an annual high. For this reason, when Friday night arrives, I know I will be drinking—and I definitely will not be alone. Last weekend, my friends and

I went to a typical residence party. If I can remember correctly, there were about 15 people noisily crowded into a room the size of a large closet, and many more were herded in the hallways. According to a study in the *American Journal of Public Health*, today's North American college students have the highest binge drinking rate of any group, even when compared to their peers who do not go to school; furthermore, alcohol is associated with many social problems on college campuses and is the most widespread and preventable health issue for the more than six million students in America (Wechsler et al., 1995, p.921).

1.1.7 Classification/Division—What Kinds Are There?

Humans, apparently by nature, tend to classify things. In **classification**, you begin with a large number of items—for example, commonly known members of the animal kingdom—and in order to write about them, you organize them into more manageable groups: mammals, birds, fish, reptiles, and amphibians. Each of the categories, such as "mammals," could in turn be organized into still smaller units, such as "rodents," "primates," "carnivores," and "cetaceans." Fast-food burgers can easily be classified according to their different kinds: hamburgers, chicken burgers, fish burgers, veggie burgers. In the example below, the writer uses classification to break down movies into five designations; the differences could then be analyzed by applying the same criteria to each category:

Ontario has five categories for rating movies: general, parental guidance, 14A (those under 14 must be accompanied by an adult), 18A (those under 18 must be accompanied by an adult), and restricted. In the "general" category, the language must be inoffensive, though words like "damn" and "hell" can occur occasionally. Violence must be limited and permissible; sexual activity includes only embracing and kissing "in a loving context"; horror is defined by genre—for example, fantasy giants, ogres, and dragons are acceptable.

—Ontario Film Review Board, http://www.ofrb.gov.on.ca/english/page6.htm

In **division**, you are more concerned with the whole than with the individual parts. You break a subject down into parts in order better to understand or explain the subject. For example, to illustrate how essay structure works, you can divide the essay into introduction, body paragraphs, and conclusion. Under 1.1.1 Definition, above, the writer divides peer-to-peer file-sharing into three different kinds.

1.1.8 Cause–Effect—What Is the Cause?

You can use the **cause–effect method** to organize an entire essay, or you can use it in one or more paragraphs to explore and analyze a main point. When you deal with causes, you consider the reasons for an occurrence. Cause–effect essays or paragraphs might focus on one effect, which would be accounted for by one or more causes. Or, you could focus on one cause and consider one or more effects or results arising from this cause. Since fast food has often been blamed for obesity in North

America, it would be possible to look at studies that link obesity (effect) to unhealthy diets (cause). Cause–effect studies are particularly common in the sciences. The **Antecedent–Consequent** organizational method uses time–order relationships in a similar way to cause–effect relationships. (Think of those "before and after" photographs.) The following essay excerpt discusses one cause for stress in first-year students.

> A major cause of stress in first-year students is the need to establish a new social base. Students not only find themselves among strangers, but also often have to rely on these strangers for moral support. Consequently, friendships tend to be forged rapidly but superficially. When students inevitably find themselves dealing with midterms, assignments, and an increasingly heavy course load, they need close friends and family for support but are forced to turn to these new acquaintances instead. Great friendships may be formed during such times, but often the stress is insurmountable, leading students to give up and head home.
>
> —Student Writer Alexis Parker

1.1.9 Question–Answer—What Is the Answer?

This method is effective when you ask the **question** in the topic sentence and then **answer** it in the paragraph. Questions—including the journalistic questions *who, what, when, where, why,* and *how?*—can be applied to almost any topic, including fast foods. Posing a relevant question is a good way to engage the reader since it directly invites his or her answer to the question. Student writer Robert Tyre began his essay by asking two questions, suggesting that his essay will focus on two related areas of foreign policy:

> In the post-Cold War era, do military solutions still have a place or is diplomacy able to solve all our foreign policy questions? Does the United Nations still have a useful purpose or will military coalitions like NATO usurp its role entirely? With increasing world tensions and the current Anglo-American-led war in Iraq, many people around the world are asking these questions.

1.1.10 Example/Illustration—How Can It Be Shown?

Using concrete **examples** is one of the best ways of supporting a point and translating an abstract claim into something the reader can understand and relate to. This method of development can often be combined with other methods, such as cause–effect, cost–benefit, or compare and contrast. (The last phrase, beginning with *such as* shows development through examples.) If you were using the cause–effect method and you wanted to develop the point that fast foods save valuable time (an effect), you might talk about the convenience of drive-through lanes at fast food restaurants as one example of this effect; another example might be the use of assembly-line workers. Providing examples is such an important element in supporting a claim that it can also be considered a kind of evidence.

Writers can cite brief examples to enable the reader to relate to an abstraction or a generality:

> Graffiti art can be seen as a political message on a sidewalk, a limerick on a bathroom wall, a doodle on a desktop, or even a digital image on the Internet.

Writers can use extended examples to explain a concept more fully. Student writer Tim Dewailly used such an example in a recent essay on the use of natural supplements by elite athletes:

> During the 2002 Commonwealth Games, Kelly Guest was suspended from participating in the triathlon by the International Olympic Committee (IOC). Guest tested positive for nandrolone, a substance banned by the IOC. Guest argued that he had never intended to use nandrolone to enhance his performance, but had ingested the banned substance through the natural supplements he was taking.

1.1.11 Problem–Solution—How Can It Be (Re)Solved?

In this organizational method, you present the **problem** then consider one or more **solutions**. As with cause–effect, this method can be used as the main organizing principle for an essay, or you could use it to develop one or more paragraphs. One problem associated with fast foods is their dubious nutritional value. After this problem is stated, you could propose ways that fast foods could be made healthier or perhaps give examples of how this is being done today; in this case, you would be combining **problem–solution** with **example/illustration**. Studies focusing on problem–solution and cost–benefit (see Section 1.1.12 below) are particularly common in the social sciences where human behaviour is the focus. In the following essay conclusion, student writer Chris Hoffart restates his thesis that Canada's Confederation in 1867 was not so much an effect, or consequence, of various causes, but the best solution to unanticipated problems.

> Politicians were not entertaining the idea of uniting the British North American colonies until numerous problems arose. Political alliances, foreign raids, railway expansion, industrial booms, and the termination of long-standing agreements would have been significant events on their own, but their convergence before 1867 helped push Canada towards Confederation. The most logical solution to these problems was union. Macdonald, Brown, and other nineteenth-century politicians did not strategically plan Confederation, but rather Confederation offered itself as a solution to the problems imposed on them.

1.1.12 Cost–Benefit—What Are the Advantages and Disadvantages?

There are many ways that something can be analyzed; one of the most common methods is to consider the advantages and disadvantages, the pros and cons. If you were to argue in favour of something, you would obviously stress the pros, and if you were arguing against it, you would stress the cons. You could apply cost–benefit analysis to fast foods by focusing on the personal, community, or perhaps even global costs or benefits. Cost–benefit analysis can be applied to almost any topic since few things in life, even those that on the surface appear to bring only benefits, come without some costs or negative consequences. In expository essays, cost–benefit analysis implies the objective weighing of pluses and minuses. If you were arguing that the benefits were more important than the costs, you might well consider the costs first and *then* the benefits and leave the strongest argument for the last. If you took the opposing position, you might begin with benefits, as student writer Jutta Kolhi does in her essay on genetically modified organisms:

> Some scientists believe that releasing GMOs into the environment could reduce pesticide use since crops could be genetically modified to produce a toxin against the pests. Unfortunately, such a toxin could have adverse effects on other organisms, such as the pollinator species of the plant. Some believe that genetic engineering could reduce hunger in third-world countries by allowing more food production. However, after growing genetically modified crops, the farmer would be unable to sow the seeds to grow more crops because GMO seeds are sterile, forcing the farmer to buy new seeds every year—an unrealistic expense. Furthermore, introducing GMOs in third-world countries would be risky as most countries have limited resources and few safety measures in place for controlling GMOs.

1.1.13 Analogy—How Is It Like Something Else?

An **analogy** is a comparison between one object and a second object that is otherwise not like the first one. Analogies enable the reader to consider the original object in a surprising and revealing light. You could compare fast foods to the fast pace of society itself. Student writer François Beaudet began his essay on water resource management by using the analogy of a desert to stress the importance of water management in North America.

> Imagine a hot, torturously dry desert. Throughout this arid wasteland, no life exists—not a tree, shrub, or animal alive. Though to many residents of Europe and North America this scenario may seem highly abstract and incomprehensible, it is the reality faced by many equatorial nations, such as China, Africa, Saudi Arabia, and parts of India. Residents of these nations have developed a keen understanding of the importance of water, and how best to manage it to enable a basic level of existence. However, residents of nations more endowed with water, such as Canada, seem largely indifferent to such a reality.

1.1.14 Compare and Contrast—How Is It Like and/ or Unlike Something Else?

To **compare and contrast** is a method of systematically drawing similarities and differences between two things. An analogy is a one-way comparison: In Shakespeare's "Shall I compare thee to a summer's day," the poet proceeds to describe how the loved one resembles a day in summer; he isn't interested in the ways that a summer's day is like the loved one. When you are comparing and contrasting, you make two-way comparisons: both objects are analyzed for similarities and/or differences (bases of comparison) and are then systematically compared for their similarities and constrasts. Analogies provide examples of non-literal (figurative) truths; comparisons are based in literal truth. In arguing that one hamburger restaurant is better than another, you could compare their prices, their food quality, their hygienic values, and the friendliness of their staff. **Compare and Contrast** is discussed as a primary method in Part Three, Section 2.2. Early in her Compare and Contrast essay, student writer Bree Stutt contrasts two different environmental philosophies by defining each, according to the beliefs of an influential philosopher:

> Conservation is a "shallow ecology" approach to viewing the environment and the role of humans within it. Conceived by Norwegian philosopher and linguist Arne Naess in the early 1970s, "shallow ecology" begins with "an assumption, often unexamined, that human beings are [the] central species in the Earth's ecosystem, and that other beings, as parts of systems, are of less importance or value." Preservation, on the other hand, is based on Arne Naess's "deep ecology" movement, which places humans within ecosystems and holds that humans are different from, but not more valuable than, other species.

—Great River, http://www.greatriv.org/de.htm

1.2 Primary and Secondary Methods

If you use one of the methods above as the **primary** method to support your thesis statement, you will likely use other methods of development in supporting roles. Some of these methods are almost always used **secondarily**. It is difficult to write an essay using *only*, or even primarily, question–answer, example/illustration, or analogy. Similarly, unless you set out deliberately to write a definition, process, chronological, or personal essay, likely none of these methods will be used exclusively in your essay. Though a good deal of writing is primarily narrational or descriptive, these methods will likely be subordinate to more commonly used methods in fact-based essays.

Exercise

Organization: Below are 15 general topics. Using at least three different organizational methods per topic, come up with at least three different topic sentences *for each topic*. Here are some examples using the topic "rap music":

1. **Cause–Effect Example**: Rap music, with its reliance on ever-changing slang, has expanded people's vocabulary; for instance, one's boyfriend is now called one's "boo."

2. **Definition Example**: Rap music is defined by some as being no more than talking over someone else's music.

3. **Description or Narration Example**: The lights were dim, and the crowd, writhing to the rhythm of the bass, was pressing forward to the stage.

Exercise

4. **Chronology Example**: The style of rap music has evolved considerably since it first gained popularity with North American youth in the early 1990s.

5. **Question–Answer Example**: How does rap music manage to offend such a broad demographic group while maintaining such a strong fan base?

6. **Problem–Solution Example**: It may seem somewhat ironic, but it is possible that many of the problems addressed in rap lyrics could be solved through this very same medium.

7. **Compare and Contrast Example**: Rap and hip hop music of the late 1980s and early 1990s, with their offensive lyrics and radical counter-cultural appeal, can be compared in terms of their sociological implications to the rock-and-roll revolution of the late 1960s and early 1970s.

8. **Personal Example**: When I first heard rap music I found the lyrics offensive and sexist.

9. **Cause–Effect Example**: Living in the ghetto, surrounded by "booty" and the "brothers," can sometimes cause young men to chant words to a particular rhythm that has no melody.

10. **Cause–Effect Example**: Rap music has been used as a vehicle for an oppressed minority to get its voice heard.

11. **Process Example**: To create rap music you need a DJ to provide the beats by mixing records, and an MC who takes the beats and contributes the vocals to make the finished product.

12. **Classification Example**: There are many different forms of rap; these include hip-hop, hard core, and R&B.

13. **Definition and Division Example**: Rap is a unique form of music that is built around heavy bass beats mixed with sharp, quick lyrics. There is a whole spectrum of rap music, ranging from slow love ballads to fast-paced dance songs.

14. **Cost–Benefit Example**: Though rap may lead young people to openly and healthily question authority and the status quo, it can lead some adolescents to commit acts of violence against society.

15. **Analogy Example**: Rap can be compared to the insistent and repetitive chants of an evangelist preacher.

Topics:

1. sports violence
2. animal rights
3. Internet piracy
4. eating disorders
5. gas prices
6. e-mail
7. exercise
8. organ transplants
9. alternative schooling
10. same-sex marriages
11. privacy
12. stress
13. public speaking
14. evolution
15. global warming

2. Essays Using a Primary Method

2.1 Definition Essays

In **Argumentative Essays** (see Part Four), defining something is often the first stage of an argument in which you go on to develop your thesis through means *other than* definition. On the other hand, definition *essays* can expand and elaborate on a subject, using a variety of organizational methods.

Definition often provides a necessary starting point for an argument. The success you have in getting your reader to agree with your definition will help establish your credibility as a writer and, in this way, strengthen your argument. Defining something also enables you, to some extent, to set the terms on which you want your argument to rest: successful definition enables you to take control of a potentially contentious, controversial, or abstract topic.

Although definition in argumentative essays can be effective, it is often an essential part of expository essays. Essays in the natural sciences and social sciences often begin by defining terms that the writer will employ throughout the essay. It may be crucial for the writer to establish the sense or connotation of one or more terms that have been subject to a variety of definitions in different studies in the writer's discipline. Many academic texts—above all, introductory textbooks—include a glossary or index of common terms that is designed to make it easier to apply terms correctly.

Definitions sometimes change over time and according to place, as well as according to cultural, national, social, and other variables. For example, the way you would define privacy today would likely be different from the way it would have been defined 25 years ago, due partly to technologies that have made it easier for others to access personal information.

In her personal essay about moths and butterflies, student writer B.I. Fischer begins by defining entomologists; she then defines and describes butterflies, using a colourful, metaphoric style appropriate for a personal essay, though probably not for an expository essay.

Entomologists are the scientists specialized in the study of insects—and like the multi-syllabic nomenclature that at first confuses the layperson, these people themselves are often misunderstood: they are passionate publicists for various hordes of tiny but potentially vicious, biting, stinging, pestilential, slimy, totally alien-looking, multi-legged, funny-faced creepy-crawlies—which often inspire screams, unpleasant words, and even killer instincts in non-entomologists like me.

Butterflies—*Lepidoptera*, in Greek, meaning "scaled wings"—are the great exception. If the spidery insect body is ignored and all attention focused on the scintillating, coloured wings, it is easy to think of flying flowers, love, dew and nectar droplets, rainbows, hummingbirds, jewels, fairies, magic, the soul escaping towards heaven, rebirth, symbolism in myth and art and literature—and these insects provide the modern urban imagination a peripheral poetic glimpse of nature. Into that happy picture of idyllic blue skies and rare beauty re-enters the entomologist—armed with a net, a jar of poison, and a pin.

The following definition paragraph also uses other methods of development. Identify two other methods, along with definition, in the paragraph:

> Vegetarianism, derived from a Latin word meaning "to enliven," was practised in ancient Greece as early as the sixth century BC by the Pythagoreans, and its reputation has spread to many other countries since then. It is a way of life in China, India, Japan, Pakistan, and even in North America with more than 14 million vegetarians. Since its beginnings, many well-known people have been non-meat eaters, including Socrates, Plato, Leonardo da Vinci, Charles Darwin, Thomas Edison, Albert Einstein, and Isaac Newton. The term "vegetarian" refers to someone who does not eat any flesh; however, there are many varieties of vegetarianism. If one eats no flesh (red meat, poultry, fish), but consumes dairy and egg products, one is said to be a lacto-ovo vegetarian (the most popular type in North America). Pesco-vegetarians eat seafood but avoid red meat and poultry. Vegans are "strict vegetarians," who not only avoid consuming any type of animal but also avoid anything manufactured from animals (soap, leather, wool, honey, gelatine). Any form of vegetarianism is a healthy way of living, which not only benefits humans but also benefits animals and the planet itself.

—Student Writer Jessica Charbonneau

2.1.1 Sample Essay

The following is a student exam essay that uses definition as a primary method. Read the essay and respond to the exercises below.

What Is Leadership?

by Andrew Fodor

An unconscious car accident victim enters the emergency room of a local hospital. Nurses, technicians, doctors and other health care providers swarm around the patient and begin administering tests and procedures. The attending physician stands back to assess, monitor, and give orders to the emergency team. The life of the patient depends on the leadership skills of the attending physician.

Leadership is a skill that actively encourages, directs, co-ordinates, and guides one or more individuals towards the completion of a goal. Leadership is a valuable attribute in nearly all areas of society, such as the military, government, business, education, as well as in families. Although a power structure is often developed to identify or assign an individual, groups of individuals, or organizations to a leadership role, this is not a prerequisite of leadership. For example, the child of a mother undergoing chemotherapy may provide hope, encouragement, and inspiration to his or her family.

A classic example of leadership is a project manager (PM). He or she has a responsibility to complete a project on time, within budget and to the requirements of the client, usually a third party or company department. The PM must provide direction (a project plan) for his or her team; delegate responsibility to team members (sub-projects); monitor team progress; communicate between management, the project team and the client, as well as manage a number of other tasks (for example, team morale).

There are numerous ways to improve an individual's leadership skills; these can often be accomplished by education (such as workshops) and on the job experience.

Leadership is the co-ordination of people, resources and tasks towards the completion of a goal. Leadership can be demonstrated in many situations, from a doctor trying to save a life in the ER to a university teacher to a military commander. Although leadership is often provided by qualified, educated persons, it may sometimes arise from unlikely sources. Regardless, leadership is a skill that can be developed through experience and education.

Exercises

A. Leadership is an abstract topic; therefore, the writer has tried hard in the limited time allotted to render it in more concrete and immediate terms. He begins the essay by narrating a scenario (an emergency room of a hospital) where leadership is urgently needed. He gives examples of other situations that evoke leadership qualities. He also gives a specific example, which is thoroughly developed as a "case study" in paragraph three. Is there anything in the essay that doesn't seem to belong, or anything else that detracts from its effectiveness?

B. Write a 300–400-word essay (about the length of the essay on leadership) on one of the following general topics:

1. tradition
2. censorship
3. multiculturalism
4. success
5. nationalism
6. justice
7. self-expression
8. freedom
9. human rights
10. consumerism

2.2 Compare and Contrast Essays

Compare and Contrast can be used as the primary organizational method in both argumentative and expository essays. From an organizational point of view, Compare and Contrast essays are the most complex; therefore, you need to be clear on method before you begin. The first step is to ensure that the topics you will be comparing are, indeed, comparable. It is not possible to compare the health care system in the United

States to the educational system in Canada. While it might be possible to compare the health care systems of the two countries, such a topic would be too broad and complex for anything much less than a full-length book. However, it might be manageable to compare the health care systems in two Canadian provinces.

After you have determined that the topics are comparable and that the essay is manageable, you must carefully choose at least three bases of comparison for the main points of your essay, ensuring again that each basis of comparison is logical and manageable.

2.2.1 Block and Point-by-Point Methods

There are two ways to structure Compare and Contrast essays: the **block** method and the **point-by-point** method. In the block method, you consider all the points that relate to your first subject of comparison. When you have finished, you consider all the points as they apply to the second subject of comparison. When you are comparing the second subject, you use the same order as you did with the first.

In the more commonly used point-by-point method, you consider one basis of comparison as it applies to each subject; you continue until you have considered all the bases of comparison. In the following, "A" and "B" represent the subjects of comparison, and the numbers represent the points (or bases of comparison):

Block Method	Point-by-Point Method

A: 1)
    2)
    3)
B: 1)
    2)
    3)
	A: 1)
	B: 1)
	A: 2)
	B: 2)
	A: 3)
	B: 3)

Below, the two methods are applied to the identical topic and bases of comparison:

Topic: Compare and contrast benefits of walking to benefits of cycling.

Block Comparison and Contrast:
A: Subject of comparison: CYCLING
         basis of comparison 1) transportation
         basis 2) exercise
         basis 3) health
         basis 4) cost
B: Subject of comparison: WALKING
         basis of comparison 1) transportation
         basis 2) exercise
         basis 3) health
         basis 4) cost

Point-by-point Comparison and Contrast:

I. basis of comparison: transportation
    A: subject of comparison: cycling
    B: subject of comparison: walking
II. basis: exercise
    A: cycling
    B. walking
III. basis: health
    A: cycling
    B: walking
IV. basis: cost
    A: cycling
    B. walking

2.2.2 Sample Compare and Contrast Essay

After reading this essay, complete the exercise that follows.

Tail of Opposites

by Barclay Katt

Meow, meow, or woof, woof?

For most people, it is an easy choice. In fact, it is not really a "choice" at all: it is simply the way it is. There are "cat people" and "dog people" in the world, and neither group speaks the language of the other. They are as separate as curds and whey, as chalk and cheese, and when a cat person meets a dog person on neutral turf, the result is a war of words in which the fur is sure to fly. It seems that each group disdains the other; in many other ways, each doggedly or cattily proclaims its separate identity.

Just by walking into a house, you can tell whether the owner is a feline fancier or a canine connoisseur. (The fact that you have made it to the front door tells you something; have you ever heard of a watchcat?) The cat owner will show you to the elegant living room. Elegant? Cat owners possess the most costly furniture, but it is invariably armoured by ugly plastic coverings with perhaps a swath of towels wrapped around sofa ends. The dog owner will conduct you swiftly to the humble kitchen table. En route, you will notice the unmistakable "odeur du chien." But in the kitchen, cooking odours will mingle with those of dog, disguising the latter, though not erasing them completely.

Talk to these two different groups of people, and you will again notice a difference. It is not that cat people are snobbish or that they believe themselves superior; the tilt of their noses has nothing to do with it. But there is one thing that they will expect of you: unremitting absorption in the object of their affection—Kitty. You had better be

---

prepared to spend much of your time gazing in adoration at the magnificent specimen. You must also suffer the fastidious attentions of the cat, if it deigns to give them—even if the tribute takes the form of the kneading of its knife-like claws on your thigh.

It is not that dog people are crude or that they have no concern for social graces. But there is one thing that they will expect of you: conviviality, even to the point of garrulousness. Be careful not to turn away from your host too often (resist the temptation to find out where that annoying series of yips is coming from). Dog owners are famous back-slappers, jabbers, and unapologetic probers of your person. But they will never ask you to share the virtues of their pet and will suddenly lose their warmth if you show too much interest. They are possessive of the bond and discourage interlopers.

Most people have been struck, at one time or another, by the way pet owners come to resemble their pets. It is strange why this is so, and never the other way around— that pets come to look more like their owners. For some reason, the face of the cat or dog is more transferable to the human face than the human face is to that of the dog or cat. Here, it must be admitted that the dog owner is at an advantage. As there are far more breeds of dogs than of cats, the observer cannot help but be impressed by the infinite variety of possible faces of dog owners—from pushed-in pug to the full-blown majesty of Irish wolfhound.

Perhaps it is due to these differences that dog owners and cat owners do not seem able to abide one another; they just never can see eye to eye on anything—or whisker to whisker, for that matter—especially where it concerns the superiority of their own pet. Certainly, the day that cat people and dog people do agree on something will be the day that world peace is finally possible.

Exercise

Identify the thesis statement, the method used for comparing, and the bases for comparison in the above essay. You can use the appropriate diagrammatic model in section 2.2.1 to show method and bases for comparison.

2.2.3 Excerpt from a Compare and Contrast Essay

The following excerpt is from the journal article "The Worlds We Live In: Gender Similarities and Differences," by Meredith M. Kimball (*Canadian Psychology/Psychologie canadienne* 35, 4: 1999). The one-paragraph introduction provides background to the topic, after which the essay is broken down into sections. The questions that follow focus on reading strategies (see Part One, Section 3) and the organization of the excerpted passage.

Throughout the history of feminism, from Wollstonecraft to the present, two views of gender differences have been advocated (Cott, 1986). In one, similarities between the sexes have been emphasized, whereas in the other women's special characteristics that differ from men's have been emphasized. These two different intellectual views have been used by feminists to support different but important political goals. Arguments proposing gender similarities have most often been used to support goals of political and social equality for women. Gender differences have been used to support the creation of special spheres or separate institutions for women. Within psychology, these two traditions of feminist thinking have been visible since the beginning of the discipline. In this paper, I will explore the tensions between them, and develop the example of moral theory as a way of exploring and using this tension.

The Similarities Tradition. The similarities tradition has focused on intellectual skills and social competencies that have been assumed to explain the preponderance of men in positions of power and prestige. By showing that gender differences in these skills and competencies are either non-existent or far too small to explain existing gender differences in the labour force, feminist psychologists have sought to provide the scientific justification for political equality. This work has occurred largely within academic experimental psychology and relies on statistical techniques as the main source of proof. Historically, this tradition can be traced to the earliest work in experimental psychology. Helen Thompson was one of the first women to obtain a Ph.D. from the University of Chicago. Her thesis, *The Mental Traits of Sex* (1903), illustrates the main arguments in the similarities tradition. These include the importance of overlap between genders, the requirement of highest methodological standards to demonstrate difference, the search for social explanations of difference, and the demonstration of the specificity of difference. In 1914 Leta Stetter Hollingworth published a series of papers that undermined the hypothesis of male superiority through greater variability (Hollingworth, 1914a) and arguments that women were dysfunctional during their menstrual cycle (1914b). Work in this tradition died out around 1920 and did not become a focus within academic psychology again until the early 1970s.

Beginning with the publication of Eleanor Maccoby and Carol Jacklin's *The Psychology of Sex Differences* in 1974, work in the similarities tradition again came to the fore of academic psychology. Feminist psychologists working within the similarities tradition have consistently emphasized the small magnitude of behavioural gender differences. Research reporting gender differences is examined for androcentric bias (e.g., Eichler, 1980; McHugh, Koeske, and Frieze, 1986; Stark-Adamec and Kimball, 1984). Statistical significance is supplemented with effect size calculations and meta-analytical techniques in order to eliminate the problem that very small and meaningless differences are assumed to be important because they are statistically significant (e.g., Hyde and Linn, 1986; Hyde, Fennema, and Lamon, 1990). Overlap between distributions of female and male scores is emphasized (Favreau, 1993). Another important theme is that it is not gender per se but the interaction of gender with situational variables that explains reported differences (e.g., Deaux and Major, 1987; Eagly, 1987; Kimball, 1989). Finally, the lack of choice and the role of coercion in determining women's behaviour are emphasized. Coercion may occur through either ideology and socialization or through violence and threats of violence (Epstein, 1988). In either case choice, especially a choice of traditional roles and behaviours, is viewed as largely illusory.

The Differences Tradition. In contrast to the similarities position, the differences tradition has focused on positive human characteristics that have been undervalued because they are associated with women and with the symbolic feminine. Central to the concerns of this tradition are the sense of connectedness, concern with human relationships, and caregiving that women, more than men, bring to human culture. The political goal is not equality, but rather the creation of a different, more humane world that incorporates traditional feminine values as a central human focus. Most of the work in this area is qualitative, and much of it exists within a psychoanalytic framework. That women and men are different is accepted; what is questioned is the traditional devaluation of women and the symbolic feminine. Historically this tradition can be traced to the early work on gender differences in psychoanalysis. Karen Horney's (1926) critique of Freud's ideas about female development illustrates the main focus of the differences tradition. She did not question that women were different from men, but did question the reduction of this difference to mere compensation on the part of women.

With the publication of Nancy Chodorow's *The Reproduction of Mothering* in 1978, a consciously feminist psychoanalytic theory began to be developed and used, which continued the tradition begun by Horney of emphasizing the importance of a particular female development and psychology that differed from the male. The three main themes of the differences tradition are present in Chodorow's work. The first is an emphasis on gender asymmetry in early child development. As a result of the social fact that infant girls are mothered by a same-sex person, issues of intimacy and autonomy become gendered. The second is an emphasis on subjective experience. For example, it is not so much mothering behaviour but rather women's desire to mother that needs explanation. Related to the emphasis on subjective experience is the theme of choice. In contrast to the emphasis on coercion and determination in the similarities tradition, theorists operating in the differences tradition emphasize and explain how it is that women make choices, in particular, choices that include traditional roles and behaviours. Indeed, Chodorow argues that mothering cannot be coerced, that the activity must be voluntary in order for a genuine emotional relationship to develop between the mother and the infant.

Tensions between the Traditions. The exchange of views and ideas between these two traditions has been minimal. The criticisms that have been levelled have an arrogant or extreme quality and thus the nature of the exchange when it has occurred has been adversarial. Feminist psychologists have, by and large, sided with one tradition over the other. Those working in the similarities tradition have tended to dismiss the differences viewpoint as empirically naïve and reinforcing of political conservatism. These criticisms are often quite extreme in assuming that work in the differences tradition is not only scientifically incorrect but politically antithetical to the goals of the women's movement (Kahn and Yoder, 1989). For example, Mednick (1989) describes Gilligan's (1982) theory as a conceptual bandwagon that lacks empirical support but remains popular because of the simplicity of the ideas. Sometimes critics do allow that difference theorists, such as Gilligan, do not intend to support conservative political views (Lott, 1989; Mednick, 1989). However, either this is not followed with an analysis of how these theories might be feminist (Mednick, 1989) or their work is described as empowering but for the wrong reasons and is therefore of dubious value (Lott, 1989). In one critique the feminist work of Gilligan (1982) on women's moral development and the work of Belenky and her colleagues (Belenky, Clinchy, Goldberger, and Tarule, 1986) on women's ways of knowing are grouped with the work of Benbow and Stanley (1980) on women's inferior math performance as examples of research biased towards differences (Kahn and Yoder, 1989) without any consideration of the differences in value that inform the work on these authors. Gender differences are not denied; however, the underlying assumption is that they are not real but rather correlates of the power differences between genders (e.g., Lott, 1990). Because "behavior has no gender" (Lott, 1990, p. 79) to think in terms of gender differences is to reinforce stereotypes (Bohan, 1992; Greeno and Maccoby, 1986; Lott, 1990).

The critique of similarities by theorists in the differences tradition is much less frequent; indeed, with a few exceptions it is absent. Sometimes there is a feeling one is experiencing an arrogance of silence, that there is a refusal to refute a view seen as so trivial or shallow. Although the reasons for silence are hard to document, the flavour of this shows in some of the criticisms. Gilligan (1986) implies that her critics reduce questions about sex differences in moral development to arguments about Kohlberg test scores, and sex differences in violent fantasies to disagreements over picture classifications (p. 331). In her psychodynamic theory of the development of mothering, Chodorow (1978) acknowledges, but then dismisses the importance of social reinforcement and ideology in constructing women's mothering. The implication is that such external factors are too shallow to be anything more than the social frosting on a psychodynamic cake.

Questions for Active Reading

Answer each of the short questions below. Then, determine and schematize the method used to compare and contrast.

1. How can the section of the article reproduced here be divided? On what basis did you determine this?

2. What assumptions about audience are evident in the first sentence of the paper?

3. Identify the thesis statement.

4. Define "androcentric" (*Similarities Tradition*, paragraph 2) and "gender asymmetry" (*The Differences Tradition*, paragraph 2).

5. What does the author consider the key work in the "similarities tradition?" In the "differences tradition?" How is this indicated in each case?

6. Explain what Kimball means by "an arrogance of silence" in paragraph 7 and consider how this concept helps shape Kimball's argument in this paragraph.

Organization

Which of the two methods for organizing Compare and Contrast essays did the writer use? Why do you think she chose this method? Construct a schematic representation of this method. You can use the appropriate diagrammatic model above (Section 2.2.1) to show method and bases for comparison.

---

3. The Design of the Essay: A Two-Part Model

3.1 Kinds of Claims: Fact, Value, Policy, and Interpretation

All essays make some kind of claim and then proceed to prove the validity of the claim by various means of support. So, there will be two main parts to an essay, whether it is argumentative, expository, or literary: the *claim* and the *support*. Generally, the claim is made in the thesis statement. The essay writer may use one or more of four kinds of claims: **fact**, **value**, **policy**, or **interpretation** (the last is pertinent to literary criticism).

3.1.1 Claims of Fact

A claim of fact is usually an empirical claim that uses the evidence-gathering methods of observation and measurement, a claim that can be proven by facts and figures or through the results of prior studies relating to the claim. Claims of fact are used in most expository essays.

3.1.2 Claims of Value

A claim of value is an ethical claim and appeals to one's sense of values or a moral system; such values could be inherent in a religious, philosophical, social, cultural, or other system. Claims of value are supported largely through a process of deductive reasoning where certain standards of good or bad, right or wrong, are accepted as premises.

3.1.3 Claims of Policy

A claim of policy is usually a call for some kind of action to rectify a problem or improve a situation. Although claims of policy do not have to be grounded in claims of value, they often are; for example, a proposed change to a law or regulation that gives people more control over something in their lives may be presented as a claim of value, and could involve the argument that the change will produce a more democratic society in which people have greater freedom to assert their rights.

3.1.4 Claims of Interpretation

A claim of interpretation is a more specialized type of claim. Literary essays often use claims of interpretation, which are supported through references to the primary (literary) text itself, as well as to secondary sources if research has been done. Writers in the disciplines of history, philosophy, and cultural studies also may use claims of interpretation if their main purpose is to weigh and interpret the evidence found in either primary or secondary sources. For example, a writer could claim that the defeat of Athens in the Peloponnesian War was inevitable due to the internal conflicts within Athens itself. In such an essay, the writer would likely use the interpretations of experts to help formulate the essay's claim. Because claims of interpretation can often be challenged, they can be considered as kinds of argumentative claims.

In general, any subject can be explored in an essay through either a claim of fact, value, policy, or interpretation, depending on the way the claim is presented. Expository essays rely on claims of fact; argumentative essays can use any claim, but more typically use claims of value or policy.

If you were asked to write an essay on homelessness, you could come up with a factual thesis statement that considered the prevalence of homeless people in society. Still using a claim of fact, you could discuss the causes and/or the effects of homelessness from many different vantages. The same subject could be the basis of a value-based claim in which you argued that homelessness is an indictment of our society; or, you could use facts and, perhaps, ethical arguments but focus primarily on workable solutions to the problem: a policy-based claim.

3.2 Support: Evidence and Credibility

Claims are not persuasive without **support**. The two major ways that claims can be supported in an essay are by presenting **evidence** (the proof) and by demonstrating the essay writer's **credibility**. Although many student writers believe that evidence is the more important of the two, the effort of evidence-gathering and arranging may be wasted if the writer is not able to present herself or himself as credible.

3.2.1 Organization of Evidence

You reveal your evidence in support of your claim through your main and subordinate points. These points function effectively when appropriate organizational methods are used and when the points are ordered logically (climax, inverted climax, or mixed order). Organizational methods include definition, division/classification, cause–effect, compare and contrast, problem–solution, and chronology. (They are discussed in detail in Part Three, Section 1.1 Essay and Paragraph Development.)

3.2.2 Kinds of Evidence

The effectiveness of your argument also depends on the specific *kinds* of evidence you use. These include the following:

- **examples and illustrations**. If one example is very important to your essay, you could set it up as a case study and proceed to examine its aspects in detail; a **case study** is both particular and representative.
- **anecdotes**, informal stories introducing or illustrating a point.
- **analogies**, comparisons.
- **precedents**, a kind of example often used by lawyers in which a prior, parallel example has been legally accepted or otherwise condoned.
- **primary sources**, such as literary texts, historical documents, surveys and questionnaires, and interviews.
- **secondary and tertiary sources**, most often, authoritative written sources, such as books and journal articles, but they also could include oral sources, such as presentations, and conference papers.
- **statistics**, facts and figures; these could be found in primary sources, such as historical or government documents, or in secondary sources.
- **personal observation**, what you personally observe and record, such as group dynamics.
- **personal experience**.

Depending on your topic, the specifications of the assignment, and the discipline in which you are writing, you may find that one or more of these kinds of evidence will be predominant in your essay. Writing for the humanities often relies on primary sources. If you write an English essay, for instance, you will probably use many quotations from literary works. The primary sources commonly used in historical research are contemporary documents such as biographies, newspapers, letters, and old records.

Social sciences writing tends to focus on facts and figures, statistics and other numerical data, case studies, interviews, questionnaires, and personal observation. Scientific studies may make use of similar kinds of evidence but frequently rely on direct methods that involve experimentation. Examples are important in just about every discipline. These methods are discussed in detail in Part Four, Section 2, The Argumentative Essay.

3.2.3 Credibility

A claim is supported through your credibility. There are three factors that contribute to credibility: *knowledge* of the topic, *reliability/ trustworthiness*, and *fairness*. Many students believe that showing their knowledge about a topic is sufficient to establish them as credible. But consider the analogy of job-hunting: when you send out your résumé, you want to impress prospective employers with your experience and knowledge; however, during the interview process, the employer will likely ask questions that pertain more to your reliability as an employee than to your knowledge—for example, *Why do you want to work for us? Where do you see yourself in five years?* Furthermore, when employers check your references, questions of your reliability are bound to arise, along with those pertaining to your expertise. Similarly with essay writing once you have conveyed your knowledge, you must convince the reader that you also are reliable.

You demonstrate knowledge through the points made in the essay and with the variety, appropriateness, and effectiveness of the kinds of evidence you use. But you can present yourself as knowledgeable without being thought reliable. You instil confidence in your reliability or trustworthiness by ensuring positive answers to questions like the following:

- Is the essay well-structured?
- Are paragraphs unified, coherent, and well-developed?
- Is the writing clear? Is the grammar correct and is the style lucid and articulate?
- Have you effectively used the conventions of your discipline?
- Is the argument (in an argumentative essay) logical or is evidence (in an expository essay) used free of bias?

You must demonstrate **fairness** in an argumentative essay, though fairness can also be a concern in expository essays in the impartial selection and evaluation of the evidence. In many argumentative essays, it is important that you consider other views, particularly those opposed to your own. A writer who is fair is impartial, objective, and discerning, and avoids slanted language that announces strongly subjective views and apparent bias. While making a case strong and effective it will help to pinpoint the shortcomings and limitations of the other side.

While you can demonstrate reliability by avoiding logical fallacies, you can demonstrate fairness by steering clear of emotional and ethical fallacies (discussed in more detail in Part Four, Sections 3 through 6).

In the following essay model, all the parts that we have considered exist in relation to the other parts; none is an isolated entity that you can simply inject into your essay mechanically or without considering where it fits into the complete design. This inter-relatedness is borne out in many places in the successful essay. An essay that demonstrates your knowledge, hence credibility, will do so partly because of the kinds of evidence that are used. Similarly, examples and analogies that have been cited as kinds of evidence in support of a point might also have been used as an organizational method. In addition to using careful and thorough research in an attempt to demonstrate knowledge, you must also convince the reader that you are reliable and fair.

The essay should be approached as a dynamic of choice and possibility; and the best way to learn how to write a successful essay is to look at it as the interweaving of your choices into a cohesive and organic whole that most fully expresses what you want to communicate to your intended audience.

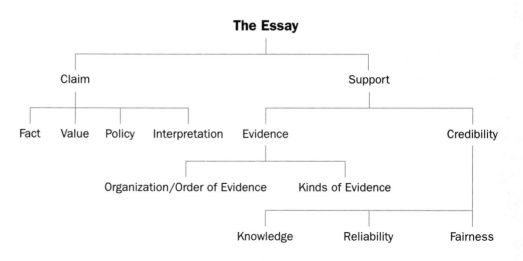

Student writers sometimes have the impression that an effective essay is comprised of discrete parts, operating more or less independently of each other. But the opposite is true: it is really an organic entity with many interdepedent parts.

Exercise

It is important to be able to distinguish between a factual claim and a value or policy claim. Although there may not always be a firm line between exposition and argument, you may be asked to write an essay that is either one or the other; and, of course, your reader should recognize what kind of essay he or she is reading. Determine whether the statements below are most suited to argument or exposition by putting an "A" or "E" beside them.

1. This paper will attempt to show that British Columbia's environmental policy is better than Alberta's policy.

2. Legislators should impose an outright ban on smoking in indoor public establishments and places of business.

3. Diplomacy and militarism are the two main approaches to foreign policy which, though sometimes used independently, are much more effective when used in combination.

4. 3M's tradition, strategy, and corporate image have helped it maintain its top-ten ranking in *Fortune* magazine year after year.

5. This essay will explore the costs and benefits of organic farming, and attempt to explain its growing popularity.

6. Hip-hop today acts as a cultural bridge for widely diverse groups of young people to communicate across racial, class, religious, linguistic, and national divisions.

7. In spite of ethical concerns, can the human race really afford to ignore the tremendous potential of embryonic stem cell research to effect cures for many major diseases?

Exercise – *continued*

8. The government should take steps to regulate the monopolistic practices of airlines today.

9. Probably nobody in the history of psychology has been as controversial —sometimes revered, sometimes despised—as Sigmund Freud.

10. What are the physical effects of artificial and natural tanning? What are the risks involved, and what can be done to educate the public about both?

Exercise

The 10 simple thesis statements below contain claims of fact, value, or policy. Identify the kind of claim and then write two sentences under the original one in which you turn the original claim into the two other kinds of claims. You may make any changes in wording you wish as long as the topic remains the same.

Example:

Thesis Statement: Cellphones are a wonderful modern convenience, but they can be dangerous in cars because they often distract the driver.

Kind of Claim: Claim of value: the statement asserts that cellphones can be dangerous (a bad thing).

A. The recent use of cellphones in cars has increased the number of accidents in many urban centres—especially during rush hour.

   Kind of Claim: Claim of fact: the statement asserts that the number of accidents has increased.

B. Cellphones in cars should be prohibited as they are dangerous both for the user and for other drivers.

   Kind of Claim: Claim of policy: the statement advocates an action, though this action is based on a value, i.e., that cellphones in cars are dangerous (bad).

1. It is increasingly necessary to be bilingual in Canada today.

2. The lyrics of rap music are inherently anti-social and an incitement towards violence.

3. Women should not be allowed to serve in the military in anything but administrative roles.

4. Whatever one may think of same-sex marriages, it is evident that they are here to stay.

5. After completing high school, it is best to travel for at least a year before proceeding to college or university.

Exercise – *continued*

6. It is necessary to provide more funding for technology in today's classroom and to spend less on teachers' salaries.

7. The current practice of appointing Supreme Court judges in Canada is undemocratic.

8. With the number of sports teams, clubs, and cultural groups on campus, students who do not participate in extra-curricular activities are not getting good value for their education.

9. School uniforms provide many benefits to students and their parents.

10. The government should subsidize organically grown food.

Collaborative Exercise

Taking one of the claims for each statement, determine how you would most effectively support it in the body of the essay. This exercise could take the form of a group discussion, or you could write out a strategic approach, referring as specifically as possible to those parts under Support in the diagram of the essay above.

Strategies to Consider: Organization of Evidence: Which patterns of organization/ development would you *likely* use? Which *could* be used?

Kinds of Evidence: Which kinds of evidence would most effectively back up your claim?

Which of the three categories of **credibility** seem the most important? Why? What general or specific strategies could you use to ensure your support was credible?

PART FOUR

The Argumentative Essay

1. Rhetoric, Argument, and Persuasion

2. Working Your Claim: Kinds of Evidence

3. Working Your Claim: The Rational Basis of Argument

4. Refuting the Opposing View

5. "Please Sign Our Petition": A Case Study

6. Categories of Faulty Reasoning

7. Organizing an Outline for Argument

8. Rhetorical Function of Parts

9. Sample Outline for an Argumentative Essay

10. Sample Essays

Argument in its many different forms is so ingrained in our lives that it might seem strange to devote space to what people do naturally and usually believe they do well—few people would say they argue poorly. A teenager argues with his parents that he is old enough to live on his own; a lawyer argues a complex point of law before a Supreme Court judge. What is the difference between these arguments? Complexity might be one difference, but another lies in the likelihood that both the teenager and the parents will present the argument at least partly in emotional terms—especially if the two sides are firmly opposed and equally determined.

This is not the case with the lawyer who knows that her credibility is built on logic, precedent, and other rational variables, not on emotional ones. It can be a good strategy for a defence lawyer to create sympathy for a defendant, but the lawyer would have to do this indirectly, perhaps through the emotional testimony of character witnesses—not by displaying emotion herself. Whereas the teenager and the parents have only a goal in mind and may be willing to use all available means to achieve it, the lawyer's goal is firmly supported by an overarching design. The kind of arguing you will do at the university level has more in common with that of the prudent lawyer than of the passionate parent.

The roots of argument are embedded in public discourse in which highly trained and proficient orators did battle with one another in assemblies, in courtrooms, and at public events in ancient Athens and Rome. Many of the argumentative strategies used today reflect these roots; even the terminology sometimes used to teach effective argumentation reveals classical origins: *argumentum ad hominem, petitio principii, post hoc,* and *non sequitur* are Latin names for some of the fallacies in argument (see Section 6.1). Although argument types have roots in antiquity, they have been adapted for an array of contemporary functions: editorials and letters to the editor, proposals advocating change, and the language of mediation all rely on argument. Advertising tries to influence us through argument, though more often by manipulating reason than by using it. When you design your résumé, you are implicitly arguing, presenting a strong case for your abilities in order to persuade an employer to hire you over someone else. The argumentative essay exercises the kind of logical and critical thinking skills you use every day.

Aristotle (384–322 BC), who laid much of the groundwork for classical and even modern argument in his book the *Rhetoric*, divided arguments into three kinds: those founded on reason (*logos*), on emotion (*pathos*), and on morality (*ethos*). Appeals to reason, to emotion, and to ethics all can be used in argument, as the following "real-life" scenario suggests:

> You are disappointed by an essay grade and arrange to meet your instructor in her office. By your effective use of reason, you try to convince her to change your mark, conceding the validity of some of her criticisms (concessions are used in many arguments). Going through the paper systematically, you focus on points that seem arguable, asking clarification or elaboration and presenting your counterclaims. As you do, you begin to come across as a responsible, conscientious student: you make an ethical appeal.
>
> You appeal to her as fair-minded, reiterating her helpfulness, your interest in the course, and your desire to do well. In this way, you succeed in

establishing common ground, as you would try to do with the reader of your essay. If you argue with integrity, you will leave a good impression. Emotional appeals, such as tearfully bemoaning your stressful life, are apt to be less successful, but subtle appeals may have influence.

In most argumentative essays, the most important appeal is to a reader's reason and logic. Ethical appeals play a secondary role, mostly in establishing your credibility as an arguer. Emotional appeals can also be useful, depending on your topic, your audience, and their placement in the essay.

1. Rhetoric, Argument, and Persuasion

Rhetoric has taken on a range of meanings today. The word can have negative connotations, as when someone speaks of empty or meaningless rhetoric—*just* words; similarly, if someone asks a question without expecting an answer but in order to produce an effect, he or she has put a rhetorical question. On the other hand, you can admire a person's rhetorical skills, meaning the clever or sophisticated way someone uses words. Aristotle intended rhetoric to stress a speaker's awareness of the choices available in any given situation to persuade an audience. He believed that a general audience would often need to be persuaded—that demonstrating knowledge was not by itself enough. Aristotle identified specific *topoi* (strategies or, literally, places) that could help accomplish this aim. Two such *topoi* are definition and comparison.

For the purposes of today's student writer, rhetoric can be defined either broadly or more narrowly. The broad definition of **rhetoric** as the use of effective modes of communication was expressed well by the nineteenth-century orator Edward T. Channing in *Lectures Read to the Seniors in Harvard College*:

> [Rhetoric is] a body of rules derived from experience and observation, extending to all communication by language and designed to make it efficient. It does not ask whether a man is to be a speaker or writer,—a poet, philosopher, or debater; but simply,—is it his wish to be put in the right way of communicating his mind with power to others, by words spoken or written. If so, rhetoric undertakes to show him rules or principles which will help to make the expression of his thoughts effective . . . in the way that nature universally intends, and which man universally feels. (31–2)

In this chapter, we will work within the narrower meaning of rhetoric as the structure and strategies of argumentation used to persuade the members of a specific audience.

Some people make a distinction between argument and persuasion, but at other times the terms "argument" and "persuasion" are used almost synonymously. If there is to be a distinction, it lies in the degree of stress on the logical argument as compared with the appeal to emotion. Faulty reasoning may, to the unsuspecting, seem convincing and may even seduce the unwary reader to a point of view; but it will not produce a good argument. It not only fails the test of logic but also would fail the test of fairness. Even so, faulty or distorted reason may persuade inattentive or uncritical readers, as Aristotle acknowledged in the *Rhetoric*.

While argument focuses on reason by employing the strategies and structures of logic, persuasion focuses on the feelings of the audience by persuasion through emotional appeals. Among ways to get people to change their minds are rewarding a change of thinking or behaviour in some way, or, more sinisterly, through coercive suggestions of physical violence, which is a form of blackmail. These methods may sound extreme, but the broadcast news frequently exposes viewers to political speakers whose persuasion stresses external effects—the dire necessity for change—more than an appeal to logical reasons for change.

Sample Argument

In the scenario below, Ivannia Herrera argued with her roommate over what might seem a trivial issue, a "Tempest in a Teapot": however, the underlying issues are not trivial. In the course of the argument, some values come to be seen as more important than others. Although this is an informal argument, it contains many of the features of a formal argument—for example, a claim, supporting evidence, and warrants that link the evidence to the claim. Refutation and concessions also are involved.

Read the argument carefully to find the appeals to reason, emotion, and ethics.

Tempest in a Teapot

Background: My roommate and I share a kitchen and utensils. Each day I make tea in a small stainless steel pot, which has a glass cover and a pouring spout with tiny holes that serve as a strainer. I pour two cups of water into the pot, let it boil, then add the leaves. When the tea is ready, I strain the tea water from the pot, leaving the tea leaves behind. I leave the pot on the counter until the next time I make tea.

The reason for the argument: My roommate has made it plain she does not enjoy seeing the pot with drenched tea leaves in the bottom.

Which points in the argument seem the most convincing to you? Why? Do you think there are any irrelevant points? Are points missing that might have been made?

My Side	Roommate's Side
If I leave the pot with the tea leaves on the counter, I can reuse them three times. Since I make the same type of tea several times a day, it makes sense that I reuse the leaves rather than throw them out, which will cost me more money in the long run.	The pot is left on the counter for many hours. Though it's okay to reuse the leaves, the kitchen looks messy. I don't like the kitchen looking dirty with an unclean pot sitting there every day. Furthermore, I can't use this pot because it is always filled with tea leaves that I can't throw away.
I bought all the pots and pans in this household, and I am happy to share them; however, if you need a pot like this to use regularly, you should consider buying one yourself.	I also bought utensils for the household—and even the computer. I share these things and understand the concept of sharing. I think that having roommates means having to compromise.

My Side	Roommate's Side
I think of myself as a clean person, and I contribute greatly to the cleanliness of the household. I think that your having to look at a small pot is a small "defect," considering. . . . Drinking tea is part of my daily life, and I enjoy it. As well, it costs me $6 per month; if I were to discard the tea each time, I would be spending $18 per month, and I can think of better ways to spend those extra $12!	I am not saying that you should throw away the tea leaves, but just find a better way to use them so they are not in sight and taking over the pot. I think that the cleanliness of my living space is a reflection on me, which is why I want a clean environment. I do not like seeing a messy pot, and that is my "defect." I also think I should be able to use the pot if I like, and I can't with the leaves in it.
We both agree on the need to compromise. I'm willing to compromise and buy a ball strainer that can hold the tea leaves inside for as long as need be. It is a small ball attached to a chain; the ball divides in half, the tea leaves are put in one half, the ball is closed, and it is placed inside a cup filled with boiling water. I suggest we compromise and each pay half for the ball strainer.	I'm happy to pay for half of it, as long as you keep the ball with the tea leaves in a cup in your own room. That way, you can bring it out anytime you want tea, but it will be out of my sight.

Exercise

Recall an argument you have had recently. Begin by briefly describing the circumstances that led to it. Then, divide a page in half vertically and summarize each point raised by "Your Side" and "The Other Side." Simply report what was said—each side's point of view and the counter-argument, if there was one. When a new point begins, draw a horizontal line to separate it from the next point. Finally, analyze the strengths and weaknesses of each point. Did the point make an appeal to reason? Did it make an emotional appeal? An ethical one? Were the points logically related to one another? Was the argument resolved? If so, how? Write a paragraph response to the argument trying to be as objective as possible to both sides.

1.1 Staking Your Claim

Like other formal essays, argumentative essays need a claim, usually made in the thesis statement near the beginning of the essay (see Part Three, Section 3.1 for types of claims). The body paragraphs should provide good reasons in support of the claim. Many kinds of evidence can be used for support, including facts, authorities, research studies, statistics, examples, and personal experience.

Since most arguments assign a positive value to something and a negative value to something else, your claim could be one of value (something is good or bad, right or wrong) or policy (something requires change through action). You can also argue a fact-based claim if you *interpret* the factual support for the claim in a particular light, rather than simply *present* the evidence as you would in an expository essay. For example, you could use a cause–effect claim to argue that aspartame is an unsafe sugar substitute. You would use the results of research but, without suppressing contradictory information, interpret the findings in a specific way that supports your claim. If you were writing an expository essay on the same topic, you would mediate the two sides of the debate, presenting the evidence and coming to an objective conclusion. Perhaps you would find that there is no conclusive evidence that aspartame is dangerous but that further research needs to be done. The following is the conclusion of an **expository** essay by student writer Rick Jew in which he objectively presented and analyzed the two sides of the debate over genetically modified organisms.

> There is no simple answer to this issue. Biotechnology is a double-edged sword. On one side, we are faced with feeding the growing population of the world, and on the other, we have to contend with the possible impact this new technology might have on our planet. Biotechnology may be able to give us the means to combat the growing malnourishment problem that persists in our world. Can we, however, turn back if we go too far by constantly modifying food to fit our needs? Does this biotechnology solution to our food shortage raise other unforeseen problems that can only be answered with another technology? The questions are many, and the answers are few. One thing certain is that genetic modification is in our future.

1.2 Arguable Claims

Many dogmatic arguments have no logical basis for argument at all; that is, they are invalid. What is needed for a valid argument? First, you need an **arguable topic**. Let's say you see two friends emerging from a showing of a recent movie. With raised voices and exaggerated gestures, friend A states categorically that Orlando Bloom is the best-looking actor in the movie. Matching friend A gesture for gesture, friend B insists that Elijah Wood is better-looking than Bloom. To support her claim, friend A cites Bloom's long locks and irresistible accent. Friend B's counter-claim is that Wood has adorable blue eyes and dimples. Who is right?

Obviously, neither is "right" because the topic is not arguable: you cannot base a rational argument on purely subjective standards. On the other hand, you could base an argument on their respective acting abilities, comparing the difficulty of their roles or how convincingly or subtly they perform in these roles.

There are other kinds of claims that are not arguable. You could not easily write an argumentative essay on the virtues of health, as there is no competing viewpoint. Similarly unarguable are obvious claims, such as "computers have changed a great deal in the last decade." A controversial subject does not always translate into an arguable one. For example, an argument that justifies computer hacking or the writing of viruses likely is not valid.

A successful claim:

1. can be tested through objective evidence, not just opinion
2. is capable of being argued; there clearly is another side.

1.3 Specific, Interesting, and Manageable Claims

You also need to ensure that the claim, like all thesis statements, is **specific**, **interesting**, and **manageable**.

1.3.1 Specific Claim

A **specific claim** states clearly and precisely what you will be arguing. The reader should know whether the claim is one of fact, value, policy, or interpretation. In addition, a specific claim is worded precisely.

> *Vague claim*: Parents of children who play hockey would like to see fighting eliminated from the game at all levels.

Although this claim technically satisfies the two conditions for an arguable topic, it is not specific enough to suggest the kind of argument to follow or even if the essay will be focused on argument rather than exposition: "parents," "would like to see," and "at all levels" are vague. Also, the phrase "eliminated from the game at all levels" doesn't seem connected to the rest of the claim. What has this got to do with the parents who presumably don't like seeing their children fight? Expanded thesis statements can be useful in arguments (see Part Two, Section 2.2), as the reader will see at a glance that you have supported your argumentative claim. In the following revised thesis statement, the claim is expressed more clearly due to specific diction as well as the inclusion of main points.

> *More specific claim*: Fighting should be prohibited in hockey, since violence gives young hockey players a negative model and reinforces a "win at all costs" mentality.

Although a claim may be specific if it is precisely worded, it is often a good idea to follow the claim by defining concepts that are central to your argument. Thus, definition is an organizational method often used in argumentative papers. In the claim above, the writer might define what is meant by "fighting." Does the dropping of hockey gloves constitute the beginning of a fight? Does overly physical contact? Does a fight begin when there is a third player involved? Definition enables the writer to narrow the topic, to make it more specific.

An "all or none" kind of claim is also non-specific. Avoid generalizing, or expressing your opinion as if it were true of everybody: "Young people today have it easy compared to the people of my generation"; "television contains too much violence"; "poor eating habits are responsible for weight gain." Where your claim is too broad, you should either use qualifiers to restrict its scope or reword it to make it more realistic. Examples of qualifiers include "usually," "often," "sometimes," "in part," "many," "some," "several," "a few," and many others. In addition, you can use verbs and verb phrases that qualify and limit, such as "may," "seems," "contribute to," and "play a role in."

1.3.2 Interesting

To help ensure the claim is interesting, it should be formulated with a specific audience in mind. In the claim about fighting in hockey, the intended audience is hockey parents as well as those in a position to institute the proposed change, such as coaches, managers, and other hockey executives. Many die-hard fans of professional hockey

Qualifying an overly broad claim can be important, but you should also be wary of diluting it by too many words and phrases like some, may, in large part, to some degree, and sometimes. You want your argument to be strong and realistic.

would not be interested in the main point of the argument, as it applies mostly to children. Those who never watch hockey or don't have children playing hockey probably would be even less interested. Similarly, an argument concerning the best measures to prevent eutrophication and growth of single-celled algae in China's lakes and reservoirs might be interesting to marine biologists, but probably not to the average reader.

Along with audience interest, an important consideration is the position of your audience towards your claim. Are most people to whom the argument is addressed likely to agree with you? Disagree? Be neutral? Will they possess general knowledge of the topic? Is the topic a current one that most will have heard of? These kinds of questions will be even more relevant when you come to structure your essay and provide support for your claim. For example, if your audience will be comprised mostly of those who disagree with your claim, it will be important to establish common ground and to convince them that you have similar values and goals. See Section 4.1.2 below for general questions about audience.

1.3.3 Manageable

Although the manageability of a claim will be determined partly by specificity and interest, it will also depend on essay length, availability of support, and the complexity of the issues as raised in the claim. Will you be using secondary sources or depending on logical premises and conclusions? Fact-based claims inevitably rely on facts, figures, and the findings of researchers and scientists. Thus, if you are not able to use these resources, the claim may not be manageable.

Policy-based claims, which try to persuade people to take action, go beyond simply proving something is bad or unfair. Often needed are realistic solutions or at least suggestions that these kinds of solutions exist. Can the proposed policy realistically be instituted? To say that a government should increase funding to post-secondary education by 25 per cent is probably not realistic given current economic conditions. If the change you advocate isn't feasible, it may be advisable to change your claim to one of value or else to amend it. Your supporting points may be complex, but the thesis statement itself must be workable and clear to the reader.

The claim about hockey violence was found to be arguable, specific, and interesting (to its intended audience), but is it *manageable*?

> Fighting should be prohibited in hockey, since violence gives young hockey players a negative model and reinforces a "win at all costs" mentality.

The issue of banning fighting throughout hockey, especially at the professional level, seems too complex to be manageable if the issues relating to young hockey players are also to be addressed. Realistically, would the fact that many hockey players act as role models for younger players sufficiently motivate those who manage the game that they would ban fighting? To make the statement manageable, the writer could focus *either* on the way that fights in professional hockey undermine hockey players as role models *or* on the consequences of fighting in minor hockey.

Value claim: Fighting in professional hockey gives young hockey players a negative model since violence reinforces a "win at all costs" mentality.

Amended policy claim: Fighting should be prohibited in minor hockey at and below the midget level since violence reinforces a "win at all costs" mentality.

Collaborative Exercise

In discussion groups, evaluate the 10 claims below, determining whether they would make good thesis statements for an argumentative essay. Are the claims **arguable**, **specific**, **interesting**, and **manageable**?

1. Cloning should be prohibited as it will mean the end of natural selection.

2. Since underage drinking is a major problem today, it wouldn't make sense to lower the drinking age any further.

3. "Friends" was a much funnier sitcom than "Family Guy."

4. Email is a very useful form of communication today as it is accessible, fast, and far-reaching.

5. Sex education needs to play a greater role in schools so that the number of pregnancies can be reduced and teenagers will practice safer sex.

6. No-fault insurance has made it easier for insurance companies to stay in business.

7. Internet dating services are an innovative, a convenient, and an affordable alternative to the singles scene.

8. It is better to have a summer job in retail than in customer service; though the pay is less, you meet nicer people.

9. Legal guidelines are needed for genetic testing as it may threaten our privacy, lead to harmful gene therapy, and have dangerous social costs.

10. Due to the dangerousness of the sport utility vehicle, people should have to prove they really need an SUV before being permitted to purchase it.

2. Working Your Claim: Kinds of Evidence

Using a variety of evidence is likely to produce a stronger argument than relying exclusively on one kind of evidence. However, it's important, especially if you are using research, that you find **hard evidence** to support your key points. Hard evidence includes facts, statistics, and authorities (experts). If you are able to find hard evidence to support your points, then a variety of **soft evidence** can enhance your argument. Soft evidence alone might make your essay readable and understandable, but it will likely not be as convincing as it would have been if you used at least some hard evidence. In fact- and policy-based claims, hard evidence usually is indispensable. It may be less important in value claims in which appeals to reason, emotion, and ethics, along with examples, analogies, brief narratives, description, or personal experience in themselves could produce an effective argument.

2.1 Facts, Statistics

It is hard to argue with facts. For this reason, factual information is the strongest kind of evidence in an essay; in addition, its effective use will enhance your credibility by making you appear knowledgeable. Although facts from reliable sources are always relevant to research essays, they can provide support in essays not involving research if you are arguing a topic you know a lot about. The student writer of the essay in Part One, Section 6.5.4 uses several facts, including references to the September 2001 tragedy in New York City as well as to works of art, artists, and art periods. When including research studies, you should check to see that the conclusions are based on factual data tested under controlled conditions. Reliable findings from research can be treated as factual.

You probably are familiar with the saying that statistics lie or with the political truism that numbers can be twisted to say whatever you want them to say. It's important that you take statistics from reliable sources. Although a statistic may not be an outright falsehood, you should be attentive to the wording of the passage from which a statistic is drawn in order to assess possible bias or distortion. Approach with scepticism statistics cited by people or organizations promoting a cause or espousing a particular viewpoint. For example, surveys conducted by special interest groups can be distorted or misrepresentative in various ways.

Consider the case of a union that wants to put pressure on the government by making its case public. The group's executive pays for a full-page ad in major newspapers, claiming 93.7 per cent support among the public. The questions to ask are, "Who were the survey's respondents?" "How many were surveyed?" "How was the survey conducted?" Perhaps in this situation a small number of people who happened to be walking by the picket lines were stopped and surveyed. Of course, the government's claims could be equally suspect due to the statistics cited at the expense of other numerical data that did not support its position. Reliable sources disclose their information-gathering methods. If you can verify the statistic through unbiased sources, however, you can treat it as accurate.

It will often be apparent whether the source is trustworthy or not. For example, although PETA (People for the Ethical Treatment of Animals) strongly opposes practices like animal testing, many statistics they publish can be considered reliable because they are obtained from reliable sources. In a PETA "factsheet" criticizing animal research, for instance, the writer cites a 1988 study that appeared in the refereed journal *Nature*, which "reports that 520 of 800 chemicals (65 per cent) tested on rats and mice caused cancer in the animals but not in humans" (Lave et al. 631). In sources like this, however, remember that statistics and factual data are being used for a specific purpose; evaluate them on an individual basis and bearing this purpose in mind.

All three student essays at the end of Part Four make effective use of facts and statistics.

2.2 Authorities, Experts

When you apply for a job, you may be asked for letters of reference. Unless your prospective employer asks specifically for a character reference, you would normally submit letters from knowledgeable experts—perhaps from your former bosses or those you have worked with. They would be considered authorities who could support your claim of competence and testify that you are a good candidate for the job.

Authorities can be used for support in an essay if they have direct knowledge of your subject. Authorities who are not experts can also be used, but they will have less authority. For example, in an essay that argues a scientific or mathematical point, citing Albert Einstein would be an example of hard evidence. In an essay about vegetarianism, citing Einstein would provide soft evidence; although he is a respected authority, he is not considered an expert on the topic. You could say that this kind of authority is the equivalent of a character reference in your job application. You will usually locate experts as you research your topic. However, it's also possible to conduct an interview with an expert, asking questions pertinent to your claim.

While hard evidence can be used directly to support your points, soft evidence indirectly supports your points and makes them more intelligible to the reader. Soft evidence tends to depend more on the writer's interpretation of facts and careful use of opinion or emotion. Kinds of indirect support include examples, illustrations, case studies, precedents, hypotheses, analogies, description, and personal experience. Of course, these kinds of evidence may incorporate various kinds of hard evidence as well.

2.3 Examples, Illustrations, Case Studies, Precedents

We use **examples** all the time in both speech and writing. To support his argument, the teenager arguing for his independence might give several examples of friends who live on their own. Examples should always be relevant and representative. The teenager's parents might refute the examples by pointing out that they are not representative—for example, that one friend, Shawn, has a full-time job and that another one, Giovanna, spent the summer travelling throughout Europe before moving out of her parents' house.

In most writing, examples bring a point home to the reader by making it specific and concrete. Examples are especially useful if you are writing for a non-specialist reader, as they make it easier to grasp a difficult or an abstract point. Illustrations, case studies, and precedents are extended examples that can be used to explain or reinforce important points.

Illustrations are detailed examples that often take the form of anecdotes or other brief narratives. In this example, student writer Graeme Verhulst uses an illustration to support his point that logic can be used to draw different conclusions from the same premise (a statement assumed to be true):

> Consider the example of the hydroelectric dam that the Urra company constructed in Colombia. The dam provides electricity to industry and profit to the companies and people who invest in it. The area flooded by the dam was inhabited by indigenous peoples. The river was a source of fresh water

and fish, and on the river's now flooded banks were food plants that sustained them. . . . If an analysis of this situation were based on the premise that all people should be treated equally and with respect, then through reason, the conclusion would be that this was a bad thing for the indigenous peoples living along the river. If, however, the basic premise was that business interests are primary, then the logical conclusion would be that the hydroelectric dam was a good thing.

Case studies are often used as support, particularly in the social sciences, education, and business; they can also be the focus of research studies. A case study is a carefully selected example that is closely analyzed in order to provide a testing ground for the claim the writer is making. Because case studies are practical, "real-life" examples, they can be used to support a hypothesis. For example, to ask if youth involvement in decision-making could produce a safer school environment, a Vancouver school planned a series of student-led initiatives and activities. When the results were analyzed, it was found that the students felt safer and had improved their pro-social and conflict resolution skills. The outcome supported the hypothesis concerning the effectiveness of youth involvement in decisions of self-governance.

Precedents are examples that refer to the way that a particular problem or situation was dealt with in the past. Judgements in courts of law establish precedents that influence decisions taken in subsequent similar situations. Once you have persuasively established some course of action as a precedent, you may then apply it to your argument. The validity of using precedents as evidence depends on your ability to convince the reader that (1) similar conditions or circumstances apply to your topic today and (2) following the precedent will produce a desirable result.

For example, if you were arguing that Canada should offer free post-secondary studies to all academically qualified individuals, you could refer to the precedent of Denmark, one of the first countries to provide universal access to post-secondary schooling. Then you must make it clear that (1) the situation in Denmark is comparable to the situation in Canada and (2) Denmark has profited from this system, therefore, that Canada is likely to benefit as well from a similar course of action.

2.4 Hypotheses, Analogies, Description, Personal Experience

These kinds of evidence are suggestive and indirect; they cannot in themselves prove a claim.

A **hypothesis** exists as an unproved assumption; it is not the same as a fact. To be valid evidence, the hypothesis must be a reasonable one that *appears capable* of being proved. Sometimes, preliminary research reinforces the validity of a hypothesis. For example, you could hypothesize that embryonic stem cell research will find cures for a number of diseases. The hypothesis would gain credibility if you discussed the successful results of preliminary research on mice. It would still, however, be an unproved assumption.

In many scientific studies, the researchers begin with a hypothesis that is rigorously tested under the controlled conditions of a scientific experiment. If the results verify the hypothesis—particularly if they can be duplicated by other researchers—the hypothesis is said to have been proved.

Analogy (comparison) and **description** can be used to make a point easier for the reader to understand and relate to. In order to explain the difference between reason and passion, student Graeme Verhulst used an analogy from Gibran's *The Prophet*:

> Khalil Gibran likened actions to a sailboat, with passion as the wind and reason as the rudder. A sailboat cannot go anywhere without wind, but is uncontrollable without a rudder. Rationality, like the rudder, can never be the sole basis for action.

Like narration, description may also play a limited role in argument, perhaps to attract interest in the essay's introduction or to set up a main point. Student writer Leslie Nelson began her essay on adolescent depression this way:

> Imagine a deep, dark hole that stretches forever without end. There is no light at either end of this hole; there is nobody else in this hole except you. Imagine living in this hole for hours, days, weeks, years. Imagine believing that you will never escape. Most teenagers find themselves in this hole—depression—at least once in their adolescent life, a time when nothing seems to go right.

Try to avoid writing on a topic to which you feel a personal connection so strong that it is likely to overwhelm reason; you may want to make emotional appeals to the reader, but you don't want to inject too much of your own emotion into a rational argument.

Personal experience could take the form of direct experiences or observations. Although this kind of evidence will enable the reader to relate to your topic, it is usual when relating personal experience to keep your voice objective. If you reveal a bias, it will undermine your credibility. Personal experience can be effective in supporting a value claim; for example, if you had witnessed a bullfight, your observations on bullfighting could be effective in supporting the claim that bullfighting is (or is not) cruel. Similarly, if you have had personal experience with homeless people by working in a food bank, you could use your experience to help support a related policy claim. Student writer Laura Benard uses personal experience to help introduce her topic (Section 10.2, Sample Argumentative Essay #2); Kerry Hinds uses it to help support her thesis (Essay #1).

3. Working Your Claim: The Rational Basis of Argument

A logical argument consists of assumptions and premises, which may or may not be explicitly stated. Two kinds of reasoning methods are used in logical arguments: through *inductive* or *deductive* reasoning, the assumptions and premises can be validated and a conclusion can be tested and confirmed. An argument, then, is a set of premises that show logical relationships with one another. Supported by various kinds of evidence, they attempt to prove a claim.

3.1 Inductive Reasoning

Induction, or **scientific reasoning**, arrives at a conclusion based on specific occurrences, which are observed and recorded. The conclusion, then, is the result of the accumulation of evidence through controlled and objective methods of evidence-gathering. Logical fallacies in inductive reasoning can develop:

1. where there is not enough evidence to make a generalization
2. where the means for gathering the evidence are faulty or biased.

People like to make jokes about the weather by using faulty inductive reasoning. How often have you heard someone say, "Whenever I wash my car, it rains," or "Every time I bring my umbrella, it's a sunny day, but the first day I forget it, it rains"?

Inductive reasoning is called scientific reasoning because scientific research frequently relies on the collection and analyzing of specific data to arrive at a conclusion. We also use inductive reasoning daily to draw conclusions. Consider the following example:

> *Recorded observations:*
> —on June 5 the sun set at 9:16
> —on June 6 it set at 9:16
> —on June 7 it set at 9:17
> —on June 8 it set at 9:17
> —on June 9 it set at 9:18

> *Prediction/Claim:*
> —on June 10, the sun will set at 9:18.

It is possible to make this prediction because we have observed specific data relating to this phenomenon. (Of course, knowledge of the motion of the Earth around the sun would also be needed to ensure the accuracy of the predictions.)

If we had simply recorded the times that the sun set on June 5 and 6, we might conclude that the sun would set at 9:16 on June 7, which would be incorrect: we would be drawing a conclusion without an adequate sample. On the other hand, if we made our first set of observations in Edmonton, Alberta, on June 5 and 6 and the second set in Regina, Saskatchewan, on June 7 and 8, the conclusions would also be incorrect because the methodology for evidence-gathering would be faulty.

Conclusions arrived at through inductive methods are said to be likely or probable, even after many observations have been made and evidence-gathering has been reliable. Most research studies focusing on causes and effects, such as clinical trials to confirm the causes of a disease or to test a new drug, work by induction, not to arrive at an absolute truth but to discover a probable cause or effect. Thus, further studies may seek to duplicate the results of the original study in order to make the findings more reliable.

3.2 Deductive Reasoning

Deductive reasoning arrives at a conclusion by assuming a general principle, the **major premise**, and applying it to a specific case, the **minor premise**. Incidents of faulty deductive reasoning can be especially insidious if they are used as the rationale for persecuting a visible minority. Many forms of stereotyping are based on faulty deductive reasoning. The major premise could take this form: "All people who live in California are in danger from earthquakes." The minor premise could be "Nancy lives in California." The logical conclusion following from the premises would be that "Nancy is in danger from earthquakes."

This logical structure is called a **syllogism**, a three-part model of deductive reasoning that presents a major premise and a minor premise to produce a conclusion. If one of the premises is wrong, as is the major premise above regarding earthquakes affecting all people in California, the conclusion will be invalid. If there is no logical relationship between the premises, the conclusion also will be invalid. The illustrative paragraph about Urra's hydroelectric dam in Section 2.3 above refers to two premises, which can be presented in syllogistic form:

Major premise: It is wrong not to treat all people with respect.
Minor premise: In building the dam, the Urra company did not treat the indigenous peoples with respect.
Conclusion: The Urra company was wrong to build the dam.

Major premise: It is right to treat business interests as primary.
Minor premise: In building the dam, the Urra company treated business interests as primary.
Conclusion: The Urra company was right to build the dam.

Even though the conclusions are contradictory, in each syllogism the conclusion is logical according to its premises.

Most logical arguments are constructed through a combination of inductive and deductive methods. However, while both inductive and deductive reasoning sound simple in theory, in practice each is fraught with potential pitfalls and perils. Successful argumentation is a difficult and sometimes slippery art, and you need to test the logic of your own reasoning as you proceed from one point to the next. The testing process will be helped by understanding the Categories of Faulty Reasoning, Section 6 below.

One of the ways of testing the logical connection between your claim, or any important point, and its support is through the underlying rationale for the claim, the **warrant**. The legal definition of a warrant is a written order issued so that a necessary act, such as a search or arrest, can be carried out. Similarly, the warrant behind your claim is a form of guarantee that, in effect, gives you the go-ahead to carry out what is announced in your claim. A warrant, then, solidifies the connection between claim and support. If the warrant will be evident to the reader, it does not have to be announced. The following warrant is clear without being stated:

Claim: It's July, and our neighbours, the Kringles, haven't put away their Christmas tree.
Evidence: I can see their tree in the middle of the room.
Warrant: Their window enables me to see into their living room.

A warrant can arise from various sources, including physical laws, human laws, assumptions, premises, common knowledge, aesthetic values, or ethical principles. For an argument to be successful, the reader must agree with the warrant. Student writer Stewart Lord announces his claim that marijuana's bad reputation is responsible for its prohibition (Section 10.4, Sample Argumentative Essay #3, below). For support he refers to actions and decisions based primarily on racial and ethnic factors. The warrant, or link between evidence and claim, is found in the tendency of socially dominant groups to impose moral standards on the activities of less powerful groups; Lord refers to this tendency as "moral entrepreneurship." The claim, then, rests on the warrant, which readers must agree with, or Lord's evidence may be discounted.

4. Refuting the Opposing View

4.1 Conditions for Rebuttal

For every valid argument there must be another side opposing the one you are arguing. You need to consider how you can respond to the opposing view. Whether and how you choose to make a **refutation** or **rebuttal** will be determined by

1. the topic itself
2. your audience
3. your purpose in arguing.

4.1.1 Topic

If the arguments on the other side will be obvious to most of your readers, it is probably unnecessary to mention them. In Laura Benard's Sample Argumentative Essay #2, Section 10.3, below, the opposing argument—that pesticides make a lawn aesthetically pleasing—needs no more than a brief acknowledgement; see Strategy A, discussed in more detail in Section 4.2.1.

If the reader is likely familiar with the topic and the major points of contention (such as arguments about legalizing marijuana), it is a good strategy to systematically raise each point and refute it; see Strategy B in Section 4.2.2. If a topic is likely to be less familiar to a reader, it may be best to acknowledge only the major counter-argument(s), while ensuring that your points are stronger and more numerous. Some would advise you not to mention the other side at all, that a refutation would weaken your argument by giving the other view the credibility of your attention. Your choice may depend on some of the other factors mentioned below.

4.1.2 Audience

You should bear in mind the stance of the audience towards your topic. If your audience is likely composed of mild dissenters and the undecided, it may be wise simply to acknowledge the other side and oppose it by a strong argument, employing Strategy A, Acknowledgement. If, however, you are addressing strong opponents, acknowledging their side and perhaps even admitting concessions would be advisable. An important aspect of rebuttal is to anticipate your opponents' objections so that you can refute such points in advance. Acknowledging the views of your opponent should show that, having analyzed them, you find them inadequate. Consider using Strategy B, Point-by-Point Refutation, then, if your audience supports the opposing view.

A related strategy in the case of moderate opponents is to stress ways that such readers can benefit—either personally or as members of a community—from considering

In refutation, consider drafting a paragraph or two in which you argue the opposing view. This can reduce your resistance to the opposing side, enabling you to understand it without bias. Your understanding of the other perspective ensures fairness. Then, draft your argument in response, revising the original version of the opposing view to ensure that your points clearly refute those on the other side.

your view. In her essay on safe injection sites (Section 10.2, Sample Argumentative Essay #1, below), Kerry Hinds addresses mild dissenters by pointing to the disadvantages drug users must overcome; when she argues that these sites would reduce health care costs, she appears to be addressing another kind of dissenting reader, one, perhaps, motivated more by practical than humanitarian concerns.

Whether the reader is undecided, mildly opposed, or strongly opposed, you should work to establish **common ground**. This can be done by demonstrating that you share basic values with your readers, though you may disagree with the action to be taken. Making concessions, agreeing in part to their argument, shows your reasonableness and willingness to compromise.

4.1.3 Purpose

The primary goal of an argumentative essay is not always to win the argument, and an argument should not be judged successful purely because it manages to silence the opposition. An argument may be an opportunity to engage in dialogue with others who share your concern about the topic, to enable your reader to see another side of a problem or another dimension to an issue in order to view it with greater tolerance. Long-lasting change is often a result of an attitude of openness and flexibility on the arguer's part, while a "pin the opponent" approach may result in nothing more than a fleeting victory. The open approach to arguing can be particularly effective with value-based claims.

4.2 Two Strategies for Refutation

4.2.1 Strategy A: Acknowledgement

Acknowledging the other side is important in most arguments. In cases where you need only acknowledge the opposition, you will have to decide on the amount of space to devote to this. In the following example, student writer Laura Benard briefly characterized the opposing viewpoint using only a prepositional phrase ("Despite their aesthetic value") ahead of her thesis statement. She presents no refutation, but treats the opposing side as generally acknowledged, i.e., as a given; the body paragraphs consist of main points relating to her thesis:

> Despite their aesthetic value, the negative impacts of maintaining lawns by means of pesticide, lawn mower, and water use are so great that lawn owners should adopt less intensive maintenance practices or consider lawn alternatives.

Writers often put the acknowledgement in the form of a dependent clause that contains the less important (opposing) information, followed by their own claim expressed in an independent clause. "Although some may argue . . . [major point of opposition argument], the fact is/I believe that . . . [your point]."

It is often necessary to provide background for the reader or a brief summation of the opposing view. In such cases, the writer can begin with this view, then follow with his or her own argument. Deciding how much space you spend on the opposing view requires striking a balance between the desire to demonstrate your willingness to be objective and the desire to present a strong argument of your own.

4.2.2 Strategy B: Point-by-Point Refutation

You should consider using a specific and thorough response to the other side if this side has considerable support or if your purpose is to arrive at a compromise between the two opposing viewpoints; in the latter case, you can seek to show that you are willing to move from your position in the interests of finding a common ground. In both cases, you would raise individual points, usually beginning with the opponent's point, and respond to the questions, implications, or flaws in the opponent's position. If your purpose is to win the argument, you will stress the opponent's inadequacies and inconsistencies, and draw particular attention to any fallacies. If your purpose is to find common ground, you will point out the inadequacies of the opposing viewpoint but assume the role of a constructive critic more than that of an antagonist. In both cases, though, your voice should remain unbiased and objective.

In the excerpt below, student writer Spencer Cleave addresses a common argument supporting the US embargo against Cuba. After a brief concession, he introduces two counter-claims, developed in the succeeding paragraph, that attempt to undercut the original claim:

> Many supporters of the maintenance of the trade embargo against Cuba contend that the Cuban government fails to uphold the human rights of its population. It is true that Cuba has had a number of human rights violations in its past. Thus, it is conceded that Cuba is also morally at fault on certain issues. However, many reforms have recently been made by the government in an attempt to remedy its human rights problems. These efforts show that the government has a desire to improve the conditions within its own nation. Furthermore, it would be in the best interest of the US to applaud the Cuban government in any human rights improvements, thus giving the image of a co-operative partner.

Because the opponents of legalized marijuana have a strong and often-debated case, student writer Stewart Lord chooses to address the main points of their argument systematically, summarizing these points and refuting them with facts and statistics (Section 10.4, Sample Argumentative Essay #3, below).

The section on the argumentative essay began by noting the importance of argument in all aspects of our lives. What follows is adapted from an information campaign of a medical service company in response to a government decision to restructure the services provided by the company. Although the form of the argument is very different from that of an essay, notice that the necessary parts of an argument are included and that in other respects, too, it conforms to the basic argumentative model discussed above. Numbers and letters have been added in order to make it comparable to body paragraphs in an outline.

5. "Please Sign Our Petition": A Case Study

As with most arguments, the claim is announced early. It is a policy claim, as the reader is asked to take an action—sign a petition; however, it is grounded in a value claim, that government plans could "compromise one of the best lab systems." To support this, the company cites various facts and statistics in their bulleted list; these purport to show that the labs provide essential services. Underlying the claim and connecting it to the evidence is the warrant: the premise that people are happy with and care about the service the lab provides. If the warrant is not accepted by the reader, the claim will be ineffective.

WE NEED YOUR SUPPORT! PLEASE SIGN OUR PETITION

The government plans to fundamentally change how laboratory services are delivered. These plans jeopardize the lab services you depend on.

These plans could also compromise one of the best lab systems there is—one that has been serving patients in communities across our province for more than 45 years.

I. WHAT THE GOVERNMENT IS PLANNING:

A. It has already announced a 20% cut in the fees it pays to community labs for the testing services we provide.

B. It is planning to dismantle the existing province-wide system and create six independent lab delivery systems—one within each of the health authorities.

C. It is planning to establish a bidding process that would see each health authority going to tender for all outpatient lab services.

The argument begins by summarizing three points of the opposing position. Systematically, the points are refuted in the next two sections. For example, point A above is countered by two points under "What this means to patient care" (point A below). The argument is developed through cause and effect: a 20% cut (cause) will affect patients and patient care.

II. WHAT THIS MEANS TO PATIENT CARE:

A. 1. Alone, the magnitude of the fee cuts will affect patients and patient care.

2. The government's other plans will bring a period of complete instability, turning today's system upside down.

B. The government's plans will result in six fragmented systems—potentially providing six levels of service and access—and six new bureaucracies to manage them.

C. Applying a competitive bidding process to laboratory medicine comes at a very high risk. Price is always a major factor in any competitive bidding process, and lowest bids come with reduced access service levels.

III. OUR CONCERNS:

A. The government based its plans on flawed, faulty, and unsubstantiated data.

B. We don't understand why the government chose to dismantle a system that works well, instead of building on its strengths.

C. We fully support the government's goals. However, we don't agree with the way it is trying to achieve those goals.

In addition to countering the major points of the government's argument, the company is concerned with establishing its credibility. Topic II addresses "patient care," focusing concern directly on the reader. Topic III Point C attempts to find common ground in an effort to show fairness to the government side: "We fully support the government's goals."

IV. WHAT WE'VE DONE

A. 1. We've told the government repeatedly that we support its goals and can help them achieve them. We've told the government to put its plans on hold so that we can talk to them about less disruptive alternatives.

2. We've told patients and physicians about the government's plans and how they could affect lab services and service levels.

WHAT WE'RE DOING NOW

B. 1. We're asking people who value the services we provide to show their support by signing our petition.

2. If you want to know more about the government's plans and our concerns, please visit our Web site.

C. *If you care about protecting the lab services you rely on—please sign our petition.*

IV. serves as a conclusion to the argument. The information in Points A, B, and C in effect summarize the claim by rewording it: in the claim/thesis, the phrase "jeopardize the lab services you depend on" is used; compare— "affect lab services and service levels," "value the services we provide," and "protecting the lab services you rely on." Point C makes an emotional appeal with its deliberate choice of the words "care" and "protect."

Community Lab Facts (statistical evidence to back the claim):
- For more than 45 years, physicians and their patients have relied on the quality cost-effective diagnostic testing and information services community labs provide.
- The testing and information services we provide help doctors diagnose, treat, and monitor their patients.
- **Every day**, the 1,600 people working in community labs:
  - provide a selection of several hundred different tests, from routine to speciality diagnostics.
  - support early discharge hospital programs by providing access to lab testing at home and in the community.
  - perform more than 55,000 tests on the 16,000 patients who visit one of our labs.
  - visit more than 700 patients in their homes and in long-term care facilities, at no charge to the patient or health care system.
  - deliver more than 5,000 specimens to public testing agencies at no cost to the patient, agency, or health care system.
  - transmit lab results electronically via PathNET to more than 3,000 physicians.
  - support our services through an extensive collection and transportation network, information technology, and analytical expertise that's taken years to develop.

Exercise

In collaborative groups or individually, analyze the argument presented above and evaluate its effectiveness, using the questions below as guidelines.

1. Consider your own position towards the issues. Do you have any knowledge about this or similar issues relating to government decisions about health care (or education)? How do government decisions affect you and/or other consumers of these kinds of services? What are the sides of the debate? Which side do you support? How might your prior knowledge and opinions affect your response to this argument or others like it?

2. Is there anything that would have made the argument more effective? Be as specific as possible.

3. Are there any questionable appeals to emotion or ethics? Are there any logical fallacies? Why do you think the company does not give specific information in main point III sub-point A: "The government based its plans on flawed, faulty, and unsubstantiated data?"

4. Analyze the refutation, bearing in mind topic, audience, and purpose. Why do the authors employ Strategy B) to refute the three points mentioned in the first main point (I), which gives background about the government's position?

5. What specific changes would you make if you were writing this argument as a formal essay? In what ways does it differ from a formal essay? (See Appendix B for some of the characteristics of informal writing.)

Exercise – *continued*

6. Imagine that one year has passed. The government is proceeding with its plans; some lab employees have lost their jobs, and there are dire predictions in newspaper editorials that our health care will be directly affected. How do you think the company's argument will change in response? Write a revised claim that reflects the new current conditions. Choose one specific form: informal brochure for distribution, letter to the editor/editorial, or argumentative essay.

6. Categories of Faulty Reasoning

6.1 Logical, Emotional, and Ethical Fallacies

Some kinds of arguments are effective; some are not. Ineffective arguments that use logical, emotional, or ethical fallacies detract from the writer's credibility. Misuse of reason affects reliability: we don't trust someone who misuses logic or reason. Misuse of emotional or ethical appeals shows unfairness to the other side: emotional fallacies *exploit* emotions so are very different from legitimate appeals to emotion.

Some fallacies are founded on faulty inductive reasoning (for example, cause–effect fallacies); others are grounded in the faulty use of deductive reasoning (where general or universal statements are made that may not be true).

Avoid these kinds of reasoning in your own writing and look for them in the argument of your opponent. Identifying them and analyzing their faulty nature will enhance your own credibility. Although these categories may enable you to identify the misuse of reason, emotion, or ethics, the categories are not all-inclusive; in many instances more than one type of fallacy may be involved.

These fallacies were categorized many years ago, and you may hear them referred to by their old Latin names. In the list that follows, their Latin names have been replaced by more modern descriptive labels.

- **Treadmill logic (circular reasoning)** argues without moving forward; circular arguments repeat, rather than evolve, by concluding with a restating of the premise in different words. Examples: "The Atlanta Olympics were designated as 'The Year of the Woman'. The title shows the great strides in women's performances as the title would not have been given otherwise." When students are asked to write about the importance of a character, incident, or setting in a literary work, they sometimes use treadmill logic by saying that without the character, incident, or setting, the story would not have been the same or could not have taken place.
- **Begging the question**. An argument based on an unproved assumption as if it didn't need proving begs [that some particular] question [be answered], meaning "pleads that an essential question be answered." You can also think of the terms as meaning that the *relevant* question has been "beggared," i.e., remains impoverished and without resources. Example: Charlotte saw a blue van drive past her house three times yesterday. She phoned the police to report the incident. This is not an

argument because the issue of whether or not the blue van is engaging in suspicious or illegal activity has not been addressed—the argument begs (asks that) the question of legality (be answered), or begs (leaves empty) the relevant issue of legality. See *name-calling*, below.

- **Guilt by association (ad hominem)** uses the fact that some supposedly disreputable person or group supports a view as an argument against it or opposes it as an argument in its favour. Example: "How bad can whale hunting be when an extremist group like Greenpeace opposes it?"

- **Name-calling** assigns base motives or a pejorative label to an individual or group (See slanted language below.) Example: Pharmaceutical companies' long hold on patents denies needed medicines to the poor and is just plain greedy. An individual or group can be assigned a negative label, which then becomes grounds for attack. Recently, the Western definition of terrorism has been challenged for its narrow applicability to subversive anti-Western groups. In such cases, applying the label of terrorist may also be **begging the question** of precisely what constitutes terrorism.

- **Red herring**: a fallacy of irrelevance that attempts to distract or sidetrack the reader, often by employing an ethical fallacy. Examples: "My honourable opponent's business went bankrupt. How can we trust him to run the country?" "I know that particular business supports the arts, but it made $1.5 billion last year."

- **Straw man**: another fallacy of irrelevance; misrepresents an opponent's main argument by substituting a clearly fallacious or minor argument in its stead. The point is to get the audience to agree with the minor argument, making it easier to criticize the opponent's overall argument. The "straw man," then, is a flimsily constructed argument that is erected in place of a valid one. Example: Thaddeus Tuttle points out that while women have not achieved wage parity with men, they often take maternity leaves, which means they don't work as much as men. Among its flaws, this argument ignores the basic principle of equal pay for equal work.

- **Name-dropping** uses the fact that some popular person or group supports something as an argument in its favour; such spurious authorities can include entertainment and sports celebrities who endorse a particular product for financial gain; compare with the **guilt by association** fallacy.

- **Authority worship** accepts unquestioningly the argument of an authority not on the basis of what is said but solely on the basis of who says it. It's important that you exercise critical thinking and do not accept claims without thinking them through, especially if bias could be involved. Example: "He spent 17 years on the Atomic Energy Board. He must know everything there is to know about his subject."

- **Bandwagon**: an emotional fallacy; argues in favour of something because it has become popular. Example: "Everyone has seen the movie. We have to see it tonight."

- **Two wrongs make a right**: a closely related ethical fallacy to the **bandwagon**. Example: "It's okay to cheat on exams; everyone does."

- **Longevity** argues the validity of something solely because it has existed for a long time. Example: "How can war be wrong when people have been fighting each other since the dawn of civilization."

- **Doubtful causes** insists that a result is inevitable and cites too few causes to support that result; basing an argument on a relationship that may not exist. Example: "He looked unhappy after the exam; he must have failed miserably." This assumes there was only one cause for his unhappiness—if, indeed, he *was* unhappy; making this assumption is also an example of a cause-effect fallacy.

- **False cause ("post hoc")**: another cause-effect fallacy; asserts that simply *because* one event preceded another one there must be a cause-effect relationship between them. Example: Neesha wears her favourite socks to class the day she fails a test; consequently, she throws the socks away. Superstitions can arise when persons assume a causal relationship when only a temporal one exists. Of course, there are causal relationships between many events; for example, if Neesha walked in front of a car and was hit, then obviously her action resulted in her injury. A false cause assumes a connection without valid evidence.

- **Hasty generalization**: forms a conclusion based on little or no evidence. Example: "I talked to two people, both of whom said the text was useless, so I will not buy it." Perhaps many people bought the text, so two people may not be a good sample.

- **Certain consequences (slippery slope)** is a common fallacy with many other names. It insists that a result will be inevitable based on an oversimplified cause-effect relationship. Example: "Without competition, society would never improve, as everybody would be happy to be like everybody else." This suggests that competition alone results in society's improvement; "If we legalize marijuana, other more dangerous drugs are going to end up being legalized as well."

- **Either/or (false dilemma)** suggests that there are only two available options. Example: "Either I borrow the car tonight or my life is over." Consider that notorious cry "you're either with me or against me," which takes the logical *either/or* fallacy and gives it a strong emotional thrust.

- **Middle ground fallacy**, in contrast to the **either/or** above, assumes that in the face of two seemingly irreconcilable options, a third option, such as a position midway between extremes, is the only one: Example: "Since Donnie wants the family pet to be a dog and Ronnie wants a cat, we'll get a bird." This could also be termed the "Solomon Solution." When two women came with a baby before the Biblical king Solomon, each declaring she was the baby's mother, Solomon threatened to compromise by cutting the baby in half! The rightful mother identified herself as being the one who protested she would rather have the other woman keep the baby so that it might live.

- **Non-sequitur ("it does not follow")** suggests that there is a logical connection (such as cause-effect) between two unrelated areas; these kinds of fallacies are so common that their Latin name has entered the English vocabulary. Examples: "If we hadn't built planes to conquer gravity, the NY tragedy of September 11 wouldn't have happened." "I worked hard on this essay; I deserve at least a B+." Unfortunately, working hard at something does not guarantee success, even if it does make it more likely.

- **False analogy** compares two things that are, in fact, not alike. Example: "How can people complain about circuses that use wild animals in their acts; we keep animals that were once wild in small spaces in our homes." Analogies can provide support for a point, but to draw a true analogy, you need to have a real basis for comparison.

- **Common knowledge** argues on the basis of what "everybody" knows or believes. Example: "In their hearts, everybody knows that capital punishment is cruel and immoral." There are few things that *everybody* knows.

- **False authority** argues on the basis of a presumed or unspecified authority: Example: "Studies show that disrespect for authority has never been greater in our society."
- **The ends justify the means** favours *product* over *process*. Often there is validity in the claim of "short-term pain for long-term gain," but the argument can become fallacious when the short-term pain is minimized or discounted—when, in effect, the *sole* concern is with the goal. The argument is also sometimes used to justify *any* means that the arguer wants to employ. It is probably safe to say that much of the suffering inflicted on humans by other humans, especially in the name of political ideology, has taken this form.
- **Fortune-telling** denies an effect as arising from a cause on the basis that it hasn't happened yet—therefore, it's not going to. In this distorted cause-effect fallacy, the perpetrator projects into the future without considering probability or other evidence. Example: "Uncle Harry has smoked two packs of cigarettes a day for 20 years, and he hasn't died yet, so smoking obviously is not that dangerous."
- **Fuzzy categories (argument of the beard)**: so named because of the difficulty of deciding how many hairs on a chin constitute a beard; insists that there is no fundamental separation between two ideas or objects, or a point where one becomes the other. This fallacy appears when terms are imprecisely defined. Example: a student argues with Professor Fuddle that there is no precise reason why his English essay was given a "C." After the professor agrees to a C+ grade, the student repeats the argument that there is no clear distinction between a C+ and a B- and eventually works his mark up to an "A."
- **Finite categories** asserts that something belongs in a certain category on the basis of only one characteristic. Example: "I'm sixteen now, so where are the keys to the car?" The illogical assumption here is that legality alone determines the right to drive a car.
- **Desk-thumping (dogmatism)** asserts without supporting evidence on the basis of what you firmly, perhaps passionately, believe. Example: "It is everyone's moral obligation to oppose the new tax." In argumentative essays, it's best to avoid the self-conscious reference to your opinion; instead, you should let your points do the talking for you.
- **Filling the void** argues that since no plausible explanation for something has been offered, the one the writer puts forward must be accepted. Example: "No one has ever been able to explain how the Pyramids got built, so obviously it must have been done with the help of aliens."
- **Tradition (or, that's the way we've always done it)** argues for a course of action because it has been followed before, even if the same conditions no longer apply. Note how this differs from using **precedents** as evidence. Example: "You shouldn't ask if you can go to Toronto for the Thanksgiving weekend. This is a time you always spend with your family."

Determining context is vital in deciding whether the writer has used fallacious reasoning or has misused emotion. There are certainly many occasions when, for example, you will be able to successfully argue that the ends do justify the means or where there may be only two alternatives to consider (**either/or**).

At other times, the fallacy represents a distortion of a legitimate and effective form of support for an argument; for example, an analogy can become a false analogy if there is no true basis of comparison between the object compared and what it is being compared to. False analogies often implicitly address the question of scale and may seek to compare the very small to the very large; for example, when a baseball strike loomed in 2002 and was scheduled to begin on 11 September, an analogy was made between the parties involved in the strike and the terrorists that perpetrated the events of 11 September 2001. As noted, the **tradition** fallacy should be carefully distinguished from the legitimate use of **precedent** as a form of evidence.

All lines of argument work most effectively when they are combined with other arguments. In fact, you could think of the fallacies as unwarranted generalizations or oversimplifications that, as such, fail to do justice to the complexities involved in an issue. Fallacies embody identifiable evidence of poor reasoning. In addition, the writer using them weakens his or her argument, as a reader could easily think, "Wait a minute; that doesn't make sense." When you use argument, you want your statements to be forceful and effective—not to provoke suspicion or mistrust. Otherwise, the reader might commit the fallacy of rejecting your entire argument (**hasty generalization**) because in one instance you misused reason.

Writers need to look closely and objectively at the *way* they argue and ensure that their arguments are always founded on logic and that their appeals to emotion and ethics are always moderate—that they do not excessively praise or condemn. Watching out for the first will make the writer appear reliable and trustworthy; watching out for the last two will make the writer appear fair.

Exercises

A. **Silencing**. Writers sometimes resort to logical or emotional fallacies because they can **silence** those against whom they are directed. They do so because there is **no logical response possible**, since the reasoning behind them is flawed. Each of the following statements is based on faulty reasoning. Try to determine why it fails the test of reason and why it would not be effective in an argumentative essay. If it seems to afford an example of one of the fallacies listed above, decide which one; in some cases, more than one fallacy might be involved. More important than being able to identify the precise label is being able to see why the statements, as they are, are not logical or make unfair appeals to emotion.

1. The premier made a promise during his election campaign that he has failed to keep. He is a liar and his word can no longer be trusted.

2. He's already a full professor, and he's only 44 years old. He must possess a brilliant mind.

3. "In our family, males have always been named 'Harold' and females 'Gertrude'; therefore, you should name your twins 'Harry' and 'Gerty.'"

4. If you don't get a degree in law, medicine, or business these days, you're never going to make any money.

5. Murder in Oman is almost non-existent because Oman has capital punishment, but murders occur every day in Canada because Canada doesn't have it.

Exercises – *continued*

6. "When I serve you dinner, it's terrible not to eat all of it when you consider that one-third of the world's population goes to bed hungry."

7. The teacher hasn't called on me to answer a question for three consecutive days; it looks like I don't need to do the reading for tomorrow.

8. Television has changed so much over the years; there can be little doubt that it will survive the invasion of the computer.

9. Believing that women should serve in combat roles in the military is like believing that men should be able to bear children.

10. "I know I went through the red light, officer, but the car in front of me did too."

B. **Find the Fallacies**: The following story by student writer Alison James contains at least five errors in reasoning. Try to classify them according to the logical and emotional fallacies referred to above:

> Last week, Tina and her boyfriend, Steve, were running late for a reservation at their favourite restaurant. They were trying to figure out the quickest route so they would not lose their table. Tina suggested taking the side streets in order to avoid the traffic lights. Steve suggested that, while there are traffic lights on the main street, there was a chance they would hit all the green lights; but if they took the side streets, they would have to stop at all the stop signs. He added that the speed limits were faster on the main street than on the side streets where the speed limit was 30 km/h.
>   Tina rebutted, "But nobody actually drives 30 on those streets!"
>   Steve replied, "But we could get stuck behind a little old lady, and everybody knows how slowly they drive. Besides, we can speed on the main street; there are never any cops on that street, so we won't get a ticket."
>   Tina said, "No, let's take the side streets: we always go that way. And there have been two accidents recently on the main street, so the side streets are safer."
>   Neither of them was convinced by the other's argument (perhaps because they were so faulty), and they missed their reservation after all!

6.2 Fallacies and Slanted Language

In addition to the misuse of logic and emotion, writers can show their lack of objectivity by using **slanted or loaded language**. Such language highlights the writer's strongly subjective views and detracts from his or her credibility. Slanted language can take various forms from extreme statements to qualifiers (adjectives or adverbs) that convey, sometimes subtly, a biased viewpoint. While slanted language is often direct and offensive, it operates more subversively when it plays unfairly on the connotations, rather than the denotations, of language—in other words, on the suggestiveness or implications of particular words and expressions, rather than on their literal meanings. A writer's careful and conscious use of a word's connotative meaning can be effective in an argument, but if the purpose is to distort the truth, then the writer's credibility will be at stake. The italicized words in the following reveal slanted language:

> In the recent election, the *reigning* political *regime was removed from office* as a result of the *atrocities they had committed* against the people of the province. The voters believed the new government would improve things, but when you achieve such easy victory there is a tendency to overlook the reason for your victory: the people who elected you. Today, the government is ignoring the middle class, *betraying* the very people who *naively* voted them into office.

Collaborative Exercise

The following paragraphs suffer from faulty logic and/or emotional appeals, as well as examples of slanted language. In groups, analyze the arguments, determine what fallacies and inconsistencies make it ineffective, and suggest improvements to make the argument stronger. More important than being able to identify the precise fallacy is being able to see that the statements are illogical or make unfair appeals to emotion.

1. Genetically engineered foods are being sold in most supermarkets without anyone knowing that we are being used as guinea pigs for the corporations developing this technology. The general public is being kept in the dark entirely, and the way that this food is being sold is through one-sided advertising. The public is being told that genetically engineered foods are a safe and effective way to grow a lot of food faster by inserting genetic material of one species into another. Though the proponents of genetically engineered foods attempt to convince the public that this technology will save lives, the reality is that major biotechnology companies are developing genetically engineered food crops to maximize their profits. Corporations would have us believe that the reason why 19,000 children starve to death daily is because of inefficient agricultural practices, but the world currently produces enough food today to provide a decent diet for every person on this planet. In spite of this fact, genetically engineered foods are being sold as the cure for Third World starvation. This, however, is simply not true. The motives of the companies selling genetically engineered foods are not to save the lives of starving people, but to line their own pockets by profiting from the biotechnological industry. As a society, we should move to force governments to ban the development of genetically engineered foods before it is too late.

Collaborative Exercise – *continued*

2. The legalization of marijuana would destroy society as we know it today. The typical Canadian would be exposed to many harsh drugs, such as coke, crack and heroin, due to the increased acceptance of drugs within the community. Rehabilitation clinics for chronic drug users would be a huge drain on the economy. There would have to be new laws and screenings implemented to prevent people from working with heavy machinery or operating a motor vehicle while impaired by marijuana. Canadian business owners would be dissatisfied with many of their employees, and then discrimination would rear its ugly head. Firing someone for smoking marijuana and not being productive at work is not discrimination; however, the point would be made that it is. Clearly, our society would sink to a despicable level if this drug were legalized.

7. Organizing an Outline for Argument

When outlining and drafting argumentative essays you should pay particular attention to the order of the main points of your argument. Ensure that they are ordered logically—i.e., from least to most important point—**climax order**—or from most important point to least important—**inverted climax**—whichever is most relevant for your argument; other orders are possible. You do not have to include all the elements listed below nor follow the same order of parts; for example, it may not be necessary to include background if the issue is well known to most readers. The refutation may not require a lot of space. Depending on the topic and other factors, you might choose to place it before your main points; indeed, in some instances, it may not be needed at all. If you use strategy A to acknowledge the other side, you could place the acknowledgement in either the Introduction or the Background section. In strategy B, you could begin a point-by-point refutation in Part III.

8. Rhetorical Function of Parts

The following pattern is based on the classical five-part argumentative model used from the time of the orators of the ancient world to the present day. Other patterns are possible, including **holding back the claim**, which can be useful if you expect strong opposition or if your opening is dramatic or memorable in another way. In this pattern, you do not announce your claim until you have provided the evidence, so your claim, in effect, would act as a conclusion. The most common pattern in formal writing, however, is the following classical model (or variants on this model):

I. INTRODUCTION
  • gains reader's attention and interest
  • includes your claim
  • may suggest the primary development method (if there is one)
  • establishes your credibility (knowledge, reliability, and fairness)

Body Paragraphs: II, III, and IV.

II. BACKGROUND
- presents background information, if relevant

III. LINES OF ARGUMENT
- presents good reasons (logical, emotional and ethical appeals) in support of thesis; draws on assumptions, premises, and warrants
- uses all relevant evidence—facts, statistics, examples, views of experts/authorities
- presents reasons in specific order related to argument

IV. REFUTATION
- considers opposing points of view
- notes both advantages and disadvantages of opposing views
- argues that your thesis is stronger than opposing view and more beneficial to the reader

V. CONCLUSION
- summarizes argument
- expands or elaborates on the implication of your thesis
- makes clear what you want reader to think or do
- may make final strong ethical or emotional appeal

9. Sample Outline for an Argumentative Essay

The following basic outline is for a five-part essay that argues against pesticide use in lawn care. The final version of the essay follows (Section 10.2).

The Grass Is Not Always Greener

I. Introduction
A. History of the lawn: Being surrounded by a large expanse of green sod has become a habit (psychological dimensions of the lawn).
B. Thesis statement (policy): With the high costs of non-essential pesticide, fertilizers, water use, and lawn mower emissions, society should adopt less intrusive lawn maintenance practices or consider lawn alternatives.

Body Paragraphs

II. Pesticide and fertilizer use
A. The toxic chemicals of lawn maintenance are significant contributors to environmental degradation.
   1. Lawn pesticides are applied on a scale rivalling agricultural toxins, accounting for about 30 per cent of all pesticides.
   2. Forty-five per cent of Toronto households use chemical pesticides or organic products on their lawns.
B. Support in reducing use of pesticides around the home is endorsed by different groups.

1. The federal government supports the idea that people should reduce their pesticide use at home as much as possible.
2. Toronto Environmental Alliance found that 82 per cent of Ontario residents supported a bylaw restricting use of cosmetic pesticides on private residential property.
3. In 1991, the town of Hudson, Quebec, adopted bylaw 270, restricting use of lawn care pesticides in its boundaries.

III. Lawn mower use

A. Fuel use and emissions factors suggest lawn mowers are significant polluters.
1. There are 4.3 million gas-powered lawn mowers in Canada.
2. Contribution to volatile organic compounds have been found as high as 13 per cent in some areas of the U.S.
3. Lawn mower pollution can be compared with that of late-model cars.
4. An estimated 5.4×10^6 litres of fuel are used per year in Canada.
B. There are sensible options for replacing gas-powered mowers.

IV. Water use and lawn alternatives

A. An average of 20 per cent of municipal water supplies go to watering lawns and gardens.
B. Options:
1. Alternative 1: Use xeriscaping to plant water-efficient lawn alternatives, such as native plants that are adapted to local weather and thus do not need watering.
2. Alternative 2: decreasing or eliminating the area of your lawn or consider lawn alternatives like clover, thyme, or flowering lawns.

V. Conclusion

A. There is a need for lawn owners to realize the negative effects of intensive lawn care practices.
B. While one can acknowledge aesthetic value of lawns (psychology), for the environment's sake, consider alternatives to current methods of lawn maintenance.

10. Sample Essays

The first of the following argumentative student essays uses minimal research. For an example of an argumentative essay that does not use research at all, see Part One, Section 6.5. The second and third essays use research extensively, so they can be considered research essays.

Annotations are given for the second essay; a series of questions follows the third sample essay. To conserve space, the essays are not double spaced and "References" and "Works Cited" sections are not on separate pages. The essays do not follow correct essay format requirements for title pages or identification information. For the correct ways of dealing with these issues, see Part Eight, Section 4, Essay Presentation.

10.1 Sample Student Argumentative Essay #1
(APA Style) (850 words)

A Case for Safe Injection Sites in Victoria

by Kerry Hinds

The 12 October 2004 edition of *The Globe and Mail* had the following headline on its front page: "107 'Safe' Overdoses at Gallery a Success." It is rare that heroin users and reports of overdoses reach the front page of a newspaper; the majority of citizens usually forget these people. Due to the city's high number of heroin users, however, Vancouver is the home to North America's only legal "shooting gallery." Recently there has been investigation into the need for and viability of a safe injection clinic in Victoria, B.C. Programs such as these raise the question of whether or not British Columbians' health care dollars should be spent on a clinic for citizens living in poverty who are not paying taxes. However, looking beyond the personal safety and health of addicts and directing our gaze towards the health of non-using citizens, it is apparent that Victoria is in need of a safe injection house. It is also important to look at this problem with foresight to avoid unneeded spending on health care for chronic disease. Opposition to spending for this and similar social programs stems from the perpetuation and misunderstanding of drug addiction and behavior.

The clinic in Vancouver is open 18 hours a day and is a safe location for heroin users to shoot up: clean needles are distributed, needles are properly disposed of, and the area is a police-free zone. There are also counseling and medically trained professionals on site. The goal of this three-year $3.7 million project is to reduce deaths by overdose and slow the spread of drug-related diseases, mainly AIDS and hepatitis. Over six months in the Vancouver clinic, there were 107 overdoses out of more than 108,000 visitors; none of these people died (Armstrong, 2004).

Victoria is an urban centre with a heroin and drug-related disease problem. This situation is easy to see when one is walking through the downtown core. The problem may not be as severe as Vancouver's, but it is necessary to take proactive actions to prevent the spread of AIDS and hepatitis. Having been involved with The Youth Empowerment Society downtown and working with street youth in Victoria, I see the need for such a program in Victoria; the personal health of users, old and young, is at stake.

Lack of support for shooting galleries comes from a prevalent conservative attitude of people believing that their tax dollars should not be spent to support people who have lived their lives in poverty and as drug addicts. Unfortunately, these people are not looking beyond their tax dollars; they do not see that safe injection clinics are also protecting their own health. Having recently met people who have been pricked by needles while cleaning their storefronts and others who have contracted hepatitis from disposing of crack pipes, I can see that safe houses are necessary for the safety of public health. Also, reducing the spread of AIDS is beneficial for everybody, not just the users who are sharing needles. If we wish to control the spread of AIDS, we cannot look at AIDS as strictly a drug-user's disease; many non-users get infected also. If money is not put into programs such as these, our health care system will be further burdened with the care of chronically ill patients, costing the tax payers even more money than the cost of opening a clinic. Without foresight and action, the health of non-users will be further compromised and our health care system will be further debilitated.

A lack of understanding of drug addiction and behaviour perpetuates a negative attitude in the general public, who may blame the addicts for their lack of self-control and motivation to get themselves out of their situations. Society should be educated in the behaviours of drug addicts; brain functioning is impaired even while a drug addict is straight; as well, many addicts justifiably see recovery as blocked by many barriers. The social, psychological, and biological barriers involved in getting straight can outweigh the benefits of being straight: weeks of withdrawal and intense introspection into their life histories and circumstances; a prolonged process of rebuilding of their self-esteem and self-worth; and the rejection of a life that is known for an unknown life of poverty and new social groups. It is important to remember that these are still people with different stories and life experiences. There are many reasons why people end up being users. For instance, people who start life in a low socio-economic family have fewer opportunities for success and lack education and self-worth. Also, people who are children of young and addicted parents are more likely to exhibit generational patterns of drug abuse. It is uncharitable to not look beyond the drug problem—we must realize that poverty and drug use are largely a social problem.

Victoria needs a safe injection clinic, not only for the health of users but also for the safety of public health. Without proactive programs such as this one, many lives will be unnecessarily lost or drastically affected, and British Columbians will be burdened with the future health costs of chronic disease. With education about drug addiction and behaviour, perhaps the stereotypes associated with drugs addicts will be eliminated and public support will increase for safe injection clinics.

Reference

Armstrong, J. 107 "safe" overdoses at gallery a success, backers say. (2004, October 14). *Globe and Mail*, A1, A8.

10.2 Sample Student Argumentative Essay #2
(APA Style) (1,350 words)

The Grass Is Not Always Greener

by Laura Benard

In the Introduction, Benard uses personal experience effectively—she draws us into the essay as an "insider," briefly acknowledging the benefits of green lawns, then stating her claim.

When I was growing up, I lived in the house with the greenest, shortest, most grub-free lawn on the block. Our lawn was the envy of the street, and our neighbours were constantly trying to figure out the secret to my Dad's lawn success. As an insider, I knew his "secret" was merely a method followed by millions of lawn owners, which included dedicated pesticide and fertilizer application, mowing, and watering. Although these maintenance practices consistently produce a lawn that can rival any golf course, the cost of such a lawn is extremely high and generally overlooked. In addition to the billions of dollars spent each year to maintain the "green carpets" that dominate most North American neighbourhoods (Levetin & McMahon, 2002), the environmental and health costs of lawns are substantial (Meyer, Behe, & Heilig, 2001). Despite their aesthetic value, the negative impacts of maintaining lawns by means of pesticide, lawn mower, and water use are so great that lawn owners should adopt less intensive maintenance practices or consider lawn alternatives.

A brief background on historical lawn "fashions" is given, which is quickly followed by statistics on their use today.

The green lawns favoured by modern society have a long history and are the result of fashion-dictated evolution. Unlike modern lawns, medieval lawns were planted to imitate natural meadows "starred with a thousand flowers" (Dawson, 1968, p. 14). These meadows were planted as features of a diverse landscape, which generally included orchards and gardens. It was not until the eighteenth century when large expanses of tended grass unadorned by any flowers or shrubs became fashionable that modern lawns were conceived (Dawson). The pure expanses of tended grass favoured in the eighteenth century maintained their popularity and continue to dominate modern landscapes today.

The struggle to maintain these pure lawns, however, has led to the reliance on toxic chemicals. A recent poll found that 45 per cent of households in Toronto use chemical pesticides or organic products on their lawns (Bashur, 2002), and it has been estimated that 50 million kilograms of chemicals are applied to Canadian lawns and gardens each year (Van Caeseele, 2000). A study by Meyer et al. (2001) found that while most homeowners felt that pesticides were harmful to the environment and human health, most participants reported pesticide use on their lawns and disagreed with the statement that their lawn was harmful to the environment. This finding illustrates the common misconception that pesticide use on lawns is not a serious contributor to environmental degradation. While individual pesticide use may appear benign, the cumulative effect of millions of lawn owners has led to levels of lawn pesticide use that rival agricultural pesticide use and that represents 30 per cent of total domestic pesticide use (Robbins, Polderman, & Birkenholtz, 2001). Effects of pesticides on wildlife and the environment can be devastating, as was illustrated by DDT in the 1960s. Additionally, many common lawn pesticides pose significant human health risks. A recent summary of findings by the Ontario College of Family Physicians found that Canadian children are "particularly at risk" from exposure to pesticides (Martin, 1998, p. 2). The study also found that pesticides used on lawns may disrupt human hormone and endocrine systems, a disruption associated with decreased immune response, alterations to the brain and reproductive system, behavioural changes, and increased susceptibility to breast and testicular cancer (Martin).

Although many homeowners subscribe to the belief that a green lawn is the only option for residential landscaping, it is becoming apparent that the costs of such lawns surpass the benefits. In 1991, Hudson, Quebec, adopted By-law 270 and became the first Canadian town to restrict the use of lawn care pesticides (Bashur, 2002). The by-law's success has compelled many municipalities to follow Hudson's lead and restrict lawn pesticides. With the effects of pesticides becoming more evident, support for cosmetic pesticide use is weakening. A 2001 Ontario-wide poll found that 82 per cent of residents would support a by-law restricting the use of cosmetic pesticides on private residential property (Bashur). While this finding is encouraging, statistics have shown that residential use of pesticides is not declining (Maynes, 2001). This discrepancy between the perceived risks of pesticide use and actual pesticide use is frequently encountered suggesting that legislation such as By-law 270 may be required to actually reduce cosmetic pesticide use.

In addition to chemical requirements, frequent mowing is another requirement of modern lawns. According to Statistics Canada, there are over 4.3 million gasoline-powered lawn mowers in Canada, which release approximately 80,000 tonnes of greenhouse gas (GHG) emissions each year (Yumlu, 1994). The harmful emissions of nitrous oxide, carbon dioxide, and hydrocarbons have significant impacts on air quality and global warming. Although the emissions of lawn mowers may seem insignificant compared to the emissions of cars, the rate at which lawn mowers emit harmful emissions is staggering. In one hour, a conventional lawn mower produces as much pollution as 40 late-model cars driving for the same amount of time (Van Caeseele,

The previous paragraph refers to the precedent of DDT; this paragraph analyzes By-law 270 almost as a case study; the writer concludes that legislation may be necessary to "reduce cosmetic pesticide use."

To argue her second main point, about gas-powered lawn mowers, Benard relies mostly on facts, statistics, and a comparison. She begins a new paragraph when she changes subpoints from toxic emissions to fuel consumption; she ends by discussing alternatives.

2002). With an estimated 4.3 million gasoline-powered lawn mowers averaging 25 hours of use per season (Yumlu), the scale of lawn-mower emissions becomes apparent.

In addition to the large-scale emissions from lawn mowers, the total fuel use by lawn mowers also occurs on a large scale, with an estimated 5.4×10^6 litres of fuel used per year in Canada. Both toxic emissions and fuel consumption could be eliminated by using alternatives to gasoline-powered lawn mowers such as electric, solar, and manual equipment. Minimizing turf areas by planting "no-mow" ground covers and other landscaping alternatives instead of grass could also reduce emissions and fuel use (Van Caeseele). The effects of GHG emissions and fuel use on global warming are becoming increasingly apparent; consequently, lawn owners should consider alternatives to gasoline-powered mowers, which are clearly contributing to the problem.

Although pesticide use and mowing are common lawn maintenance practices, watering is the most important step in modern lawn maintenance (Harris, 1996). On average, 20 per cent of municipal water supplies are dedicated to lawns and gardens (Deering, 2002). This high figure is likely due to the position Kentucky bluegrass, the most common North American grass, holds among the top water guzzling plants (Harris).

As innocuous as watering lawns may appear, the fact that North America is currently undergoing desertification faster than areas of Africa indicates that measures must be taken to reduce water consumption. Water is a valuable resource and excessive water use results in increased costs of water supply, treatment, and disposal. Although the water supply may appear infinite, it is a finite resource that must be used conservatively. The strain of watering lawns on local reservoirs has led to the development of xeriscaping, a method of low-water landscaping that can be used to plant water-efficient landscapes by selecting drought-tolerant plants or indigenous plants that have evolved to the climate of the region and thus require less water input. Lawn alternatives favoured by xeriscaping include clover lawns which, in addition to having reduced water requirements, do not require pesticides or mowing, thyme lawns, flowering lawns, or local ornamental grass lawns. Replacing or reducing lawn size in favour of water-efficient lawns can have significant positive economic and environmental effects. If lawn alternatives are not suitable, proper watering of lawns by watering early in the morning and only when the soil is completely dry can save a lawn owner thousands of gallons of water annually. With their ability to withstand summer droughts and watering restrictions, xeriscaped lawns are becoming increasingly popular and are predicted to dominate twenty-first century landscapes (Harris, 1996).

Benard's method of development in the final body paragraph clearly changes from cost-benefit to problem-solution. Note the absence of statistics here and her reliance on one source—both contrast with previous paragraphs.

The efficient conclusion summarizes the main points and looks ahead to future lawn practices.

Lawns are undeniably the dominant feature of modern landscaping. Lawns are so widespread that the desire to be surrounded by a plot of green grass has become habitual. Despite the dominance of lawns in our society, the implications of such lawns should not be overlooked. The labour required to keep grass weedless, shortly cropped, and green is endless and requires excessive and non-essential pesticide use, mowing, and watering. Although it may be difficult to envision abandoning modern lawns and the maintenance practices of such lawns, the effects of lawn maintenance on the environment and human health are so grave that it is difficult to justify intensive lawn maintenance practices. Modern lawns are the result of fashion-dictated evolution and, like any evolving entity, are not static. It is to be hoped that the future evolution of lawns will be dictated not by fashion but by our environmental and health conscience.

References

Bashur, S.V. (2001). *Playing it safe: Healthy choices about lawn care pesticides.* Toronto: Toronto Public Health Agency.

Dawson, R.B. (1968). *Practical lawn craft.* London: Crosby Lockwood and Son.

Deering, A. (Winter 2002). "Defining the naturescape concept." *BC Naturalist*, 12–13.

Harris, M. (1996). *Ecological gardening: your path to a healthy garden.* Toronto: Random House of Canada.

Levetin, E. and K. McMahon, (2003). *Plants and society.* 3rd ed. New York: McGraw-Hill.

Martin, K. (1998). *Environmental health committee newsletter for family physicians: Pesticides and human health.* Toronto: Ontario College of Family Physicians.

Maynes, C. (2001). Pesticide free naturally. Retrieved November 18, 2001, from http://www.gca.ca/pesticides.htm

Meyer, M., H. Behe, and J. Heilig (2001). The economic impact and perceived environmental effect of home lawns in Minnesota. *Horttechnology*, 11, 585–590.

Robbins, P., A. Polderman, and T. Birkenholtz. (2001). Lawns and toxins. *Cities*, 18, 369–380.

Van Caeseele, R. (2002). Climate change and your yard. Retrieved September 28, 2002, from http://www.climatechangeconnection.org/pages/yardcare.html

Yumlu, S.V. (1994). *Lawn mower use and emissions in Canada.* Ottawa: National Printers.

10.3 Sample Student Argumentative Essay #3 (MLA Style) (1,400 words)

Numbered footnotes are permitted in MLA style, but they should provide additional information, suggested reading, and similar functions—not just bibliographical information. For another example of an essay using MLA style, see Part Six, Section 16.3. The following essay was written in 2003, prior to recent developments in the decriminalization of marijuana in parts of Canada.

The Prohibition of Marijuana: A Legacy of Moral Entrepreneurship

by Stewart Lord

How many times have you, your friends or family enjoyed a cold beer on a hot day, a glass of cabernet sauvignon with dinner, or a nightcap of single malt scotch? Whether or not you regularly consume alcohol, imagine if it were illegal to do so. Consider for a moment the implications of this and the value of being able to make your own decisions about alcohol. Unfortunately, this freedom does not extend to marijuana. Its use has long been a subject of dispute; the arguments on both sides of this issue are long and complex. What is true of this debate, however, is the tendency to avoid the real subject of ethics and to introduce less important discussions. Opponents of marijuana's legalization generally focus on its negative health effects or addictive and gateway tendencies, while proponents herald its medicinal and practical applications. Although these digressions have their place, in this vein of the debate they only serve to draw away our attention from the fundamental injustice of its prohibition. The criminalization of this substance robs us of our innate liberty, the freedom to choose. The recreational use of marijuana is shrouded in disrepute due to the unfounded and arbitrary imposition of moral entrepreneurship.

Moral entrepreneurship can best be defined in sociological terms from a conflict theorist's perspective. It is the legislation of subjective moral standards by those in a position of considerable power or influence over society. In Canada, our drug laws concerning marijuana have a particularly dubious origin. The Opium Act of 1908, which itself was formed with the racist agenda of curbing the freedoms of Asian-Canadians, set the precedent for all laws concerning illicit drug use that would follow (Dion).[1] By outlawing substances not typically favoured by European cultures, minority groups were effectively targeted for harassment and deportation. This basis of racism played a

---

1 See Dion for further analysis of this relationship with racism.

significant role in the eventual criminalization of cannabis. It was Emily Murphy, Canada's first female judge, who, under the pen name of Janey Canuck, wrote exposés on the drug trade that helped to swing public opinion against marijuana. These articles depicted hemp smokers as "the lowest class of yellow and black men" and found such strong support from many of Canada's white Christians that they were later published in a book titled *The Black Candle*. In this form, they served as powerful government propaganda, spreading fears and lies. In 1927, on the heels of similar decisions south of the border, Canada passed laws banning the use and trafficking of cannabis (Bruce B2). Numerous extensive and well-funded studies concerning the effects of marijuana, such as the La Guardia report and Le Dain Commission report, have found no link between its use and crime or violence.[2] Despite these results and the urging of lobby groups, welfare agencies, and medical associations to decriminalize the substance, its consumption still constitutes a criminal act. Although the deceptions spread through media such as *The Black Candle* and *Reefer Madness* have subsided, current programs continue to proliferate unsubstantiated fears.[3] In the impressionable minds of many, this misinformation, coupled with the illegal nature of recreational marijuana use, only serves to reinforce the stigma that surrounds it.

There is little that justifies the legal distinction between this drug and other "soft" narcotics such as alcohol, tobacco, and coffee. Tetrahydro-cannabinol, the active ingredient in cannabis sativa, is a unique substance and, as such, may pose distinct health concerns. That said, alcohol, tobacco, and coffee are equally dubious and, in some cases, considerably more dangerous. Statistics on the consequences of abusing these socially accepted agents bring the issue into sharp focus. An estimated 6,507 Canadians died in 1995 due to alcohol consumption, while another 82,014 were admitted to hospital. During the same year, the percentage of vehicle accidents attributed to drinking was 43 per cent (MADD 3).

Even more alarming is that tobacco is the number one preventable cause of death in Canada with 45,214 recognized fatalities in 1996. That amounts to roughly three times more victims than car accidents, suicides, drug abuse, murder, and AIDS combined. Statistics regarding marijuana-related fatalities, reliable or otherwise, are hard to obtain. Health Canada does, however, report that an estimated 804 Canadians died in 1995 due to drug abuse (Health Canada). What fraction of these deaths is attributable to marijuana

---

2 Refer to the "Crime" subsection in "The Mental Attitude of the Marihuana Smoker chapter of La Guardia report and "Cannabis" (166) under "A Review of Selected Drugs" in the Le Dain Commission report.

3 *Reefer Madness* (1938) is possibly the most famous exploitation film ever, depicting marijuana smokers as murderous villains.

is speculation, but many contend that the reason no mortality statistics are available is because use of the substance does not constitute a direct health threat. Clearly, any responsible user should acknowledge not only the obvious consequences of smoke inhalation but also the possibility of unknown long-term effects. There is a fine line between the use and abuse of any substance; therefore, conscientious habits are essential. Whatever the circumstance, neither "potheads" nor casual smokers should commit any direct or indirect offence against any other person. Beyond that, we must all recognize the right of each individual to define his or her own ethical and moral boundaries.

When faced with this argument many react in moral panic and rhetorically ask, "why don't we legalize all drug use?" This question of where to draw the line is admittedly difficult to answer. Ultimately, no definitive conclusion can be formulated, as the problem is subjective and qualitative in nature. Yet, specific criteria could be established and each drug evaluated according to these merits. Concerns such as short-term effects, user dependence, long-term consequences, and correlations with crime and violence would need to be addressed, but eventually a consensus should emerge. As a result, we may find softer legal substances at one end of a scale with legal, yet controlled ones in the middle, and hard drugs that bring strict criminal sentences at the other. Whatever form such a system might take, it is clear that direct comparisons with currently legal substances would place cannabis on the non-criminal side of the scale. By nearly all accounts, it is a milder substance than alcohol or nicotine, particularly in terms of its addictiveness. It is true that marijuana users can become psychologically addicted, but they do not form the physical dependencies that accompany excessive alcohol and tobacco consumption.[4]

This point commonly spurs opponents of legalization to ask, "why not prohibit drinking and smoking as well?" By reversing the short-sighted "all or nothing" argument, the circular nature of the argument becomes apparent. Furthermore, this approach has been tried in the past and notoriously failed. In 1920, the United States introduced prohibition. The lifting of the ban in 1933 coincided with the height of the Depression (Thornton). Although it is unlikely that this decision had much to do with the economic upturn of the mid-1930s, it does raise a strong point. In 1998–9, the taxation of alcohol amounted to $3.6 million in proceeds for the Canadian government (CCSA). Through upholding the outdated legislation regarding recreational marijuana, our government has forced the industry underground and is therefore missing out on significant revenue.

---

4 See "Cannabis" (179) under "A Review of Selected Drugs" in the Le Dain Commission report.

In addition to the positive direct impact that this industry could have on our economy, legalization would indirectly alleviate stress on our judicial system. An estimated 2,000 Canadians are jailed for marijuana possession every year. At an average cost of $150 per inmate per day (not taking into account legal expenses or the cost of finding and apprehending these individuals), it is clear that fighting the use of marijuana constitutes a heavy burden (CCSA). The funds obtained from legalization would be more than just profit-taking. This money would be needed to fund research initiatives, establish strict production standards, and restructure existing organizations to accommodate and control the sale of cannabis. Users would no longer need to associate with a criminal element of society to obtain the drug. They could either grow it themselves or purchase it from a licensed retailer. This would bring a level of safety and security not present in the current black market. Buyers could be confident of a product's purity, quality, and potency.

The main reason why marijuana is still illegal and socially marginalized today is the haunting legacy of racial and ethnic snobbery that founded its prohibition. There is no rationale or validation for outlawing the recreational use of cannabis while condoning alcohol, tobacco, or even coffee. We must all push for the legalization of this substance both for the benefits of our economy and judicial system, and most fundamentally to protect the rights and ensure the safety of those who use it.

Works Cited

Bruce, Harry. "The Real Janey Canuck." *The National Post* 15 April 2000: B2.

Canadian Centre on Substance Abuse. *Cannabis Control in Canada: Options Regarding Possession*. CCSA Ottawa, May 1998.

Canadian Government Le Dain Committee. *The Commission of Inquiry into the Non-Medical Use of Drugs*. Canada, 1970.

City of New York La Guardia Committee. *The Marihuana Problem in the City of New York*. City of New York, 1944.

Dion, Guy. "The Structure of Drug Prohibition in International Law and in Canadian Law." *Canada's Parliament* August 1999. Special Committee on Illegal Drugs. 31 October 2002 http://www.parl.gc.ca/37/1/parlbus/commbus/senate/com-e/ille-e/witness-e.htm

Health Canada. *Deaths in Canada Due to Smoking*. Health Canada, January 1999.

Mothers Against Drunk Driving. *The Real Facts on Alcohol Use, Injuries and Deaths*. MADD Canada, 22 August 2002.

Thornton, Mark. "Alcohol Prohibition Was a Failure." *The CATO Institute* 17 July 1991. Policy Analysis No. 157.31 October 2002 http://www.cato.org/pubs/pas/pa-157.html

Questions to consider in a critical and analytical reading of "The Prohibition of Marijuana: A Legacy of Moral Entrepreneurship":

1. In his Introduction, how does Lord attempt to distinguish his essay and his argument on legalizing marijuana from the many others on this topic?
2. What two methods of development does the writer use in his first body paragraph (paragraph 2)? Identify two different methods used in paragraphs 3 and 4.
3. Do you believe that Lord successfully demonstrates his credibility? (Is he knowledgeable? reliable? fair?) In what ways does he succeed (or fail to do this)?
4. Of the two strategies for handling opposing views discussed in Part Four, Sections 4.2.1 and 4.2.2, which did Lord choose to use? Do you think he adequately considered his topic, audience, and purpose in arguing in his approach? Specifically, what shows you he did this (or failed to do this)?
5. In the paragraph preceding his Conclusion, Lord discusses some advantages of legalizing marijuana. Do you believe this paragraph fits well with the rest of the paper? Why or why not? What order of points do you think he used?

10.4 Reading #1 (APA Style)

Exercise

A. **Pre-reading**:

1. According to the abstract, the writer will be using the ideas of Derek Parfit in his essay. Look up "Derek Parfit" on reliable Internet sites, such as links provided by universities. Find reviews of his book *Reasons and Persons* (1984) in order to discover what you can about his work in the field of personal identity.

2. How might the name of the journal that the article appears in enable you to anticipate the writer's general approach? "Cloning and Identity" is divided into six sections. Note the section headings and lengths. Which do you think will be the most important? Why?

Cloning and Identity[1]
Nicholas Agar

ABSTRACT

Critics of human cloning allege that the results of the process are likely to suffer from compromised identities making it near impossible for them to live worthwhile lives. This paper uses the account of the metaphysics of personal identity offered by Derek Parfit to investigate and support the claim of identity-compromise. The cloned person may, under certain circumstances, be seen as surviving, to some degree, in the clone. However, I argue that rather than warranting concern, the potential for survival by cloning ought to help protect against the misuse of the technology.

Keywords: cloning, personal identity, psychological connection

I. INTRODUCTION

Recent discussions of cloning are riddled with references to identity. Commentators fear that if successes with sheep, cows, and mice lead the technology to be applied to us, then human identities must inevitably be compromised. Take the following passage from Leon Kass:

> The cloned person may experience concerns about his distinctive identity not only because he will be in genotype and appearance identical to another human being, but, in this case, because he may be twin to the person who is his "father" or "mother" [. . .] The cloned individual, moreover, will be saddled with a genotype that has already lived. He will not be fully a surprise to the world. People are likely always to compare his performances in life with that of his alter ego. (Kass, 1997, p. 22)

An array of disparate allegations about cloning appear in Kass' article. Much of the difficulty in making explicit the charge of identity-compromise stems from the multifaceted nature of our commonsense concept of identity.[2] Sometimes when we talk about identity we mean identical similarity; at a first approximation any two objects are identically similar when they share all non-relational properties. Other times we intend something specific to persons. The issue of personal identity, in turn, encompasses questions both about the metaphysics of our survival over time and about our subjective senses of who we are.

The first question we must ask is whether any of these strands of our commonsense notion of identity pick out attributes of persons capable of being affected by cloning. Unless we can show this there is no question of identity-related harm. Some tempting wrong turns present themselves. For example, emphasis on identical similarity seems to motivate most fictional portrayals. The typical Hollywood clone is unsettling chiefly because she is so similar to the cloned person as to be indistinguishable in terms of both appearance and thinking. The bad news for Sci-Fi movie enthusiasts is that this depiction misunderstands the process. Experts do not tire in pointing out that cloning is not copying (see Butler & Wadman, 1997; Evers, 1999; R. Wright, 1997). Traits of individuals result not from the *action* of genes alone, but rather from the complex *interaction* of genes and environment; and unless we could replicate exactly the womb of the donor's mother and the external environment we would expect many of the clone's genes to express themselves in ways different from the way they did in the original.[3]

Some commentators suppose that to clear up the genetic determinist confusion is to dispel any fears surrounding cloning and identity (e.g., Butler & Wadman, 1997; R. Wright, 1997). I argue that matters are more complicated than this. I will examine cloning against the backdrop of the well-mapped philosophical terrain of the metaphysics of personal identity. There are two views about the impact of cloning on personal identity. On one view cloning is *reproduction* (see e.g., Kahn, 1997). If this is true, then cloning raises the same kinds of concerns as any other of the techniques for providing children potentially furnished by the new genetics, and debate about moral implications will be best not cluttered with references to identity. On the alternative view, a clone is not the child of the DNA-donor, but some extension of her, and cloning is more properly characterised as *self-perpetuation* than reproduction.

I argue that neither the view that cloning is self-perpetuation nor the view that cloning is reproduction captures the entire truth about human cloning. Cloning is a technology with two faces. Under some circumstances the products of the technology will be best viewed as children of their DNA-donors. In other contexts it produces individuals who can be described as partial extensions of the donors of their DNA. I appeal to Parfit's (1984) version of the widely accepted psychological continuity account of the facts underlying a person's existence over time to explain what it might mean for my clone to be a partial extension of me. Any chance of the Parfitian survival of the DNA-donor in the clone will require that the DNA-donor have the goal of self-perpetuation and that she have some control over the environment in which the clone is to be reared.

Though the question of whether or not a person is a clone bears on her identity, there is a further issue as to whether the effects of cloning should be seen as damaging to her. I address this issue towards the end of the paper, arguing that precisely the tendency toward identity-compromise provides some protection against the reckless cloning of humans.

II. THE PSYCHOLOGICAL CONTINUITY THEORY AND SELF-PERPETUATION

Earlier I said that the term "personal identity" is used in two ways. Metaphysicians of personal identity set out to determine what conditions must obtain if someone is to survive over time. In contrast, those with an interest in the subjective strand of our commonsense notion of personal identity wonder about the psychological facts that underlie our sense of self. They ask what it is that gives an individual a feeling of distinctness from other people as well a sense that her projects and commitments are her own (see Heyd, 1992, chap. 6).

Should we pass our concerns about cloning over to the metaphysicians or to the psychologists? In the earlier quoted passage, Kass appears to state his fears in terms of the subjective strand of the concept. Continual comparisons with the clone's alter ego stand to impair her sense of self; despite her manifest youth she has the feeling of already having lived.

Although the subjective strand seems likely to point to facts more immediately related to harm, my discussion is directed at the metaphysics of personal identity. If cloning turns out to have no implications for the metaphysical identities of either the clone or the donor of its DNA then I suggest we have an argument against any impaired sense of self. Consider cloning alongside a case with a reversed mismatch of metaphysical and subjective identities. On most views about the metaphysics of identity, each of the "selves" in a case of Multiple Personality Disorder belongs to the one person. Though current practice is notorious for sometimes departing from this aim, the therapist ought to attempt to cull down the many subjective identities so that they accord in number with the single metaphysical identity.[4] Similar could be said about the clone's alleged fractured sense of self. Full independence from the DNA donor would make subjective angst about identity the symptom of no underlying metaphysical disorder. The illusion of compromised identity may be difficult to shake but shake it we should.

On the other hand, if it is true, as I shall claim, that the clone can lack full metaphysical independence from the donor of his DNA then these facts ought to be represented in her sense of self. We will need to address the psychological implications of the overlapping identities.

According to modern thinking about personal identity, persons are objects extending through time composed out of time-slices of persons, or person-stages. An account of the metaphysics of identity will say what relation must obtain between person-stages for them to belong to one person rather than to more than one. Earlier I pointed out that cloning is not copying. The self-perpetuation hypothesis certainly does not demand that we think of it in this way. Whatever the personal identity relation turns out to be it is clearly capable of withstanding a fair amount of environmental modification of genetically identical person-stages. The growing of a goatee or the varnishing of fingernails make later person-stages qualitatively dissimilar to earlier ones. So the fact that no stage of the clone is qualitatively identical to any stage of the DNA-donor does not, by itself, rule out the survival of the DNA-donor in the clone.

Psychological continuity theories have long been the most popular accounts of personal identity.[5] According to these theories, claims about identity or survival over time are true in virtue of facts about continuities of memories and other psychological features. Parfit's widely discussed presentation of the view will form the backdrop for the following discussion.

Before I describe Parfit's theory I note that his selection as a contemporary advocate of the psychological continuity theory immediately forces us to refocus our inquiry. According to Kass and others, cloning is dangerous because, amongst other effects, it compromises identity. Parfit's theory seems ill-equipped to illuminate this kind of damage, as on his view identity is *not* what really matters in a person's survival over time. Parfit argues that focus on psychological continuities makes indefensible our customary concern for preservation of our identities. To replace identity in our affections he offers Relation R, a relation which we find when two person-stages are psychologically connected. Psychological connections, in turn, obtain whenever particular psychological features such as memories or beliefs continue to be held. If an earlier person-stage has a memory of a tractor ride, a later person-stage possesses that same memory and both states are causally linked. It follows that the two stages are psychologically connected. In all likelihood the two person-stages will also be bound by myriad other connections in the form of persisting beliefs, desires, and other memories. According to Parfit the holding of such connections is what matters in survival. Our customary identity-related concern ought to be reconfigured so as to accord with Relation R.

I will explain how Relation R is supposed to diverge from identity. However, first I want to say a little about how the truth of this claim should make us adjust our goals.[6] The self-perpetuation hypothesis certainly makes sense once Relation R is substituted for identity. We will not be asking whether the cloned person is identical to the clone, but instead whether what matters in survival is transmitted from the DNA-donor to the clone, where Relation R captures what matters in survival.[7]

So, why is Relation R different from identity? Parfit considers two types of cases with particular relevance to cloning.

First are the fission cases. Parfit wonders how we should react to a story in which a person divides into two later persons. The logic of identity prevents us from saying that the pre-fission person is identical with either of the later persons. They are plainly not identical to each other and so cannot both be identical to the single pre-fission person. Yet in spite of the non-identity of pre- and post-fission persons it would seem a mistake for the pre-fission person to be entirely indifferent to the fates of either post-fission persons. Intuitively he should respond to the threatened torture of either person in the same kind of way that he would to threats to a unique future self. Relation R obtains between the pre-fission person and both post-fission persons and thereby can account for what we deem the right pattern of concern. What matters in survival carries over to both post-fission persons.

The lives of donors of DNA may overlap in time with those of their clones making it strange to say that the donor survives in the clone. If we accept Parfit's claims about the logic of survival and, most importantly, can show that donor and clone are psychologically connected, then we may trace this reluctance back to the mistaken idea that "survival" and "personal identity" are synonyms. Cloning will be viewed as fission transformed from science fiction to near science fact. My pre-cloning person-stages will be psychologically connected both to later stages of my conventional self and to those of the clone. As we shall see, though less of what matters in survival is transmitted to person-stages of my clone than to later stages of my conventionally acknowledged self, some is transmitted nonetheless.

On to the second difference between identity and Parfitian survival with interesting implications for cloning. The self-perpetuation hypothesis demands an account of personal identity or survival sufficiently flexible to permit a weakened reading. Differences in upbringing stand to make person-stages of my clone vary from person-stages that are uncontroversially recognised as mine to a greater degree than person-stages of my conventional self vary from each other. The account we are after will make it legitimate, under these less than optimal circumstances, for me to feel *some* identity-related concern for my clone.

Parfit's is such an account. His separation of identity from survival allows him to tell a rather undemanding story about the conditions under which someone survives. Identity is all or nothing; person A is either fully identical with person B or fully non-identical with him. In contrast, what matters in survival, or Parfitian survival, comes in degrees; different person-stages of a single conventionally recognised person may be linked by differing numbers of psychological connections and thereby carry over what matters in survival to varying degrees. The young Lauren Bacall shares more memories, desires, and beliefs with the forty year old Bacall than she does with the seventy year old. This means that the seventy year old carries over less of what matters in survival from the young actor than does the forty year old.

So, the fact that not all psychological features will be carried over will be no decisive objection to the possibility of self-perpetuation by cloning. If we accept Parfit's view of survival and can show that clone and donor of DNA are psychologically connected then we discover that my clone can be a successful, if less than perfect continuer of me.

III. ARE CLONE AND DONOR OF DNA PSYCHOLOGICALLY CONNECTED?

Partit's claim that survival need not be one to one, or all or nothing is good news for the self-perpetuation hypothesis. However, unless clone and cloned turn out to be psychologically connected there is no question of carrying over what matters in survival. To see whether psychological connections could obtain between clone and donor of DNA we need to subject to closer scrutiny Parfit's notion of a psychological connection.

Parfit holds that the normal functioning of the brain is the usual, but not exclusive explanation for the holding of psychological connections. He describes a Star Trek-style teletransportation device that first records all of the physical information about a person's body, then destroys it, producing an exact replica out of different matter (Parfit, 1984, section 75). Parfit appeals to the psychological connections linking the pre- and post-teletransported person-stages to support the claim that the original person survives the process. Such stories lead him to claim that *any cause* of psychological connectedness between person-stages suffices to transmit what matters in survival (Parfit, 1984, section 79).

In order for cloning to resemble teletransportation in counts as a non-standard means of carrying over what matters in survival, the transfer of adult DNA into a host egg must succeed in establishing psychological connections between two largely physically discontinuous human bodies. Since the teletransporter produces an exact copy of the original person the transmission of all key psychological states is guaranteed. Things are less clear when only some part of the original, in this case her genes, are copied.

Some indication that cloning might resemble teletransportation in this respect comes from many studies of monozygotic twins reared in different environments. The case of Jack and Oscar is an impressive story of psychological similarities showing up despite divergent upbringings. Jack was raised as a Jew in Trinidad and Oscar as a Nazi in Czechoslovakia. When reunited both were wearing shirts with shiny epaulets, enjoyed sneezing in lifts to startle other passengers and habitually flushed the toilet before and after using it. Another reunited pair, both called Jim, chain smoked, were described by their wives as ostentatiously romantic and had woodworking woodshops in their garages. The two Jims also owned Chevys and had served as sheriff's deputies. On first meeting two female twins both were wearing seven rings and had sons named Richard Andrew or Andrew Richard.[8]

A philosopher of personal identity must be cautious when dealing with such cases. The structure of the argument in the next pages can be summarized as follows. Some people take split twin cases to demonstrate that sameness of genotype guarantees substantial psychological similarity. I argue that if this genetic determinist claim is true then there can be psychological connections between clone and cloned, supposing that the existence of clone-psychology causally depends on the decision to be cloned. I then propose that survival by cloning does not require the truth of the thesis of genetic determinism. A partially environmental explanation will require an upbringing conducive to psychological connections between clone and DNA-donor. I argue that, though far from guaranteed, such an environment stands a reasonable chance of obtaining.

As it happens monozygotic twins are often referred to in the cloning debate, but by those seeking to head off surprising conclusions about the impact of cloning on identity rather than by those seeking to support them (Evers, 1999). Twins don't survive in each other, so how could the cloned person survive in the clone? I think that we should both say that while there is no realistic prospect of psychological connections between twins, split twin cases can constitute evidence for such connections between clone and genetic original.

First, why are there no psychological connections between twins? Certainly in both the twin case and the cloning case we can trace chains of causes linking psychological states. These chains can be pointed to in explanations of psychological similarities between twins, on the one hand, and between clone and cloned, on the other. How can we say that in the one case the chain can underwrite psychological connections and in the other it will not, while squaring this claim with Parfit's view that any cause is sufficient for connectedness?

The answer is to be found by focusing on the structure of the respective causal chains. In order to underwrite a psychological connection the relationship between content-similar psychological states will need to be substantially by *direct* cause and not solely by *common* cause. Suppose, for point of illustration, the thesis of genetic determinism, according to which genes are responsible for the production of psychological and other traits with no, or very little, contribution from the environment. The similarities of the psychological states of monozygotic twins would then be explained by common cause. In such cases, soon after fertilisation an embryo splits, forming two genetically identical cell masses that go on to develop into distinct persons. The genotype of the pre-split embryo will be seen as the common cause of both twins' psychologies. Oscar's psychological states will not be directly causally responsible for Jack's content similar states, nor vice versa, and it follows that we would be wrong to think of Oscar carrying over what matters in survival from Jack or of Jack carrying over what matters in survival from Oscar. Their causally explicable close psychological similarities will not be any manner of psychological connections.

The self-perpetuation hypothesis requires direct causal links between clone and cloned. If we stick, for the time being at least, with the hypothesis of genetic determinism we can find such links. Take the clone produced with the aim of self-perpetuation. The DNA-donor's decision to self-perpetuate by cloning will be causally linked to others of his psychological states. The decision leads to the generation of a human being genetically identical to the donor, and this genetic identity, in turn, suffices to produce copies of many of the donor's psychological features. The causal link may seem somewhat tortuous. However, if we accept Parfit's point that psychological connections can be secured by *any* cause, it should not matter that these causal paths are traced by way of the cloning decision, genes and developmental processes, to the corresponding features in the clone.

The preceding paragraphs assumed a genetic determinist interpretation of split twin cases. If this highly controversial interpretation turns out to be true identity of genotype would underwrite connectedness as efficiently as teletransportation. Some modern studies have seemed to confirm that if monozygotic twins are reared in one of the many varying environments that count as normal for humans there will be substantial psychological similarities between them.[9] Critics of the study argue that twin similarities can often be traced back to shared environmental influences (see Farber, 1981; Lewontin, 1992). Indeed, it is sensible to doubt that any genetic mechanism could realistically dictate the numbers of rings worn.

The outcome of the debate over whether split twin similarities are primarily environmental or genetic has important implications for survival by cloning. The genetic determinist view of human psychology that some see as the only explanation for Oscar and Jack and the Jims makes connectedness in cloning a possibility. It goes far beyond the scope of this paper to decide whether any version of genetic determinism is true. In what follows, however, I suggest that the self-perpetuation hypothesis can be upheld even if we reject genetic determinism and allow that developmental significance is roughly equally apportioned between environment and genes.

Clones differ from the products of sexual reproduction in having nuclear DNA identical to that of a single parent or DNA donor. If genetic determinism were the case we would have a significant relationship between DNA-donor and clone that does not obtain between parent and conventionally conceived child. While it would be astronomically unlikely that the child would be identically similar to either parent, the clone would be guaranteed to be identically similar to the DNA-donor in most significant respects. Deprived of the hypothesis of genetic determinism we need other reasons for saying that what goes for the clone does not go for the conventionally conceived child. I will argue that survival by cloning depends on a cooperative environment – the DNA-donor must exercise some control over environmental inputs to generate psychological connections between him and clone.

A parent also selects environmental inputs for a conventionally conceived child in a way that produces some psychological similarities. If donors of DNA can transfer to clones what matters in survival by manipulating their environments then can parents make their children vehicles of their Parfitian survival? An interesting version of the self-perpetuation hypothesis requires some way of distinguishing the DNA-donor desirous of cloned survival from the domineering parent, who, perhaps inspired by Parfit's theory, imposes her personality on her daughter.

I suspect that once the "any cause" view about psychological connections is combined with the claim that survival can be by degree it is hard to deny that some of what matters in survival is transmitted from parents to children, thereby vindicating the overlap that some writers have detected between motives behind reproduction and self-perpetuation (see e.g., Heyd, 1992, chap. 6). My environment may be manipulated so as to ensure the transmission of some of what matters to either my clone or my conventionally conceived child. I will give reasons for thinking that the degree of my Parfitian survival is likely to be greater in my clone than in any product of sexual reproduction. Clones are more likely to pass any threshold of connectedness before identity-related concern is warranted. This makes the technology of human cloning better suited to the purpose of self-perpetuation than sexual reproduction. While far from an ideal tool it offers the best bet for would-be self-perpetuators.

IV. THE PROBLEM OF MEMORY

Memories are the psychological features that have loomed largest in discussions of identity. They are also perhaps the most serious obstacles to the possibility of the survival of the DNA-donor in the clone. Early versions of the psychological continuity theory were essentially memory theories. Autobiographical memories, apparent replayings of events from a person's past, certainly make up [a] substantial part of the story about that person's awareness of his survival over time. Now, if genetic determinism about psychological states such as desires and affections is implausible, it is insane for memories. Whatever other features they may share, separation at birth seems sufficient to ensure that Oscar and Jack do not share memories.

The idea that memories might be transmitted by cloning does seem to be part of popular understanding of the process. For example, the most recent *Alien* movie, *Alien Resurrection*, involves the cloning of Ellen Ripley, the character played by Sigorney Weaver in the first three Alien movies. The Ripley-clone, again played by Weaver, appears to remember key events from "her" past lives as depicted in the first three movies. Yet, a commonsense model of how memories are produced and how they are stored makes it unlikely in the extreme that memories could be transmitted from Ripley-DNA-donor to Ripley-clone. Memories are generated in response to events in a person's life-time. The idea of memory-transfer from Ripley-DNA-donor to Ripley-clone seems to rest on the biological heresy of reverse-transcription. It is an established part of biological orthodoxy that changes to an organism's phenotype cannot lead to modifications of genes.

The first thing to note is that Parfit's is not a memory theory. Together with memories, judgements about survival must take into consideration psychological features such as beliefs, desires, and hopes. This move away from exclusive focus on memory seems well motivated. Suppose we did encounter a person with global amnesia. Though we might agree with Parfit that the pre-amnesiac does not survive entirely in the post-amnesiac we would want to use the continuities of hopes, desires and other psychological dispositions do [*sic* to] allow that the pre-amnesiac does survive to some degree.

In what follows I show, without assistance from an auxiliary hypothesis of genetic determinism, that although their transfer is not guaranteed, psychological features including memories have a fair chance of being carried over from the DNA-donor who desires to self-perpetuate, to the clone. Psychological connections will require a cooperative environment. I give reasons for thinking that this cooperative environment is more likely to obtain for clones produced with the goal of self-perpetuation than either for clones produced without the goal of self-perpetuation or for conventionally produced children. Memories, the psychological features that seem most recalcitrant to transfer by cloning, will be my focus. I claim that the self-perpetuation hypothesis can accommodate memory while avoiding the heresy of reverse transcription.

A widely held view of memory emphasises its reconstructive nature (see Schacter, 1989; Dennett, 1991, chap. 5–6; Smyth, 1994). On this view memories are not exact recordings of every aspect of initial experiences. What are stored are schemata of experiences, later fleshed out with suitable detail in the act of remembering. Of particular interest is the role this model gives to background information in the encoding, reshaping and retrieval of memories (Dennett, 1991, pp. 115–126; Smyth, 1994). Our starting beliefs about the world help determine which aspects of a remembered event get encoded in memory schemata. Information presented after the remembered event can often be integrated into a schema.

The malleability of memory has been widely commented on in connection with eye-witness testimony. Witnesses have starting expectations about the kinds of people who commit certain crimes and when later asked unknowingly make adjustments in response to subtle hints and suggestions from the questioner.

In order for this malleability to lend support to the hypothesis of survival by cloning I will need to establish two things. I must demonstrate that the family and educational environment of the clone produced with the goal of self-perpetuation can be such that at least some memories of the clone will not only be causally connected to memories in the DNA-donor, but they will be phenomenologically convergent with them. Further, I will need to show that these points apply to significant experiences rather than only to ones peripheral to our senses of who we are. Such experiences will be heavily weighted in judgements about whether or not the DNA-donor might survive.

The phenomenon of False Memory Syndrome may show that reconstructions that deviate quite markedly from initial experiences can be quite central to our senses of ourselves (see Ross & Wilson, 1999). In the cases in question patients begin therapy with no accessible memories of childhood abuse. After therapy they have detailed apparent memories of traumas inflicted by family members. There is no consensus amongst psychologists about what to say about such cases. However, on one interpretation well-meaning therapists inadvertently implant in patients memories of nonexistent abuse. Psychologists use the term "interrogative suggestibility" to help explain this transfer of memories (see Gunjonsson, 1992). John Kihlstrom says that the generation of false memory relies on

> . . . a closed social interaction consisting of just the patient, therapist, and like-minded supporters; therapeutic premises that, however plausible, may be ill-founded or uninformed; a relationship based on interpersonal trust, which forms a catalyst for leading questions to be interpreted as plausible or believable; uncertainty on the part of the patient about what happened in the past; a suggestive stimulus including leading questions about trauma; a professional relationship, with at least the veneer of science, which allows such questions to be perceived as appropriate; and the shared belief that techniques being employed will succeed in recovering valid memories of the past. (Kihlstrom, 2000)

Kihlstrom is concerned with the transfer of memories of abuse. We will need to make appropriate adjustments before we can apply these points to the hypothesis of survival by cloning. The first issue concerns the label "false memory". In the cases of apparent remembered abuse much hangs on the psychological plausibility of genuine memories of traumatic events being buried in such a way as to be recoverable by therapists' targeted questions. If the apparent memories cannot be traced back to any genuine episode of abuse then we should call them false. In the cloning case apparent memories may be traced back to genuine events in the DNA-donor's life. They will be false if we fail to uphold the self-perpetuation hypothesis; they will be accurate if we can show that the clone is a Parfitian survivor of the DNA-donor.

There are some grounds for thinking clones produced with the goal of perpetuating DNA-donors may be quite interrogatively suggestible. The DNA donor with a serious interest in survival by cloning will treat the clone as an extension of himself. Stories about significant exploits will be appropriately packaged. He will take care to provide schooling and broader upbringing similar to his. The physical resemblance of clone to donor will also influence the social interactions of others with the clone. His appearance ought not to trick us into thinking that the clone and the donor are in all significant respects identically similar. Nevertheless, this appearance combined with an environment in which others take seriously the possibility of survival by cloning could induce some who interact with the clone to supply information and ask questions that, at least in some cases, will lead him to form and flesh out his memory schemata in ways convergent with the memories of the original. For example, friends and relatives may find uncanny resemblances between the fifteen-year-old clone and school photographs of the DNA-donor. Such perceived similarities may well influence their treatment of the clone.

The theory ladenness of memory explains how there might be some convergence in phenomenology between acts of remembering of clone and DNA-donor. Why do many reported lake monsters tend to follow the single Loch Ness monster design? Suppose we consider only sincere reports. It seems likely that the initial experiences of the misrecognised objects, be they logs, swimming deer, or odd shaped waves will be quite different from one another. Widely publicised views about what lake monsters look like can either influence schemata as they are being laid down, or can be integrated into schemata later. The result is considerable convergence in rememberings despite quite different initial experiencings of these objects. Something like this could account for convergence in memory phenomenology between clone and DNA-donor.

Doubtless the clone's remembering of a given event will often differ in phenomenology from rememberings of that same event by the DNA-donor. This phenomenological variation need not rule out counting the two mental events as the same memory, however. The reconstructive nature of memory makes exact identity of phenomenology too demanding a requirement for two rememberings to count as tokens of the same memory. The most we can demand is that there be phenomenological overlap between instances of remembering. Clone's and DNA-donor's rememberings will be causally connected to the same event. In such a case the interrogative suggestibility of the clone could generate some phenomenological overlap between the two instances of remembering.

The above environmental story describes a non-genetic determinist way of generating a degree of psychological convergence. It provides the direct causal links between states of clone and cloned required for psychological connections.

My emphasis on the environment enables us to see the real problem with the *Alien Resurrection* story. It may make sense that Ripley-clone's appearance and some aspects of her behaviour are reminiscent of Ripley-DNA-donor. However, the environment she finds herself in should be very hostile to the formation of psychological connections. She is reared and her growth accelerated in isolation on board a space ship two hundred years after the death of Ripley-DNA-donor. These are in all probability, surroundings most unlike those enjoyed by the young Ripley-DNA-donor. It is only once freed from relative isolation that she encounters people who treat her as the Ripley-DNA-donor, asking her about that life. If the genetic determinist is right about any psychological states then these may be held in common by Ripley-clone and Ripley-DNA-donor. However, it seems unlikely that connections that require a cooperative environment could obtain between clone and original.

V. CONVENTIONALLY PRODUCED CHILDREN, CLONES, AND PSYCHOLOGICAL CONVERGENCE

I might rearrange my environment so as to generate psychological connections between me and my clone. Earlier I suggested that there is nothing to stop my undertaking a similar project in respect of my conventionally conceived child. I now argue that cloning stands at an advantage over sexual reproduction as a means of self-perpetuation in respect of both genetic and environmental inputs into development.

Some will balk at the idea that a single memory connection suffices to transfer even the tiniest amount of what matters in survival. They will argue that there is a threshold of connectedness below which no identity-related concern is appropriate. I claim that clones are more likely to pass any such threshold than conventional children.

First the genetic side of the ledger. Genetic determinists may overstate the significance of genes. Yet, even a picture of development that places roughly equal importance on genes and environment will allow that cloning offers a significantly better chance of transferring psychological traits than sexual reproduction. The reason is simply that in selecting cloning over sexual reproduction we are choosing to hold approximately half rather than a quarter of developmental influences fixed.

I suspect that an environment ideal for establishing psychological connections is more likely to obtain for a clone than for a normal child. This is because the products of sexual reproduction are likely to be less interrogatively suggestible when faced with the identity-constitutive experiences of parents.

Conventionally conceived children whose parents seek to impose their psychologies on them have other children to serve as reference points. We are not accustomed to viewing normal children as ontological offshoots of parents and think that there is something wrong with parents who treat them as such. This helps protect against viewing parents' anecdotes as describing things that happened to them.

At least initially, similar reference points are less likely to exist for the clone simply because cloning is a new technology. The first human clones will be viewed as novelties. Others will treat them as something different from the products of sexual reproduction. It would be wrong to make too much of this novelty. Louise Brown, the world's first test tube baby, was, at the time of her birth, seen as something entirely new, but test tube babies are now looked upon as ordinary children. There is a difference between IVF babies and clones, however. Our language of identity and familial roles provides no alternative way of viewing test tube babies and so we have come to recognise the individuals that IVF helps create as normal children of their genetic parents. Widespread fears that test tube babies might somehow be less human or spookily more "manufactured" than normal children could not be given rational expression. If the argument in this paper is correct then Kass's suspicions about cloning's impact on identity may be made sense of. The similarity of genetic inputs into clone and cloned make psychological connections more likely to obtain between them. This fact combined with the widespread fear that cloning bears on identity helps generate a broader social environment that could encourage psychological connections between clone and DNA-donor.

VI. CLONING AND HARM

I have sought to show that cloning can enable the survival of the DNA donor. As a consequence the identity of the clone will sometimes be compromised. By this I mean that it will often be more accurate to say of the young child conventionally borne and reared than of the clone produced with the goal of self-perpetuation, that she is a genuinely new person. I now address the further question whether this propensity for cloning to prolong the life of the donor harms the clone.

If psychological connections obtain between clone and cloned then we have grounds for thinking that pleasures or miseries of the clone are in some sense property of the donor. I have a reason not to drink all day and everyday, bequeathing to my future selves an alcohol-ravaged existence. Supposing we accept Parfit's account, this is not because I am, strictly speaking, identical with my future selves – but because they are Parfitian survivors of my current person-stage. I have the same manner of reason for not placing my cloned future selves in miserable circumstances.

Here is a genuine difference between clones and other proposed human products of the new genetics. Eugenicists will not feel inhibited in their efforts to redesign persons into super-soldiers by identity-related reasons. There is no similar sense in which the future miseries of the super-soldiers will be property of the eugenicists.

So, contra Kass, it may be that rather than constituting harm, the propensity for cloning to compromise identity provides protection against harm. We will need to look elsewhere to justify a ban on cloning humans.

Notes

1. I am grateful to referees for this journal and Jeff McMahan for detailed comments on this paper.
2. For discussion of different concepts of identity and their relevance to cloning see Evers (1999).
3. For discussion of the status of genetic explanations of traits given this interactionist picture of development see Sterelny & Kitcher (1988).
4. For book-length discussion of the philosophical implications of Multiple Personalities, see Hacking (1995).
5. For recent presentations of the view see Lewis (1976), Parfit (1984), Shoemaker in Swinburne & Shoemaker (1984).
6. Lewis (1976) contends that Relation R and Identity can be reconciled by understanding the latter concept in a tensed way.
7. If compromise to identity is as ubiquitous as Parfit thinks, then perhaps we should reject uncritical acceptance that it is harmful. Indeed, Parfit draws salutary moral implications from his rejection of identity. Freed from the illusion of identity we recognise that the barriers between us and other people are far from absolute and a utilitarian morality becomes more appealing. It may even be the case that the advent of human clones, with identities compromised more than the norm, will bring Parfit's preferred impersonal morality closer. I raise Parfit's important conclusions about the relationship between identity and morality in this note only to put them to one side. They will play no role in my argument that cloning is unlikely to be damaging.
8. For excellent recent discussion of twins see L. Wright (1997).
9. See Bouchard, Lykken, McGue, Segal, & Tellegen (1990) for description of the widely discussed Minnesota twin study.

References

Bouchard, T.J., Lykken, D.T., McGue, M., Segal, N., & Tellegen, A. (1990). Sources of human psychological differences: The Minnesota study of twins reared apart. *Science*, 250, 223–228.

Butler, D., & Wadman, M. (1997). Calls for cloning ban sell science short. *Nature*, 386, 8–9.

Dennett, D. (1991). *Consciousness explained*. Boston: Little, Brown.

Evers. K. (1999). The identity of clones. *Journal of Medicine and Philosophy*, 24, 67–76.

Farber, S.L. (1981). *Identical twins reared apart*. New York: Basic Books.

Gunjonsson, G. (1992). *The psychology of interrogations, confessions, and testimony*. Chichester: Wiley.

Hacking, I. (1995). *Rewriting the soul: Multiple personalities and the sciences of memory*. Princeton: Princeton University Press.

Heyd, D. (1992). *Genethics: Moral issues in the creation of people*. Berkeley: University of California Press.

Kahn, A. (1997). Clone mammals . . . Clone man? *Nature*, 386, 119.

Kass, L. (1997, June 2). The moral repugnance of cloning. *The New Republic*.

Kihlstrom, J. (2000). *Memory, autobiography, history*. Address presented at the annual meeting of the Rocky Mountain Psychological Association, Tucson 2000 [On-line]. Available: http://socrates.berkeley.edu/%7Ekihlstrm/rmpa00.htm

Lewis, D. (1976). Survival and identity. In: A. Rorty (Ed.), *The identities of persons*. Berkeley: University of California Press.

Lewontin, R. (1992). *The doctrine of DNA: Biology as ideology*. London: Penguin.

Parfit, D. (1984). *Reasons and persons*. Oxford: Clarendon Press.

Ross, M., & Wilson, A. (1999). Constructing and appraising past selves. In: D. Schacter and E. Scarry (Eds.), *Memory, brain, and belief*. Cambridge, MA: Harvard University Press.

Schacter, D. (1989). Memory. In: M. Posner (Ed.), *Foundations of cognitive science*. Cambridge, MA: MIT Press.

Smyth. M. (1994). *Cognition in action* (2nd ed). East Sussex: Erlbaum.

Sterelny, K., & Kitcher, P. (1988). The return of the gene. *Journal of Philosophy*, 85, 339–361.

Swinburne, R., & Shoemaker, S. (1984). *Personal identity*. Oxford: Basil Blackwell.

Wright, L. (1997). *Twins and what they tell us about who we are*. New York: Wiley.

Wright, R. (1997. March 10). Can souls be Xeroxed? *Time*.

Source: Agar, N. (2003). *Journal of Medicine and Philosophy*, 28(1). Address correspondence to: Nicholas Agar, Ph.D., Philosophy Program, Victoria University of Wellington, PO Box 600, Wellington, New Zealand. E-mail: Nicholas.Agar@vuw.ac.nz

Exercise – *continued*

B. **Reading for Content**: See Part Five, Section 8 on Summarizing. Try to summarize as concisely as possible; your summary should be shorter than the original.

1. The heading in Section II introduces two terms. Summarize what is meant by "The Psychological Continuity Theory" and "Self-Perpetuation." For Agar's purposes, who is the principal proponent of this theory? What is "Relation R?"

2. Summarize the difference between the "genetic determinist" interpretation of split twins and the environmental interpretation. Why are these differences important to Agar's argument?

C. **Critical and Analytical Reading**:

1. Definition is an important method of development; for example, Agar gives two different definitions of "identity" (p. 138). Where else is definition employed? What other methods of development are used in the essay?

2. Consider how Agar bridges the different stages of his argument to make it easier for the reader to follow him. You could consider the ways he refers to what he has discussed and anticipates what he will discuss. Why does he use the first-person ("I") so often? From a reader's point of view, do you think the level of language contributes to the complexity of the subject matter or makes comprehension easier?

3. Much of the evidence Agar provides is unconventional; for example, following Parfit, he refers to a "Star Trek-style teletransportation" and to the movie *Alien Resurrection* (p. 141, p. 146). Do you think these analogies are valid as evidence?

4. Paraphrase the final two paragraphs and analyze the logic of Agar's assertion that "Eugenicists will not feel inhibited in their efforts to redesign persons into super-soldiers by identity-related reasons" (p. 148).

D. **After reading**: Write a short response to Agar's article in which you address what you consider the major issue in cloning: the issue of scientific feasibility (i.e., can humans actually be cloned successfully)? What are the ethical ramifications? What is the identity issue that Agar discusses? Is there another related issue?

PART FIVE

The Expository Essay

1. The "Three-Part" Essay: Exposition, Research, Synthesis

2. What Is Research?

3. Who are these experts . . . and where can you find them?

4. A Note about the Internet

5. Research Proposals

6. Researching Your Topic

7. Sources of Research Material

8. Summarizing Your Sources

9. Outlines for Research Essays

10. Integrating Secondary Sources

11. Documentation: Citations and References

12. The Formal Précis

13. A Method for Summarizing

14. Sample Précis

15. Sample Student Essays

16. Reading #2 (APA Style): "Marketing Movies on the Internet"

1. The "Three-Part" Essay: Exposition, Research, Synthesis

The main difference between an argumentative essay, discussed in Part Four, and an expository essay is that the former seeks to convince the reader, to change his or her mind about a subject. The expository essay doesn't seek to change the reader's view, but it does seek to convince the reader that the thesis statement is valid by using factual information, such as statistics and the findings of research, to support its thesis. In this sense, argument is involved in expository writing.

Exposition means "put forth." Exposition is an inclusive term for writing concerned with *explaining*, as distinct from arguing or persuading. **Research** comes from the French *rechercher*, "to seek again." Many student researchers can attest to the fact that when they conduct research, they look and *look again*—exploring, checking, and re-checking are integral to research. **Synthesis** means "put together." You put together the evidence provided by your primary and secondary sources to create a new entity: your essay.

In expository research essays, **claims of fact** are generally used, and you don't set out to argue for one side or the other; instead, you analyze and assess the validity of the conclusions of various researchers on a topic and, on the basis of their positions, come to a reasoned conclusion.

In an argumentative essay, the **effectiveness** of your **argument** is vital to your success; in an expository essay, the **presentation** of your **information** is vital to your success. As expository essays often lack the driving thrust of an argument, however, you should find ways to make the essay interesting and appealing to the reader. Ensure that your essay is not merely a mechanical assemblage of dry facts; as defined below, exposition involves much more than finding out what someone else says or thinks about something, and then rewriting it in your own words. At the university level, exposition usually involves research.

Knowledge is cumulative, and the increments account for what we call "progress" in the sciences, the social sciences, and the humanities. The most knowledgeable experts depend on the findings of others to help in their own explorations; the research they do, in turn, adds to their store of knowledge, enabling them to contribute to their chosen field.

The in-depth training you receive in your discipline will prepare you for specialized work. Part of that training will no doubt involve research: exploring topics and finding out what conclusions other researchers have come to. However, if you went no further, if you contented yourself *only with finding out*, your training would not be complete. You might know a lot, but you would not necessarily be able to apply your knowledge unless you also are able to synthesize, or integrate, your new-found learning. Thus, while exposition implies research, research, in turn, implies synthesis—putting together what you have learned.

As a term applied to philosophy, the synthesis is the third, higher stage of truth that results from the combination of thesis and antithesis. In chemistry, synthesis refers to the formation of a more complex compound from two or more chemical elements. This suggests what you do when you use the findings of others to help explain your topic: you create a synthesis, or "a higher stage of truth."

The comprehensive scope of the expository essay is reflected in the discrete tasks or mental operations involved in its production. These tasks can serve as chronological

> In the successful expository essay, the writer synthesizes or interweaves his or her main ideas, structure, and language with the ideas, structure, and language of the sources to make a contribution to the field of knowledge.

steps in writing the expository essay; however, the step-by-step approach should not imply simple linearity. For example, although adding and checking citations will probably be the last step for most student writers, writing down all the bibliographical details of the sources is a vital part in step 2, **assimilation**. Writers may find themselves going back to steps 1 and 2 when they are integrating sources during the outline or first draft stages (steps 3 and 4) if they discover they have overlooked or minimized an important aspect of research, perhaps a significant study.

Although the writing process is not always a linear one, it can be thought of as cumulative. As you undertake work during these different stages in the process, there are specific questions you can ask yourself—perhaps using the answers as a checklist. Before moving on to each successive stage, you should feel that you have gained something to build on. You will then be able to proceed with greater confidence.

1.1 Research—Finding and Exploring

This step involves determining your topic and relevant sources. At this early stage, it is helpful to construct a *research proposal* (Section 5), which includes a summary of your purpose (what you expect to prove), as well as a tentative list of source material. To help you reach this stage, of course, you will have had to think about the topic and use the pre-writing strategies you find the most effective.

Questions to ask:
- Where do my interests lie?
- Do I have a knowledge base I can use to explore a topic thoroughly?
- If the area I would like to explore is unfamiliar, how can I obtain background information?
- What am I hoping to contribute to this subject area?
- Whom am I writing for? Who is my audience?
- What kind of sources would be appropriate given my topic and my audience?
- Where will I find my source material?
- Do I know of the major authors in the field, or how can I find these authors?
- Have I given myself sufficient time to research, synthesize, organize, compose, document, and revise?

1.2 Synthesis (I)—Assimilation

After you have found your sources, your mental process becomes one of **assimilation**; by taking notes and summarizing where appropriate, you are demonstrating that you can accurately represent another person's ideas and use them (assimilate them) with your own ideas. This vital stage of the research essay is discussed here; summaries are discussed in Section 8, below. When you have done these tasks, you are ready to express these ideas in the expository essay.

Questions to ask:
- Is my research geared towards supporting my points?
- Have I understood the results of the studies I've looked at and/or the positions of the experts whose works I have read?

- Are all my sources credible? Are there many recent ones?
- Have I summarized adequately and/or quoted accurately all sources I might use?
- Which sources are the most important?
- How do the different experts' views or conclusions fit together?
- Are there opposing positions? Do some findings challenge other ones, for example?
- How do they help me in my exploration of the topic?
- Has my research changed my view of my topic? If so, how? Do I need to change my thesis?

1.3 Organization—Arranging

Every essay needs a structure; usually this will take the form of an outline, a kind of blueprint for the writing stage. Outlines for expository essays are discussed below in Section 9.

Questions to ask:
- Do I have enough support to begin an outline? If so, what kind of outline should I use?
- Is there a natural organizational method I should use? (chronological? cause and effect? problem-solution?)
- Do my points thoroughly explore the topic?
- Are some points inadequately developed to produce substantial paragraphs?
- Are all areas of my research relevant to the points I want to make?
- What points are most essential and what sources are most relevant?
- Am I off topic anywhere?
- Does the structure I choose reflect my purpose? Does it reflect my audience? Is it logical?

1.4 Synthesis (II)—Integration

During the first-draft stage—as you are now concerned with integrating your sources into your essay—synthesis takes place at the linguistic or the textual level. Thus, how you use direct quotations, summary, and paraphrase will be important (see Section 10).

Questions to ask:
- Am I overusing my sources? Under-using them?
- Which sources should be summarized, which paraphrased, and which quoted directly? (This will depend on various factors including length, importance, and phrasing of the source)
- Am I using my sources effectively?
- Can I use ellipses to omit less important parts of the source?
- Am I providing smooth transitions between them and my own writing?
- Is the language level roughly the same throughout? Is it appropriate for my audience?
- Are direct quotations grammatically integrated and easy to read?
- Have I double-checked them for accuracy?
- Is my own writing clear, grammatical, and effective?

1.5 Documenting: Following Procedures

In this final stage of the research essay, you follow the directives for scholarly style in documenting sources as laid down by the authority of the pertinent discipline. The three main scholarly formats for referencing are those of the Modern Language Association (MLA), the American Psychological Association (APA), and the Chicago (Note) style. These resources should be available in your college library or bookstore (see Section 11).

Questions to ask:
- What documentation style is expected for this essay?
- Where is information on documenting to be found?
- If I am using electronic sources, am I clear on acceptable methods for documenting them? (Has my instructor given me guidance or directed me to specific sites/sources?)
- Do I know what needs to be documented and what does not?
- Is it possible that the reader could confuse my own ideas or observations with information taken from a secondary source?
- Have I carefully documented other people's words and ideas but without cluttering the essay with unnecessary citations?

2. What Is Research?

Research should be familiar to most students. It is unlikely you will have made many important decisions in your life without researching them beforehand, whether deciding which brand of MP3 player to buy or deciding which post-secondary schools to apply to. In the case of an MP3 player, you may have asked friends or simply browsed through the selection on the store shelves, noting the features of each. In the case of schools, you may have read brochures, talked to other people—perhaps current students, graduates, or school counsellors—and considered various academic and non-academic criteria. However, you probably placed the highest value on *factual evidence*: programs, prerequisites, tuition fees, housing, and campus size. You may have consulted objective experts, such as people who have researched the different schools (or the models of MP3 players), ranking them according to different criteria.

Decision-making on the basis of research is a life skill, and the critical skills of analysis, judgement, and evaluation are involved in the decision-making process. Research assignments in college or university ask you to analyze, compare, assess, and/or synthesize the scholarship of experts in your subject area, generally by discussing multiple positions on a problem. Simply rephrasing these sources is not necessarily research, nor is a summary of your own opinions or experiences. One common approach to organizing a research paper is to compare and contrast the similarities and differences between two or more ideas. Another method is to evaluate the strengths and/or weaknesses of a point of view based on criteria that you create or borrow from experts. The following example involves both compare/contrast and evaluation.

1. Identifying a problem:

    Scientists report that holes have appeared in the earth's ozone layer in the past two decades.

2. Stating a claim or the thesis about this problem (what the writer will explore or prove):

    Acid rain is causing holes in the earth's ozone layer.

3. Describing the points made by one or more "experts" concerning the claim:

    Scientist one claims his research demonstrates that ozone holes did not exist before 1983. He presents information gathered from weather balloons that shows acidic particles in the air over North America in the same time period.

    Scientist two asserts that ozone layer holes are not new phenomena, and should not be attributed to acid rain. Since she began viewing ozone holes by telescope in 1983, she has measured ozone holes as they have increased in size.

4. Reaching a decision on the merits of these experts' approaches to the thesis:

    Scientist one's arguments are more convincing than those of scientist two. Scientist one claims to have information that shows that the holes in the atmosphere appeared at a particular time. Scientist two is able to demonstrate an increase in size, but cannot pinpoint the onset of these holes in the Earth's ozone layer.

5. Concluding with your judgement on the thesis, either by rating the experts' approaches or by suggesting a new way of thinking about the problem:

    Scientist one has convinced you that there is a relationship between acid rain and holes in the ozone layer. His experiments began before such holes were identified, and he has data that show their existence in 1983. However, scientist two's work should not be completely discounted, as these ozone holes may have existed much longer but were not recognized until the mid-eighties.

3. Who are these experts . . . and where can you find them?

Authorities, or experts, are people who are highly experienced or highly educated, who have published or produced significant work about a subject. A documentary filmmaker may be an expert; watching his or her film will enable you to gather information for your essay. A writer for a magazine or newspaper may also be an expert;

so, too, could a person interviewed on radio or television be very familiar with a topic, either through his or her research, knowledge, or personal experience. The shelves of libraries are laden with the publications of experts, and the Internet may be another source of expertise. Since the number of these experts may be enormous, you need standards for screening the quality of their information. In the case of the filmmaker, you could consider the following criteria for credibility:

- An important part of research is to select sources whose work has been scrutinized by their colleagues. Anyone who can run a camera can make a documentary film. Are there any reviews in journals or other comments you can read about the film? This will help you know what the filmmaker's colleagues think about this film.
- Is the film part of your institution's collection or available through a reputable organization like the National Film Board?
- Since you are writing a research paper in an educational context, you may wish to consider the filmmaker's academic credentials.

Another criterion used to measure the usefulness of research material is **publication date**. Since attitudes and analyses change over time, more recent information allows you to consider the latest developments in your field. A further advantage in beginning with recent material is that the source often will refer to previous studies that might be useful. Sometimes just scanning the Works Cited or References section at the end of a recent work will suggest potential sources. However, it is also wise to consider the most enduring experts in your subject area alongside the latest trends in order to help you understand why or how outlooks about the subject have changed, if they have.

4. A Note about the Internet

When it comes to assessing the credibility of a secondary source, especially an Internet source, you could consider the words of the porcine dictator in George Orwell's *Animal Farm*: "[S]ome animals are more equal than others." The ease with which anyone with basic computer skills can publish on-line has created both new opportunities and new challenges for researchers.

Surfing the Web for MP3 prices and using it for academic research require different criteria; research is focused on the trustworthiness of the author(s). Because the Internet is a compilation of the efforts of countless individuals, companies, and institutions, with very few controls to guarantee the accuracy or fairness of the information placed on-line, to ensure the quality of the information you download, you must assess the reputation of a site's creator(s) and double-check the information in other sources. Many thoughtful and well-respected authors use the Internet to reach others who share their interests; however, it is important to judge a Web-site author's motivation carefully. Some of the information available on the Web is of limited value due to the promotion of the author's point of view or due to inaccurate information. Ask yourself, "Is the author I'm reading providing a reasoned argument or just an opinion about the subject being discussed?" Be aware that personal Web pages and listservs are, by and large, designed for conversation and opinion rather than with the rigorous deliberation of various points of view that characterizes academic research.

University Web sites provide a wealth of accurate scholarly information, so an excellent strategy for beginning researchers is to allow university or library sites to guide you towards appropriate on-line material. The final part of a Web site's Universal Resource Locator (URL) directs you to these Web sites. The addresses of degree-granting American educational institutions always end with the domain name ".edu." Canadian schools' Web sites generally contain a shortened version of their name, followed by ".ca."

5. Research Proposals

5.1 Purpose

Proposals are common to university research and the working spheres of science and business. Non-profit organizations and individuals also use them to apply for financial support. A writer's ability to make the proposal sound worthwhile may convince the agency that the writer is the best person for the project. Similarly, as an essay writer, you want the subject you investigate to demonstrate its worth and you want to be perceived as credible.

In the professional world, proposals can be detailed and complex. They can be divided into introduction/overview, background information and/or statement of the problem, goals and objectives, methods, available resources, needed resources, and conclusion. Because there is much variability in what instructors look for in research proposals, what you are asked to write might be different from the following minimal two elements: a statement of purpose and a statement about your planned research.

Even if you are not asked to submit a proposal and have it approved before beginning your essay, choosing to write one yourself can clarify your thinking about your topic and provide a rough plan. Sometimes writers include dates for the completion of specific parts of the process—for example, the date to be finished preliminary research.

5.2 Format

In the research proposal, you state your topic and what you hope to prove about it. Proposals can take the form of questions that you expect to answer or statements you will be considering related to your topic. You also should consider the kinds of sources you are likely to use and where you will find them. The following summarizes the aims of the research proposal and the way it is set up:

What could be included in the proposal?
- topic and tentative thesis statement
- relevant background (if any)
- kinds of sources you are likely to use
- main organizational method
- your main points

Part One—Purpose
1. Announce the area you want to explore. You can also briefly state why you want to explore this area, why the topic interests you, and/or why it might interest other people or be of concern to them. A good way to approach this is to consider a few

essential questions about the subject that you hope to answer. This can also help develop your thesis statement and main points.

2. Include a tentative thesis statement; of course, you can amend it later.
3. Try to outline at least 2–4 main points in addition to your thesis. Some proposals also include a more complete outline, especially if the proposal is written after you have located your sources and are more certain about your main points and the essay's structure.

Part Two—Research Methodology

1. Relevant background could include anything you need to find out about before you begin writing.
2. You may not have to refer to specific sources but to the *kinds of sources* you will likely be using; what kinds of resources does the discipline related to your topic offer? Which are likely to be most useful to you: books, journals, magazines, Internet sources, interviews? What kind of preliminary research are you planning?
3. You should anticipate what organizational methods (cause/effect, compare and contrast, division, problem-solution, etc.) and evidence (in addition to secondary sources) will best support your factual claim.

5.3 Sample Research Proposals

Here are three sample research proposals of increasing levels of complexity written by student writers; they range between 175 and 250 words. They use different methods, but all satisfy the essential functions of proposals.

Proposal for Research Essay on the Effects of Stimulants

by Danielle Harvey

Topic: The use of physical enhancers to lengthen and improve study sessions for students.

Purpose: To investigate the use of caffeine (pills or beverages) and other supplements, such as ginkgo biloba, to determine effect on academic performance and health. Some students are trying to prolong late-night study sessions through the use of caffeine. Others believe that taking supplements such as ginkgo biloba will enhance their memory capability. As a student, I am curious about whether these products actually work or whether they are just hoaxes with long-term health costs.

Central Questions: How effective is caffeine for lengthening study sessions? Does ginkgo biloba actually enhance memory capabilities as advertised? How do they work as stimulants? Are these methods helpful for students in the long term? What are benefits/costs of both in terms of health and studying proficiency? Do many students use these products?

Projected Research: Research actual products as advertised on selected Web sites as well as in scientific journals/papers in the school library; evaluate experimental data and scientific conclusions; look to see if the different sources reveal discrepancies between advertising claims and findings about specific products; conduct interviews with students.

Proposal for Essay on Obsessive Compulsive Disorders in Children

by Kasey Chittenden

I would like to explore obsessive compulsive disorders (OCD) among children. I want to explore the symptoms, diagnosis, and treatment of this disorder. I chose OCD because I'm extremely interested in psychology, and I always love learning about new psychological disorders. Another reason is that when I was younger I had many of these symptoms, which I eventually outgrew, and my younger cousin was recently diagnosed with this disorder as well. I thought that this topic might be interesting for others to read about since many people are interested in, though uninformed about, the details of psychological disorders. Driven by anxiety-evoked ideas, OCD interferes with children's daily routines, leaving them to seek help through medication or psychotherapeutic treatment.

I need to find out the symptoms, how they vary in different children, and the treatment for those symptoms. I have found some books that are extremely helpful, but I am going to search through journal articles as well to see if I can find more recent methods of treatment. I'm planning on presenting this essay in a problem-solution format to recognize the problems these children have and how they can attempt to control this disorder.

Proposal for Compare and Contrast Essay on Traditional

Chinese Medicine versus Western Medicine

by Grace Chau

Years ago, Western conventional medicine was seen to be infallible. Recently, more people have turned to alternative remedies including Traditional Chinese Medicine (TCM). I would like to explore the nature and origins of these two different approaches. First, I would need to define the elements of these systems and, using chronology, briefly trace their developments. Clearly, two different models are involved, the Western method focusing primarily on problem-solution and TCM on a more holistic approach to the body. In addition, while Western medicine typically attempts one method of treatment and measures its effectiveness (before possibly trying something else), TCM more typically uses more than one method of treatment. Finally, I want to look at what kind of people prefer to use TCM and why they are drawn to it. From this, it may be possible to generalize about the future of TCM versus Western medicine.

My preliminary research has revealed that there are a few studies in such journals as *The Journal of the American Medical Association* that assess TCM as a treatment method. My research will include books and articles that define TCM and explain how it works. Since I am familiar with Western methodology, I need to look closely at the information from these texts in order to differentiate between the two models. I hope to be able to interview a practitioner of TCM in Victoria to gain a further understanding of the underlying principles of the methods used.

6. Researching Your Topic

6.1 Exploring

The first stage in researching a topic is to determine the major authors in your subject area and what they say about your topic. As well, you need to know where they provide this information so that you can quote or paraphrase what these experts have to say and so that you can accurately document your sources.

Finding important authors and works in your area may be easier if your instructor can recommend them. However, in most cases, especially if you are free to choose your own topic, beginning and narrowing the search will be something you do yourself. Looking for a general work, such as a textbook, in your subject area is a useful first step. General works frequently include extensive bibliographies (alphabetical listings of works used or consulted), which you can scan for relevant titles and authors. Consult works in the library's Reference section, such as indexes, encyclopedias, dictionaries, and comprehensive guides in your area. Most books in a library's reference section can't be taken out of the library, but they can direct you to more specific sources that can be taken out. Internet search engines and subject directories can also provide excellent starting points, providing you with general topics that you can narrow down.

When you find potentially useful sources, you can add them to your **working bibliography**, a list of books and articles you plan to look at. When you find these works, skim the index and the table of contents to determine how helpful the source will be. If it looks promising, but you're still uncertain, read the writer's Introduction, Preface, or Foreword. The author often summarizes his or her approach and,

When you are taking down this information, don't forget to record your own observations, comments, and queries. You will need the bibliographical details, of course, but you will also need to synthesize the ideas of the source with your own ideas as your essay develops; you will have to relate it to other sources and to your own thesis statement. It's important to keep source material separate from your own comments—by writing your responses on another piece of paper or by writing your own comments in pencil or with a different coloured pen. *Always give clear directions to yourself when you take down this information.*

sometimes, provides chapter-by-chapter summaries in the introductory section. With articles, read the abstract (abstracts are short summaries that precede journal articles in the sciences and social sciences). Your working bibliography will not necessarily look much like the final list of works you actually use; the principle of a working bibliography is to lead you to directly relevant sources. Remember to note the date of the work's publication on the copyright page of books (the other side of the title page). Prefer more recent works not only because they will be up to date but also because they may draw on relevant previously published works and provide you with other useful sources.

6.2 Research Note-Taking

Keeping constructive and methodical records during the research phase of the essay-writing process will allow you to read material efficiently as well as save time (and your sanity) when you write your paper. You should make notes as you research your sources, ensuring that you record the following information:

1. A direct quotation, a summary or a paraphrase of the writer's idea; *if it is a direct quotation, make sure you put quotation marks around it*
2. The complete name(s) of the author(s)
3. The name(s) of editor(s) or translator(s), if applicable
4. The name of the book, journal, magazine, newspaper, or Web site
5. The name of the specific article, chapter, section, or Web site
6. Full publication details, including date, edition, or translation
7. The name of the publisher and the company's location (including province or state) for books
8. In the case of Internet sites, the day you viewed the page
9. The call number of a library book or bound journal for later reference, if needed
10. The page numbers you consulted, both those from which specific ideas came and the full page range (or some other marker for unnumbered Web documents)

6.3 Organizing Research Notes

One time-honoured method is to write these notes on index cards (just don't forget to number them). You can also record notes in a journal and use tabs to section the book into particular headings. If you have regular access to a computer you can create a record-keeping system, either using a database program like *Access* or by simply creating multiple document files in a folder. In addition, there are a number of software programs available that can assist you in organizing your research. Programs such as *Scribe* (http://www.scribesa.com/) imitate the card file system. Others, like *EndNote* (http://www.endnote.com/), *Bibliographix* (http://www.bibliographix.com/), and *Nota Bene* (http://www.notabene.com/) are databases. Learning these programs takes time, but they generally offer beneficial extra features like the automatic formatting of citations and references/bibliographies. If you choose a computer-based note-taking method, you should back up your work onto disk regularly in case of a technical failure.

6.4 Cross-Referencing

Writing or underlining in library books themselves is both destructive and inefficient as a note-taking method because you should be able to refer to your notes without re-reading an entire text again.

The utility of any form of note-taking can be significantly increased by cross-referencing, which means creating a list of central or key words, names, or themes and recording where in your notes these occur. You can cross-reference by writing notes in a margin or by using either index cards or computer files. Some students draw themselves a visual aid like a mind map (graphic organizer) on a large sheet of paper to connect their key words. Some word-processing programs include a cross-referencing feature for single documents (in Word XP, for example, this is found under Insert, then Reference, in the drop-down menu). The computer databases mentioned previously often have built-in, key word-based cross-referencing systems.

6.5 Some Useful Research Strategies

6.5.1. Assimilating

- Begin the research by gathering definitions of the key words in your thesis statement.
- Read or view everything with the thesis statement always in mind. Resist getting sidetracked by reading unconnected material, however interesting it might seem.
- Judge whether or not a book will be worth your time by looking up your cross-referencing key words in the index at the back of the book. Read the abstracts (condensed summaries preceding many journal articles) of articles to similarly determine their usefulness.
- Consider how the information you take from your sources can be strung together using transitional words and phrases like "because," "as a result of," "on the other hand," or "in contrast." This will help you select points that flow logically.
- Try to find an example to support every major statement you wish to make. An example can be a quotation, a paraphrased reference, or a larger concept like an author's comment on or solution to your thesis statement.

6.5.2. Arranging

- When you've finished your first round of research, write an outline that lays out the structure of your paper by creating primary and secondary headings corresponding to the major elements of your thesis statement. Under the headings, list the lines of reasoning that support these points and the examples that support each of them.
- Decide how many pages you will allot for each section of the paper, taking the instructor's requirements for paper length into serious account.
- Look over your outline. Do you have sufficient examples to support all your major statements? Then review your page allotment. Do you have enough material in your study notes to fill the pages? If neither of these things appears to be true, perhaps you need to do more research. On the other hand, if you have too many key points and several examples for each one, now is the time to choose the strongest ones in order to meet length stipulations.

- Consider laying out your paper in a word-processing program according to the suggested page number count. If you use the manual "page break" option (under "Insert" in most programs) to create document sections that follow your outline, you'll easily be able to judge whether you're writing too much or too little for any portion of the paper.
- Design a time line for each of the steps in your paper if you haven't done so in a research proposal. This will help ensure that you don't spend a disproportionate time on any segment of the paper.

6.6 Using Contradictory Evidence

In the initial research stage, you look for sources relevant to your topic; however, not all studies on a given topic arrive at the same conclusion. If your primary purpose is to explain or investigate a problem, you will have to assess the validity of the different findings, trying to account for their differences, perhaps by analyzing their respective strengths and weaknesses. Thus, assessing is a fundamental part of the research process.

In the humanities, where your claim is often one of interpretation, you must carefully delineate the interpretations of other academics from your own. It can be an excellent strategy to acknowledge another interpretation and use it as a springboard into your own interpretation. Contradictory interpretations should not simply be dismissed without explanation; it is better to acknowledge them and qualify them, possibly by briefly discussing their limitations.

Scientific experimentation often involves the attempt to test the results of previous findings. Through continual testing and retesting, our knowledge grows incrementally. In the sciences and social sciences, researchers using inductive methods may, though appearing to observe and measure data under controlled conditions, draw different conclusions. For example, there have been many recent studies that attempt to show the health benefits of vitamins. If you are investigating the benefits of Vitamin E in preventing heart disease and have found that credible evidence exists, you still need to acknowledge contradictory studies and explain how these findings fit into your claim about the value of Vitamin E.

Researching a topic can be a challenging and rigorous process—possibly a trial run for the kind of work you will do later in your academic or professional career. If you experience doubts or uncertainties at any stage of the process, talk to your instructor as soon as possible. Don't wait until the day before your paper is due!

7. Sources of Research Material

Until a generation ago, a student began the process of researching a paper by going to a library and checking out books written about the topic. In this digital age, limiting your research to the texts available on a single library's shelves seems, at the very least, unimaginative. However, although research sources have become more various, they are more confusing and contentious than in the past. The main dilemma revolves around the choice between doing library-based research and gathering information on-line. However, this "library versus Internet" dichotomy is rapidly blurring into irrelevancy, since almost all research can now be described as electronically mediated in some way, and libraries have progressed from being physical repositories of paper into new roles as interactive and virtual clearinghouses of information storage and distribution. Thus, a "library source" today doesn't always mean a hard copy version but one that could also exist electronically as a library holding—or perhaps exists only electronically.

7.1 The Range of Sources

Rather than dividing the world of knowledge into cyber versus paper categories, we can define some types of information sources used for research, which may be available either on-line or at a library. There are many different kinds of source materials available; most of the important ones are discussed below.

7.1.1 Primary and Secondary Sources

The distinction between primary and secondary sources is crucial to you as a student researcher for two reasons. A major goal of university-level research is to read or view original material, known as **primary sources**. The ability to analyze and integrate **secondary sources**, the literature that has grown up in response to the original work, is also a principal goal of post-secondary learning. You need to be able to distinguish between **original** authors and the **commentary** on their work. Sometimes authors function in both roles, as authors of primary literature and as commentators on other original works. Essay assignments frequently include a requirement that both primary and secondary sources be identified and referenced.

Primary sources are the original compositions of authors. The First Folio edition of Shakespeare's plays published posthumously in 1623 provides the earliest available text of *As You Like It* by William Shakespeare and would be considered the primary source for this play. A particular scholarly edition of the play, such as one in the Oxford series of Shakespeare's works, will be acceptable as a primary source in most cases affecting undergraduates because the First Folio editions are rare. Personal documents, such as letters and other material created at the same time as an event, and initial scientific articles reporting on a work are also considered primary sources. A secondary source for *As You Like It* would be another writer's analysis and commentary on the play, books about Shakespeare's theatre, books about Elizabethan English, and so on. An encyclopedia entry is also considered a secondary source.

It's possible to obtain a copy of a primary source like *As You Like It* by searching a library's catalogue (in person or on-line) and taking the book home to read. *As You Like It* and other Shakespeare plays also are available in "full-text versions" from several different sources on the Internet.

7.2 Start Your Research by Looking at Secondary Sources

An efficient way to construct a general framework of research from your thesis statement is to access reference sources such as indexes, almanacs, encyclopedias, dictionaries, and yearbooks. These compendiums can provide you with concise summaries of statistics, definitions, and biographies, and they also generally provide a reading list of the principal primary and secondary sources. As mentioned, the

When using texts accessed on-line, it is important to remember that multiple translations/editions often are available, and the on-line version may not be the most accurate or accepted one. In addition, the majority of e-books are what could be described as classics, since Canadian copyright restricts the free publication of works for the life of an author plus 50 years. Check with your instructor before you go ahead and use Internet material as a primary source.

paper copies of these books are found in the Reference section of a library and usually can't be taken home. This restriction is mediated by the fact that this type of broad-spectrum information is widely available on the Internet. For instance, a Google search of "black hole" and "encyclopedia" returns results that include the *Encyclopaedia Britannica*, the *Columbia Encyclopedia*, *Encarta Encyclopedia*, and numerous library-based sites offering further links to information on the subject. The *Britannica* entry includes a listing of relevant books, articles, Web sites, magazine articles, and videos on black holes.

7.2.1 Books

Once you've developed a basic understanding of your topic, you can look for books and journal articles that refer specifically to your thesis statement. Continue your research by locating either books or periodicals mentioned in your preliminary search of reference materials. A book can be written on a single theme; a compilation of articles, essays, or chapters by a number of authors around a topic; or a collection of pieces by a particular author that have already been published individually. Books that are available to you can be located by searching a library's card catalogue or sometimes can be found on-line by doing an author or title search or by using a database. For instance, Project Gutenberg has digitally republished more than 6,000 e-books (http:// promo.net/pg/), ranging from the contemporary *Human Genome Project, Y Chromosome*, by The Human Genome Project, to the nineteenth-century novel *The Hunchback of Notre Dame*, by Victor Hugo.

7.2.2 Periodicals

Periodicals are published regularly—for instance, monthly, yearly, or daily. Examples include newspapers, magazines, journals, and yearbooks. Unless you are writing about an extremely current aspect of contemporary culture, you will probably be concentrating on periodicals called **journals**, which publish articles written by academics, scientists, and researchers. The most respected journals are **peer-reviewed**, which means that other experts in that field have assessed the work prior to its being published. Peer-reviewed journal articles are expected to describe the authors' original research.

7.2.3 Locating Journal Articles

The articles published in scholarly journals are the "products" that researchers and graduate students produce in order to advance their ideas—and their careers. As a result, there are thousands of scholarly journals publishing a wealth of current and authoritative research on just about any topic you can imagine. However, finding these articles can be a challenge because the journals generally are distributed only through very expensive subscriptions. University libraries subscribe to some of the journals that they consider most valuable and then allow students, faculty, and staff access to them either in paper editions or on-line.

Locating a **hard copy** (paper copy) of a journal article generally begins with a library's electronic card catalogue, whether you are physically at the library or use an Internet connection to view it. Let's say you have located an article from the bibliography of a well-known textbook on your topic. In order to find the article, you'll need some detailed information that makes up what is called a **citation**, which includes much more than the author's name and the name of the journal. The following components of a citation illustrate what you will need:

Author(s) Name(s): Ellsworth, E.
Publication Year: 1989.
Article Title: "Why doesn't this feel empowering? Working through the repressive myths of critical pedagogy"
Journal Name: *Harvard Educational Review*
Volume and Issue Number: 59(3)
Page Numbers: 297–324.

The complete citation written in APA style (Section 11.4 below) looks like this:

Ellsworth, E. (1989). Why doesn't this feel empowering? Working through the repressive myths of critical pedagogy. *Harvard Educational Review*, 59(3), 297–324.

Most card catalogues are designed so you can select "journals only" in the search limiters and then search for the journal name (as opposed to the article title or author name). You'll be given a call number that will direct you to a location in the library where you'll find either unbound or bound (into a book) journals. Look up the volume month or issue, and then follow the page numbers to the article.

7.3 Internet Searches

What happens if your university doesn't subscribe to a paper version of the particular journal you want? This is where the Internet has revolutionized the research process in recent years. University libraries now generally subscribe to databases and indexes that contain the full texts of journal articles, which you can gather directly onto your computer's hard drive. Supplied by private companies, these services are called **aggregator databases** since they collect or aggregate many different journals together in searchable interfaces that give you access to many more journals than any individual library could ever afford to subscribe to or find the space to store.

The information contained in the full-text journal articles accessed through a database is almost always the same as what appears in the print version of the journal. Databases also may house a blend of scholarly and non-scholarly information, including popular magazines, newspapers, and non-peer-reviewed journals, along with government-produced documents. In addition, databases supply links to the growing number of journals that don't publish a paper version at all, and are available only online: electronic journals, or e-journals.

Although database interfaces can vary, most function on the principle of key words (including authors' names). For instance, the database EBSCOhost provides links to several thousand journals and millions of articles by using a combination of key words, search limiters, and search expanders. The search window for EBSCOhost looks like this:

EBSCO HOST Research Databases

New Search | View Folder | Preferences | Help

Basic Search | Advanced Search | Choose Databases

UNIV OF BRITISH COLUMBIA

Sign In to My EBSCOhost

Keyword | Publications | Subject Terms | Idexes

Cited References | Images

Database: Academic Search Premier

Database Help

Find: [   ] in Default Fields   Search   Clear

and [   ] in Default Fields

and [   ] in Default Fields

Search Tips

Folder is empty.

Refine Search | Search History / Alerts | Results

Limit your results: Limiters | **Expanders**   Reset

Full Text ☐

References Available ☐

Scholarly (Peer Reviewed) Journals ☐

Published Date   Month   Yr: [   ]   to   Month   Yr: [   ]

Publication   [   ]

Publication Type
Periodical
Newspaper
Book
Primary Source Document

Document Type
Abstract
Article
Bibliography
Book Entry

Number Of Pages [   ]

Cover Story ☐

Articles With Images
PDF
Text with Graphic

Expand your search to: Limiters | **Expanders**   Reset

Automatically "And" search terms ☐

Top of Page

Brought to you by The University of British Columbia Library.

This database screen shows how databases typically organize research information. By entering a word or phrase in the **find** box, you can retrieve any article that contains your key words in either the title or the body of all of the thousands of periodicals available through EBSCOhost. Needless to say, this list can be enormous and somewhat overwhelming. For this reason, EBSCOhost allows you to select **limiters** on your search, including a time period of publication and the option to search only peer-reviewed journals. There is also an advanced search window, which permits you to define various combinations of key words and **search limiters** or **expanders**. Each academic discipline has specialized databases and indices that concentrate on publications that are particularly relevant to that field. You can ask your instructor to direct you to the most appropriate databases or search your library's Web site for discipline-related listings. All databases have a link to on-line help. When you need help in your search, use the **help** button.

Boolean operators are used to customize your search. Search limiters include the words "AND" and "NOT." If you type the word "AND" between two or more search terms, your results will include both search terms; if you type the word "NOT" between search terms, your results will omit what follows "NOT." If you use "OR" as a search expander, your results will include **at least one** of the terms.

Let's say you were undecided about the topic you wanted to explore but were seriously considering either caffeine or alcohol. A database search on "caffeine OR alcohol" using EBSCOhost turns up 27,388 entries. This is far too many to be useful, so you then enter only one search term, "caffeine"; this yields 1,658 entries. Thinking that you might want to compare caffeine and alcohol, you use the limiter "AND," which produces 116 results. In order to exclude "tobacco" from your search, you add a second limiter, "NOT tobacco" and hit Search. Using the two limiters (caffeine AND alcohol NOT tobacco) produces 93 results—a more manageable start.

> Depending on your search engine, you can narrow or expand your search by using specific symbols. For example, putting words between double quotation marks will restrict the search to text in which the words appear in the order you place them; for example, typing in "fair trade coffee" (using quotation marks) will greatly reduce the number of entries you get because they will exclude results that contained the three words in a different order or separated by one or more words.

7.3.1 Some Popular Databases

EBSCOhost is a comprehensive "gateway" database service for more than 9,500 journals on a vast range of discipline areas, with an Internet style (Boolean logic) search interface. EBSCOhost is the inclusive academic database operating at this time. It is widely available through university library sites; see your institution's library site for login directions.

Ingenta is an excellent source for journals in the humanities, sciences, social sciences, and education. It features "full texts of about 15,841,801 articles from 28,351 publications."

ProQuest describes itself as an "on-line information service" that provides access to thousands of current periodicals and newspapers that are updated daily; it contains full-text articles from as early as 1986.

Lexis-Nexis Academic Universe contains full-text articles from nearly 2,000 sources such as company reports, newspapers, transcripts of broadcasts, wire services, newsletters, journals, legal case law, government documents, as well as some valuable reference texts.

Project Muse offers full-text articles from at least 100 scholarly journals in the humanities, the social sciences, and mathematics. Articles are available from 1995.

InfoTrac describes itself as a source for "research in academic disciplines as well as current news and general interest articles." It provides indexing and abstracts for 1,550 journals, along with full-text articles from more than 500 social sciences, technology, and humanities journals.

WorldCat, operated by a consortium of more than 9,000 universities, libraries and colleges, allows users to view or borrow audiovisual materials, books, films, government documents, computer files, and research reports in 400 languages. This "database of databases" has thousands of full-text articles and an interlibrary loan service for non-digitalized items.

ERIC (Educational Resources Information Centre): This large database pertains to education and is best known for its sizable series of short synopses on pertinent topics (ERIC Digest Records) written by educational experts under the auspices of the U.S. Department of Education. In addition to this education-oriented information, the ERIC Social Sciences Citation Index provides a multi-disciplinary directory of more than 1,725 social and behavioural sciences journals published after 1995.

Newspaper Source allows access to a range of full-text articles from 18 international newspapers, including *The Christian Science Monitor*, 6 newswires, and 139 regional American newspapers.

CANSIM (Canadian Socio-economic Information Management) Database (Statistics Canada) is a comprehensive database from Statistics Canada containing nearly 18 million government documents.

Health Source Nursing/Academic Edition offers full-text articles from more than 500 health and medical journals and indexes the abstracts of more than 850 publications.

BioMed Central indexes hundreds of journals offering peer-reviewed research about biology and medicine.

Business Source Elite is a database assembled for business schools and libraries, which incorporates 2,804 scholarly journals and business periodicals relating to marketing, economics, and accounting.

PsycINFO is operated by the American Psychological Association and offers citations (not full-text articles) for reports, articles, dissertations, and book chapters relating to psychology in fields such as education, business, medicine/nursing, and sociology.

IEL (IEEE/IEE Electronic Library) makes available full-text access to more than 125 technical journals and 600 conference proceedings in engineering, physics, computer science, and materials sciences.

7.4 Some Notes on Library Research

With the wealth of research information available electronically, it may seem redundant to go to a university or public library in person. In reality, libraries continue to be valuable resources for researchers at all levels of expertise, partly because they have books not available on-line and they are staffed by professionals who understand how information is organized and inter-related. Most libraries have reference librarians who can save you time and direct you to sources you might never come across on your own. Furthermore, libraries hold many important records, including the following:

- Indices for many periodicals, images, films, microfiche files, and videos
- Theses and dissertations (book-length documents written by university students as part of their advanced degree requirements)
- Historical documents, including maps and public records
- Collections of textual and graphic material on special subjects, sometimes including original documents
- Clipping files from newspapers and magazines
- Bound volumes of journals
- Collections of audio and film/video recordings

In addition, libraries store print information that has been gathered, sometimes over centuries, that is too expensive or fragile to digitize. Even for documents that are considered essential, the gradual transition to electronic record-keeping means that many important compilations of information made before 1985 are available only in paper form at a library.

Using electronic sources to access journals that publish paper versions has another wrinkle that can frustrate inexperienced researchers: these publications often hold their latest year's editions from databases in order to maintain their subscription lists. This means that it's still necessary to view the most current issues in person; and remember, accessing recent studies is vital, especially if your subject is a topical one.

Although the nature of research has changed dramatically with the increasing availability of on-line resources, the best way to think of the cyber–paper relationship is to consider it a complementary one. Relying *only* on the Internet is inadvisable and some instructors may specify how much—if any—electronic research is allowable.

7.5 Alternative Information Sources

Although this section has emphasized research information available by way of the written word, many disciplines accept support for your thesis statement from visual or audio media, such as television, film, video, works of art, performances, surveys/questionnaires, interviews, and observations. Using these alternative sources of information requires the same attention to detail in note-taking as when using traditional materials, and most citation styles provide instructions for citing and referencing non-textual research information. As these approaches to research are more acceptable by some disciplines than by others, it is wise early in the writing process to review with your instructor an essay paper outline that emphasizes alternative information sources.

7.5.1 Interviewing

If you have direct access to a noted authority in your field, interviewing can be an effective form of research. The principle advantage of an interview, whether face-to-face, by telephone, or by e-mail, is that you can ask questions specific to your research rather than having to search many potential sources for this particular information. Interview subjects can be treated the same way as other expert sources of knowledge; that is, their words can be summarized, paraphrased, or quoted directly. There are also specific methods for documenting interviewees. The college or university community—including, perhaps, one of your professors—is an ideal place to look for experts.

8. Summarizing Your Sources

When you summarize from a secondary source, you take the important parts of somebody else's work to use in your own essay—always ensuring that you give credit to your source. During the research stage, it is a good idea to write out the summaries from all the main sources you plan to use, as well as to carefully record significant direct quotations. It is a great nuisance to try to find again books and pages and lines once you have returned them to library shelves. Summarizing a book, article, or Internet source puts the main points before you when you come to write your essay, enabling you to *demonstrate your understanding of the source and its applicability to your thesis statement*. Summarizing the content of a source also avoids the unfortunate practice of *too much* direct quotation.

Apart from the summarizing you will do as part of the research process, summaries of essays and articles are often assigned as projects independent of essay-writing, because the ability to summarize is an important skill in itself. In such cases, you will probably have to write to a specific word length.

When summarizing, the writer is acting partly on behalf of the original writer. Scrupulous representation of these ideas is the hallmark of good summarization.

8.1 Summary

A **summary** is a general term for the rephrasing of somebody else's ideas essentially or completely in your own words. Summaries can range from a sentence (occasionally less) to many pages. Summaries rephrase main ideas. The précis and the abstract are specific kinds of summaries.

8.2 Précis

A **précis** is a condensed summary of the main points of an article or essay. A précis is generally 20 to 25 per cent the length of the original. The précis is discussed below, Section 12.

8.3 Abstract

While a research proposal states your purpose in exploring a topic and, perhaps, what you hope to find out about it, an **abstract** is an overview of your purpose, methods, and results; you write it *after* you have finished your essay, or, at least, after you have arrived at your conclusions. However, abstracts physically precede the essay; they are placed after the title and author notation and before the Introduction, enabling readers to decide whether they wish to read the full work that follows.

An abstract should be able to stand on its own, clearly but briefly representing the entire essay. It should include most or all of the following: background or overview of the field of study; the specific problem and your purpose in investigating it; methods or procedures; results; and a discussion of the results. It may end with a brief consideration of the significance or implications of the findings. An essay abstract should be 75–100 words, unless your instructor tells you otherwise. The abstracts for scientific papers are typically at least twice as long (150–250 words). Many abstract writers incorporate key phrases or even complete sentences from the full work into the abstract. The following abstract by student writer Kathy Dawson preceded her essay that compared the usefulness of two on-line sources of information. It includes the topic, problem, criteria for evaluation, and findings.

This report compares and contrasts the quality of two on-line sources as academic research tools. They were chosen for their information on endangered languages and the increasing concern with language extinction and conservation. Maffi's (2002) journal article "Endangered language, endangered knowledge" and Crawford's (1996) Web site article "Endangered Native American languages: What is to be done, and why?" were evaluated on their credibility, organization, and content. While Maffi's essay was found more credible, Crawford's Web-essay was better organized. Both provided excellent content and proved equally valuable as research sources. *(88 words)*

8.4 Annotated Bibliographies

An **annotated bibliography** is an *expanded* bibliography (annotate = to + note). Annotated bibliographies often accompany large research projects, such as books, dissertations, or major compilations relevant to a particular field. They can take the form of critical surveys, demonstrating the variety of approaches that other writers/ researchers have taken to the subject, as well as the relationship of the work in which the bibliography is situated to the research area being studied. While abstracts concisely summarize your own work for potential readers, annotated bibliographies concisely summarize similar works in the field of study—they tell your readers where the writer's particular piece of the puzzle fits into the whole.

Generally, each entry in an annotated bibliography provides a very brief summary of content, focusing primarily or exclusively on thesis statement and major points and findings. If the entry refers to a book-length study, the main points may take the form of major section or chapter headings. Frequently, annotated bibliographies contain an appraisal of the study's usefulness or contribution to the field of study.

8.5 Paraphrase

A **paraphrase** is usually about the length of the original. You would normally paraphrase an important part of a text, perhaps as much as one paragraph or even, occasionally, more. A strict paraphrase is entirely in your own words and in a different order from the original. Because paraphrases don't omit anything of substance from the source, they are unlike summaries whose main purpose is to condense the original, retaining its essence.

9. Outlines for Research Essays

How do you know when you have sufficient support for your points and can begin an outline? The answer may depend on the assignment itself, as your instructor may be expecting a specific or minimum number of sources. Otherwise, as suggested above, you should probably have at least one citation (direct quote, paraphrase, or idea) to support each of your major points. Whereas an argumentative essay depends on effective reasoning and various kinds of evidence—including examples, illustrations, analogies, anecdotes, and *perhaps* the findings of secondary sources, the expository essay relies heavily on outside authority as support. Therefore, your outline may benefit from such sources. Being specific in your outline will make it easier to write your first draft, where your principal concern will be with integrating the sources with your own words.

The excerpt below is from a detailed outline of an essay on children affected by AIDS in South Africa. The writer, Meghan McLeod, began her outline by citing relevant statistics relating to the problem of AIDS in Africa. She quickly narrowed her focus to young children in South Africa, describing some of the debilitating effects on children and using current AIDS statistics. The outline for her *first two body paragraphs*, given here, includes her main point and sub-points, along with supporting details from credible sources. Note that she has used many direct quotations from these sources. In her final version, she might choose to paraphrase some of them. At the outline stage, her priority is to determine where they will fit into the structure of her essay. For an example of a complete formal outline that uses secondary sources, see Part Four, Section 9.

Outline of Essay on Children Affected by AIDS in South Africa

II.   Broken family pattern in South Africa

    A.   A broken family environment is partly a legacy of the past in South Africa and is caused by "the history of displacement of people as a way of implementing the racially segregated society envisaged during the years of apartheid, combined with the migrant labour system" (*Children on the Brink*, a video released at the XIV International AIDS conference in Barcelona, Spain, published in 2000).

    B.   AIDS is dramatically contributing to the phenomenon of the broken family, "unravelling decades of gain in child survival and development" (UN secretary general, Kofi Annan).

III.   How AIDS further undermines family structure

    A.   Children are orphaned after watching their parents and other older relations suffer and eventually die, leaving them to care for their brothers and sisters.

    B.   They become heads of the households at early age inheriting responsibility that comes with it. "[C]hildren without parental protection lose opportunities for school, health care, growth, development, nutrition, shelter, and even their rights to a decent and humane existence itself" (Sibongile Mthembu-Mkhabela, CEO of the Nelson Mandela Children's Fund); even if these children don't get AIDS or have parents, aunts, or uncles die of the disease, they are adversely affected as they are surrounded by "ill parents or [are] living in households that have taken in orphans. They are often just as vulnerable" (Carol Bellamy, exec. dir. of UNICEF).

10. Integrating Secondary Sources

All secondary sources require parenthetical citations and an alphabetical listing in the *Works Cited* section at the end of your essay (MLA) or the *References* section (APA). You must cite secondary sources —whether you quote from them directly, summarize them, paraphrase them, or just refer to them in passing—by using the appropriate style of your discipline.

The judicious use of quotations from your secondary sources enables you to support your argument and demonstrate your familiarity with source material. A synthesis essay, interwoven with textual citations in the correct format, reveals your competence as a discerning reader, researcher, and writer.

You can treat secondary sources in any of three ways:

1. you can summarize the source, or the section of the source that is most directly relevant to your point;
2. you can paraphrase the source;
3. you can cite from the source directly.

10.1 Plagiarism

Remember that plagiarism does not apply just to the words of the source, but also to any idea you obtain from a source. You also are plagiarizing if you use the language of the source without enclosing it in quotation marks or if you closely imitate the structure of the material cited—even if you changed the words.

Plagiarism is the unacknowledged borrowing of someone else's words or ideas. Intentional plagiarizing is considered by many the most serious academic crime, for which there are equally serious repercussions. Unintentional or inadvertent plagiarising usually leads to the same repercussions, even if the reason for the plagiarism was careless note-taking, improper documentation, or a lack of knowledge about plagiarism itself.

However, you don't need to reference anything that falls under the category of "general knowledge," even if you obtained the information from a specific source. If in doubt about what constitutes general knowledge, refer to the "sunrise–sunset rule of thumb": you don't need to cite the fact that the sun rises in the east and sets in the west.

In reality, of course, the rules for source acknowledgement are not quite as strict as that, *but if there is a reasonable presumption that a typical reader would not know it, then cite the reference*; if, however, a fact would be *easily obtainable* by a reader from a number of different sources (even if a typical reader wouldn't know it), it may not be necessary to cite it. Your instructor may be able to tell you how many sources constitute "easily obtainable" information; a minimum number often given is three.

Remember, though, that general knowledge can vary according to audience: if you are writing for an audience with a scientific or medical background, for example, you may not need to cite the fact that the active ingredient in marijuana is tetrahydrocannabinol; if you are writing a paper for historians or political scientists, you may not need to cite the fact that British Columbia became a Canadian province in 1871 because your readers could easily obtain this information. If the general knowledge or the easily obtainable standards do not apply, make the citation.

In addition to failing to cite an idea, paraphrase, or summary, you plagiarize if your rephrasing uses the language of the source without putting it in quotation marks; you should also avoid using the identical structure of the original. Italicized words below indicate sections of the original that are plagiarized.

Original:

Anybody who will look at the thing candidly will see that the evolutionary explanation of morals is meaningless, and presupposes the existence of the very thing it ought to prove. It starts from a misconception of the biological doctrine. Biology has nothing to say as to what ought to survive and what ought not to survive; it merely speaks of what does survive.

—Stephen Leacock, "The Devil and the Deep Sea: A Discussion of Modern Morality"

Language of the source unchanged:

A person willing to see *the thing candidly* would realize that morals cannot be accounted for through evolution.

Sentence structure unchanged:

Biology does not distinguish between *what should and should not survive; it simply tells us "what does survive."*

Acceptable paraphrase:

An honest appraisal can tell a person that morals cannot be accounted for through evolution . . . . Biology tells us only "what does survive," not what should and should not survive (Leacock 57).

A good strategy for avoiding plagiarism (and consciously integrating the information) is to carefully study the passage you want to use; then, close the text and write the passage from memory completely in your own words. Finally, look at the passage again, ensuring that it is different in its structure as well as in its language—and that you have accurately restated the thought behind it.

10.2 Summary, Paraphrase, Direct Citation, Mixed Citation

One of the choices you will have in using secondary sources is the way you decide to integrate the information with your own ideas. Using a variety of methods is usually best. However, there are general guidelines that can help you make choices. In all cases, remember that the source must be identified either in a signal phrase (see below), or in a parenthetical reference if you do not use a signal phrase (MLA and APA styles). In Chicago (Note) documentation style, you will need to cite each reference by a footnote or endnote.

10.2.1 Summarize

Summarize if you want to use a source's main idea(s) to provide background information, to set up a point of your own (to show similarity or difference, for example), or to explain one or various positions relevant to your argument. You can summarize passages of just about any length—from one sentence to several pages of a source.

10.2.2 Paraphrase

Paraphrase restates the source's meaning using only your own words. Paraphrase when you want to cite a relatively small amount of material that is directly relevant to the point you wish to make. When you paraphrase, you include **all** of the original thought, but rephrase it.

10.2.3 Direct Quotation

Direct quotation is used when the **source** itself is important *and* the **exact wording** is important. This could be due to specialized vocabulary in the cited passage or the particularly appropriate way that the source uses language or expresses the idea. You can use direct quotations for small amounts of text or for larger ones. If you choose to quote four or more consecutive lines, use the **block format** in which you indent 10 spaces from the left margin (five spaces in APA style). You double-space the text, **but do *not* use quotation marks**. The usual procedure is to introduce the block quotation by a complete sentence followed by a colon. See also Section 10.2.4, "Mixed Citation."

Use single quotation marks to indicate a word or passage in your source that is in quotation marks:

> "In a number of narratives, the (usually female) character finds herself at a significant crossroad between home and a problematic 'elsewhere'" (Rubenstein 9).

The single quotation marks around 'elsewhere' inform the reader that quotation marks were used in the original.

Avoid direct quotations if there is no compelling reason to use a direct quotation; use summary or paraphrase instead. Direct quotations are most effective when used *selectively* for one of the reasons stated above. You demonstrate your ability to understand and synthesize sources when you summarize and paraphrase.

Avoid using direct quotes if:

- the idea in the passage is obvious, well-known, or could be easily accessed;
- the material is essentially factual and does not involve a particular *interpretation* of the facts;
- it can be readily paraphrased.

Avoid large blocks of quoted secondary material. Some instructors discourage this practice by not including direct quotations in the total word count. Do make direct quotations used *selectively* an essential part of most essays.

The following are examples of direct quotations that are unnecessary or ineffective. The preferable alternatives are given after them.

> "About one-third of infants are breast-fed for three months or longer."

Paraphrase: Approximately 33 per cent of infants receive breast-feeding for at least three months (Statistics Canada).

"The greenhouse effect is the result of gases like carbon dioxide, nitrous oxide, and methane being trapped in Earth's atmosphere."

Paraphrase: The accumulation of such gases as carbon dioxide, nitrous oxide, and methane in the atmosphere has led to the greenhouse effect.

The following are examples of direct quotations that are necessary or effective.

Albert Einstein once said, "It always seems to me that man was not born to be a carnivore."

Although this quotation is easily paraphrased, the fact that you are quoting as well-known a personality as Einstein, although he is speaking not from expertise but from personal predilection, would make a direct quote a good choice—though not an essential one. However, in the following instance, precise wording matters:

Neither capital punishment nor life imprisonment without possibility of release shall be imposed for offenses committed by persons below 18 years of age—UN Convention on the Rights of the Child.

10.2.4 Mixed Citation

Using a mixture of paraphrase and direct quotation can be an effective means of demonstrating familiarity with the source and displaying confidence in your ability to integrate words and ideas seamlessly into your argument:

Although in his tribute to Pierre Elliott Trudeau in *The Globe and Mail*, Mark Kingwell recalls the former Prime Minister as "the fusion of reason and passion, the virility and playfulness, the daunting arrogance and wit, the politician as rock star," underneath all this he finds "the good citizen."

Compare with the original:
It's hard to say anything about Trudeau now that has not been said a thousand times before: the fusion of reason and passion, the virility and playfulness, the daunting arrogance and wit, the politician as rock star. All true; all banal. But underneath all that I find a more resonant identity, one which is at once simpler and more profound: the good citizen.

When you use direct quotations, you have to ensure that the quoted material is integrated grammatically, clearly, and gracefully. For information on how to use brackets or ellipses to integrate quotations, see Section 10.3 Signal Phrases, Ellipses and Brackets.

When you integrate a direct quotation using a mixed citation, you can remove the quotation marks and just look at the portion of quoted text as words, phrases, or sentences that must be made grammatical in the context of your own encompassing sentence. Don't forget to put the quotation marks back in when you've integrated it grammatically, and also ensure that any changes you made to the original are indicated through brackets or points of ellipsis.

Examples:

Ungrammatical:
Charles E. Taylor discusses the efforts of scientists "are defining a new area of research termed artificial life" (172).

Grammatical:
Charles E. Taylor discusses the efforts of scientists to "[define] a new area of research termed artificial life" (172).

Unclear:
Art critic John Ruskin believes that the highest art arises from "sensations occurring to *them* only at particular times" (112).

Clear:
Art critic John Ruskin believes that artists produce the highest art from "sensations occurring to *them* only at particular times" (112).

10.3 Signal Phrases, Ellipses, and Brackets

10.3.1 Signal Phrases

The examples above under Mixed Citation use **signal phrases** to introduce direct quotations. Signal phrases contain the source's **name** (Kingwell, Taylor, Ruskin) and a **signal verb**, such as "recalls," "discusses," or "believes"). Signal phrases alert the reader to exactly where the reference begins. They can also guide the reader through the complexities of an issue that involves different findings or interpretations. The following example contains two direct citations; the first citation employs a *signal phrase*:

> *Richard Goldbloom states* that a surveillance video taken in Toronto showed that in more than 20 per cent of incidents where bullying was involved, peers actively became part of the bullying (2). Furthermore, recent statistics show not only the pervasiveness of the problem but that outsiders perceive bullying as a problem in schools today (Clifford 4).

The reader of this paragraph would easily be able to separate the two sources, so a second signal phrase is unnecessary, though certainly not incorrect. Signal phrases are not always necessary if the context is clear without them; they can clutter an essay and make the writing seem mechanical if they are overused. However, it's often helpful to "signal" your intentions.

The example above uses MLA documentation style. If you are using APA style, the signal phrase will include the year of the work's publication as well as the author's name; a comma will separate name and year, and if a page number is required, another comma will be used along with the abbreviation for page, "p."

APA Style:

Asch and Wishart (2004) state that the Slavey communities had grade schools by the 1960s and people left their homes to live in communities so as to retain social benefits (p. 186). As children and parents were reminded, a half-dozen absences from school could result in fines and jail for the parents and the loss of family allowance payments (*The Catholic Voice*, p. 5).

10.3.2 Ellipsis (plural: *ellipses*)

In direct quotations, you can use points of ellipsis (. . .) to indicate that you have omitted one or more words within the sentence of the original writer. Three spaced dots (periods) show an ellipsis. Four dots with a space at the beginning of the sequence (childhood requires . . . .) indicate that the omitted text includes all of the remaining words up to the period at the end of the sentence. Four dots preceded with no space (childhood requires. . . .) means the first dot is a period and ends the sentence of the original, but that an indeterminate amount has been omitted between that sentence and the one that follows. Note that some word processing programs do not acknowledge this distinction.

You can use points of ellipses before or after the original punctuation to show exactly where you have dropped material:

Jane was an heiress . . . ; her friend Elaine was a woman of inferior means.
Running beneath the stars, . . . to meet the stars.

When you omit significant amounts of material, such as an entire paragraph, or line(s) of verse, the points of ellipsis should occupy a line to themselves:

. . . but were there one whose fires
True genius kindles, and fair fame inspires;

. . .

View him with scornful, yet with jealous eyes,
And hate for arts that caus'd himself to rise;
Damn with faint praise, assent with civil leer,
And without sneering, teach the rest to sneer; . . .

—Alexander Pope, "Epistle to Dr. Arbuthnot," ll. 193–4, 199–202.

Use an ellipsis to omit unnecessary words. Do *not* use an ellipsis *before* a direct quotation, except, as in the example above, when part of a line of poetry has been omitted. With prose, the reader assumes that there is text before the quotation begins. In general, also do not use an ellipsis *after* a direct quotation. However, if what follows the end of the direct quotation is significant in the meaning of the sentence—as was the quotation above from Pope in the context of the writer's discussion of Pope's influence on the values demonstrated in contemporary journalistic writing—use an ellipsis in order to avoid a potentially incomplete or misleading statement.

10.3.3 Brackets

Generally, brackets are used to indicate a change or addition made to the original passage. Use brackets to indicate a stylistic change (e.g., upper case to lower case), a grammatical change (e.g., the tense of a verb), or a change for clarity's sake (e.g., adding a word to make the context clearer). The following illustrates these kinds of changes, although you would probably paraphrase a passage that contained as many brackets and ellipses as this:

> The text states that "[a]ll secondary sources require parenthetical citations and an alphabetical listing . . . at the end of [the] essay . . . . [Students] must cite secondary sources, whether [they] quote from them directly, summarize them, paraphrase them, or just refer to them in passing by using the [MLA, APA, or Chicago] style."

The original text:
> All secondary sources require parenthetical citations and an alphabetical listing in the *Works Cited* section at the end of your essay (MLA) or the *References* section (APA). You must cite secondary sources—whether you quote from them directly, summarize them, paraphrase them, or just refer to them in passing—by using the style preferred by your discipline.

You may occasionally use brackets to explain an unfamiliar term within a direct quotation:

> Emergency room nurse Judith McAllen said, "We triage [prioritize by severity of injury] patients if it's a non-emergency, and don't treat them on the basis of their arrival time."

Avoid the use of brackets any more than is strictly necessary.

Inserting "sic" (which means "thus") between brackets: [sic], tells the reader that what immediately precedes [sic] occurs in the original exactly the way it appears in your quotation. One use of [sic] is to call attention to an error in the original:

> As people often say, "vive le différence" [sic].

[Sic] here calls attention to the article error: "le" should be "la." In APA and Chicago documentation styles, italicize "*sic*" within brackets: [*sic*].

Punctuate a direct quotation exactly as it is punctuated in the original, but do not include any punctuation in the original that comes *after* the quoted material. Note the omission of the original comma after "recklessness."

Original:
> "Any accounting of male-female differences must include the male's superior recklessness, a drive, not, I think, towards death . . . ."

Directly Quoted:
> In his essay "The Disposable Rocket," John Updike states that "[a]ny accounting of male-female differences must include the male's superior recklessness."

Parentheses would be incorrect in the passages to the right. Parentheses, like dashes, are a form of punctuation (or may explain or expand on something, as here); square brackets (usually just called "brackets") tell the reader that a change has been made to the original passage or that something has been inserted.

11. Documentation: Citations and References

11.1 Choosing Your Citation Style

The purposes of citations and references are:

- To give appropriate credit to the work of others
- To enlarge on a matter (in a footnote or endnote) that would be a digression if placed in the text
- To establish your own credibility as a researcher
- To show where your own work fits into other work in the field
- To avoid plagiarism, a form of theft, and certainly one of the most serious academic crimes with severe penalties for anyone who knowingly or unknowingly plagiarizes
- To enable readers (especially markers) to trace or verify your sources
- To find the reference again if you need it for further research

The guidelines for specific citation styles are made available to writers in manuals published by the editors of university presses and research associations. The dilemma attached to any style is that new editions of these manuals are released every five years or so, meaning second-hand copies may not provide accurate rules. Public and university libraries provide a range of current style manuals in their reference sections. The rapid development of Internet-based scholarship has caught many of these style designers by surprise, so that most manual publishers maintain official Web sites advising researchers about revisions concerning electronic citations.

Each area of academic research favours one (or more) citation styles, and your instructor will generally inform you of his or her preferred formats. Broadly speaking, APA style is used by writers in education, business, psychology, political science, other social sciences, and many sciences. Chicago and MLA styles are widely used in the humanities, including English, religion, philosophy, cultural studies, classical studies, and history. A common style in some scientific writing is known as CBE (Council of Biology Editors, although the council has changed its name to the Council of Science Editors). Guidelines are laid out in *Scientific Style and Format: the CBE Manual for Authors, Editors, and Publishers*, 6th ed. (New York: Cambridge University Press, 1994). A more comprehensive seventh edition is forthcoming.

In addition to the major styles, some subject areas have their own style specifications. Generally, these discipline-specific styles are adaptations of one of the major styles, and you will not need to know the specific modifications until you are familiar with the major style favoured by your discipline. An exception is journalism, which has one major style of its own, along with several variants. Subject areas with their own stylistic specifications include anthropology, archaeology, chemistry, law, mathematics, medicine, music, political science, sociology, and specific areas of engineering.

Although there are many subtle differences among the various styles, the main elements of a citation usually include

1. the author(s) name
2. the page number or a similar locator of the information cited
3. the year of publication
4. details of publication

Most citation styles require an abbreviated citation in the sentence where the acknowledgement appears and fuller mention in an alphabetized list at the end of the paper under a heading such as "References," "Works Cited," or "Bibliography." The following references have been styled according to the rules of each handbook or manual.

Humanities: <u>MLA Handbook for Writers of Research Papers</u>, 6th ed. (New York: MLA, 2003).

Social Sciences: American Psychological Association. (2001). *Publication manual of the American Psychological Association* (5th ed.). Washington, D.C.: American Psychological Association.

University of Chicago Press: *The Chicago Manual of Style* 15th ed. Chicago: University of Chicago Press, 2003.

11.2 Necessary versus Unnecessary Citations

Above we discussed *what* needs to be documented in your essay; below you will find some basic guidelines for the MLA, APA, and Chicago formats—the *how* of documentation. However, students who understand both the *what* and *how* of documentation can be confused about the *where* and *when*. This confusion can easily come about after students are told that they must thoroughly document all outside sources, whether a direct quote, summary, paraphrase, or idea. When they have done this and receive their graded essays, they are sometimes surprised that the instructor has commented on an excessive number of in-text references.

Parenthetical references are intended to convey to the reader as *much* information as possible about the source while interfering as *little* as possible with the essay's content and readability. The general rule is that you reference enough to give the reader the information needed, while avoiding redundancy. If it is clear what specific source is being referred to without a reference, then don't give one.

Don't use a parenthetical reference for every statement or fact from a source if you use that one source for consecutive references. In fact, you can often combine quite a few references from the same source in one comprehensive citation. For example, let's say you used three pages from your source Jackson; when you were finished drawing from that source, you could indicate this in your text this way: (Jackson 87–89). This citation would tell the reader that you used that one source continuously for three of her pages—perhaps one idea from page 87, two facts from page 88, and a paraphrased passage on page 89.

In both APA and MLA styles, in the interests of efficiency you can combine two or more sources in the same citation, using a semicolon between the names of the sources:

Constant public protests and political regulations have caused a general mistrust of GM foods, biotech companies, and science itself (Carlson, 2001; Danforth, 2000). [APA style]

Note that this applies to MLA style where you cite direct quotations and all other references by page number; APA citations include publication date as well. However, what is true for both formats, as well as for the Chicago format, is that, in general, you shouldn't acknowledge the source by name until you are finished with that source, unless you decide to use a signal phrase to set up the source, in which case you will name the source before you give the information from the source.

11.3 The Major Documentation Styles

The basic standards for documenting sources are given below with examples to illustrate format. The examples are as close as possible to one another so you can easily compare and contrast the differences among them. Because of the vast number and range of resources available to the researcher today, especially Internet resources, it is impossible to include all of them. However, the most common formats and most of the usual variants on these formats are included. Students should consider buying the manual that applies to the discipline they are planning as their major. For examples that aren't given below, you can also check updates on the APA, MLA, and Chicago Web sites. As well, you can consult your instructor for hard-to-find citation specifications.

Many libraries and university departments across Canada and the U.S. offer information themselves or provide links to information about source citation. However, these sources aren't always updated to reflect the most current standards. If you use one of these sites for help, always double-check the information with one or more other sites, taking note of when the Web site was updated, if this is available. If you have run out of resources, or simply don't have more time to spend on the citations chase, common sense suggests you adapt the rule closest to your particular case.

11.4 APA Citation Style

In the social sciences, the principle documentation style has been developed by the American Psychological Association (APA). The Association publishes a manual (*Publication manual of the American Psychological Association*, 5th ed.) and maintains a Web site (http://www.apastyle.org/) that offers updates, FAQs, and specific information on Internet citations.

APA style is parenthetical, meaning that where an author is quoted or paraphrased in your essay you create a note within the sentence that lists the author(s), the year of publication, and, sometimes, page number(s). Then, you provide a more complete description of the source on the final page(s) of your paper, titled "References."

11.4.1 APA In-Text Citations

Guidelines
1. Use the abbreviation "p." for "page" or "pp." for "pages" with numbers to show page citation.
2. Retain redundant tens and hundreds digit in final page number (e.g., pp. 52–55, *not* 52–5; 212–247, *not* 212–47).

3. Use commas to separate items in a parenthetical reference.
4. If your instructor prefers underlining to italics, underline punctuation that ends titles; for example: <u>The beginner's guide to academic writing and reading: A new approach.</u> <u>Reading Research Quarterly.</u>

Specifics:

1. **Citation including a direct quote:** last name of author(s), a comma, year of publication, a comma, and page number(s) in parentheses.

   During World Wars I and II, the Canadian government often employed masseuses because surgery and medical care were insufficient "to restore severely wounded men" (Cleather, 1995, p. ix).

   You can use a signal phrase to set up your reference (see Section 10.3.1). Since a signal phrase names the author(s) and year, the citation includes only the page designation:

   Bochner (2000) says that this intellectual state of multiple identities, blurred genres, and displaced totalities spoils his appetite for "generalizable abstractions and unified knowledge" (p. 734).

2. **Block quotation:** A quotation that is more than 40 words long is placed on a new line and indented five spaces from the left margin. Quotation marks are not used, and the quote should be double-spaced. The author's name, the year of publication, and the page number appear in parentheses at the end of the quotation and *after* the final period.

   (Ellis & Bochner, 2000, pp. 81–82)

3. **A citation including a specific paraphrased idea.** State the last name of author(s), year of publication and the page number(s) in parentheses.

   Some autoethnographers (Reed-Dahany, 1997, p. 3) highlight the goal of researcher transparency, while others concentrate on revealing and resisting cultural norms (Kenny, 2000, p. 27).

   Using a signal phrase:

   Reed-Dahany (1997) highlights a goal of researcher transparency (p. 3), while Kenny (2000) concentrates on revealing and resisting cultural norms (p. 27).

4. **A citation for a general, paraphrased idea or summary.** Give the last name of author(s), and the year of publication in parentheses.

   Conservation biologists agree that protecting habitats is the most effective way to conserve biological diversity (Primack, 2000).

5. **A citation referring to a third-party source.** Include the original author in the sentence, along with the third-party name(s) in parentheses with the phrase "as cited in" and year of publication.

Content knowledge encompasses what Bruner (as cited in Shulman, 1992) called the "structure of knowledge"—the theories, principles, and concepts of a particular discipline.

6. **Personal communication, including interviews.** Give the author's name, including first initial(s), the phrase "personal communication," and a date in parentheses.

(J. Derrida, personal communication, September 20, 2000).

Note that personal communications are cited only in the text of your essay; they are not listed in the References section.

11.4.2 APA In-Text Citations by Format

1. **Kinds of Authors**

   A. **Work by one author (book or article). In parenthesis:** author's last name, a comma, year of publication, a comma, page number(s) (if direct quotation or specific paraphrase). Note that a book with an author and an editor will be cited by author.

   (Bloom, 2002, p. xviii).

   B. **Work by two authors.** State the last names of both authors with an ampersand (&) between them, a comma, a date, a comma, and a page number; in parentheses.

   (Higgins & Wilson-Baptist, 1999, p. 44).

   When naming the authors *in the text* of your essay, use the word "and" instead of an ampersand:

   Higgins and Wilson-Baptist (1999) argue that "a tourist exists outside of experience. A traveller, though, submerges herself in the new" (p. 44).

   C. **Works by three, four, or five authors.** List the last names of all authors in parentheses for the first citation. Later citations need the last name of the first author followed by the abbreviation "et al." with the publication year; in parentheses. If the authors are mentioned more than once in a paragraph, the year of publication is not included.

   (Higgins, Wilson-Baptist, & Krasny, 2001)
   subsequent citations: (Higgins et al.)

D. **Work by six or more authors.** State the last name of the first author followed by the abbreviation "et al.", a comma, the publication year; in parentheses.

(Bermondsey et al., 1892)

E. **Two or more works by the same author.** Give the author's last name, a comma, the year of publication perhaps with a lower case letter, a comma, and the page; in parentheses. If the author has published more than one work in the same year, add an alphabetical letter in lower case (a, b, c) to distinguish works chronologically in that year.

. . . self enforced discipline (Foucault, 1980a, p. 37).

F. **Two authors with the same last name.** Cited like "B" above with the addition of the the authors' first initials:

(Sinkinson, S. & Sinkinson, B., 2001, pp. 225–237).

G. **Group or organization as author (corporate author).** Documents published by companies and government departments may not list an author. If the group title is long, or is well known by an acronym or abbreviation of the name (for example, The United Nations Children's Fund is commonly known as UNICEF), for the first citation include, in parentheses, the entire title where the author's name would appear, give the acronym in square brackets, a comma, and the year of publication. For subsequent citations use the abbreviation with the year of publication throughout the rest of the paper.

(American Educational Research Association [AERA], 2001); succeeding citations: (AERA, 2001)

H. **Work with an unknown author** (including many dictionary and encyclopedia articles). The first few words of the title of an article or chapter in quotation marks, a comma, the year of publication; in parentheses.

("Plea to City Hall," 2003)

An author designated as "Anonymous" is cited in the same way as a named author:

(Anonymous, 1887, p. 12)

11.4.3 APA In-Text Citations: Internet Sources

The most challenging aspect of citing on-line documents is that they usually lack page numbers. In order to pinpoint a quote or paraphrase as closely as possible, APA recommends counting by paragraphs and using the symbol ¶ or the abbreviation "para." to identify parts of a Web document. In long documents, it is permissible to use identifiers such as section titles. If materials like journal articles have page numbers, use the original numbers rather than the numbers of the printout.

A. **Standard Internet citation. In parentheses:** author's last name, a comma, the year the site was mounted or updated, and a descriptive locator.

(Blaukind, 2000, ¶ 5)

B. **Private or personal Web site.** Give author's name, a comma, the year the site was mounted or updated, a comma, and a descriptive locator; in parentheses.

(Sung, 2002, ¶ 7)

C. **Internet site without an author or without a date.** Use the title or an abbreviated form of the title, a comma, the year the site was mounted or updated, a comma, and a descriptive locator; in parentheses. Use the abbreviation "n.d." if the date that the site was created is absent.

(Muchinfo's poll, 2002, para 16)
(Hannak, n.d., para. 2)

11.4.4 APA In-Text Citations: Non-Textual Sources

Film, video, audio, TV broadcasts, and musical recordings: use the most senior production person's name, a comma, and the year of public release or broadcast; in parentheses.

(Coppola, 1979)

Installation, event, performance, or work of art: use format followed by other non-textual resources, such as artist(s) name, a comma, and a date of showing or creation.

(Byrdmore, 2006)

11.4.5 APA Citations in the References Section

APA style requires you to list your sources beginning on a new page at the end of your paper (keep your page numbers continuous). The title of this element of a paper is "References."

Guidelines
1. The title is centred, an inch from the top of the page.
2. The list is alphabetized by author's last name; each entry begins flush left with the margin; subsequent lines are indented five spaces from the margin.
3. The standard APA citation begins with the author's last name followed by initial(s), not given name(s). Capitalize the following elements of work titles: the first word, the first word after a colon, all proper nouns, and acronyms like NFB or CBC,

regardless of how the original is capitalized. Titles of *journals* do not follow the capitalization rules for book and article titles.

4. List book data in the following sequence: author, date of publication, title of book, place of publication, publisher; for example: Fries, C. C. (1962). *Linguistics and reading*. New York: Holt, Rinehart & Winston.

5. List journal article data in the following sequence: author, date of publication, title of article, title of journal, volume number, inclusive pages; for example: Booth, W. C. (1977). The limits of pluralism. *Critical Inquiry*, *3*. 407–423.

1. **Kinds of Authors**

   A. **Work by one author (book):**

   Butler, J. (1997). *Excitable speech: A politics of the performative.* New York: Routledge.

   B. **Work by two authors:**

   Luckner, J. & Nadler, R. (1992). *Processing the experience.* Dubuque: Kendall/Hunt Publishing.

   C. **Work by three, four, or five authors.** List all the authors.

   Festial, L., Ian, H., & Gomez, S. (1956). *When economics fails.* Minneapolis: University of Minnesota Press.

   D. **Work by six or more authors.** List the first six authors and add the abbreviation "et. al." after the last name.

   Rosher, I., Crewdeshell, J., Lamb, L., Miracle, M., Crown, K., Berstein, R., et.al. (1976). *Teen spirit and crowd behavior.* Cambridge, Mass.: Harvard University Press.

   E. **Two or more works by the same author.** Works by the same author are arranged chronologically, earliest to latest. Works with the same publication year are identified by letters after the year, arranged chronologically.

   Foucault, M. (1977). *Discipline and punish: The birth of the prison.* A. Sheridan (Trans.). New York: Random House.

   Foucault, M. (1980a). *The history of sexuality*, (Vol. I). R. Hurley (Trans.). New York: Random House.

   Foucault, M. (1980b). *Power/Knowledge: Selected interviews and other writings 1972–1977.* C. Gordon (Ed.), L. Marshall, J. Mepham, C. Gordon K. Soper (Trans.). Brighton, Sussex: Harvester Press.

F. **Work by two authors with the same last name:**

Sinkinson, A., & Sinkinson, B. (2002). *Art history: A feminist perspective.* Turin, Italy: Turin Press.

G. **Group or organization as author (corporate author):**

Call Ontario. (1997). *KPMG/Boyd call centre study.* Crown Publications: Toronto, Ontario.

H. **Work with an unknown author (non-electronic source).** If no author is given, list alphabetically by the selection's title. When an author is listed as "Anonymous," alphabetize by the letter "A."

Interveners. (1993). In *Canadian Encyclopedia* (Vol. 11, pp. 344–348). Ottawa: Smith Press.

2. **Source Type**

A. **Work by author with an editor or translator.** Formats are the same, except that with a translator the abbreviation "Trans." replaces "Ed." and original publication date should also be indicated in parentheses after the final period (Original work published 1948.). "Eds." is used for two or more editors.

Hawthorne, N. (1995). *The scarlet letter* (J. S. Martin, Ed.). Peterborough, Ontario: Broadview Press. (Original work published 1850.)

B. **Chapter or other type of selection, such as an essay, in edited volume:**

Bergen, D. (2003). Lucy in the sky. In T. S. Kane, L. J. Peters, & M. R. Legris (Eds.), *Writing prose: Techniques and purposes* (pp. 353–354). (3rd Canadian ed.). Don Mills: Oxford University Press.

C. **Multivolume work (referencing one volume):**

Bosworth, A. B. (Ed.). (1995). *A historical commentary on Arrian's history of Alexander* (Vol. 1). London: Oxford University Press.

D. **Second or subsequent edition of a work:**

Suzuki, D. T., Griffiths, A. J., & Lewontin, R. C. (1989). *An introduction to genetic analysis* (4th ed.). New York: W. H. Freeman.

E. **Article in a journal that uses continuous pagination.** Page numbers in journals are not preceded by "p" or "pp." Include volume number but not issue number.

Garner, R. (2003). Political ideologies and the moral status of animals. *Journal of Political Ideologies, 8,* 233–246.

F. **Article in a journal that is paginated by issue.** Include both volume and issue number.

> Trew, J. D. (2002). Conflicting visions: Don Messier, Liberal nationalism, and the Canadian unity debate. *International Journal of Canadian Studies, 26*(2), 41–57.

G. **Article in a Newspaper.** List author if author is given; if no author, begin with title. The abbreviation "p" or "pp" is used for newspapers. A letter to the editor follows the same format and includes the following in brackets after title: [Letter to the editor].

> Lawyer seeks mistrial for client accused of illegal midwifery. (2003, April 20). *National Post*, p. A8.

H. **Third-party source.** List the work the citation comes from, not the original text.

I. **Personal communication.** Because they cannot be reproduced or verified, personal communications (including e-mails, phone calls, interviews, and conversations) are not included in the list of references.

3. **APA Internet Citations**

Internet sources can be fleeting, and, as a result, the 5th edition of the APA manual notes that "if no archives are maintained, then the message will not be retrievable and should not be included in the reference list. At best, it can be cited as a 'personal communication'" (APA, 2001, p. 277). Confirm Internet links before including them in your paper. More information on electronic reference formats recommended by the APA is available at http://www.apastyle.org/elecref.html.

A. **Standard electronic reference:**

> Jiminez, K. (2000, ¶ 5). *Freudian dreams.* Retrieved June 7, 2003, from www.rbi.edu/~ vttsc/frdream.html.

B. **An Internet document with no author and/or no date:**

> My unfounded opinions. (n.a.). (n.d.). Retrieved Jan. 3, 2004, from http://www.notallthatreliable/ca

C. **Private or personal Web site.** Cite no reference, following the APA guidelines above.

D. **Group or organization (corporate) Web site:**

> American Educational Research Association [AERA] (2001). *Sources of health insurance and characteristics of the uninsured* (Issue Brief No. 123). Washington, DC. Retrieved January 24, 2001, from Columbia

University, Institute for Learning Technologies Web site: http://www.ilt.columbia.edu/ publications/papers/newwine1.html

E. **On-line book:**

Radford, B. (2000). *Soil to social*. Retrieved July 1, 2000, from http://on-line-books.ora.com/mod- bin/books.mod/javaref/javanut/index.htm

F. **Article in on-line-only journal:**

Gingras, J. (Oct. 21, 2002). *Body matters*. The Journal of Radical Dietary Health. Retrieved August 6, 2003, from http://www.vespro.com/

G. **Internet article based on a print source:**

Van Nygen, G., & Carre, F. (2001). Goals of nursing teams in tertiary care. [Electronic version]. *Journal of Nursing Research*, *5*, 117–122.

H. **Article from a database:**

Brother, W., & Avery S. (1993). Summer school: practical performance outcomes. *Journal of Applied Pedagogy*, *78*, 143–149. Retrieved October 1, 2000 from EBSCOhost database
(Internet address not required but can be put in parentheses here).

I. **Message posted to on-line forum or discussion group:**

Bal, M. (April 3, 1995) Amino acids definition. [message 734]. Message posted to Science-Links electronic mailing list, archived at http://www.sci.rg/mail-archive/am-link/msg00068.html

4. **APA Citations for Non-Textual Sources**

A. **Film, video:**

Coppola, F.F. (Producer), (1979). *Apocalypse now*. [Motion picture]. USA: Zoetrope Studios.

B. **TV broadcast:**

Zickermann, O. (Executive Producer). (1993). Absent minds. [Television broadcast]. In Smith, L. (Producer), Zickermann, O. (Producer), & Levinson, F. (Director), *The life of the mind*, Los Angeles, Calif.: Annenberg/CPB Collection.

C. **Music:**

Morrison, V, (1993). On *Too long in exile*. [cd]. UK. Polydor.

11.5 MLA Citation Style

The Modern Language Association of America (MLA) publishes two manuals that define its MLA style. The *MLA Style Manual and Guide to Scholarly Publishing* is designed for use by publishing academics. The MLA *Handbook for Writers of Research Papers*, 6th edition (2003) is compiled specifically for student researchers in the humanities, including cultural studies, English, and modern languages. The Association also maintains a Web site (http://www.mla.org) that offers guidelines on Internet citations and updates.

As a style that uses parenthetical referencing, the MLA system appears quite similar to that of the APA, apart from MLA's additional requirements for footnotes and endnotes. However, there are many small but important differences between the two styles, one being that MLA parenthetical references do not include dates. MLA-style footnotes and endnotes are not meant to be a method of citing authors throughout the text (see Section 11.5.1 following). A more complete description of your sources is provided on the final pages of your paper, entitled "Works Cited."

11.5.1 MLA In-Text Citations

Guidelines: In contrast to the APA style,

1. Do *not* use page abbreviations ("p," "pp").
2. Do *not* use the redundant hundreds digit in final page number (e.g., 212–47, *not* pp. 212–247). Do use both tens digits (e.g., pp. 34–37.)
3. Do *not* use commas to separate items in a parenthetical reference.
4. Underline titles, but don't underline punctuation at the end of titles. (MLA recommends underlining for graded essays, but your instructor may permit italicized titles.)

Specifics
1. **Citation including a direct quote.** Give the last name of the author and the page number in parentheses.

   During World Wars I and II, the Canadian government often employed masseuses because surgery and medical care were insufficient "to restore severely wounded men" (Cleather ix).

   You can use a signal phrase to set up your reference (see Section 10.3.1). Since a signal phrase names the author, the citation requires only the page number:

   Bochner says that this intellectual state of multiple identities, blurred genres, and displaced totalities spoils his appetite for "generalizable abstractions and unified knowledge" (734).

2. **Block quotation.** In MLA style, a quotation that is longer than four typed lines is indented (ten spaces or one inch). Quotation marks are not used, and the quote should be double-spaced. The author's name and page number appear in parentheses at the end of the quotation and *after* the final period. (Ellis and Bochner 81–82)

3. **A citation including a specific paraphrased idea.** Cite the last name of author(s) and the page number(s) in parentheses.

> Some autoethnographers (Reed-Dahanay 3) highlight the goal of researcher transparency, while others concentrate on revealing and resisting cultural norms (Kenny 27).

Using a signal phrase:

> Reed-Dahany highlights a goal of researcher transparency (3), while Kenny concentrates on revealing and resisting cultural norms (27).

4. **A citation including a general paraphrased idea or summary** requires the last name of author(s) and the page number in parentheses.

> Conservation biologists agree that protecting habitats is the most effective way to conserve biological diversity (Primack 183).

5. **A citation referring to a third-party source.** Name the original author in the sentence, along with the third-party name(s) in parentheses with the phrase "qtd. in," along with page number(s):

> Content knowledge encompasses what Bruner (qtd. in Shulman 43) called the "structure of knowledge"—the theories, principles, and concepts of a particular discipline.

6. **Personal communication, including interviews,** needs the author's last name only, in parentheses:

> (Derrida)

11.5.2 MLA In-Text Citations by Format

1. **Kinds of Authors**

   A. **Work by one author (book or article).** Give the author's last name and page number in parentheses. Note that a book with an author and an editor will be cited by author.

   > (Bloom xviii)

   B. **Work by two authors** needs the last names of both authors with the word "and" between them, in addition to a page number in parentheses:

   > (Higgins and Wilson-Baptist 44).

When naming the authors in the text, the word "and" also appears, along with a page number in parentheses:

Higgins and Wilson-Baptist argue that "a tourist exists outside of experience. A traveler, though, submerges herself in the new" (44).

C. **Work by three or more authors.** The last names of all authors, commas between them. When following this format for citing multiple authors, the word "and" is placed between the second and third names in the list in addition to page number(s) in parentheses. It is also acceptable to give only the last name of only the first author with the abbreviation "et al.," and page number(s); in parentheses.

(Higgins, Wilson-Baptist and Krasny 102); (Higgins et al. 102)

D. **Two or more works by the same author.** The author's last name, along with a shortened version of the work's title (underlined) and a page number.

"self-enforced discipline" (Foucault, Power/Knowledge 37).

E. **Two authors with the same last name.** The author's first initials along with page number(s).

(S. Sinkinson and B. Sinkinson 225–37).

F. **Group or organization as author (corporate author).** Documents published by companies and government departments may not list an author. MLA style recommends including the entire name of the organization in the body of the sentence in order to identify it as a source. For example, the organization commonly known as UNICEF would appear as The United Nations Children's Fund (along with a page number in parentheses). However, it is also acceptable to shorten the organization's name and place it in parentheses, accompanied by the page number in the same manner as a standard author citation.

The United Nations Children's Fund reports that indigenous children are at exceptional risk of becoming refugees (204).

Some child protection advocates suggest that indigenous children are at exceptional risk of becoming refugees (UNICEF 204).

G. **Work with an unknown author** (including many dictionary and encyclopedia articles). The title if it is short followed by the page number, in parentheses. When the title is extremely long, a condensed version can be used. Distinguish articles from complete works by placing the name in quotation marks.

("Plea to City Hall," Manifesto 22).

Note: The MLA has specific guidelines for citing literary works (see Part Six, Sections 16.2 and 16.3, Sample Student Literary Research Essay).

11.5.3 MLA In-Text Citations: Internet Sources

Directing readers to the specific location of your citations is difficult in on-line documents because they rarely have page numbers. The *MLA Handbook for Writers of Research Papers*, 6th edition (2003) suggests placing the author's name within a sentence without any other locators if your source is the entire Web site. If you are citing a specific quote or paraphrasing, paragraph numbers or document sections (for example, the abbreviation "Introd.") can identify parts of a Web document. If materials such as on-line journal articles have page numbers, use the original numbers rather than the numbers of the printout.

A. **Standard Internet citation.** Give the author's last name within the sentence.

> Jiminez claims that "The Friendly Giant" is sorely missed.

B. **Internet site without an author.** In MLA style, authors are required to cite "what is available" (MLA 221). Following this logic, a site without an author's name adheres to the guidelines for a document without an author and uses the site title to direct readers to the source of any information.

> (MLA "FAQS")

11.5.4 MLA In-Text Citations: Non-Textual Sources

Film, video, audio, TV broadcasts, installations, events, performances, works of art and musical recordings. The most senior production person's or artist's name is given within the body of the sentence. The underlined title of the work can be included for clarity.

> Francis Ford Coppola's film The Conversation explored the psychology of surveillance.

11.5.5 MLA Citations in the Works Cited Section

In MLA style, the "Works Cited" document containing complete retrieval information appears at the end of your paper and on a new page that continues the numbers of your essay. The "Works Cited" list is double-spaced, with a one-inch margin. Omit words like "Press," "Inc.," and "Co." after publisher name (but university presses should be abbreviated "UP" for "University Press." Chapter seven of the handbook lists abbreviations acceptable in MLA style, including those for publishers and locations. Some of the most common include Assn. (Association), ch. (chapter), ed. (editor[s], edition), fwd. (foreword), introd. (introduction), P (Press), par. (paragraph), pt. (part), rev. (revised), rpt. (reprint), sec. (section), trans. (translator), U (University), vol. (volume).

Guidelines
1. The title is centred, an inch from the top of the page without underlining or bolding.
2. This list is alphabetized by author's last name; each entry begins flush with the margin with subsequent lines indented half an inch.

3. The standard MLA citation begins with the author's last name, followed by a complete first name (unless the author has published only initial[s]). Titles are underlined. All key words in the title are capitalized, even if the initial source did not do so. Punctuation after title is not underlined.

Specifics

1. List book data in the sequence: author; title of book; place of publication; shortened version of the publisher's names created by removing articles like "A" or "The" and abbreviations; year of publication, thus:

   Fries, Charles, C. Linguistics and Reading. New York: Holt, Rinehart and Winston, 1962.

2. List journal article data in the sequence: author, title of article (within quotation marks), title of journal (underlined), volume number, year of publication, inclusive pages, thus:

   Booth, Wayne. C. "The Limits of Pluralism." Critical Inquiry 3 (1977): 407–23.

3. **Kinds of Authors**

   A. **Work by one author (book):**

      Butler, Judith. Excitable Speech: A Politics of the Performative. New York: Routledge, 1997.

   B. **Work by two or three authors.** Second and third authors' names are not inverted.

      Luckner, John, and Reldan Nadler. Processing the Experience. Dubuque: Kendall/Hunt, 1992.

   C. **Work by four or more authors.** MLA styling provides two possibilities: the complete names of all authors, reversing the name of the first author only and including a comma between the authors' names; or give the complete name of just the first author plus the abbreviation "et al.":

      Festial, Lawrence, Harold Inch, Susan Gomez, and Komiko Smith. When Economics Fails. Minneapolis: U of Minnesota P, 1956.

      or:

      Festial, Lawrence, et al. When Economics Fails. Minneapolis: U of Minnesota P, 1956.

D. **Two or more works by the same author.** Works by the same author are arranged chronologically from earliest to the most recent publication. The author's name appears in the first listing only, with three dashes substituted for it in the additional citation(s).

Foucault, Michel. Discipline and Punish: The Birth of the Prison. Trans. Alan Sheridan. New York: Random, 1977.

———. The History of Sexuality. Trans. Robert Hurley. 3 vols. New York: Random, 1978.

E. **Work by two authors with the same last name:**

Sinkinson, Susan, and Barbara Sinkinson. Art History: A Feminist Perspective. Turin, Italy: Turin, 2002.

F. **Group or organization as author (corporate author):**

Call Ontario. KPMG/Boyd Call Centre Study. Toronto, ON: Crown, 1997.

G. **Work without an author, publisher, or publication location (non-electronic).** If the work being cited doesn't provide an author's name, it is preferable to list it alphabetically by the title. MLA style makes provisions for missing elements of a citation other than the author's name using the abbreviations "N.p." and "N.d." as substitutes. Use square brackets to identify the information that isn't from the source.

1. **No author name:**

   "Interveners." Canadian Encyclopedia. 1985 ed.

2. **No publisher:**

   N.O Webb. The Great Haileybury Forest Fire. N.p. 1971.

3. **No publishing date:**

   M.J. Case. Opus Dei. N.p. N.d.

4. **Uncertain source:**

   [Ascribed to William Shakespeare]

4. **Source Type**

   A. **Work by author with an editor or translator.** Formats are the same as for APA: for translator the abbreviation is "Trans.";"Ed." is used for one or more editors:

   Hawthorne, Nathaniel. The Scarlet Letter. Ed. John Stephen Martin. Peterborough, Ontario: Broadview, 1995. (Originally published 1850.)

   B. **Chapter or other type of selection, such as an essay, in edited volume:**

   Bergen, David. "Lucy in the Sky." Writing Prose: Techniques and Purposes. Ed. Thomas S. Kane, Leonard J. Peters, and Maurice R. Legris. 3rd Canadian ed. Don Mills: Oxford UP, 2003. 353–54.

   C. **Multivolume work (referencing one volume):**

   Bosworth, A. B., ed. A Historical Commentary on Arrian's History of Alexander. Vol. 1. London: Oxford UP, 1980.

   D. **Second or subsequent edition of a work:**

   Suzuki, David, Aaron Griffiths, and Rebecca Lewontin. An Introduction to Genetic Analysis. 4th ed. New York: Freeman, 1989.

   E. **Article in a journal that uses continuous pagination.** Include volume number but not issue number:

   Garner, Robert. "Political Ideologies and the Moral Status of Animals." Journal of Political Ideologies 8 (2003): 233–46.

   F. **Article in a journal that is paginated by issue.** Include both volume and issue number.

   Trew, Johanne Devlin. "Conflicting Visions: Don Messier, Liberal Nationalism, and the Canadian Unity Debate." International Journal of Canadian Studies 26.2 (2002): 41–57.

   G. **Article in a newspaper.** Cite author if author is given; if no author, begin with title. Give day, month, and year; give page number preceded by section number or letter if more than one section. A letter to the editor follows the same format and includes "Letter" after title:

   "Lawyer seeks mistrial for client accused of illegal midwifery." National Post 20 April 2003. A8.

   H. **Third-party source.** Cite the work where you found the citation rather than the original text.

   Evans, Robely. J.R.R. Tolkein. New York: Warner Books, 1972.

I. **Personal communication, including interview.** Include a description of the communication.

Carr, Emily. Letter to Lawren Harris. 12 December 1940.

11.5.6 MLA Internet Citations

The Modern Language Association has developed an intricate series of guidelines in response to contemporary scholarly activity in cyberspace. Although complex, these procedures for citations are structured on the eminently practical principle of "citing what is available" (MLA 216). Your instructor may well wish you to provide specific information in your citations, so it could be wise to seek clarification before handing in your paper. Note that angle brackets surround the URL in MLA style.

A. **Standard electronic citation:**

Jiminez, Delmi. Freudian Dreams. 2000. 7 June 2003.
<http://www.rbi.edu/~ vttsc/frdream.html>.

B. **An Internet document with no author and/or no date** is probably not a reliable source for your paper according to the criteria established for expert and reliable information. Sites without uploading or update dates are more common, but often a visit to the main page will help you locate this information. If necessary, cite an authorless Web page in the following manner:

"My Unfounded Opinions." 2001. 3 Jan. 2004 from:
<http://www.notacademicwriting/ca>.

C. **Private or personal Web site with no title:**

Tan, Li. Home Page. 1999. 18 June 2002. <http://www.tan-li/~oscar/
reviews.html>.

D. **Group, organization (corporate) Web site:**

American Educational Research Association. Sources of Health Insurance and Characteristics of the Uninsured (Issue Brief No. 123). 2001. 24 Jan. 2001. <http://www.ilt.columbia.edu//publications/papers/newwine.html>.

E. **On-line book:**

Radford, Barbara. Soil to Social. New York: Random, 2000. 1 July 2000.
<http://on-line- books.ora.com/mod-bin/books.mod/javaref/javanut/index.htm>.

F. **Article in on-line-only journal:**

Gingras, Jacqui. "Body Matters." The Journal of Contemporary Dietary Health 10.2 (2001). Oct. 21, 2002 <http://www.vespro.com/>.

G. **Internet article based on a print source and retrieved from a database:**

Van Nyugen, Gayle and Frances Carre. "Goals of Nursing Teams in Tertiary Care." Journal of Nursing Research, 5.2 (2001):117–122. EBSCOhost. <http://journal.nur.edu/tert- /contents.html>.

H. **Message posted to on-line forum or discussion group:**

Bal, Mac. "Amino Acids Definition." On-line posting. 3 Apr. 1997. Science-Links Electronics <http://groups.yahoo.com/group/melectronics/message/25>.

11.5.7 MLA Citations for Non-Textual Sources

MLA style has been updated to include specific citation formats for a plethora of non-textual information sources. As a general rule of thumb, the person(s) most relevant to your discussion should be featured in your citation, along with an abbreviated description of their role. For example, if your paper is about actors, you can cite their contribution in a film either alongside or instead of naming the director.

A. **Film**

Apocalypse Now. Prod. Francis Ford Coppola. Zoetrope, 1979.

B. **Video or DVD**

To Sir With Love. Perf. Sidney Poitier. 1967. DVD. Columbia/Tristar, 1996.

C. **TV broadcast**

"Absent Minds." The Life of the Mind. Prod. Oliver Zickermann. Annenberg/CPB. 2 June 1993.

D. **Music**

Morrison, Van. Too Long in Exile. Polydor, 1993.

E. **Installation, event, or performance**

Romeo and Juliet. By William Shakespeare. Dir. John Gielgud. Stratford Theatre, Stratford, ON. 2 April 1963.

F. **Work of Art**

Escher, M.C. Drawing Hands. Cornelius Collection, National Gallery of Art, Washington.

11.5.8 MLA Footnotes

MLA allows either footnotes (at the bottom of the page) or endnotes (at the end of the document) as a way of including information you feel is valuable but doesn't fit well within the text. You may footnote in order to further explain a point, to suggest additional reading, or to cite related points of interest. These notes are designated by a superscript number directly to the right and above the word most related to the note, or at the end of a phrase; they run consecutively through your paper. Format the notes to match the rest of the document by double-spacing and indenting each note. For an example of a student essay that uses MLA style with footnotes, see Part Four, Section 10.3.

11.6 Chicago Citation Style (Note)

Students writing papers in the humanities (including history, art history, and religion) and, sometimes, in business, communications, or economics, are asked to adhere to the Chicago style, as found in 15th edition of *The Chicago Manual of Style*[1] published by the University of Chicago Press. There are actually two Chicago styles. Since the scientific form closely resembles APA with an MLA-style bibliography, the humanities version will be outlined here. It uses footnotes (at the bottom of each page) or endnotes (at the end of the paper) to direct readers to the sources of the information cited. Most word-processing programs will format these notes for you (under Insert— Footnote/Endnote); creating your notes manually can be tedious.

There is a perception that Chicago style doesn't categorically require a "Bibliography" listing at the end of a paper to accompany these footnotes or endnotes. However, the 15th edition of the *Chicago Manual* clearly states that a "Bibliography" *should* follow the last page of any paper.[2] The *Manual* editors maintain a questions and answers page at <http://www.press.uchicago.edu/Misc/Chicago/cmosfaq/cmosfaq.html>.

11.6.1 Chicago Style In-Text Citations

A. **Citation including a direct quote from author(s)** needs a superscript number (one that is raised above the level of the rest of the sentence and has a smaller point size) directly after the last word and quotation mark surrounding the author's words. This number refers to a note, either at the bottom of the page or at the end of the document. Notes are single-spaced with the first line indented five spaces (a half-inch) from the rest of the text.

> During World Wars I and II, the Canadian government often employed masseuses because surgery and medical care were insufficient "to restore severely wounded men."[1]

---

1 University of Chicago Press, *The Chicago Manual of Style* 15th ed. (Chicago: University of Chicago Press, 2003).
2 Ibid., 612.

1. **First reference.** The footnote or endnote begins with the author's first name followed by last name:

   1. Joan Cleather, *Head, Heart and Hands: The Story of Physiotherapy in Canada* (Toronto: Canadian Physiotherapy Association, 1995), ix.

   (a) **Second citation from the same source.** Once you've provided the full publication details for each source the first time, Chicago style allows you to condense later citations. Later references to a source you have already cited need only the author's last name, an abbreviation of the work's title, and the specific page numbers. Italicize a shortened book title and put an abbreviated article's title in quotation marks.

   12. Cleather, *Head, Heart and Hands*, 14.

   (b) **Successive notes from the same source.** Chicago style also allows the use of the abbreviation "Ibid." (Latin for "the same place") plus a page number when you have two consecutive notes from the same source. Use "Ibid." *alone* if the page number is the same as in the previous note.

   13. Ibid., 17.

2. **Block quotation.** In Chicago style, a quotation that is longer than four typed lines may be indented (five spaces or half an inch) from the rest of the text, **without quotation marks.** The footnote number follows the period at the end of the quotation.

3. **A citation including a specific paraphrased idea** needs the same information as a direct quote. Paraphrasing, or putting another author's ideas into your own words, is customary practice in the disciplines that use Chicago style. In areas of study such as history, there are so many secondary (interpretative) sources available that student researchers need to take special care not to inadvertently borrow the ideas of other historians.

   Some autoethnographers[2] highlight the goal of researcher transparency, while others concentrate on revealing and resisting cultural norms.

   Using a signal phrase:

   Reed-Dahany[3] highlights a goal of researcher transparency, while Kenny[4] concentrates on revealing and resisting cultural norms.

4. **A citation including a general paraphrased idea or summary** requires a footnote or endnote. The only exceptions to this rule are what the University of Chicago editors call "commonly known facts, proverbs and other familiar expressions."[3]

---

3 Ibid., 445.

Conservation biologists agree that protecting habitats is the most effective way to conserve biological diversity.[5]

The footnote for this example appears this way:

5. Richard B. Primack, *A Primer of Conservation Biology* (Sunderland, England: Sinauer Associates, 2000): 183.

5. **A citation referring to a third-party source** needs a footnote for the original author in the sentence, along with the third-party name(s) in brackets with the phrase "quoted in," along with page number(s):

Content knowledge encompasses what Bruner[6] called the "structure of knowledge"—the theories, principles, and concepts of a particular discipline.

The footnote for this example appears this way:

6. Jerome Bruner, *Actual Minds, Possible Worlds* (Cambridge, Mass: Harvard University Press, 1986), quoted in Lee Shulman "Ways of Seeing, Ways of Knowing, Ways of Teaching, Ways of Learning about Teaching." *Journal of Curriculum Studies*, 28 (1992): 43.

6. **Personal communication, including interviews,** needs a footnote:

Derrida[7]

The footnote for this example:

7. Jacques Derrida, letter to author, 27 May 2001.

11.6.2 Chicago Style Footnote/Endnote Citations by Format

Notice that citations use the order: given name(s)-last name; name of work; and parentheses around city, publisher, and date. Notes include the page(s) of the specific citation, whereas the bibliography gives complete page ranges.

A. **Kinds of Authors (book)**

1. **Work by one author** needs the author's first name followed by his or her last name, the title of the book (in italics), and then the location of the publisher, the publisher's name and publication date in parentheses. The page number(s) appear last, outside of the parentheses.

   Harold Bloom, *Genius* (New York: Warner Books, 2002), xviii.

2. **Work by two to three authors** needs the first and last names of all authors with commas between them and the word "and" between second last and last

name, in addition to the name of the work (in italics). The location of the publisher, the publisher's name and the publication year follow in parentheses. The page number(s) appear last, outside of the parentheses.

Chris Higgins and Karen Wilson-Baptist, *Accidental Tourist* (Toronto: Imagination Press, 2000), 44.

3. **Work by four or more authors** needs the name of the first author only, along with the phrase "and others." The name of the work in italics follows, with the location of the publisher, the publisher's name, and the publication year in parentheses. The page number(s) appear outside the parentheses.

Lawrence Festial and others, *When Economics Fails* (Minneapolis: University of Minnesota Press, 1956), 402.

4. **Two or more works by the same author.** Chicago style includes the full or an abbreviated name of the work in the footnote, which makes straight-forward the tracing of which one of an author's works is being cited.

5. **Two authors with the same last name.** Confusion over authors with the same last name is eliminated in Chicago style through the use of both first and last names in footnotes and endnotes.

6. **Groups or organizations as authors.** The editors who compile the Chicago style suggest using the name of the organization as the author of a work if an individual is not mentioned. Provide the full name of the group or organization in the first footnote, and then follow the standard format for second and subsequent citations.

"Suffragettes were regarded by many social service groups as fascinating phenomena, as long as one's own family members did not succumb."[8]

The footnote would appear this way:

8. The London Men's League, *The Men's League Handbook on Women's Suffrage* (London, 1912), 23.

7. **Work with an unknown author (including many dictionary and encyclopedia articles).** Begin with the title (in italics) followed by the year of publication and page number, in parentheses.

9. *Manifesto* (1987, 22).

B. **Kinds of Works (periodical)**

1. **Work by one author (article).** Give the author's first name followed by last name, and then the title of the article in quotation marks. The title of the journal in italics, the volume and the issue (if paginated by issue), which is specified

with the abbreviation "no." followed by the issue number. The year of publication (in parentheses) precedes a colon and the page number(s).

continuous pagination journal: include volume number but not issue number.

10. Robert Garner, "Political Ideologies and the Moral Status of Animals," *Journal of Political Ideologies* 8 (2003): 235.

journal paginated by issue: include both volume and issue number.

11. Johanne Devlin Trew, "Conflicting Visions: Don Messier, Liberal Nationalism, and the Canadian Unity Debate," *International Journal of Canadian Studies* 26 no.2 (2002): 51.

2. **Footnote/endnote citations—Internet sources**
Guiding readers to your citations precisely in on-line documents is a challenge because sites rarely have page numbers. The *Chicago Manual of Style* distinguishes between formal and informal publication, with the URL in the same position as other publishing information. Personal Web pages and electronic mailing lists are considered informal, and should include a descriptor like "photo gallery" or "e-mail to mailing list." If materials such as on-line journal articles have page numbers, use these rather than actual numbers provided on your hard drive or printout.

3. **Standard Internet citation.** Use the author's last name as signal phrase.

Jiminez[12] claims that "The Friendly Giant" is sorely missed.

The footnote would appear this way:

12. Carlos Jiminez, e-mail to CBC listserv, 5 April 2003.

4. **Internet site without an author.** In Chicago style, authors can be substituted for the name of the site owner if no individual's name is available.

The Association of Canadian Dental Technicians reports that chewing gum can increase concentration.[13]

The footnote would appear this way:

13. The Association of Canadian Dental Technicians, "Chewing Gum" <http://www.acdt.can.org/guides.html>.

C. **Footnote/Endnote: Non-Textual Sources**

1. **Film, video, audio, TV broadcasts, and musical recordings.** Cite the most senior production person's or artist's name to begin the footnote, followed by

the piece's title in italics. Publication details including location, corporate information, and year of release are placed in brackets, followed by a descriptive word like "slides." Chicago style offers little consistency in the citations of non-print sources, so checking the manual itself is recommended.

Francis Ford Coppola's film *The Conversation* explored the psychology of surveillance.[14]

The footnote would appear this way:

14. Francis Ford Coppola, *The Conversation* (Zoetrope, 1974), video.

2. **Installations, events, performances, artworks** are not discussed in detail in the 15th edition of *The Chicago Manual of Style*. Follow guidelines for other non-textual sources.

11.6.3 Chicago Style Bibliography

In Chicago style, the Bibliography pages appear at the end of your paper on a new page that continues the numbers of the text. The Bibliography is single-spaced with a double space between each entry and a one-inch margin around the page. The title is centred an inch from the top of the page without underlining or bolding. This list is alphabetized by the author's last name, and each entry begins flush with the left margin, with subsequent lines indented half an inch. The standard Chicago bibliographic citation begins with the author's last name, followed by a complete first name (if only initials are given, use those). The italicized title of the work follows with a publication location, the publisher's name, and the year of publication. All key words are capitalized, even if the original source did not do so.

A. **Kinds of Authors**

1. **Work by one author (book):**

   Bloom, Harold. *Genius*. New York: Warner Books, 2002.

2. **Work by one author (article):**

   Garner, Robert. "Political Ideologies and the Moral Status of Animals." *Journal of Political Ideologies* 8 (2003): 233–46.

3. **Work by two or three authors:**

   Higgins, Chris and Karen Wilson-Baptist. *Accidental Tourist*. Toronto: Imagination Press, 2000.

4. **Work by four or more authors:**

   Festial, Lawrence and others. *When Economics Fails*. Minneapolis: University of Minnesota Press, 1956.

5. Two or more works by the same author are arranged chronologically from earliest to the most recent publication. The author's name appears only in the first listing, with three dashes substituted for the name in the remaining citations.

> Foucault, Michel. *Discipline and Punish: The Birth of the Prison*. Translated by Alan Sheridan. New York: Random, 1977.
>
> ———. *The History of Sexuality*. Vol. 3. Translated by Robert Hurley. New York: Random, 1978.

6. **Work by two authors with the same last name:**

> Sinkinson, Susan and Barbara Sinkinson. *Art History: A Feminist Perspective*. Turin, Italy: Turin Press, 2002.

7. **Work authored by an organization:**

> Call Ontario. *KPMG/Boyd Call Centre Study*. Toronto, ON: Crown Press, 1997.

8. **Work without a publication location or date (other than electronic).** If the work being cited lacks a publication location or an author's name, Chicago style allows the use of the abbreviations "n.p." and "n.d." as substitutes.

9. **No author name (encyclopedia or dictionary).** Precede entry title by "s.v." (sub verbo, "under the word").

> *Canadian Encyclopedia*. 1985 ed., s.v. "Interveners."

B. **Specific parts of a source**

1. **Chapter or other type of selection, such as an essay, in edited volume:**

> Bergen, David. "Lucy in the Sky." In *Writing Prose: Techniques and Purposes*, 3rd Canadian ed. Edited by Thomas S. Kane, Leonard J. Peters, and Maurice R. Legris, 353–4. Don Mills: Oxford University Press, 2003.

2. **Multivolume work (referencing one volume):**

> Bosworth, A. B., ed. *A Historical Commentary on Arrian's History of Alexander*. Vol. 1. Oxford: Oxford University Press, 1980.

3. **Second or subsequent edition of a work:**

> Suzuki, David, Aaron Griffiths, and Rebecca Lewontin. *An Introduction to Genetic Analysis*. 4th ed. New York: Freeman, 1989.

4. **Third-party source.** Cite the work where you found the citation rather than the original text.

5. **Personal communications.** In Chicago style, personal communications are not included in the bibliography.

C. **Chicago Internet Bibliographic Citations**

The editors of the Chicago Press have decided that the citation of Internet-based information should follow the same general patterns as traditional sources, with the URL considered to be another form of publication information. However, they are somewhat restrictive in what they consider a publication to be, with anything other than peer-reviewed journals, magazines, and newspapers being grouped into a category known as "informally published material."[4] In response to the transitory nature of some on-line sources, Chicago style doesn't require you to provide an access date, but suggests that as much information as possible be given about authors.

1. **Standard electronic bibliographic citation:**

Jiminez, Karinna. "Freudian Dreams." Personal Website. <http://www.rbi.edu/~ vttsc/frdream.html>

2. **An Internet document with no author and/or no date.** Academic work that is being graded should be supported by the most reliable sources available to you. Sites without uploading or update dates are common, but often a visit to the main page will help you locate this information. If necessary, cite an authorless Web page in this way:

"My Unfounded Opinions." Anonymous Web Blog. <http://www.notacademicwriting/ca>

3. **Private or personal Web site with no title:**

Tan, Li. Home Page. Personal Web site. <http://www.tan-li/~oscar/ reviews.html>

4. **Group or organization (corporate) Web site:**

American Educational Research Association. "Sources of Health Insurance and Characteristics of the Uninsured." Issue Brief No. 123. <http://www.ilt.columbia.edu//publications/papers/newwine.html>

5. **On-line book:**

Radford, Barbara. *Soil to Social*. New York: Random, 2000. Also available on-line at <http://on-line-books.ora.com/mod-bin/books.mod/javaref/javanut/index.html>

---

4 Ibid., 707.

6. **Article in on-line-only journal.** Chicago style allows the inclusion of access dates for electronic material if you wish.

> Gingras, Jacqui. "Body Matters." *The Journal of Contemporary Dietary Health* 10.2 (2001). <http://www.vespro.com/> (accessed Oct. 21, 2002).

7. **Internet article based on a print source and retrieved from a database:**

> Van Nyugen, Gayle and Frances Carre. "Goals of Nursing Teams in Tertiary Care." *Journal of Nursing Research*, 5.2 (2001): 117–22. <http://links.ebscohost/jouranl.nur.edu/tert-/contents.html>

D. **Chicago Bibliographic Citations for Non-Textual Sources**
Chicago style includes ways to reference some, but not all, non-textual information sources. Works of art, performances, and installations are not addressed. The manual offers the option of creating a discography for audio-visual material, but does not provide very specific guidelines concerning this listing method. In keeping with the rest of the style, the name of person(s) involved in creating the piece should be obvious in your citation, along with an abbreviated description of the material.

1. **Film, video, or DVD:**

> Coppola, Francis Ford. *Apocalypse Now*. Video. Directed by Francis Ford Coppola. Burbank, CA, Zoetrope Studios, 1979.

2. **Music:**

> Morrison, Van. *Too Long in Exile*. Compact disc. Polydor, 1993.

Exercises: Integrating and Documenting Sources

The following exercises ask you to apply information from Section 11. They test your knowledge of paraphrase, direct quotation, mixed quotation, block format, signal phrases, ellipses, brackets, and the rudiments of MLA and APA parenthetical citation.

I.   Integrating Sources

   A.   Following precisely the instructions that have been given in this text, use sections from the excerpt below to compose sentences that show your understanding of effective ways to integrate secondary sources. The excerpts are from the Web site article "Comets May Have Led to Birth and Death of Dinosaur Era," by Hillary Mayell (National Geographic News, May 16, 2002); the information for part 1 is taken from paragraphs 1 and 2 of the source; part 2 is taken from paragraph 4; part 3 is taken from paragraph 3.

Exercises: Integrating and Documenting Sources – *continued*

B. Paraphrase the following using one or two sentences (do not use any direct quotations). Use the MLA style of parenthetical referencing:

> Comets slamming into the Earth may be responsible for both the birth and the death of the dinosaur era, an international group of researchers report. There is a considerable amount of evidence that a bolide [a comet or asteroid] collision with Earth triggered the end of the dinosaur era 65 million years ago.

C. Rewrite this sentence so that it includes a signal phrase (MLA style—includes source's name and signal verb) and a direct quote that is no more than eight words (choose the most appropriate words for the direct quote).

> "We have been able to show for the first time that the transition between Triassic life-forms to Jurassic life-forms occurred in a geological blink of an eye," said Paul Olsen, a geologist at the Lamont-Doherty Earth Observatory of Columbia University.

D. Using square brackets, integrate grammatically into the sentence the following direct quotation:

> The cause for the end of the dinosaur age might have been "a giant ball of ice, rock, and gases smashed into the supercontinent Pangaea."

II. Integrate the passage below according to the directions in each of A, B, and C.

A. Use a **signal phrase** and follow APA style, which includes source's name, year, and signal verb followed by a direct quote of the entire passage—but see C

B. **Format the quote** in the most appropriate way—i.e., either as part of the text or in block format.

C. **Omit the last phrase in sentence three** ("just to mention a few") and indicate to the reader that material is omitted.

> (The author is David Suzuki; the name of article is "Saving the Earth"; the date of publication is June 14, 1999; the quotation is from page 43 of *Maclean's* magazine.)

> In this century, our species has undergone explosive change. Not only are we adding a quarter of a million people to our numbers every day, we have vastly amplified our technological muscle power. When I was born, there were no computers, televisions, jet planes, oral contraceptives, transoceanic phone calls, satellites, transistors or xerography, just to mention a few. Children today look at typewriters, vinyl records and black-and-white televisions as ancient curiosities.

Exercises: Integrating and Documenting Sources – *continued*

1. Paraphrase the passage below, which is from the same Suzuki essay, using the directions given in (a) and (b), and document using APA style:

    (a) you **may** use a maximum of **one direct quote**. Remember that a paraphrase includes all the information in the source put only in your own words—but for this exercise, you can make one direct citation as part of the paraphrase;

    (b) do **not** use a signal phrase.

    > (The author is David Suzuki; the name of the article is "Saving the Earth"; the date of publication is June 14, 1999; the quotation is from page 45 of *Maclean's* magazine.)

    > In biological terms, the globe is experiencing an eco-holocaust, as more than 50,000 species vanish annually, and air, water and soil are poisoned with civilization's effluents. The great challenge to the millennium is recognizing the reality of impending ecological collapse, and the urgent need to get on with taking the steps to avoid it.

12. The Formal Précis

Précis are specific kinds of summaries. They contain the main ideas of the source, so can be thought of as miniaturized versions of their longer, more detailed originals. Making such summaries sharpens your reading and analytical skills. As you read a work for summarization, you will first be concerned with understanding its meaning. The process you follow will be similar to that described above in Section 10.2.2, Paraphrase. The difference is that you must not only understand and synthesize the information—as you need to do any time you read for content—but also distinguish the most important ideas from the less important ones.

12.1 Main Features of the Précis

The précis:

1. retains the essence of the original piece;
2. includes all the main ideas;
3. includes only the most important developments of these ideas (a shorter précis wouldn't include any developments);
4. omits examples and illustrations, unless very important;
5. uses the same order as the original;
6. does not add anything that wasn't in the original;
7. uses succinct prose;
8. is mostly your own words, but you may use some words from the original (though no more than you strictly have to). You *must place quotation marks* around any phrases or sentences that you cite directly; if you cite more than **three** consecutive words, you should place them in quotation marks;

9. is approximately 20 per cent to 25 per cent the length of the original, unless you have been told otherwise.

12.2 Rhetorical Stance

If the purpose of the essay is to persuade its reader, rather than present factual information, you need to acknowledge its rhetorical purpose. In such cases, you should carefully distinguish between fact and opinion. For example, this is the way that one professional writer began an essay:

> In the course of two years' research for a book on how we think about pain, I've spoken to neurologists, doctors, artists, therapists of every stripe, as well as psychologists—the frontline workers. And frankly, I preferred the people selling healing magnets to most of the psychologists. They were bad communicators. They couldn't make eye contact. They seemed more interested in certain folds in the brain than in helping human beings cope with pain.
>
> –Marni Jackson, "Every Breath You Take: A Former Hospital Pain Specialist Puts His Faith in the Powers of Meditation," *Maclean's* (Aug. 16, 1999).

If, in such a case, you did not acknowledge the writer's words as opinion, you would seriously misrepresent her:

> Psychologists generally communicate badly and are shifty-eyed.

However, you could acknowledge the author's rhetorical purpose this way:

> Marni Jackson preferred "the people selling healing magnets" to the majority of psychologists she spoke to.

12.3 Signal Phrases

Signal phrases (see also Section 10.3.1) can be used to clearly attribute a statement to one or more people. Carefully choose a signal verb that reveals the writer's rhetorical purpose—verbs like "prefer," "believe," "claimed," and "argued" all suggest opinion, whereas "says," "states," "described," and "found" do not. In expressing rhetorical purpose, whether through appropriate verbs or phrases like "according to," you are showing the writer's attitude towards the subject. But do not explicitly characterize the writer's stance as negative or make assumptions from what you know about the writer's background that refer to his/her possible bias. Summaries should "represent," not judge. Therefore, it is sufficient to represent opinion through appropriate diction. The writer may be opinionated; when representing those opinions, you should not express your own opinions.

Be especially careful *not* to:

Two Cheers for Brevity
To précis—
be as brief as you can
without omitting any main
ideas from the original.

- become too general or vague; be *specific* but *not detailed*;
- distort the writer's meaning in any way; use *your words* but *the writer's ideas*.

13. A Method for Summarizing

You can summarize using three steps:

1. Read the work for the first time to learn its purpose, thesis statement, intended audience, rhetorical stance, etc.
2. When you re-read it, note its major points, along with the most important sub-points and/or key examples, and from these points write an outline.
3. Following your outline closely, write a summary that includes the thesis statement and all the main points. If you are writing a summary of a specific length and have room for more than the main points, pick the most important sub-points or developments of ideas to reach the required word range.

A précis, at its minimum, should contain the work's thesis statement and main ideas; logically, the place to look for these is at the end of the introduction (thesis statement) and in the topic sentences of major paragraphs (main ideas). Remember that not all topic sentences are the first sentences of paragraphs—indeed, not all paragraphs in all writing have topic sentences. Furthermore, not every paragraph will contain a major idea, so there will not necessarily be a predictable relation between the original's number of paragraphs and the number of points in your outline. When you have written the summary, check it over to ensure that it is essentially in your own words and that you have put quotation marks around words and phrases taken directly from the source.

14. Sample Précis

In the first example, the main ideas are presented in the form of an outline, and then a summary was written from these ideas. In the second example, the outline stage was omitted. The summaries are approximately 20–25 per cent of the length of the originals. "How Should One Read a Book?" is excerpted from Virginia Woolf ("How Should One Read a Book?" *The Second Common Reader* [New York: Harcourt, 1986] 258–70).

How Should One Read a Book?

by Virginia Woolf

The chapters of a novel—if we consider how to read a novel first—are an attempt to make something as formed and controlled as a building: but words are more impalpable than bricks; reading is a longer and more complicated process than seeing. Perhaps the quickest way to understand the elements of what a novelist is doing is not to read, but to write; to make your own experiment with the dangers and difficulties of words. Recall, then, some event that has left a distinct impression on you—how at the corner of the street, perhaps, you passed two people talking. A tree shook; an electric light danced;

the tone of the talk was comic, but also tragic; a whole vision, an entire conception, seemed contained in that moment.

But when you attempt to reconstruct it in words, you will find that it breaks into a thousand conflicting impressions. Some must be subdued; others emphasized; in the process you will lose, probably, all grasp upon the emotion itself. Then turn from your blurred and littered pages to the opening pages of some great novelist—Defoe, Jane Austen, Hardy. Now you will be better able to appreciate their mastery. It is not merely that we are in the presence of a different person—Defoe, Jane Austen, or Thomas Hardy—but that we are living in a different world. Here, in *Robinson Crusoe*, we are trudging a plain high road; one thing happens after another; the fact and the order of the fact are enough. But if the open air and adventure mean everything to Defoe, they mean nothing to Jane Austen. Hers is the drawing room, and people talking, and by the many mirrors of their talk revealing their characters. And if, when we have accustomed ourselves to the drawing room and its reflections, we turn to Hardy, we are once more spun around. The moors are round us and the stars are above our heads. The other side of the mind is now exposed—the dark side that comes uppermost in solitude, not the light side that shows in company. Our relations are not towards people, but towards Nature and destiny. Yet different as these worlds are, each is consistent with itself. The maker of each is careful to observe the laws of his own perspective, and however great a strain they may put upon us they will never confuse us, as lesser writers frequently do, by introducing two different kinds of reality into the same book . . . .

But a glance at the heterogeneous company on the shelf will show you that writers are very seldom "great artists"; far more often a book makes no claim to be a work of art at all. These biographies and autobiographies, for example, lives of great men, of men long dead and forgotten, are we to refuse to read them because they are not "art?" Or shall we read them but in a different way, with a different aim? Shall we read them in the first place to satisfy that curiosity which possesses us sometimes when in the evening we linger in front of a house where the lights are lit and the blinds are not drawn, and each floor of the house shows us a different section of human life in being? Then we are consumed with curiosity about the lives of these people—the servants gossiping, the gentlemen dining, the girl dressing for a party, the old woman at the window with her knitting. Who are they, what are they, what are their names, their occupations, their thoughts, and adventures? Biographies and memoirs answer such questions, light up innumerable such houses; they show us people going about their daily affairs, toiling, failing, succeeding, eating, hating, loving, until they die.

(650 words)

When you decide on the main points of the source you are summarizing, you can paraphrase them either as you construct an outline or after you have your outline in place. Remember that the final summarized version must be essentially in your own words and that words and phrases quoted directly must be placed in quotation marks. In the example below, most of the paraphrasing was done *after* the outline stage.

Outline:
—a novel is "an attempt to make something as formed . . . as a building"
—words are "more impalpable than bricks"; "reading is a longer and more complicated process than seeing"
—to understand "what a novelist is doing" try to take a strong personal impression and write about it
—when you try to reconstruct it you will probably lose the sense of the emotion you felt at that moment
—if you then start reading a novel by a great writer his/her "mastery" should soon be apparent
—each world "is consistent with itself," and the maker "observes the laws of his own perspective," never baffling the reader by presenting two worlds in the same book
—most books, such as biographies and autobiographies, don't pretend to be "art"
—we read biog. differently from novels, to satisfy our curiosity about the lives of individuals; they answer the questions we ask about the lives of others

Note that there is much omitted from the lengthy second paragraph: paragraph length is not always a reliable clue when summarizing; in this instance, the second paragraph contained much descriptive detail and many examples—but few main points.

Summary:
Woolf says a novel is "an attempt to make something as formed . . . as a building"; but bricks are easier to grasp than words, and to read something is more difficult than to see it. To understand the novelist's art, Woolf suggests you write about a personal experience; as you write, you will probably lose the emotion you felt; however, if you start reading the work of great novelists you will then appreciate their ability to render different worlds. The "master" novelist respects the "laws of his own perspective," so never baffles the reader by presenting more than one world. In contrast, most books, such as biographies and autobiographies, don't pretend to be "art." We read them differently, to satisfy our curiosity about the lives of real people.
(125 words)

Exercise

Summarize the following in about 100–110 words; a summarized version follows the original. The essay is excerpted from Charles E. Taylor's "Life As We Don't Know It" (Reprinted with permission from *1993 Yearbook of Science and the Future*, © 1992 by Encyclopaedia Britannica, Inc. 172–87).

Life as We Don't Know It

by Charles E. Taylor

What is alive and what is not? How large is the class of objects that possess life? The answer from humankind's deep past—from its oldest myths and ancient religions and cosmologies—has been that life extends beyond plants and animals and permeates all nature and the universe. "We are part of the earth and it is part of us. The perfumed flowers are our sisters. The bear, the deer, the great eagle, these are our brothers. The rocky crests, the juices of the meadow, the body heat of the pony, and man, all belong to the same family," said Seattle, chief of the Suquamish. As far as can be determined, most hunter societies have similar beliefs.

For Western culture that traditional view began to change with the Greek philosophers, particularly Aristotle. Animate and inanimate came to be viewed as fundamentally different. Over the centuries the separation continued to grow, culminating in the theory of vitalism, which lasted well into the 20th century. During the 17th and 18th centuries, building on the discoveries of Galileo, Newton, and others, Descartes and other philosophers made various attempts to view animals as "nothing but" machines. None of their theories proved satisfactory, however, especially for biologists.

The trend toward separation has now reversed itself. The distinction between living and nonliving is thoroughly blurred. In fact, scientists are building artificial systems—some of them far removed from the common perception of living organisms—that possess most or all of the properties and behaviours that traditionally have been associated with life. These characteristics include self-assembly and self-reproduction, development and differentiation, adaptation and evolution, and complex ecological interactions. Such scientific efforts are defining a new area of research termed artificial life, or a-life. The field attempts to extract the logical properties from naturally occurring organisms and then to provide them to characteristically nonliving systems, like computer processes or robots. It has also begun to seek signs of life in such unlikely places as the abstract realm of ideas and theories.

A variety of human-made systems now being studied have properties that one commonly attributes to living systems. Investigating these systems is making it possible to understand life in the broader sense, that is, life-as-it-can-be, and through this effort to better appreciate life-as-it-is. The consequences of research in artificial life are likely to be profound: they will challenge, perhaps fundamentally alter, our view of humankind's place in nature; they will dramatically enhance our ability to control our environment; and they may even endow other systems with the ability to control us.

(423 words)

Précis

What is life? According to the most ancient traditions, life pervades nature and the universe. For Western culture, this view changed with the Greek philosophers who distinguished between the animate and the inanimate. Seventeenth- and eighteenth-century philosophers and scientists saw animals simply as machines, but biologists didn't agree, and now the line between the living and non-living is unclear.

Today scientists are building "artificial systems" with properties previously associated with life, creating a new era of research called "a-life." The "logical properties of life" are taken from natural organisms and applied to "non-living systems," like robots and computers and even thought. Such investigations will challenge our place in nature.

(108 words)

Note that most of the first paragraph is omitted; its main purpose was to attract the reader's interest. The long quotation by Seattle is poetic—but would not be included in most summaries of this passage. As the longest, most developed, and most relevant paragraph, paragraph three is given the most attention, while the speculative fourth paragraph is greatly condensed.

15. Sample Student Essays

Annotations are given for the first essay; a series of questions follows the second essay. To conserve space, the essays are not double spaced and "References," "Works Cited," "Notes," and "Bibliography" sections are not on separate pages; in addition, the essays do not follow correct essay format requirements for title pages or identification information (see Part Eight, Section 4, Essay Presentation).

15.1 Sample Student Expository Essay #1 (APA Style) (1,400 words)

This essay is an example of an important kind of research essay: a review of the literature available on a topic. Such survey essays are typical of student research assignments at the advanced undergraduate level, particularly in the natural sciences and social sciences. They deal with the findings from research, placing them in a logical order (usually chronological), evaluating them, and arriving at a fact-based conclusion. Many studies featuring original research in the social sciences and the natural sciences begin with a review of the literature, after which the writer states his or her thesis. Grant uses APA documentation style.

See Sections 15.2, below, and Part Six, Section 16.3 for examples of research essays that use MLA style; see Section 15.3, below, for an example of an essay that uses Chicago style.

In the Introduction, the writer uses the chronological method of development, culminating in a summary of the direction and aims of the research done to date—as is typical of this kind of research essay, the summary serves as the thesis statement.

Creatine: An Effective Ergogenic Supplement

by Andrew Grant

Athletes have used ergogenic aids for thousands of years to improve such things as strength, speed, and stamina. One such ergogenic chemical that has gained popularity within the last decade is creatine. Creatine was discovered to be a nutrient found in the flesh of animals more than 150 years ago. However, its use as an ergogenic aid was not considered until the 1960s when it was discovered that, as a constituent of human muscle tissue, it played an important role during exercise recovery. As a result of this discovery, in the 1970s small groups of elite athletes and scientists began experimenting with creatine supplementation to improve athletic performance, but were only able to provide anecdotal evidence regarding its efficiency. In the late 1980s, Olympic athletes such as Linford Christie and Sally Gunnell reportedly began using creatine despite the lack of empirical evidence supporting the efficacy of its supplementation, and eventually won gold medals in the 1992 Barcelona Olympics in the 100-meter sprint and 400-meter hurdles, respectively. Continued claims about the efficacy of creatine supplementation based on anecdotal evidence prompted many supplement companies to begin mass producing creatine powders to market to the general public, and consequently, creatine, in the form of powdered creatine monohydrate, became one of the most popular nutritional supplements worldwide. By the early 1990s, scientists such as Robert Harris finally began to study the efficacy of creatine supplementation using carefully designed and controlled experiments. Their research revealed exactly how creatine played a crucial physiological role during exercise recovery, revealed how oral creatine supplementation could be used as an

The end of paragraph citation shows that the information was summarized from one source.

The writer's first main point concerns the role of creatine in recovery from exercise; the second point examines creatine as an aid to improved athletic performance; the third explores safety concerns. Compare with the thesis statement.

This paragraph uses examples, cause and effect, and analysis to develop the main point.

ergogenic aid to improve athletic performance, and also addressed concerns regarding the safety of creatine supplementation (Williams, Kreider, & Branch, 1999).

ATP (adenosine triphosphate) is the high-energy molecule, formed from the breakdown of ingested fuels such as fats, carbohydrates, and proteins, that supports muscle contractions, and is the primary source of energy for cellular functions within the body, including exercise from recovery (Brooks, 2000). ATP is structured with an adenosine molecule attached to three phosphate groups that are bound to each other by high-energy bonds. When one of the high-energy bonds between the phosphate groups is broken, ADP (adenosine diphosphate) is formed, and energy that can be used by cells is released. Creatine acts as a phosphate carrier that is capable of shuttling phosphate formed from the breakdown of ATP back to ADP. The phosphate group carried by creatine can then be reattached to the ADP molecule to form ATP, which once again can be broken down to create energy. The cyclic manner of the breaking of the phosphate bonds and the shuttling of unbound phosphate groups being carried back to ATP by creatine results in the most readily available source of energy used by muscles because the process does not depend on a long series of reactions, oxygen is not needed, and ATP and creatine are stored in close proximity to the muscles. However, the supply of creatine in muscle cells at any given time is limited, and, consequently, the creatine phosphate-ATP system can provide energy only for short periods of exercise lasting up to roughly 30 seconds until the supply of creatine is depleted temporarily (Vander, Sherman, & Luciano, 2001).

Despite this depletion, the concentration of creatine stored in muscles can be increased by 10–40 per cent by ingesting powdered creatine supplements with any beverage in the following manner: 20 grams per day divided into four or five equal doses daily for five days (loading phase), followed by two to three grams per day for four to twelve weeks (maintenance phase). The ingestion of creatine powder during the loading phase performs a function similar to the standard practice of carbohydrate loading employed by aerobic endurance athletes prior to competition (Williams et al., 1999).

Increasing the creatine stores in muscle tissue by supplementation improves muscular strength and power by allowing quicker recovery from intense exercise such as weight/strength training, but creatine supplementation itself does not *directly* improve strength (Corbin, Lindsey, & Welk, 2000). This occurs due to the increased availability of ATP (as previously described). The ability to rapidly recover during training enables trainees to work at intensities close to their maximum level of output. For example, this would translate into a trainee being able to lift a weight closer to his or her maximum for multiple repetitions while less time would be required to allow the muscles to be repaired and adapt between sets and consecutive workouts. As a result, the trainee would quickly be able to use progressively heavier weights and would consequently become stronger much more rapidly than he or she would be able to without the use of creatine supplementation (Urbanski, Vincent, & Yaspelkis, 1999). Such a training effect plays a vital role for athletes who perform rapid, powerful, single repetition movements such as swinging a baseball bat, and is why former "home run king" Mark McGwire allegedly used creatine as an ergogenic aid en route to breaking Roger Maris's long-standing single season home run record of 62 in 1997.

While creatine supplementation potentiates an improved recovery time during training, translating into improved performance, it also has a more direct impact on improving sprinting speed. Most sprinting events involve an acceleration, maintenance, and deceleration phase despite the appearance that the runners are accelerating the entire time. Because sprinting, lasting no longer than 30 seconds, is an anaerobic activity, the creatine phosphate–ATP system provides the most readily available supply of energy to the muscles. With increased creatine stores in muscle tissue, ATP can be re-synthesized rapidly and for a longer time than would otherwise be possible without creatine supplementation. Therefore, both the acceleration and maintenance phases during a sprint can be prolonged, and the deceleration phase can be minimized (Sahelian & Tuttle, 1997). In an event such as the 200-meter sprint, which typically lasts about 20 seconds, the effect of creatine supplementation proves particularly useful because it pushes the limits of the anaerobic alactic energy system.

Creatine can prove beneficial for improving athletic performance, but its use may come at a cost. Williams et al. (1999) point out that one significant side effect of creatine supplementation is weight gain through increased water retention caused by osmosis as creatine enters the muscle cells. For aerobic endurance athletes such as marathon runners, this weight gain can have a negative impact as it increases the amount of internal work that must be done to move a heavier body. Because the benefits of creatine supplementation work only for anaerobic exercise, aerobic endurance athletes cannot reap the benefits of creatine use, and their performance may, in fact, be hindered by its use.

According to Williams et al. (1999), most scientific research conducted on the potential deleterious side effects of creatine supplementation has concluded that there are few, if any, negative impacts on the body if creatine is administered according to the method outlined above. However, many apparently healthy athletes who have used creatine as a supplement have complained about side effects including renal and liver damage,

---

Grant is treating the achievement of McGwire as common knowledge and easily obtainable from various sources.

In this paragraph, the writer reports on "anecdotal" evidence (in other words, evidence that the research has not confirmed); personal experience is also included.

dehydration, severe muscle cramping, diarrhea, increased blood pressure, gastrointestinal discomfort, headache, anxiety, nausea, and sexual dysfunction (Sahelian & Tuttle, 1999). In fact, last year a friend of mine confided to me that he was suffering from premature ejaculation without ever reaching orgasm during sexual intercourse. He associated this problem with his recent use of creatine monohydrate supplements, and after discontinuing his creatine supplementation, his sexual dysfunction ended within two weeks. It should, however, be noted that claims regarding the potential negative side effects of creatine supplementation are purely anecdotal and lack scientific support at this time.

The first sentence of the conclusion is a carefully phrased summary; it is followed by an acknowledgment of the limitations of current findings and the need for caution.

Clearly, the discovery of how creatine supplementation provides an ergogenic effect has provided athletes with a means to legally improve their athletic performance. Currently, creatine has not been banned by an athletic organization, including the IOC, because it is classified as a nutritional supplement and not a drug, and is therefore not subject to the strict testing and regulation that drugs are. However, as creatine supplementation has only been studied seriously for the last decade, little is known about its long-term side effects, and many health professionals are hesitant to take a stance on the safety of its supplementation (Williams et al., 1999). Therefore, anyone considering using creatine as an ergogenic supplement should read all the available literature on the topic, and then, only after consulting a physician, determine whether creatine is an appropriate supplement for him or her.

References

Brooks, G.A. (2000). *Exercise physiology: Human bioenergetics and its applications* (3rd ed.). Mountain View, Calif.: Mayfield Publishing Company.

Corbin, C.B., Lindsey, R., & Welk, G. (2000). *Concepts of physical fitness* (10th ed.). Boston: McGraw-Hill.

Sahalein, R., & Tuttle, D. (1997). *Creatine: Nature's muscle builder*. Garden City Park, New York: Avery Publishing Group.

Urbanski, R.L., Vincent, W.J., & Yaspelkis, B.B. (1999). Creatine supplementation differentially affects maximal isometric strength and time to fatigue in large and small muscle groups [Electronic version]. *International Journal of Sport Nutrition, 9*(2), 136–145.

Vander, A., Sherman, J., & Luciano, D. (2001). *Human physiology: The mechanisms of body function* (8th ed.). New York: McGraw-Hill.

Williams, M.H., Kreider, R.B., & Branch, J.D. (1999). *Creatine: The power supplement*. Champaign, Ill.: Human Kinetics.

15.2 Sample Student Expository Essay # 2 (MLA Style) (1,650 words)

Multiculturalism in Canada: Controversial Consequences of

the *Multiculturalism Act*

by Reneé MacKillop

What does it mean to be Canadian? The act for "the preservation and enhancement of Multiculturalism in Canada" declares recognition and promotion of understanding racial and cultural diversity as important parts of the Canadian identity (Bissoondath 36–37). The *Multiculturalism Act* allows all Canadians to freely safeguard and develop their cultural heritage (36). This act, however, has evoked questions concerning its validity, acceptance, and limits as well as questions of national unity and identity. According to supporters of multiculturalism, being Canadian means being a part of a cultural mosaic in a pluralistic society; according to critics of the Act, there is no conclusive answer to what it means to be Canadian because multiculturalism hinders the national quest for unity and identity. The *Multiculturalism Act* has required government involvement in cultural affairs and has extended accommodations to immigrants. The absence of restrictions on multiculturalism has blurred lines between what is acceptable and what is not. The ambiguity of the Act has forced questions about what unites Canadians as a national community and what makes this country Canadian.

The validity of government involvement in the cultural affairs of Canadians is a debatable issue. Opponents of the *Multiculturalism Act* believe that, similar to religion, culture should be a private matter left to individuals and families (Bissoondath 112). They argue that the state has no jurisdiction in the cultures of Canadians. Opponents refer to Canada's past foundation based on "white supremacy" and on the shift from Canada as an "ethnic nation" to a "civic nation" (Kymlicka 25). After World War II, individuals became included in the national community by becoming legal citizens as opposed to past inclusion based on ethnicity; the Citizenship Act of 1946 provided a new way to be Canadian (James). Therefore, in the declaration that Canada is a "civic nation," ethnic and cultural neutrality in the government is implied. Supporters believe that government involvement, namely the *Multiculturalism Act*, is vital to ending racism and discrimination. They feel that it is the Canadian government's duty to redress past wrongs by ensuring equality to present-day ethnic minorities. However, both opponents and supporters agree that the true motives behind government involvement in the cultural affairs of the nation are unclear.

Although the policy of multiculturalism was established with the equality of all Canadian citizens in mind, Richard Gwyn has accused policy-makers of creating a "slush fund to buy ethnic votes" (as cited in Bissoondath 25). Moreover, due to "internal globalization" and the neo-liberal shift in Canadian society, emphasis is diverted from the original intentions of the policy to national competitiveness and economic gain (Abu-Laban and Christian 119–23). Ethnic entrepreneurs provide valuable trading and investment connections to the global community (111). The government issued an evaluation of the *Multiculturalism Act*, the *Brighton Report*, in 1996, which reviewed the program through literature, media coverage, and interviews, along with providing a statistical analysis of funding for the policy. The *Brighton Report* stated that past funding reinforced attendance to special interests and not to all Canadians (113). However, the Report did not mention ulterior motives for government funding of multiculturalism. Nonetheless, some Canadians are questioning whether the support and funds for multiculturalism are government strategies for attaining an international competitive advantage and not primarily for nation-building.

The *Multiculturalism Act* is a renegotiation of immigrant integration (Kymlicka 37). Critics feel that the policy has created excessive accommodations for immigrants, instead of integration, while advocates feel that accommodations are necessary. Critics hold the opinion that immigrants expect integration and that newcomers are responsible to learn an official language, abide by Canadian laws, and accept Canadian society (Bissoondath 23). However, advocates believe that multiculturalism is not intended to create new nations within Canada for individual cultures (Kymlicka 37). Proponents of multiculturalism feel that in response to problems of social marginalization and historically stigmatized communities' political inequality, it is necessary to redress past injustices and ensure a better and more equal future; the *Multiculturalism Act* encourages victims of stigmatization to seek redress (Dyck 117). After progress recognizing ethnic minorities, providing funding, and confronting past wrongs (wrongs frequently authorized by the government) ethnic minorities had endured in Canada, critical opposition surfaced in the 1990s (Dyck 120–21). Critics of multiculturalism believe that immigrants are threatening job security. They cite as an example the "instant Liberals" who were welcomed into the party based solely on their ethnicity, which undermined hard-working members who had been active in the party for considerable lengths of time (Dyck 121). Opposition has grown as Canada continues to increase accommodations for ethnic minorities. Political and legal protections of cultural expression allow the open-ended policy constantly to be stretched (Bissoondath

134). Some critics fear the direction that multiculturalism is taking in Canada by legitimizing all forms of cultural expression.

The official recognition of minority contribution, personal freedom, and diversity, namely pluralism, has declared that society is best served by the contribution of varied components (Bibby 2). Tolerance and respect are enforced, and coexistence has become a national objective. Canadian critics do not consider pluralism beneficial, however, because it entrenches relativism, "the inclination to see the merits of behaviour and ideas as universal or absolute, but as varying with individuals and their environments, and, in the end, as being equally valid because they are chosen" (Bibby vi). According to the critic, "pluralism establishes choices; relativism declares the choice valid" (10). The essential concern is the lack of restrictions limiting what is socially acceptable in Canada.

The thorny question of restrictions is difficult because relativism has validated all viewpoints, eliminating cultural expectations (Bibby 10). Hopeful advocates of multiculturalism believe that boundaries would enable the multiculturalism policy to be successful. However, critics continue to caution the "slippery slope" of relativism that is leading towards acceptance of all forms of cultural expression and away from civic and political integration, regardless of the impact on Canada (Kymlicka 60). They believe that "rights [are] outstanding rules" and "relativism has slain moral consensus" because there are no authoritative instruments capable of measuring Canadian social life (Bibby 10–11). On the contrary, a pluralistic nation, which entails relativism and individualism (the tendency to stress the individual over the group), is notably rewarding because Canadians are free to live out their lives as they see fit, resulting in high standards of living, peaceful existence, and, ultimately, freedom (Bibby 90). However, what is best for Canada is no longer relevant because everything is equal and, therefore, no particular way can be better than another, according to opponents (14). A clear example of the feared results of relativism is the continued practice of female circumcision by some African minorities in Canada. In spite of western society's view of female circumcision as a form of mutilation and a health risk, it is a vital, traditional rite of passage to womanhood for some African women (Bissoondath 134–35). The questions are whether this practice should be acceptable in Canadian society and how far, in the Canadian context, should Canada go in accommodating these kinds of cultural expressions? Detractors of the *Multiculturalism Act* believe that the policy ends where notions of human rights and dignity commences (135). Critics fear that Canadians are "not differentiating between being judgemental and showing sound judgement and between exhibiting discrimination and being discriminatory" (Bibby 101).

Despite the concerns over relativism and individualism in a pluralistic society, supporters of multiculturalism claim that the policy provides external protection to minorities, possibility for redress, access to mainstream institutions, and protection from discriminatory and prejudiced conduct (Kymlicka 65). These advocates believe that, despite the lack of explicit restrictions limiting the policy, the preamble to the Act emphasizes human and individual rights and sexual equality (66–67).

Multiculturalism encourages accepting the rights of others to be different and, consequently, national togetherness (Bibby 90). However, critics pose the following question: "If what we have in common is our diversity, do we really have anything in common at all?" (92). There is freedom for the individual, but how are people brought together into the national community? This implicit criticism suggests that a group needs an identity because individualism brings freedom and equality, but it also removes persons from the guidance of the group and the security of tradition. Thus, the identity of merely being an autonomous Canadian is forced upon citizens (96). Whereas proponents advocate the policy's ability to instil pride in Canadians and a sense of belonging to a mosaic of cultures, opponents call the policy a "song and dance" affair that encourages stereotyping and national divisiveness (96–98). Proponents acknowledge multiculturalism as officially recognizing the reality that Canada has never been unicultural; opponents see it as extenuating national minorities. Aboriginal and Francophone Canadians, two national minorities, are offended by being categorized with other minorities and not being recognized as founding peoples (James). René Lévesque called multiculturalism "folklore" and named the policy a "'red-herring' . . . devised to obscure the 'Quebec business', to give an impression that we are all ethnics and do not have to worry about special status for Quebec" (Bissoondath 37). Some Canadians propose officially declaring Canada multinational along with multicultural as a solution to the problem of national unity. The problematic criticism remains, however, that multiculturalism is divisive and prevents Canadians from establishing a national identity.

The *Multiculturalism Act*, like all political policies, is not above criticism, and the concept of multiculturalism has both supporters and detractors. It is essential that a democratic state be constantly analyzed, critiqued, and questioned. Diversity is a reality in Canada; however, government involvement in immigration integration is controversial. The outcomes of a pluralistic society, officially recognized as being polyethnic, are uncertain as Canada diverges from the melting pot standard. Not surprisingly, there have been unexpected consequences of The *Multiculturalism Act*, such as relativism, individualism, and division. In the words of the *Brighton Report*, critics "misunderstand and misrepresent Canada's multiculturalism policy." However, the report concluded that the policy is in need of amendments (Abu-Laban and Christian 113). In summary, the *Multiculturalism Act* is progressive, yet in need of revision to allow Canada to flourish as a unified country with a strong national identity.

Works Cited

Abu-Laban, Yasmeen and Gabriel Christian. Selling Diversity: Immigration, Multiculturalism, Employment Equity, and Globalization. Peterborough, Ontario: Broadview, 2002.

Bibby, Reginald. Mosaic Madness: The Poverty and Potential of Life in Canada. Toronto: Stoddart, 1990.

Bissoondath, Neil. Selling Illusions: The Cult of Multiculturalism in Canada. Toronto: Penguin, 1990.

Dyck, Rand. Canadian Politics: Critical Approaches. 4th ed. Toronto: Thomson Nelson, 2004.

James, Matt. Political Science 101 Lecture. University of Victoria. 25 Nov. 2004.

Kymlicka, Will. Finding Our Way: Rethinking Ethnocultural Relations in Canada. Don Mills, Ontario: Oxford UP, 1998.

Questions to Consider

Questions to consider in a critical and analytical reading of "Multiculturalism in Canada: Controversial Consequences of the Multiculturalism Act":

1. Summarize the arguments of the two sides as they are presented in the first body paragraph (paragraph 2).

2. In sharp contrast to the writer of the previous student essay, MacKillop uses direct and mixed citation to support her points, along with some paraphrase and summary. Why does she choose to use a variety of methods? What is the role and importance of direct quotation in an essay that presents two opposing views of a topic?

3. Explore the writer's credibility. Does her essay demonstrate knowledge, reliability, and fairness?

4. Explain her use of secondary sources. Do you think she uses them well (for example, is there an over-reliance on any source)? Do the sources themselves appear reliable?

5. MacKillop's essay compares and contrasts two positions on multiculturalism and the *Multiculturalism Act*. Which of the two methods for organizing compare and contrast essays does she use (Part Three, Section 2.2.1)? Are the two positions always clearly differentiated from one another?

Questions to Consider – *continued*

6. Does the first paragraph function satisfactorily as an Introduction? Does the last paragraph provide a satisfactory Conclusion? What kind of Introduction does the writer use? What kind of Conclusion? Do they work well together? (See Part Two, Sections 1 and 5).

15.3 Sample Excerpt from Student Essay (Chicago Style)

In the following 500-word excerpt, the writer, Anna-Marie Krahn, mediates a debate among classical scholars concerning the description of the Greek hero Aias's (Ajax) shield in Homer's epic poem the *Iliad*. Scholars long have pondered the existence of Mycenaean elements in the poem and have turned to the descriptions of shields in an effort to determine to what extent the poem embodies this older heroic age. The writer uses endnotes, which are set up under the heading "Notes" on the page(s) following the text of the essay. At the end of the essay under the heading "Bibliography," the writer lists secondary sources alphabetically.

Shield Descriptions in the *Iliad*: Proof of a Mycenaean Poetic Tradition?

(Excerpt)

by Anna-Marie Krahn

One theory suggests that the discrepancies in shield descriptions arise from the conflation of two different types of shields.[1] According to this theory, the large Mycenaean body shield, which seems to have been used until the end of the fourteenth century BC, provides the basis for Homer's descriptions of Aias's "tower shield." The *Iliad*'s more usual description of smaller "[bronze]-bossed" and "well-rounded" shields comes from the smaller shields that were common from the late Mycenaean period until the seventh century.[2] The body shield descriptions could have originated with Mycenaean bards and been passed down to the eighth century BC through bardic tradition. This is certainly possible since Homer, like other bards, used standard epithets and formulae that were passed from one bard to another. These elements were invented to allow poets to tell long stories without memorizing huge amounts of information word for word, or constantly having to search for new words.[3] Although poets modernized most epithets and formulae as social and political conditions changed, some, including those who describe large shields, could have originated with bards in the fourteenth century BC or even earlier. Poets seem to have kept some lines that no longer made sense to them. In one case, a line in which Hektor carries a body

---

shield is followed by a line describing the shield as if it were a later round shield (*Iliad* VI.117–8). According to T.B.L Webster, the first line is quite old, while the second line represents the failure of a later poet to visualize the situation.[4] Epithets and formulae related to Aias's and Hektor's shields could show that Homeric poetry preserves elements of a Mycenaean bardic tradition.

A more recent theory claims that apparent inconsistencies in shield descriptions are not inconsistent at all. Hans Van Wees argues that passages describing the shields of Aias and Hektor refer to a consistently described "fantasy shield" that is "round, man-sized and covered with bronze."[5] According to Van Wees, Homer found it irrelevant that such a shield would be useless for a regular human being; his protagonists are not regular humans, but heroes. Aias kills a man by throwing a gigantic rock. If he could perform such a feat, why could he not carry an oversized bronze shield? As Van Wees argues, such "superhuman strength" would simply emphasize his superior capabilities. Poets could have created this "coherent fantasy" from memories of the Mycenaean tradition of large shields or from inventing shields suitable for heroes.[6] The idea for the shields' bronze facing could have come from the smaller historical shields, which were sometimes bossed with bronze, or a poet may simply have added the bronze as a description fit for a hero, since bronze was considered valuable in the epics. Van Wees's interpretation shows that the references to larger-than-life shields are not necessarily relics of the Mycenaean past: "Its demotion from a certain instance to merely a possible one would be a serious blow to the theory of Mycenaean origins [for some Homeric elements]."[7]

Notes

1. E.S. Sherratt, "'Reading the Texts': Archaeology and the Homeric Question," *Antiquity* 64, no. 4 (1990): 810.

2. J.V. Luce, *Homer and the Heroic Age* (London: Thames and Hudson, 1975), 26.

3. Hans Van Wees, *Status Warriors: War, Violence and Society in Homer and History* (Amsterdam: J.C. Gieben, 1992), 12.

4. T.B.L. Webster, *From Mycenae to Homer* (London: Methuen & Co., 1960), 92.

5. Van Wees, *Status Warriors*, 18.

6. Ibid., 19–20.

7. Ibid., 21.

Bibliography

Luce, J.V. *Homer and the Heroic Age*. London: Thames and Hudson, 1975.

Sherratt, E.S. "'Reading the Texts': Archaeology and the Homeric Question." *Antiquity* 64, no. 4 (1990): 807–24.

Van Wees, Hans. *Status Warriors: War, Violence and Society in Homer and History*. Amsterdam: J.C. Gieben, 1992.

Webster, T.B.L. *From Mycenae to Homer*. London: Methuen & Co., 1960.

16. Reading #2 (APA Style)

Exercise

Pre-reading

1. The question in the article's title indicates the primary method of development will be comparison, and this is borne out in the abstract. What other important method of development is suggested in the abstract? Do you think that an essay as short as this one needs headings? What function do they provide? Without reading the article, determine whether the authors use the "point-by-point" or the "block" comparison method.

2. To get a sense of the nature of the topic, go to one Canadian studio site and one Hollywood studio site mentioned in the essay to gather your impressions about the appeal and comprehensiveness of the two sites (URLs are given in the essay). Jot down a few observations and compare them to the relevant paragraphs in "Canadian studio sites" and "Major Hollywood studio sites" after you have read the article. (Remember that the article was published in 2000.)

Marketing Movies on the Internet: How Does Canada Compare to the U.S.?
Adam Finn, Nicola Simpson, Stuart McFadyen, Colin Hoskins

Abstract: Canadian filmmakers have had little success competing with Hollywood in the domestic market. Canadian films do not have the marketing budgets needed for the saturation television and newspaper advertising used by the Hollywood majors. But if Canadian film producers and distributors marketed their products as effectively as their Hollywood competitors, they would be expected to be quick to take advantage of a new, relatively low-cost marketing tool that is particularly suited to reaching niche audiences, namely, the Internet. In this paper, we compare the way Canadian, Hollywood major, and U.S. independent producers and distributors use the Internet to communicate with their target audiences.

Introduction

For years, Canadian filmmakers have had little success competing with Hollywood in the domestic marketplace. Canadian films' share of Canadian box-office is only about 2% (Department of Canadian Heritage, 1998). Many scholars (e.g., Gasher, 1992; Pendakur, 1990) blame the low market share for Canadian films on Hollywood's dominance of the film distribution and theatrical exhibition market structure in Canada, the so-called "structural deficiency" paradigm (Hoskins, McFadyen, & Finn, 1998). Supporters (e.g., Globerman, 1991) of a "commercial forces" paradigm argue that Canadian distributors recognize that Canadian films lack market appeal for Canadian audiences and, in order to avoid throwing good money after bad, provide only token marketing support.

Clearly, Canadian producers and distributors, taken together, place far less relative emphasis on the marketing and promotion of Canadian films. Houle (1997) reports that even with Telefilm providing most of the funds, marketing expenditures for Canadian films were usually less than $150,000, only 6% of the average production budget of $2.5 million. This compares with North American promotion budgets for the Hollywood majors of U.S. $20 million, or 50% on top of the average U.S. $40 million production budget.

It is understandable that low-budget Canadian films lack the marketing budget needed for the saturation television and newspaper advertising that the Hollywood majors use to support the blanket roll-out of their movies. Moreover, this strategy is rarely appropriate for the niche audiences for typical Canadian films. But if Canadian film producers and distributors marketed their products as effectively as their Hollywood competitors, they would be expected to be quick to take advantage of a new, relatively low-cost marketing tool that is particularly suited to reaching niche audiences, namely, the Internet.

Marketing on the Internet

Hofacker (1999) identifies four levels of marketing activities which firms can undertake on the Internet. In the current context these can be interpreted as follows:

1. *communicating* promotional messages for conventional products and services like any other media – A film-related site could include display ads like newspapers and directory-like information on where films are playing, and provide access to movie reviews. However, the Internet can also enrich communication through interactivity, for example, by allowing the potential audience members to choose a film trailer they would like to download and view.
2. *on-line selling* of traditional products and services – A film industry site could sell physical products such as film posters, stills, toys, and other licensed items that provide revenues for filmmakers. It could also become an alternative channel for "later window" sales of videocassettes or videodiscs, which could be shipped direct to customers. Direct electronic distribution of films via the Internet is a likely future extension of this activity.
3. *providing content* as a new media service for narrower market segments than the traditional broadcast medias – For film, examples might include providing access to insider information, such as edited footage or a database of stills, and on-line interactive games involving film characters.

4.   *networking* a widely distributed population as a new service function – For film, examples might include interaction amongst members of the audience for a genre, such as an on-line science fiction film convention or chat group, or a forum for a character's fan club.

If the "structural deficiency" paradigm holds, we expect Canadian producers and distributors to actively and effectively market Canadian films by:

1.   using more sophisticated communicating, clearly targeting niche audiences;
2.   making relatively less use of on-line selling, as niche products lack the mass market promotion needed to generate profitable interest in licensed product, etc.; and
3.   making relatively greater use of networking, because of its greater potential value for a thinly distributed niche audience, compared with a mass audience.

This paper compares the Web sites of Canadian film distributors with those of Hollywood studios to determine whether their use of the Internet demonstrates the effective marketing that is consistent with the "structural deficiency" paradigm. Sites were examined in Summer 1998, and then revisited in January 1999 and in June 2000. While the studios invariably make and distribute television programs, our examination focused on feature films.

Canadian studio sites

The 2000 edition of the Alliance Atlantis Web site (URL: http://www.allianceatlantis.com) shows the company is making greater efforts to reach audiences and offer interactive marketing features. First, an on-line "Studio Store" now offers retail merchandise such as Alliance Atlantis-logo clothing, books, and other paraphernalia, but these relate to popular Atlantis television shows. The most visible merchandise is videocassettes and DVDs of popular Hollywood films that Alliance distributes in Canada (URL: http://www.allianceatlantis video.com). Second, "Web Cinema" now offers contests for Alliance releases and entrance to popular movie Web sites, such as the highly anticipated *Lord of the Rings*. These two new features are marked improvements in on-line selling and niche marketing. However, Canadian films are unlikely to benefit greatly from this on-line marketing, as Alliance Atlantis does little for Canadian productions. Individual Alliance Atlantis films do not have their own Internet presence, or at least no links are provided from the main studio site. There continue to be no links to other Canadian film Web sites or to partner Web sites (such as Miramax), no content provision, and no networking features.

The Lions Gate Films Web site (URL: http://www.lionsgatefilms.com) in June 2000 shows more effort to market films effectively and to provide content to audiences, despite its lack of on-line selling, content provision, or networking in 1998. The site is visually appealing and focuses on the films, not the company. A collage of stills from current Lions Gate releases adorns the main page, and offers links to individual sites for these films. Lions Gate has chosen to use a new domain name based on the title for each new film it is promoting (e.g., URL: http://www.americanpsycho.com) This means that audiences who only know the film's title can access its Web site and, from there, surf to the Lions Gate site to peruse other products.

Amongst other formerly important Canadian distributors, Cineplex-Odeon and Astral Films do not have corporate Web sites (though Astral Media's site is located at URL: http://www.astral.com), while Malofilm and Cinephile have disappeared due to bankruptcy.

Major Hollywood studio sites

Columbia/Tri-Star's Web site can be accessed through its parent company, Sony (URL: http://www.sony.com or http://www.spe.sony.com for Sony Pictures Entertainment). The 1998 Columbia/Tri-Star site was colourful and well laid out, but the text was often very small and the frames format sometimes made manoeuvring difficult. By June 2000, the site had undergone major renovations. It now offers more interactive features than before. It is very successful in providing all four of Hofacker's marketing functions to audiences, and takes full advantage of the unique interactive environment. Content does not simply mirror print and television advertising, and networking is encouraged within the site (through chat boards, contests, etc.).

Disney's Web site (URL: http://www.disney.go.com) in 1998 and in 2000 continues to target children and their parents as the main consumers. The emphasis on the children's market is not limited to design and content; there are no immediately visible links to Touchstone, Hollywood Pictures, Buena Vista, ABC, or other Disney entities that produce entertainment for more mature audiences. Though the site effectively targets the younger market that the company is famous for tapping into, as a movie marketing tool the Disney Web site could be described as somewhat limited in scope, and does not effectively promote Disney products/services to a wide audience.

For Metro-Goldwyn-Mayer and United Artists (MGM/UA) (URL: http://www.mgm.com) in 1998 the visitor could choose to visit the "regular" site or the Java Script site (with enhanced graphics). This showed an early recognition of consumer differences; not every Internet user has a high-speed computer or advanced Web browser. As a promotional tool, MGM Online in 1998 provided a clearinghouse of information rather than encouraging real interactivity with the consumer. In June 2000, it appears that MGM is striving to do more on-line selling and promoting of products already guaranteed an audience (such as entries in the James Bond franchise).

The Paramount site (URL: http://www.paramount.com) in 1998, though informational and easily navigable, did not encourage a great deal of consumer interactivity with the exception of the trivia game. Significant additions to the site in 2000 promote networking in the form of a prominently featured chat/BBS link (including "chats" with stars from popular Paramount television shows) as well as interactive promotions in the form of contests and quizzes.

In 1998 the Twentieth Century Fox Web site (URL: http://www.fox.com) appeared initially similar to that of Paramount and Columbia/Tri-Star but became much more complex as the visitor navigated further into the site. The first noticeable change in the June 2000 version is the animated promotion of a Fox television program before the visitor even accesses the index page. Now focusing almost entirely on promotion of the Fox television network, the most prominent features of the site are pictures and links to Fox programming and contests. The July 2000 edition of Fox Movies only offers links to individual Web sites for current Fox releases and a link to "Fox Auction"; there are no other links. This evolution is a little disappointing. The 1998 version seemed to make greater efforts to reach audiences with original content and interesting promotional items (such as the downloadable press kits). In order to get any detailed information or promotional material on Fox products, visitors are now forced to leave the main Web site, which may not help cement brand identification.

Universal's Web site (URL: http://www.mca.com or http://www.universalstudios.com), like MGM's, gave visitors the initial option of a "full graphics" or "quick access" site in 1998. The links were numerous and comprehensive, but the initial site had no separate promotion of current or upcoming feature films, and the promotional links were skewed towards multimedia products and overall studio public relations. Although the Universal site was a good marketing tool, it was deceptively shallow and offered little real information about upcoming releases. In June 2000, the technological demands of the Universal site had diminished – no more plug-ins are required to access the graphics or main sections. The index page now promotes Universal films (at least one current or upcoming release), but the "Movies" site has not changed in its basic design. Pages such as "Shop," "Win Prizes," and "Cool Sites" make use of on-line selling and networking features, but the Universal site overall remains fragmented and not as effective as it could be in promoting the company's feature film products.

According to Media Metrix and RelevantKnowledge, Warner Bros. Online (WB Online; URL: http://www.warnerbros.com) was consistently in the top three most-visited studio sites on the Web in 1998. Also, WB Online was ranked the number two site on the Web in concentration of women aged 18–49, a demographic group highly valued by advertisers ("Warner Bros. Online's...," 1998), Though the site's basic design has changed in June 2000, it maintains a high level of interactivity and unique content. The main site offers more content than the 1998 version, but allows easy access to subpages for specific WB products. Networking features include chats, bulletin boards, WeB cards, and ACME City. The WeB cards are on-line greeting cards that feature Warner Bros. cartoon and television characters, and may be a very effective way to entice new visitors to the site. ACME City is another new feature, which gives the users up to 20MB of free Web hosting space with which to create their own sites featuring their favourite WB television shows, music, movies, or DC comic books. ACME City is significant because it is a positive reaction to the popularity of unlicensed fan Web sites, and it allows the studio to promote fan sites within their own legal space. Other studios have simply dealt with the copyright infringement of some fan sites by threatening legal action; Warner Bros.'s ACME City is a terrific compromise and costs the studio little in transactional or site construction costs. Another unique feature of WB Online is the Web-casting of celebrity-studded premieres of its films, so that the viewer can watch their favourite stars arrive on the red carpet. This is a highly effective way of bringing people to the site, despite its demand for high-speed connections and technological savvy with which to navigate.

Warner Bros. is still the leader in providing unique and sophisticated content, networking, and communicating experiences in major Hollywood studio Web sites.

U.S. independent studio sites

New Line Cinema's Web site (URL: http://www.newline.com) in 1998 encouraged little interaction with the user. Much of the material was out of date and there was little lead-in material for upcoming films of interest. Some additions and design changes in the 2000 version make the site more appealing to visitors. For example, a trivia game and the on-line auction of memorabilia from New Line movies shows an effort towards giving visitors a different experience than traditional print or television advertising. With the surge in popularity of on-line auction sites (such as eBay), studios would be expected to anticipate greater demand for these services, and may provide them on their own sites.

Between July 1998 and June 2000, Miramax's Web site (URL: http://www.miramax.com) dubbed the "Miramax Cafe," has not changed at all in design or features. It remains design heavy with numerous text and iconic links, which are closely packed and sometimes difficult to distinguish from advertising. This page is a better marketing tool than that of New Line Cinema, with more contests and interactive opportunities (e.g., one can become a "member" of the Miramax Cafe). Within each separate movie page are "about" sections and "download" sections. However, it is difficult to return to the main site once the visitor has left it and the visitor has to click on "back" several times before the shift occurs.

Comparison of Canadian and U.S. studio sites

Table 1 summarizes the communication characteristics of these sites in January 1999 and June 2000. It is clear that the Canadian distributors have not fully exploited this new marketing channel. Moreover, Canadian sites have not been employed in ways consistent with the "structural deficiency" paradigm. Canadian distributors do not engage in more sophisticated communication targeting niche audiences. They do not make relatively greater use of networking to better reach an audience thinly distributed over a wide area, compared with a mass audience. They do attempt less on-line selling, but this does not seem to be due to the audience targeted, but rather to a lack of audience. Where Canadian distributors are attempting on-line selling, it is for Hollywood products.

Table 1: Summary of Film Company Web Site Characteristics

Distributors	Communicating Traditional		Communicating Interactive		On-line Selling Films		On-line Selling Other		Providing Content		Providing Chat		Networking Other	
	1999	2000	1999	2000	1999	2000	1999	2000	1999	2000	1999	2000	1999	2000
Canadian														
Alliance	Yes	Yes	No	Yes	Yes	Yes	No	Yes	No	No	No	No	No	No
Lions Gate	Yes	Yes	Yes	Yes	No	Yes	No	No	No	Yes	No	No	No	No
Hollywood														
Columbia/Tri-Star	Yes	Yes	Yes	Yes	Yes	Yes	Yes	Yes	No	Yes	No	Yes	No	Yes
Disney	Yes	Yes	Yes	Yes	Yes	Yes	Yes	Yes	No	Yes	No	Yes	No	Yes
MGM/UA	Yes	Yes	Yes	Yes	Yes	Yes	Yes	Yes	Yes	Yes	No	Yes	No	Yes
Paramount	Yes	Yes	Yes	Yes	Yes	Yes	Yes	Yes	No	Yes	Yes	Yes	No	Yes
20th Century Fox	Yes	Yes	Yes	Yes	Yes	Yes	Yes	Yes	Yes	Yes	No	Yes	Yes	Yes
Universal	Yes	Yes	Yes	Yes	Yes	Yes	Yes	Yes	No	Yes	No	Yes	Yes	Yes
Warner Bros.	Yes	Yes	Yes	Yes	Yes	Yes	Yes	Yes	Yes	Yes	Yes	Yes	Yes	Yes
U.S. Independent														
Miramax	Yes	Yes	Yes	Yes	Yes	Yes	Yes	Yes	No	No	Yes	Yes	Yes	Yes
New Line	Yes	Yes	Yes	Yes	Yes	Yes	Yes	Yes	No	No	No	No	No	Yes

The U.S. majors use their sites as marketing/promotional tools that emphasize items of interest to moviegoers. The Columbia/Tri-Star, Fox, and Warner Bros. sites encourage interactivity and are particularly effective. While the New Line and Miramax sites are less effective, they do target moviegoers rather than investors. In contrast, the Alliance site still appears aimed at investors. The "motion picture" section of the site has little for the average moviegoer. Alliance has enjoyed a box-office share that puts it in the same league as the Canadian distribution arms of the U.S. majors. Yet it offers little effective marketing content on the Alliance site; it has changed very little over the last two years. The Lions Gate site works better, but it still lacks higher level communication characteristics and links to other film-related sites. Cineplex Odeon's site (URL: http://www.cineplexodeon.com) provides interesting content (such as trailers) and links to movie sites, but it is an (American-owned) exhibitor, not a Canadian distributor of Canadian product.

Marketing movies on the Internet in 2000

The success of *The Blair Witch Project*, with 56 million people visiting its site within months of the film's release (Graser & Hayes, 2000), suggests that on-line marketing campaigns will work best for films that target a technologically literate demographic—young males who like horror, science fiction, and action films. Internet marketing makes up 3–5% of overall promotional budgets (Graser & Hayes, 2000). That means a Hollywood movie's Web site could cost up to $1.5 million—a huge jump from the $20,000 budgeted a few years ago, and 10 times the entire marketing budget for the average Canadian film.

Downloadable trailers are an effective way to build buzz for a picture far in advance of its release. The Internet trailer for *Star Wars Episode I: The Phantom Menace* was downloaded 3.5 million times within the first five days of its appearance on the Internet. The trailer for *Lord of the Rings* was downloaded 1.7 million times in the first day (Morris, 2000).

Conclusion

The World Wide Web is an important new vehicle for the promotion of feature films for the Hollywood studios. Their Web communication has moved well beyond traditional advertising to interactive features, such as on-line selling, provision for fan networking, and even providing new forms of content. Major feature film projects now include the development of interactive CD-ROM and digital products, not just promotional lunchboxes, toys, and T-shirts. Studios now plan for the interactive market when developing a project, not just as a cross-promotional tool after film completion.

Canadian producers and distributors had the same opportunity. If the "structural deficiency" paradigm held, we would expect to see Canadians make more use of sophisticated communication and of networking, while engaging in less on-line selling. However, only the latter is true. While Canadian studios have made efforts, they lag behind both the Hollywood studios and the U.S. independents in this new form of communication, demonstrating no evidence of confidence in even the niche market potential of Canadian films. This lack of confidence is cemented by what on-line selling is available – the products most promoted are American films, not Canadian. There is a preponderance of investor information and a relative lack of material attractive to the average moviegoer. Thus, our results provide support for the "commercial forces" paradigm rather than for the "structural deficiency" paradigm. Canadian producers' and distributors' assessment of the commercial appeal of Canadian films has led them to minimize marketing expenditures including Internet communication. If they believed Canadian movies had market appeal, it would be shortsighted not to invest in sites and the technology to communicate with their niche audiences. Weak Internet marketing provides more evidence of their lack of faith in the commercial viability of Canadian films.

Acknowledgement

The authors wish to acknowledge the financial support provided by a Social Sciences and Humanities Research Council grant to three of the authors.

References

Department of Canadian Heritage. (1998, February). *A review of Canadian feature film policy.* Discussion paper. Ottawa: DCH.

Gasher, Mike. (1992). The myth of meritocracy: Ignoring the political economy of the Canadian film industry. *Canadian Journal of Communication, 17*(3), 371–378.

Globerman, Steven. (1991). Foreign ownership of feature film distribution and the Canadian film industry, *Canadian Journal of Communication, 16*(2), 191–206.

Graser, Marc, & Hayes, Dade. (2000, March 2). "Witch" hunting: Studios fail to match "Blair" flair on 'Net. *Variety*, p. A1.

Hofacker, Charles F. (1999). *Internet marketing*, Dripping Springs, TX: Digital Springs.

Hoskins, Colin, McFadyen, Stuart, & Finn, Adam. (1998, June). *Distribution problems in the marketing of Canadian feature films.* Paper presented to the Tenth International Conference on Cultural Economics, Barcelona, Spain.

Houle, M. (1997, July). *Report on the production and distribution of Canadian films.* Report prepared for Telefilm Canada.

Morris, Mark. (2000, May 10). The big picture. *The Guardian.* URL: http://www.guardian unlimited.co.uk/Archive/Article/0,4273,4016474,00.html

Pendakur, M. (1990). *Canadian dreams and American control: The political economy of the Canadian film industry,* Toronto: Garamond.

Warner Bros. Online's Entertaindom channel creates co-branded site with the Internet Movie Database: Warner Bros. Online presents the most comprehensive film reference available on the World Wide Web. (1998, April 6). *PR Newswire.*

Reading for Content:

1. In the "Introduction," two "paradigms" are briefly defined. Paraphrase what is meant by the "structural deficiency" paradigm and the "commercial forces" paradigm. (See Section 8.5)

2. What is a "niche audience" ("Introduction," par. 3)?

Critical and Analytical Reading:

1. The authors don't explicitly state why they include U.S. independent studio sites in the comparisons. Why do you think these sites are included?

2. What is the reason for including Hofacker's "four levels of marketing activities" ("Marketing on the Internet," par. 1) before comparing the studio sites?

3. Why do the authors choose to test the validity of the "structural deficiency" paradigm and not the "commercial forces" paradigm? Specifically, what would the authors expect to find if the "structural deficiency" paradigm accurately accounts for Canadian marketing of movies? What inference do the authors draw from the results of the comparisons?

4. Although the authors strive for objectivity in their study, what comments suggest that argument is at least slightly involved? See in particular "Major Hollywood studio sites," pars. 4 and 6).

After reading:

Write a short response based on the concluding sentence: "Weak Internet marketing provides more evidence of [Canadian producers' and distributors'] lack of faith in the commercial viability of Canadian films." Consider how the phrase "lack of faith" might apply to any aspect of Canadian culture (not necessarily movies) that competes with U.S. culture.

PART SIX

The Literary Essay

1. Common Ground
2. Literature as a Unique Encounter
3. Kinds of Literary Essays
4. Text-Centred and Context-Centred Approaches
5. Evaluating Student Essays
6. On the Road to the Rough Draft
7. When You Write about Literature
8. Theory into Practice: A Sample Poetry Analysis
9. The Literary Genres: Poetry, the Short Story, the Novel, and Drama
10. How to Approach the Poem
11. Fiction Forms
12. The Short Story
13. The Novel Tradition
14. How to Approach Fiction
15. How to Approach Drama
16. The Literary Research Essay
17. Reading #3 (MLA Style): "The Urban Working Girl . . ."
18. A Brief Glossary of Literary Terms

1. Common Ground

In today's diverse literature classes, you might study poems, short stories, plays, novels, biographies, autobiographies, journals, diaries, songs, myths, or movies. The close relationship between the works you read (or view) and your writing is a defining feature of literature classes.

Although literary essays have unique characteristics, they have features in common with other kinds of essays you have written or will write. In its structure, the literary essay is like an argumentative or expository essay. It begins with an introduction that contains a thesis statement, includes several well-developed body paragraphs, and ends by summarizing your main points and reiterating your thesis. Attention to grammar, punctuation, and mechanics is important. You will also need to pay close attention to diction (word choice), syntax (word order), and sentence structure. In sum, you will need to give as much thought to clarity, coherence, and concision as you do with other essays.

A literary essay argues for the validity of a claim. You will need to adopt a specific viewpoint to the work(s) you analyze and express this in your thesis statement. The claim you make will not be one of fact or policy or value (unless you are evaluating a work as you would in a book report); rather, it will be one of interpretation. In the body paragraphs, much of the supporting evidence for your claim will come from the primary text(s) you are analyzing. You will support your points also through researching the authorities on your text, i.e., through secondary sources.

2. Literature as a Unique Encounter

In responding to a literary work, you are expected to acknowledge a long-established tradition—a kind of tacit agreement between writer and reader—to "willingly suspend your disbelief." In other words, we agree to treat the events that occur in a novel, play, or poem as something that *really could have occurred* to people like us. Although in 1817 poet Samuel Taylor Coleridge applied the phrase "willing suspension of disbelief" to his own poetry, today the phrase still is used to explain the foundation on which we become receptive to works of fiction.

In reading literature, you will experience feelings evoked by a poem, by the thoughts or behaviour of a character in a novel or play, or by a significant moment in the life of a character in a short story. One of the reasons for studying literature is to learn a more complex response. When you write an essay about the work, you will focus both on the particular and specific, as well as on the universal qualities of the work. By learning to particularize—exploring what is unique about a character, setting, situation, or condition—and by learning to synthesize and to recognize universals in counterpoint to particulars—you are recognizing or making meaning and you are creating significance.

The American poet Emily Dickinson once described the experience of reading good poetry: "If I feel physically as if the top of my head were taken off, I know *that* is poetry." Responding to good literature can be a physical experience. Sometimes you feel as though you were at the mercy of two gravitational forces, one pulling you towards the familiar and the specific, the other tugging you towards the unfamiliar and the abstract or universal.

You should refer to a work's **meaning** or its **theme**, rather than its *message*, which implies a direct ideological focus. Literary works seldom are written with the *explicit* goal of getting across a message.

Many of the challenges of writing about literature are related to the practices and procedures of literary analysis. Unless you are writing a personal response to a work, you will need to be familiar with the terminology used in analyzing literature. As with other disciplines, a vocabulary and a methodology have developed over the millennia enabling those who analyze literary texts to converse in a specialized—though certainly not a privileged—linguistic environment.

As is often not the case with students studying younger disciplines, like psychology, anthropology, or women's studies, for the first time, many students of literature already are acquainted with the rudiments of this vocabulary and with the essential practices of literary interpretation through English courses in high school or, perhaps, through discussions with family or friends of stories, poems, or novels. Most students also are familiar with current movies, which, of course, have plots, settings, characters, and themes similar to those of literary texts. Studying literary works, then, is not so much a question of learning an entirely new category of discourse as of expanding and refining what you know to adapt to the more sophisticated analyses you will do at the post-secondary level.

3. Kinds of Literary Essays

Although the kinds of assignments will vary considerably from instructor to instructor, generally literary essays are expected to be one of three types: a response, an evaluation of a work, or a literary or critical analysis.

3.1 Response

A **response**, such as a journal entry, is concerned with your personal or "gut" reaction to a work: the ways it affects you or makes you feel, or the ways it leads you to reflect on your own attitudes, values, or life experiences. You could be asked to keep a record of your responses to various works you study throughout the term. Although such assignments may not be a required component of a course, they can still be worthwhile. When you have to choose a topic to write on, looking back at your personal responses can remind you what interested you or what you enjoyed most— where your motivations lie—and perhaps provide a starting point for a more complex analysis.

For example, a student responded to a poem about an elderly woman knitting ("Aunt Jennifer's Tigers," by Adrienne Rich) by recalling his feelings about his grandmother, and the security and comfort he felt when around her. Asked to analyze the poem for an assignment, the student returned to his journal entry and, beginning with the feeling that the poem had first evoked, began to explore its ironies and complexities; this led him far beyond his first response to develop a thesis statement related to the traditional roles of women and their creative outlets in a patriarchal society.

3.2 Evaluation

Although **evaluations** often have a subjective element, they should use primarily objective criteria to judge the quality of a work. Because a successful evaluation is based largely on *informed* opinion, it is necessary to support the claims you make about the work's worth or relevance. This can be done by referring directly to the work as well as by basing your comments on such accepted standards for assessing a work's achievement as plausibility, quality of writing, originality, or universal appeal. In an evaluation, the focus is on the work's meaning and its significance to the reader. It attempts to answer the questions, *What is the importance of this book? How is it like or unlike other works? Should I recommend this work?* In answering these questions you will be concerned more with the "what" than with the "how." An evaluation is usually shorter than an analysis and deals much less with technique. The most common form of an evaluative essay is a book report.

While a response implies a highly personalized engagement with the work, an evaluation typically is written for many readers, usually for people who have not read the work. Because successful evaluations may tread a fine line between opinion and analysis, they fulfill a function between highly personal responses and objective literary analysis.

3.3 Literary or Critical Analysis

Literary or critical analysis is writing directed to the knowledgeable reader. Critical analyses are concerned with the writer's technique—the strategies and methods a writer uses to create the work—and are comparable to the analytical level in 3-D Reading (Part One, Section 3). A critical analysis might show how figurative language contributes to the interpretation of a work, how imagery contributes to a work's mood, or how the first-person voice enables us to identify with the narrator. The aim of analysis is to support a claim about some aspect of the work. Like an evaluation of a work, a critical analysis comes round to its theme, but it will get there via a more complex route, giving us a more technical, multi-layered understanding of the work. Because an analysis is objective, you should avoid the use of quantitative words like "great" or "amazing"; in most analyses, you should avoid first-person references entirely: "I believe. . . ," "I will show . . . ," "it seems to me . . . ."

In a literary analysis you support your thesis statement in part by citing what others have said about the work. In a literary research essay, you try to use reviews, commentaries, articles, and books that analyze the same work you are analyzing and whose approaches are similar to your own. You may also consider approaches to the primary text that are different from yours in order to broaden your own approach or argue against these approaches. As in all essays involving research, you will be concerned with integrating your own ideas and language with the ideas and language of others.

4. Text-Centred and Context-Centred Approaches

Two of the most common approaches to a literary analysis are text-centred and context-centred approaches.

1. A text-centred approach involves a close, detailed reading[1] of the work, treating it as a self-sufficient entity. A text-centred approach could explore a work's structure and the way that the parts function separately yet form a whole, or it could analyze the techniques that the writer uses in one or more isolated passages and relate them to a specific claim about the work.

2. A context-centred approach pays careful attention to the text but is as much concerned with its relation to the bigger picture. It views the work within an established context of some kind: historical, biographical, ideological/political, aesthetic, sociological, cultural, psychological, feminist, mythic, or sources-based. Context-centred approaches could also refer to a theoretical model and analyze the work within its framework. Although text-centred approaches may or may not need to be bolstered by secondary sources, context-centred approaches likely will refer to important work(s) in the field.

The text-centred and the context-centred approaches are discussed in detail below. The three complete essays in this section illustrate these different approaches: the essay on "Stopping by Woods on a Snowy Evening" (Section 6) and the student-essay on "Metamorphosis" (Section 11.4) illustrate the former; the student-essay on "The Yellow Wallpaper" and "My Papa's Waltz" (Section 17.3) is a research paper that combines text- and context-centred approaches.

5. Evaluating Student Essays

Take a moment to consider the following objections frequently heard from students:

"There aren't really any objective criteria for grading a literary essay!"
"I can say whatever I want as long as I back it up!"
"There seems to be one reading of a work—and it's the prof's!"

For the most part, instructors do arrive at grades using objective standards, even if these standards are not clear to the student and are not comparable to those in disciplines where there are right or wrong answers. Some readings of texts are superior to others. It is the purpose of this text to help you to assess the characteristics of excellence. Although the grading of an English essay may not be as straightforward as in disciplines where knowledge can be quantified or where compilation is a goal, nonetheless literary standards can be defined. Three standards that pertain to your use of primary texts are discussed in the sidebars, pp. 243–4.

The 3 C's of Criticism; or, How *Not* to Get a "C" on Your Essay
The best readings of a work are those that demonstrate coherence, consistency, and complexity using the tools you are given to analyze works of literature.

It is essential that you support your points by referring directly to the literary work itself, but that alone may not be sufficient support for a point. To ensure that you have used the text logically and effectively, and to persuade the reader that you have, you must show that your reference is representative and relevant.

Representative and relevant references clearly illustrate the point you are trying to make. In the first example below, the writer has not provided a strong enough context for the quotation; in the second, the quotation does not bear out the claim the writer makes for it.

---

1 "Reading" is a term that can refer to the cognitive act of processing words (the familiar sense of reading a book). It is also used to refer to the perhaps more analytical process of interpreting a literary work's meaning.

Coherence: the reading makes sense; the points are clearly made, are well expressed, and can be followed easily by a reader. *Consistency*: the reading contains no apparent contradictions nor is one aspect of the whole given greater prominence at the expense of other equally important elements; it takes into account the entire work. Inconsistent readings may result when the writer seizes on an isolated element, such as a particular image, and builds a reading around it. *Complexity*: the reading is not superficial or simplistic but is detailed and multidimensional, within such guidelines prescribed by your teacher as length in words.

A.

> In Dickinson's "Because I could not stop for Death," adulthood is depicted in the line, "The Dews drew quivering and chill."

How, specifically, does the line depict adulthood? The statement needs elaboration:

> In Dickinson's "Because I could not stop for Death" the poet's metaphor for life is a carriage ride that passes through childhood, passes fecund life in the image of "Fields of Gazing Grain," and arrives, after the sunset of life ("We passed the Setting Sun"), at an age in adulthood where the falling of the dew draws from the body quivering and awareness of chill: "The Dews drew quivering and chill."

B.

> The longer that the narrator is confined to the room the more obsessed with the yellow wallpaper she becomes: "It makes me tired to follow [the pattern]."

The quotation intended to illustrate her obsession reveals only her weariness.

A work's meaning is a function of the complex interplay of many factors. Unlike a didactic work (one with a clear message), literary works do not always have a fixed, determinate meaning; instead, they may offer numerous, but certainly *not limitless*, possible readings.

Insight and originality also are important, but should be incorporated into an analysis of a work that is coherent, consistent, and complex. These three factors pertain to your reading and handling of the primary work. Obviously, other factors will have a bearing on your grade, such as whether you wrote on topic or strayed from it, or whether you gave equal consideration to all the texts relevant to your subject. Furthermore, paragraphing, grammar, punctuation, sentence structure, appropriate level of language, and mechanics of form and presentation will be determining factors, as they are in all essays you write. If you conducted research for your essay, your effective use of secondary sources and correct documentation methods will also contribute to a good grade.

6. On the Road to the Rough Draft

Although there are many ways to proceed to explore the meaning of a literary work, having some guiding principles in mind can be useful. What follows is a step-by-step approach to analysis, but you can go about the steps in any order you wish or omit certain steps. You are always the best judge of your own best method.

You may be assigned a specific topic to write on, you may be given a list of topics from which to choose, or you could be asked to come up with a topic based on classroom lectures, class or group discussions, or your own interests. The guidance given in Part One, Sections 3, 4, and 5 can help you in the choice of a topic as well as guide you through the initial stages of thinking about a topic—typically, the most difficult stage for many writers—and in developing the topic from a rough formulation to the outline and draft stages. To review those steps briefly:

6.1 Method for Developing an Outline or Draft

1. *Read and re-read* the work without preconceptions.

2. *Commit your thoughts and feelings to writing* if necessary to give you confidence when it comes to the more formal stages of the analysis. If you have been keeping a response journal, review it and supplement it with fresh perceptions or expand on what you wrote about earlier.

3. *Consolidate your impressions of the work.* Ask the kind of questions referred to in the "How to Approach the Poem/Fiction/Drama" sections that follow to help you formulate a tentative thesis statement. If you don't think you have firmly grasped the content of the work, try paraphrasing or summarizing it. In novels, plays, long poems, and even short stories, you might construct a section-by-section, chapter-by-chapter, or scene-by-scene breakdown, clarifying precisely what happens to whom when and where, but also so that you can locate important textual references later on.

4. Briefly consider information about the author, the age he or she lived in, nationality, philosophy, beliefs, or other works he or she has written. Review your class notes about the writer and the work(s). Briefly review some commentary—even article titles can be useful—or peruse chat rooms and on-line discussion groups to consider how others have approached the work.

5. Remember that your task as a student writer is *not* to say everything you know or that might be said by an expert about a text or to consider every important detail. *Selection* is expected. Therefore, try to focus on *one or a limited number of important areas*—for example, structure, point of view, imagery, tone, mood, symbolism—whichever seem important. As you proceed to analyze, you may find yourself exploring more of these areas, but, for now, choosing one or two areas can help you focus on a possible thesis statement.

6. *Make connections and find patterns to formulate a thesis statement.* Looking for connections and patterns in a work of poetry, drama, or literary prose is the way to work towards a reading that is coherent, consistent, and complex. Literary conventions, such as structure and organization, imagery, poetic devices, locales and settings, points of view, treatments of historical connections, consciousness of philosophical issues, to mention a few, suggest many patterns through which a work can be explored. Explaining the connections and patterns you have found in terms of the specific literary conventions is what is meant by analyzing that work.

   For example, if you find a striking image in a work, see if you can find similar images; once you find a pattern of such images, describe the connections to the character(s) or structure or location or ideas in the work; now you are well on your way to explaining the patterns of these images in terms of the work as a whole. Next, you should be able to write a tentative sentence or two that includes the main point/theme of the work that is related to the main point/theme that you want to focus on for your analysis.

7. Although your personal responsiveness might have been important in your early reading and thinking about a work, it is now time to step back, to *make the transition from personal feelings and associations to objective, critical analysis.*

8. Do your research.
   A. Decide on a method of organized note-taking. See Part Five, Sections 6.2 and 6.3 for help with research note-taking.

B. Don't worry too much if your language isn't keeping pace with your ideas at this point. Finding the right words, or even the best *terminology,* for critical analysis is less important than getting your ideas down. Precise and/or correct word choice, style, and grammar can follow. It is important, though, that you jot down examples and page references as you write; often, just the page, paragraph, or line number is sufficient.

    Move from the general to the specific; moving back and forth as required, from concept to detail, from the large-scale to the small-scale, and from general claims to textual references, may help strengthen and support your points and weave the wording of your first draft even as you assemble an outline.

C. Continually test your points against your thesis. Work towards expanding points that support and enhance your thesis, but don't necessarily discard what seem to be valid and important points that don't directly support your thesis; the main point of your analysis may be flexible enough for you to amend or expand it.

D. Technique is the means by which the poet, the dramatist, or the writer of fiction expresses his or her artistic vision. Therefore, your literary analysis should include a consideration of the kinds of devices the writer has used. The technical aspects of the text you are analyzing will vary according to:

1. The genre you are analyzing—for example, a poem *may* (but will not always) rely more on stylistic and figurative devices than other genres do; fiction writers rely on specific structural devices and narrative techniques.

2. The formal properties (conventions) of a tradition to which the work belongs (the sonnet, elegy, ode, or initiation story, for example). Texts within a tradition can be explored in part through the conventions of the tradition, which the author may follow closely, disrupt, or adapt to suit his or her purposes.

3. The topic you have been given; you may be required to write on imagery, setting, point of view, or dramatic structure.

9. You may now have enough information to begin constructing an essay outline or a first draft. Since much of your support likely will come from the primary work itself, sometimes just a scratch outline with page numbers from the literary work beside your main points is all the structure you need, though formal outlines are usually very helpful. (See Part One, Section 5.3.)

7. When You Write about Literature

A. Avoid telling what happens in the work; assume your reader knows the work and has read it recently. Give as much information about plot, character, and setting as necessary to provide an adequate context for the point you are making. A summary is not the same thing as an analysis; summarizing too much wastes space.

B. When you refer to the text, *use the present tense* to describe action and character; this is known as the **literary present**. This convention applies generally to the arts. For example, if you were looking at Leonardo DaVinci's *Mona Lisa*, you would say that she *has* an enigmatic smile on her face. Remember, however, that though the work is considered timeless, the author *lived and wrote* at a specific time. The following passage, from a student essay on Ted Hughes's poem "Hawk Roosting," illustrates the way that the literary present is used to represent the actions in the poem and their textual significance. In the last two sentences, Darcy Smith uses the past tense to depict actions in the past outside of the poem.

> The hawk's flight "direct / Through the bones of the living" *is* a particularly sinister image, reinforcing the hawk's vision that he *controls* all life. All these images *project* a sense of divine, or more likely demonic, power. The imagery in the last stanza *suggests* how the hawk's egotism *represents* human nature. In the first line of this stanza, the hawk *observes* "The sun is behind me." The sun *was considered* a god by many ancient civilizations. Ancient Egyptian pharaohs, for instance, *claimed* their divine right to rule *originated* in being descended from the sun.

C. Use the present tense, also, to refer to the words of critics: "Levin *claims* . . . ."

8. Theory into Practice: A Sample Poetry Analysis

Frost's poem is often included in poetry anthologies as an object of critical analysis. You may want to look at Section 10 below "How to Approach a Poem" before reading the analysis here.

Assignment: The *assignment* was to write a 500–700-word textual analysis of "Stopping by Woods on a Snowy Evening." A textual analysis focuses largely on the text itself, paying attention to the poet's technique and the relations between techniques and theme.

Stopping by Woods on a Snowy Evening
by Robert Frost

Whose woods these are I think I know.	˘ / ˘ / ˘ / ˘ /	**a**
His house is in the village though;	˘ / ˘ / ˘ / ˘ /	**a**
He will not see me stopping here	˘ / ˘ / ˘ / ˘ /	**b**
To watch his woods fill up with snow.	˘ / ˘ / ˘ / ˘ /	**a**

My little horse must think it queer
To stop without a farmhouse near
Between the woods and frozen lake
The darkest evening of the year.

He gives his harness bells a shake
To ask if there is some mistake.
The only other sound's the sweep
Of easy wind and downy flake.

The woods are lovely, dark and deep.
But I have promises to keep,
And miles to go before I sleep,
And miles to go before I sleep.

Preliminary Considerations: "Stopping by Woods on a Snowy Evening" presents particular challenges to the student writer: its simplicity is deceptive. When you read it over (especially if aloud), you might find its simplicity appealing, its regularity captivating, or you might find it a boring poem and wonder how you will be able to write so many words about it. You could begin by asking questions about the poem, first to record your impressions and then to consolidate them, to discover patterns from which you can formulate a tentative thesis statement.

What first strikes you about the poem? Perhaps its regularity strikes you. The structure of the poem consists of three four-line stanzas with an identical rhyme scheme and a fourth stanza with identical end-rhymes. In creating the poem, the poet has imposed a strict formal pattern on the poem: stanza length, rhyme, metre are regular and predictable.

What actually is happening in the poem? Remarkably little is occurring. Surprisingly, there is as much about the poet's horse as there is about the poet himself, who seems lost in his thoughts, having fallen into a kind of trance as he looks into the woods. The poet is portraying an everyday kind of experience. Its ordinariness is noteworthy, though. Most readers at one time or another will have experienced a similar feeling to the poet's: being momentarily arrested by a strong, perhaps undefined or untranslatable feeling on their way somewhere or while performing some worldly task. This might be a good place to begin exploring the poem.

If you chose to begin your analysis this way, your notes about the poem might attempt to connect the experience that the poem's speaker is describing with similar experiences you've had. Perhaps you are daydreaming now as you succumb to thoughts about something other than the poem. If so, it might be useful to write down associations with daydreaming or perhaps to freewrite on the topic. *What one main area should you focus on?* Rather than being overwhelmed by possibilities at this stage, you should try to narrow your focus. In the poem, an act of contemplation seems important. Since contemplative thought may involve a mood, one area to explore might be the mood the poem evokes. Mood can be defined as the predominant tone of the poem created by the poet's language or approach to character and/or setting. To develop this theme, you might want to focus on the way that language and setting combine to evoke a tone of solemnity. Remember, you can always return to the thesis statement and refine it later—or even radically change it if you need to.

Tentative thesis statement: *The speaker draws the reader into the poem by creating, through simple rhythms, diction, and the device of repetition, a familiar mood of solemnity while contemplating something mysterious or enticing.* This probably wouldn't serve as the final version of a thesis statement; for one thing, it doesn't explain why mood is important or how the mood of the poem contributes to meaning (thus it would probably fail the tests of consistency and complexity). But it does identify important elements that you can expand on. It specifies mood, setting, and three technical devices: rhythm, diction, and repetition.

Here are some rough notes about the poem. In the final version that follows, you can see that the writer hasn't used all the points, but has applied the principle of selection, using those points that seem most suitable in supporting the thesis statement.

Stanza 1:
—metre is perfectly regular: there are four iambs (metrical unit with one unstressed followed by a stressed syllable) in each line, making it iambic tetrameter. The rhyming scheme is, likewise, quite regular: aaba bbcb ccdc dddd. Diction: simple words: mostly one-syllable words and a few two-syllable ones

—"His house," "his woods": repetition suggests importance of ownership; "He will not see me stopping here": would not approve?

—sets up opposition between woods and the house in the village: do the woods really "belong" to the man in the village? Nature vs. civilization? Narrator vs. owner?

Stanza 2:

—horse seems to think speaker's behaviour is unusual, not his customary habit to stop like this; he is a man of routine or business, perhaps— horses, too, are creatures of habit, under control of humans: a *work* horse?? Action vs. thought?

—setting is particularized: "*between* the woods and the frozen lake": alternatives?

—time is particularized: significance of "darkest evening of the year": winter solstice; the word "dark" recurs in final stanza; but in contrast to the "dark" is the snow: whiteness

Stanza 3:

—"harness" suggests captivity, containment: "bells" suggest celebration: Christmas?

—speaker attributes human qualities to the horse: "thinking" (l. 5), "asking" (l. 10): personification

—the sound of the shaking bells contrasts with the "only other" sound, that of the wind

—"easy" suggests the easy way, the simplest choice? It is easy to give way to what you desire, not so easy to give way to what you *must* do

—"downy" conveys softness, comfort, like a pillow: you don't usually think of wind as "easy," and snowflakes are in reality cold, ice crystals

Stanza 4:

—line 13 contains two repeated words: "woods" and "dark"; besides being "dark," the woods are "lovely" (appealing? tempting?) and "deep"; these words suggest seduction, being drawn towards something potentially dangerous and deceptive; or is he in fact being drawn towards something beautiful, profound, and truthful? Alternatives again! "Lovely" is used abstractly—why are they "lovely?" Is it because they are "dark and deep" or for some additional reason not specified? "Deep" and "dark" are likewise not very specific: deep as what? Dark as what? In what sense is "dark" also "lovely" and "deep" also lovely? Do you feel as a reader that your emotional commitment to the implications of these words leaves you hanging over an abyss?

—the speaker abruptly reminds himself that he has "promises to keep": what kind of promises and to whom? to what?

—literally, he has distance to travel before he can sleep; sleep can refer to literal sleep (when the journey is done) or perhaps to death—the end of life's journey?

—why does the speaker repeat the last line? Is he confidently and securely repeating what must be done (reinforcing its importance and his choice) or does the repeated line further the idea of a kind of spell or enchantment that he can't break away from? This seemingly simple poem poses alternatives and tensions throughout!

These notes suggest that the poem is built not just on regularity but also on contrasts, on oppositions between two worlds. In the essay itself, the writer stressed both these elements but decided that one is more important than the other. This analysis, of course, is far from the only one possible; nevertheless, it is well-supported by the text and is coherent, consistent, and complex, within the 500–700-word requirement.

Mystery or Mastery? Robert Frost's "Stopping by Woods on a Snowy Evening"

Though most of us prefer a planned and orderly life, we may at times surrender to a spontaneous impulse. The first-person narrator of Robert Frost's "Stopping by Woods on a Snowy Evening" yields to such an impulse, stopping by woods to "watch [them] fill up with snow" and falling deeper into their mystery—or, some would say, their mastery. Similarly, the poet draws the reader into the poem by creating a familiar mood of solemn contemplation, using simple diction and basic rhythms.

By constructing a seemingly straightforward poem that employs a regular iambic tetrameter metre with a relatively predictable rhyming scheme of aaba bbcb ccdc dddd, the poet stresses the ordinariness of his experience. Despite this ordinariness, the poem relies on tensions or oppositions to suggest how our perception can at times transcend the ordinary. However, in the end, the poem's regularity affirms a commitment to worldly routine: although the woods hold a mysterious temptation, "lovely, dark and deep," they do not hold mastery, "But I have promises to keep . . . ."

One of the tensions configured by the poem is between the village, representing civilization, and nature. In the first stanza, the poet tentatively identifies the owner of the woods, but since the man lives at some distance, he will not see the poet "stopping here / To watch his woods fill up with snow." Already, a tension is established between the private world of the poet, who has access to nature, and the public world of ownership or business, which separates even the owner from his legacy in nature. Even the horse seems part of the world the poet has left behind. The horse "thinks" his stopping is "queer" and "ask[s] if there is some mistake." The poet hears the harness bells shaking, but the impatient call to routine is opposed by the subtler sound, "the sweep / Of easy wind and downy flake." The adjectives "easy" and "downy" could convey comfort, relaxation, sleep—the "easy" succumbing to his tranquil feeling; or the lure of the woods, could suggest a treachery in nature, the temptation to drop his responsibilities and simply give himself up to sleep, and inevitable death through exposure to cold, in the winter woods at night.

End rhyme also supports the idea of being drawn to the woods: in stanzas one to three, the rhyme in the third line is picked up in the stanza that immediately follows, creating a mesmeric effect. But as the poet falls deeper under the spell of the woods, he abruptly recalls he has "promises to keep." What are these promises? The "darkest evening" might refer to the winter solstice, and the image of the shaking bells suggests it is near Christmas. Are his "promises" connected to religious or familial duties? Or is he facing some other darkness, a disappointing relationship, awareness of advancing age, sorrow or pain associated with a loved one?

The repetition of lines 15 and 16 could suggest the progressive intensifying of the spell; more likely, though, they consciously reassert his need to complete the journey and fulfil his obligations. The poem's regular structure, rhyme, and metre, along with simple diction, suggest that he remains committed to his routines even while he is lured by the woods. Like most people, worldly responsibilities restrain him from falling under the power of an undefined impulse; his deeper commitment, like ours, is to duty to the world he knows. As he continues his physical journey and reaches his goal, he may well recall his "stopping by woods" much more than the journey. Our respites from routine are usually more memorable than the routine itself.

9. The Literary Genres: Poetry, the Short Story, the Novel, and Drama

Much of what has been discussed to this point relates to what the genres of literary writing have in common. The sections on poetry, fiction (the short story and the novel), and drama that follow focus on their unique characteristics and some of the challenges they present to the student researcher and writer. Various ways to approach your reading and study of the genres are discussed.

Most of us are more familiar with the conventions of prose than of poetry; after all, we use prose to communicate every day. However, we may not be able to identify the conventions we are using when we write in prose or may not recognize that in analyzing literary prose we are using many of the conventions of everyday writing. Learning to analyze literary prose means that you can use the conventions *more consciously*. The awareness of conventions and special techniques applies perhaps more to the analysis of poetry, which typically is more formal and compressed than prose and usually makes greater use of stylistic and figurative devices.

10. How to Approach a Poem

10.1 Intuitive Approach

Approach a poem, if you can, without preconceptions or expectations; read it in spite of what you know *about* it or have been taught to look for *in* it. Read it as if you are the first person to discover it, to engage with it, to catch its moods, its vagaries—to sound its depths. As discussed above in the Method of Organizing an Outline or Draft, Section 6.1, the intuitive approach should enable you to respond in a personal way to what the poem has to offer. Two other approaches, the text-centred approach and the context-centred approach, apply to all the literary genres, so some of the comments below apply to the literary genres in general.

10.2 Text-Centred Approach (the inside-out approach)

The text-centred approach limits itself to the wide range of strategies and poetic devices available to the poet to make the poem. Because it explores the connections between the formal elements of a work and its meaning, it is called the **formalist** method. Following are some strategies that you as a reader and writer can apply to analyze the poem "from the inside out."

Those terms related to poetic techniques and devices (in bold face) that cannot be defined concisely as they arise in the text are defined in the glossary at the end of Part Six, in Section 18.

Structure refers to the arrangement of parts, to the way they work separately yet contribute to the whole. Is the poem divided into parts? How is it put together? Are there distinct divisions? What are their functions? Do the parts suggest contrast? Do they suggest a movement or progression of some kind? Do they parallel one another? What can you say about the poem's structure?

Stanzas are a type of division into parts. Within these larger parts there are smaller but significant structures such as **parallelism** (simple repetition or "echoing") or **juxtaposition** (words or images placed beside another for effect); **anaphora** (repetition of words or phrases at the beginning of lines or clauses) and **chiasmus** (inversion in the second of two parallel phrases of the order followed in the first) are specific kinds of parallelism. Examples of smaller structural elements in lines of poetry are the **caesura**, a pause in the middle of a line, and **enjambment**, in which the sense of one line runs into the next one, rather than being **end-stopped** (having a logical and syntactic stop at the end of a line).

Remember:
Prose is written in sentences; poetry is written in *lines*.
Prose is written in paragraphs; poetry is written in *stanzas*.

- Listen to the poem. You discern speaker and voice by listening to what is *between* the lines (see below); you determine sound patterns by looking at and hearing the *lines themselves*. Read the lines aloud. What kind of **rhythm** do they have? Is the rhythm regular, with repeated units recurring at predictable intervals? If so, can you characterize the poem's **metre**? *Scansion* is the reading of a line of poetry to determine the pattern of stressed and unstressed syllables. Are there departures from a regular metre? If so, what purpose might they serve? The names for the most frequently occurring patterns of rhythm can be found in the glossary, Section 18, below.

- If the poet uses **rhyme**, where are the rhymes? At the end of each line? Are they ever in the middle of a line? Do the words rhyme exactly, or do they just sound similar? If there is a distinctive pattern of rhyme, what is it? Are there other aural features in the poem, such as closely placed words with repeated sounds at their beginning: **alliteration**? Or with rhyming vowels in their midst: **assonance**? Are there examples of **onomatopoeia** (words that sound like their meanings— "buzz," "splash")?

- Look at the poem's *speaker* (the main *voice* in the poem) or *narrator* (if the poem is narrated—told as a story). Can you determine the speaker? Not just *who* it is, but what is his/her perspective? How is the poem told? Does the poet seem to be addressing anyone or anything? Is the person or object absent, as in an **apostrophe**? What is the **mood** of the poem, and how does it make you feel? Is a predominant emotion expressed? Is it constant, or is there a shift at some point? What is the poem's **tone**? Does the poet use **irony**? What kind and for what effect? Is **hyperbole** used (extreme exaggeration)? **Understatement**? (drawing attention to something by minimizing it): they may help convey a work's tone; use of hyperbole is common in comic works; either can be used to convey irony.

- Remember that the "voice" in the work is not necessarily that of the poet. It may be that of a "persona" adopted by the writer. One cannot assume that a literary work is a reliable form of autobiography. Writers may use facts or apparent truths about themselves, but from the standpoint of criticism, these facts are subordinate to the poem as poetic art. The aspect of the poetic work that concerns the critic is the poet's impulse towards creativity and art, more than autobiography.

- Pay close attention to stylistic and rhetorical devices. Some of the more important devices are **diction**, **syntax**, and such **figures of speech** as **metaphors**, **metonymy**, **synecdoche**, **similes**, **allusions**, and **personification**. Rhythm and structure are also related to style. Other rhetorical elements are logic-centred; they include **paradox** and **oxymoron** (the verbal juxtaposition of contraries, as in "darkness visible" or "terrible beauty"). Oxymoron is also considered a device of compression. Another similar device is **ellipsis**.

- Look at the poem's **imagery**. Try to discover patterns of images. What kind are they? Can you characterize them? Do they refer to the senses? Which ones? How do the images connect with other elements referred to above to lead you to a more complex reading of the poem? Does the poet use one or more **symbols**? Some symbols resonate as **archetypes**, while others combine with narrative elements to create **allegory**.

10.3 Context-Centred Approach (the outside-in approach)

The context-centred approach is another beginning point for a textual analysis. The context-centred analysis employs all of the technical terminology of textual criticism, but relates it to an encompassing context. Literary works can be explored through biographical, historical, cultural, racial, gender-based, or theoretical perspectives. Although the formalist (text-centred) critic tends to take an "art for art's sake" approach to poetic analysis, the context-centred critic employs connections between literary art and the "real" world, and considers many of the oppositions between life and art erected by the text-centred critic to be artificial, arbitrary, or, at the very least, limiting. Some of the most common contexts are discussed briefly following this developed example of poetry.

You may be concerned primarily or even exclusively with viewing a poem in a larger context, perhaps that of a poetic tradition or a specific poetic form with its **conventions** (set of formal requirements or expectations). You could look at the ways that the poem conforms to conventions, the ways that it departs from them, or the ways that the writer adapts the conventions for his or her own purposes.

Broadly speaking, poetry can be classified as lyric, narrative, or dramatic: **lyric** ("song") poetry expresses strong emotions or thoughts in relatively brief form. By contrast, **narrative** poetry tells a story and tends to be longer—it may run to book length; **dramatic** poetry has drama-like qualities, such as a speaker who addresses an imaginary listener (**dramatic monologue**).

The voice in lyric poetry can be referred to as "the poet" (which is not, however, synonymous with the actual author); in narrative poetry, the voice can be referred to as "the narrator"; in dramatic poetry, the voice can be referred to as "the speaker." Both narrative and dramatic poetry can also be lyrical in places; as well, a lyric could have narrative or dramatic elements. Although these three divisions were introduced by Aristotle in 350 BC, they are used today.

Other traditional poetic forms include the ode, the elegy, the sonnet, the villanelle, the haiku (examples of lyric poetry); the ballad and the epic (examples of narrative poetry); and the dramatic monologue (an example of dramatic poetry). Each form employs specific conventions. For example, the **sonnet** always has 14 lines and has two possible stanzaic arrangements: the Italian or Petrarchan form with an eight-line octave and a six-line sestet, and the English or Shakespearean form with three quatrains (four lines each) and a couplet (two lines); others, like the haiku and the villanelle, have an even stricter and more exacting form than the sonnet. All three are examples of **fixed forms**, which allow for little flexibility. Still others, like the elegy and the ode, may vary widely in their characteristics from one era to another and from poet to poet. At the other extreme from fixed forms are **open forms**: free verse is an open form that does not conform to any set conventions of **stanza**, **rhyme**, or **meter**.

The Biographical Context: What was the poet's childhood like? Who/what were major influences in his or her life? Does the poem appear addressed to someone the poet knew or does it mention names or places connected with the writer's life? Does the poem focus on a family member or friend? An **elegy** mourns the death of a well-known person or someone the poet knew, providing consolation and usually celebrating that life.

Although the poet is viewed critically as the creator of the work, not the autobiographical equivalent of the voice, speaker, or narrator, in **confessional poetry** an autobiographical sensibility is produced through the expression of strong emotions and intense personal experiences characterized by revelations of painful honesty and unsettling rawness. The tone can range from despair to anger. Nonetheless, you should not assume that the voice of the poem is *identical* with the poet of biography.

Historical/Cultural Context: What historical or cultural factors can be brought to bear on the poem? Does the poem reflect a particular time period? Can it be studied as a historic, social, or cultural document? In the following excerpt, student writer Rory Wizbicki explores Al Purdy's poem "The Country North of Belleville" in a historical context. The poem details the hardships of poor, immigrant, nineteenth-century farmers, who travelled to Canada in the hope of finding prosperity and freedom in a new country.

Although, geographically, the plots north of Belleville are every farmer's nightmare, within this shallow soil lies their blood, sweat, and tears produced from endless days of work and toil. A farmer becomes so connected to his land, "plowing and plowing [his] ten acre field" that the "convulsions [begin to] run parallel with his own brain" (57). The land is both his greatest enemy and his most respected companion. Despite his plot's stubborn resistance to human cultivation, a man of this area "might have some / opinion of what beauty / is and none deny him / for miles" (5–8). This timeless beauty and respect for the land is paralleled by the lasting cultural values engraved into the farmer's stony fields.

Cultural, Racial, Gender-Based Context: Awareness of the culture that the poet is part of has been instrumental in extending and broadening the canon of literature in the last few decades. For example, the fact that Dionne Brand and George Elliott Clarke are of black heritage and that Adrienne Rich and Margaret Atwood have strongly identified with the feminist movement can be important in analyzing the ways in which their works give voice to the concerns of the marginalized. Was the poet a member of a well-defined group that shared certain values? Did she or he contribute intellectually to a social, political, or aesthetic movement? Was the poem written as a radical response to a contemporary reality; does it protest something? Cultural, racial, gender, socio-economic, and class issues can serve political ends in poems of protest or resistance; their object may be to express collective or personal empowerment. See the sample literary research essay Section 17.3.

The **traditional (Western) canon** was based on the opinion of critics and readers —mostly, white, middle-class, and male—that particular works exemplified high artistic standards and were the most worthy objects of study and scholarship. Due to the increasing interest today in the productions of other individuals and groups, publishers have become responsive to a broader range of human experience. The **literary canon** is now more inclusive of varied cultural, racial, ethnic, economic, and gendered perspectives.

Theoretical Perspective: Was the work written from within an established theoretical tradition or does it try to establish a new theoretical position? Theoretical approaches to literature can be divided into two types: those formulated by artists themselves who have sought to explain their own goals by theorizing about them, and approaches that represent particular schools of critical thought.

Attempts to systematize poetry and other literary genres have brought about what might seem a confusing array of critical approaches today. The profusion of -*isms* began around the turn of the twentieth century through the attempts of writers and critics to categorize technical innovations of that time. Some of these innovations came to be associated with *literary movements*—for example, **imagism**, with its focus on the concrete image, and **surrealism**, with its focus on the subconscious.

Today, the widely divergent schools of criticism may represent the collaborative efforts of educated theorists whose original training was in non-literary fields. Their theories may seek to incorporate theory and practice from other disciplines—for example, linguistics, visual art, history, education, philosophy, psychology, anthropology, economics, and mythology. If there is a collective goal of modern literary theories, it is to break down the notion of a "centre," to stress the ways that all literary art is dependent on and engages with aspects of language and culture. The interdisciplinary approach to literature enables us to study it from many different angles and viewpoints. These kinds of approaches are common in literary criticism today.

10.4 Sample Student Literary Analysis

The following student essay features a close textual reading of a poem by Canadian poet Leona Gom. (700 words)

Metamorphosis

Something is happening
to this girl.

She stands on one leg
on the third block
of her hopscotch game,
lifts herself forward
to the next double squares,
and, as she jumps,
something changes.

Her straight child's body
curls slowly in the air,
the legs that assert themselves
apart on the squares
curve in calf and thigh,
angles become arches;
her arms pumping slowly
to her sides adjust
to a new centre of gravity,
the beginnings of breasts
push at her sweater,
her braids have come undone
and her hair flies loose around her.

Behind her
the schoolhouse blurs,
becomes insubstantial
and meaningless,
and the boys in the playground
move toward her,
something sure and sinister
in their languid circling.

Slowly she picks up the beanbag.
When she straightens,
her face gathers
the bewildered awareness
of the body's betrayal,
the unfamiliar feel
of the child's toy
in her woman's hand.

From *The Collected Poems* by Leona Gom, 1991, Sono Nis Press, Winlaw, BC.
Reprinted by permission.

A New Game: Leona Gom's "Metamorphosis"

by Melissa Lee

The most intimate experiences of human existence occur every day, to all of us. Art allows us to publicly engage in these without vulnerability; it recognizes their profound impact on human life without taking away their personal value. Leona Gom's poem "Metamorphosis" is an example of how art can reveal the significance of common life events. The appeal of this poem is universal because it deals with maturation and change, something all humans experience. Gom focuses attention on details with several techniques. Aspects that may first appear unimportant become essential to understanding. In particular, diction, alliteration, and imagery help create the effect of a time-lapse photograph commonly used to show organic growth. Gom's subtle use of such techniques echo the theme of sensing the amazing in the mundane.

Gom's diction relates to the changes the girl undergoes. Thus, words such as "straight," "squares," and "angles" appear to represent feelings of childhood. They are straightforward, systematic, and even mathematical. There is nothing confusing about them; things are black and white. As the girl moves through the game, the diction shifts. The words "curls," "curve," "arches," "undone," "loose," "circling," and "blurs" are used to symbolize maturation. Her body is literally changing from straight to curvaceous, while her mind is changing from concrete to flexible. The diction is complex and chaotic, reflecting the lack of rules for growing up. A grey area exists now where definitive lines used to be.

In the beginning, the girl "lifts herself forward," expressing her agency in the changes. The use of alliteration in the poem draws attention to pivotal points. Though she is not yet aware of the meaning of her actions (moving towards maturity), she is actively participating. "The beginnings of breasts" represent the changes, signalling a new beginning, not only an end (to childhood). As her changes are public, her societal role must change. Describing the boys' attraction to her as "something sure and sinister" reveals her feelings of newfound power. At the same time, her "bewildered awareness / of the body's betrayal" suggests her resentment of new burdens and responsibilities that come with changes. Cumulatively, these images show an emerging self-consciousness as she begins to reflect on her identity.

The imagery that Gom uses also represents the girl's passage into womanhood. The fragmented body parts, "leg," "calf," "thigh," "arms," "breasts," "hair," "face," and "hand" throughout the poem suggest feelings of not being fully formed yet. There are many pieces to her, but they are not quite connected. This awareness of being incomplete is the girl's first step towards maturation. She recognizes that she now must find a force within herself to put the pieces together, in a higher order. Thus, at the end we see phrases suggesting action and decisiveness: "she picks up the beanbag," "she straightens," and "her face gathers." These show the girl taking control over her situation and, at some level, accepting her new role in life: she puts things together with a new insight.

The image of reaching higher resonates throughout the poem and can be seen in the phrases "lifts herself," "she jumps," "curls slowly in the air," "new centre of gravity," and "flies loose around her." Such images evoke the activity of rising up to challenge one's limits. As the poem continues, the take-off gets easier, which is reflected by the diction ("lifts" becomes "jumps," which becomes "curls slowly" and "flies loose"), suggesting the desire of the girl to push her limits and thus change. It is a very positive and optimistic image, showing that while change may close one chapter in a life, it opens many others. She begins to trust her abilities and takes a leap of faith in herself. Without self-doubt holding her down, she experiences a new gravity; she is transformed, undergoes a metamorphosis.

While change is essential for life to continue, it can also cause great unease. When people adapt to challenging changes in their lives, they gain meaningful insight into what they can accomplish. A poem like "Metamorphosis" acknowledges these private experiences and their deep impact, enabling people to stay connected to what matters most.

11. Fiction Forms

The model that follows can apply to any literary work; however, it is most applicable to fiction, which is often analyzed according to what you can call the *comfort categories*. In fiction, the comfort categories include the traditional areas of plot, character, setting,

Plot: **What** happens in the novel?

Character: **Who** thinks and acts in the work?

Setting: **Where** does the work take place? **When** does it take place?

Point of View: **How** is the work told?

Theme: **Why** is this work important?

point of view, and theme. Essentially, the comfort categories relate to basic questions you often ask of a work of fiction or narrative poem in order to begin analyzing it: what, who, where and when, how, and why.

Explaining or analyzing a work involves exploring its theme(s), or controlling idea(s), along with the other elements mentioned above. A novel's or short story's characters may seem unusual, its plot unlikely, and its setting unfamiliar, but there will always be something familiar about its theme(s): it might focus on love, death, suffering, renewal, human relationships, social injustice, or spiritual longing. Through the work's theme(s), the reader can make connections with his or her own experience—themes universalize the writer's work.

A Model for Reading and Interpreting Fiction

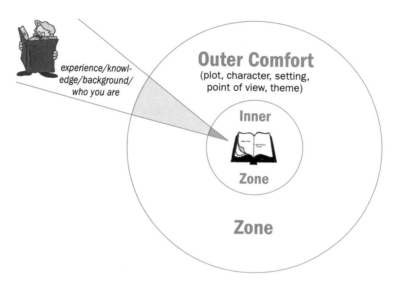

As the diagram shows, one reader's response to a work of fiction will depend partly on his or her experience, knowledge, and background. Because each one brings a different set of experiences and expectations to a work, no two analyses will be identical. Even though we share the critical tools for analyzing fiction (that "outer zone" containing the comfort categories of plot, character, setting, point of view, and theme), in the "inner zone" one can apply the more complex tools for analyzing fiction discussed below. Being familiar with the many resources for analyzing fiction will enable you to respond more fully and sensitively to the work, to produce an in-depth reading.

12. The Short Story

Whether a work of fiction is called a *short story*, a *novella*, or a *novel* depends on its length. In approximate terms, a **short story** is a fictional narrative of fewer than 15,000 words; a *novella* is 15,000–40,000 words; a *novel* is more than 40,000 words, often much more.

The following creative definitions by students in a fiction-writing workshop draw attention to other elements of successful short stories, expanding the definition so you can see what a short story *does*, not just that it is short and a story.

1. It should provide some kind of continuous dream which the reader can enter, commune with, and leave having felt something.
2. It is a fully realized world. After passing through this world, the reader sees his or her own world differently.
3. It is a narrative wherein a character absorbs an experience.
4. It is a slice of life—the thinner the better.

Definition 1: stresses the effect of stories on their readers; stories are a shared experience that evoke feelings;

Definition 2: is "a fully realized world," despite brevity; the short story renders a complete picture of something;

Definition 3: conveys the importance of character; furthermore, the character undergoes an experience; the reader is offered an opportunity for learning, either what the character did or what the character did not.

Definition 4: suggests that a story represents universals in as succinct or condensed way as possible by showing us an important example ("slice") of the whole.

12.1 The Single Effect

One of the earliest developers of the short story, Edgar Allan Poe (1809–49), claimed that, unlike the novel, the successful short story should be of a length to be read at one sitting and should focus on one effect that serves to unify its elements. According to Poe, writers of short fiction should decide what this single effect is to be and select incidents that help bring it about. Such a dictate stresses a necessary *economy* of the story—the judicious use of atmosphere, dialogue, **mood**, **imagery**, etc. that results in a unified effect. In many short stories, the single effect relates to a discovery a character makes about nature, society, other people, or about himself/herself.

Novella (novelette): Since a novella occupies the middle space between a short story and a novel, it's not surprising that it shares some of the characteristics of the short story as well as some of those of the novel. A novella usually is more fully developed in one or more areas of plot, character, and setting than a short story, but is less developed than a novel in all these areas.

13. The Novel Tradition

A **novel** is an extended fictional prose narrative involving one or more characters undergoing significant experiences over a span of time. The term is from the Italian *novella*, a short, realistic prose work popular in the late medieval period. The word "novel" means "new," and the fictional works of Daniel Defoe brought to English a new prose form, very different from the popular romances of the middle ages that depicted the imaginary exploits of heroes, such as Beowulf and King Arthur and the Knights of the Round Table. The English novels were notable at first for their realism: Defoe's *Journal of the Plague Year, Robinson Crusoe, Moll Flanders*; for their efforts at psychological detail: Richardson's *Pamela* and *Clarissa*, and Fielding's *The History of Tom Jones, a Foundling*. Yet the novel is not always a realistic form. In France the *roman* retained its connection to the romance of the middle ages (Voltaire's *Candide*; Dumas's *Three Musketeers*) through anti-heroes of the influential writers of the nineteenth century (Balzac's *Père Goriot*, Flaubert's *Madame Bovary*) evolving towards modern preoccupations with various sorts of ideals and anti-ideals, especially the political and social, and that were approached through irony and satire (Camus's *The Plague*; Sartre's *Nausea*) and the *nouveau roman* (new novel), which breaks from many of the conventions of the form itself (Robbe-Grillet's *Jealousy*).

The two words *novella* and *roman* suggest two directions for the novel: towards realism and towards romance or idealism. However, one should not overlook the Russians, Tolstoy and Dostoevsky, who weigh in with novels composed of both these traditional threads combined with a generous vein of moralism. For a further discussion of realism in fiction, see Section 15.5.

The English novel's early appeal to the rising numbers of middle-class readers was based partly on its depiction of real-life characters with whom readers could identify. The English novel has proven an adaptable form, and many different kinds of novels have flourished in its roughly three centuries of development. A necessarily brief overview of prominent novelistic forms in English follows:

The Picaresque Novel (seventeenth and eighteenth centuries) tells a story composed of loosely related, realistic incidents or episodes featuring a low-born, usually male, hero called a *pícaro* (*picaroon* if the hero is female), a merry rogue on a journey who survives by his wits; though often deceptive and dishonest, the hero is not immoral, but his encounters reveal the corruption of others and of society.

The Epistolary Novel (novel of letters) (eighteenth century) uses letters to advance the plot and reveal depth and variety of characterization; it features a middle- or upper-class, usually female, protagonist in social settings like drawing rooms or salons, and at social assemblies. The epistolary novel flourished for a time but then experienced a decline in readership. Inevitably, though, elements were absorbed into emerging forms, such as the eighteenth-century sentimental novel, which stressed character and feeling over incident.

The Gothic Novel, an immensely popular form from 1790 to 1820, possessed typical features related to plot, setting, and mood. Making liberal use of the supernatural, the Gothic novel featured entrapped heroines dominated by tyrannical older males who represented the repressions of political, social, or religious authorities. Many of the elements of Gothic novels were absorbed into later novelistic forms—its influence today is felt in popular horror films and television shows like *Buffy the Vampire Slayer*.

Historical Romance, popularized by Sir Walter Scott early in the nineteenth century, exploited conventions of romance, including larger-than-life characters performing heroic deeds of historical significance. Later in the century, such writers as Robert Louis Stevenson and Rudyard Kipling maintained the genre's popularity under the gradually diminishing glow of British imperialism.

The Victorian Novel (mid- to late-nineteenth century) represented a culmination of the previous styles with its elaborate plot development and profusion of characters.

One kind of Victorian novel is the **bildungsroman**, or novel of self-education; Charlotte Brontë's *Jane Eyre* and Charles Dickens's *David Copperfield* and *Great Expectations* are examples. Elizabeth Gaskell, Dickens, and others also wrote **social-problem novels**, which drew the attention of their readers to contemporary social and political issues.

The twentieth-century novel, owing to the influence of psychological theories, is often concerned with exploring psychological and perceptual states; many novelists of the modernist period (1895–1945), such as James Joyce and Virginia Woolf, sought through technical innovation to disrupt the conventions of the Victorian novel. Modernist novels tended to be more experimental, open-ended, and morally ambivalent than their Victorian predecessors.

14. How to Approach Fiction

Remember to avoid plot summary unless it is specifically assigned. Elements of plot, however, can be an important part of your analysis.

Some tools for analyzing stories, novellas, and novels are discussed below. Many of the terms also are useful in analyzing drama and narrative or dramatic poetry.

14.1 Plot

The plot is the arrangement or sequence of actions in a story, novel, or drama.

Plot Structure. You may be familiar with the pyramidal division of plot into *rising action*, *climax* (the high point of the conflict), and *falling action* (*resolution* or *denouement*). In most dramas, novels, and in many stories, the rising action is preceded by the *exposition*, which introduces background information. The *initiating incident* begins the rising action. *In medias res* describes the strategy of beginning a story in the midst of an important action.

Fiction involves one or more kinds of **conflict**, which usually takes the form of obstacles the character must overcome to achieve a goal. Conflict—the initiator of and driving force behind the actions or events of a short story, novel, or drama—may arise from the character's motivation or through forces lying outside the character. The conflict is usually introduced early and instigates the rising action.

Many other structural devices offer coherence to a story; for example, authors may use a *framing* technique in which the beginning and the end mirror one another in setting or situation. In some novels, a character narrates the beginning and the end with the story of the main character evolving within this narrative frame. Other forms of *parallelism* can be used to suggest similarities or differences between characters, or to show the development in a character at different points in a novel.

Plots may be closed or open-ended. A traditional way to provide *closure*, especially in novels of social interaction, such as the *novels of manners* of Jane Austen, is through a marriage. The actions or events of the plot may be unified (closely related) or only loosely related, as in the episodic plot of a picaresque novel, in which case, the overarching structure may take the form of a journey. A *quest* is a journey with a specific goal, usually a valuable object. The quest is completed when the hero/heroine overcomes all the obstacles and has brought the object back to his or her society. However, the *quester* may fail in the quest; invariably, the failed quester undergoes an important learning experience while trying to satisfy the terms of the quest.

The incidents that comprise a plot can be ordered in various ways: most simply, they may be arranged chronologically (time order); even in the chronological order, however, other devices or effects can be used—for example, the writer may use such *chronological telescoping* as *foreshadowing*, creating suspense through the anticipation of a future action or result, or *flashbacks*, moving back in time to narrate important events perhaps as a character recollects them.

14.2 Character

Henry James was one of the earliest writers to treat the novel as an art form, one that combined meticulous technique with moral vision. In "The Art of Fiction" (1893), James asked "What is a picture or a novel that is *not* of character?" Through point of view, said James, the author can keep in focus the character's consciousness. Writers' fidelity to the consciousness of the protagonist produced the *psychological realism* of many English novels of the late-nineteenth and early twentieth centuries.

Character Type. Novels usually have at least one *rounded* (fully developed and complex) and several *flat* (one-dimensional, undeveloped) characters. The main character in a work of fiction or drama is called the *protagonist*. One expects the protagonist to be the rounded character. The novel may also have an *antagonist*, who opposes the protagonist. An antagonist often reveals hidden or submerged aspects of the protagonist. The *doppelgänger, double,* or *shadow self* is used by some authors to express a character's alter ego or alternate, usually diametrically opposite, expression of the self, as Hyde is to Jekyll in Robert Louis Stevenson's *The Strange Case of Dr. Jekyll and Mr. Hyde.* A *foil* is a character who *provides contrast to* another character, though the two characters don't necessarily oppose one another, such as Bertha Mason, the first wife of Edward Fairfax Rochester, who provides every sort of contrast to the nature and condition of the heroine Jane, in *Jane Eyre,* but with whom Jane hardly interacts.

Character Development. Character may be disclosed through direct narration, in description or exposition, or indirectly through dialogue or action. A character's development may be represented primarily through his or her thoughts or through that character's actions. Character development usually occurs through a learning experience: in an *initiation story,* a young protagonist makes the transition to adulthood, from innocence to experience. The learning experience could be one of suffering, resulting, as it often does in drama, especially tragedy, in an intense moment of recognition or insight. In short fiction, James Joyce talked about the concept of the *epiphany,* a character's sudden recognition in an ordinary event or object of something personally illuminating.

14.3 Setting

Setting is the place and time of the work. In contrast to short stories, there is usually more than one main setting in novels, and the time may span several days (occasionally less) to several years or, in the case of some nineteenth-century novels, generations. Setting can be shown through concrete detail conveyed through diction and imagery. Selective use of imagery can also create a specific atmosphere, which may be important in creating a mood. *Regionalism* is the realistic portrayal of the beliefs and behaviours of characters from a distinct part of a country; examples include William Faulkner (Mississippi), Stephen Leacock (Orillia, Ontario), Alice Munro (Southwestern Ontario), and Jack Hodgins (Vancouver Island).

14.4 Narrative Point of View

Narrative Point of View is the personal perspective or unique angle of vision from which the narrative is told.

Narrator (field of vision). An *omniscient* ("all knowing") *narrator* sees and tells the whole story in the third-person, moving to different scenes, and in and out of the minds of characters; a *limited omniscient narrator* can move in and out of the minds of one or more characters, but often is limited to the consciousness of the main character; *first-person narrators* report from their own experiences (using the first-person "I" voice).

Narrator (involvement). First-person narrators do not always reflect the most subjective viewpoints; they can be relatively detached, narrating events from the first-person *observer* or uninvolved perspective. First-person narrators can also, of course, be involved in the action. First-person *involved* narrators may narrate events in which they play a significant role. Writers may choose to utilize special techniques to represent internal consciousness—such as *inner monologue* or *stream of consciousness* to show the mind in flux or the transient emotions, thoughts, and sensations of a character; both these techniques attempt to represent raw perceptions at the pre-verbal or subconscious levels.

Narrator (reliability). Narrators may be reliable or unreliable. A reliable narrator can be trusted to relay a truthful picture of events and character. Most third-person narrators can be considered reliable, but you should still be aware that this kind of narrator is not necessarily the voice of the author per se.

An *unreliable narrator* may be naïve; that is, he or she may not be in possession of all the facts or may be too young or inexperienced to see things as they are or to make sound judgements. The *naïve narrator*, then, may be limited in his or her capacity to understand and explain. On the other hand, a narrator may consciously or unconsciously deceive the reader in order to avoid confronting unpleasant facts about himself/herself or due to a bias or prejudice. Unreliable narrators can vary greatly in their unreliability. A writer's use of an unreliable narrator will produce **irony**, as there will be a discrepancy between the narrator's perceptions and the reality of a situation. Through unreliable narration, writers convey the complexity of perception and the human capacity for (self-) deception.

14.5 Orientation to Reality

"My task . . . is, by the power of the written word, to make you hear, to make you feel—it is, before all, to make you see. That—and no more, and it is everything."
                                                                    –Joseph Conrad

Realism. The popularity of the novel from its inception has been due in part to its ability to portray ordinary people, places, and circumstances. Realism in the novel has produced many sub-genres, including social realism, psychological realism, and historical realism. Because the term *realism* is so broad, it is difficult to define. In the general sense, it refers to the need of the fictional writer to portray things as they really are, "to make you see," as Conrad says.

Realism also can be considered a distinct literary tradition that began in Europe as a response against *romance* and to contemporary scientific discoveries and theories about the place of humans in the universe—for example, the theory of evolution that gained prominence after Charles Darwin published *On the Origin of Species* in 1859. Such theories looked back to other mechanistic views of humans and their world, such as those of Copernicus and Newton. Since it seemed less and less truthful for artists to dwell on idealized human traits, writers turned increasingly to the everyday interactions among ordinary people, showing middle-class characters in a recognizable environment and using an accumulation of realistic detail to do so. Editor Wayne Grady has called realism the "most characteristic feature" of the Canadian short story. Some critics see realism primarily as a technique or method, viewing *naturalism*, rather, as the school of realistic writing applicable to fiction and drama.

Naturalism. An outgrowth of realistic writing in the late nineteenth and early twentieth centuries that stressed humanity's helplessness before external forces, such as those of one's society or natural environment, or before internal ones, such as heredity. French novelist Émile Zola drew an analogy between the naturalistic writer and the laboratory scientist, both of whom examine phenomena dispassionately and draw conclusions based on evidence. Frequently, naturalistic writers portray their protagonists as victims of fate.

Romance. The romance may be distinguished from the novel. Romance deals with imaginary, though usually conventional, heroes and heroines. However, characters may be exalted and their goals idealized. American novelist Nathaniel Hawthorne (1851) called his works romances because they owed an allegiance not to "the probable and ordinary course of man's experience" but to "the truth of the human heart." Like realism, romance is a term that has been made complex by overuse.

Departures from the Realism/Romance Divide. "Reality" is not an absolute term. A work may be oriented to reality, while utilizing a symbolic framework, though, on the surface, **symbols** and realistic detail might seem incompatible. Similarly, *science fiction* and *fantasy* may invert or subvert some of the standards of objective reality and still be considered real; in this case, the relevant question would not be "could it happen in our world?" but "could it happen *given the world created by the writer?*" *Magic realism* combines the objectively real and the surprise of the unreal or unexpected; in magic realism, the created world is magical and real at the same time. *Metafiction* defines its own boundaries of the real by focusing on the story itself as the testing ground of the "real"; one of the themes in a work of metafiction is the status of fiction and fiction-making; metafiction uses the work itself to explore this status.

Much critical writing today attempts to examine the many faces of *postmodernism*. Postmodernism is certainly not restricted to fiction; indeed, it incorporates diverse aspects of contemporary culture. Although notoriously difficult to define, postmodernism in literature tends to reject such assumptions as the authority of the author, univocal (one-voice) perspectives, unifying narratives, and other "absolutes"; in their place, it stresses plurality, possibility, and "play."

For other terms used in the analysis of poetry, fiction, and drama see "A Glossary of Poetic Terms," below, Section 18.

15. How to Approach Drama

When you think about drama, you may recall plays you studied in high school, including those by William Shakespeare. Most of Shakespeare's plays are classified as tragedies or comedies, but the general term "drama" (from the Greek *dran*, "to do" or "to perform") refers to a story acted out by actors on a stage, or, nowadays, in front of a camera. The creator of drama is called a dramatist or *playwright*. The second syllable, "wright," refers to a *maker*, as in "wainwright," not a "write-r," and it is important to remember that, in the truest sense, plays are "wrought," carrying a connotation of construction in their making, because the intention is not just that they be written and read, but that they be mounted as productions and observed. Thus, when you read a play, it is essential to imagine it as performance and spectacle—not just as dialogue on a page.

Aristotle (384–322 BC) called drama an "imitated human action." He declared that dramas should observe the three *unities* of time, place, and action. By unity of time he limits the play's action to approximately one day; by unity of place he limits it to one setting; and by unity of action he limits it to a single set of incidents that are related as cause and effect and "having a beginning, a middle, and an end." Although the unities are not strictly observed by playwrights (for example, most of Shakespeare's plays depart from this rule), their observance does help create dramatic focus and intensity, necessary elements in theatre where the audience must remain attentive for at least two hours to absorb the full experience of the spectacle.

Drama in Western cultures dates back to Ancient Greek and Roman drama, which had its beginnings in ceremonial rites. Comedy evolved from fertility rites, while tragedy originated from rites connected with the life-death cycle. The three major ancient Greek playwrights, Aeschylus, Sophocles, and Euripides (all circa 525–400 BC), used Greek myth and legend to fashion tragedies that centred on the downfall of noble figures. Their plays featured heroes or heroines in their struggle against an unavoidable destiny. A group of people forming a *chorus* commented on the action. Aeschylus' main concern was with the cosmic significance of tragic destiny; Sophocles and Euripides focused more on the psychology of the protagonist in his or her struggle with that destiny.

William Shakespeare (1564–1616) exemplifies Elizabethan drama, considered "the golden age" of English drama. Elizabethan dramatists combined elements from ancient drama with newer, native forms to produce a wide variety of dramatic forms, from histories and chronicle plays, to comedy, romance, and tragedy. The Puritan government that replaced the Stuart monarchy disapproved of the theatre and closed London playhouses in 1642. When the theatres re-opened in 1660, comedies of manners and domestic tragedies prevailed and drama became more a form of entertainment exclusive to the educated classes during the Restoration period and into the eighteenth century.

As does the modern novelist, the modern dramatist is likely to locate the principal action of the play within the minds of the characters; psychological interest and the contemporary theme of alienation are reinforced by experimental techniques that made the drama relevant to contemporary audiences. Several modern playwrights sought to revive traditional dramatic practises: in the twentieth century Eugene O'Neill attempted to update the commentator function of the Greek chorus in *Mourning Becomes Electra* (1931); Arthur Miller in *Death of a Salesman* (1949) wrote a modern American tragedy in the classical tradition.

Although certainly not all works of drama can be classified as comedies or tragedies, the divisions between them have traditionally defined, for the playwright, the boundaries of human experience, because comedy and tragedy are concerned with human limits.

15.1 Comedy

In viewing human limits as weaknesses, comedy celebrates the lesser—the carnal or physical—self. Comedy uses laughter as a form of displacement, enabling its audience to identify the "other" as debased, silly, pretentious, or unimportant.

Low comedy traditionally draws its characters from low-life figures, that is, socially or morally inferior stereotypes: servants, shopkeepers, prostitutes. Low comedy lacks a serious moral purpose and may be used, as in many of Shakespeare's plays, to divert temporarily the attention of the audience from weightier matters (*comic relief*); low comedy as *farce* depends on the idea of the absurd and draws attention to events that appear meaningless or valueless out of context, the pratfall, for example.

High comedy is more sophisticated and traditionally uses characters from a higher socio-economic class; the humour of high comedy appeals more to the intellect (characterized as *wit*, *wittiness*), having such targets as social pretensions and character inconsistencies. It typically has a more complex function than low comedy, dealing with serious issues like human relationships—even dealing with the subjects of tragedy from a perspective of lightness and humour.

Satire can be considered a genre apart from comedy or tragedy, but its use of ironic humour aligns it to high comedy. In addition to humour, satire uses ridicule and irony to undercut, critique, or attack human institutions, ostensibly for the purpose of improving them. Satire may be mild, intended to make society's members more aware (*Horatian satire*) or harsh, intent on attacking these institutions (*Juvenalian satire*). Related to satire is *parody*, in which the writer imitates another literary work, poking fun at it and/or revealing its weaknesses.

Comic plot. Fortune, chance, and coincidence are the major external forces that drive the plot of comedy; inner forces that determine comic action include such instincts and motivations as physical desire, greed, envy, ambition, and concern with appearances. In the end, base human desires usually are punished, while continuity is suggested by a marriage between the most worthy and virtuous characters.

Comic theme. One of the most important themes in drama is that of identity, perhaps because in drama the onstage character is isolated in a way that he or she usually is not in a novel—because all drama is character-driven due to limitations of time and space necessitated by the stage. *Asides, monologues,* and *soliloquies*—speeches in which a character reveals his or her own thoughts for the ears of the audience alone—can be used to underscore this sense of isolation. Comedy may revolve around exchange and multiplicity of identity. In most of Shakespeare's comedies, for example, there are frequent changes of identity and/or mistaken identities.

15.2 Tragedy

Tragedy celebrates the greater, ennobling self by viewing the limits to human strengths tested against more powerful forces; tragedy involves cataclysmic change from prosperity to intense suffering and, usually, the death of the protagonist (the *denouement* or *catastrophe*). This suffering arouses a complex mix of emotions in its audience in which fear and pity are particularly strong. Traditionally, the characters of tragedy were high-status individuals, royal personages; this, however, is not the case with most tragedies written in the last 200 years. It is essential, though, that we see the tragic protagonist as admirable in some way.

Tragic plot. The exterior forces of fate or destiny are associated with tragedy; the inner force that drives the protagonist in classical tragedy is pride (*hubris*) or some such trait that exists in an extreme or distorted form (*tragic flaw*, or *hamartia*).

Tragic theme. The theme of identity is important in tragedy, also, but from the perspective of the tearing away and negation of identity. In both ancient Greek and Shakespearean tragedy, the protagonist was a king or high-status figure, making the fall from the greatest height as devastating as possible for an individual and in social terms as well, for the loss of the monarch would overturn the entire society. Shakespeare's King Lear falls from kingship, to an old man divested of kingly power, to a madman in a storm in a wilderness (heath) prior to his death.

16. The Literary Research Essay

Since information about conducting research (Part Five, Sections 2–7), using secondary sources effectively (Part Five, Sections 8–10), and documenting them correctly (Part Five, Section 11) has already been given, the section below will focus on specific strategies for dealing with literary sources.

16.1 Primary and Secondary Sources

Primary sources are the literary works that you are analyzing; *secondary sources* are studies (books, articles, and other media) that comment on or analyze one or more aspects of the primary work. Secondary sources include criticism relating to the work itself or to the writer's life (biographical criticism), as well as historical, cultural, linguistic, and other kinds of discourse that incorporate literary works. Using secondary sources in your analysis will broaden your paper; it will show how your observations about a work relate to what others have said. Researching the views of other readers and critics should also serve to strengthen your analysis.

16.1.1 How to Use Secondary Sources

1. Use a source to provide general information or to introduce something you will be discussing:

   General information. Gerald Vizenor, a contemporary critic and Native American spokesperson, writes that "movies have never been the representations of tribal cultures; at best, movies are the deliverance of an unsure civilisation" (179).

   Introduce. Author Miriam Bird once said, "travel is more than the seeing of sights; it is a change that goes on deep and permanent, in the ideas of the living" (11). Similarly, the journeys the two characters undergo leave an indelible effect on them, changing the way they see the world and respond to others.

2. Use a source to support, explain, or expand your point:

   Support. It is not vanity that drives the protagonist, an unproven knight, in Browning's narrative poem "Childe Roland to the Dark Tower Came," and he is far from idealistic as well. As James Stonewall states, "it is a simple desire to finish his quest, to finally put an end to his journey, that motivates Roland" (76).

   Explain. Dick tries to teach Rosemary that the values she has adopted are corrupt, immature, and over-simplified. Post-World War I American prosperity had already promoted the doctrine that youthfulness and wealth could buy one's social position, but, as Stern argues, it was the movies that "midwifed into full birth" this American mythology (115).

   Expand. The wreck itself is a dense image, and through its complexity, Rich is able to illustrate the complexity of myths. The wreck represents "the history of all women submerged in a patriarchal culture; it is that source of myths about male and female sexuality which shape our lives and roles today" (Mcdaniel par. 7).

3. Use a source to disagree or to qualify:

   Disagree. Donohue's fixation on the "elfin child" Pearl places undue emphasis on the ways we redeem our (innocent) children, rather than on the novel's more important concern with the ways society judges sin.

   Qualify. Herb Wyile asserts that Chance "displays . . . insidious racism. His vision for his epic is grounded in a self-exculpatory, racist triumphalism characteristic of the western" (3). This may be the case, but since it is Chance's perspective, he likely considers it the truth.

16.1.2 Reliability of Sources

As with secondary sources for expository research essays, you must be careful with the kinds of sources you use, especially if you use the Internet for research; university- or college-related Web sites are the most reliable.

Reliable. Critical studies of the work (books, articles in journals or from essay collections, etc.); other media and online resources affiliated with universities and officially designated agencies or organizations.

Unreliable. Internet sites that feature essays on specific literary works by unnamed authors, or writers who give their name but include no accreditation or biographical data; discussion groups, and other unofficial postings, such as the home pages of enthusiasts or unofficial postings of student essays.

Questionable. SparkNotes, Coles Notes, KnowledgeNotes, Cliff Notes, etc. Remember that these quick-fix approaches to literature invariably present mechanical and superficial treatments of generic topics; they are seldom insightful or offer a reading that you wouldn't be more than capable of yourself. But, of course, if you do use one, you must acknowledge it.

16.1.3 Currency

Unless you are specifically commenting on the reception of the work in the time it was written or the cultural/historical conditions that affected the work, prefer current sources to older ones as you would in other disciplines where older sources often become outdated. Another advantage of beginning with recent criticism is that such sources often refer to useful older criticism. Sometimes just scanning the Works Cited section at the end of a recent article will provide you with potentially useful sources.

However, there may be a classic commentary on your subject, such as Aristotle and Plato on poetry and drama, Samuel Johnson on Pope (and others in his *Lives of the Poets*), Matthew Arnold on Wordsworth, T.S. Eliot on Yeats, Northrop Frye on Blake; your instructor can steer you towards secondary sources that may be considered fundamental or monumental on a topic.

Many post-secondary institutions offer access through their library systems to on-line versions of scholarly journals. Libraries may provide this through large electronic subscription services such as *Project Muse* or *Literature Online (LION)*, enabling students to access full-text articles in a wide variety of literary journals, from general ones to those specializing in the literature of a specific time period (such as *Victorian Studies, Journal of Modern Literature,* and *Studies in English Literature 1500–1900*); literature of a particular country or region (such as *Scandinavian Review, Canadian Literature,* and *New England Quarterly*); literature categorized by genre (such as *Poetry, Studies in Short Fiction,* and *Studies in the Novel*); literature associated with movements (such as *American Transcendental Quarterly, Modernism/Modernity,* and *Feminist Studies*); literature and culture (such as *African American Review, Folklore,* and *Journal of Popular Culture*); literature on an individual author (such as *Shakespeare Studies, Dickens Quarterly,* and *Emily Dickinson Journal*); and interdisciplinary studies (such as *Biography: an interdisciplinary quarterly, Literature and Psychology*, and *Mosaic: a journal for the interdisciplinary study of literature*).

Most library arts and humanities databases allow you to search by author, subject, title, keyword, and journal, as well as to limit your search (see Part Five, Sections 7.1, 7.2, 7.3, 7.4).

16.2 Revising the Literary Essay

Student writers need to be careful with essay presentation, grammar, style, documentation, and related areas when revising their essays. The points below represent common problems for students editing their own literary essays.

- Convey your ideas clearly and objectively. The work(s) you are using as primary and secondary sources are written differently from your own tone and style—they may be stylistically dense with many figures of speech and, perhaps, unfamiliar words. You need to write in a direct and straightforward fashion to manage and integrate these other voices. Dealing with the complexities of literary texts can present legitimate problems of style and readability, but complex (or convoluted) language or sentence structure impedes understanding of complex thought; it also wastes words.

- Integrate direct quotes effectively. The challenge in writing literary essays, because you will probably refer often to the text to support your points, is to weave them logically and gracefully into your sentences. In the student research essay (Section 17.3 below), the writer effectively integrates both primary and secondary sources into her analysis.

- When citing from primary texts, check all your references carefully. Poetry citations should refer to line number(s) rather than page number(s). If the poem is divided into sections, precede the line number by the section number, separating the two by a period. Thus, a parenthetical citation for the last four lines of Samuel Taylor Coleridge's "The Rime of the Ancient Mariner" would look like this: (VII.622–25). For short poems, such as Robert Frost's "Stopping by Woods on a Snowy Evening," line numbers usually are considered optional, but you should check with your instructor. For works of fiction in various editions, you should cite the page number(s) in your edition, then follow with a semi-colon, a space, and chapter (ch.) or section (sec.) number. Plays should be referenced by act number, scene number, and line number(s) with no spaces in between.

Examples:

In the end, Tess acknowledges her punishment: "'I am ready,' she said quietly" (417; ch. 58).
"The rarer action is / In virtue than in vengeance" (*The Tempest* 5.3.27–28).

- Students sometimes have a harder time coming up with a title for a literary essay than for an expository one. Be especially careful that your title isn't too broad; it should refer directly to the work(s) you analyze.

Too broad:

"Humanity's Quest"; "The Desire for Freedom"; "Distortion of Reality in Modern Literature"; "The Theme of Race." By specifying the titles of the individual work(s), the writers could have made their essay titles more meaningful and useful.

On the other hand, a title may be specific but uninformative.

Uninformative:

"An Essay on Stephen Crane's 'The Monster'"; "Ted Hughes's 'Hawk Roosting.'"

Informative and Interesting:

"A Frankenstein of Society's Making: Stephen Crane's 'The Monster'"; "A Hawk's Guide to Megalomania."

See Part Five, Section 11.5 for MLA documentation.

16.3 Sample Student Literary Research Essay (MLA style) (1,500 words)

The following essay explores a theme common to a short story and a poem, using the texts and secondary sources for support. The short story, "The Yellow Wallpaper," is summarized, and the poem, "My Papa's Waltz," is reproduced below.

Summary of "The Yellow Wallpaper," by Charlotte Perkins Gilman, first published in 1892. "The Yellow Wallpaper" is comprised of journal entries of an unnamed woman narrator over a period of three months, during which her husband, John, has leased "a colonial mansion." The couple has a new baby, looked after by a nanny, and the narrator is forbidden any activity, including writing, while she recovers from "nervous depression." Although she believes that work and change would do her good, she complies with her husband's wishes, except for writing in her journal, which she hides from her husband and sister-in-law. Confined to an upper room she believes was once a nursery, she is repelled by its yellow wallpaper, but for lack of anything to do studies it intently, becoming more and more obsessed by it.

Over time, she discovers a pattern beneath the surface pattern; and what begins as "a formless sort of figure" later becomes a woman or several women "creeping behind the pattern." The woman shakes the bars of the outer pattern, which are revealed by moonlight; during the day, the trapped woman, like the narrator, is "subdued." The narrator's physical health improves as her obsession deepens; she suspects John and his sister also take an interest in the wallpaper. In the week before the expiry of the lease, the narrator thinks she sees the woman creeping about the grounds. On the last day, the narrator is determined to free the woman forever and, to do so undisturbed, locks the door and throws the key out a window.

Armed with rope to tie up the woman if she tries to get away, the narrator completes the job by ripping off the wallpaper. In the final scene, the narrator is creeping around the room's perimeter as John enters, then faints. Stepping over him, the narrator says, "I've got out at last . . . . And I've pulled off most of the paper, so you can't put me back!"

"My Papa's Waltz"
by Theodore Roethke

The whiskey on your breath
Could make a small boy dizzy;
But I hung on like death:
Such waltzing was not easy.

We romped until the pans
Slid from the kitchen shelf;
My mother's countenance
Could not unfrown itself.

The hand that held my wrist
Was battered on one knuckle;
At every step you missed
My right ear scraped a buckle.

You beat time on my head
With a palm caked hard by dirt,
Then waltzed me off to bed
Still clinging to your shirt.

Gilman's "The Yellow Wallpaper" and Roethke's "My Papa's Waltz":

An Exploration of Ambivalence

by Kiyuri Naicker

Using the logical method, the writer quickly narrows the focus to the "grey areas" of domestic relationships. The last sentence makes it clear that she will be using, in part, a context-centred approach in her readings of the works.

We often look at our world in terms of opposites or dualities. Only the bravest writers attempt to explore the grey areas of life where binaries converge and borders are not clearly defined. Some have persevered and created scenarios in which our traditional methods of perception fail us, forcing us to peer into this undefined area. Much can be uncovered about human nature in these instances. Two authors, in particular, have excelled in examining these interstices as they occur in domestic relationships:

Naicker uses biography sparingly, choosing to devote most of her commentary on the story to the social construction of the feminine in the late nineteenth-century and, in particular, on the authority the medical community exercised over women.

Charlotte Perkins Gilman and Theodore Roethke. The works analyzed here investigate what lies between the poles of sanity and insanity, abuse and affection. The ambiguous situations they have created draw our attention to societal concerns and ultimately urge us to question how we interpret the world around us.

At the turn of the century, relatively little was understood about the progression of mental disorders. In her story "The Yellow Wallpaper," Gilman takes us on one woman's journey into madness through a first-person perspective. The story describes the transitional period between sanity and insanity, during which reality slips away and disorder slowly takes over. This fictitious account is based on Gilman's own experiences with neurasthenia and depression, which she underwent early in her marriage. A widespread belief during this period was that mental illness in women stemmed from moral deviance, and it was treated accordingly. In Gilman's case, her physician concluded that she needed to live as domestic a life as possible and limit herself to two hours of "intelligent" life a day. "The Yellow Wallpaper" was written to challenge the prevalent "domestic ideology" of the time; it is largely regarded as a feminist work. In this blurry region of conflicting realities, issues concerning the role of women in a patriarchal society, especially in relation to the medical world, began to surface. The narrative Gilman created "chronicles how women have been socially, historically, and medically constructed as not only weak, but sick beings" (Suess 61). The character never overtly accuses her oppressors for the state she finds herself in, but the story places the blame for the narrator's insanity on her situation rather than on herself. Jeannette King and Pam Morris explain that early feminist readings such as this were important because they "rectified the tendency to enclose the heroine's problems within her own abnormal psychological state" (37). This story forces one to look at what has actually transpired in the mind of the narrator, something that was generally avoided at the time in the treatment of mental disorders. As is evident in the narrator's interactions with her physician husband, the capacity of women to assess their own mental health was not taken seriously, and their concerns regarding their conditions were often marginalized. The outcome of this story points to the dangers of inadequate communication between physician and patient. Paula A. Treichler, for instance, reads the story as "an indictment of the complex and unhealthy relationship between women and medical language" (72).

It is also an indictment of the view towards women and creativity at the time. The narrator's writing was seen to be the cause of many of her problems, and any attempts she made to continue with her craft were done in a furtive and guilty manner. Conrad Schumaker believes that it demonstrates "what happens to the

Note the way that Naicker provides a transition between the works by pointing to an element they have in common: the way that love and trust in a domestic relationship can lead to abuse.

imagination when it is defined as feminine (and thus weak) in a patriarchal Victorian society that values only the practical" (591). The original purpose of this piece was therefore to change the view of the prescribed "rest cure" for women with neurasthenia; however, the cure itself had roots in a patriarchal medical realm that came under the magnifying glass as a result. The imposed confinement that Gilman underwent and the negative effects she consequently suffered are apparent in the story; the physician husband acts lovingly but succeeds in imprisoning his wife and driving her over the brink of sanity. Apart from providing an early feminist perspective, this story also illustrates how easily we can hurt those we love, and how trusting we can be of our aggressors.

Roethke explores this balance between affection and abuse more thoroughly in "My Papa's Waltz." Through his carefully ambivalent description, he has created a piece in which the two coexist in the same energetic scene. Roethke went to considerable lengths in his word choice to create ambiguity. Original poetic manuscripts reveal many revisions, the most drastic occurring in the fourth stanza. The first two lines originally read, "The hand wrapped round my head / Was harsh from weeds and dirt," but were changed to, "You beat time on my head / With a palm caked hard by dirt" in the printed version (McKenna 38). The diction in the revision is much more strongly ominous. In contrast, one of the earlier titles was "Dance with Father," but the title was later changed to "My Papa's Waltz"(39). The final title has more affectionate, lighthearted overtones. This has the effect of "plung[ing us] into the comic and tragic tension" of the poem (Janssen 44). Speculation on the tone of this poem has divided many readers. This effectively illustrates the extent to which interpretation depends on an individual's perspective. According to H.R. Swardson,

In the topic sentence of this paragraph, the writer states that she will explore the balance between love and abuse "more thoroughly" in the poem. Accordingly, in her analysis, she refers extensively to the text, to manuscript revisions, and to several critical studies of the poem.

> The words of a poem create a series of filters that eliminate possible meanings. In the universe of possible readings, comparatively few precipitate through all the filters. But in a poem like "My Papa's Waltz," several different readings do succeed in making their way through. At that point, the "preferred reading" is not found in the text, but in the interaction of reader and text. (4)

Two quotations of four lines or more in this essay are set up in the block format.

Those who see the joy in the poem place much emphasis on the rhythm and simple rhyme of the piece, and take the image of the waltz literally. The drunken father is seen as playfully tipsy, lavishing affection on the boy, which readers may have experienced with their own usually reserved fathers after they have had a few drinks. However, those who see the darker side of the poem view the waltz and rhythm ironically. These elements set a dizzying pace for the succession of fearful images remembered by the boy. The whiskey on his father's breath, the shaking room, his frowning mother, and the marred hand of his father (possibly from previous beatings) all flash past him on this terrifying journey around the kitchen. Words like "battered," "scraped," "death," and "beat" are implicated in recounting fear rather than joy. The element of alcohol also enhances the potential for violence and loss of control, according to many. As Bobby Fong observes, "The poem is like a seesaw, where the elements of joy . . . are balanced against the elements of fear . . . . A seesaw tips easily, and 'My Papa's Waltz' is susceptible to the pressure of personal experience" (80).

Given that both elements are present, it is more pertinent to question why they are there rather than argue for one perspective over the other. The ambivalence of the poem illustrates the extent to which the poles of affection and abuse converge, especially for those in dependent relationships. For example, it is possible that the child knows on some level that a terrifying incident has transpired, but in recalling the incident has "regressed into areas of the psyche where powerful thoughts and feelings—the raw materials and driving power of our later lives—remain under the layers of rationale and of civilized purpose" (Snodgrass 81). According to Snodgrass, he is therefore, out of civility and self-preservation, refraining from mentioning the abuse that has occurred. However, it is more likely that the boy himself does not know where the rapture ends and the terror begins. He has difficulty in separating the abusive monster from the loving father, and perhaps does not view them as distinct, opposing forces, as we tend to do. When the "waltz" ends, he still clings to his father who carries him up to bed. Roethke seems to be suggesting that the two extremes are perhaps not as distant as we would like to imagine. Blurring the lines in such a volatile situation makes it easy to understand how domestic violence is perpetuated through generations. The boy in this case has not attached solely negative connotations to the event and may find himself interacting with his own future son in this manner. The whole scene lends itself well to the idea of perpetuity, as stated by Ronald Janssen:

> As an image of still larger patterns, the idea of the waltz raises the image of the dance of death, the dance of life, and we are led to think not only of the succession of daily experiences but also the succession of generations as a kind of pattern as the younger generation moves into the older. (45)

In contrast to her use of other secondary sources, the writer quotes Snodgrass to voice her disagreement with this critic's reading.

Despite the indefinite tone and imagery of the poem, it still succeeds in conveying the nuances of a very complex scene. The tone manages to avoid being deliberately condemning in addressing a highly sensitive subject, and as a result invites honest interpretation and introspection.

Both the works discussed above provide complex and subtle social commentaries. Gilman and Roethke have explored everyday domestic life that exists between the dualities around which we tend to cluster. Their force lies in what they have left unsaid, leaving room for interpretation and, through it, self-examination. By leading us into areas we would normally never venture, they raise issues in feminism and domestic violence that are still pertinent today. As these authors' works suggest, relationships are seldom simple or polar.

Works Cited

Fong, Bobby. "Roethke's 'My Papa's Waltz.'" College Literature 17 (1990): 79–82.

Janssen, Ronald. "Roethke's 'My Papa's Waltz.'" Explicator 44.2 (1986): 43–44.

King, Jeannette, and Pam Morris. "On Not Reading Between the Lines: Models of Reading in 'The Yellow Wallpaper.'" Studies in Short Fiction 26.1 (1989): 23–32.

McKenna, John J. "Roethke's Revisions and the Tone of 'My Papa's Waltz.'" ANQ 11.2 (1998): 34–39.

Schumaker, Conrad. "'Too Terribly Good To Be Printed': Charlotte Gilman's 'The Yellow Wallpaper'". American Literature: A Journal of Literary History, Criticism, and Bibliography 57 (1985): 588–99.

Snodgrass, W. D. "That Anguish of Concreteness—Theodore Roethke's Career." Theodore Roethke: Essays on the Poetry. Ed. Arnold Stein. Seattle: University of Washington Press, 1965. 81.

Suess, B.A. "The Writing's on the Wall: Symbolic Orders in 'The Yellow Wallpaper.'" Women's Studies 32.1 (2003): 79–97.

Swardson, H. R. "The Use of the Word Mistake in the Teaching of Poetry." ADE Bulletin 91 (1988): 4–13.

Treichler, Paula. A. "Escaping the Sentence: Diagnosis and Discourse in 'The Yellow Wallpaper.'" Tulsa Studies in Women's Literature 3.1–2 (1984): 61–77.

17. Reading #3 (MLA Style)

Exercise

Pre-reading

1. What do you know or assume about the conditions or experiences of North American working women around the turn of the twentieth century? Using a prewriting technique, explore your associations with this topic.

2. This essay contains descriptive section headings, each of which is followed by a brief excerpt. What functions do the headings and excerpts serve?

The Urban Working Girl in Turn-of-the-Century Canadian Fiction
LINDSEY MCMASTER

The eyes of the women met. They smiled at one another. Fellow-workers – out in the world together. That's what their eyes said: Free!

– Jessie Georgina Sime, *Sister Woman* (40)

At the turn of the twentieth century, the relatively new figure of the independent urban "working girl" represented for many writers the modern city: its opportunities but also its potential for immorality and cultural disruption. At a time when women – in particular young single women – were entering the paid workforce in unprecedented numbers, there emerged in social commentary and fictional narrative the recognized figure of the working girl – the representational counterpart of society's new female wage earners. It is to this culturally constructed figure that I refer in the following discussion of the working girl in Canadian literature.

While many American writers seized upon the working girl as a heroine through which to explore the dubious social repercussions of modernity, Canadian writers were more hesitant to address this female harbinger of change. In a literary market dominated by historical romance, the texts of social realism more likely to depict the working class were often neglected, but a more specialized suppression seemed to apply to representations of the urban working girl. Subject to exploitation both economic and sexual, the working girl had the potential to take on universal meaning as the innocent working-class victim of unprincipled capital, and in some texts this is her role. But the confidence and enthusiasm with which young women were entering the urban fray in Canada significantly undermined the appraisal of them as unwilling sacrifices to industrialism. Not easily fixed in categories of innocence or corruption, the working girl's elision from Canadian literature may in part reflect an unwillingness to face the complex social changes that she embodied.

Notably, the works of the few writers who did take up the figure of the working girl seem to fall into two distinct genres: either issue-oriented social realism or lighthearted popular romance, both often neglected in criticism then and today. While journalists and social reformers of the day voiced concern about the plight of working women, it seems that literature directed at the middle-class literary audience was not expected to foreground social injustice too insistently, and it is this literature that entered the canon. There are, of course, myriad reasons for one text to be canonized and not another, but the coincidence that saw urban themes, working-class issues, and gender politics all frequently sidelined suggests a palpable resistance to acknowledging precisely those cultural conditions epitomized in the working girl. Those works that do address this figure were thus engaged in a politics of representation wherein even to depict the working girl was to invest meaning where it had long been denied. Just as working women were contributing to the industrial economy in a whole new way, so too working girls in literature were doing cultural work in figuring social transformation and gender transgression, and, considering the momentous changes in gender expectations occurring in the twentieth century, the narratives that lent meaning to the wage-earning woman are social documents of great importance.

Social Realism and Working Women
in Canadian Literature

> And so, by force of cruel fate, as it seemed, this girl was as truly chained by invisible fetters to her daily toil among those relentless wheels and pulleys, as if she were a galley-slave.
>
> – Agnes Maule Machar, *Roland Graeme* (67)

In 1919, Jessie Georgina Sime published *Sister Woman*, a collection of short stories that addressed the "Woman Question" by portraying, in stark realist mode, the struggles of Montreal's working-class women. Reviews of the work were not hostile, but they betray a marked ambivalence: "It is an attractive and clever book, but the constancy of the point of view in the tales gives a certain monotony. But one doesn't need to read them all at once" (Donovan). More intriguing than mere dismissal, however, is the opening statement of the anonymous *Canadian Bookman* review, which situates its evaluation in terms of the national literature: "There are qualities about the collection of short sketches entitled 'Sister Woman,' by Miss J.B. [sic] Sime, which make us hesitate to describe it as belonging to Canadian literature" (57). The reviewer admits that the writer has lived in Montreal for several years, and the setting is likewise Canadian, but "it is not a book for a young country. It is lacking in sentimentality and optimism, which we seem to demand from purveyors of fiction on this North American continent" (58). Despite these reservations, the review is not otherwise negative; the reviewer describes the story "Munitions" as "one of the most effective presentations in modern literature of the desire of the modern woman for economic independence" and the whole volume as one "which should take rank among the best of the current work of English writers" (58). The hesitation to embrace the text as part of Canadian literature, then, seems to be based not on any lack of quality but on a feeling that, partly because of its dearth of optimism and sentimentality, the work was atypical of Canadian literature and unlikely to be appreciated by Canadian readers. The degree of ambivalence betrayed by these reviewers, and in particular the articulation of that ambivalence in terms of the national literature, are indicative of the reluctance to accept social criticism as part of Canadian literature. But that nationalist bent further suggests a reluctance to acknowledge contemporary social problems in Canada or to see fiction as one part of the debate needed to address social inequity.

In her introduction to the 1892 novel *Roland Graeme, Knight*, Carole Gerson notes that "In nineteenth century Canada. . . realistic social fiction was generally rejected in favour of historical romance inspired by the example of Sir Walter Scott. So rare was the literary acknowledgement of social problems that for *Roland Graeme*, one of the most sustained examinations of socio-economic issues to appear in Canadian fiction before the First World War, Machar chose an American setting" (xiii). Gerson explains that this may have been careful planning by Machar, who knew that America and Britain would likely hold the majority of her audience, while Canadian readers would more readily accept a social critique set outside Canada. *Roland Graeme* appeared in the late nineteenth century, but the Canadian distaste for socially engaged fiction persisted into the twentieth century as "scores of writers produced lyrical tributes to place and youth. . . or penned tender historical romances" (New 140). As William H. New points out, this predilection for historical romance was concomitant with a rejection of urban narrative. Despite the rapid expansion of Canadian cities, literature remained rural in setting and theme. Representing problems of social inequity may not demand an urban setting, but in literature of social critique the city, as the spatial manifestation of modernity, often provides the milieu in which questions of social injustice are represented in most detail. Furthermore, the most sustained challenges to the social order in terms of gender configuration were taking place in the city as women's increasing entrance into the paid workforce brought about fundamental shifts in gender relations. As New points out, there was also a gendered aspect to the taste for rural themes in Canadian literature: "The general resistance to 'city themes' was perhaps a refusal to recognize social inequities in Canada, perhaps part of a continuing rejection of women's newly visible role in literature and (urban) politics. The city was in some sense figuratively theirs, just as received versions of 'Nature' were extensions of male myths of control" (140). The rejection of urban social themes in Canadian literature, then, was not merely a genre preference but a refusal of those media that might allow for gender contestation. As one of the most visible and troubling figures of urban modernity, the working girl embodied precisely those conflicts that Canadian literature sought to avoid. It is not surprising, then, that Sime's *Sister Woman*, despite its acknowledged merit and its realist innovation, was excluded from established notions of what constituted Canadian literature, for it centred on the urban working girl.

While feminist critics such as Sandra Campbell and Lorraine McMullen have brought to light writers who, like Sime, have often been neglected in the canonization of Canadian literature, novels of socially engaged fiction are still largely marginalized, meaning that narrative representations of Canada's urban working women have been all but buried. In the United States, the tale of the working girl is a much more recognized institution, with landmark texts such as Theodore Dreiser's *Sister Carrie* and Dorothy Richardson's *The Long Day* standing out from a crowd of lesser-known popular works and serialized fiction. Indeed, at the end of the nineteenth century in America, the prolific serial-fiction writer Laura Jean Libbey made the working-girl story into a formula romance and guaranteed best-seller, and her works may have influenced to some degree the Canadian writers who did portray the working girl in their fiction. In fact, the few texts that do revolve around this figure reveal a degree of class tension and social turbulence that is all the more fascinating for its Canadian context. One 1912 novel even has its working-girl heroine suddenly awaken to class hierarchy as she looks for work: "It had never before occurred to her that in applying for this place she had forfeited some of the rights of caste. Social distinctions had troubled Christine as little as they trouble most sensible Canadian girls. She had thought as little about her position as a duchess might: now, for the first time, she felt troubled and uneasy" (Mackay 66). This passage draws on the Canadian myth of a classless society, a myth that often went unchallenged by mainstream literature, which curtailed class commentary by excluding social fiction. As Christine's troubling realization demonstrates, the struggles of the working girl are inextricably bound to class inequity, and the Canadian reader of working-girl fiction was likely, like Christine, to feel "troubled and uneasy" when literature brought that conflict to light.

The four texts that I discuss in detail here feature themes of gender and labour, and, though they differ greatly in their treatment of the social questions involved, the various depictions of the working girl suggest her representational power. Since the texts are seldom read today, what follows are brief summaries to clarify the content and genre positions of the texts.

As with the Canadian working girl's realization of class in the quotation above, Agnes Maule Machar's *Roland Graeme, Knight* is a novel designed to elicit precisely this kind of awakening to social injustice. Published in 1892, it centres on a young, middle-class woman, Nora Blanchard, who comes to sympathize with her working-class sisters and subsequently embarks on a number of philanthropic projects to help them. The catalyst in her moral awakening is Roland Graeme, a member of the Knights of Labour and a Canadian, who introduces Nora to labour politics and thus educates the reader. With its focus on middle-class characters, the novel clearly addresses a middle-class reader as well, urging sympathy for the working class in the form of maternal feminist philanthropy for women and fair labour practices for men. Two minor characters are working girls employed at the town mill: Lizzie Mason, who supports an ailing mother and a wayward brother, is chronically overworked and on her way to an early grave by the end of the novel; Nelly Grove, meanwhile, the more spirited incarnation of the factory girl, displays the good looks and fancy dress that portend her fate as a fallen woman. These two versions of the working girl are recognizable tropes in both fiction and social commentary of the day, figures meant to evoke the pity and humanitarian impulses of a middle-class readership.

While the novel remains largely conservative in that it does not mount an overt challenge to class hierarchy, the way in which Machar executes her moral project is interesting in terms of gender politics. While the title character and ostensible hero is male, the central character is undoubtedly Nora, whose awakening to class inequity provides her character with the most development; Roland, by contrast, is virtuous but static. In this narrative of labour unrest, the presence of the Knights of Labour and the event of a strike suggest a male conflict, but the only working-class characters of any prominence are the working girls; meanwhile, what causes the major reforms for the mill workers are the complaints to the mill owner by his wife and daughter, who, like Nora, are appalled by the working conditions of the young women. The working girls, then, appear to stand in for the whole working class, since their exploitation is the most visible and the most likely to elicit middle-class moral indignation; and the middle-class women, albeit by pestering their men, are the primary agents of social change. The novel is thus very much about the role of women in labour politics, even though in 1892 a relation between these two would seldom have been thought to exist.

Novels aimed at a more popular audience represented the working girl differently. Bertrand Sinclair's most popular novel, *North of Fifty-Three* (1914), and Isabel Ecclestone Mackay's *The House of Windows* (1912) both depict the working girl as adventurous and capable. *North of Fifty-Three*'s Hazel Weir is twice subjected to unwanted physical advances by men, and both times she successfully slugs the offender and proves herself both physically and morally superior. The novel sold 340,000 copies, and Sinclair followed it with several more novels also set in British Columbia, few of which, however, featured female characters so prominently or sold so well. In many ways, *North of Fifty-Three* depends on gender stereotypes, but a major part of Sinclair's project is a critique of urban industrialism, and it is significant that for this Sinclair chose the working girl as the pivotal figure. Hazel

Weir starts the novel as a stenographer in an eastern city and is engaged to a young man in real estate, who breaks their engagement when he believes a false rumour that she has had an affair with her boss. Hazel moves out to British Columbia to teach, where she gets lost in the woods and is found by Roaring Bill Wagstaff, who promptly kidnaps her to spend the winter in his isolated cabin. In many ways, this episode echoes the rumours of bride-ship girls brought out from Britain and whisked off by wilderness men to backwoods weddings; it is as though the novel's working-girl formula is being highjacked by western Canadian folklore. Wagstaff, ever the gentleman, does not lay a finger on Hazel, and come spring he yields to her demand to be released, escorting her to Vancouver and leaving her there. Hazel plans to pick up where she left off by finding work as a stenographer, but the bustle of the city is now alien to her: "She had her trade at her finger ends, and the storied office buildings of Vancouver assured her that any efficient stenographer could find work. But she looked up as she walked the streets at the high, ugly walls of brick and steel and stone, and her heart misgave her" (158).

Just as the city thus threatens to overwhelm her, she encounters her ex-fiancé, Jack Barrow, on the corner of Seymour and Hastings. He is full of apologies for his past behaviour and begs her to take him back. Hazel cannot resist comparing him in her mind to Wagstaff: "And she could not conceive of Bill Wagstaff ever being humble or penitent for anything he had done. Barrow's attitude was that of a little boy who had broken some plaything in a fit of anger and was now woefully trying to put the pieces together again. It amused her" (161). Soon after, Hazel makes her way back to Wagstaff's cabin, and she and Wagstaff are married instantly. Her moral choice between the rugged wilderness life, considered here to be more honest, and wage work in the city is represented as a romantic choice between the hypermasculine mountain man and the vacillating city boy.

As a working girl engaged to a real estate man, Hazel begins the novel as a representative of the corrupt urban life: subject to harassment in the economically and sexually exploitative workplace and a victim of false innuendo, she is betrayed by her fiancé and ostracized by a hypocritical society. Here the working-girl figure is clearly the touchstone for judgements on city life and the moral cesspool of urban industrialism. Her journey to the West Coast, then, is a moral one as well as a physical and romantic one. However, since redemption here is contingent upon rejection of city and workplace hypocrisies, and valorization of the explicitly masculine wilderness life, Hazel must renounce her role as a worker and become the devoted backwoods wife. The romance, of course, naturalizes this transition, but an extended section of the novel involves her reluctance to give up the pleasures of the urban social scene for the isolation of rural BC. By positing her redemption, figured as romantic fulfilment with Wagstaff, on renunciation of city life, the novel demonstrates the tendency for moral arguments on urban life to coalesce around the working girl, whose independence in a setting of moral indeterminacy is considered unmanageable and so demands containment.

Also aimed at a popular audience, Mackay's *The House of Windows* shares many attributes with the formulaic working-girl romance, including sinister plots and kidnappings, a hidden family lineage, an almost-thwarted romance, and a heroine whose flawless beauty is exceeded only by her perfect virtue. While still a baby, Christine is discovered abandoned in the Angers & Son department store. One of the shop girls takes her home and, together with her blind sister, raises the child as if she were their younger sister. When she is sixteen, Christine and her adoptive sisters fall on hard times, and Christine also becomes a shop girl at Angers & Son. Meanwhile, a fallen-woman subplot rises to unusual prominence, incorporating strong judgements on women's wages and labour conditions: before Christine appeared as a baby at Angers & Son, a shop girl there had turned to prostitution because of overwork, low wages, and the need to support an ailing mother. The shop girl died, but her mother recovered and swore vengeance upon the owner of Angers & Son, Adam Torrance, whose indifference to the plight of his shop girls indirectly caused the downfall of the daughter. The avenging mother therefore kidnapped Torrance's baby girl and left her in the department store, the child being none other than our heroine Christine. Sixteen years later, with Christine a shop girl, the old woman fulfils her scheme of poetic justice by kidnapping Christine and imprisoning her in a brothel, where she is every moment in danger of experiencing the same fate as the hapless daughter. The ensuing detective narrative has Christine rescued by Torrance's nephew, who has loved her all along. The novel concludes with a merging of upper and lower classes: Christine engaged to the nephew and the blind adoptive sister engaged to Torrance. Although the novel is set in an unnamed city in eastern Canada, Mackay wrote it in Vancouver, and she includes a subplot that sends the shop owner's nephew to Vancouver, where he comments on the charm and sophistication of the city's young women. The romance formula tends to have the hero sent away as an obstacle to the eventual union with the heroine, and it is interesting that Mackay uses this convention to add a commentary on life in her own city of Vancouver, lending the tale a degree of West Coast character.

Undoubtedly the most serious work of fiction regarding the working girl in early-twentieth-century Canada is J.G. Sime's *Sister Woman*, set in Montreal and published in 1919. As Sandra Campbell points out, Sime intended the form of her writing to reflect the character of modern urban life, and for this reason she used the short story: "one feels in the cities, I think, the potentials of quite another kind of art – disjointed, disconnected art that finds its expression in thumb nail sketches, short stories, one-act scrappy plays and the like" (qtd. in Campbell 43). The stories in *Sister Woman* revolve around the many incarnations of the urban working woman: seamstresses, secretaries, munitions workers, domestic workers, and so on. Many of the narratives also explore female sexuality by representing the relationships of working women with men, drawing special attention to illicit relationships popularly known as "irregular unions": a secretary's secret relationship with her boss, a housekeeper's with her employer, an unwed couple faced with an unplanned pregnancy. All of these relationships are represented with a sympathetic yet unapologetic candour very unusual for the time. Employing the fragmentary form of the short story collection, Sime's writing carefully connects the tone of urban life with the struggles of the working woman, and, by further focusing on gender relations, her fiction places the working girl at the forefront of cultural transformation.

All four of these texts depict the working girl in narratives of social unease, with economic exploitation and sexual danger everywhere. In fact, as with the boss who gets socked in the teeth in *North of Fifty-Three*, or the mill owner's son who flirts with factory girls in *Roland Graeme*, the two are often conflated. In stories of the working girl, the pressures of the labour economy are closely bound to a coercive sexual economy fraught with shifting implications for gender politics in urban society. When the working-girl narrative functions as the subplot for a middle-class morality tale, as in *Roland Graeme*, it operates in a very different way than it does when it is the centre of popular romance such as *The House of Windows*, in which working-class virtue guarantees wealth and happiness. The fact that the figure of the working girl can act as a recognizable trope in a variety of texts, yet a trope with multiple possible meanings, is indicative of the cultural significance of this neglected figure of Canadian literature.

Class Cross-Dressing in *The House of Windows*

> Again he took the small hand extended to him and again it seemed to change
> miraculously from the hand of Miss Brown into the hand of some delectable princess.
> – Isabel Ecclestone Mackay, *The House of Windows* (180)

Isabel Ecclestone Mackay moved to Vancouver in 1909 and wrote a number of novels, primarily romantic in tone and aimed at a popular audience, but she was better known for her poetry, which was grouped with that of Pauline Johnson. Published in 1912, *The House of Windows* draws on the dime novel tradition of the working-girl romance, a formula popularized in late-nineteenth-century America by Laura Jean Libbey, whose serialized narratives were devoured by America's female working class. In Canada, a writer of comparable popularity was May Agnes Fleming, but her romances featured primarily middle-class characters, while the working-girl romance always had a working-class heroine. So, while the works of Libbey and her counterparts were likely read in Canada, there was no equivalent trend in Canadian literature. *The House of Windows*, then, was unusual for Canadian literature of the day; with its urban setting and shop-girl characters, it represented a side of Canadian life not usually addressed in literature. Far from Sime's direct realism, however, Mackay's novel mixes realist depictions of working women's hardships with romantic fantasies of danger, adventure, and wealth. Nan Enstad examines the genre of working-girl fiction at length in her book *Ladies of Labor, Girls of Adventure: Working Women, Popular Culture, and Labor Politics at the Turn of the Twentieth Century*, and these plots of mystery, intrigue, and Cinderella romance characterized the working-girl formula popular in America: "The stories invoked the difficulty of working-class women's lives – toiling at jobs that offered little hope for advancement – and offered them fabulous fantasies of wealth, fashion, success, and love" (19). In some ways, this popular-culture form, closing with wealth and marriage, which remove the young heroine from the working sphere, seems to reinscribe a traditional vision of female success. But as critics of the genre have pointed out, there is a noticeable current in such narratives running counter to readings that would thus circumscribe the meaning of the texts, especially as representations of class.

In *Roland Graeme*, the factory girl, Nelly, engages in a flirtation with the mill owner's son, Harold Pomeroy, already engaged to another girl. This relationship signifies the moral degradation of both characters, but it is Nelly who fares worse in the end with the implication that she becomes a fallen woman. Working-girl narratives often feature an involvement between the working girl and the boss's son, sometimes representing the latter as hero but more often as wicked seducer. As Michael Denning points out in *Mechanic Accents: Dime Novels and Working-Class Culture in America*, such narratives render class conflict as the direct, personal confrontation of sexual intrigue or harassment (196), but how that conflict unfolds may also indicate the social agenda of the writer: "Unlike the seduction novels that occasionally occur in middle-class fiction, which focus on the fallen woman, the Libbey stories [working-girl dime novels] are tales of the woman who does not fall, despite drugs, false marriage, physical violence, and disguise. Against middle-class sympathy for the fallen is set working-class virtue" (192). *Roland Graeme* is very much a novel of "middle-class sympathy," in which working girls are pitiable victims of industrial and sexual exploitation; while middle-class philanthropy might ease their suffering, there is no question of their class position changing or of the women themselves successfully resisting their treatment. By contrast, in the popular working-girl narrative established by Libbey and played on by Sinclair and Mackay, the sexually charged class confrontation of working girl and upper-class man unfolds quite differently. In

North of Fifty-Three, Hazel capably punches her boss in the nose and even somewhat enjoys it: "It seemed unwomanly to strike. But the humour of the thing appealed to her most strongly of all. In spite of herself, she smiled as she reached once more for her hat. And this time Mr. Bush did not attempt to restrain her" (21). Hazel's able self-defence here is a precursor of her ultimate rejection of class exploitation, represented through her relationship with the socialist hero. In *The House of Windows*, the gentleman seducer hovers around the heroine's workplace, virtually stalking her, until Christine confronts him: "'I do not know you,' she said quietly, 'but if you are a gentleman you will annoy me no further. I do not wish to appeal to the police.' . . . It was a defeat as complete and unexpected as Waterloo!" (151). Christine is the embodiment of working-class virtue, and the introduction of this would-be seducer seems to be almost an offhand way to highlight the impossibility of her being tempted. She does, however, strike up a romance with the boss's adopted son, here the hero, who must actually masquerade as a working-class piano salesman so that her initial attraction to him remains unsullied by questions of class aspiration. These popular depictions of the working girl appealed to a working-class readership, who might well have been insulted if the working girl were represented as morally weak. Where narratives aimed at the middle class may invite sympathy for the downtrodden working girl, her vulnerability to seduction and her exploitation in the workplace seeming to go hand in hand, they nevertheless leave class divisions intact. The moral and physical strength of the working girl who ably fights off her assailants, meanwhile, suggests a working-class resistance to exploitation, sexual or class based. The endings of working-girl novels in turn reward their feisty heroines with secret inheritances and propitious marriages that defy class boundaries.

What both the middle-class and dime novel modes of fiction demonstrate, then, is that, in narratives of working-class womanhood, class identity and sexual purity are inextricably intertwined: in *Roland Graeme*, Nelly's vulnerability to sexual degradation is a product of her class-specific environment, while in *The House of Windows* Christine's unassailable purity is, depending on one's reading, a testimony to working-class virtue or evidence that Christine is really a "lady" all along. This connection between class and sexuality, and the dual readings that arise from it, are part of a debate central to the working-girl narrative. As Denning points out, "in the rhetoric of the late nineteenth century bourgeois culture, a working woman could not be virtuous, regardless of her virginity" (191). To contend, as working-girl novels did, that the working woman was indeed a figure of unquestionable virtue was to assert that she was as good as any "lady." Hence the central question in these narratives: "Key to the dime novel plot is the question: Can a worker be a lady? That is, does work indeed degrade, spoil one's virtue, make one coarse and masculine?" (Enstad 74).

Concerned with the proper public deportment of the working woman, a 1903 article by Annie Merrill in *Canadian Magazine* dispensed the following fashion advice for the "Serious Woman in Business": "She is careful to avoid being conspicuous in her manner. Dresses plainly. Does not try to ape the 'lady,' with gaudy imitations in gowns and jewels" (408). Accompanying this admonition is an illustration of the modestly dressed working woman, the caption reminding us that "She dresses plainly" (408). Merrill's advice manifests the middle-class desire to clarify class divisions, especially when working-class women were at issue, and fashion was a major system of signification for female class hierarchy. In fact, the tendency of working-class women "to ape the 'lady,'" as Merrill puts it, was a common middle-class complaint about working girls. Enstad documents working women's consumer culture and describes turn-of-the-century working women who were notorious for their fashion sense, choosing clothes that many thought were inappropriate for their class:

Working women dressed in fashion, but they exaggerated elements of style that specifically coded femininity: high-heeled shoes, large or highly decorated hats, exceedingly long trains (if trains were in style) and fine undergarments. . . . By appropriating and exaggerating the accoutrements of ladyhood, working women invested the category of lady with great imaginative value, implicitly challenging dominant meanings and filling the category with their own flamboyant practices. (78)

Enstad draws a connection between this fantasy of ladyhood enacted through dress and the fantasies afforded to working women in novels, in which the working girl similarly becomes a lady. The heightened femininity of their attire, meanwhile, responded to the notion that work was masculinizing for women: class and gender definitions, then, were clearly both at stake. Mackay describes the shop girls in *The House of Windows* engaging in this exaggerated and decorative femininity through their hairdos:

The fashion in hairdressing had also changed, and the young ladies behind the counters, who in Celia's day had been content with neatly coiled or braided tresses, were now resplendent in towering structures which held the eye with the fascination of the wonderful. It was all simple enough to one who understood the mysteries of rats and buns and turbans and puffs and curls, but to the uninitiated the result was little short of miraculous, for even supposing that Nature, in lavish mood, had supplied such hair – how did they get it to stick on? (123)

That the hairdos here are extravagant, defy nature, and include fake stick-on hair demonstrates the trend toward excess described by Enstad. Shop girls, in fact, whose work had everything to do with fashion and display, were thought to be particularly guilty of this kind of accessorizing overkill. In *Counter Cultures: Saleswomen, Managers, and Customers in American Department Stores 1890-1940*, Susan Porter Benson describes how shop girls, working in the world of style and consumerism, often displayed their expertise through their dress, a practice that also narrowed the class gap between them and their customers, sometimes to the dismay of the latter (235). For Christine in *The House of Windows*, it is interesting that, even before she starts working in the stores, she is categorized with shop girls because of her appearance. Following her failed attempt to get work in a home reading to the lady of the house, the maid sums up her chances elsewhere:

"She'll have some trouble getting anything respectable with that face," she remarked. "In her walk of life I always say that beauty is a drawback as often as not." . . .

"And what would you say Miss Brown's walk in life might be, Martha?"

The maid shook her head slowly. "Oh, she's got airs and graces enough! But you never can tell. Shop girls are getting very dressy, these days, what with their false hair and all! And ladies don't go about looking for work." (75)

In other words, Christine resembles either a lady or a shop girl, according to her good looks (her hair in particular is often mentioned), her dress, and her demeanour; the only reason not to classify her as a lady is that ladies do not need work. This scene has everything to do with identity and the class and gender markers that supposedly reveal that identity, but the working-girl figure poses a significant challenge to her interpreters; undermining the maid's apparent accuracy here is the dramatic irony – though the characters are not aware of it, the reader knows that Christine really is a lady. Mackay is thus deliberately playing on the class and fashion ambiguities that make the shop girl hard to distinguish from the lady, foregrounding class indeterminacy and so gesturing to the possible breakdown of class division.

Enstad has examined the frequent objections made by middle-class commentators such as Merrill to the "tastelessness" of working women who were thought to be aping the lady through their fashion choices. In fact, turn-of-the-century social critics, especially those concerned with prostitution, such as John Shearer, not only judged fashionable working women's attire as tasteless but also predicted that it was the first step toward immorality – where class ambiguity led, aspersions of sexual impropriety followed. At the end of *Roland Graeme*, the fate of the factory girl who flirted with the boss's son is rendered in a shorthand that the nineteenth-century reader would have understood instantly when Roland says "I met that poor Nelly, the other day, very much overdressed. I don't think she works in the mill, now" (283). In *The House of Windows*, the stores have a policy of "employing only such girls as have homes and other means of support" (144). When questioned about this, the owner, Torrance, explains: "Because long ago I investigated and found out that, as a matter of fact, a girl, entirely alone and dependent upon herself, would find it hard to get along comfortably upon her wage. This, in the cases of some girls more fond of display, etc., etc., led to a – ah – deplorable state of things. Things which I need not discuss" (144). Here, once more, a taste for clothes or a fondness of display essentially stands in for the less mentionable sexual downfall of the working woman. But in addition, this assumed connection between dress and sexuality influences not only attitudes toward the working woman but labour policies as well. Mackay's is an informed depiction here, for in Vancouver and elsewhere it was common business practice to hire only girls who lived at home and had other means of support, a policy that drew on the prevalent view that young women worked for "pin money" and thus did not deserve or require a living wage (Kealey 36). This practically institutionalized preoccupation with working women's consumer habits, especially in the heavily symbolic area of dress, suggests the widespread anxiety over their potentially transgressive desires. In the scene noted above, Torrance is upbraided by his sister, who mocks his euphemism ("fond of display, I think you said" [145]), and his redemption in the novel involves a "reformation of his labour practices. The way in which working girls' fashion was considered an index of their morality signals the conceptual bond between class position and sexual purity: dressing above one's station was a moral failing. With working women's dress signifying so much, it is no wonder that, like the novel, it became one terrain on which questions of ladyhood and respectability were repeatedly played out.

In the class narrative of *The House of Windows*, Mackay seems to oscillate at certain points between extolling working-class virtue and reinscribing class essentialism by reminding us of Christine's hidden birthright. When Christine is kidnapped by the evil old woman who intends to make a fallen woman of her, the detective assures the girl's rich long-lost father that Christine will never fall because "blood tells. Don't you ever believe but that good blood tells" (195). Yet her goodness is elsewhere ascribed to the devoted upbringing given by her working-class adoptive sisters. She herself never thinks of her own class position until she looks for work, and the class indifference ascribed to Christine, who "thought as little about her position as a Duchess might" (66), is also used to describe Vancouver girls, mentioned in a letter by the travelling hero, Mark: "One's notions of caste get a sharp knock out here. . . . These girls, for instance, whose mother waited at table and whose father worked as a navvy, would be quite undismayed in shaking hands with a princess. It would not occur to them that there was any reason for undue diffidence" (138).

Mackay's repeated representation of young women whose self-respect defies class distinctions suggests her endorsement of this tendency ascribed to "most sensible Canadian girls" (66). Meanwhile, the upper-class characters such as Mark and Torrance have interactions with such women that shake their class-defined assumptions, and Torrance eventually marries one of Christine's poor sisters, thereby transcending class division. Mackay seems to relish the moment when class distinctions are unexpectedly rendered visible and through that visibility shown to be unnatural and undesirable. By endorsing the views ascribed specifically to young Canadian women, even to shop girls, Mackay destabilizes class categories while giving her novel a Canadian specificity. To lend the working girl the voice of authority in matters of class was bold for Canadian literature, and perhaps the contradictions and inconsistencies in the class terminology of the novel indicate a hesitancy to fully challenge a conservative readership. Nevertheless, by situating the working-class woman at centre stage of her narrative, Mackay was already defying convention for Canadian literature, and by choosing the highly visible shop girl as the heroine, and titling the novel *The House of Windows*, perhaps Mackay sought to lend greater social recognition to the working girl and her struggles. Considering Merrill's admonition to avoid being "conspicuous," and the moral imputations concerning those "fond of display" or "making a spectacle of themselves," to insist that women and especially working women deserved greater social prominence was to protest against codes of both gender and class. And in this way, the project of writers such as Mackay and Sime cannot be underestimated.

Sex and the City

> There was the Factory – the Factory, with its coarse, strong, beckoning life – its noise – its dirt – its men. Its men! And suddenly into Bertha Martin's cheek a wave of colour surged.
> – Jessie Georgina Sime, *Sister Woman* (44)

Representations of the working girl often mediate the cultural transitions of urban industrialism. As Suzanne Mackenzie points out, "It is not a simple coincidence that periods of urban transition happen simultaneously with periods of gender role alteration. . . . Changes in the city and in women's activities are inextricably linked" (24). Literature that represented the urban working girl took a great interest in her social life, for, despite long hours and low wages, young working women were known for their pursuit of leisure, and the city offered new kinds of pleasures, many targeted at the growing demographic of single working women. One area of leisure that underwent rapid change soon after the turn of the century was the practice of dating. Not surprisingly, Annie Merrill had advice on this activity as well:

> This Serious Woman in Business will not allow men to squander money upon her, remembering the admonition of her good old grandmother, that such a course would be vulgar. She insists upon bearing her share of the expense when going about with her men friends, and the nice man will appreciate her position, amiably permitting her to feel a comfortable independence which to-day is making real comradeship between men and women such a delightful possibility. . . . It proves to him that she values his friendship and companionship for its own worth; that she is not accepting his attentions merely for the "good time" he is able to give her, in the way that the mercenary girl "makes use of" many a generous-hearted and blindly-devoted man. (408)

Two versions of the working girl appear here: the "Serious Woman in Business" who listens to her grandmother's advice and "the mercenary girl" who uses men to have a good time. Meanwhile, the question of who pays for dinner was clearly as much an object of debate one hundred years ago as it is today. Merrill was reacting to the changing codes of dating, which may have been dictated in part by young women eager for amusement but low on spending money; Joanne Meyerowitz documents the habits of American "women adrift" living on their own and working in the city: "Adopting new urban dating patterns, they relied on men for entertainment, luxuries, and sometimes necessities. By the early twentieth century, many 'women adrift' belonged to urban subcultures in which women gave men sexual favours in return for limited economic support" (xviii). These may have been the mercenary girls of whom Merrill speaks; however, whether exchanging a few favours with men or insisting on paying their own way, working women were playing an active role in changing the rules of dating and the associated rules of gender relations. Merrill even makes a utopian gesture in her assertion that women who pay for themselves will enable a "real comradeship" to exist between men and women. Her advice signals the interest taken in the social practices of single working women and the dual vision that opposed the morally upright woman who shuns vulgarity to the mercenary vixen out for a good time — a contradiction that fuelled the imaginative fire surrounding the sex life of the working girl.

North of Fifty-Three's Hazel Weir has no family in the novel, and she manages all of her relationships on her own, without chaperones or advice. Working girls in literature tend to lack the traditional family and so have to fend for themselves. This was increasingly typical of actual single working women, who came from the countryside or from overseas to find work in the city. Often living on their own in rooming houses or hostels, they conducted their social lives free of family structure and according more to their own preferences than to conventional standards, and their influence on social codes was unmistakable: "By the 1920s, young middle-class flappers romanticized and imitated the working-class women who lived on their own and socialized with men. And popular movies and pulp magazines used the overt sexual behaviour of some 'women adrift' to spread a new stereotype of women as sexual objects. In these ways, the wage-earning women who lived apart from family were a vanguard in the decline of Victorian culture" (Meyerowitz xxiii).

Signalling society's familiarity with the independent working girl as a romantic figure, Sime opens one of her stories with "A bachelor girl! What visions of cigarettes and latch-keys – and liberty!" (272). The reader here is expected to recognize the "bachelor girl" instantly along with the accessories that symbolize her independence. The unconventional relationships of single working women made possible by this independence feature in many of Sime's stories, and the intentionality of the female characters in entering into these relationships is often reaffirmed – they are not innocents seduced but women whose social circumstances afforded them new choices: "And so they had – not drifted into it, not at all. They had entered perfectly open-eyed into an irregular union: into one of those unions with which our whole society is honeycombed to-day. Marion Drysdale had gone on working. She had taken nothing from David Winterford but his love" (95). In a literary context in which the depiction of women engaging in illicit relationships was either completely absent or couched in the assertion of moral imperatives, to represent this choice in such an unflinching way was bold. But there is a series of choices represented here, the connection of which is noteworthy; Marion will engage in a socially unsanctioned sexual relationship, she will keep working, and she will remain financially independent. In a sense, then, the basis of the relationship and the suggested equality of Marion and David are posited on the economic independence of the woman, made possible by her work. Women's wage work was thus a determining factor in new types of relationships between men and women, and the immediate connection in this passage between work and sexual choices demonstrates the profound influence of women's work in the cultural handling of gender.

Sime elaborates on how working women conceived of their relationships and distinguished their behaviour from that of socially stigmatized mistresses or "kept women," and the difference has everything to do with their position as workers. In "An Irregular Union," a secretary who has a secret relationship with her boss makes a point of continuing to work and taking nothing material from her lover:

> In plain words, she didn't take any money for the gift of herself.
>
> It is queer how a little practical fact like that can make an old episode seem new – a new thing in the history of the world. . . . The little insignificant fact that she was able to "keep herself," as it is called, changed for her the whole complexion of her love episode. It gave her confidence and self-respect. She could feel with perfect accuracy that she was not a "kept woman." (79)

For this character, the fact of working colours her view of sexual relationships. Yet her need to justify her actions in her own mind and to separate herself from traditionally censured versions of female sexuality also demonstrates the difficulties faced by women who challenged social codes of gender and sexuality. Working women may have been pioneering new kinds of relationships, but destabilizing gender systems was not work to be taken lightly. The working classes may have readily rejected a certain degree of middle-class prudery, but enduring codes of female chastity and working-class honour still had influence and in many cases contributed to working women's self-definition. Given middle-class administrators eager for evidence of moral degradation among working women, often the affirmation of purity was important not only to working women's pride but to their political activism as well. The niceties of an irregular union or the degrees of supposed impropriety, then, were considerations of some importance. Sime, though she often focuses on the sense of liberation and independence among working women, also represents some of the subtleties and contradictions that beset women who took advantage of newfound freedom. The secretary in "An Irregular Union," for instance, spends the story in her room waiting for the phone to ring because her lover is in the hospital, and, unable to visit him because of the nature of their relationship, she has to await news of his condition from a nurse. The new world of urban dating was an important manifestation of the desires of working women, but it was also a world of many pressures and constraints.

The freedom to enact new kinds of desire as well as the challenges involved in so breaking with tradition were both linked in important ways to working women's residence in the city. In "An Irregular Union," the single working girl rents her own room and is therefore able to engage in her secret relationship unchaperoned and unnoticed; the narrative likewise depends on the telephone, a relatively new form of technology that came first to urban centres and thus marks the urban setting of the story. As in "Munitions," which takes place on a streetcar carrying women to the factory, Sime's other stories lend prominence to urban technologies, suggesting their significance to her representation of modern women. In "A Woman of Business," the narrator repeatedly mentions the electric light beneath which she hears the life story of a woman who made a career of wealthy lovers:

Madame Sloyovska has led what we call a bad life. She is thoroughly disreputable from head to heel. She has walked in the shadiest paths, and there are few dirty tricks that her hands haven't dabbled in. The snatches of her life, as she gave them to me hurriedly in the glare of that unprotected light, sounded like something you might read in a dime novelette. . . . Madame Sloyovska had had lovers galore, and when she had had one lover's money she had gone on to the next one and she had had his money. (204)

Sime uses the electric light here perhaps as a metaphor for the illumination of things usually kept dark and hidden. But it is striking that she specifically uses a modern technology to provide her metaphor, for in this way she links Madame Sloyovska's way of life to the conditions of modern urban settings. That her way of life depends on a type of sexual conduct wholly condemned by polite society thus suggests a link between urban life and illicit sexuality. The use of this metaphor is another instance of a writer highlighting the existence of figures usually rendered invisible by both social custom and literary convention. In fact, the mention in this passage of the "dime novelette" is telling. The realist short-story genre in which Sime is working is far from the dime novel, yet by using this reference she signals the only other literary milieu in which Madame Sloyovska might be encountered. This gestures subtly to the exclusion of certain women – working-class women or in this case sexually suspect women – from mainstream representation. Sime was highly aware of the form of her writing, choosing the short story for its ability to mimic the fragmentation of urban life, so her thematization of technology is perhaps part of her insight into her own technology of writing. In a sense, then, her story, like the electric light that figures in it, renders suddenly visible what was previously thought too sordid for exposure.

Sime's writing reveals the critical links between modern technology, urbanism, and women's work, and in this way her writing is highly sensitive to the social transformations taking place in part through the agency of working women. Sime could clearly imagine that the urban conditions allowing working women a wholly new independence could lead to the creation of wholly new kinds of women. Although some of her characters fall into feminine stereotypes in their relationships, evincing a self-sacrificing devotion to their lovers that is somewhat essentialized by Sime as a woman's nature, one story depicts a woman wholly separate from the heterosexual system. "The Bachelor Girl" focuses on a single working woman named Tryphena, whose way of life has always been free of men. Orphaned early, raised by a maiden relative, and educated in a convent, Tryphena now earns her own living as a masseuse for female clients only. The result, we are told, is a total indifference toward men:

Men for Tryphena really don't exist. She does not so much dislike them – she simply feels an absolute indifference for and about them. They don't exist for her. . . . This liberty to look past men she buys with work – hard, honest work. Her work is, as she says herself, "just rubbing arms and legs." . . . She knows her work – and she is popular. Women like her quiet ways. . . . And they admire her too – Tryphena is emphatically a woman's woman. (273-74)

For this character, the ability to support herself and live on her own has made possible a way of life and a perception of reality that render traditional gender relations completely obsolete. The narrator points out that "Old Maid is what they would have called her fifty years ago" (272), but Old Maids tend to be defined as women who have failed to find a husband; Tryphena, however, is not just indifferent to men but even finds the thought of marriage preposterous. Seeing her excited one day, the narrator wonders if she has a suitor: "'Oh *no*,' she said. 'Not that.' She looked at me reproachfully. 'How *could* you think,' she said, 'I'd ever marry!' I felt a positive criminal" (276). The narrator's embarrassment here signals her feeling that she has blundered, her mistake being the heterosexist assumption that Tryphena would ever be interested in men or marriage. Although the narrator does not draw further attention to it, this moment of realization – that not all women want men – takes place as Tryphena is giving her a massage, suggesting a more sensual level to this female dialogue. But the desire that Sime elaborates on in the remainder of the story is more maternal in nature; Tryphena is excited because she has bought a baby from the nuns, who were watching for an appropriate orphan for her to adopt. Now that they have found her a baby girl ("A *boy*! No, sir! What do you take me for?" [279]), Tryphena is engrossed in making financial plans for single motherhood. Sime closes the story with Tryphena's intention to name the baby Tryphosa, alluding to the twin sisters from the New Testament. The reference is perhaps a suggestion that Tryphena will raise the child in her own image to relish sisterly female bonds and dismiss heterosexual conventions. Although many of Sime's stories address unconventional relationships of various kinds, this is the only one that suggests the possibility of rejecting heterosexuality outright, and it is striking how explicit the link is – almost cause and effect – between earning one's own living and the "liberty to look past men." Here work provides a degree of freedom that will influence women on fundamental levels of identity and sexuality. Moreover, in 1919, the idea that a woman might intentionally set out to become a single mother would certainly have been unfathomable to many people; indeed, it remains so to many people today. By representing the many possible forms that the working girl might take, Sime shows an awareness of how subtle shifts in gender norms would give way to profound upheavals in the social fabric.

In *Toronto's Girl Problem: The Peril and Pleasures of the City, 1880–1930*, Carolyn Strange describes how "The issue of sexual morality loomed like a dark cloud over discussions of woman's work in the industrializing city, casting waged labour as a test of chastity rather than an economic or political issue" (22). Sime, however, resolutely sees the silver lining here, and, in a society eager to condemn any increase in the sexual licence of women, she demonstrates in the tone of her writing a way to recognize women's sexual choices without castigating them. In a similarly utopian way, where many women virtually drew knives over who could be deemed a lady, Sime advocated a feminist sisterhood that would cross class boundaries. Although Mackay does not write with the same degree of political conviction, her working-class heroine similarly suggests the possibility of transcending class divisions. In fact, it seems that, where representations of the working girl lead, sexual transgression, class breakdown, and gender instability soon follow. A denizen of factories, city streets, and department stores, the single wage-earning woman represented to her contemporaries everything that was unnatural and unnerving about modern life. Those who were watching closely could see her potential to unravel social codes and critically redefine what it meant to be a woman in Canadian society. This is where writers entered into the cultural work initiated by these women: by representing this often disregarded figure, they insisted on new distributions of social respect, and they validated the cultural innovations of independent women. Middle-class critics may have wished that

Sime's characters were not quite so "extreme" in their reactions to economic freedom, but her unapologetic heroines were as striking in their realism as in their actions, making Sime's book a prescient social document.

Works Cited

Benson, Susan Porter. *Counter Cultures: Saleswomen, Managers, and Customers in American Department Stores 1890–1940*. Chicago: U of Illinois P, 1986.

Campbell, Sandra. "'Gently Scan': Theme and Technique in J.G. Sime's 'Sister Woman' (1919)." *Canadian Literature* 133 (1992): 40–55.

Campbell, Sandra, and Lorraine McMullen, eds. *New Women: Short Stories by Canadian Women 1900–1920*. Ottawa: U of Ottawa P, 1991.

Denning, Michael. *Mechanic Accents: Dime Novels and Working-Class Culture in America*. New York: Verso, 1987.

Donovan, Peter [Tom Folio]. Rev. of *Sister Woman*, by J.G. Sime. Saturday Night 28 Feb. 1920: 9.

Dreiser, Theodore. *Sister Carrie*. 1900. New York: Norton, 1970.

Enstad, Nan. *Ladies of Labor, Girls of Adventure: Working Women, Popular Culture, and Labor Politics at the Turn of the Twentieth Century*. New York: Columbia UP, 1999.

Gerson, Carole. Introduction. *Roland Graeme, Knight: A Novel of Our Time*. Ottawa: Tecumseh, 1996. vii–xx.

Kealey, Linda. *Enlisting Women for the Cause: Women, Labour, and the Left in Canada, 1890–1920*. Toronto: U of Toronto P, 1998.

Mackenzie, Suzanne. "Building Women, Building Cities: Toward Gender Sensitive Theory in the Environmental Disciplines." *Life Spaces: Gender, Household, Employment*. Ed. Caroline Andrew and Beth Moore Milroy. Vancouver: UBC P, 1988. 13–30.

Machar, Agnes Maule. *Roland Graeme, Knight: A Novel of Our Time*. 1892. Ottawa: Tecumseh, 1996.

Mackay, Isabel Ecclestone. *The House of Windows*. Toronto: Cassel, 1912.

McMullen, Lorraine, ed. *Re(Dis)covering Our Foremothers: Nineteenth-Century Canadian Women Writers*. Ottawa: U of Ottawa P, 1990.

Merrill, Annie. "The Woman in Business." *Canadian Magazine* 21 (1903): 407–10.

Meyerowitz, Joanne. *Women Adrift: Independent Wage-Earners in Chicago, 1880–1930*. Chicago: U of Chicago P, 1988.

"A Montreal Woman on Women." *Canadian Bookman* Apr. 1920: 57–58.

New, W.H. *A History of Canadian Literature*. London: Macmillan, 1991.

Richardson, Dorothy. *The Long Day: The Story of a New York Working Girl*. 1905. Women at Work. Chicago: Quadrangle, 1972.

Sime, J.G. *Sister Woman*. 1919. Ottawa: Tecumseh, 1992.

Sinclair, Bertrand. *North of Fifty-Three*. [Toronto]: n.p., [1914].

Strange, Carolyn. *Toronto's Girl Problem: The Peril and Pleasures of the City, 1880–1930*. Toronto: U of Toronto P, 1995.

Source: McMaster, Lindsey. "The Urban Working Girl in Turn-of-the-Century Canadian Fiction." *Essays on Canadian Writing* 77 (Fall 2002). Reprinted with kind permission.

Exercise – *continued*

Reading for Content:

Using a handbook of literary terms, look up "trope" (283, 284) and "dramatic irony" (14). Using a reliable dictionary, look up "indeterminacy" (282, 287); think of a synonym for "indeterminacy."

1. Paraphrase "politics of representation" (279) (see also "mainstream representation" [291]).

2. What label does McMaster frequently use to characterize novels with working-class females as characters. Who is the major American writer of these kinds of novels?

Critical and Analytical Reading:

1. What audience do you think McMaster is addressing in her essay? Why? What strategies does she employ to help the reader understand content?

2. In her introduction (278–9), how does McMaster try to convince her audience that her study of these neglected texts is important? Identify her thesis.

3. Consider the order of primary texts analyzed. Why does the author use this order? Why does she spend so little time on the first of the four main texts, *Roland Graeme, Knight*?

4. McMaster uses primary texts and secondary sources extensively. Explain the importance of the prolonged discussion of fashion, hair, and dress (285–7). Why does she refer at such length to a short essay on deportment that appeared in *Canadian Magazine* in 1903 (285, 288–9)?

After reading:

Browse through a collection of stories by Canadian women around the turn of the twentieth century. Write a brief response to one of these stories, focusing on the portrayal of women in the story. Examples of collections: Sime, J.G. Sister Woman. 1919. Ottawa: Tecumseh, 1992; Campbell, Sandra, and Lorraine McMullen, eds. New Women: Short Stories by Canadian Women, 1900–1920. Ottawa: U of Ottawa P, 1991. The following anthology contains many stories by women: Dean, Misao, ed. Early Canadian Short Stories: Short Stories in English Before World War I. Ottawa: Tecumseh, 2000.

18. A Brief Glossary of Literary Terms

Although most of these terms can be applied directly to poetic analysis, many can be used in analyzing fiction and drama as well.

allegory A narrative in which characters, actions, places, and objects are given abstract qualities; thus, there is a one-to-one correspondence between the literal and the symbolic. In allegory, the symbolic relationship is clear, often through names: in John Bunyan's religious allegory, *The Pilgrim's Progress*, the pilgrim is named "Christian," and he is on a journey from the "City of Destruction" (the state of sin in the fallen world) to the "Celestial City" (heaven). Many other works have allegorical elements, but are not pure allegories (for example, George Orwell's *Animal Farm* and William Golding's *Lord of the Flies*). See **Symbol**.

allusion   A historical, religious, mythic, literary, or other kind of outside reference used thematically or to reveal character in a work; allusions can also be used to broaden a work's focus: "This man had kept a school/And rode our *wingèd horse*"—W.B. Yeats's allusion to the mythological horse Pegasus, associated with poetry.

alliteration   The repetition of like sounds, usually consonants, at the beginning of words in close proximity: "O *w*ild *W*est *W*ind, thou *b*reath of Autumn's *b*eing" (P.B. Shelley). (Note that it is appropriate to speak of examples of alliteration but not of "alliterations.")

anaphora   A device of repetition; repeated words or phrases at the beginning of lines or clauses: *"I love thee* freely, as men strive for Right;/*I love thee* purely, as they turn from Praise./*I love thee* with the passion put to use/In my old griefs. . . ."* (E.B. Browning).

apostrophe   An address to an absent person, animal, object, or concept: "Thou wast not born for death, immortal Bird!" (John Keats).

archetype   A "primordial image" that, according to psychologist Carl Jung, represents part of the collective unconscious of human beings; archetypal symbols appear in myths, dreams, rituals, and other collective experiences; writers often use them in literature to give depth and resonance to the literary work. Examples include the shadow ("other") self, the old man, the wise mother, the guide, the journey, descent to the underworld, and other cross-cultural images, characters, settings, and occurrences. See **Motif**.

assonance   The linking of words by similar sounds (a) of their accented vowels (but not consonants) repeated by their proximity: "Up to the sw*a*llow thr*o*nged l*o*ft by the sh*a*dow of my h*a*nd" (Dylan Thomas) or (b) of their identical consonants (with different vowels) frequently used instead of true rhyme; in these lines from John Milton's "Lycidas" we see both true rhyme ("head" with "shed") and assonance ("wears" with "tears"):

> The musk-rose, and the well attir'd woodbine,
> With cowslips wan that hang the pensive head,
> And every flower that sad embroidery wears:
> Bid amaranthus all his beauty shed,
> And daffadillies fill their cups with tears,
> To strew the laureate hearse where Lycid lies.

Hint: the first two letters of "assonance" spell "as," meaning similar but not identical.

chiasmus   The reversal in the order of words in two otherwise parallel phrases: Example—"Beauty is truth, truth beauty" (John Keats).

conceit   An extended comparison or metaphor, usually complex and ingenious, such as John Donne's comparison in "A Valediction: Forbidding Mourning" of separated lovers to a compass.

consonance   The repetition of like consonant sounds especially at the end of adjacent words. Ben Jonson's "Ode to Himself" gives us the consonance of "st" in "crusts" and "nasty" among other spitting sibilants to deride plays formed of scraps: ". . . and stale / As the shrieve's crusts, and nasty as his fish—."

diction   Word choice; could refer to specific words or to the level of language used in the work—formal, elevated, informal, colloquial, abstract, concrete, etc.

ellipsis   The omission of one or more words, which the reader can assume are implied, for the sake of brevity. Ellipsis contributes to the compression—the poetic intensity—of a work: "If ever two were one, then surely we [are one]. / If ever man were lov'd by wife, then thee [(thou) art loved]" (Anne Bradstreet); square brackets indicate the words supplied by the reader. Also, in quoted material, the use of three periods to indicate where some words within the quotation have been omitted. If the omitted words follow the end of a sentence, the sentence has the closing period followed by the three points of ellipsis; if the omitted words include the end of a sentence, the last word is followed by a space, the points of ellipsis, and then the period; if the omitted words are within a single sentence, then the three points of ellipsis have space on either side but no fourth point (or period) is used.

figure of speech   An implicit comparison between two objects; figurative (non-literal) language makes reference to the *connotations* (suggestiveness) of language, not their literal (*denotative*) meanings; metaphors, similes, metonymy, and synecdoche are figures of speech.

imagery   Words conveying sense impressions, particularly sight, used in almost all literary writing. Images may occur in descriptive passages where their primary focus is on the physical world, or they may be used in figurative (non-literal) language; of course, an image can function descriptively *and* figuratively.

irony   A device of *indirection* as well as an example of a speaker's tone (see **Tone**). Irony is the condition of two levels of meaning, the apparent (literal or surface) meaning and another intended (non-literal or deeper) meaning. Irony may differ in degree according to its purpose (see below, verbal irony), and traditionally is divided into three types.

1.   In **verbal irony**, the discrepancy is between the literal and intended meanings of language. Verbal irony resembles sarcasm, but irony is usually more indirect than sarcasm, which simply states something as its opposite. Sarcasm: Mr. Bennet in Jane Austen's novel *Pride and Prejudice* refers to his worthless

son-in-law: "I am prodigiously proud of him." Verbal irony: "Yet graceful Ease, and Sweetness void of Pride, / Might hide her Faults, if *Belles* had Faults to hide" (Alexander Pope). The last clause is ironic since the "belle," Belinda, is mortal and, as such, does have faults. In his anti-war poem "*Dulce et Decorum Est*," the irony intended by Wilfred Owen is much harsher. His graphic images of a youth dying from a gas attack render ironic the patriot's claim that "dulce et decorem est"—it is "sweet and right to die for your country." While the title affords an example of verbal irony, the poem, as an indictment of war and the "lie" of those who promote its glory, exemplifies situational irony (see below).

2. In **dramatic irony**, the reader/audience possesses an awareness about the character or situation that the character doesn't have. For example, in many of Shakespeare's comedies, people are disguised, and while the audience is aware of these disguises, most of the characters are not. **Tragic irony** exists if the reader/audience is aware of a situation that the hero is oblivious to and that will lead to disaster, as when the audience for Shakespeare's *Othello* learns long before Othello does of Iago's treachery. Dramatic irony can also be found in poetry and fiction—as when in Roethke's short lyric, "My Papa's Waltz," irony is expressed in the desperate love of a child for his father despite the father's drunkenness and abuse: "Then [you] waltzed me off to bed / Still clinging to your shirt."

3. In **situational irony**, a situation appears to point to a particular outcome but results in the reverse of the expected or intended one. Situational irony is often found in drama, fiction, and narrative poetry. It is ironic that Pip, the protagonist of Charles Dickens's novel *Great Expectations*, discovers that his benefactor is not the wealthy Miss Havisham but the convict Magwitch.

metaphor   An implicit comparison between two things not usually considered similar; metaphors call attention to an object in an unexpected comparison: "Love . . . is the star to every wandering bark" (Shakespeare). Love is compared to a star and the lover is implicitly compared to a "bark" or ship; "star" and "bark" are metaphors for love and the lover, respectively. Metaphors can be divided into the *tenor* (the object being compared—"love," the lover) and the *vehicle* (the image to which the tenor is linked—"star," "bark"). See **Conceit**, **Simile**.

metonymy   The substitution of an object or idea for a related one: "A *goose's quill* has put an end to murder" (Dylan Thomas). The poet refers to a document signed by a king; it is in reality the person, not the quill, who "put an end to murder." See **Synecdoche**.

metre   The pattern or arrangement of feet in a line of poetry. Metre usually refers to the repetition of stressed and unstressed syllables. The name of the metre is determined by the basic unit of measurement (the foot) and the number of feet in a line. The four most common feet are:

iamb (unstressed + stressed syllable make up the unit) ˘ ´

   "On either side the river lie" (Alfred, Lord Tennyson) ˘ ´ ˘ ´ ˘ ´ ˘ ´

trochee (stressed + unstressed syllable) ′˘

"Tyger, Tyger, burning bright" (William Blake) ′˘ ′˘ ′˘ ′

anapest (two unstressed syllables + stressed syllable) ˘˘′ ˘˘′ ˘˘′ ˘˘′

"When the voices of children are heard on the green" (Blake)

dactyl (stressed syllable + two unstressed syllables) ′˘˘ ′˘˘ ′˘˘ ′˘

"lurching through forests of white spruce and cedar" (Alden Nowlan)

>   **Truncated rhythm** occurs when a syllable is omitted from the beginning or end of a line; in the example from Blake and the example from Nowlan each last foot omits the final unstressed syllable.
>   A line that contains three feet is called a **trimeter**, one that contains four feet is a **tetrameter**, and one made up of five feet is a **pentameter**. Thus, a poem with lines composed of five iambs would be written in **iambic pentameter**. **Blank verse**, the closest to the rhythms of everyday English speech, is written in unrhymed **iambic pentameter**. Blank verse is used in much narrative and dramatic poetry, including the epic poem *Paradise Lost*, by John Milton, and parts of Shakespeare's plays.

mood   A particular emotional response produced by the elements of a poem, play, or work of fiction—for example, suspense, fear, empathy, humour.

motif   A distinctive element or narrative feature in literature, art, or music that occurs in numerous works, such as a magic ring, a Christ figure, a whore with a heart of gold.

paradox   A statement that appears impossible on the surface but turns out to be true when examined closely: "Take me to you, imprison me, for I, / Except you enthrall me, never shall be free" (John Donne). The poem's context resolves the apparent contradiction of imprisonment and freedom.

personification   The attributing of human qualities to the non-human: "The hills, like giants at a hunting, lay, / Chin upon hand" (Robert Browning).

rhyme   The repetition of identical sounds at the end of lines (*end rhyme*); in the middle of a line it is known as *internal rhyme*; in *masculine rhyme*, the identical sound occurs on a final stressed syllable ("bells," "shells"), while in *feminine (double) rhyme*, the identical sound is heard on the stressed syllable and on the unstressed syllable ("battle, rattle"); *near rhyme (slant rhyme)* repeats the final vowel sounds *or* consonant sounds, not both: "Tell all the Truth but tell it slant— / Success in circuit lies / Too bright for our infirm Delight / The Truth's superb surprise"—(Emily Dickinson): lines 2 and 4 illustrate end rhyme (masculine); lines 1 and 3 provide an example of near rhyme; "bright" and "Delight" illustrate internal rhyme. A rhyme scheme is a distinctive pattern in which letters are assigned to the end rhymes; for example, in an *aabb* rhyme, the first two lines and the last two lines would rhyme. See also **Stanza**.

rhythm   The rhythm of poetry in English is determined by the arrangement of stressed and unstressed syllables; the rhythmical pattern in most traditional English poetry can be classified according to its metre.

simile   A comparison using "like" or "as" or a similar word/phrase: "The holy time is *quiet as a Nun*" (William Wordsworth).

stanza   A structural unit of poetry consisting of a group of lines, usually with a distinctive metre and rhyming scheme and a line break between one stanzaic unit and another; it is very roughly equivalent to the paragraph in prose. Three-line stanzas (*tercets*) and four-line stanzas (*quatrains*) are common arrangements. A *couplet* consists of a two-line rhyming unit; it is usually part of a larger stanzaic unit.

symbol   An image referring to a person, place, thing, or action that is given importance in a work due to the way the author uses it and/or because of its associations. A *traditional symbol*, such as the sea, star, or heart, has specific cultural or cross-cultural associations; *see* **Archetype**. The importance of a *contextual symbol* resides in the way the author uses it; contextual symbols are announced and their significance suggested through context—for example, a symbol can be announced in a work's title: "The Raven" (Edgar Allan Poe), "Mending Wall" (Robert Frost).

synecdoche   A kind of substitution wherein the part stands for the whole or the whole for the part: "By *mourning tongues* / the death of the poet was kept from his poems" (W.H. Auden). It is not the "tongues" that mourn but the people who speak about the poet's death.

syntax   Word order; poets may invert or disrupt normal syntax for surprise or emphasis: "Berries or children, patient she is with these" (Irving Layton).

tone   The emotional or intellectual register of the work, that is, the way that the author conveys attitude towards subject matter and/or audience: serious, comic, distant, intimate, contemplative, ironic.

PART SEVEN

Sentence Essentials

1. Grammatical Groundwork

2. Introducing . . . the Parts of Speech

3. Introducing . . . the Sentence

4. Introducing . . . Phrases and Clauses

5. Punctuation

6. Apostrophes

7. Agreement

8. Pronouns at Work

9. Sentence Construction Errors

10. Summary Exercises

Here are the basic concepts you need in order to understand and use English grammar and punctuation. First you will meet the constituents of a sentence, including the parts of speech, phrases and clauses, and the sentence itself. In the second part, you will find guidelines for using commas, semicolons, colons, and apostrophes. The third part will introduce you to subject–verb agreement, pronoun–antecedent agreement, pronoun reference, pronoun consistency, pronoun case problems, misplaced modifiers, dangling modifiers, and parallelism.

1. Grammatical Groundwork

There are many contemporary definitions of grammar. For practical purposes, grammar can be defined this way:

Grammar comprises a set of conventions governing the linguistic units that make up a sentence, including their order and the relationships among them.

For some, grammar is simply a set of rules to be learned; for students, it is a means to an end, perhaps an improved or a good grade; for students interested in careful thought, it is a way not only to improve their writing but also to further their understanding of how the English language is put together. What correct grammar will *always* do is help create a channel of clear communication between writer and reader.

A convention, which means *come together*, is a recurring pattern that we follow in our everyday lives by common consent and for the purpose of clear communication and understanding. Conventions depend on culture and context. For example, a North American who meets someone from Japan at a business luncheon would likely prefer to talk using first names: "Hi, I'm Todd." The Japanese custom, or convention, would be to use last names: "Hello, I'm Mr. Daisuke Yahamae."

Since languages develop within cultures, grammatical conventions are determined partly by the development of that culture's written language. Many languages, for example, don't have articles ("the," "a," "an"), so learning to write in English will involve learning the conventions governing English use of articles—along with many other conventions. For those who have been speaking, reading, and writing in English for years, learning grammar is mostly a matter of refining and honing—making conscious—the conventions of written prose.

As you know from considering the roles of purpose and audience in the planning and shaping of your essay, context plays a vital part in all communication. In general, the conventions of grammar apply to all written discourse across the academic disciplines. That means you will adhere to these conventions, some of which have defined acceptable academic writing for generations. Some of the conventions of language apply to written discourse but not to spoken discourse (speech). The conventions of punctuation and spelling, for example, aren't applicable to speech. Consider the following sentence:

Our pear tree is losing its leaves; I think it's sick.

The sentence has two main ideas. The writer has two options for punctuating it: to put a period after "leaves" and begin a new sentence with "I" or to place a semicolon after "leaves." However, when one speaks the two thoughts, one does not state "semi-colon" or "period"; one simply pauses between the expressions of the two ideas:

Our pear tree is losing its leaves   I think it's sick.

1.1. Grammar and Usage

The sentence about the sick pear tree illustrates the way we rely on the conventions of spelling and punctuation in written discourse. However, adhering to most of the conventions of grammar and usage is necessary to communicate clearly and unequivocally in both speech *and* writing. For example, in the sentence below the writer uses an incorrect form of the verb:

Our pear tree are losing its leaves.

To a listener or reader familiar with the grammatical rule for subject–verb agreement, the verb would sound or look wrong and raise issues of meaning. Did the speaker intend to refer to one pear tree or many? "Our pear trees are losing their leaves" has a meaning different from "Our pear tree is losing its leaves."

The conventions of usage and grammar, then, unlike spelling and punctuation, apply both to speech and writing. Yet the conventions governing both usage and grammar can vary according to context, according to whom you are speaking and writing and the form(s) you use to address your audience.

The conventions of grammar and usage are determined partly by level of formality. In usage, we can distinguish several levels of discourse—from the freest level of ordinary speech to the most formal level of academic writing. Many usage dictionaries since Henry Fowler's *A Dictionary of Modern English Usage* have attempted to *describe* more than *prescribe*, and to leave most choices up to the writer. The authors of *Guide to Canadian English Usage*, Margery Fee and Janice McAlpine, explain this principle in their introduction:

Usage conventions arise precisely in areas where choice is possible, and though usage guides are expected to approve one choice as "correct" and the others as "incorrect," sloppy, or vulgar, this guide—perhaps to the frustration of some readers—is more likely to lay out the possibilities and to discuss the contexts where different choices might be effective.

Although writing can be informal, or even conversational, in *Writing by Choice* we are concerned with formal or semi-formal writing intended as a *written* record of some kind. Most journalistic prose would be considered semi-formal, along with much business and technical writing. The most formal level would include writing intended as a *permanent written* record, such as formal speeches and academic prose, from the essays written for college and university courses to the articles written for publication in scholarly journals—the level that is often referred to as *edited English*.

It may seem strange to consider the essay you write "on demand" for a class assignment a permanent record; after all, you may never see it again after it is handed back, or it may be relegated to storage with other dusty relics of university life. However, as an instance of academic discourse it needs to be written precisely as a permanent record.

Examples of informal writing might include memos, advertising copy, or letters to friends; conversational writing is the equivalent of everyday speech. In the works of creative writers you can see examples of both informal writing and conversational writing (which, depending on the speaker or character, could be formal, semi-formal, or informal.) For example, here is a brief passage from Ann-Marie MacDonald's novel *Fall on Your Knees*:

> By Hallowe'en she was big as a house. One evening he came home to find her sitting at the kitchen table with a bowl of molasses-cookie dough, for that was what the ingredients lined up on the table indicated. He was delighted. Her first attempt at cooking. He even gave her a kiss to show just how pleased he was, but when he went to dip a finger in the dough the bowl had been licked clean.
> "What in God's name are you doing?"
> She just looked queasily straight ahead.
> "Answer me."
> She just sat there, bloated.
> "What's wrong with you? Don't you think? Haven't you got anything to say for yourself?"
> The blank stare, the flaccid face. He grabbed the bowl.
> "Or are you just a lump of dough?"
> No answer.

Evidence of informal usage appears in the first sentence: "big as a house" wouldn't be acceptable in formal writing; the word "as" is omitted after "was"—an omission unacceptable in formal writing where ellipsis (omission of one or more words) should be avoided. But in the excerpt above, a specific grammatical rule also is broken repeatedly—the passage contains three sentence fragments. Of course, there are other conventions in the passage that characterize narrative, as opposed to expository, prose—for example, the writer's dependence on dialogue.

1.2 A Choice-Based Grammar

The reason for studying grammar and style is to enable one to write by *choice*, rather than by *chance*. But choice should not imply arbitrariness. As is true with any other element of the writing process, you can make informed choices only if you are aware of the choices available to you—"to break the rules, you have to know what the rules are." The old saying holds true for grammar, though we are not really talking about breaking—or even *bending*—rules, but about applying practices according to audience and form. Matters of choice, whether they pertain to essay format and documentation, style, or even grammar, are guided by your audience, purpose in writing, the form of your written communication, and, of course, the message itself—what it is you wish to communicate.

Because most academic writing across the disciplines today is formal writing, the section on *Sentence Essentials* approaches grammar formally, though without encumbering the student writer with excessive terminology. Although formal grammatical conventions are stressed throughout this section, instances where choice may be involved are noted; usually, these choices apply to less formal writing—certain kinds of business, technical, or journalistic writing. However, since you will inevitably encounter some documents that are written less formally, you should be aware of options available for some writers in specific contexts. Again, since disciplines sometimes differ in the accepted level of informality, your instructor should be the final arbiter in such matters.

> ## Collaborative Exercise
>
> Find examples of formal and informal prose: an excerpt of each from a magazine, newspaper, or book. Share your excerpts in groups, considering how each could be changed into informal prose or how it could be rewritten as acceptable formal prose. Consider such factors as vocabulary, sentence length and variety, tone of voice, and audience. Then, consider which ones might be rewritten as conversation.
>
> To help you identify these three writing styles, think in terms of different kinds of audiences, but particularize—you can think of a specific person or persons whom you are writing for: e.g., a friend, for informal prose or conversation; a workplace acquaintance, such as your boss, for semi-formal prose; and the chairperson of the English Department for formal prose.

1.2.1 The Grammar of Reading and Writing

As we read a communication, our understanding of grammar helps us to determine the relationships among the various syntactical units in a sentence and to make sense of (decode) the message, whether it takes the form of a simple declarative statement or a much more complex statement of a theory or ideology.

As a reader, especially if English is your first language, you can decode meaning partly due to your recognition, though not necessarily your complete understanding, of grammatical and other linguistic indicators and conventions because they are embedded in the language (see Fishing for Grammar sidebar, pages 307–8). The processing of grammatical structures and syntactic conventions is, therefore, embedded in the act of reading, also.

As a writer, though, you are responsible for ensuring that readers can decode your message; therefore, you need to make the encoding process as clear and efficient as possible for your intended audience. Writing usually is a more self-conscious act than reading, and so part of your consciousness needs to include familiarity with grammatical conventions, if you are to write effectively. To apply grammatical principles and rules properly is to assure the reader's accurate decoding of the message. This is a part of what you can do to open up the channel of communication through which you transmit your message.

Experienced writers seldom need advice in *applying the rules* of grammar, but they may have forgotten *the basis* for these rules. They may attend writing workshops not because they need to know *what* is correct but because they want be reminded of *why* it is correct. Students may be in the enviable position of having studied the rules more recently and may more easily learn, with repetition, how to write grammatically flawless sentences.

The fastest, least complicated way to learn English grammar is to familiarize yourself with the basic *concepts* that underlie the rules of grammar. The pages that follow teach a concept-based grammar, beginning with the smallest semantic units in the sentence: the parts of speech. From there, we look at what constitutes a simple sentence and conclude by looking at the complex additions of phrases and clauses.

2. Introducing . . . the Parts of Speech

CONCEPTS and TERMS *NEW* to this section

- abstract noun
- appositive
- adjective
- adverb
- auxiliary (helping) verb
- collective noun
- common noun
- concrete noun
- conjunction
- conjunctive adverb
- co-ordinating conjunction
- correlative conjunction
- count noun
- demonstrative pronoun

- direct/indirect object
- indefinite pronoun
- intensive pronoun
- interjection
- interrogative pronoun
- intransitive verb
- linking verb
- main verb
- modal
- modifier
- non-count noun
- noun
- object
- object of a preposition
- parts of speech

- personal pronoun
- preposition
- prepositional phrase
- proper noun
- pronoun
- reciprocal pronoun
- reflexive pronoun
- relative pronoun
- subject
- subjective complement
- predicate noun/adjective
- subordinating conjunction
- transitive verb
- verb (action word)

The seven major parts of speech are nouns, pronouns, adjectives (including articles) verbs, adverbs, prepositions, and conjunctions.

Before considering what constitutes a **sentence**, the basic unit of written communication in English, you need to be able to identify the units that make up a sentence. The sentence can be divided into individual words, which, in turn, can be categorized as different parts of speech; there are seven principal parts of speech. Phrases and clauses are larger units than individual words; being able to identify the forms and functions of the parts of speech will help you understand these larger units, too. The seven major **parts of speech** are nouns, pronouns, adjectives, verbs, adverbs, prepositions, and conjunctions.

Articles, such as *a*, *an*, and *the*, and determiners, such as *this* an *her*, may precede nouns and can be considered to function adjectivally. *Interjections*, such as "oh!" and "hey," are not grammatically related to the rest of the sentence. They express surprise or emotion, and should not be used in formal writing unless they form part of a quotation. Many words can be used as more than one part of speech. For example, the word *fish* is a noun (a thing), but *fish* also is a verb (to perform the act of fishing). When "fish" as a noun is placed in front of another noun, as in a *fish* market, it functions as an adjective (modifying the concept, "market").

2.1 The Parts of Speech at Work

When you are hired by an organization, given a job title, and a detailed job description, the job title is what you will be called; but the full job description explains your responsibilities, duties, or functions within the organization. Similarly with the parts of speech, all have specific, assigned roles within their organizational structure, the sentence. Remember that words may have many meanings and may even serve as different parts of speech. "Cause" may be a noun and used as the subject of a sentence; "cause" may also be a verb and used as the predicate of a sentence. For example, in the sentence, "Justin's cause caused a ruckus," the first "cause" is a noun meaning "a belief or crusade" and the second is a verb meaning "made or created." When one meaning of a part of speech is assigned to a function in a sentence, *that meaning* cannot be used as a different part of speech in the same clause. For example, when a noun is the subject of the verb in a clause, it cannot also be

Fishing for Grammar
When words have meanings that allow them to function as many different parts of speech, sorting the meanings and their functions usually is quite easy. For example, in "Fish want to fish for fish," you quickly gather that one meaning probably is that "Larger fish seek as their prey other and smaller fish." Can you explain, in terms of grammar, how to come to this conclusion? One possible way of reasoning is as follows:

It is not **the part of speech**, i.e., a particular noun, which cannot function simultaneously as another part of speech in the same sentence, but a particular **meaning of a word as a part of speech** that cannot simultaneously serve in another part of speech in the same sentence. The defining of relationships among words **according to their use in the sentence, that is, as different parts of speech** imposes different meanings on the word "fish." The first word "Fish" derives its meaning from its function as the **subject** of the sentence, not alone from its being a noun. The second "fish" is identifiable as a

object of the verb in the same clause. This is clear in the following: "Frasier has gone to see Frasier." Evidently the second "Frasier" must refer to a different person of the same name, or, perhaps, to a television program or a town, or some other thing. But the distinction is less clear in "Thomas adores Thomas" or "London is London and always will be, the hub of their universe." The identical nouns must be intended in some way that is not really identical. In the first case where action is reflexive we usually substitute a pronoun for the noun and understand that the subject "Thomas" is taking action towards a limited meaning of "Thomas," namely, "the concept that he has *of himself*." In the second case, "London" as the subject noun has a more general meaning than the subjective complement noun "London," a city that retains its essential character despite other changes inevitable over time, essences to which certain persons adhere as "the hub of their universe."

The chart below identifies the parts of speech, along with their major functions. Moving from the ability to identify the categories of the parts of speech to being aware of their semantic functions (denotations and connotations) within the sentence will enable you to apply the conventions of grammar.

2.2 Substantives: Nouns and Pronouns

Identification	Functions
Noun (*nomen*: "name"): name of a person, place, or thing. *Proper* nouns refer to names and begin with a capital letter; *common* nouns refer to class or a general group and are not capitalized; *concrete* nouns refer to physical objects and things experienced through the senses; *abstract nouns* refer to concepts, ideas, and abstractions; *count* nouns name things that can be counted; *non-count* nouns refer to things that can't be counted; and *collective* nouns refer to groups comprised of individual members.	1. **Subject**: performs the action of the verb (the *doer* of the action); sometimes called the "simple" subject to distinguish it from the complete subject that includes the "simple" subject plus its modifiers 2. **Object** (also called the **direct object**): receives the action of the verb 3. **Object of a preposition** (also called the **indirect object**): is preceded by a preposition 4. **Subjective Complement** (also called the **predicate noun**): follows an intransitive (linking) verb (a form of *to be* such as *is, are, was, were*) and completes this verb 5. **Appositive**: is grammatically parallel to the previous noun or noun phrase
Pronoun (*pro* + *nomen*: "in place of the noun"): a word that takes the place of a noun in a sentence. For a list of kinds of pronouns, see below.	Since pronouns generally replace nouns, they share the functions of nouns (see "nouns" *above*).

2.2.1 Functions of Nouns and Pronouns (Substantives)

Nouns and pronouns are the *substantive* words in a sentence because they name substantial entities: people, places, and things.

1. **Subject.** The subject noun is the doer or performer of the action.

In the following examples the subject is in bold face; the action word, the verb, is italicized.

Dan *stood* at the front of the line-up; **She** *awoke* before dawn; The **rain** in Spain *falls* mainly on the plain.

verbal noun because it includes the meaning of an *action* that can be predicated about a subject (such an action is a verb) and from its proximity to "to," which we recognize as the infinitive form of the verb meaning "to catch fish" and because as a verbal noun (i.e., the infinitive of a verb used as if it were a noun) it is the **object of the verb** "want." The third "fish" appears as the **object in a prepositional phrase** that modifies the verbal noun "to fish," which makes it **adjectival** in reference to "to fish": thereby we understand that the third "fish" is of a kind that differs from the first "fish" and we can surmise how—as prey—and why—likely, size.

The subject usually precedes the verb, but sometimes follows it, as, for example, with some questions: *Was* the final **exam** difficult?

2. **Object (of the Verb)** also called **Direct Object.** The object of the verb is the receiver of the action of the verb.

   In the following examples the object is in boldface; the verb is italicized.

   James *beat* **Dan** into the movie theatre. Erin *let* **him** into the house.
   They *chopped* the **logs** for firewood.

3. **Object of the Preposition (**also called **Indirect Object).** The noun/pronoun is usually preceded by a preposition.

   In the following example the object is in boldface; its preposition is italicized.

   She awoke *before* **dawn**. The rain *in* **Spain** falls mainly *on* the **plain**.
   I never heard *of* **it** before.

4. **Subjective Complement (Completion).** The noun or pronoun that "completes" (renames) the subject after an intransitive (linking) verb.

   In the following example the subjective completion is in boldface; the intransitive linking verb is italicized; the subject is underlined.

   Rayna *was* the first **person** to get a job after graduation.

5. **Appositive.** A noun, noun phrase, or pronoun that is grammatically parallel to a preceding noun/pronoun and that rephrases or (re)names the preceding noun.

   In the following example the appositive is in boldface; the preceding noun is italicized.

   Madeline's *cats*, **Evie**, **Peachy**, **and Nanny**, have very different characters.

   The subject of the sentence is "cats"; the names of the cats are **in apposition to the subject** (the names are not part of the subject).

2.2.2 Kinds of Pronouns

Personal pronouns refer to people and things; in the possessive case, they can function as adjectives. *He* ran all the way to the sea. She sat down because *her* feet were blistered.

Relative pronouns introduce dependent clauses that *relate* the clause to the rest of the sentence; these clauses usually function adjectivally. *That, which, who.*

Aspen, *who* had become disconsolate, departed.

Interrogative pronouns introduce questions. *How, what, which, when, why, who, where.*

Demonstrative pronouns point to nouns; they can function as adjectives. *This, that, yonder.*

> **This** is the *day* of reckoning.
> "**Yon[der]** Cassius hath a lean and hungry look."

Indefinite pronouns refer to unspecified individuals or groups; they do not require an antecedent and form their possessives in the same way as nouns. *Any, some, whoever.*

> It is *anyone's* guess when the boat will arrive.

Reflexive pronouns have the form of personal pronouns with the *-self* suffix; they refer back to the subject as the receiver of an action. In the following example the subject is italicized and the reflexive pronoun is in boldface.

> *Ben* congratulated **himself** on his successful election.

Intensive pronouns also have the form of personal pronouns with the *-self* suffix; they serve to reinforce their antecedents:

> The *teacher herself* was often late for class.

Reciprocal pronouns refer to the separate parts of a plural antecedent. In the following example the reciprocal pronoun is in boldface and the antecedent is italicized.

> *People* need to accept and tolerate **one another**.

2.3 Verbs

Identification	Functions
Verb (*verbum*: "word"): conveys an action, state, or condition, or precedes another (main) verb. The three different kinds of verbs have different functions.	1. **Transitive verbs** convey some kind of *action*, not necessarily physical, towards, or in some sense passed onto, a direct object. 2. **Helping or auxiliary verbs** precede a *main verb* to form more complex *tenses* (indications of the time, continuance, or completeness of the action) or to express a *mood* such as obligation, necessity, probability, or possibility; or *voice*, i.e., whether the relation of verb to subject is active or passive. 3. **Intransitive (linking)** verbs do not take or require a direct object (whether expressed or implied).

Functions of Verbs The various tenses of English verbs are illustrated in Appendix A.

Verbs express action, condition, or a state of being. Some kinds of action are not necessarily visible—*think, imagine,* and *suggest* are examples of action verbs in which the "action" is interior or mental. Verbs may be modified by adverbs or adverbial phrases.

Helping Verbs (also called **Auxiliary Verbs**) combine with main verbs. The two most common helping verbs are *to be (am, are, is, was, were, will be,* etc.) and *to have (have, has, had,* etc.) Forms of *to be* are used in the *progressive* tenses; forms of *to have* are used in the *perfect* tenses (see Appendix A).

Modals are verb forms placed before the main verb to express necessity, obligation, possibility, probability and similar conditions: *can, could, will, would, shall, should, may, might, must* and *ought to* are modals.

Intransitive (Linking) Verbs. *To be* is used as a **linking verb** to connect subject and predicate in one of six ways:

1. expressing identity: e.g., Today is Saturday.
2. expressing condition: e.g., I am upset.
3. expressing state: e.g., These are my colleagues.
4. expressing opinion: We are for freedom of speech.
5. expressing total: One and one are two.
6. expressing cost: The fundraiser is $200 a plate.

These instances do not express an action; they are *not* modified by adverbs but *link* the subject to a *noun* that renames the subject. In the above examples, "Saturday" is the *subjective completion* in 1.; "$200 a plate" is the subjective completion in 6. The verb links the subject in 2 and 4 or to an *adjective* or *adjectival phrase* that describes the subject ("upset" in 2.; "for freedom of speech" in 4.). Without the noun or adjective, the sentence would seem incomplete.

As nouns can take different meanings as parts of speech, some verbs can be transitive or intransitive, depending on their function in a sentence. "To taste" may be transitive, as in "Hakim tastes the dill in his falafel filling" or may be intransitive, as in "Honey tastes sweet."

In many uses of verbs involving a comparison, the traditional use of "to be" has been dropped in speech and even in formal prose, so that the intransitive application of the verb "to be" has become obscured:

> She seems [to be] well; he appears [to be] ill; Wendy looks [to be] fabulous [i.e., a woman of fabled beauty].

The formal expression that has been avoided sometimes is the complex comparison of conditions: "This *as if it were to be* that."

> Bark smells [as if it were to be infected with must] musty; Berue acts [as if she were one who is] crazy.

Verbs that imply "to be" also may function as intransitive verbs:

> Mildred becomes [begins to be] faint as the night grows [continues to become] cold.

Compare: "He *acted* splendidly as Hamlet in Shakespeare's play." "He **acted** sick by staying home from school."

In the first sentence "acted" is used as a transitive verb—there is a direct object of this activity: "as [in the role of] Hamlet"—and is modified by the adverb "splendidly." In the second sentence, "acted" is used intransitively —he acted [behaved as one who *is*] sick—the verb implies "to be"—and thus is followed by a subjective complement in the form of a predicate adjective "sick" (see below).

2.4 Modifiers: Adjectives and Adverbs

Adjectives and adverbs modify, or give more information about, the major parts of speech—nouns and verbs.

Identification	Functions
Adjective (*ad* + *jectum*: "put near to"): a word that modifies a noun or follows an intransitive verb; it answers the questions *which* or *how many?*	1. **Adjectival modifiers** describe or particularize a noun and precede it. 2. **Subjective complement** (also called the *predicate adjective*) follows an intransitive verb (see "nouns" above) and completes the verb.
Adverb (*ad* + *verb*: "to the verb"): a word that modifies a verb, adjective, adverb, or even the entire sentence; it often ends in *-ly* and answers the questions *when, where, why, how, to what degree,* or *how much?*	1. **Adverbial modifiers** describe or particularize a verb and may precede or follow it; an adverb may also modify an adjective or another adverb; a *sentence* adverb may be the first word of the sentence and modify the entire sentence. 2. **Conjunctive adverbs** are a specific group of adverbs that may be used to connect two independent clauses.

Adjectives modify nouns and usually precede them. Adjectives also follow intransitive verbs, where they *complete* the subject, as *subjective completions* or *predicate adjectives*. In the following examples the adjective is in boldface and the modified noun is italicized.

> They attended the **delightful** *party*.

In the following example the predicate adjective is in boldface, the intransitive verb is italicized, and the subject is underlined.

> The party *was* **delightful**.

Adverbs modify verbs, adjectives, and adverbs.

1. In this example the adverb, in boldface, modifies the verb, italicized.

    > Jake *turned* **suddenly**.

2. In this example the adverb, in boldface, modifies the adjective, italicized.

    > That looks like a **very** *contented* cow.

3. In this example the adverb, in boldface, modifies another adverb, italicized.

> They lived **quite** *happily* together.

Some adverbs can also act as **conjunctions** to connect two independent clauses:

> Richard was hired by the publicity firm on Monday; *however*, he was fired on Tuesday.

Note the semicolon separating the clauses and the comma after "however."

2.5 Joiners: Prepositions and Conjunctions

Prepositions and conjunctions are classed together here as they connect different parts of a sentence.

Identification	Functions
Preposition (*pre* + *ponere*: "to put before"): a small word/short phrase that often refers to place or time.	1. **Prepositions** join the noun or pronoun that follows to the rest of the sentence.
Conjunction (*con* + *junction*: "join together"): a word/phrase that connects words, phrases, and clauses of equal or unequal weight or importance. For a list of common subordinating conjunctions, see page 317.	1. **Co-ordinating conjunctions** join *equal* units, including independent clauses; there are seven co-ordinating conjunctions. 2. **Subordinating conjunctions** join *unequal* units, including independent and dependent clauses. 3. **Correlative conjunctions** join *parallel* units; they join in pairs.

Commonly Used Prepositions

about, above, across, after, against, along, among, around, as, at, before, behind, below, between, beside, besides, beyond, by, despite, down, during, except, for, from, in, inside, into, like, near, next (to), of, off, on, onto, out, outside (of), opposite, over, past, regarding, since, than, through, throughout, to, toward(s), under, until, up, upon, with, within, without

Prepositions join nouns and pronouns to the rest of the sentence and add information to subject or predicate. Their functions are *adjectival* or *adverbial* depending on what part of speech they are modifying. Where there is a preposition, you will usually find an object of the preposition (noun or pronoun) following (see Section 2.2, Substantives, object of preposition). Prepositions introduce prepositional phrases. In the following examples the preposition is in boldface, the object of the preposition is italicized, and the prepositional phrase is underlined.

> You will find the letters **in** the *attic*. She worked **during** the summer *vacation*. They laughed **at** *him*.

Commonly Used Prepositions. The noun or pronoun that follows a preposition cannot ever be the subject of the clause, but will function as the object of the preposition. Many prepositional phrases, such as *as well as, in spite of, on account of*, are not listed here, but can often be recognized by the fact of a noun or pronoun following.

Conjunctions
Co-ordinating conjunctions join *equal* units—words to words, phrases to phrases, clauses to clauses. An important use of co-ordinating conjunctions is to join *independent*

clauses in compound sentences. In the following example the co-ordinating conjunction is in boldface:

> Tanya objected to their new roommate, **but** Bronwyn liked her.

Note the comma before the conjunction.

Subordinating conjunctions join *unequal* units, usually a *dependent* clause, which it begins and is part of, to an *independent* clause. In the following examples the subordinating conjunction is in boldface. Note the comma in the second sentence.

> He plans to exercise his option **once** the season is over.
> **Once** the season is over, he plans to exercise his option.

Correlative conjunctions are conjunctions that occur in pairs and require parallel structure. In the following examples the correlative conjunctions are in boldface:

> **Either** you will support me **or** you will not be able to borrow my car.
> **Both** Ali **and** his father work at the community centre on Saturdays.

3. Introducing . . . the Sentence

Because the sentence is the basic unit of written (though not of spoken) communication, you need to know how to identify incomplete sentences in your writing so you can make them complete in formal writing. In order to know what an incomplete sentence is, you need to first consider the concept of the sentence.

CONCEPTS and TERMS *NEW* to this section

• add-on fragment	• gerund	• predicate
• clause	• independent clause	• sentence
• dependent clause	• imperative sentence	• subject (complete)
• (sentence) fragment	• infinitive	• subject (true or simple)

3.1 What Is a Sentence?

If you think that a sentence is easy to define, consider which of the following is a sentence:

> Write!
> Right!

Now, consider this pair:

> Seeing As Believing.
> Seeing Is Believing.

Although you may have been able to correctly identify "Write!" and "Seeing Is Believing" as complete sentences, the examples show that the typographical appearance of a word or group of words does not guarantee a sentence, but may be something less. In commands, the subject "you" is implied (see Section 3.2, below); therefore, "Write!" means "You write!" and is a complete sentence. A **sentence fragment** is the term for a less-than-complete sentence. "Right!" and "Seeing As Believing" are examples of fragments; "Right!" is missing both subject and predicate: "You are right!" "Seeing As Believing" is a noun phrase; there is no predicate.

Some textbooks define a sentence as a complete thought. This somewhat philosophical definition is helpful but limited. If we define a sentence simply as a complete *thought,* we need to know what a thought is. What is an *incomplete* thought and how does it compare with a complete one? As well, sentences certainly can contain more than one thought.

Which of these word groups is a sentence?

Rules of grammar.
Grammar rules!

If we accept "rules" in the second example as a colloquialism (an informal expression) that means "helps students get high grades," then the second word group would qualify as a sentence. The first, however, is not a sentence because nothing is happening: there is a subject but not a predicate. No comment *about* the rules of grammar is being made; the noun and its prepositional phrase represent an abstraction. Some groups of words can be recognized as sentences because a word or words suggest something is happening or a relationship is being observed.

The word "rules" in the second sentence tells us something the writer is observing about "Grammar." The first word also is necessary to make the sentence complete; it indicates *what* "rules." So, you can say that complete sentences need two things: a *subject* (answering the reader's question "What or who is this about?") and a *predicate* that tells us something the subject is doing or some condition or state of existence of the subject.

A sentence, then, is a word or group of words that expresses a complete thought, but it can also be defined grammatically: a sentence is a group of words that contains at least one subject and one predicate and needs nothing else to complete its thought. To determine the subject of a sentence, you can ask, "Who or what is doing the action in the sentence?" Consider the very simple sentence,

Dogs bark.

The answer is "Dogs." So, "Dogs" is the subject of the sentence. A subject must be a *noun* or a *pronoun.* In some sentences, the subject is implied (see Section 3.2, below).

To determine the predicate of a sentence, you can ask the question, "What does the subject do?" The answer is "bark." A predicate will always include a *verb.* The line in the sentence below divides the subject from the predicate.

Dogs │ bark.

The sentence "Dogs bark" is extremely brief. This information can be modified by making the sentence longer. The line between subject and predicate will not change; the difference will be that a reader will know more about the dogs *and* about their barking.

Dirty, dangerous dogs | bark balefully behind the barn.

The reader has been informed that the dogs are "dirty" and "dangerous." The predicate also has been enlarged: the reader has been told *how* the dogs barked ("balefully") and *where* they barked ("behind the barn"). The longer sentence illustrates that more complex statements can be constructed by adding words or phrases, *modifiers*, to the subject and to the predicate. The subject together with its modifiers is called the **complete subject**; the main noun or pronoun is sometimes called the **simple subject** to distinguish it from the complete subject.

Another way you can give more information in a sentence is to add more subjects and/or more predicates. When you add one or more subjects and predicates, the sentence is no longer simple. While simple sentences convey one complete thought, more complex sentences can convey more than one complete thought.

The first thing to check in your writing is that you are writing in complete sentences, which means you must make sure that the sentence you write has two parts, a subject and a predicate.

3.2 The "Invisible-Subject" Sentence

The need for a subject and a predicate in every complete sentence suggests that the minimum English sentence must contain at least two words. There is one exception: an **imperative sentence**, which is a command, may consist only of a predicate (verb). The subject, which is always implied, is the pronoun "you," although it is invisible. For example, in the imperative sentence, "Listen!" the subject "you" is understood to be the subject: "[You] listen!" In the command, "Go to the store!" "you" is understood to be the subject: "[You] go to the store." Notice that "you" could be plural, i.e., the command could be to more than one individual; indeed, all readers of the work could be implied.

Exercise

Which of the following are complete sentences? Draw a line between the subject and the predicate. Mark with "S" those that contain only a subject and with "P" those that contain only a predicate.

1. The cat on the window ledge.

2. The kind of doughnut that doesn't have a hole in the middle.

3. Wanted to bury his treasure where it would never be found.

4. Dropped the ball with only ten yards to go.

5. A sweet-smelling fragrance.

Exercise – *continued*

6. Opportunity knocks.

7. Is willing to give a presentation.

8. On a mountaintop in the remotest region of the Yukon.

9. Send in the clowns!

10. Hundreds of geese in the field.

3.3 Four Errors of Incompletion

Fragment 1—lacks subject or predicate. In example 10 above, "Hundreds of geese in a field" something essential is missing. What about geese in a field? Do they exist? Are the geese doing something? What did they look like? Who saw them? To answer any of these questions is to complete a thought—and the sentence. For example,

Hundreds of geese in a field | were resting before the next stage of their long journey.
Mr. Elford | imagined hundreds of geese in a field.

In the first example, a predicate has been supplied. In the second example a subject, Mr. Elford, and a verb, "imagined," have been introduced and the "hundreds of geese in a field" have become part of the predicate, the direct object of the verb "imagined."

Exercise

To the remaining fragments in the previous exercise add a subject and/or predicate to create grammatically complete sentences.

Fragment 2—add-on fragment. Add-on fragments contain neither subject nor predicate. They may begin with *such as, like, for example, including, also, as well as, except (for), besides,* and *especially*; with an incomplete verb form such as the infinitive; or with a prepositional phrase. Writers can mistake phrases beginning with these words for complete sentences because in speech a major pause is usual between them and the sentence that precedes them. The easiest way to fix them is to make them part of the previous sentence or to supply missing essentials such as subject and/or predicate. Punctuation may not be needed; at other times, you can use a comma or a dash.

Fragments:
Exaggerated images of fitness are everywhere. Especially in teen-oriented magazines.

Corrections:

Exaggerated images of fitness are everywhere, especially in teen-oriented magazines.

Exaggerated images of fitness are everywhere—especially in teen-oriented magazines.

Fragment:

Emily placed the picture of Stefan beside the picture of Drew. To see whether the twins still looked alike.

Correction:

Emily placed the picture of Stefan beside the picture of Drew to see whether the twins still looked alike.

Fragment:

On a mountaintop in the remotest region of the Yukon.

Correction:

She│stood *on a mountaintop in the remotest region of the Yukon.*

Fragment 3—"-ing" fragment. A third kind of fragment occurs when an incomplete verb form ending in *-ing* is mistaken for a complete verb. In such cases, the writer may believe that the sentence contains a predicate when it does not. An auxiliary verb is missing in this example:

Holiday crowds *milling* around shopping malls.

What are the crowds doing? If you said "they are milling," you have changed the fragment into a complete sentence by adding the helping verb *are*:

Holiday crowds│*are milling* around shopping malls.

Fragment 4—dependent clause fragment. A dependent clause fragment is the most common. Independent clauses are equivalent to simple sentences: they have a subject and a predicate and need nothing else to complete them. Dependent clauses also contain a subject and a predicate, but they express incomplete thoughts because the information they contain is *dependent on* the information in the independent clause. Another way that dependent clauses can be identified is by the word they begin with—a subordinating conjunction. The following includes the major subordinating conjunctions, words and phrases that introduce dependent clauses:

after, although, as, as if, as long as, as soon as, as though, because, before, even though, ever since, if, if only, in case, in order that, once, rather than, since, so that, that, though, unless, until, what, whatever, when, whenever, where, whereas, wherever, whether, which, whichever, while, why, who, whom, whose.

Dependent clause fragments sound incomplete and leave us wondering about the missing part. Consider this fragment:

> Because his car wouldn't start this morning.

This sentence fragment leads you to wonder what happened because his car wouldn't start. When you provide that information in an independent clause, you have a complete sentence. You can test a sentence for completeness by asking whether the word group is true or false. "Because his car wouldn't start this morning" can be neither true nor false due to missing information. Adding information completes the example sentence:

> Because his car wouldn't start this morning, he was late for his first day of work.

The subordinating conjunction that is used to introduce the dependent clause indicates the relationship of that clause to the independent clause, such as one of cause-effect (*as*, *because*), time (*since*, *when*, *while*), or contrast (*although*, *though*, *whereas*). If you take away the subordinating conjunction, you are left with a subject and a predicate and a sentence that expresses a complete thought. Another way to fix a dependent clause fragment, then, is to take away the subordinating conjunction; you will be left with a simple sentence that expresses one idea. However, it may not be the idea you intended to convey. "His car wouldn't start this morning" is a complete sentence, but does not explain why, the consequences of the situation, etc.

Exercise

The following may, or may not, be sentences. If they are not, identify what kind of fragment they illustrate. If they are fragments, make them into complete sentences with a subject and a predicate and needing nothing else to complete them.

1. Ensuring that you write in complete sentences.

2. Huge tears rolled down his cheeks.

3. Whenever they called her into work.

4. He promised to call on her tomorrow. To see if she was still all right.

5. He must be guilty. Since he's already confessed.

6. I won't vote tomorrow. Unless I hear something that makes me change my mind.

7. Introducing our next prime minister.

8. A row of stately elms interspersed with sprightly cedars.

9. Swimming on her back.

10. Walking beside the tracks, he eventually reached the town.

11. Because spiritual values are more enduring than material ones.

12. A leader is one who has charisma and poise. One who is capable of motivating others.

Exercise – *continued*

13. Stress can make us victims of illnesses. Including mild to life-threatening ones.

14. The student sauntered into class. After he opened the door and cautiously peeked inside.

15. Which leads to another popular argument for lowering the drinking age.

16. For example, the famous TV show "Friends."

17. This is the information age. A time when ideas are literally at your fingertips.

18. The opposition to Kyoto is a manifestation of fear. A fear that big business will come to bear the major burden for Kyoto.

19. Enabling students to learn about people from different ethnic groups.

20. Stress can have devastating effects on many groups of people. Such as depression in those who fail to meet the expectations of demanding figures of authority.

Exercise

The following passage contains four sentence fragments. Underline them; correct them by joining them to complete sentences or by adding information. Of the four kinds of fragments discussed above, which is *not* present in the passage?

Although it is known that the people who inhabited the island were of Polynesian descent. In 1994, DNA was extracted from 12 skeletons found on the island, and it was proven to be from people of Polynesian descent. Furthermore, it was suggested that these Polynesians came from Southeast Asia. From the fact that the crops grown by the indigenous people were native to Southeast Asia. For example, bananas, sugarcane, taro, and sweet potato. For more than 30,000 years prior to human settlement of the island, the area was a subtropical forest of trees and woody bushes. Towering over a ground layer of shrubs, herbs, and grasses.

4. Introducing . . . Phrases and Clauses

Having learned the parts of speech and the concept of the sentence, you will find it easier to consider **phrases** and **clauses**—units within the sentence that are larger than one of the parts of speech by itself but no larger (and usually smaller) than a complete sentence.

Prepositions join nouns and pronouns to the rest of the sentence, while conjunctions handle the other joining functions. **Co-ordinating** conjunctions join two or more independent clauses while **subordinating** conjunctions join dependent and independent clauses. By joining dependent and independent clauses, you can form different sentence types.

CONCEPTS and TERMS *NEW* to this section

- adjectival (relative) clause
- comma splice (fault)
- complex sentence
- compound predicate
- compound sentence
- compound–complex sentence
- noun clause
- prepositional phrase
- phrase
- run-on (fused) sentence
- simple sentence

4.1 Phrases

4.1.1 Prepositional Phrases

A phrase is a group of two or more grammatically linked words that, lacking a subject or predicate, or both, can be thought of as functioning as a single part of speech.

A group of words that includes more than one part of speech can, as a unit, modify a verb. If it does, it is said to be functioning **adverbially** (as an adverb) within the sentence. Similarly, a group of words can modify a noun or pronoun, in which case it is functioning **adjectivally** (as an adjective). Prepositional phrase units will act as either adverbs or adjectives.

> She drove me *into town* so I could do my laundry.

The prepositional phrase "into town" begins with the preposition "into" and is followed by the noun "town," the object of the preposition. But if you look at the phrase as a unit, you can see that "*into town*" is functioning as an adverb modifying the verb "drove" by explaining where the action took place: drove *where? Into town.*

Consider the prepositional phrase in this sentence:

> Some *of the injured passengers* had to be hospitalized.

The phrase, "of the injured passengers," begins with the preposition "of," has as its object, "injured passengers," and modifies the indefinite pronoun "Some"; therefore, it is functioning adjectivally in the sentence.

4.1.2 Noun and Verb Phrases

In the previous example, the indefinite pronoun with its modifier makes a **noun phrase**. Notice that "Some of the injured passengers" also constitutes the subject in this sentence because it tells us who or what is the subject of the predicate, "had to be hospitalized."

> Some of the injured passengers | had to be hospitalized.

Phrases, then, can act also as nouns in the sentence.

Consider the following sentence:

> We *will be looking* carefully for the person with a red flag on her backpack.

In this sentence "will be looking" conveys the action of the subject "We" and is made up of more than one word; therefore, it is called a verb phrase.

4.2 Clauses

Word units larger than phrases that can be broken down into two grammatical units, each with a subject and a predicate, are called **clauses**. In the following sentence the subjects are in boldface, the verbs are italicized, and the conjunction is underlined.

> **Frances** never *answers* questions in class unless the **teacher** *calls* on her.
> *First clause*: Frances never answers questions in class
> *Second clause*: unless the teacher calls on her.

The first part of this sentence could stand alone as a sentence, as it has a subject, "Frances," a predicate, "answers," and needs nothing else to complete its thought. The second part could not stand alone as a sentence—the word "unless" makes it a dependent clause fragment. Thus, this sentence illustrates two different kinds of clauses: the **independent clause**, which can stand alone as a sentence, and the **dependent clause**, which cannot stand alone as a sentence. A noun clause is a particular type of dependent clause, and the relative—or adjectival—clause is another kind of dependent clause. It is especially important to be able to distinguish an independent clause from a dependent clause in order to avoid writing a sentence fragment.

A clause is a group of words containing both a subject and a predicate.

As discussed under "Fragment 4" (page 317), a dependent clause contains an idea subordinate to the idea of the main clause.

4.2.1 Using Conjunctions to Join Clauses

An independent clause standing by itself is equivalent to a *simple sentence*. "Frances never answers questions in class" is a simple sentence consisting of an independent clause. Clauses are used as building blocks to construct more complex sentences. The function of co-ordinating conjunctions is to connect equal units, such as two independent clauses; the function of subordinating conjunctions is to connect unequal units, such as an independent clause and a dependent clause. Different rules for punctuation apply to independent and dependent clauses connected this way.

The seven co-ordinating conjunctions are *and, but, for, or, nor, so,* and *yet.* Only these seven words can be used (with a comma) to join two independent clauses.

Co-ordinating conjunctions connect *co-ordinate* or *equal* units, such as two independent clauses; **subordinating** conjunctions connect clauses of *unequal weight,* an independent clause and a dependent clause.

Sentences formed by two or more independent clauses joined by a co-ordinating conjunction are called **compound sentences**. We can see these kinds of conjunctions (italicized) operating as joiners in the following examples:

> The woodwinds warbled *and* the strings sang sweetly.
> Our profits in the first quarter showed a ten per cent increase, *but* in the second quarter they dropped again.
> Not rich am I, *nor* am I powerful.
> He has rung, spoken to her, *and* they will go to dinner.

A sentence can have two subjects or two verbs and still be a simple sentence. Co-ordinating conjunctions join equal units. They often join two verbs governed by one subject. Such compound-predicate constructions can occur in simple sentences.

However, a compound *sentence* contains two independent clauses, *each* with a subject and verb.

Examples

Simple sentence with compound subject:

> *Nassim* of a bright mind and *Kayla* of a kind heart redoubled their efforts to help the family.

Simple sentence with compound predicate:

> Jason *awoke* before dawn and *listened* happily to the sounds of the new day.

Note that there is no comma before the conjunction *and* because the two verbs it connects are parts of the same clause.

A sentence formed by one independent clause joined by a subordinating conjunction (see Fragment 4, above) to a dependent clause is called a **complex sentence**. In a complex sentence, two or more subordinating conjunctions may connect two or more dependent clauses to an independent clause. We can see these kinds of conjunctions operating as joiners in the following examples:

> Plagiarism is a problem at many universities *where* much research these days is conducted through the Internet.

> *Although* much work has gone into developing artificial organs, the results, to date, have been disappointing.

> Ena began taking night classes *after* her company announced *that* there would be layoffs in the near future.

In the first sentence, *where* can clearly be seen as the subordinating conjunction that begins a dependent clause and joins it to the preceding independent clause. In the second sentence, the dependent clause comes first, but the subordinating conjunction *although* nevertheless joins the dependent to the independent clause. (You can just as easily start a sentence with a dependent clause as an independent one.) The third sentence contains an independent clause followed by two dependent clauses; *after* and *that* are the subordinating conjunctions that join them.

A sentence that combines a compound sentence (independent clause + co-ordinating conjunction + independent clause) with a complex sentence is a **compound-complex sentence**. It will contain two independent clauses along with one or more dependent clauses. For example,

> The woodwinds warbled, the brass bellowed, *and* the strings sang sweetly, *though* the timpani thundered, almost drowning out the other instruments.

Exercise

To demonstrate your familiarity with the different kinds of clauses and joiners, construct compound, complex, and compound-complex sentences from the independent clauses (simple sentences) below. When you've joined the clauses in the most logical way, identify the sentence type: compound, complex, or compound-complex. Ensure that you have at least one example of each type of sentence.

1. They intended to eat at Benny's Bistro.
   They saw a long line-up outside Benny's.
   They went to Kenny's Kitchen instead.

2. There may be nearly two million kinds of plants in the world.
   There are likely at least as many different kinds of animals.
   No one can know how many species have evolved, flourished, and become extinct.

3. Timothy Findley's story "Stones" takes place in Toronto.
   Norman Levine's "Something Happened Here" takes place in northern France.
   Both stories describe the tragic assault by Canadian troops on Dieppe during World War II.

4. We may suspect that Earth is not unique as a life-bearing planet.
   We do not as yet have any compelling evidence that life exists anywhere else.
   We must restrict our discussion of the pervasiveness of life to our own planet.

5. Drug-testing procedures for Olympic athletes are becoming more and more elaborate.
   Athletes often feel they have to boost their performance.
   They want to compete at the same level as their competition.

4.3 Errors of Combining

The second frequent error in sentence construction is created by combining two independent clauses incorrectly. A fragment in formal writing suggests the writer does not fully understand what a sentence is. But sometimes writers run one sentence into another, suggesting they don't know where to end the sentence. The two major errors in ending a sentence are the **run-on sentence** (sometimes called "the fused sentence") and the **comma splice**, or the comma fault.

4.3.2 The Run-On Sentence

The writers of run-on sentences simply join two sentences without stopping. This is analogous to running a stop sign without changing speed. They charge through the end of the first main idea and into the second one without separating their statements, that is, without coming to a full stop—without placing a period at the end of the first one and without capitalizing the first letter of the word that should begin the second sentence.

A sentence may contain one, two, or more subject–predicate units, and these units (independent clauses) must be joined correctly so that the reader can distinguish one main idea from another. The problem with the sentences discussed below is that the subject–predicate units are not joined correctly.

> Sean | put on a set of headphones to do his homework // that way he | could get it all done and be entertained too.
> Toxic chemicals and pollutants | do not disappear // they | accumulate in our natural resources.

The run-on sentences above contain two complete thoughts, or two main ideas. Lines indicate the division between subject and predicate; double lines show where the first sentence ends and the second begins, and where a period should be placed.

4.3.2 The Comma Splice

An error more common than the run-on sentence is the comma splice—the "fusing" of two complete sentences by a comma. The person who commits the comma splice joins two "sentences" with a comma. This error is analogous to slowing down at a stop sign without coming to a full stop, then charging through. By itself, a comma cannot be used to connect two sentences.

> *Incorrect:*
>
> Learning to function in a busy office environment was completely new to her, she had always worked at home.
> Censorship does not just mean getting rid of swearing and nudity, it can also mean blocking an idea or viewpoint.

As you will see, a co-ordinating conjunction plus a comma or a "stop" form of punctuation—a semicolon or a colon—is needed to join two independent clauses. The rules under commas, semicolons, and colons illustrate how these forms of punctuation can be used to connect two separate thoughts, or two subject–predicate units.

Exercise

Fix the sentences by using a period to make two separate sentences, or if you already know the rules for using other forms of punctuation to join independent clauses, you can use them.

1. I took two buses to get downtown it was a long way.

2. Our neighbour's dog howled all last night, it was just impossible to get a night's sleep.

3. I was frightened during my first driving lesson the instructor yelled at me.

Exercise – *continued*

4. It's easy to punctuate sentences, just put a comma whenever you pause.

5. Janne ate as quickly as he could then he went upstairs to finish his homework.

6. The incidence of breast cancer has increased, it takes the lives of many women today.

7. Homelessness has existed for centuries, literature on the subject dates back to the feudal period in Europe.

8. Humans are imitators, conforming is something they are good at.

9. Mozart composed his first minuet at the age of five he wrote his first symphony before he turned nine.

10. Asthma is a common problem among Canadians, exposure to second-hand smoke in public places can intensify this condition.

Exercise

Determine what is wrong in the following sentences; then, make the correction.

1. He managed to pass the year though he seldom did his homework, what will happen to him next year is anyone's guess.

2. The opening ceremonies were delayed. On account of rain.

3. She went to France for the summer. It being a fine opportunity to learn another language.

4. Though they both liked to read, they usually read different books, she read adventure stories while he liked detective stories.

5. While books are still the main source for acquiring knowledge.

6. The only way a person can learn. To pay attention to what is going on in class.

7. He was too tall and thin to excel at sports. Except basketball, of course.

8. The concept that "bigger is better" is part of our culture, it is promoted by both advertisers and the media these days.

9. Understanding the theory of relativity and its impact on our daily lives.

10. Martin Luther King led protests during the civil rights movement, his enthusiasm and his will to end discrimination made him a leader.

11. The Romans were willing to change their religious beliefs quite easily, the Greeks, however, were less willing to do this.

Exercise – *continued*

12. Although TV can corrupt the minds of innocent children if it is not monitored closely.

13. The computer is not the only way to access e-mail today, telephones and palm pads may come equipped with e-mail capability.

14. It seems that the North American mass media prescribes two roles for women, they can be sex objects or passive housewives.

15. Martial arts are attracting more people than ever before. Especially those who want to gain self-control and self-awareness.

5. Punctuation

CONCEPTS and TERMS *NEW* to this section

- attributive noun
- comma
- co-ordinate adjective
- direct address
- interrupter
- non-co-ordinate adjective
- non-restrictive phrase or clause
- parentheses
- parenthetical material
- restrictive phrase or clause
- sentence adverb
- serial comma

5.1 Commas

Comma Chaos Theory

Does the precise placement of those visually challenged marks on paper really matter? As a student, you will be writing essays or reports for many of your classes; as a working professional, you may write letters, reports, summaries, memoranda, or other documents that need to be punctuated; therefore, the short- and the long-term answers both are, "Yes." Correct comma use guides the reader through the syntax of the sentence, clarifying the relationships among some of the parts of the sentence.

Myths about comma use abound, such as the "one breath rule," which asserts that where in speaking you naturally stop and pause for a short breath, you should insert a comma. However, commas are there to assist the average silent reader more than the one who reads aloud. If you are coaching yourself to read a speech effectively, you may want to place commas where you plan to pause for breath, but in formal writing, the "one breath rule" is simply too vague to be of any use; in fact, it can lead you astray.

The word "comma" comes from the Greek word *komma*, meaning "cut" or "segment." In general, commas separate (segment) the smaller or less important units in a sentence; working with co-ordinating conjunctions, however, they are used also to separate large units, independent clauses. Commas separate in a sentence: (1) items in a series, (2) independent clauses, (3) parenthetical material, and (4) miscellaneous items, such as adjectives, dates, addresses, and titles. These rules embrace special cases of various kinds, so that they should be thought of as "rules of thumb" or categories of practice.

5.1.1. Use Commas to Separate Items in a Series

This rule category applies to three or more grammatically parallel items, such as nouns, verbs, or adjectives—whether single words, phrases, or clauses. For example:

A series of three nouns:

> It doesn't matter whether the items in the series are words, phrases, or clauses.

A series of three predicates:

> Every Saturday, Davina gets up, drowns herself with coffee, and stumbles to the door before she realizes what day it is.

A series of three clauses:

> Come to the Broadmead Art Tour tomorrow: view artworks in a variety of media, add to your collection, and meet with talented artists on their doorstep.

A note on "**the serial comma**": the comma before the last item in a series of three or more items, referred to as "the serial comma," is sometimes omitted in informal writing. There are instances where its use is essential to the sense of the sentence; therefore, for formal, academic writing, it's best to use it consistently to eliminate the need to consider in each instance whether it can be omitted. The final, or *serial,* comma should not be omitted when the final element or the one that precedes it is compound. In this example, the last item in the list is compound, a single thing, "toast and jam" comprised of two elements: "toast" and "jam."

> She ordered orange juice, an omelette with cheese, and toast and jam.

The serial comma is especially helpful to the reader where the second-last or the last item is a phrase or is significantly longer than the other items:

> The two-year specialization includes 10 half-courses, two full courses that involve internships in health care facilities, and a research paper.

5.1.2. Use Commas to Separate Independent Clauses

The rule category applies to three related situations: (a) two independent clauses joined by a co-ordinating conjunction, (b) introductory words, phrases, or clauses when an independent clause follows, and (c) some conclusions when an independent clause precedes the conclusion.

(a)   Use a comma after an independent clause when that clause is followed by another independent clause and joined by a co-ordinating conjunction. In other words, use a comma before the conjunction in a compound sentence: the co-ordinating conjunction joins while the comma separates the two main ideas.

I was about to go out for a walk, *but* it started to rain.
He forgot to order paper plates for the picnic, *so* people had to eat from their laps.
Dyana was the best dancer on the cruise ship, *and* there is nothing more to be said.

Short Independent Clauses: Exceptions to this rule may be made if the second clause is very short or if the clauses are so closely related that they could be considered compounds (i.e., the ideas are hard to separate). For example, the comma may be omitted between "dress" and "I":

"She wore the dress and I stayed home," sang Jack Lemmon in the movie *Some Like It Hot*.

(b) Use a comma after an introductory word, phrase, or clause when an independent clause follows it.

Hardly daring to breathe, Martin carefully opened the oddly wrapped box.
After six years as committee chair, it was time for her to retire.
In order to get the maximum enjoyment from his stereo equipment, Curtis put it in a room where the acoustics were excellent.

In the following instance, the introduction is one word, a **sentence adverb**, an adverb that modifies the independent clause that follows it:

Unfortunately, we have run out of mineral water.

In complex sentences (consisting of one independent and at least one dependent clause), when you begin the sentence with the dependent clause, a comma follows the dependent clause introduction:

While the drinking age is 19 in most provinces, it is only 18 in Alberta.

Compare with rule (c), below.

(c) Use a comma before a concluding word, phrase, or clause when an independent clause precedes it, unless the concluding phrase or clause gives essential information

W.J. Prince wrote to his client Larry Drucker, asking direction in the case.
He gave a gasp of horror, then fainted dead away.

Rule (c) will apply when a previous statement is attributed to an individual or group:

Students who participate in sports or social activities at school are more likely to consider themselves satisfied with their lives compared to those who do not, according to a recent study.

The rule sometimes applies to complex sentences ending with a dependent clause.

1. He seldom visits the zoo, though he lives only one block away.
2. He often visits the zoo when he is in town.

In sentence 1, the dependent clause gives additional information; such information may be interesting and important, but it is not essential to the main idea of the sentence. The main idea is that *he seldom visits the zoo*. But in sentence 2, the dependent clause completes the thought, giving us essential information. Without the dependent clause the sentence itself would have quite a different meaning: the information in the dependent clause is essential.

Some authorities make it simple by giving you two separate rules, depending on whether you begin the sentence with a dependent or an independent clause: in the former case, you should use a comma to separate the clauses; in the latter case, you do not use a comma. If you wish to follow this simple distinction, you should be aware that, in some instances, such as when the dependent clause begins with *although, though, even though,* or *whereas,* you will have to consider nevertheless whether or not the information in the concluding dependent clause is essential before you decide whether to use a comma before the concluding dependent clause.

First clause dependent, use comma:

Because it was warm there, the sleek Siamese cat lay on the sofa.

First clause independent, omit comma:

The sleek Siamese cat lay on the sofa because it was warm there.

Dependent clause of ambivalent importance, decided to consider it of less importance:

The sleek Siamese cat continued to lie on the sofa, though it was no longer warm there.

If in doubt about using a comma to separate an independent clause from a dependent concluding clause, omit the comma (as in this sentence one is omitted) as it is usually not required.

5.1.3. Use Two Commas to Separate Parenthetical Information

When you place something in parentheses, you signal to the reader that this information is less important than what is not in parentheses. Commas operate similarly to partition less from the more important information in the sentence.

(a) **Use commas before and after non-restrictive (non-essential) phrases or clauses**. The information in non-restrictive clauses is not essential to the primary meaning of the sentence. Though this information may be important, it *can* be left out without changing the essential meaning or the grammar of the sentence (i.e., by making it ungrammatical). By contrast, a restrictive clause is *essential* to the meaning of the sentence; in this sense, it *restricts,* or limits, its meaning. If you left it out, the sentence would mean something different or would be ungrammatical. These distinctions are important also for the uses of the words "that" and "which." "That" introduces restrictive clauses and does not take a comma; "which" introduces non-restrictive clauses and is preceded by a comma.

1. Tony, who often wears a leather jacket, was identified as one of the rescue team.
2. A man who wore a leather jacket was identified as one of the rescue team.

The main idea in sentence 1 is that Tony was identified as part of the rescue team. Tony's leather jacket may be important elsewhere in a larger narrative, but in this sentence it is of secondary importance; therefore, the information is parenthetical and enclosed by commas. Note that *two* commas are required, just as two parentheses would be required; to use only one is not correct. In sentence 2 the information about the jacket is essential to the identification of this person on the team. If you were to leave out the clause "who wore a leather jacket," the sentence would say simply that a man, not a woman, was on the rescue team.

(b) **Use commas to set off appositives**—words or phrases that share a grammatical function with a preceding noun or phrase; they name, rephrase, specify, or explain the noun or noun phrase that comes just before.

Her first work, a short story collection called *Drying the Bones*, was given outstanding reviews.

You need to ensure that you use commas for true appositives and not to separate a modifier, such as an *attributive noun*, from the noun it modifies (nouns can be used adjectivally and placed before other nouns, though the practice is often considered too informal for academic writing). If in doubt, take the second noun or noun phrase out of the sentence and see if the sentence is complete and makes grammatical sense.

Incorrect:
At the heart of the conservation movement was the renowned forester, Gifford Pinchot.

Titles: Be particularly careful about using unnecessary commas where a work's title follows. For example, no commas are needed in this sentence because the poem's title is essential information:

Michael Ondaatje wrote the poem "The Cinnamon Peeler" in 1982.

(c) **Use commas to set off adverbs and adverbial phrases** that interrupt the flow of the sentence from subject to predicate, from verb to object or subjective completion. See Section 5.3.1 for a list that includes *indeed, after all, however, needless to say,* etc.

Use commas to set off the person you are addressing directly:

"I must say, Frank, that your performance on the aptitude test demonstrates, beyond a doubt, that you would make an excellent engineer."

It is never wrong in formal writing to use two commas to separate an interruption. However, there are times, especially in informal or semi-formal writing, when to do so may produce comma chaos. Except in the most formal writing, commas around adverbial interruptions can be omitted if they directly follow a co-ordinating conjunction, such as "but," to avoid three commas in close proximity.

Leslie worried about her driver's test, but in fact she aced it.

5.1.4. Miscellaneous and "Comma Sense" Uses

Stylistic convention more than grammar dictates that you use commas between co-ordinate adjectives before a noun, with dates, addresses, titles, and before and after direct quotations.

1. Adjectives modify nouns and usually precede them. When the adjectives are *co-ordinate*, or equal and interchangeable, you separate them by a comma. When the adjectives are *non-co-ordinate*, or unequal and not interchangeable, you do not use a comma.
2. Co-ordinate adjectives: big, friendly dog; tall, white tower; proud, condescending man
   Non-co-ordinate adjectives: white bull terrier; welcome second opinion; incredible lucky break
3. To separate quotations from the rest of the sentence:

   The sign says, "trespassers will be prosecuted."

   "I am not a crook," said Richard Nixon.

4. To distinguish names and locations in addresses:

   Charter House, 1313 Mockingbird Lane, Los Angeles, California

   Convention also dictates that you place a comma *after* the name of the province or state if the sentence continues:

   I lived in Los Angeles, California, until I moved back to Transylvania.

5. Dates:

   October 7, 1951 or October 1951 or 7 October 1951

   A comma is not used with the month and year alone, nor is it used if you begin with the day and follow with the month and year.

6. Degrees, Titles, and Similar Designations:

   Sabrina Yao, M.D., Ph.D., F.R.C.P.S.

7. Numbers:
   Under the metric system, there is a space rather than a comma between every three digits in a number of more than four digits (the space is optional with four-digit numbers). You will sometimes see the non-metric format where a comma separates every three digits starting from the right.

   The output of chemical wastes was 13,890,457 kilolitres per day for that factory.
   In 2001, the population of Nunavut was 26,745, according to Statistics Canada.
   The US Defence Department listed 2,356 casualties earlier in the year.

8. Generally, the convention in North America is to place commas and periods inside quotation marks. Other marks of punctuation are placed outside quotation marks.

   "You should always put periods and commas inside quotation marks," said Professor LeGuin.
   The new topic, "Where Ecological Ends Meet," has been posted.
   Although the company has paid for transportation, we are assured that our meals "are not gratis."

9. In some cases, you will have to apply "comma sense." If a sentence sounds confusing when you read it over, it may be necessary to insert a comma. Commas in the following sentences ensure the sense intended.

   In 1971, 773 people were killed in an earthquake in Peru.
   He told the student to come now, and again the following week.
   The year before, a deadly virus ravaged half the outlying area.

Exercise

Naming the rule categories discussed above, add commas to the following sentences, if and where required.

1. I had planned to go to Calgary but my bus was delayed for more than four hours so I decided to go back home.

2. Jessica Julep the mayor of Nowhere Nova Scotia provided inspirational leadership.

3. After her inaugural speech several members of the house rose to congratulate her.

4. The optional package includes bucket seats dual speakers and air-conditioning.

5. We have collected more than $20,000 and there is a week remaining in our campaign.

6. Metaphors similes and personification all are examples of figurative language.

7. As one can see the tower is leaning some four-and-one-half metres to the south.

8. Hardly daring to breathe Nelson took a quick look at the valley far below him.

9. Although many are called few are chosen and even fewer make it to the top.

10. The magnificent country estate is hidden behind a long elegant row of sweeping silver birches.

11. Juliet studied medicine at The University of Western Ontario in London Ontario before becoming a doctor near Prince Albert Saskatchewan.

12. "After all" he said bitterly "we can't achieve peace in our time if we assume war is inevitable."

13. Her apartment building was a newer one with dark wood trim and large open rooms.

14. As well as the Irish many Africans were forced to leave their families behind during times of famine.

15. Nick and Nicole were married on April 20 1995 but they separated two years later.

16. The simple sentence as we've seen is easily mastered by students but compound sentences necessitate an understanding of various forms of punctuation.

17. The waste of our resources including the most precious resource water is a major environmental problem that Canada is facing today.

18. The committee studying the proposal is a mixture of health officials journalists and politicians.

19. British general Sir Frederick Morgan established an American-British headquarters that was known as COSSAC.

20. The book with the fine red binding on the highest shelf is the one I want.

21. The types of RNA required for protein synthesis are messenger RNA transfer RNA and ribosomal RNA.

Exercise – *continued*

22. Agnes Campbell Macphail the first woman elected to Canadian Parliament served for 19 years beginning her career in 1921.

23. People have immigrated to Canada from countries in Asia Europe the Middle East and Central and South America.

24. The first steam-powered motorcycle known as the "bone-shaker" led to the bikes we use today.

25. Following successful completion of the English test another skills test is taken which is in a written format.

26. He combed through directories of professional associations business and trade associations and unions looking for possible contributors to his campaign.

27. Oliver Wendell Holmes an American was known as a master essayist but Canadian Barry Callaghan is also internationally respected as an essayist.

28. Handwriting of course is a major problem for dyslexics and there are few who can adopt a neat legible script but the prevalence of computers today has helped alleviate many if not all such difficulties for them.

29. After visiting her ancestral homeland China and meeting her sisters from her mother's first marriage Amy Tan wrote *The Joy Luck Club*.

30. The soldier with the red coat in the picture fought on the side of our enemies the Americans.

Exercise

The following excerpt from a book review illustrates the use of many of the comma rules explained above; commas, appropriately placed, make a complex writing style easier to understand. Identify the following rules by placing the corresponding number beside the comma (or absence of a comma) that illustrates the rule:

1. commas to separate items in a series (2 examples)

2. a comma separating an introduction from an independent clause

3. a comma to separate independent clauses in a compound sentence

4. serial commas (2 examples)

5. a restrictive clause

6. a non-restrictive clause

7. appositives (3 examples)

8. co-ordinate adjectives (5 examples)

Exercise – *continued*

9. non-co-ordinate adjectives (2 examples)

Anne Hébert was born in Quebec in 1916, published her first book of poetry in 1942, and has lived mainly in France since the mid-1950s. Her often violent, dramatic psychological novels have generally been interpreted as symbolist or surrealist accounts of the psychic struggle of Quebec in the 20th century that also explore the conflict between Jansenist and Gnostic views of the universe.

Whether an interpretation can be firmly attached to Hébert's latest novel, *Burden of Dreams*, which won the Governor General's Award for fiction in French in 1992, is perhaps not within the province (so to speak) of this reviewer, a lapsed Protestant Ontarian. Yet from its very first page, the reader is acutely conscious of entering a strange, unruly, and disquieting world.

The book begins with the arrival of Julien, a Québécois, in Paris just after the Second World War, and it is immediately clear that his voyage is one of flight as much as discovery.

Anne Denoon, "Review of Anne Hébert's *Burden of Dreams*," *Books in Canada*, Feb. 1995. Reprinted by permission of the author.

5.2 Other Forms of Punctuation

The most common mark of punctuation is, of course, the comma. However, the discriminating use of semicolons, colons, dashes, and parentheses gives your writing polish and precision. The colon and semicolon, along with the dash and parentheses, are stronger, more emphatic marks of punctuation than the comparatively mild-mannered comma. For stronger breaks, longer pauses, and to convey a greater emphasis, learn where to use these marks in your writing.

CONCEPTS and TERMS *NEW* to this section

- apostrophe
- colon
- compound
- contraction
- dash
- joint ownership
- possessive case (possession)
- semicolon
- transitional phrase

5.3 Semicolons

One of the major functions of commas is to separate independent clauses in a compound sentence. Three rules for semicolon use also involve joining independent clauses; the fourth function is to separate items in a series that contain commas.

5.3.1 Semicolon with Independent Clause

A. You may use a **semicolon** rather than a comma and a **co-ordinating conjunction** to join independent clauses if there is **a close relationship between the**

clauses. Using a semicolon to join two independent clauses, rather than a comma + a co-ordinating conjunction, signals to the reader the close connection between the ideas in the two clauses. Consider the following examples:

1. Strong economies usually have strong school systems, and investment in education is inevitably an investment in a country's economic future.

2. Strong economies usually have strong school systems; weak economies generally have weak school systems.

In sentence 1, the second clause is logically related to the preceding one; however, they have different subjects and are not so closely related that a semicolon would be called for. In sentence 2, however, both clauses are concerned primarily with the relationship between economic strength and school systems. That focus, despite the contrasting elements in each clause, justifies the use of a semicolon.

1. Scott was impatient to get married; Salome wanted to wait until they were financially secure.

2. Although unfamiliar with the requirements of the position, he sent in his application. He was hired the following week.

In sentence 1, the subjects of the clauses are strongly linked—individuals in partnership considering marriage—justifying the use of the semicolon. In sentence 2, the second clause is closely related to the preceding one logically, but implicit is the passage of time between the two actions described. Although there is no break in topic or change in subject, a semicolon is not needed because of the separateness in time of two circumstances.

B. The rules for independent clauses we have looked at so far demonstrate many options for connecting important ideas.
   1. You can simply begin a new sentence after you have expressed your first idea. This is particularly useful if you are conveying very complex material or information that is difficult to absorb if too condensed or too closely linked.
   2. You can join the two clauses by using a comma + a co-ordinating conjunction.
   3. You can use a semicolon in place of a period and a new sentence or in place of a comma plus a co-ordinating conjunction (*and, but, for, or, nor, so, yet*) if you want to stress the closeness of the ideas in the independent clauses.

A fourth option is **the use of a semicolon with a conjunctive adverb or a transitional phrase followed by an independent clause**. Conjunctive adverbs and transitional phrases are too numerous to list in their entirety, but all are used to connect two clauses.

1. My roommate lacks charm, friendliness, and humour; *still*, he is an excellent cook.

2. A recent study has found a surprising correlation between a rare form of sleeping disorder and those with telephone numbers that include the

Here are some of the most common conjunctive adverbs and transitional phrases:
accordingly, afterward, also, as a result, besides, certainly, consequently, finally, for example, if not, in addition, in fact, in the meantime, further(more), hence, however, indeed, instead, later, likewise, meanwhile, moreover, namely, nevertheless, next, nonetheless, otherwise, similarly, on the contrary, on the other hand, still, subsequently, that is, then, therefore, thus, undoubtedly

number six; *however*, the conclusion is being challenged by several researchers.

A common error is to miss the distinction between adverbs like *however* and *therefore* acting as ordinary adverbs (interruptions) and these same words acting as **conjunctive adverbs** (joiners). The following sentence pair illustrates this distinction. In sentence 1, commas are required because the adverb occurs in the midst of the clause as an interruption between the subject "he" and most of its predicate "[will] . . . be making." In sentence 2, a semicolon is required before the conjunctive adverb because of its location as a joiner of two independent clauses:

1. Dr. Suzuki will not be in his office this week; he will, *however*, be making his rounds at the hospital.

2. Dr. Suzuki will not be in his office this week; *however*, he will be making his rounds at the hospital.

C. Use a semicolon for clarity between independent clauses when a co-ordinating conjunction is used and when there is considerable internal punctuation within the clauses. In such cases, you will use the semicolon for the strongest break in the sentence (i.e., to separate independent clauses). This is an optional rule that makes a potentially confusing sentence easier for the reader to follow:

He purchased some rare, valuable antiques, including several jewellery items, a candelabra, and a Queen Anne chair, without having so much as a nickel in his wallet; and he had no idea how, when tomorrow came, he would be able to pay for them.

5.3.2 Serial Semicolon

A semicolon should be used **between items in a series if one or more of the elements contain commas**. Without semicolons, these sentences would be confusing:

Her company included Alex Duffy, president; Marie Tremble, vice-president; John van der Wart, secretary; and Chris Denfield, treasurer.

Bus number 1614 makes scheduled stops in Kamloops, BC; Valemont, BC; Jasper, Alta.; and Drayton Valley, Alta., before arriving in Edmonton.

You may also use semicolons to separate **items in a list** when each item is a long phrase or clause, especially where there is internal punctuation. The following sentence would be difficult to read if the items in a series were not separated by semicolons:

1. The success rate of organ transplants has increased steadily due to the use of stronger, more effective drugs to combat infection; the skill of nursing staff to respond quickly to complications; and the growing recognition, supported by recent studies, that psychological factors contribute to patient recovery.

2.   The role of the vice-president will be to enhance the university's external relations; strengthen its relationship with alumni, donors, business and community leaders; implement a fundraising program; and increase the university's involvement in the community.

Note that this is the only rule for using semicolons that does not involve independent clauses. Next to commas, semicolons are probably the most abused form of punctuation. You should use them *only* to join independent clauses in one of the three ways discussed above or to separate items in a series where, otherwise, confusion might result.

5.4 Colons

It is often said that while a semicolon brings the reader to a brief stop or a rhetorical pause, the colon leads the reader on. The colon has three main uses: (1) to introduce quoted material, (2) to set up or introduce a list or series, and (3) to answer, complete, or expand on what is asked or implied in the preceding independent clause.

5.4.1 Formal Uses

1.   To introduce quoted material.

The Oxford English Dictionary defines the word "rhetoric" this way: "The art of using language so as to persuade or influence others."

Direct Quotations: When you use direct quotations in your essays, you can set them up formally with a colon.

Health Canada has made the following recommendation for dentists: "Non-mercury filling materials should be considered for restoring the primary teeth of children where the mechanical properties of the material are safe."

Direct quotations can also be set up less formally. In such cases, a comma may be required or no punctuation at all. To determine which, treat the complete sentence as if it contained no quotation and see if one of the rules for using commas is applicable:

According to the American Academy of Dermatology, "a tan is the skin's response to an injury and every time you tan, you accumulate damage to the skin."

The most general definition of evolution is "any non-miraculous process by which new forms of life are produced" (Bowler 2).

In the first sentence, a comma rule dictates the use of a comma before the quotation; in the second sentence, there is no rule that would necessitate a comma before the quotation.

2. To set up or introduce a list or series.

    In 1998, the CBC outlined three challenges for the future: to attract more viewers to Canadian programming, to increase the availability of "under-represented" categories, and to direct its resources towards this kind of programming.

    Avoid the temptation to insert a colon just before you start a list unless what precedes it is completely expressed. Normally, you would *not* use a colon after *including* or *such as*, or right after a linking verb like *is* or *are*, though these words are often used to set up a list or series.

    Incorrect:
    Caffeine withdrawal can have many negative effects, such as: severe headaches, drowsiness, irritability, and poor concentration.

    One of the questions my essay will attempt to answer is: Does our current public health system work?

3. The colon may begin the answer, completion, or expansion of what is asked or implied in the preceding independent clause. Like the comma and semicolon, then, the colon can be used to separate independent clauses; however, its use is restricted to places in which the second clause clearly amplifies, expands on, or illustrates the first, or completes something implied or stated in the previous clause:

    There is only one quality you omitted from the list of my most endearing characteristics: my modesty.

    David's driving test was a memorable experience: he backed over a curb, sailed through two stop signs, and forgot to signal a left turn.

    If what follows the colon is at least the equivalent of an independent clause, you may begin with a capital letter. It is perfectly acceptable to begin with a small letter, however, as in the two examples above.

> Remember that unless you are using semicolons to separate items in a series, what *precedes and follows a semicolon* should be an independent clause.
>
> What *precedes a colon* should be an independent clause that makes a complete statement.

5.5 Dashes and Parentheses

Although some people use dashes and parentheses interchangeably, their functions are dissimilar. Imagining this scenario might help: you are in a crowded room where everyone is talking. Somebody takes you aside and begins speaking in an unnaturally loud voice about some scandalous event. You look around. People are listening, and that, of course, is the design of the person talking. A couple of minutes later, somebody else approaches and very discretely begins whispering the same information in your ear.

Using dashes is like giving information that is meant to be overheard, to be stressed. But parentheses are more like asides: they are used to convey additional information which, while relevant, is not important enough to be included in the sentence proper.

Dashes, then, set something off and can convey a break in thought. You can use dashes sparingly to emphasize a word or phrase; two dashes (one dash if the material comes at the end of a sentence) will set off the text and draw the reader's attention to what is between the dashes. You can type two hyphens to indicate a dash—if you don't leave a space after the second hyphen, your computer may automatically convert the hyphens to an *em*-dash like this: —.

> Lee wasn't about to let her brother Nigel get the better of her—even if he was at least a foot taller than she was.

Use parentheses sparingly to include a word or phrase, even occasionally a sentence, that isn't important enough to be included as part of the main text; where dashes emphasize, parentheses de-emphasize.

> "Crayolas plus imagination (the ability to create images) make for happiness if you are a Child" (Robert Fulghum).

You will also use parentheses to reference a source after a quotation if you use a parenthetical method for documenting sources, which also is illustrated in the previous example and extensively in Part Five, Section 11.

Deciding how to punctuate material enclosed by parentheses can be tricky. If the parentheses enclose *a complete sentence*, its period or other closing punctuation should be placed *inside* the second parenthesis, as it pertains only to what is between parentheses.

If there should be a mark of punctuation attached to the encompassing sentence and immediately following the parentheses, it will be placed *outside* the second parenthesis. (In other words, punctuate the entire sentence just as you would if there were no parentheses there.) The previous sentence affords an example of terminal punctuation of a complete sentence enclosed by parentheses. The following sentence illustrates punctuation that has nothing to do with the parenthetical insertion, but is required to separate independent clauses. Notice the absence of a capital letter:

> Cassandra wanted to be an actress (her mother had been an actress), but she always trembled violently as soon as she stepped on a stage.

Use dashes and parentheses sparingly. Many writers seem to prefer dashes to parentheses, or vice versa, and use either one or the other too often—especially in first drafts. Consider using other forms of punctuation if you use more than four dashes or two sets of parentheses per page. However, counting the number of times you use one or the other can also point towards one or more areas to work on as the essay takes final form. Overuse of dashes may suggest ideas that are not well connected, while overuse of parentheses could indicate that you are trying to say too much at once.

Exercise

Using the rule categories discussed above, replace commas in the sentences below with the most appropriate form of punctuation. In some cases, the commas are correct and should not be replaced.

1. April showers bring May flowers, May flowers bring on my asthma.

2. A developing salmon goes through four stages, the alevin, the fry, the smolt, and the adult.

3. The opening sentence of *Moby Dick* introduces us to an unusual narrator, "Call me Ishmael."

4. Every essay needs three parts, an introduction, a body, and a conclusion.

5. She lay down, utterly exhausted, in the middle of the parking lot.

6. He paused to admire the splendid sight before his eyes, the ruins of Montgomery Castle.

7. Mayumi tended to look on the good side of things, Glenn usually saw the bad side.

8. The tour includes visits to the following museums, the Prado in Madrid, the Louvre in Paris, and the Rijksmuseum in Amsterdam.

9. It's easy to punctuate sentences, just put a comma wherever you pause.

10. It is probable, though not certain, that she will be promoted to the rank of corporal next year.

11. It was the best of times, it was the worst of times.

12. Marselina has a fine ear for music, unfortunately she can't sing a note.

13. In my health sciences class, we studied the four main food groups, dairy products, meats, carbohydrates, and fruits and vegetables.

14. Brian never tired of misquoting Shakespeare, "the quality of mercy is not stained."

15. First advice to those about to write a novel is the same as Punch's to those about to wed, don't. —Victor Jones

Exercise

Using the rule categories discussed above, replace commas in the sentences below with the most appropriate form of punctuation. In some cases, the commas are correct and should not be replaced.

1. The Romans were willing to change their religious beliefs quite easily, however, the Greeks were less willing to do this.

2. There are two ways to pursue fabulous wealth, to inherit it and live a restrained lifestyle or to work like the devil and play for the highest stakes.

3. His plans for the new development included the following, an apartment complex, single-family residences, a 60-store mall, and a multi-use recreation centre.

4. Union members voted overwhelmingly to return to work, there was a consensus that they had achieved almost all their objectives.

5. It was the ideal summer job, you were outdoors in lovely weather, you were active, and the pay was more than reasonable.

6. If you want to remain well-liked, not to mention alive, among members of a motorcycle gang, there are two things you need, a love of motorcycles and a hatred of authority.

7. In compound sentences, use a comma to join independent clauses where there is a co-ordinating conjunction, use a semi-colon where two such clauses are not joined by a co-ordinating conjunction.

8. This year's conference on the environment is intended to focus concern on three main areas, global warming, pollution, and the destruction of natural habitat.

9. Andrea could hardly keep her eyes open after studying microbiology for 14 hours straight, therefore, she decided she would switch to organic chemistry for the next 14 hours.

10. Virginia Woolf had this to say about the essay, "Of all forms of literature it is the one which least calls for the use of long words."

11. The art of writing the news lead is to answer as many of the following five questions as possible, Who?, What?, Where?, When?, and How?.

12. The current figures of mercury absorption have been announced by the ADA, however, the group's review has been criticized as misleading.

13. Diogenes looked for the one moral person with a lantern, today you would need a megawatt searchlight.

14. Jarrett rushed to the airport only to discover that his flight had been cancelled, a heavy fog had descended on the region.

15. W.B. Yeats believed that the Irish people should govern themselves, they did not have to be subject to English authority.

16. As rainwater travels downwards through the soil, it may collect a number of pollutants, furthermore, an extended period of time may elapse before this pollution is discovered.

17. There is one basic fact about beginning to write that you should bear in mind, whether it aims to entertain, inform, or persuade, or aims at all of these, good writing has a purpose that guides the writer.

18. Freewriting can be a useful means of overcoming blocks, it can help you write when you're not in the mood, it can generate ideas, even if you are the kind of writer who has a hard time coming up with main points, and it can energize your writing.

Exercise

The poem that follows is Edward Lear's nonsense poem "The New Vestments."
Write it in paragraph form, making sense out of nonsense, by punctuating it
for correctness and effectiveness. Most of the original end-line punctuation
has been taken out, and some internal punctuation also has been omitted;
some of the nineteenth-century spellings have been changed.

There lived an old man in the kingdom of Tess
Who invented a purely original dress
And when it was perfectly made and complete
He opened the door and walked into the street

By way of a hat he'd a loaf of Brown Bread
In the middle of which he inserted his head
His Shirt was made up of no end of dead Mice
The warmth of whose skins was quite fluffy and nice
His Drawers were of Rabbit-skins but it is not known whose
His Waistcoat and Trousers were made of Pork Chops
His Buttons were Jujubes and Chocolate Drops
His Coat was all Pancakes with Jam for a border
And a girdle of Biscuits to keep it in order
And he wore over all as a screen from bad weather
A Cloak of green Cabbage leaves stitched all together.

He had walked a short way when he heard a great noise
Of all sorts of Beasticles Birdlings and Boys
And from every long street and dark lane in the town
Beasts Birdles and Boys in a tumult rushed down
Two Cows and a half ate his Cabbage-leaf Cloak
Four Apes seized his Girdle which vanished like smoke
Three Kids ate up half of his Pancaky Coat
And the tails were devoured by an ancient He Goat
An army of Dogs in a twinkling tore up his
Pork Waistcoat and Trousers to give to their Puppies
And while they were growling and mumbling the Chops
Ten boys prigged the Jujubes and Chocolate Drops
He tried to run back to his house but in vain
Four Scores of fat Pigs came again and again
They rushed out of stables and hovels and doors
They tore off his stockings his shoes and his drawers
And now from the housetops with screechings descend
Striped spotted white black and gray Cats without end
They jumped on his shoulders and knocked off his hat
When Crows Ducks and Hens made a mincemeat of that
They speedily flew at his sleeves in trice
And utterly tore up his Shirt of dead Mice
They swallowed the last of his Shirt with a squall
Whereon he ran home with no clothes on at all
And he said to himself as he bolted the door
"I will not wear a similar dress any more
"Any more any more any more never more!"

5.6 Punctuation Prohibitions

No-Comma Rules

Do **not** use a comma to separate simple compounds (two of something with a word like *and* between). Writers sometimes generalize this non-rule from the items in a series rule: remember that a list comprises *three or more* items and that a separate rule applies to compound *sentences* where a comma is required before the co-ordinating conjunction.

> *Incorrect:*
> Some of the heaviest damage from steroid use occurs to the heart, and the liver.
>
> Logging reduces the number of old-growth forests, and destroys these habitats.
>
> We live in a culture that celebrates thinness, and condemns those who do not conform to this standard.

Do **not** use a comma to separate the subject and the predicate. This non-rule is probably the result of writers mistakenly applying the "pause" non-rule.

> *Incorrect:*
> The only way our society is going to be fixed, is if we change our laws.
>
> One advantage in using helicopters to fight fires, is the accuracy of their drops over the scene of the fire.

It is easy to be distracted by parentheses and mistakenly insert a comma between a subject and a predicate:

> *Incorrect:*
> The American College of Sports Medicine (a body that advances research into exercise and sports), considers all physically active females at risk for developing eating disorders.

Do **not** use a comma alone to join independent clauses; this produces a comma splice, a serious grammatical error.

> *Incorrect*:
> Football is one of the most popular sports in North America, it is also one of the most brutal of all sports.
>
> You must use the buttons provided at the bottom of the pages to navigate through the application, otherwise you could lose your connection.
> —*from an on-line application form*

No Semicolon Rules

Do **not** use a semicolon if what follows the semicolon is a fragment.

Incorrect:

When the media portrays minorities, it often stereotypes them; leading audiences to reinforce the stereotype through their behaviour.

For many years, Canada has been a leader in multiculturalism, along with a few other countries; such as the United States and England.

Do **not** use a semicolon to introduce a list or series; a *colon* is correct.

Incorrect:

Shakespeare's last plays are sometimes called romances and include the following; *Cymbeline*, *A Winter's Tale*, and *The Tempest*.

6. Apostrophes

Technically, the apostrophe isn't a mark of punctuation; it is an internal change that indicates the possessive case of nouns. It is also used to show the omission of one or more letters. The apostrophe, then, has two main uses: (1) to indicate the possessive and (2) to show where letters have been omitted, as in contractions.

1. **Apostrophes for Possession in Nouns.** The possessive case in nouns and pronouns indicates ownership and similar relationships, such as association, authorship, duration, description, and source of origin. So, the possessive form is a short form indicating that the second noun is "of" the first noun; the first noun owns or is associated with the second noun. When a noun adds an apostrophe to express the possessive, it is then functioning adjectivally and can be replaced by the corresponding possessive adjective. Most pronouns, however, do not show the possessive through an apostrophe:

the hard drive of the computer = the computer's hard drive (*its* hard drive)

the landlady's apartment (ownership) (*her* apartment)

the tenants' rights (association) (*their* rights)

Dvorak's *New World Symphony* (authorship) (*his* symphony)

Singular Nouns. The usual rule with *singular* nouns, including proper nouns (nouns that begin with a capital letter) ending in *s, ss,* or the *s* sound, is to *add 's*:

the attorney's portfolio, Mr. Price's car, the week's lesson

There are a few plural nouns not ending in *s* that are treated as singular nouns because of their ending: *children, women, men, people*:

the popular children's book, the women's group

Plural Nouns. With plural nouns, including plural proper nouns ending in *s*, an apostrophe alone is added:

the companies' profits, the islands' inhabitants, the Hansons' children, the Gibbses' marriage certificate, two weeks' lessons, the readers' perceptions

Proper nouns ending in "s." Because it may look and sound awkward to add an apostrophe + an *s* to a proper noun ending in *s*, some authorities convey "the book of Tracy Jarvis" as "Tracy Jarvis' book," though others add an apostrophe + *s* = Tracy Jarvis's book. Whichever rule you follow, it's important to be consistent in applying it.

Joint Ownership. In the case of *joint ownership*, where both nouns share or are equal parties in something, only the last noun should show the possessive; ensure from the context that both nouns reflect a truly equal, shared relationship. In the following sentences, the assumption is that Salem and Sheena shared duties as hosts at one party, but that the general manager and the district manager were paid separate wages.

I attended Salem and Sheena's party.

Morana raised the general manager's and the district manager's wages.

The following would be *incorrect* as the individuals do not share the same belief or theory:

Piaget and Montessori's beliefs about how children learn were similar in many ways.

Correct:
Piaget's and Montessori's beliefs . . . .

2. **Contractions.** The second main use of the apostrophe is to denote missing letters. Generally, contractions don't give people too much trouble. However, there are two main exceptions: the contraction *it's (it is)* is often confused with the possessive form of the pronoun *its* (as in *I gave the dog its bone*); and the contraction *who's (who is)* is sometimes confused with the possessive form of *who* (the man *whose house I'm renting*). Contractions are not generally used in formal writing. You should check with your instructor to see if they are acceptable in such assignments as personal essays.

    The apostrophe also is **not** used to indicate the possessive of *pronouns* except for indefinite pronouns, such as *one's opinion, nobody's baby*.

Exception: Apostrophes can be used for clarity with numbers, letters, or symbols to indicate the plural: Adrian got two A's and three B's on his transcript.
In general, *avoid the possessive form with inanimate objects* in formal writing.

"People can develop a tolerance to the effects of caffeine" is preferable to "People can develop a tolerance to caffeine's effects."

Exercise

Decide which nouns in the following sentences require the possessive; then add apostrophes (and "s" in some cases), as appropriate.

1. The Smiths and the O'Neils are going on a trip together.

2. The introductory paragraph should capture the readers interest while developing the writers credibility.

3. Parents and teachers often complain about televisions influence in todays society.

4. The Crosses house is up for sale, and its list price is $179,000. (The last name is Cross.)

5. Its a shame that Lennys parents werent able to attend their sons graduation ceremonies. (Lenny is an only child.)

6. The course I took required two hours homework a day.

7. The mayors biggest asset is her commitment to the citys future growth.

8. This weeks classifieds had several jobs for legal secretaries, all requiring three years experience in solicitors work.

9. Ryans and Jessicas birthday is on the same day.

10. Apples, oranges, mangoes, and tomatoes are the stores specials today.

11. A citizens education should not depend on the financial resources of that persons parents.

12. I don't know whether this etching is his or hers, but theres no doubt its worth a lot in todays market.

13. Its true there are four "ss" and four "is" in the word "Mississippi," but there are only two "ps."

14. In anorexia nervosa, a patients fingernails and teeth may be damaged due to a lack of calcium.

15. Zebra stripes always make me homesick for my Uncle Filbert, whos in jail for stealing his brothers life savings.

16. "Heres looking at you, kid," said Theas father to her twin cousins pet goat.

17. As a child whose parents were relatively well off, I thought all my relatives lives were as easy as mine.

Exercise – *continued*

18. The desire of Pip in Charles Dickens *Great Expectations* to find his place in the world illustrates the works main theme.

19. James Joyces, Amy Tans, and Alistair MacLeods short stories will be analyzed to explore the development of their child protagonists. (The last names are Joyce, Tan, and MacLeod.)

20. The young man stated his churchs mission is to spread Jesus message to people throughout the world.

Exercise

Punctuate for correctness and effectiveness, using commas and other forms of punctuation as appropriate. Minimal punctuation has been provided in places to aid in understanding; however, the punctuation may not be correct. Correct all errors in apostrophe use. The passage concerns the response to an investigative article entitled "Spin Doctors," posted on the Canadian news and information Web site CANOE.

Reader reaction was swift and impassioned. The sites traffic which averages 65 to 70 million views each month experienced an additional 50,000 page views within the first 10 days of the posting. The investigation drew more than 400 letters to the editor hundred's of emails to the message boards and more than 16,000 responses to an online poll.

The intensity of the response surprised veteran investigative journalist Wayne MacPhail the articles author. Although the sheer volume of letters was unexpected it proved to him that there was an audience for online journalism in Canada. MacPhail has experimented with hypertext reporting since the late 1980s but outside of "Spin Doctors" he believes that by and large newspapers have done a "woeful job" of building an audience for Web-based investigative reporting . . . .

Unlike it's media rivals CANOE has never made journalism it's only or even its most important focus. A headline announcing the top story of the day appears underneath the CANOE banner but there are so many other things to do, shopping email contests Web utilities and lifestyle tips all compete with the news.

The CNEWS section isnt necessarily the first place people are expected to go on the network though it is usually at the top of the highlighted sections. It is also part of the site that changes the most during daylight hours. In other words when CNEWS changes the entire home page changes. A "This Just In" feature was recently added but theres no set schedule for posting stories. Despite this expansion of the news section CANOEs promotional material drives home the message that the site is about much more than current events. One recent ad reads, "shop chat email read, in that order."

7. Agreement

7.1 Subject-Verb Agreement

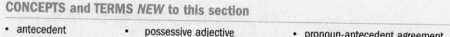

CONCEPTS and TERMS *NEW* to this section

- antecedent
- gender bias
- possessive adjective
- pronoun-antecedent agreement
- subject-verb agreement

7.1.1 Verbal Disputes: Subject–Verb Agreement

A verb must agree in number, person, and gender with its subject; similarly, *a pronoun must agree in number, person, and gender with its antecedent*. These forms of agreement reinforce the close connection between a subject and the verb it governs, along with the close connection between a noun and the pronoun that replaces it.

Because adhering to the principle with both person and gender is usually straightforward, it's not necessary to remember specific rules. But ensuring that a verb agrees with its subject can be more difficult when it is not apparent whether a subject is singular or plural. In the specific instances explained below, the rules assist the writer in applying the principle of subject–verb agreement.

7.1.2 Finding the Subject

The subject of a sentence or clause is the noun or pronoun that performs the action of the verb, or that exists in the state or condition expressed by the subjective complement. In most cases, the subject precedes the verb and is easy to find:

> *Kevin and Nigel* are happy that they passed the exam.

Sometimes the subject is harder to spot for one of the following reasons:

(a) the sentence begins with *here is/are* or *there is/are:* the subject follows the verb, not precedes it, and you will have to look ahead in the sentence to determine whether the subject is singular or plural.

> There *are* many *reasons* for supporting the legalizing of marijuana.

> Here *is* one *person* who supports raising the drinking age.

(b) the sentence asks a question: you may need to look ahead to determine the number of the subject.

> What *is* the main *reason* for legalizing marijuana?

> Where *are* all of the *people* who are in favour of raising the drinking age?

(c) the subject is delayed: because the sentence begins with a prepositional phrase, the noun(s) in the phrase will *seem* to form the subject, but the verb has a different subject later in the sentence.

With the dependence on caffeine *come withdrawal symptoms.*

Among Graham's favourites *was the recent CD* by Nickelback.

(d) the subject is governed by an intransitive verb that has a plural complement: don't be distracted by what follows the verb; the subject alone determines plurality of the verb.

Tanning *salons are* the safest way to get a tan these days.

The *topic* for discussion tomorrow *is* the pros and cons of indoor tanning.

(e) the subject is followed by one or more prepositional phrases that contain nouns and/or pronouns that are *not* the subject. People sometimes forget that the common word "of" is a preposition and that the following noun or pronoun will be the object of the preposition, not the subject.

A long *list* ~~of items, including vegetables, fruits, meats, and several kinds of bread~~, *was* handed to Tao.

The *roots* ~~of his dissatisfaction with the course~~ *go* very deep.

7.1.3 Mistaking the Subject

In the examples with (c), *above,* the nouns *dependence* or *caffeine* in the first sentence and *favourites* in the second sentence could be mistaken for the subjects of *come* and *was,* respectively; however, they are preceded by prepositions. A noun or pronoun that directly follows a preposition can not act as a subject; it will be the object of the preposition.

Incorrect:
By choosing to take a few correspondence courses may afford a student athlete greater flexibility in meeting academic requirements.

Correct:
Choosing to take a few correspondence courses may afford a student athlete greater flexibility.

Incorrect:
With the development of the computer saw automated robots on the production line.

Correct:
The development of the computer saw automated robots on the production line.

In the following sentence, a dependent clause is mistaken for a subject:

Incorrect:
Although Edna thinks of her children at the last moment before her death does not change the fact she is still willing to leave them.

Correct:
Although Edna thinks of her children at the last moment before her death, still, she is willing to leave them.

Edna thinks of her children at the last moment before her death, though this does not change the fact she is willing to leave them.

7.1.4 Rules for Subject–Verb Agreement

Compound Subjects. A compound subject contains two nouns, two pronouns, or a noun and a pronoun (recall that a compound sentence consists of *two* independent clauses).

1. Compound subjects linked by the conjunction "and" require a plural verb form.

   Thanh *and* his friend *are* visiting Ottawa.

   At times, you may want to use a compound subject that expresses a single idea.

   Rhythm and blues was always popular with younger audiences

   To compare and contrast the roles of setting in the novels is sure to be a question on the exam.

   In both examples, the compound subject can be treated as a singular subject since both elements are so closely connected that they can't be separated or their meaning would change.

2. When the compound subjects are linked by the conjunctions *or* or *nor,* along with the correlative (or paired) conjunctions *either . . . or* or *neither . . . nor,* the verb form is determined by the element of the compound **nearest the verb**. These conjunctions suggest singularity, or a choice of alternatives, much more than *and,* which clearly suggests duality requiring the plural verb.

   The chairs *or the table is* going to auction.

   Neither famine nor *floods are* going to force the people to leave their homes.

   If you changed the order of the nouns making up the compound subject in the above sentences, you would need also to change the number of the verb.

3. Prepositional phrases can also be used to join two nouns in a compound subject. *As well as, along with, in addition to, together with,* and *combined with* are examples of such phrases. These phrases do not have the strength of the conjunction *and*. The corresponding form of the verb where prepositional phrases join compound subjects is *singular* if the first element of the compound is *singular*. Logically, the noun or pronoun before the prepositional phrase is considered the most important, or true, subject, while the noun or pronoun following is considered less important. If the writer of the following sentence wanted to stress equality, the sentence should read: "The instructor *and* her students *are* . . . ."

The *instructor, as well as* her students, *is* going to be attending the symposium on the environment.

The Australian *prime minister, along with* the minister for foreign affairs, *is* set to arrive tomorrow.

4. **Collective nouns** refer to groups. They are singular in form, but may be either singular or plural in meaning, depending on context. If the context suggests singular, then the verb form is singular; the same applies, of course, for plural. Examples of collective nouns include *band, class, family, audience, committee, jury, team, gang, group, congregation, staff,* and similar nouns.

   Whenever the context suggests the members of the group are to be thought of as *one unit*, all doing the same thing or acting together, the verb form is *singular;* when the members are considered as *individuals,* the corresponding verb form is *plural.*

   The jury *is* out to consider the evidence before it.

   After the lecture, the class *are* going to be able to ask questions of the guest speaker.

   Most often, collective nouns are considered singular, so, if in doubt, choose the singular form. If a plural verb with a collective noun sounds odd, you can rephrase the subject so that the collective noun functions adjectivally before an appropriate plural noun.

   After the lecture, class members are going to be able to ask questions of the guest speaker.

5. In the following phrases, the verb form will be singular, even though the noun or pronoun that follows will be plural: *one of, each of, either/neither of, every one of,* and *which one of.* The verb form following *the only one who* also will be singular.

   One of our 115 students *has* written an A+ essay.

   Alec is *the only one of* those attending who *has* difficulty speaking before a large group.

6. Most indefinite pronouns are considered singular and take a singular form in agreement. *Each, either, neither, one, no one, everyone, someone, anyone, nobody, everybody, somebody, anybody, anybody, anything, everything, nothing* are singular indefinite pronouns. Unlike other pronouns, indefinite pronouns use the apostrophe to express the possessive: *Everybody's* opinion is welcome. *Compare with:* His or her opinion is welcome; *their* opinions are welcome.

   Some authorities believe that when context clearly warrants the use of plural agreement with the antecedents "everyone" and "everybody," as in the second sentence below, you may use the plural pronoun.

   Everyone is going to stand when the opening ceremonies begin.

   When the pepper was spilled, *everyone* blew *their* noses.

7. There is a separate rule for portions and fractions, such as *any, none, some, part, much, all, more, most, plenty, a lot + of, a variety + of, a number + of,* and *(one-) half + of.* The form of the verb depends on whether the noun or pronoun following "of" is singular or plural.

   None of the missing **pieces** *have* been found yet.

   Some of the **losses** incurred with the companies' merger *are* being absorbed by the shareholders.

   Half of the **pie** *is* gone.

   One-third of the **employees** *are* out on strike.

8. Subjects referring to *distance, time, money, weight, or mass* will be *singular;* also, when the subject is **the** *number of,* the verb is *singular* (contrast with rule #7).

   Twelve miles is not a great distance to an experienced hiker.

   The number of people attending the courses *has dropped* in the last two years.

9. Some nouns end in *s,* but because they usually refer to a singular concept or subject, they require the singular form of the verb: Examples include *politics, economics, mathematics, statistics, physics, billiards, darts, athletics, gymnastics, measles, mumps,* and *news.*

   Statistics is an inexact science; no *news is* good news

   Depending on their context, many of these nouns can be considered plural and should then take a plural verb form. For example, *statistics* could refer to a set of facts, rather than to one subject:

   The *statistics* on global warming *are* alerting politicians to the need for worldwide action.

Whether the titles of artistic works or the names of companies are singular or plural in form will not affect the verb: a singular verb will be needed to agree with the subject.

Montreal Stories is a recent collection of Mavis Gallant's fiction; McClelland & Stewart *is* the publisher.

10. Logically, the following will be plural and will require the plural form of the verb: *both, few, many, several, parts of.*

A well-educated *few seem* to care about correct grammar and punctuation these days, but *both are* essential parts of the writing process.

Be especially wary (1) *when you use a compound subject,* (2) *when an indefinite pronoun is the subject,* and (3) *when there are intervening words between the subject and the verb.* Most errors in subject–verb agreement are due to one of these three situations.

8. Pronouns at Work

8.1 Pronoun–Antecedent Agreement

The **antecedent** of a pronoun is the noun it replaces, and a pronoun must agree with its antecedent noun in number. Most of the rules for subject–verb agreement also apply to pronoun–antecedent agreement. If you have difficulty finding the antecedent, see if it, or an equivalent form, can be substituted for the pronoun in the sentence:

The first thing that usually strikes us about *a person* is his or her (a person's) physical appearance.

Their is an adjectival form derived from the pronoun *they.* The rule for pronoun-antecedent agreement also applies to such possessive adjectives, which are formed from pronouns.

Compound antecedents require the plural form of the pronoun and adjectives formed from pronouns.

Connie *and* Steve *have* invited me to *their* cottage.

If the compound subject includes the words *each* or *every,* the singular form should be used.

Each book and magazine in the library *has its* own entry.

When two antecedents are joined by *or* or *nor,* the pronoun agrees with the closest antecedent.

Neither the prime minister *nor his advisors were* certain how to implement their proposal.

As with subject–verb agreement, collective noun antecedents require the singular pronoun form if they are thought of in the collective sense, as a unit; if the context suggests that individuals are being referred to, the pronoun will take a plural form.

Our hockey team will play *its* final game against *its* arch-rivals. (The team will be playing as a unit.)

The team will be receiving *their* new jerseys Friday. (Individual team members each will be given a jersey.)

With pronouns referring to portions and fractions, agreement depends on whether the noun following *of* is singular or plural.

Studies show that *a* large *number of college and university students are* cheating on their exams and essays; however, a much larger number are not.

If the pronoun has an indefinite pronoun antecedent such as *anybody* or *someone*, the singular form will apply, as it does with subject–verb agreement.

Incorrect:
One should be careful about pronoun agreement, or *his* teacher will certainly point out the error to *him*.

8.2 Problematic Pronouns: Inclusive Language

In recent years, the efforts of many to avoid forms of language perpetuating gender bias have driven them to a gender-neutral, but grammatically incorrect, use of "their" with the singular indefinite pronoun. The inclusion of both correct pronouns in the form "his/her" or "his or her" is awkward compared to the "inclusive him," but is preferable to an erroneous "their" and far better than a form that may appear sexist. Rewriting the sentence to avoid "one" may produce a smoother-sounding result.

A student must footnote *his* or *her* references or the teacher will expect *him or her* to correct the oversight.

Teachers will return papers without references so that students may correct *their* oversights.

The problem of pronoun–antecedent agreement is especially common among student writers when the antecedent noun is either an indefinite pronoun such as *anybody* or *someone* or a singular noun referring to a person where gender is unspecified— a generic noun such as *reader, writer, student, teacher, individual, character,* or *person*.

Option 1: Replace the plural pronoun with both singular personal pronouns (or possessive adjectives). This option is nearly always acceptable in academic writing, but can be seen as awkward and repetitive in much journalistic and workplace writing.

Incorrect:
Anybody not willing to put in long hours for little pay should give up *their* idea of becoming a writer.

Possible solution:
Anybody not willing to put in long hours for little pay should give up *his or her* idea of becoming a writer.

Option 2: Change the singular antecedent into the equivalent plural form and use the plural pronoun.

> *Those* not willing to put in long hours should give up *their* ideas of becoming writers. (Note the plural on "ideas" to agree with "those" and "their.")

Option 3: Revise the sentence so that you don't need a pronoun to replace the noun. This option is not always possible and may occasionally sound too informal for academic writing.

> If you are not willing to put in long hours for little pay, you should give up the idea of becoming a writer.

Exercise

Chose the correct form of the verb and/or pronoun in the sentences and make any other necessary changes in agreement. Rewrite the sentence if that will produce a better result.

1. Everybody who supported the motion raised (his/her/their) hand.

2. Neither the film's director nor its producers (was/were) on hand to receive (his/her/their) prestigious award.

3. The instructor as well as the students (thinks/think) the room is too small.

4. It is unfortunate when a person no longer cares what others think about (him/her/them).

5. One should never expect to succeed unless (one/they) (is/are) willing to persist—even against the odds.

6. It is the tried and true that (provides/provide) the ultimate refuge in mediocrity.

7. Everyone who works during the year (is/are) obliged to file (his/her/their) income tax return.

8. Her set of baby teeth (was/were) complete when she was only eighteen months old.

9. He was one of those few candidates who (was/were) able to win re-election.

10. None of the company's products (requires/require) testing on animals.

11. Lining the side of the highway (is/are) a lot of billboards advertising fast food restaurants.

12. Every specimen of the horned grebe (has/have) a distinctive tuft on each side of (its/their) head.

13. Media and information technology training (provides/provide) students today with important communication skills.

14. Neither team members nor their coach (expects/expect) the season to last another game.

15. The maximum number of people allowed on this elevator (is/are) 30.

Exercise

Most of the following sentences contain one or more subject–verb agreement and/or pronoun–antecedent agreement errors. Correct them.

1. Every person in the community should have the right to attend a university and create new opportunities for themselves.

2. Especially unique to adolescent depression are physical symptoms, such as headaches.

3. The tonal quality of Amati's violins are excellent, but not perfect.

4. Over the past week, there has been some unexplained occurrences on the girls' floor of the residence.

5. Small class sizes and a low student population means few opportunities to meet new people.

6. A typical poem by Emily Dickinson leaves the reader searching for another line or even another stanza to satisfy their craving for closure.

7. Use of the leaves of the coca plant for its stimulant effects dates back thousands of years.

8. A coalition of neighbourhood organizations, students, and unions are currently forming to oppose the University's proposed plan.

9. Everyone who has purchased tickets is eligible for the grand prize, but they must be residents of Canada to claim their prize.

10. If a child is denied the opportunity to play, how can they develop emotionally and physically?

11. Participation and public education is necessary in a true democracy.

12. When a person contracts jaundice, their skin as well as the white part of their eyes turn yellow.

13. Another round of intense labour negotiations have not produced a settlement, so each union member has been told to do his duty on the strike line.

14. Before rendering its unanimous verdict, the jury was polled individually.

15. Almost nothing shapes a person's true character as much as their home.

16. The nature and role of human resources in organizations have undergone tremendous change in the last two decades.

17. In P.K. Page's poem, it is apparent that the landlady's prying nature and lonely life has made her forget her place.

18. Stereotyping and the use of degrading language in the book serves to reinforce its theme.

19. His overriding concern with rules and regulations, together with his excessive neatness and demand for order, suggests a mild obsessive–compulsive complex.

Exercise – *continued*

20. A person who continually disregards others' feelings will pay for their neglect sooner or later.

21. The encouragement of curiosity, questioning, and discussion is vital to the success of today's school environment.

22. In Japanese culture, a person's reputation along with their social standing depend on the concept of "saving face."

23. Medieval universities established a system of education and academic credentials that continue to function in today's universities.

24. The give and take in any relationship is the most important factor in sustaining it.

25. Although the Canadian Forces is still one of the best-trained military in the world, the training standards and morale of the forces is declining, according to some people.

8.3 Pronoun Reference

In addition to agreement problems, there are other potential pronoun pitfalls: errors in *pronoun reference, pronoun case,* and *pronoun consistency.*

CONCEPTS and TERMS *NEW* to this section

- ambiguous pronoun reference
- broad pronoun reference
- comparisons
- demonstrative adjective
- elliptical construction
- gerund

- missing antecedent (no reference)
- objective case
- participle
- person (of pronoun)
- (pronoun) case

- (pronoun) consistency
- (pronoun) reference
- remote pronoun reference
- subjective case
- syntax

For a moment, consider life without pronouns.

A Lost Loonie Leads to a Lesson Learned

Alex and Alex's lawyer, Alan, left in Alex's limousine for Loonies Unlimited to buy Alex's landlady, Alice, a litre of light lemonade. Alice told Alex and Alan to also buy a litre of light lemonade for Alice's long-time lodger, Alison. When Alex and Alan alighted at Loonies Unlimited, Alex and Alan were alarmed that Alex had left Alex's loonie in Alex's loft. So Alphonse, of Loonies Unlimited, allowed Alex and Alan only one litre of lemonade, along with a length of limp licorice, and Alphonse loudly lamented Alex's and Alan's laxness.

As you know, pronouns take the place of nouns, and the noun that the pronoun replaces is called the *antecedent*—literally, the one that "goes before" the pronoun. *Each pronoun you use in your writing should refer clearly to its antecedent.* Formal writing requires your adherence to this principle; more informal writing often permits its looser application (especially with *Broad Reference,* section 8.3.4 below). Pronouns replace specific nouns; *the relationship between pronoun and antecedent must always be clear.* There are four kinds of pronoun reference errors, which can be repaired in different ways.

8.3.1 No Reference (missing antecedent)

This error occurs where the pronoun has no apparent noun antecedent. Consider this sentence:

> Following the prime minister's speech, *he* took several questions from reporters.

The personal pronoun *he* apparently replaces *prime minister's,* which is merely an adjective. Pronouns replace nouns, not adjectives. In the following sentence, the noun antecedent is implied but not actually stated; grammatically, the reference is missing:

> One thing that Canadians are especially proud of is *its* national health care system.

Where there is no antecedent, one must be provided or the pronoun changed into an appropriate noun.

> After the *prime minister* spoke, *he* took several questions from reporters.

Or:

> After speaking, the prime minister took several questions from reporters.

> One thing that *Canadians* are especially proud of is *their* national health care system.

A tendency in speaking, and sometimes in informal writing, is the use of the impersonal third-person pronoun *it* or *they* to refer vaguely to some unmentioned authority. In formal writing, you should avoid this habit:

> *They* say there's nothing like a nice car to make you popular.

Don't begin a sentence with a preposition, such as *at, by, for, in, on,* or *with,* and then follow it with a pronoun with an antecedent that is the object of the preposition. In such a construction, the grammatical antecedent will be missing, and the sentence will have to be revised to include an antecedent/subject of the clause. The examples below illustrate this problem (and its solutions), which sometimes occurs in rough drafts when a writer is trying to get ideas down quickly.

Incorrect:
With the new Formula One scoring system, *it* keeps fans excited throughout the season.

Correct:
The new Formula One scoring system keeps fans excited throughout the season.

Or:

With the new Formula One scoring system, fans remain excited throughout the season.

8.3.2 Remote Reference

A reader should not be expected to connect a pronoun to a noun when they are separated by more than a sentence.

In George Orwell's prophetic book *1984,* people's lives were watched over by television screens. These screens, along with brainwashing techniques, enabled people to be kept under firm control. *It* is an example of dystopian fiction.

The personal pronoun *It,* in sentence three, takes up the thread too late. Many nouns have intervened, causing the reader to have to hunt for the antecedent. Repetition of the noun is often the best solution where the antecedent is far away from the pronoun.

8.3.3 Ambiguous (Squinting) Reference

This error occurs when the pronoun seems to refer to two or more nouns, either of which could be the antecedent.

When *Peter* gave *Paul his* driver's licence, *he* was very surprised to see that it had expired.

Who was surprised in this sentence? The pronoun *he* could refer to either Peter or Paul.

Other Examples:
The problem for readers aspiring to look like the models in women's magazines is that *their* photos have been airbrushed. (*Their* has two grammatical antecedents: *readers* and *models.*)

In 1916, a member of the Russian parliament denounced Rasputin before *his* colleagues. (Does *his* refer to the member's colleagues or to Rasputin's?)

While it is sometimes possible to correct ambiguous reference by repeating the noun intended to act as the antecedent, the result is not always pleasing:

When *Peter* gave *Paul* his driver's license, *Peter* was surprised to see that it had expired.

Rewriting may be the better solution:

On giving his driver's license to Paul, Peter was surprised to see that it had expired.

The problem for readers aspiring to look like the models in women's magazines is that the models' photographs have been airbrushed.

In 1916, a member of the Russian parliament denounced Rasputin before the house.

8.3.4 Broad Reference (Vague Reference)

This error occurs when the pronoun (often *this, that,* or *which*) refers to a group of words, an idea, or concept, rather than *one specific noun*.

Children these days are too prone to lazy habits, such as watching television. *This* shows we have become too permissive.

This replaces too much—in effect, the whole preceding clause. The following, though, would be quite acceptable in anything but the most formal writing, even though the pronoun *which* doesn't replace a specific noun here, but rather the fact that she *received top marks*. The meaning of the sentence, however, is unambiguous.

She received top marks for her final dive, *which* gave her the gold medal in that competition.

In the following sentence the pronoun *this* appears to refer to an idea, rather than a noun antecedent; as a result, the precise meaning of the second independent clause is unclear.

Many older drivers are re-tested if they have had medical problems, but *this* needs to go further.

Broad reference often requires that a sentence be rewritten. Sometimes, the easiest way is to provide a noun and change the demonstrative pronoun into a demonstrative adjective. (Demonstrative adjectives have the same form as demonstrative pronouns—*this, that, these, those*—but, as adjectives, they precede nouns as modifiers, rather than take their place.)

Children these days are too prone to lazy habits, such as watching television. *This tendency* shows that we have become too permissive.

Many older drivers are re-tested if they have had medical problems, but *this re-testing* needs to go further.

Broad pronoun reference errors are particularly distracting when they occur repeatedly as a writer tries to develop an important point. The following paragraph provides an example:

Genetically modified foods have been engineered to flourish in harsh environments. *This* will help alleviate the need for usable farmland as *this* will enable farming to occur on lands once considered unsuitable for growing crops. *This* will be a major benefit to many nations in Africa, Asia, and South America where there is a shortage of food and available land.

While there is perhaps a "broad" allowance for broad reference error, depending on the level of formality required, *it* is a personal pronoun, and, like all personal pronouns, must always have a clear noun referent.

Poor:
We try not to mention specific businesses by name in our article; however, it can't be avoided in some situations.

Better:
We try not to mention specific businesses by name in our article; however, we can't avoid names in all situations.

Exercise

Working backwards: To reinforce the principle that pronouns require clear antecedents, make up antecedent nouns for the pronouns to replace and construct sentences/clauses containing the nouns to precede these sentences/clauses.

Example: He just shrugged off all she had to say in her defence.

Preceding sentence: Lucinda explained her behaviour to Ted, but he just . . . .

1. She had long, brown hair down to her waist. (antecedent for *She*)

2. He found him sleeping soundly on the kitchen floor the next morning. (*He, him*)

3. They lived as if nobody else mattered but themselves. (*They*)

4. This will be her chance to prove whether she is good enough to make the team. (*she*)

5. They have a responsibility to educate the public. (*They*)

Exercise – *continued*

6. His attorney decided on a "not guilty" plea. (antecedent for possessive adjective *His*)

7. She awoke suddenly to the sound of gunfire. (*She*)

8. They make a delightfully odd couple. (*They*)

9. She will eat only the most expensive kind of deluxe cat food. (*She*)

10. After hearing their protests for a long time, he finally agreed to take them along. (*their, he, them*)

Exercise

Identify the kind of pronoun reference errors in the following sentences; then, correct the errors by making necessary revisions. In the first five sentences, the pronoun that needs to be changed is italicized.

1. *It* says in my textbook that pronouns should always have a clear referent.

2. Whenever a staff meeting is called, *they* are required to attend.

3. Racism is a disease that will continue to plague society until *it* is non-existent.

4. Sixty per cent of our pesticides are used on cotton, and *this* is our major ground water pollutant.

5. During Roosevelt's Pearl Harbor speech, *he* identified the U.S. as a peaceful and tolerant nation.

6. I know it said *No Parking*, but I went ahead and parked there anyway. They gave me a $20 fine.

7. Her second novel was far different from her first. It was set in the remote Hebrides.

8. Previous Afghan successes were significant victories; for example, they last waged war against the powerful Soviet Union.

9. Some psychologists and researchers believe in the "innate" theory of prejudice, which purports that ingrained prejudice is cross-cultural and that awareness of race is one of the earliest social characteristics to develop in children. These two claims seem to add credence to its popularity.

10. During the dinosaur age, they lived in a rapidly changing environment.

11. It is the right of everybody to have access to knowledge, and this means access to the education of choice.

12. In Chapter 21 of my textbook, it analyzes the success of the Liberal party in Canada.

Exercise – *continued*

13. Supervisors may discourage workers from reporting injuries since they receive annual bonuses for low injury rates.

14. Children often hide their compulsive behaviours from friends and family due to feelings of shame, causing them to remain undiagnosed.

15. To experienced "gamers," the quality of the video card is crucial; this is because the latest games require a high standard of video card.

16. The Catholic kings of Spain rallied the country to fight their enemies, the Moors. This became known as the "Reconquista."

17. Huck Finn was the physically abused son of Pap, who harasses Judge Thatcher when he is drunk. This creates sympathy in the reader, which makes him more likeable.

18. By teaching today's youth safe and healthy approaches to sexuality, it will elevate their self-esteem.

19. Part of the appeal of driving an SUV is that they are big and look impressive beside the "merely mortal" car.

20. Japanese smokers consume more than twice the number of cigarettes as American smokers do, and it continues to increase steadily.

8.4 Pronoun Forms (Case)

Compared to many other languages, English is not highly inflected. In many European languages, such as the Germanic languages, which included Old English, the major parts of speech change their forms to reflect their function in the sentence; for example, a noun acting as a subject would usually have a different ending from a noun acting as an object of a verb or of a preposition. The inflected form would convey its function within the sentence and help determine the meaning of the sentence itself.

There are a few instances of *inflection* in English—for example, the possessive form of nouns (Jermaine's) and pronouns (hers), and the third-person singular form of verbs in the present tense (he/she/it *goes*)—but, for the most part, a writer indicates a word's function by **syntax**: the order of words in the sentence. (This principle will be important when we consider misplaced modifiers.) However, there is another important example of inflection: some forms of the personal pronoun along with the relative and interrogative pronoun *who*.

8.4.1 Personal Pronoun Forms: Case

Personal pronouns refer to persons. The *first person* refers to the one *doing* the speaking or writing; *second person* refers to the one *spoken to*; *third person* refers to the one *spoken about*. All nouns are considered third person.

The following chart can be used to distinguish between one group of pronouns and another group. It's important to be able to distinguish between them because the role that a personal pronoun plays in a sentence will determine whether you use the pronoun form from the first group (subjective) or from the second one (objective). Notice that the second-person pronoun *you* doesn't change its form, so it's the first- and third-person pronouns you will be concerned about—the inflected forms.

Pronoun Person	Subjective-Singular	Subjective-Plural	Objective-Singular	Objective-Plural
First person	I	We	Me	Us
Second person	You	You	You	You
Third person	He, She, It	They	Him, Her, It	Them

On the chart, consider the pronoun forms under *Subjective–Singular* and *Subjective–Plural*:

He was swimming in the pool.

He is subject of the sentence, the third-person singular masculine form of the pronoun.

He is the correct form because it is the subject of the clause/sentence, so it is said to be in the **subjective case**. The following sentence illustrates what happens when the pronoun plays a different grammatical role from that of subject:

I was swimming in the pool with *her*.

The subject *I* is first-person singular. But the other pronoun in the sentence is acting as object of the preposition *with*. When it acts as the object of a verb or of a preposition it is in the **objective case**.

If you are in doubt about the correct form of a personal pronoun, determine the grammatical role it is playing in the sentence and then use the corresponding case form.

She spoke so softly to the teacher that it was difficult for *him* to understand *her*.

She is *subject* of the verb *spoke*; *him* is *object* of the preposition *for*; *her* is *object* of the infinitive *to understand*.

Notice the different pronouns in these two sentences:

Anna, the King, and *I* are going out for Chinese food tonight. (*I* is part of the subject.)

Anna arrived late for her dinner with the King and *me*. (*Me* is part of a prepositional phrase; it is object of the preposition *with*.)

The way to decide which form to use is (1) to determine the grammatical relationship involved: Is the pronoun subject of a clause/sentence, or the object of a verb, preposition, or infinitive? (2) to choose the appropriate form (subjective or objective); until the forms become familiar, you can refer to the pronoun chart above.

> The first and third forms of the personal pronoun and two other pronouns ("who" and "whom") change their form, or *case*, to express their grammatical function in the sentence.

Special Situations. Although the principle of pronoun case with personal pronouns is quite straightforward, there are special instances that can easily confuse writers.

1. With compounds that include a noun and when the first-person plural pronoun precedes a noun.

    Strategy: isolate the pronoun from the noun to determine the correct form:

    ~~Tina and~~ I plan to attend Mavis's wedding on May 15.

    Mavis's wedding will be a joyous occasion for ~~Tina and~~ me.

    We ~~students~~ believe firmly that our rights should be given back to us.

    Our rights should be given back to us ~~students~~.

2. With appositives.

    Strategy: Since appositives are grammatically parallel to the noun or noun phrase that precedes them, it is logical to look to the grammatical function of that noun or noun phrase to decide on the case of the appositive:

    Only two *friends*, Nina and *he*, saw Cindy off on her journey.

    Cindy saw her *friends*, Nina and *him*, off on their journey.

3. When an intransitive verb precedes a personal pronoun. Intransitive verbs include all forms of the verb *to be* and verbs that express a condition or state of being rather than an action. These include verbs that refer to the senses, along with other verbs followed by nouns or pronouns that *complete* the subject. Logically, when a pronoun completes the subject, i.e., acts as a *subjective completion*, it will be in the *subjective* case. Other examples of intransitive verbs requiring subjective completions may include *seem, appear, act, become, get, grow, remain*, although they may have transitive meanings as well. Contrast this situation with the one where the pronoun that follows an action verb acts as the object of the verb and therefore must be in the objective form.

    Strategy: When a pronoun follows a verb, check to see if the verb is an intransitive (linking) verb, in which case the pronoun will require the subjective case.

    It *was he* who betrayed *her* after promising faithfully to help.

    He is a subjective complement following the intransitive verb *was*; *her* is the object of the transitive verb *betrayed*.

4. With comparisons using *than* or *as.* When these conjunctions are used with the second object of a comparison, the second clause does not always need to be fully

expressed. An **elliptical construction** is one in which one or more words are omitted. For example, in the following sentence, it would be quite acceptable in informal or formal writing for the writer to use an elliptical construction and end the sentence after *eyelid piercing*.

> My new Jon Bon Jovi hairstyle gets more attention than my eyelid piercing (gets attention).

> When I'm short of money, I would rather choose Eliot than Ellen as a dinner companion because he has more money than *she* (has money). —*She* is the subject of the verb *has*.

> It goes without saying that I choose Eliot as a dinner companion more often than (I choose) *her.*—*Her* is the object of the verb *choose*.

8.4.2 Possessive Pronouns

Another example of inflection is the possessive (adjectival) form of nouns and pronouns (e.g., my *uncle's* pet alligator; *his* pet alligator).

> The book doesn't belong to Anthony but to Kristy; it is *hers*.

Hers is the noun form of the possessive pronoun replacing the antecedent *Kristy*. The adjectival form is seen in the following sentence:

> The book doesn't belong to Anthony but to Kristy; it is *her* book.

The following chart completes the first one by including the possessive forms of pronouns.

Pronoun Person	Adjectival-Singular	Adjectival-Plural	Subjective Complements, Singular	Subjective Complements, Plural
First person	My	Our	Mine	Ours
Second person	Your	Your	Yours	Yours
Third person	His, Her, Its	Their	His, Hers, Its	Theirs

8.4.3 Gerunds and Participles

Gerunds. There isn't much danger of your confusing the possessive (adjectival) form of pronouns with the subjective or objective cases. However, the previous sentence illustrates one such possible confusion: "confusing" is **a gerund**, an "-ing" form of a verb acting as a noun. You should always use the possessive adjectival form of a pronoun before a gerund since gerunds function as nouns.

Incorrect:
There isn't much danger of you confusing the twins, Mother.

Correct:
There isn't much danger of *your confusing* the twins, Mother.

Participles. Note the difference between the two sentences that follow, the first of which illustrates the use of the possessive adjective before a gerund, the second of which illustrates the use of the objective case before an *–ing* form acting as an adjective.

1. *His pretending* to know nothing didn't fool me. (gerund)
2. I saw *him pretending* to be surprised. (participle)

In sentence 1, *pretending* is the subject. *Pretending* is a gerund, which requires the adjectival possessive form of the pronoun. In sentence 2, *him* is the object of the verb *saw*, so the objective case of the pronoun is required; *pretending* is a participle and adjectival—a verb form acting as an adjective is called a **participle**—and modifies the pronoun *him*.

8.4.4 Relative Pronouns

Relative pronouns *relate* the dependent clause they introduce to the rest of the sentence. A relative clause usually functions as an adjective, modifying a preceding noun. Of the major relative pronouns (*who, whoever, which, whichever, that*), only *who* and *whoever* inflect (change their form) depending on whether they are being used as the subject of the clause, or as object of either the verb or a preposition in the clause.

To determine the case of a relative pronoun, look at *the role the relative pronoun plays within the clause*; in other words, the answer to whether you use *who* or *whom* will be found *in the clause that the relative pronoun introduces*.

If either the pronoun *who* or *whoever* is subject of the clause or is the subjective completion, use the subjective form. If the pronoun is acting as an object of the verb or of a preposition in the clause, use the objective form: *whom (whomever)*. Consider these two sentences; italics indicate the dependent (relative) clause:

1. The old man harangued *whoever happened to be within listening distance.*
2. The old man should be free to harangue *whomever he chooses.*

In sentence 1, it is of secondary importance that *whoever* is object of the verb *harangued*. It is the *subject of the clause it introduces* (*whoever happened to be within listening distance*) that is the determining factor in pronoun form.

In sentence 2, *he* is subject of the clause, and the relative pronoun is in the objective case. If you see that the relative clause has a subject, you can be certain that the relative pronoun will *not* be the subject of the clause. In sentence 2, *he* does the choosing and is the subject of the verb; *whomever* is the object of the verb.

One test for case is to substitute the third–person form of the personal pronoun for the relative pronoun in the relative clause. *Whoever* (relative pronoun) *happened to be within listening distance* would become *he/she* (personal pronoun) *happened to be within listening distance.* In sentence 2, the relative clause would read, *he chooses he,* which most speakers of English recognize to be incorrect.

Determining pronoun case with relative pronouns always involves determining the function of the relative pronoun that begins the clause. Which is correct?

1. Jeong-Gyu is someone who, we firmly believe, will go far.

2. Jeong-Gyu is someone whom, we firmly believe, will go far.

Answer: sentence 1 is correct. *Who* is the subject of the relative clause *who will go far.* *[W]e firmly believe* is not part of the relative clause but part of another clause (with another subject) that interrupts the relative clause.

Jeong-Gyu is someone who, ~~we firmly believe,~~ will go far

8.4.5 Interrogative Pronouns

The interrogative pronouns (*who, whoever, which, whichever, what*) are those which ask questions. Once you know how to determine the case of the relative pronouns, *who/whom,* the interrogatives shouldn't give you too much trouble; again, you need to determine their function to determine pronoun case. Of the three interrogatives, it is *who* and *whoever* that change, depending on their function in the sentence.

With whom did you go out on Saturday night? (object of the preposition)

Who says you should never reveal your feelings? (subject of the verb)

Whom would you recommend for the new opening? (object of the verb)

At one time, some grammarians prohibited the ending of a sentence with a preposition; consequently, that construction may sound incorrect to some people. If you end a sentence with a preposition, the pronoun that would ordinarily follow it will now precede it. In such instances, remember that the *objective case* must be used for the pronoun:

Whom did Professor LeGuin direct the question *to*?

The more formal usage makes it easier to determine case:

To whom did Professor LeGuin direct the question?

It is now clear that *whom* is the object of the preposition *to*.

Exercise

Choose the correct form of the pronoun.

1. Management often forgets about the needs of (we/us) wage-earners.

2. (Who/whom) should run for office this election?

3. I have no intention of speaking to (they/them).

4. The person (who/whom) finishes first will be rewarded.

5. You recommend (who/whom) for the position?

6. As she entered the room, a mysterious feeling came over (she/her).

7. Margaret Laurence was a novelist (who/whom) entertained her readers with well-developed plots and realistic characters.

8. (Him/His) deciding to run for office will throw the election process into chaos.

9. The instructor explained the different cases of pronouns to Gail and (I/me).

10. "Hey, buddy, (who/whom) did you mean to refer to when you used that insulting term?"

11. (Whoever/whomever) fails to address the most important issue—unemployment—will find themselves among the unemployed.

12. Liv Tyler is, without any doubt, the actress (who/whom) I most admire.

13. My fifth grade teacher always let her favourite students—Mallory, Cindy, and (I/me)—help her with clean-up.

14. I wanted to ask her (who/whom) the note should be addressed to.

15. The young narrator's goal is to bring back a present for his friend's sister (who/whom) he admires from afar.

16. Chris's rival, Mike, lasted longer in the ring than (he/him).

17. We were allowed to invite (whoever/whomever) we wanted to the party.

18. I proposed that Geordie and (I/me) would stack chairs after the meeting.

19. The only "mother" (who/whom) the kitten has known is Madeline, (who/whom) rescued it from traffic.

20. The newly renovated house is a very pleasant place for my brother and (I/me) to live.

21. Elizabeth's prejudice becomes apparent when (she/her) and Darcy converse at the ball.

22. Nora tires of being married to someone (who/whom) she always has to put on an act for.

23. Christy so drastically changes his personality that his own father can barely believe it is (he/him).

Exercise

24. It seems that the government has again forgotten about the needs of (we/us) students.

25. Choose the grammatical poem:

(a.) Roses are red,
Butterflies are free;
You must choose
Between him and me.

(b.) Roses are red,
Birds can fly;
You must choose
Between he and I.

8.5 Pronoun Consistency

A pronoun must agree in number, gender, and person with its antecedent. There will be many occasions in which you will refer to different persons in the same sentence, and it's acceptable to do so, as long as the change isn't arbitrary. On the other hand, if you want simply to replace a preceding noun with a pronoun, the pronoun should be the same *person* as its antecedent. Remember that all nouns are third-person.

Incorrect:
During final exams, if *students* must go to the washroom, raise *your* hand so *you* can be escorted there. (*Students* is third-person; *your* and *you* are second-person.)

Correct:
During final exams, if *students* need to go to the washroom, *they* should raise their hands . . . .

or, more informally:
During final exams, if *you* need to go to the washroom, raise *your* hand . . . .

Further examples:

Incorrect:
It is possible that *our* desire to make life easier for *ourselves* will, in fact, make *humans* redundant.

Our and *ourselves* are first-person; *humans* is third-person.

Correct:
It is possible that *our* desire to make life easier for *ourselves* will, in fact, make *us* redundant.

It is possible that the desire to make life easier for *humans* will, in fact, make *them* redundant.

Incorrect:

Educators today should teach *students* learning skills, such as how to manage your money.

Correct:

Educators today should teach *students* learning skills, such as how to manage *their* money.

Remember not to change the *person* of the pronoun unnecessarily.

The following is an example of an unneeded change:

If *one* goes to watch a body-building competition, it is unlikely *you* will see a competitor with hair on his chest.

One, an indefinite pronoun, is third-person; *you* is second-person. Either of these is correct:

If *one* goes to watch a body-building competition, it is unlikely *one* will see . . . .

If *you* go to watch a body-building competition, it is unlikely *you* will see . . . .

Exercise

The following paragraph contains errors in pronoun consistency, along with some awkward use of third-person pronouns. When you rewrite the paragraph, strive for correctness and effectiveness. The first thing you should decide is which person you want to refer to consistently; this decision might be based on the level of formality you want to use (first- and second-person pronouns are considered more informal than third-person pronouns).

You can definitely learn a lot from educational TV; we can learn things that we cannot learn from written texts. If one is a major in Commerce, for example, and if he or she watches the business news, he or she can understand the commerce textbook better by applying what he or she learns from the news. Similarly, I think that watching sports programs can provide people with excitement. Watching sports can also give us a better understanding of the game. On the other hand, if one chooses to watch comedy all the time, people are not going to gain any real benefits. I feel comedies are generally meaningless.

9. Sentence Construction Errors

Writing in complete sentences and using the appropriate conjunctions to join clauses will help you to construct grammatical sentences; however, there are other potential problems in constructing sentences. Maintaining parallelism in the use of modifiers is an important part of the writing process. By looking at the sentence as a complex unit made up of specific parts properly ordered, you will be able to write sentences that are both complete and well-constructed.

These kinds of errors result from forgetting two basic principles in English grammar:

1. Modifiers should be placed as close as possible to the words they are intended to modify.
2. Co-ordinate elements in a sentence must be grammatically parallel and complete.

Major sentence construction errors are discussed below under four categories: (1) misplaced modifiers; (2) dangling modifiers; (3) faulty parallelism; and (4) faulty comparisons.

Misplaced modifiers and dangling modifiers are examples of errors that can result when the first principle is not adhered to. Faulty parallelism and faulty comparisons result when the second principle is not followed (see sidebar, left).

9.1 Misplaced Modifiers

CONCEPTS and TERMS *NEW* to this section

- dangling modifier
- misplaced modifier
- participial phrase (participle)

The primary function of adjectives is to modify nouns, while the primary function of adverbs is to modify verbs. Prepositional phrases can also function as adjectives or adverbs. Misplaced modifiers, then, can be either adjectives or adjectival phrases, or adverbs or adverbial phrases. They are misplaced when mistakenly placed next to a part of speech they are not intended to modify.

The meaning of a sentence in English is heavily dependent on word order, or *syntax*; it is partly through syntax that a speaker encodes his or her meaning and that the reader decodes the meaning.

9.1.1 Adjectival Modifiers

The usual position for an adjective is immediately before the noun it is intended to modify; however, adjectival phrases and clauses usually follow the noun they modify. Consider the following examples of misplaced modifiers:

Incorrect:
They headed for a child in the front row *with a long overcoat.*

It is the child, not the front row, wearing the long overcoat. The adjectival phrase should follow the noun *child*.

They headed for a child with a long overcoat in the front row.

Consider:
The furnace thermostat is located upstairs, *which displays the temperature settings.*

In this sentence, the adjectival (relative) clause, *which displays the temperature settings,* is placed next to the **adverb** *upstairs* instead of closest to the noun *thermostat*.

The furnace thermostat, which displays the temperature settings, is located upstairs.

9.1.2 Adverbial Modifiers

Misplaced adverbs and adverbial phrases are even more common than misplaced adjectives and adjectival phrases because the conventions of syntax are a little more fluid with adverbial modifiers. It is safest, especially with one-word adverbs like *only*, *almost*, *just*, *not*, and *even*, to place them right before the word or phrase they are supposed to modify. See below, Section 9.1.4, *One-word Modifiers*.

The meaning of the following sentence could be misconstrued:

Students should buy this book because it will give them all the information they need to know about writing *in a convenient form*.

Presumably, the writer did not want to highlight "convenience in writing," but that the book "will give them . . . information . . . in a convenient form." Correctly,

Students should buy this book because it will give them, *in a convenient form*, all the information they will need to know about writing.

Consider:
The conviction carries a penalty of eight to 10 years *in two provinces*.

Because of the misplaced prepositional phrase, the writer seems to be saying that on being convicted, the criminal will have to "do time" in two provinces. Either of the following re-phrasings is correct:

In two provinces the conviction carries a penalty of eight to 10 years.

The conviction carries a penalty in two provinces of eight to 10 years.

9.1.3 Fixing Misplaced Modifiers

When the misplaced modifier *in two provinces* in the last sentence is placed before or after the verb it should modify, *carries*, the problem is fixed. The solution to misplaced modifiers, whether an entire clause, a phrase, or a single word, is simple: **move them**.

The following misplaced modifier makes the sentence awkward or misleading:

Incorrect:
The instructor marked the essay I wrote *unfairly*.

Correct:
The instructor *unfairly marked* the essay I wrote.

Or:

I thought the instructor *marked my essay unfairly*.

When you are writing quickly, trying to get your ideas down, misplaced modifiers can can occur anywhere in a sentence; however, they often occur at the end, almost as an afterthought. That is the place to begin checking:

> *Incorrect:*
> Cars today produce large amounts of toxic chemicals that can damage human cells *if inhaled*.

> *Correct:*
> Cars today produce large amounts of toxic chemicals that, if inhaled, can damage human cells.

9.1.4 One-Word Modifiers

One-word adverbial modifiers, though, can occur just about anywhere in the sentence. As noted above, you need to be especially careful with limiting adverbs like *only, almost, just, even, nearly, barely, merely*, etc. They need to be carefully placed before the word they are intended to modify.

Does one little word out of place *really* affect the meaning of the sentence? Consider how the meaning of the following statement changes, depending on where the "little" word *only* is put: *Jared didn't do his homework yesterday.*

Seven Answers to the Question:
Is Jared a Lazy Student or a Conscientious One?

1. *Only Jared* didn't do his homework yesterday.

Everyone but Jared did his or her homework; *only* is an adjective modifying *Jared*.

2. Jared *only didn't do* his homework.

The meaning of this sentence is ambiguous. It could mean the same as sentence 1 or that Jared did other things—but not his homework. It could also mean that the fact Jared didn't do his homework wasn't important.

3. Jared didn't *only do* his homework yesterday.

Now *only* is an adverb modifying the verb *do* and suggests that Jared did do his homework and other things as well.

4. Jared didn't do *only his homework* yesterday.

Placing *only* before *his homework* means that Jared definitely did his homework and other things as well. It might also mean that Jared was involved in doing someone else's homework in addition to his own.

5. Jared didn't do his *only homework* yesterday.

Placing only between *his* and *homework* implies that Jared might under other circumstances have had much more homework, but yesterday had only a lesser amount, which he nevertheless did not do.

6. Jared didn't do his homework *only yesterday*.

Either Jared normally does his homework but only yesterday did not, or as recently as yesterday, Jared did not do his homework, the implication being that his refraining from that activity is frequent.

7. Jared didn't do his homework *yesterday only*.

Perhaps Jared is not such a lazy student after all: the only day he didn't do his homework was yesterday!

9.1.5 Dangling Modifiers

Misplaced and dangling modifiers both appear to modify nouns or verbs they are not intended to modify. Misplaced and dangling modifiers can be the grammatical equivalent of life's most embarrassing moments: modifiers that are misplaced or dangling can give the communication a quite different, sometimes humorous, meaning from the intended one, such as the Precocious Parents of this writer:

> When only seven-years-old, my parents decided to enrol me in a Highland dancing course.

Then, consider the "Résumé Ruiner," which stated in an application to the Grammar School:

> When not working or attending classes, my hobbies are gardening, doing macramé, and bungie-jumping.

As dangling modifiers are often "-ing" participle (adjectival) phrases with nothing to modify, they are sometimes called **dangling participles**. The reader is forced to assume they modify the closest noun. These adjectival phrases, then, are dangling because the intended noun or noun phrase is not in the sentence. Therefore, it doesn't help to move the modifier.

The way to correct dangling modifiers is (1) by providing the noun or noun phrase in the independent clause to give the modifier something to modify, or (2) by turning the dangling phrase into a dependent clause with a subject.

> When only seven-years-old, I was enrolled by my parents in a Highland dancing course. (1)

> When I was only seven-years-old, my parents decided to enrol me in a Highland dancing course. (2)

When not working or attending classes, I enjoy several hobbies, including gardening, doing macramé, and bungie-jumping. (1)

When I am not working or attending classes, my hobbies include gardening, doing macramé, and bungie-jumping. (2)

While misplaced modifiers frequently appear at the end of a sentence, dangling modifiers usually are found at the beginning—somewhat less often at the end—of a sentence, and even occasionally in the middle. With misplaced modifiers, the needed information is in the sentence, and the modifier needs to be moved as close as possible to the word or phrase it is intended to modify. With dangling modifiers, the essential information *is not in the sentence.* The examples below will show you how to identify dangling modifiers by asking the appropriate questions.

In this example, poetic description is undercut by the assertion that the clouds are arriving in Calgary, when more likely the writer is describing his or her arrival.

When arriving in Calgary, the clouds had scattered, and the sky was aglow with bands of pink and red.

In the next example, the book seems to have written itself.

Though a well-known writer, his latest book failed to make the best-seller's list.

The question to ask in the first example is, *Who is arriving in Calgary?* In the second, we don't know, *Who is the well-known writer?* Since the answers are not in the sentences, the modifiers must be dangling. In both cases, the missing information needs to be provided in the independent clause, or the dangling phrase needs to be turned into a dependent clause that can modify the independent clause that follows. The above sentences may be corrected:

When arriving in Calgary, I saw that the clouds had scattered, and the sky was aglow with bands of pink and red. (1—information has been provided in the independent clause)

When I arrived in Calgary, the clouds had scattered, and the sky was aglow with bands of pink and red. (2—dangling phrase has been changed to a dependent clause)

Though a well-known writer, he failed to make the best-seller's list with his latest book. (1)

Though he was a well-known writer, his latest book failed to make the best-seller's list. (2)

The following example has a dangling modifier at the end of the sentence:

Verbal and non-verbal skills are greatly enhanced when living in a foreign country.

Who is living in a foreign country? This information is missing, so the participial phrase *when living* is dangling. To correct it, add information:

When living in a foreign country, you are able to enhance your verbal and non-verbal skills. (1)

Verbal and non-verbal skills are greatly enhanced when you live in a foreign country. (2)

Collaborative Exercise

The intended meanings of the following sentences are obscured or distorted due to modifier problems. Working in groups, identify the particular problem (misplaced or dangling modifier) and determine the grammatical (incorrect or ambiguous) meaning(s) of the sentences. Then, fix the sentences using one of the methods above.

1. A striped hat was on his head that came to a point.
2. As we were leaving, he promised to visit us with tears in his eyes.
3. Although unambitious and downright lazy, I have never known Sam to break his word.
4. His ego was further inflated by being awarded first prize in the Ben Affleck look-alike contest.
5. Every character has a purpose in Shakespeare's play, big or small.
6. When asked what my favourite sport is, I usually say that it is running without any hesitation.
7. Stepping out of the airplane, the fresh air was most invigorating.
8. Gabriel Kolko describes peace in Vietnam after the war in his book.
9. Opening the door unexpectedly, his eyes fell upon two of his employees in a passionate embrace.
10. Teacher Laurie McNamara posed for the photographer with Principal Dan Saunders, who gave her a kidney last month, in the Cloverdale Elementary School hallway.

Exercise

Correct the following sentences, each of which contains a modifier error; in some instances, it will be necessary to reword the sentence for clarity and correctness.

1. In our fair city, shady characters lurk on quiet corners that offer a variety of drugs.
2. Over the years, several world-class cyclists have had spectacular careers, such as Eddie Merckx and Greg LeMond.

Exercise – *continued*

3. Running down the street without a care in the world, two pedestrians had to quickly move out of his way.

4. Being a member of the Sikh community, my paper will be given a strong personal focus.

5. Built in mere minutes, you will have a fully interactive Web site for your business or for your personal use.

6. Benefits will only result from a smoke-free environment.

7. Germany has built an extensive network of highways through its countryside, known as the Autobahn.

8. Trying to find a job today, employers are stressing verbal and written communication skills more than ever before.

9. People's rights to privacy should be forfeited when caught in criminal behaviour.

10. This species of snake will eat frogs, mice, and small pieces of meat in captivity.

11. Walking through the streets of Srinigar, devastation and fear are immediately evident.

12. As a beginner, my instructor taught me about the respect one karate student must show to another.

13. Tylenol and Aspirin effectively reduce pain when experiencing a fever.

14. Speaking from experience, tans that dye the top layer of the skin last for about one week.

15. Moving to Nebraska at the age of 10, Jim Burden's narrative reveals the reflections of one his age.

16. Being an Elizabethan playwright, I am certain that Shakespeare would have been a major influence on Marlowe.

17. Adolescents essentially experience the same depressive symptoms as adults do.

18. As a serious snowboarder, it is exciting to observe the growth of this sport.

19. In John Donne's "Death, Be Not Proud," Death has a personality that is usually only given to a human being.

20. The boy in "Araby" returns home empty-handed without the highly valued object, in this case, a gift for Mangan's sister that most quests require.

21. Darwin's theory of evolution may be contested on the grounds that species may cease to appear abruptly.

22. Another example of imagery of light and dark in "Heart of Darkness" occurs when Marlow encounters an African dying in a clearing with a white scarf.

> **Exercise** – *continued*

23. Based primarily on the work of Karl Marx, socialists see the creation of profit as a complex process.

24. Having an emotional personality, Beethoven's music identified him as a nineteenth-century Romantic.

25. A mother and her daughter were recently reunited after 18 years in a checkout line.

9.2 The Parallelism Principle

CONCEPTS and TERMS *NEW* to this section

- co-ordination
- incomplete comparison
- incompatible comparison
- parallelism
- subordination

Co-ordinate elements in a sentence must be grammatically parallel and complete.

Elements in a sentence exist in relationships that could be pictured geometrically or architectonically. Balanced constructions give a sentence grace and strength, while unbalanced constructions make a sentence weak and unstable in the context of the whole piece of writing, as a misaligned wall in a building undermines a building's stability. A sentence must be constructed so that words and phrases parallel in the logic of the sentence are parallel in the grammatical structure of the sentence.

Co-ordinate elements are *equal* elements. Checking for parallelism is checking to ensure that the elements in a sentence that have the *same grammatical function* are expressed in parallel structures.

When studying paragraph coherence (Part Two, Section 4.4), you looked at using repetition and balanced structures. Learning the fundamentals of parallelism in this section will help ensure that your writing is both grammatically correct and aesthetically satisfying. Apply the principle of parallelism carefully to ensure grammatical correctness, and work to ensure that the grammatically parallel structures you use lend clarity, smoothness, and elegance to the writing.

When you have checked to see that the syntactical units have the same function, you should then check the style: (1) could the sentence be *written more efficiently*? (2) Does the sentence *sound balanced*? In asking such questions, you are moving beyond the concern with correctness into the realm of successful and appealing prose writing, a realm where the conscious choices you make as a writer will become a vital part of the composing act.

Experienced writers have mastered the principles of parallel structures and use them routinely in their writing; balanced structures are rhetorically effective structures. Consider, for example, the following excerpt from Francis Bacon's essay "Of Youth and Age" (1601), which is made up almost entirely of parallel words, phrases, and clauses:

A man that is young in years, may be old in hours, if he have lost no time. But that happeneth rarely. Generally, youth is like the first cogitations, not so wise as the second. For there is a youth in thoughts, as well as in ages . . . .

Young men, in the conduct and manage of actions, embrace more than they can hold; stir more than they can quiet; fly to the end, without consideration of the means and degrees; pursue some few principles, which they have chanced upon absurdly; care not to innovate, which draws unknown inconveniences; use extreme remedies at first; and, that which doubleth all errors, will not acknowledge or retract them; like an unready horse, that will neither stop nor turn. Men of age object too much, consult too long, adventure too little, repent too soon, and seldom drive business home to the full period, but content themselves with a mediocrity of success.

Student writer Allison McClymont was able to utilize parallel structures to create a dramatic opening for her essay on school uniforms:

In the hallways of today's high school, students congregate in various cliques, using their dress as an indicator of their conformity: there are the "jocks" in their letterman jackets, the "nerds" in their high pants and suspenders, the "cheerleaders" in their short skirts and sweaters, and the "arties" in their paint-covered hippie clothes. Other easily identifiable cliques include the "gangsters," the "preppies," the "moods," the "punks," the "weirdos," and "the band geeks."

Read the following sentences. Although their meanings are clear, they don't *sound* balanced. In fact, they're not balanced because the important words in the compound or list aren't all the same part of speech: each sentence contains an error in parallel structure. The words you need to pay attention to are italicized:

1. Ian would rather *snack* on some chips than *eating* a regular dinner.
2. The basic human needs are *food, clothing, shelter* and *having a good job*.
3. After her 10-kilometre run, she felt *weak, tired*, and *she badly needed water*.
4. Our cat enjoys *watching* TV, *looking* out the window, and *to sleep* at the foot of our bed.
5. Neither a *borrower* be, nor *lend* to others.

9.2.1 Identifying and Fixing Parallelism Problems

Use a two-stage approach to identify and fix parallel structures in your writing:

1. Be alert to places where there should be parallelism in these kinds of syntactical structures: *lists, compounds, correlative conjunctions,* and *comparisons*. For example, in the following sentence there is a compound object of the verb *prefer*:

   Ian would prefer *to snack* on some chips rather than *eating* a regular dinner.

2. To fix elements that are not parallel, identify the parts of speech that should be grammatically parallel and make them so. The two objects of the verb *prefer* are not expressed in parallel fashion: *to snack* and *eating*. Either the verbal noun (infinitive

form of the verb acting as a noun) or the gerund can function as objects, so either of these changes is correctly parallel:

Ian would prefer *to snack* on some chips than *to eat* a regular dinner.

Ian would prefer *snacking* on chips to *eating* a regular dinner.

Identify in the following sentences the parts of speech that have the same functions:

1. The basic human needs are *food, clothing, shelter* and *having* a good job.

Now, use four nouns in the list to make it grammatically parallel.

2. After her 10-kilometre run, she felt *weak, tired,* and *she badly needed water.*

Now, using three predicate adjectives, make this list parallel. You could also fix the sentence by using three independent clauses: *she felt weak,* etc.

3. Our cat enjoys *watching* TV, *looking* out the window, and *to sleep* at the foot of our bed.

Use three gerunds (*–ing* verb forms acting as nouns) to make the list parallel. Next correct the sentence using three infinitives.

4. Neither a *borrower* be, nor *lend* to others.

Using two verbs after the correlative (paired) conjunctions *neither* and *nor* makes the sentence parallel. You could also follow Shakespeare's example in his play *Hamlet* and use two nouns after the conjunctions: Neither a *borrower* nor a *lender* be.

When checking for parallel structure, consider first the structurally essential words like nouns and verbs (not their modifiers). Second, see that adjectives or adverbs *by themselves*, without words to modify, also are in parallel form. Third, look at the larger grammatical units, such as prepositional phrases, which also should appear in parallel relationships with other prepositional phrases—dependent clauses with dependent clauses, and independent clauses with independent clauses.

The examples below apply the two-step method to lists, compounds, correlative conjunctions, and comparisons.

9.2.2 A List or Series

A list or series comprises three or more items. So, whenever you list something, you need to check for parallel structure. For example, if you use an expanded thesis statement that lists your essay's main points, you need to ensure that the items in the list are grammatically parallel.

Incorrect:
Research into cloning should be encouraged as it could lead to cures for diseases, successful organ transplants, and put an end to infertility problems.

Correct:
Research into cloning should be legalized as it could lead to *cures* for diseases, successful organ *transplants*, and *solutions* to infertility problems.

The elements are now parallel; notice that to avoid repeating the word *cures*, a word with a similar meaning has replaced it.

Note: Length is not necessarily a factor in parallelism: for example, a simple noun would normally be considered parallel with a noun phrase (but not with a prepositional phrase), because they have the same grammatical function. You may be asked to write sentences in which all items in a series have the same form as well as function, and, while this criterion is useful when you start out learning about parallel structure, it is often not heeded in longer, more complex constructions. As a general rule, ensure that the function of parallel elements is the same and be conscious of the sound and rhythm of each element in the construction when deciding about matching form.

The following sentence contains two nouns preceded by adjectives and a noun followed by an adjectival (prepositional) phrase. All the elements are parallel, though their form is not identical:

Discipline in single-sex schools has been shown to directly affect regular *attendance*, good *grades*, and *standards for dress and behaviour*.

The following thesis statements include lists where the items are not parallel:

Incorrect:
The major forms of eating disorders involve the compulsion to count calories, to constantly exercise, and the need to alter one's appearance.

Correct:
The major forms of eating disorders involve the compulsion *to count* calories, *to* constantly *exercise*, and *to alter* one's appearance.

Incorrect:
Buddhism teaches that one's karma can be affected by many things: your generosity to those less fortunate, your behaviour to strangers, and if you treat even your enemies with respect.

The list of "noun, noun, clause" needs to be changed to "noun, noun, noun":

Buddhism teaches that one's karma can be affect by many things: your *generosity* to those less fortunate, your *behaviour* to strangers, and *respect* even for your enemies.

You also need to be careful that items in a list are *logically*, as well as grammatically, parallel. The following list contains five nouns/noun phrases, but not all of the items are logically parallel. Which item does not belong in the list? Why?

Common injuries in the meat-packing industry include chemical burns, broken bones, lacerations, amputations, and even death.

More informal lists that use bullets, numbers, or point form also require parallel structure. Choose a set up or starting point; then, ensure that each bulleted item has the same grammatical function and, if necessary, form.

Before choosing a graduate program, a student should investigate:

- the number of graduate students who receive financial support
- the expertise of faculty in the student's desired specialty
- course work required
- do research opportunities exist for graduate students?

Electing to start all items in the list with a noun or noun phrase would make the list grammatically parallel:

- financial support . . .
- expertise of . . .
- course work . . .
- research opportunities . . .

9.2.3 Compounds

Correct comma use requires you to separate items in a list or series by commas; two items (compounds) are not generally separated by a comma. But you do need to apply the principle of parallel structure to compound elements. Co-ordinating conjunctions, such as *or, and,* or *but,* can signal a compound, as can prepositional phrase joiners such as *as well as;* in comparisons, *than* or *as* may join the two elements of a comparison.

Once you've identified a compound, look at the important word or phrase in the first element of the compound and ensure that the second element that follows the joiner uses the parallel grammatical structure. Several examples of compounds follow.

As you can see from the example (right), an infinitive (to + verb) is not considered grammatically parallel with a gerund.

Incorrect:
It is actually cheaper *to convert* a used vehicle into an electric vehicle than *buying* a new gas-powered model.

Correct:
It is actually cheaper *to convert* a used vehicle into an electric vehicle than *to buy* a new gas-powered model.

Some compounds that cause trouble are those with auxiliary verbs. In these cases, it may be helpful to draw a line where the first element begins and another where the second begins (after the conjunction); then, see if both parts line up with the main verb that follows; you can draw a line there too. The main verb in the sentence below is *worked:*

Incorrect:
The prohibition of marijuana and the laws in place for it |*do not* and |*have never*|worked.

Test:
The prohibition of marijuana and the laws in place for it | *do not* . . . worked and *have never* worked.

Correct:
The prohibition of marijuana and the laws in place for it *do not* **work** and *have never* **worked**.

Sometimes compound phrases ending in prepositions don't line up with what follows. Here is an example of a compound in which the words that follow the verbs are not aligned with the object. Again, the presence of a co-ordinating conjunction can alert you to these tricky kinds of compounds:

Incorrect:
Most people under thirty *are familiar or have heard of* the rapper Eminem.

Correct:
Most people under thirty | *are familiar with or* | *have heard of* | the rapper Eminem.

Incorrect:
"We have to change our production methods to make sure the products we sell are *as good or better as* any in the world," said the Minister of Agriculture.

Correct:
"We have to change our production methods to make sure the products we sell are | *as good as* | or *better ~~as~~ than* | any in the world," said the Minister of Agriculture.

9.2.4 Correlative Conjunctions

A specific kind of compound involves correlative conjunctions. These are joiners that work in pairs (*either . . . or, neither . . .nor, both . . . and, not . . . but, not only . . . but also*). Logically, the part of speech that follows the first half of the compound should also follow the second half. It might be helpful to draw a line after each conjunction:

Incorrect:
A college degree today is an investment *not only* | in students' financial resources *but also* | their time.

What follows *not only* is a prepositional phrase that begins with *in*; therefore, a prepositional phrase, not just a noun (*time*), must follow the second member of the pair:

A college degree today is an investment *not only* | in students' financial resources *but also* | in their time.

Incorrect:

The lack of classroom availability means *either* constructing new buildings *or* lower the number of students accepted into programs.

Correct:

The lack of classroom availability means *either contructing* new buildings *or lowering* the number of students accepted into programs.

Here's a slightly more complicated sentence that includes correlative conjunctions and a compound joined by *and*:

Success is determined *not*|by the amount of money you have, *but*|the happiness in your life and |the goals you achieve.

Success is determined *not by* the amount of money you have, *but by* the happiness in your life *and by* the goals you achieve.

9.2.5 Comparisons

Under *Compounds* we looked at comparisons as compound structures requiring parallelism. However, sometimes faulty comparisons have less to do with grammar than with logic.

Because comparisons are always made between one thing and another thing, both these elements must be fully expressed for the comparison to be complete. Often either the comparison is left incomplete or the terms being compared are incompatible; that is, they cannot be compared because there is no basis for comparison. Note: *Than* is the word for comparisons, not the adverb related to time, *then.* Other words and phrases can also signal comparisons: *compared to, similar (to), different (from), as, like,* etc.

Writers, when they use comparisons, need to ask if the two parts of the comparison are grammatically parallel; if both parts of the comparison are fully expressed; and if the two objects of the comparison can logically be compared. Are the two parts of the comparison grammatically parallel in this sentence?

Willem had bid greedily on a yacht grander than any made previously by his former partner Stoat.

Incomplete:
An unfortunate stereotype is that males are more scientific and less intuitive.

In the first example, the comparison is complete. But in the one following, the reader is left to assume whom males are being compared to.

Complete:
An unfortunate stereotype is that males are more scientific and less intuitive *than females.*

Incompatible:

I have found that students are less judgmental at university compared to high school.

You can ask what precisely is being compared to what and if the comparison is logical; in this case, the writer is comparing a perceived trait of *students* at university to . . . high school. People must be compared to people.

Compatible:

I have found that people are less judgmental at university than they are at high school.

The two sides of the comparison are now complete and compatible.

Incompatible:

Edgar Allan Poe's story "The Purloined Letter" is a precursor of the modern detective story and bears striking resemblance to Sherlock Holmes.

What is being compared here? Are the terms comparable? The writer is comparing a *story* to the *character* Sherlock Holmes.

Compatible:

Edgar Allan Poe's story "The Purloined Letter" is a precursor of the modern detective story and bears striking resemblance to Arthur Conan Doyle's Sherlock Holmes stories.

Exercise

In the word groups that follow, there are three or four main points related to a topic. Build parallel structures in thesis statements for each topic. Make whatever changes are necessary to achieve parallelism and use whatever order of points seems natural.

Topic 1: Why I like toe socks:
   –warm and comfortable
   –they are the latest fashion in socks
   –come in many colours and designs

Topic 2: The advantages of yoga:
   –to relax and reduce stress
   –to exercise
   –also can meet people in yoga classes

Topic 3: The importance of computers to students:
   –they provide entertainment
   –cutting down on homework time is important
   –you can obtain a wealth of information quickly

Topic 4: Living with roommates:
   –they can create a lot of mess
   –invade your personal space
   –you can talk to them about your problems

Exercise – *continued*

Topic 5: The benefits of coffee:
–coffee helps you wake up
–its rich, satisfying flavour
–it improves your concentration

Topic 6: The comparison of two recreational drugs:
–their possible dangerous side effects
–who uses them
–the effects they produce in the user

Topic 7: The facts about organically grown food:
–the way organically grown food is farmed
–the cost of these kinds of foods
–their nutritional value

Topic 8: The advantages of home birthing:
–allows the parents to maintain control over their surroundings
–a positive and friendly place for the child to be born
–is as safe as a hospital birth if common sense is used

Topic 9: School uniforms are beneficial:
–promote school identity and school pride
–they save parents money and hassle
–reduce the pressure of students to conform to the latest fashions
–to make it easier for school authorities to enforce discipline

Topic 10: The legalization of marijuana:
–it is less addictive than some other illegal drugs
–the Canadian government has already made it legal under certain circumstances
–governments could increase their revenue by selling it
–making it legal would reduce crime since people wouldn't have to obtain it illegally

Exercise

The sentences below contain parallelism errors. Identify the kind of error (series, compounds, correlative conjunctions, or comparisons) and fix the errors.

1. A good journalist is inquisitive, persistent, and must be a good listener.

2. Music can directly affect your thoughts, emotions, and how you feel.

3. In this essay, I will be looking and writing about the role of women in the military.

4. Tiddlywinks is not only a game of considerable skill but also strategy.

5. Television can affect children in a variety of negative ways since children often lack judgment, are naturally curious, and easily influenced.

6. There are three main qualities that a leader must possess: a leader must be enthusiastic, organized, and have creativity.

7. Aman never has and never will be good at golf.

8. She was not only the best teacher I have ever had, but also I was impressed by her wardrobe.

9. Tremors may occur on either or both sides of the body.

10. A recent study has found that Caucasian children acquire self-awareness at an earlier age than other ethnic groups.

11. There are many reasons why people choose to or enjoy watching television.

12. My trip to London involved such pleasures as Buckingham Palace, feeding the pigeons, visiting my relatives, and those quaint London accents.

13. I enjoyed watching *The Last Samurai*, *The Last of the Mohicans*, and *Braveheart* was also enjoyable.

14. I want to emphasize that my work as MP in this riding has not, and will not, be affected by political developments.

15. When Jim has the choice of either jumping or to stay on the doomed ship, he chooses to jump.

16. Physical education teaches children not only to work well together but also patience and discipline.

17. "Providence" is a short story about the protagonist's failed marriage and living with her daughter after the divorce.

18. Users of ecstasy report feeling euphoric, energized, intensified pleasure, and increased sensory awareness.

19. What made Beethoven's music different from other composers was his expressive style.

20. Recent studies suggest that wellness depends on three main factors: feeling good about yourself, your everyday eating habits, and being comfortably active.

21. Although two very different American writers, Nathaniel Hawthorne and Mark Twain's works are nevertheless similar in many ways.

22. Differing viewpoints in a work of fiction not only add conflict, but they can also reveal differences in characters' ages, genders, and upbringings.

23. Those who exercise regularly show a decrease in anxiety, depression, fatigue, and elevated vigour.

24. In Sonnet 130, Shakespeare stresses the reality of his mistress rather than portraying her as something she is not.

25. According to a recent poll, US president George W. Bush has more support among US college students than the general public.

10. Summary Exercises

Summary Exercises

The following five paragraphs contain various errors that have been discussed in Part Seven, Sentence Essentials. Identify the errors indicated and then make corrections.

1. Identify one instance of each:
   a) comma splice
   b) 1 comma use error
   c) error in pronoun case
   d) broad pronoun reference
   e) missing pronoun antecedent
   f) 2 pronoun-antecedent agreement errors
   g) apostrophe omitted
   h) ambiguous pronoun reference
   i) failure to use gender-neutral language

   In my family, my father and sister play video games as much as me. They have become very complex, and can even improve problem-solving in children. By progressing through increasing difficulty levels, it can help childrens thought processes. On the one hand, if the child goes straight to the hardest setting, they may feel discouraged, on the other, if the child tries to systematically progress through increasing levels, they can learn the mechanics of the game step by step. This can help in the study of math, as the child may learn to persevere until he finds the solution.

2. Identify one instance of each:
   a) comma error
   b) subject-verb agreement error
   c) fragment
   d) 2 parallelism errors
   e) misplaced modifier
   f) dangling modifier
   g) pronoun inconsistency
   h) comma splice

   Having a job and earning one's livelihood is a necessary goal in life, it is one of the reasons you acquire an education. At the place where I work however, many people come in expecting to find a job lacking presentation skills. Many are poorly dressed, do not know how to behave, and they may not speak grammatically. Untidy, disorganized, and unprepared, I still have to match them with a prospective employer. They lack the skills to present themselves to others and knowing what to do in public. Although they may be highly intelligent people.

3. Identify one instance of each:
   a) comma splice
   b) misplaced comma
   c) parallelism error

Summary Exercises – *continued*

d) 2 apostrophes omitted
e) fragment
f) 2 pronoun-antecedent agreement errors

Logic can be defined as "the science of the formation and application of a general notion." Meaning that logic is apt to vary according to ones way of seeing certain things as important. A vegetarians logic, asserts that it is completely unnecessary—not to mention cruel—to eat animals in our day and age. Today's meat eater also has their logic. For them, meat is to be enjoyed, the taste of the food and the social interaction involved is to be cherished. We need to allow time in our busy lives to eat more and feeling guilty about it less.

4. Identify one instance of each:
a) 4 comma errors
b) one error in use of a semi-colon
c) comma splice
d) pronoun case error
e) error in apostrophe use
f) dangling modifier

The Myers-Briggs personality test is based on the work of Swiss psychologist, Carl Jung, and two Americans; Isabel Briggs Myers, and her mother Katharine C. Briggs. Myers developed the tests, and tried them out on thousands of schoolchildren; she wanted to see how the test results would correlate with vocation. Consisting of a series of questions requiring a yes or no response, she tested a group of medical students, who she followed up on 12 years later and who confirmed the test's validity. Variations of Myer's test are sometimes given by employers today, however, the results should not be the sole means for a hiring decision.

5. Identify one instance of each:
a) comma splice
b) 1 other comma error (missing or misplaced)
c) 1 punctuation error other than comma
d) parallelism error
e) 2 apostrophe errors
f) subject-verb agreement error
g) pronoun-antecedent agreement error
h) broad pronoun reference error

According to the principle's of Buddhism, neither sensual pleasures nor self-mortification bring about enlightenment, instead, the "Middle Way" is the path between these extremes; this can be understood through the "Four Noble Truths." These truths are: the truths of suffering, of the origins of suffering, of the cessation of suffering, and finding the path to end suffering. The Buddhas teaching asks each individual to examine their own conscience, and to come to a conclusion about the nature of truth.

PART EIGHT

Achieving Clarity and Depth for 3-D Writing

1. Effective Style: Clarity
2. Providing Depth: Variety and Emphasis
3. Proofreading: Perfection Is Possible
4. Essay Presentation
5. Common Words That Confuse: Guide and Exercise

CONCEPTS and TERMS *NEW* to this section

- absolute phrase
- cumulative sentence
- emphasis
- euphemism

- faulty predication
- infinitive phrase
- intensive
- nominal

- nominalization
- participial phrase
- passive voice (construction)
- periodic sentence

---

1. Effective Style: Clarity

What is style? If you have used secondary sources in an essay, you will know that the word *style* is applied to the standardized formats for citing references, such as the conventions of the MLA, APA, or Chicago documentation styles. Style is also a broad term applied to the writing of individual writers—especially to works of poetry, fiction, or drama. Thus, if someone tells you she prefers the fiction of Margaret Atwood to that of Katherine Mansfield, you might suppose she enjoys the condensed, multi-layered prose of Atwood more than the sparer, epigrammatic prose of Mansfield. Of course, there could be many other reasons for her preference, yet the works of those two writers, like those of many writers, are characterized by their author's personal writing styles.

Although everyone has a unique writing style, when you are writing factually with a specific purpose for a specific audience, you need to stress clarity, if necessary, at the expense of your personal style or distinctive voice. More than a half-century ago, Wendell Johnson wrote about clarity:

> For writing to be effective . . . it may or may not be grammatically correct, but it must be both clear and valid. It can be clear without having validity, but if it is unclear its validity cannot well be determined . . . . We ask of the writer, "What do you mean?" before we ask, "How do you know?" Until we reach agreement as to precisely what he is writing about, we cannot possibly reach agreement as to whether, or in what degree, his statements are true. ("You Can't Write Writing")

Clarity depends on various factors. If you were writing for a general audience on a specialized topic and used words that were unfamiliar to most readers, you would not be writing clearly, though your thought might be clear to a specialist. Word choice and level of language are important factors in clear and effective writing. Achieving an effective style is not a matter of following rules but of being aware of the choices you can make in your writing.

It is seldom evident how much judgement, polish, and experience go into writing that is straightforward and concise. What lies behind the art of making things simple is hard work and attention to detail. Few writers—experienced or inexperienced—are capable of writing clear prose without making several revisions. Much of the revising process, in fact, consists in bringing the language in precise alignment with the ideas.

One of the differences between experienced and inexperienced writers is that the former expect to spend much of their time revising their prose; they ask not just *Is this clear?* but also *Can this be put more clearly?* Student writers should ask the second question, too.

You should work towards clarity as you revise, but you can also focus on clarity during your first draft by rephrasing important points as you write to see if they can be expressed more clearly. You can consciously use transitional phrases like *in other words, in sum, in effect, that is,* or *specifically* and follow by restating what you've said. The purpose is not necessarily to develop a point but to ensure that it is clear to you—if it is, there is a good chance it will be clear to the reader. However, if you find it difficult to paraphrase what you originally wrote, it could be a sign the passage is indeed hard to understand and that you need to work to make it clearer and open to paraphrase.

But when student writers are told to aim for clarity, they may not know where to begin. When they see *unclear, awkward, wordy, clarify, expression* or *?* in the margins of their graded essays, they may ask, "Why is this marked 'unclear?' I know what it means!" Although the easiest way to get an answer might be to ask the instructor, the best option is to try paraphrasing it (putting it in other words). Can you do this readily? Does your paraphrase express the point more clearly? When you paraphrase something you've written, you often find that the second version is closer to what you intended to say.

What, then, is clear writing? Certainly, writing is clear that is grammatical, concise, direct, precise, and specific. When you revise, you can ask yourself not just *Is the writing clear?* but also the following questions:

- *Is it grammatical?* Part Seven has provided most of the information a writer needs to make the arrangements of the words he or she knows into intelligible sentences.
- *Is it concise?* Do you use as many words as you need and no more than you have to? Have you used essential terms and simplified structures that reflect what you want to say?
- *Is it direct?* Have you used straightforward language and avoided circumlocutions (circumlocutions "speak around")? Is the structure of your sentences as simple as possible given the complexity of the point you are trying to express?
- *Is it precise?* Does it say exactly what you want it to say? When you are writing for a reader, *almost* or *close enough* is *not* enough. Would another word or phrase more accurately reflect your thought?
- *Is it specific?* Is it as detailed as it needs to be? Is it definitive and concrete—not vague or abstract?

Writers who carefully work to make their writing more grammatical, concise, direct, precise, and specific will likely produce an essay that is exemplary in its clarity. However, experienced writers aim also for writing that is sophisticated, forceful, and resonant. To these ends, they may introduce variety and emphasis.

Why should so much effort be devoted to concise and direct writing? For one thing, such writing is likely to be easier to follow and to keep the reader's interest. Redundancy and unnecessary detail may cause the focus of your essay or a point to lose its sharpness.

Concise and direct writing affects your credibility, making you seem reliable and knowledgeable; on the other hand, wordy, indirect writing may give the impression that you lack confidence in what you're saying, that you are just trying to impress the reader, or that you are trying to use more words to reach an assigned word limit. Finally, when you use more words than you have to or express yourself in a round-about way, you greatly increase the odds of making grammatical and mechanical errors.

American author Edith Wharton's advice to a journalist friend sums up the goals and strategies of effective writing: "Drop . . . your Latinisms . . . mow down every old cliché, uproot all the dragging circumlocutions, compress, diversify, clarify, vivify."

1.1 Cutting for Conciseness

The word *concise* comes from the Latin *caedere*, meaning *to cut*. The prefix *con* intensifies the meaning of the root word *cise*. To achieve conciseness, you cut what is inessential. How do you determine what is unnecessary? The simple test is whether you can leave something out without changing the meaning and effectiveness of your statement.

Many common stylistic patterns that student writers adopt, especially in their early drafts, are described below under specific categories. Those who correct, grade, or revise your paper may simply strike out words or put parentheses around what is unnecessary. Such criticism is directing you to more effective and readable writing.

Under *Concision* and *Directness*, we consider patterns student writers use unconsciously that end by displacing the stress from the main nouns and verbs. Certainly it is not always wrong to use two of the same parts of speech consecutively or to use an intensive. And to banish all passive constructions would unreasonably limit writers, especially in the social and natural sciences. Context will usually determine usefulness.

1.1.1 Doubling Up: The Noah's Ark Syndrome

Writers sometimes suffer from a form of double vision. They may know clearly what they want to say, but when they write it, two words automatically pop up: two verbs, two nouns, two adjectives, or two adverbs. Experienced editors offer this formula: one + one = one-half. In other words, when you use two words when one is enough, you are halving the impact and effectiveness of that one word. When you do choose to use two of the same parts of speech, ensure that the two words don't convey the same thing and that the repetition creates a valid emphasis.

> Ann came up with an ~~original,~~ innovative suggestion for cost-cutting. (Anything innovative is bound to be original.)

> The event will be held at ~~various~~ different venues.

Ensure that one of the words doesn't incorporate the meaning of the other, as does *different* in regard to *various* in the second sentence example. This applies to phrases with words that are unnecessary because the meaning of the phrase can be understood without them. Be especially wary of verb-adverb combinations; ensure that the adverb is necessary.

> The airport was ~~intentionally~~ designed for larger aircraft. (Can a design be unintentional?)

> She ~~successfully~~ accomplished what she had set out to do. (The word *accomplished* implies success.)

Here are some common pairings of adverb-verb and other combinations that usually are redundant:

combine/join (together)	unite (as one)
fill (completely)	finish (entirely)
refer/return (back) to	emphasize/stress (strongly)
examine (closely)	sob (uncontrollably)
hurry (quickly)	drawl (lazily)
(anxiously) fear	(suddenly) interrupt
(totally) eradicate/devastate	(eventually) evolve (over time)

(strictly) forbid
rely/depend (heavily) on,
(harshly) condemn
protest (against)
(symbolically) represent
vanish (without a trace)
descend (down)
climb (up)
(clearly) articulate
(successfully) prove
(completely) surround

dwindle (down)
praise (in favour of)
gaze (steadily)
ponder (thoughtfully)
plan (ahead)
estimate/approximate (roughly)
gather/assemble (together)
dominate (over)
(carefully) consider
progress (forward/onwards)
(better/further) enhance

Be wary, too, of such repetitive adjective–noun pairings as the following:

powerful blast
fiery blaze
dead carcass
advance warning
past memory
mutual agreement
total abstinence

sharp needle
terrible tragedy
positive benefits
timeless classic
future plan
brief encapsulation
knowledgeable specialist

Redundancies are evident in such familiar phrases as *end result, end product, consensus of opinion, this point in time, time frame, time period, time span, in actual fact, years of age,* etc.

Unnecessary nouns are redundant. These nouns steal the thunder from other parts of speech, including other nouns and verbs.

The world of politics demands that you kowtow to the ineptitude of others.

The efforts of conservationists in the fields of ecology and biodiversity are leading to renewed efforts to save old-growth forests.

In each sentence above, the most important noun has been displaced by a weaker noun. In sentence 1 we are not really talking about a *world*, but about *politics*; in sentence 2 the noun *fields* is redundant because *ecology* and *biodiversity* are fields of study.

1.1.2 Phony Phrases

Phony phrases are superfluous prepositional phrases. Look for them after verbs and nouns.

Unnecessary:
For now, her kidneys are functioning at a normal level.

Better:
For now, her kidneys are functioning normally.

The prepositional phrase *at a normal level* can be replaced by the adverb *normally*:

Here the phony phrase is introduced by the preposition *for*.

> The bill was legislated in 1995 for a brief period of time.

Better:
The bill was briefly legislated in 1995.

A cluster of non-specific nouns are connected to phony phrases beginning with *on*, *to*, or other prepositions. Watch for prepositional phrases that include *level, scale, basis, degree,* and *extent,* for example, *on/at the international level, on a regular basis, on the larger scale, to a great/considerable degree/extent.* The phrase likely can be replaced by an appropriate adverb. For example,

> Jindra checks her answering machine on a regular basis.

Can be revised:
Jindra checks her answering machine regularly.

Relative clauses are adjectival and may sometimes be replaced by a corresponding adjective preceding the noun, as in the following:

> Most body-builders follow a strict diet that is high in protein.

[T]hat is high in protein is a relative (adjectival) clause modifying *diet*.

> Most body-builders follow a strict, high-protein diet.

1.1.3 The Small but Not-So-Beautiful

Even small words, such as prepositions and articles, may be omitted. Writers sometimes seem to think they make an ordinary phrase sound just a little bit more impressive. In the examples below, parentheses indicate words that can be omitted:

> He was (the) last out (of) the door.

> (The) taking (of) life can never be condoned.

Look at the following passage and consider what can be deleted—big words and small—without changing the meaning of the sentence:

> The city of Toronto has one of the most ethnically diverse of cultures in all of North America. The city has a population of 2,500,000 people, and is also the home of a variety of sports teams that play in professional leagues.

The word *that* can be used as a pronoun (demonstrative and relative), an adjective, and a subordinating conjunction. It can often be omitted if the subject of the second clause introduced by *that* is different from the subject of the preceding clause.

By methodically checking your first draft for unnecessary *thats*, you can often improve sentence flow.

> I thought (that) Silas was going to go to the same school (that) his brother went to.

Unravel the meaning of the following statement:

> It's certain that that "that" that that person used was wrong.

1.1.4 Those Un-Intensives

An *intensive* is a word or phrase that adds emphasis to the word or expression it modifies but has little meaning on its own. In all levels of formal writing, intensives should be rooted out whenever they do not truly add emphasis. The intensives in the following sentence are unneeded:

> She is ~~certainly~~ a(n) ~~very~~ impressive speaker.

Words like *certainly* and *very* have been overused and may add nothing to the sentence. Many intensives are adverbs modifying verbs or adjectives. In some instances, you can simply use a stronger verb in place of a weak verb and an intensive, or a stronger adjective in place of the intensive plus a weak adjective; or, you can just eliminate the intensive, as in *it was a ~~very~~ unique idea.*

> He was very grateful for his warm reception.

> He was gratified by his warm reception. *or* He appreciated his warm reception.

Words and prepositional phrases that may clutter:

whilst
thusly
amidst
so as to
amongst
oftentimes
in terms of
in regard to
irregardless
cognizant of
pertaining to
inasmuch as
analogous to
as a result of
with regard to
consequent to

Hackneyed intensives include the following: absolutely, actually, assuredly, certainly, clearly, completely, considerably, definitely, effectively, extremely, fundamentally, highly, in fact, incredibly, inevitably, indeed, interestingly, markedly, naturally, of course, particularly, significantly, surely, totally, utterly, very.

Hackneyed qualifiers: apparently, arguably, basically, essentially, generally, hopefully, in effect, in general, kind of, perhaps, quite, rather, relatively, seemingly, somewhat, sort of, virtually.

the majority of
subsequent to
in reference to
whether or not
with respect to
each and every
aforementioned
in comparison to
in connection with
in conjunction with
in accordance with
due to the fact that
in the final analysis
at this point in time
despite the fact that
in view of the fact that
notwithstanding the fact that

1.2 Writing Directly

Writing should get straight to the point. Indirect writing stresses the less important parts of the sentence. Passive constructions tend to indirectness, although they may be acceptable or even preferable when you do not want to stress the subject of a clause or if the exact subject is unknown.

1.2.1 Passive Constructions: The Lazy Subject

In a passive construction, the subject of the sentence is *not* doing the action. Ordinarily, the subject *is* acting, as in the following:

> Ezra placed the book on the table.

To change the sentence so that the object becomes the (non-active) subject:

> The book was placed on the table by Ezra.

The sentence now has a passive subject, one being acted on rather than itself acting. Notice that the passive subject sentence requires more words to provide the same information. In a passive construction the subject *receives* the action. Effective, direct English is geared towards the *active*, not the passive, voice.

The passive voice uses a form of the verb *to be* followed by a past participle. If the actor is named, it will be the object of a prepositional phrase that begins with *by*, e.g., *by Ezra*. Although you can identify the passive by the verb forms that compose it—the past, present, or future form of *to be* plus a past participle—don't confuse the identifying verb forms of the passive with a construction in which a form of the verb *to be* is used along with the past participle as a predicate adjective. For example, in the following sentence, the subjects are clearly the actors; you can't add the preposition *by* after *determined* or after *pleased*:

Dana was determined to succeed at any cost; I am pleased to see him succeed.

In the following sentence, there are three indicators of a passive construction:

The door was opened by a tall, sinister man.

1. The subject (*door*) is not doing the action expressed by the verb *open*;
2. The preposition *by* precedes the actor (*man*);
3. The simple past of *to be* combines with the past participle of the main verb to form the passive voice of the verb.

To change a passive to an active construction, (1) move the subject so that it follows the verb as the direct object; (2) move the object of the preposition *by*, the actor, to the beginning of the clause to replace the passive subject; and (3) get rid of the identifying passive forms of the verb and the preposition *by*:

A tall, sinister man ~~was~~ opened the door ~~by~~.

Here's a slightly more complicated example:

Passive:
The special commission was informed of its mandate by a superior court judge last Monday.

Active:
A superior court judge informed the special commission of its mandate last Monday.

In its active form, the sentence contains fewer words, and the thought is expressed more directly. As a general rule, *don't use the passive voice if the active will serve.* However, these are times when the passive is acceptable, or is even the better choice:

1. When the subject isn't known or is so well known it doesn't matter.

   Pierre Trudeau was first elected Prime Minister in 1968.

   It is unnecessary to mention that *the voters* or *the electorate* elected him.

2. When passivity is implied, or if the context makes it seem natural to stress the receiver of the action.

   When a cyclist completes a hard workout, massages are usually performed on the affected muscles.

   In this sentence, the massages are more important than the person giving them.

Acceptable passive:
The woman was kidnapped and held hostage by a band of thugs.

Questionable passive:
Several of the thugs were picked out of a line-up by the woman.

In the first sentence, the woman obviously is the passive recipient of the action of the thugs; in the second sentence, she is doing the action. Therefore, in the second sentence, the active is preferred:

Active:
The woman picked several of the thugs out of a line-up.

Occasionally, you may choose the passive voice because the rhythm of the sentence requires it, or because it is rhetorically effective.

The books obviously had been arranged by a near-sighted librarian.

In this sentence, the librarian's near-sightedness is important; the placement of the adjective near the end of the sentence gives it emphasis.

There are cases in academic writing, especially in the sciences, in which it is unnecessary to mention the author of a study or the researcher; the passive may be used to stress the object of the study or the method of research.

Through case studies, a comparison of two common methods for treating depression will be made.

In the following examples from academic writing, the passive is preferred either because the actor doesn't matter or because the writer wants to stress the receiver of the action:

In 1891 the science of embryology was shaken by the work of the cosmopolitan German biologist and vitalist philosopher, Hans Driesch (Bowring, 2004, p. 401).

The emergence of second-hand smoke (SHS) [as a cancer hazard] has been offered as a viable explanation for the increased enactment of local smoking restrictions (Asbridge, 2003, p. 13).

Exercise

The following sentences use passive constructions. Determine which are appropriately in passive voice and which are inappropriately in passive voice. Change unnecessary uses of the passive voice to form active constructions. Be prepared to justify your decisions to leave some sentences as passive constructions.

1. I was given two choices by my landlord: pay up or get out.

2. It was reported that more than 1,000 people were left homeless by recent flooding.

3. Theo's protest was heard by the fairness committee.

4. The tree was buffeted by the wind, which tore off one of its lower branches.

5. Beethoven's Third Symphony, *The Eroica*, originally was dedicated to Napoleon, but the dedication was erased after Napoleon proclaimed himself emperor.

6. Education needs to be seen by the government as the number one priority.

7. Many acts of self-deception were committed by Bertha, the protagonist of "Bliss."

8. The belief in a powerful and infallible Creator is commonly held today.

9. Poverty in First Nations communities must be addressed by the federal, provincial, and First Nations' governments.

10. There are two ways of looking at rights-based ethics that were put forward by Emanuel Kant.

1.2.2 Black Hole Constructions

Inappropriately passive constructions not only use too many words but also place the stress where it doesn't belong; consequently, they are weak constructions. Several kinds of indirect constructions create similar weakness. You can consider them the black holes of writing: they swallow up the substance of the sentence.

1. It was . . . .

It was Mary Shelley who wrote *Frankenstein* in 1816.

As simple as this sentence is, it begins weakly by displacing the logical subject, *Mary Shelley*, and substituting the bland and unnecessary *It was*. The sentence is stronger and more direct when the most important noun is made the subject:

Mary Shelley wrote *Frankenstein* in 1816.

If a relative pronoun (who, which, or that) follows the displaced subject, consider getting rid of the "empty" subject (*It was, There is, Here is*) and the relative pronoun to make the statement more direct and concise. Occasionally, you may want to use this and similar constructions for rhetorical effect. In such cases, emphasis, rather than directness, may determine your choice.

Unnecessary:
There are a variety of different strategies that you can use to reduce excess verbiage in your writing.

Better:
You can use various strategies to reduce verbiage in your writing.

2. *one of*—A redundancy to be avoided:

    Poor:
    The path you have chosen is one of danger and uncertainty.

    Better:
    The path you have chosen is dangerous and uncertain.

    You have chosen a dangerous, uncertain path.

3. Perhaps more notorious is the structure *the reason . . . is because*, which is both illogical and redundant:

    Incorrect:
    The reason Jessica is lucky is because she studied for the test.

    Correct:
    Jessica is lucky because she studied for the test.

1.2.3 Numbing Nouns

Writers sometimes fall into the habit of using a weak verb and a corresponding noun rather than a verb that directly expresses the meaning. In these cases, a weak verb phrase supplants the more direct alternative:

1. I *had a meeting* with my staff, and I am now asking you to *provide a list* of all your clients.
2. Inexperienced writers *have a tendency* to be wordy.
3. She *made changes* to the document, *making clear* what was ambiguous.
4. Sam *offered comfort* to Amanda, who *received a failing grade* on her essay.
5. Canada *made a significant contribution* to the war effort in France and Belgium.

Stronger constructions:

1. I *met* with my staff, and now ask you to *list* all your clients.
2. Inexperienced writers *tend* to be wordy.
3. She *changed* the document, *clarifying* ambiguities.
4. Sam *comforted* Amanda, who *had failed* her essay.
5. Canada *contributed significantly* to the war effort in France and Belgium.

Note: in the weak phrase *has an effect on*, where *has* is the verb and effect is the noun, remember that the corresponding verb form is *affect*.

Global warming *affects* shifting major weather patterns.

Nouns that pile up in a sentence can create a numbing effect. This is especially true with *nominals*, nouns formed from verbs. There is nothing wrong with using a polysyllabic noun formed from a verb—unless a more concise and direct alternative exists.

Verb	Nominal	Example
accumulate	accumulation	The (accumulation of) evidence is overwhelming.
classify	classification	We will now proceed with the classification of Vertebrata; we will now classify Vertebrata.
intend	intention	Our intention is to complete the installation of the new system this month; we plan to finish
install	installation	installing the new system this month.

Clear expression in literary essays is sometimes a challenge to students due to their lack of familiarity with terminology or to the temptation to make a point sound complex and, thereby, significant.

> The conflict between Billy and Claggart ultimately serves as a device in the interruption of the reader's attempts at a coherent interpretation of the novel as an ideological message. In addition to problematizing definitive interpretations, this technique effectively secures a lasting relevance for the novel.

The thought in these sentences can be expressed more directly and clearly by omitting words and reducing the number of nominals.

> The conflict between Billy and Claggart challenges a coherent ideological reading of the novel, making definitive readings difficult and ensuring the novel's relevance.

Writing in academic journals is not immune from excessive nominalization, as this Internet example, featured in a bad writing contest, illustrates:

> It is the moment of non-construction, disclosing the absentation of actuality from the concept in part through its invitation to emphasize, in reading, the helplessness—rather than the will to power of its fall into conceptuality.
> (Paul Fry, *A Defense of Poetry*, 1995)

1.2.4 Euphemisms

Many ancient cultures used euphemisms to avoid naming their enemies directly. They believed that naming gave power to those they feared, so they invented ways around saying their names; the word *euphemism* comes from the Greek word that means "to use words for good omen." We sometimes do the same today out of consideration and kindness to those who may be suffering, as a way of speaking about taboo subjects and objects, or as a form of satire or irony. For example, the euphemisms for *die* are numerous: *to expire, to pass away* (or *on*) *to cross over, to meet one's Maker, to graduate, to croak, to go west, to kick the bucket, to bite the dust, to go to the great beyond, to buy the farm, to turn up one's toes,* etc. Although euphemisms can be used to protect us from the unpleasant, they can be used also to falsely reassure. For example, *urban renewal* avoids the implications of *slum clearance, revenue enhancement* has a more positive ring than *tax increase,* and *collateral losses* attempts to sidestep the fact that civilians have been killed during military action.

We also sometimes use euphemisms to try to give more dignity and a sense of importance to special objects, actions, or vocations: *pre-owned automobile* for *used car* and *job action* for *strike.* The Plain English Campaign recently awarded a Golden Bull Award to the writers of a document that described the act of laying a brick in a wall as "install[ing] a component into the structural fabric."

The following classified ad uses some verbose and euphemistic language:

> We are seeking an individual who possesses demonstrated skills and abilities, a sound knowledge base coupled with the experience to provide service to mentally handicapped teenagers with "unique" and significant challenging behaviours.

The requirements of the position could have been written in half the words:

> Applicants need proven skills, knowledge, and experience to serve mentally handicapped teenagers with challenging behaviours.

A special category of "acceptable euphemisms" are those that we, as a society, agree should be substituted for expressions that have acquired inappropriate connotations. For example, to refer to someone in a wheelchair as a "cripple" inappropriately stresses the disability and its limiting attributes. More sensitively and more accurately, this person is *physically disabled* or *physically challenged.*

Exercise

Rewrite the following paragraphs, aiming for concise, direct writing.

1.

Dear Employers,

The Youth Resource Centre, in conjunction with the Federal Human Resource Department of Canada, has opened the Hire-A-Student office once again this summer, staffing Summer Employment Officers working towards finding the best possible student employees for any jobs that you may have available to post with us at the Centre.

Our service, conveniently situated at 147 High Street, is a totally free service to both employers posting jobs in the Centre and to students and youths trying to secure employment opportunities throughout the community. The service is a means for you the employer to help advertise any positions you may have available, and is additionally a way to assist students who are showing initiative in finding possible long-term or limited-term seasonal employment.

We are not a solicitation firm, and this is the point that we need to emphasize to the greatest extent. Our service is absolutely free of charge, and our intention is first and foremost to try and find employment for students who seem serious about working, as well as to offer a free alternative to posting jobs in newspapers and ad agencies that could end up costing you an excessive amount of money through advertising ventures.

Exercise *– continued*

2.

In medieval English universities, such as Oxford and Cambridge universities, chest loans were made available to students who were able to demonstrate their financial neediness. Students would make use of an item, usually a book, as a form of collateral against an interest-free loan that was taken from a chest of money that had been put in place by a benefactor. Nowadays, the only thing that resembles the concept of the benefactor is the branch of government that disburses loans and grants for students who are lacking in sufficient funding resources.

Recent studies have conclusively demonstrated that the vast majority of Canadian students over 26 years of age have an average debt of in excess of $20,000 relating to their overall education. The bulk of these costs relates to the expenses incurred by tuition fees and ordinary, everyday cost of living expenses. These expenses do not generally take into account the very high cost of student textbooks, which are required purchases for most of a student's courses at university. In regards to textbooks, students may have the option of buying brand new textbooks or purchasing less expensive used texts, and in some instances they are able to borrow required readings from a library.

Exercise

The following sentences can be revised for greater concision and directness. Make whatever changes you believe are necessary and be prepared to justify these changes.

1. Tanya has been invited to provide us with a summary of the significant main points of her findings.

2. The unexpected eruption of the volcano changed the Western Samoan island into a fiery, blazing inferno.

3. Gretta was decidedly overjoyed after being the unexpected recipient of an income tax refund in excess of $1,000.

4. The protagonist of *Life of Pi* was confronted with the necessity of making the decision about whether he wanted to continue on living or not.

5. It was in 1964 that the Beatles first made their inaugural tour of the North American continent.

6. The disappearance of even one single species at the lower end of the food chain can have dire adverse effects in many instances on the survival of various other species.

7. Although Copernicus's radical idea that the Earth made revolutions around the Sun was once considered an extreme heresy and was ridiculed mercilessly by his peers, the idea eventually gained gradual acceptance.

Exercise – *continued*

8. The fact is that for a great many years now antibiotics have been utilized on a regular basis by many people as a cure for each and every symptom that they develop over the course of their entire lifetimes.

9. Perhaps in the heat of emotion the act of capital punishment would seem to be a feasible idea, but when you come to think of it rationally, this act would accomplish virtually next to nothing at all.

10. In protest of their salary freeze, all of the teachers who teach at the high school in Oak Bay have made the unanimous decision not to undertake any tasks of a supervisory nature until the school board has conducted a fair and impartial salary review.

11. Vehicles that have the four-way drive feature option are an extremely practical and pragmatic form of transportation for the majority of the Canadian population in this day and age.

12. There are many people in our society today who have serious drug addictions that take complete and utter control over their lives.

13. From the beginning of its conception, Canada has been a country concerned with promoting an active multicultural society, although the reality of unity within the country is still a large, unanswered question in the minds of most of the people of Canada.

14. A French scientist by the name of Louis Pasteur was the first individual to make the discovery that microbes were harmful menaces to the well-being and healthy functioning of the human body.

15. The reason yoga allows us to live a healthy lifestyle is due to the fact that it provides a strong basis for the efficient functioning of the body's endocrine system.

1.3 Working towards Precision: Wise Word Choices

For most writing assignments in college and university, you will be required to use formal writing. Accordingly, you will avoid contractions, unless your instructor tells you otherwise. Also, avoid slang, colloquialisms, and jargon. For example, you would not use any of the following in a formal essay: *mindset, lifestyle, price tag, quick fix, down side, upfront, stressed (out), okay, do drugs, give the green light, grab the reader's attention, put (someone) down, fall for, obsess (about something), pan out, put on hold, put a positive spin (on something), opt for, tune out, no way, the way to go, go to great lengths, go overboard, way more* (of something—*a lot* is also colloquial). Avoid merely quantitative words and phrases, such as *great, incredible, beautiful, terrible*, and the like; they are non-specific. Of course, you also should refrain from using words and expressions that might suggest to some readers a gender, sexual, racial, cultural, or other kind of bias.

Effective writers choose their words and phrases carefully. In the following three examples from student essays, the writers did not choose carefully. If in doubt, use a dictionary; don't rely on spell checker, which would not have caught these errors.

The mass production of plastics and ready-to-use products is growing at a *stagnating* [sic *staggering*] rate.

Note: *staggering* is informal; the writer could have used *rapid*, *rapidly increasing*, or *exponential*, or a specific number, such as *doubling every year*.

The Shakespearean sonnet is an *oppressed* [sic *compressed*] form of poetry.

After successfully completing police officer training camp, the applicant can finally *swear* [sic *be sworn in*] and become a police officer.

Rather than making extreme blunders, more often you choose a word that is not quite precise for your purpose. These kinds of "near misses" can distract or confuse the reader. Of course, you should not let the search for the exact word prevent you from fully expressing your ideas in a first draft. But during revision, you should look up the meanings of all words you're in doubt about—even those you're only a little uncertain about.

You can use a thesaurus to look for words similar in meaning. Some writers also use a thesaurus to replace hackneyed words. But a thesaurus should be used to jog your mind, not to create something out of nothing. Since a thesaurus is not a "synonym dictionary," it should always be used along with a reliable dictionary; most thesauruses, such as the ones that come with word-processing programs, simply list words similar in meaning; they do not provide connotations for the words.

Some dictionaries help you to be precise not only by defining the main entry but also by providing distinctions among similar words. In addition to illustrating the way a word is used by providing examples, many mid-sized dictionaries distinguish the main entry from other words with similar meanings. For example, the *Gage Canadian Dictionary*, which lists more than six meanings for the adjective *effective*, also defines two words similar to *effective* in meaning but different in connotation:

> *Syn. adj.* **1. Effective, effectual, efficient** = producing an effect. **Effective,** usually describing things, emphasizes producing a wanted or expected effect: *several new drugs are effective in treating serious diseases*. **Effectual,** describing people or things, emphasizes having produced or having the power to produce the exact effect or result intended: *his efforts are more energetic than effectual*. **Efficient,** often describing people, emphasizes being able to produce the effect wanted or intended without wasting energy, time, etc.: *A skilled surgeon is highly efficient*.

Similarly, the *Student's Oxford Canadian Dictionary*, which lists seven meanings for the adjective *nice*, offers the following examples of words that may be more appropriate or more forceful than *nice* in certain contexts:

> we had a **delightful/splendid/enjoyable** time
> a **satisfying/delicious/exquisite** meal
> a **fashionable/stylish/elegant/chic** outfit
> this is a **cozy/comfortable/attractive** room

When you read books and articles in your courses, you get used to looking up unfamiliar words as an essential part of the learning process. Checking out the precise meanings of the words you write should become a habit. Although knowing some common roots of English words can increase your vocabulary, the most efficient way to add to your store of words is to use a reliable dictionary.

she is **kind/friendly/likeable/amiable**
our adviser is **compassionate/understanding/sympathetic**
a **thoughtful/considerate/caring** gesture

1.3.1 Precision and Logic

Choosing your words carefully will help make your writing precise. But sometimes, imprecision may be more the result of illogical thinking or of writing down an idea before it is fully developed. To determine if something you've written really makes sense, you need to look carefully at the relationship among the syntactical units in the sentence, especially at the relationship between the subject and predicate. **Faulty predication** exists if a verb cannot be logically connected to its subject. In general, avoid the phrases *is when* and *is where* after a subject in sentences that *define* something. For example, in the following sentence *faulty predication*, which is a thing, is illogically referred to as a time or a place.

Incorrect:
Faulty predication is when/where a verb cannot be logically connected to its subject.

Correct:
Faulty predication *occurs where* [i.e., in a sentence] a verb is not logically connected to its subject.

Faulty predication *is* an illogical juxtaposing of a subject and a verb.

Consider this comment on the setting of Joseph Conrad's *Heart of Darkness*:

The Congo represents an inward journey for the character Marlow.

The Congo is a country as well as a river. How can a country or a river represent a journey? Of course, a *trip* through a country or on a river could represent an inner journey.

In one kind of faulty predication, an inanimate object is falsely credited with an action.

Ibsen's play *Ghosts* struggles with the tensions of an unacknowledged spiritual inheritance.

The play itself doesn't *struggle*, though characters in the play do.

Ibsen, in his play *Ghosts*, explores the tensions of an unacknowledged spiritual inheritance.

The characters in Ibsen's play *Ghosts* struggle with the tensions of an unacknowledged spiritual inheritance.

Sound should also play a role in word choice. You should avoid placing words with similar sounds in close proximity (the "echo effect").

Endorphins enable the body to heal itself and *gain pain* relief.

You should also be wary of unintentional puns in a work of scholarship:

The first experiments in music therapy were *noted* during World War I.

Exercise

Circle every example of informal diction in the following paragraph; then, rewrite using formal diction. There may be one or two places where the word or phrase is colloquial but necessary due to context or the fact it can't be rephrased easily.

Having the winter Olympic Games held in Vancouver is a once-in-a-lifetime opportunity, and it seems like a great idea. It would create world recognition for this world-class city, helping to really put it on the map. On top of that, it would be a fun and exciting time for the citizens of BC. However, after sober second thought, it is clear that while the Games might pay for themselves, who will pay for the upgrades necessary to get Vancouver in good shape for the Games? Even with both the provincial and federal governments chipping in for a fair amount of the costs, because we are dealing in billions of dollars, even a small chunk of that cost is a lot of money. These small chunks will come from the pockets of the taxpayer, some of whom are not big fans of the Games at all. But although these direct costs are bound to be steep, it is the hidden costs of the Games that are the real killer. Because of the direct and the hidden costs involved in this affair, the Games should not be held in Vancouver.

1.4 Working towards Specificity

You can make your writing specific through the detail you choose to support your points: examples, illustrations, descriptions, statistics, quotations from experts, etc. Another important strategy is the choice of vivid verbs and pertinent nouns describing detail. Compare the following passages. The second is taken from the autobiography of the Irish poet, Louis MacNeice; the first is the same passage rendered into duller prose, using common verbs and non-specific nouns, adjectives, and adverbs:

A.

During the holidays my sister and I were taken to the salt-mines. We went on a car, and I listened to the sounds the horses made and saw the sun shining, but my sister and I were anxious to get there; we had always wanted to go under the earth to see the caves beneath the ground. We went down, and at the bottom was a cross along with a big area where the miners worked.

B.

> During one summer holidays my father took us to the salt-mines. We went on an outside car, clopping of hoofs and scuttling of pebbles, the country a prism for the sun was shining on the patchwork, but Elizabeth and I were impatient till we got there; we had always wanted to go down under the earth to the caves of crystal and man-made thunder, to the black labyrinth of galleries under the carefree fields, under the tumbledown walls, the whins and the ragweed. We descended a pitch-black shaft in a great bucket; at the bottom was a cross of fire and there sure enough was the subterranean cathedral and men like gnomes in the clerestories, working with picks.

1.4.1 Verbs with Vitality

Verbs are the action words in a sentence. Look at the verbs in your sentences. Can you replace them with stronger, more descriptive verbs? Can you replace verbs, like *be* and *have*, which convey a state or condition, with verbs of action? Common verbs, such as *do*, *make*, *go*, and *get*, are not specific. Can you replace them with more precise or emphatic verbs?

Exercise

Read the following paragraph and underline places where you would revise verbs to make them more expressive and descriptive.

> By the 1800s, inventions were beginning to put people out of work. One of the first inventions that resulted in rebellion was in the craft guild. In 1801, Joseph Jacquard became known as the inventor of the Jacquard loom. This loom was capable of being programmed by pre-punched cards, which made it possible to create clothing design patterns. This invention led to the creation of the Luddites, who were a group made up from the craft guild. These people were against any type of manufacturing technology and went about burning down several factories that were using this new technology. The Luddites were around only for a couple of years, but the name Luddite is still used to describe people who are resistant to new technologies. The Jacquard loom was, in effect, an invention that replaced people. It could do great designs quickly and without making any errors. The replacement of people by machines was beginning.

The most used verb in English, *to be*, takes many different forms as an irregular verb: *am*, *is*, *are*, *was*, *were*, *will be*, etc. and appears frequently as an auxiliary verb. Your prose may be made more emphatic if the verbals *being* or *to be* can be pruned from your sentences.

> The results of the study can be interpreted as ~~being~~ credible.

> She dreamed of a carriage ~~being~~ pulled by two fine horses.

> Hypnosis has been proven ~~to be~~ an effective therapy for some people.

Verbs expressing uncertainty, like *seem* and *appear*, can weaken your point or make your thesis appear tentative. Be wary of overusing them.

In AD 313 Christianity was declared ~~to be~~ the official religion of Rome.

If you can easily omit a form of *to be*, do so.

As people put on the spot by journalists and the public, politicians have sometimes chosen vague language to avoid committing themselves to statements they may regret later. A more cynical view suggests that taking refuge in abstract, indefinite language enables them to say little while appearing informed and in control of a great deal. Notice the lack of specificity in the following comment by American politician Colin Powell, reported by the Associated Press:

> "We knew that the ICRC had concerns, and in accordance with the matter in which the ICRC does its work, it presented those concerns directly to the command in Baghdad. And I know that some corrective action was taken with respect to those concerns."

Exercise

Suggest how the following passage could be improved by using more specific language and by omitting unnecessary words and phrases:

> The time period between 1985 and 1989 was a difficult one for graffiti artists in New York City. This was a time when graffiti barely stayed alive because of the harsh laws and efforts of the Metropolitan Transit Authority, which is known as the MTA. This period was called the period of the "Die Hards" because of the small number of die-hard artists who were able to keep graffiti from dying out completely. As a result of the measures of the MTA against graffiti art and artists, there was a lack of paint available for use and the level of enforcement was extremely high. The only important thing that happened during these years was the use of markers for tagging. These tags were usually small, of poor artistic quality, and were finished quickly by the artists. These tags can be seen today at some bus stops and in some washrooms throughout the city.

1.4.2 Prepackaged Goods: Clichés

Expressions considered "clichés" today were in their prime a veritable breath of fresh air. If commentary on the cliché were to be made in clichés, you would find the prose wordy, cloying, and fraught with irrelevant connotations:

> However, with the passage of time (more years than you can shake a stick at), they became the stuff of idle minds until after time immemorial they assumed the mantle of respectability and were accepted verbatim as par for the course. Writers worth their salt should avoid clichés like the plague or they will stop all readers with a good head on their shoulders dead in their tracks (to call a spade a spade and to give the devil his due).

Clichés are overworked, hackneyed phrases. Writers reach for them in a vain attempt to "spice up" their writing. Clichés tend towards *dead metaphors*: expressions whose novelty or aptness once carried dramatic or poetic force that dissipated through overuse. Clichés descend to informality unacceptable in formal writing; they are unattractive substitutes for informative, imaginative words.

Exercise

In this short passage adapted from a travel feature, find evidence of tired and predictable writing, citing particular words and phrases that could be made more effective. Although newspaper features use informal writing, it should be descriptive and concrete. How could you make this passage more interesting?

> We're up and about at the crack of dawn, and from outside our cabin we can see the peak of a small mountain looming in the distance. Our ship glides effortlessly over the fathomless blue sea, and soon the mountain's craggy features come into view.
>
> "It's breakfast, honey," my wife, Jen, sings from inside the cabin, and soon our impeccably dressed waiter knocks softly on our door. As we sit down to partake of the delectable repast, I feel as though I could pinch myself. Yes, here we are, aboard a luxurious liner, about to drop anchor off the coast of one of the world's most fabled isles.

---

2. Providing Depth: Variety and Emphasis

When you revise an early draft to improve clarity, you will find opportunities to make your prose more sophisticated and appealing. Variety and emphasis in your writing will make what is competent also *compelling*. Variety and emphasis are worthwhile goals in all forms of essays: personal, literary, argumentative, and expository.

2.1 Sentence Variety

2.1.1 Length

You can vary the lengths of sentences for rhetorical effect. Just as short paragraphs suggest underdeveloped points, a succession of short, choppy sentences could suggest a lack of content. On the other hand, a succession of long sentences may confuse a reader—even if the sentences are grammatical.

That doesn't mean you should write only sentences that are between 15 and 20 words long. The previous sentence has 16 words and on the Flesch scale of readability, which includes word and sentence length—received a score of 80, an excellent rating on a scale available with many word-processing programs. However, a "sentence" in which the same words were arranged randomly received the identical score. Although sentence length alone is no measure of readability, consider revision if you find you have written several very short or several very long sentences in a row.

To connect short sentences you can use appropriate conjunctions. Simple sentences can be joined by one of the seven co-ordinating conjunctions. If the idea in one sentence is less important than the idea in the sentence before or after it, use the subordinate conjunction that best expresses the relationship between the sentences. You can join independent clauses by using a semicolon or a colon.

You can also join independent clauses by using a conjunctive adverb or transitional phrase, ensuring that a semicolon precedes the connecting word or phrase. You may be able to grammatically connect phrases or clauses through a parallel relationship, such as one of apposition. The second phrase or clause could also modify the preceding word, phrase, or clause—for example, a relative (adjectival) clause could give information about a preceding noun clause.

Generally speaking, you waste space when you begin a new sentence by repeating part of the previous sentence, or by beginning a new paragraph by recapitulating part of the previous one. Although repetition can be used to build coherence, it should not create redundancy.

In 1970, Gordon O. Gallup created the mirror test ~~This test was~~, designed to determine whether ~~or not~~ animals are self-aware.

Exercise

The following paragraph consists of too many short sentences. Using the strategies mentioned above, revise the paragraph to make it more effective.

(1) During the earth's long history, there have been various periods of glaciation. (2) This fact is well known. (3) There is also evidence of one great glacial event. (4) It is possible that the earth was once completely covered by ice and snow. (5) Skeptics argue this is impossible. (6) They say that the earth could never have become this cold. (7) The idea of the tropics being frozen over is unlikely, they believe.

When checking your work for overly long sentences, consider breaking up sentences with more than two independent clauses or one independent clause and more than two dependent clauses. See if the relationships between the clauses are clear. If they are not, divide the sentences where clauses are joined by conjunctions, by transitional words and phrases, or by relative pronouns.

Exercise

The following paragraph consists of sentences that are too long. Using the strategies mentioned above, revise the paragraph to make it more effective.

(1) Finding a definition for "the homeless" is difficult, but the most common definition, which is used both in the media and in current research, defines the homeless as those who lack visible shelter or use public shelters. (2) Literature about homelessness is sparse, and it was not until the 1980s that the incidence of homelessness began to be reported in the media, but homelessness has existed for centuries, and literature on the subject dates back to the feudal period in Europe.

2.1.2 Structural Variety

You can experiment with phrasal openings to sentences. Consider beginning the occasional sentence with a prepositional phrase, a verbal phrase, or an absolute phrase.

Prepositional phrases begin with a preposition followed by a noun or pronoun; they are adverbial and modify the closest verb. A **participial phrase**, which ends in *–ing*, *–ed*, or *–en*, is a verbal phrase acting adjectivally. An **infinitive phrase**, which is preceded by *to*, can act adjectivally or adverbially as a sentence opener. An **absolute phrase**, consisting of a noun/pronoun and a partial verb form, modifies the entire sentence.

In this short excerpt from an essay about the death of a moth, Virginia Woolf uses a prepositional phrase opening, an absolute phrase (a phrase that is syntactically independent) that introduces an independent clause, and two verbal phrase openings:

> *After a time*, tired by his dancing apparently, he settled on the window ledge in the sun, and **the queer spectacle being at an end**, I forgot about him. Then, looking up, my eye was caught by him. He was trying to resume his dancing, but seemed either so stiff or so awkward that he could only flutter to the bottom of the window-pane; and when he tried to fly across it, he failed.

Note the types of modifiers: *After a time*: prepositional phrase; *tired by his dancing*; *looking up*: verbal phrases; **the queer spectacle being at an end**: absolute phrase.

Make sure that when you use a participial phrase at the beginning of a sentence that you include the word it is intended to modify so that it does not dangle.

2.2 Creating Emphasis

Writers may create emphasis by presenting main points or details in a particular order. Two kinds of sentences can be distinguished according to their rhetorical effect: **periodic** and **cumulative** sentences.

Periodic sentences begin with modifiers—words, phrases, or clauses—before concluding with an independent clause. Cumulative sentences work the other way: they begin with an independent clause and are followed by modifying or parallel words, phrases, and clauses. While periodic sentences delay the main idea, creating the tension of anticipation, cumulative sentences develop the main idea by drawing it out, stressing its complexity or multiplicity. Many sentences are slightly or moderately periodic or cumulative, depending on whether the writer has begun with modifiers or ended with them. However, a writer can employ either periodic or cumulative sentences to create a specific effect.

Periodic:
Unlike novelists and playwrights, who lurk behind the scenes while distracting our attention with the puppet show of imaginary characters—and unlike the scholars and journalists, who quote the opinions of others and take cover behind the hedges of neutrality—the essayist has nowhere to hide (Scott Russell Sanders, "The Singular First Person").

Cumulative:
The root of all evil is that we all want this spiritual gratification, this flow, this apparent heightening of life, this knowledge, this valley of many-colored grass, even grass and light prismatically decomposed, giving ecstasy (D.H. Lawrence, *Studies in Classic American Literature*).

When the subject is delayed in this kind of construction, ensure that the verb agrees with the subject, which will follow the verb rather than precede it.

A writer can delay the main idea generating tension also by beginning with a prepositional phrase:

Behind the deconstructionists' dazzling cloud of language lie certain more or less indisputable facts (John Gardner, *The Art of Fiction*).

Other ways to achieve emphasis include parallel structures and repetition—techniques that also help in paragraph coherence—and rhythms that call the reader's attention to important ideas. The end of a sentence in itself provides emphasis, since a reader naturally slows down when approaching the last part of a sentence and pauses slightly between sentences.

The two paragraphs below employ parallel structures, repetition, and rhythm for emphasis.

A.

My professors, many of whom were to become very famous, did not tend to be philosophic and did not dig back into the sources of the new language and categories they were using. They thought that these were scientific discoveries like any others, which were to be used in order to make further discoveries. They were very much addicted to abstractions and generalizations, as Tocqueville predicted they would be. They believed in scientific progress and appeared (there may have been an element of boasting and self-irony in this) to be convinced that they were on the verge of a historic breakthrough in the social sciences, equivalent to that scored in the sixteenth and seventeenth centuries in the natural sciences . . . . These teachers were literally inebriated by the unconscious and values. And they were also sure that scientific progress would be related to social and political progress (Allan Bloom, *The Closing of the American Mind*).

Bloom employs the most common structural pattern of subject–verb–object in all his sentences, establishing a predictable rhetorical pattern that complements the predictability and uniformity of his professors that he wants to stress. Thus, *My professors*, the subject in the first sentence, is replaced by the pronoun *they* in the following three sentences; in the fourth sentence, *they* is the subject of two clauses. To avoid too many identical openings, Bloom continues with the same rhythm but varies the subject slightly: the last two sentences begin with *These teachers* and *And they*, respectively.

B.

Tales about Pythagoras flew to him and stuck like iron filings to a magnet. He was said, for example, to have appeared in several places at once and to have been reincarnated many times. Taken literally, this idea can be consigned to the same overflowing bin which contains the story that he had a golden thigh; but taken figuratively, it is an understatement. Pythagoras—or at least Pythagoreanism—was everywhere and still is (Anthony Gottlieb, *The Dream of Reason* 21).

The most obvious technique in paragraph B is the use of figurative language: Gottlieb uses a simile in the first sentence (*like iron filings to a magnet*) and a metaphor in the third sentence (*overflowing bin*). However, he effectively uses sentence length and rhythm to make the paragraph more appealing still. The paragraph is framed by short simple sentences that stress Pythagoras's prominence. The middle sentences develop the main idea through examples. Gottlieb's final sentence, though the shortest, contains strong stresses: the use of dashes allows the writer to repeat the name Pythagoras without seeming redundant, while heavy accents fall on the final two words.

3. Proofreading: Perfection *Is* Possible

In businesses related to publishing the written word, "editing" refers to the revising of the author's work before it is typeset, whether for a book, a newspaper, a magazine or journal, or some other print medium. Proofreading refers to the further checking of the typeset material that usually is in the form of paper "proofs" that have been printed from the typesetter's computer files.

While someone who edits and suggests revisions to a document is primarily concerned with improving and correcting it, the proofreader is looking for mistakes. The proofreader is the document's last line of defence before it falls under the public eye. Ironically, inadequate proofreading may be the first thing noticed in the published document.

In spite of its importance, the last proofreading to ensure that the "i"s are dotted and the "t"s are crossed is usually one of the neglected stages for student writers working under deadline to submit an essay. Exhausted from the final efforts of putting the essay together, students may think that tiny errors are inconsequential beside other parts of the process. However, distracting errors may strike your instructor in a completely different light. They could be interpreted as a symptom of carelessness and, as such, cast a poor light on your entire essay; worse, the marker could become annoyed by a succession of small mistakes and become unfairly critical of other parts of the essay.

Whether or not proofreading is seen as tedious, it is best performed as a mechanical process. By taking a disciplined, thorough, and systematic approach to the essay at this stage, students can be more confident that their work of many hours, days, or even weeks will be more readable to the person who assesses it.

3.1 Proofreading Methods

Documents may be read **in teams** with one person reading aloud while the other follows the printed copy silently. When it is your work being proofread, it's best if you read aloud since you may more easily catch errors you've missed as a writer. This method works on the principle that two readers are twice as likely to spot errors as one person; and it may be more enjoyable for some people than working alone. Clearly it works only if a second reader is available and both readers are knowledgeable about grammar and committed to the task.

Reading forward is the method of reading the paper aloud more slowly and carefully than you would usually do, paying attention both to the words and to the punctuation. Because it can be hard to concentrate solely on the words to the exclusion of the meaning, it's best to read through the essay at least once for meaning and then at least once again for spelling and other errors.

Reading Backwards is the method by which you start at the end and read to the beginning word by word or sentence by sentence. This technique forces a great deal of attention on the writing; it works well for catching spelling errors. However, it is time-consuming, may miss some punctuation and other "between the words" errors, and may miss some words because their context is harder to grasp.

Reading syllabically, you read from the beginning, breaking every word into its syllables. Of the four methods discussed, this is faster than reading backwards, works well for catching internal misspellings, is quite effective for catching missing and extra words and for correcting word endings (which may be overlooked when you read forward); however, it is a slower method than reading forward word by word, requires some discipline to master, and can be hard on the eyes if done for a prolonged time.

3.2 Guidelines for Proofreading

- Probably the main reason for essays with careless errors is that not enough time was allotted for proofing. The half hour *not* set aside for proofreading can undo the work of several hours.
- Plan, if possible, to let some time pass before you look at the essay for the final time (overnight is recommended).
- Having someone else go over the essay can be helpful but is no substitute for your own systematic proofing. Instructors are not likely to be sympathetic to the cry of baffled frustration, "But I had my roommate read it over!"
- Use Spell Checker but don't rely on it. Remember the poem that made the rounds on the Internet a few years ago: *Eye halve a spelling chequer / It came with my pea sea / It plainly marques for my revue / miss steaks eye kin knot sea . . . .* Spell checker will not see any difference between *there house is over their two* and *their house is over there too.*
- Experiment with the different proofreading methods discussed above and use the one(s) you feel most comfortable with and works best for you. When you start proofreading using one particular method, though, you should use it until you finish reading.

3.3 Common Errors

Here are categories of typical errors to watch for and correct in your writing.

- All areas where consistency is required—spelling, capitalization, abbreviations, hyphenation, numbers, internal punctuation, and other places where choices pertaining to the mechanics of writing may be involved
- Proper nouns (especially unfamiliar names), acronyms, etc. Are all references to authors and titles spelled correctly?
- Middles and endings of words, for spelling and for agreement
- Small words, such as articles and prepositions (*a, an, the, of, to, in, at, and, or, as, if, it,* etc.)
- Font style (Italic, bold, Roman: applied correctly and consistently? applied to *all* necessary words?) Have you used underlining (or italics—check with your instructor) for complete works, such as books and films, and placed works within larger works, such as essays, articles, short stories, and poems, within quotation marks?

- End punctuation (periods and question marks)
- Quotation marks applied appropriately? both "opening" and "closing" quotation marks present? Have double and single quotation marks been alternated correctly? periods and commas inside; colons and semicolons outside? Similar checks can be made for parentheses.
- All citations, both in-text and on the final page of the essay. Check both for accuracy (author, title, journal name, date, and page numbers) and for consistency. Are all citations documented according to the style of your discipline—including capitalization, punctuation, and other conventions?

4. Essay Presentation

Your audience and purpose are relevant to how you present your essay; for example, a scientific or engineering report probably would look quite different from an essay for English class—for one thing, it might have standardized headings, whereas the English essay would probably not. A research essay, too, must conform to the documentation style of your discipline; on the other hand, if you are writing a personal essay and not using references, presenting your essay may mostly be a matter of following directions for title, typeface, margins, spacing, indentation, page numbering, and appropriate identifying information.

Although there can be considerable variability in document design, there is one thing you can be sure of: if your professor asks you to format your essay a certain way, he or she will look to see that you followed these instructions. Therefore, if you are unsure about essay presentation, seek clarification by asking.

Unless you are told otherwise, you can refer to the following; it is based on MLA guidelines:

- Most instructors require essays to be typed. Use good-quality white paper, printing on one side. If you wish to conserve paper by printing on both sides, check with your instructor first; one-sided printing generally is considered to look neater and more professional.
- Leave 1-inch margins (2.5 cm) on all sides. The first page should include identification information positioned flush left (i.e., starting at the left margin). List information in the following order: your name and student ID, if applicable; instructor's name (use the title that your instructor prefers—e.g., Professor Carl Leggat, Dr. K. Blanco, Ms. J. Winestock, etc.); course number and section, if applicable; submission date. Double space, then insert the essay's title, centred.
- Double space the text of your essay; this makes it much easier for the instructor to correct errors and add comments. *Also double space* any Notes, the Works Cited page, and block quotations.
- Indent each paragraph five (5) spaces—do *not* use additional spaces to separate paragraphs, and leave a single space (not two spaces) after each period before beginning the next sentence.
- Number pages using Arabic numerals in the upper right-hand corner preceded by your last name; place about one-half inch (1.25 cm) from top and flush right; you can probably create this kind of header automatically using the "Insert" or a similar

function on your computer. If you need to include prefatory pages (such as a Contents page or a formal outline), use lower-case Roman numerals for those pages.

- Title pages are optional usually, though some instructors ask for title pages. Position the essay's title down one-third of the page with your name about half-way down; near the bottom of the page include course number, instructor's name, and submission date. All items should be centred. Begin your essay on the second page (numbered 1) under the centred title.

- No illustrations or colours, other than black and white, should be on any pages unless you use graphics directly relevant to your essay—for example, charts or diagrams for a scientific study. Use a paper clip to attach the pages (some instructors ask for stapled pages)—especially, don't dog-ear them. Don't use folders, clear or coloured, unless asked for. (If you do use a folder, the left-hand margin should be slightly wider than the other margins to enhance readability.)

- Prefer common fonts, such as Times New Roman, Arial, or Garamond (not Courier New or cursive ones). Use 10- to 12-point type size. *Do not* justify lines to the margins in academic papers or reports (i.e., set the paragraphing for flush left and use a *ragged* right line at the margin). Finally, ensure that the text of your essay is easy to read. An essay printed in draft mode or from a cartridge that is almost out of ink will not be easy to read.

5. Common Words That Confuse: Guide and Exercise

English has many word pairs that are confusing either because the two words look similar (for example, *affect* and *effect*) or because they have similar, but not identical, uses (for example, *amount* and *number*)—or both. In most cases, the dictionary is the best resource for unravelling difficulties that pertain solely to meaning, but usage can be a more complex matter. The words below are among those that continue to give student writers the most trouble. The "Top Twenty-five" have been distinguished and clarified in hints and examples.

Using a good dictionary and reliable guide to English usage, provide similar definitions, hints, and examples for the pairs below that are merely listed. For a guide to spelling, there is no better resource than the dictionary; if you have the slightest doubt about the spelling of a word, consult a dictionary—don't rely on a spell checker.

1. **Accept, Except—Accept** is a verb meaning "to receive, to take what is offered." **Except** is a preposition meaning "other than" or "leaving out."

   Hint:
   Think of the "crossing out" connotation of "x" in "except" to remind you that "except" means "leaving out."

   Example:
   The bargaining committee accepted all the terms except the last one.

2. **Affect, Effect—Affect** is a verb meaning "to influence or have an effect on." **Effect**, a noun, means "a result." As a verb, effect is less often used; it means "to bring about" or "to cause"—not "to have an effect on."

Hint:
Try substituting "influence" in the sentence; if it fits your intended meaning, "affect" is the word you want.

Example:
The news of Michael Jordan's return to basketball greatly affected his fans. The effect was also felt at the box office; an immediate hike in ticket prices was effected.

3. **Allot, A lot**—**Allot**, a verb, means "to portion out"; **a lot** can be an adverb (I sleep a lot) or a noun (I need a lot of sleep) meaning "a great deal." "A lot" is too informal for most academic writing; you should use the more formal "a great deal," "much," "many," or similar substitutes. The one-word spelling, "alot," is incorrect.

Example:
My parents allotted me $500 spending money for the term, which was not a lot considering my shopping habit. (informal)

4. **All right, Alright**—**All right** is all right, just as "a lot" is a lot better than "alot"; **alright** and "alot" are not words.

5. **Allude, Elude**—Both are verbs, but they mean different things. **Allude** (to) means "to refer to something briefly or indirectly"; **elude** means "to avoid or escape, usually through a clever manoeuvre or strategy." "Allude" should be followed by "to": e.g., "In the poem, Hardy alluded to the end of the century."

Hint:
"Allude" is the verb from which the noun "allusion" (a kind of reference, see *Allusion*) is formed; you can associate the "e" in "elude" with the "e" in "escape."

Example:
In his prison memoirs, the bank robber alluded to the time in the desert when he eluded capture by disguising himself as a cactus.

6. **Allusion, Illusion**—You may have come across the literary use of **allusion**, meaning an historical, religious, mythic, literary, or other kind of outside reference used thematically or to reveal character in a work. An **illusion** is something apparently seen that is not real or is something that gives a false impression.

Hint:
Since the most common mistake is misspelling "allusion" as "illusion" in literary essays, you could remember that "allusion," meaning an outside reference, *al*ways begins with "*al*."

Examples:
The title of Nathanael West's novel *The Day of the Locust* is an allusion to the Book of Exodus in the Bible.

Optical illusions often use graphics to fool our senses.

7. **Among, Amongst**

8. **Among, Between**—The simple distinction is that **between** refers to two persons or things and **among** to more than two.

   Example:
   The Senator found himself between a rock and a hard place.

   Ms. O'Grady stood among her adoring students for the school picture.

   Between may be the obvious choice even if more than two things are involved. For example, "Interlibrary loans are permitted between campuses." Even though a number of campuses may be part of the interlibrary loan system, any one exchange takes place between two campuses.

9. **Amount, Number**—Use **amount** to refer to things that can't be counted; **number** refers to countable objects.

   Hint:
   Think of using numbers when you count.

   Example:
   The number of errors in this essay reveals the amount of care you took in writing it.

10. **As, Like**

11. **Attain, Obtain**

12. **Beside, Besides**—**Beside** is a preposition meaning "next to," "adjoining"; **besides** has several meanings as a preposition; as an adverb **besides** means "in addition (to)."

    Hint:
    Think of the extra "s" in besides as an additional letter to remind you of "in addition to."

    Example:
    Beside the telephone was the telephone book, besides which she had an address book.

13. **Bias, Biased**—**Bias** is a noun that refers to a "tendency to judge unfairly"; **biased** is an adjective that means "having or showing a preferential attitude." A person can have a bias (a thing); be a biased person (adjective modifying "person"); or can be biased (predicate adjective after a linking verb). A person cannot be bias. Also, a person is biased or has a bias *against* (not *to* or *for*) something or someone.

Example:
His bias against the Gothic style applied to science fiction made him overlook the clever plot twists in *Dune*.

14. **Cite, Sight, Site—To cite**, a verb, is "to refer to an outside source." (The complete naming of the source itself is a citation.) **Sight** (noun or verb) refers to seeing, one of the five senses. **Site**, when used as a noun, is a location or place (usually of some importance). The most common error in essays is the use of "site" when "cite" is meant.

Hint:
Remember that "cite" is a verb referring to "the act of giving a citation"; "site" is "where something is situated or sits."

Example:
She said the ruins were excavated in 1926, citing as proof the historic plaque that commemorated the site.

15. **Compare With, Compare To**

16. **Complement, Compliment**

17. **Comprise, Compose**

18. **Conscience, Conscious**

19. **Continual(ly), Continuous(ly)**

20. **Could Of/Would Of, Could Have, Would Have**

21. **Different From, Different Than**

22. **e.g., i.e.—E.g.** is an abbreviation for the Latin *exempli gratia*, meaning "for the sake of example"; **i.e.** is an abbreviation for the Latin *id est* meaning "that is." Use "e.g." ahead of one or more examples; use "i.e." if you want to elaborate on or clarify preceding statements. In both cases, use a period after each letter and a comma after the abbreviation. Because they are abbreviations, they should be avoided in formal writing.

Hint:
The first letter in "example" tells you that examples should follow "e.g.".

Examples:
J.K. Rowling defied the common formula for success in the children's book market by writing long novels, e.g., *Harry Potter and the Goblet of Fire*, *Harry Potter and the Order of the Phoenix*. Some of Rowling's novels have episodic plots that contain many well-developed characters, i.e., their structures tend towards length.

23. **Farther, Further**

24. **Fewer, Less—Fewer** is the quantitative adjective of comparison and refers to things that can be counted; **less** is the qualitative adjective of comparison, referring to amount and things that can be measured.

    Examples:
    Don't believe the notice on the mayonnaise jar: "Contains 40% less calories." Calories can be counted.

    There were fewer than a dozen people at the nomination meeting.

    The less said about his defection, the better.

25. **Former, Latter**

26. **Good, Well—Good** may be an adjective, noun, or adverb. When used as an adjective, it should clearly modify a noun (e.g., a good story) or be used as a subjective complement (predicate adjective, e.g., the child was good until bedtime). It cannot be used as a predicate adjective after verbs that express an action, although it is frequently heard in speech, especially in sports ("I was hitting the ball good"). The association of "good" strictly with moral value ("I feel good" must mean "I am feeling virtuous") or worth ("That watch looks good" must mean "that watch looks to be a good one") and in that way distinct from "well" has become eroded. "I feel good" may refer to feeling healthy; "That watch looks good" may refer to its satisfactory or attractive appearance.

    Incorrect:
    She beat the batter good.

    Correct:
    She is a good cook and beat the batter well.

    The hat looks well on her. The dress looks good, too. The outfit makes her look like a model.

    As an adjective, **well** means "in good health" or "satisfactory." As an adverb, it has several meanings, including "thoroughly" and "satisfactorily," as in the *Correct* examples above.

    Hint:
    Do not use "good" as a predicate adjective after an action verb; you may use it before a noun or right after an intransitive (linking) verb.

    Examples:
    Making a good donation to the Children's Hospital made the corporation look good (i.e., "appear altruistic" *not* "appear good-looking").

Although just having come out of the hospital, she looked well and continued to feel well during her recovery. (i.e., "well" is used as an adjective after the intransitive, or linking, verbs and means "healthy.")

27. **Imply, Infer**

28. **Its, It's**—**Its** is a possessive adjective meaning "belonging to it." Remember that a pronoun possessive form is never spelled with an apostrophe. **It's** is the contraction for "it is," the apostrophe indicating that the letter "i" is left out.

    Hint:
    Try substituting "it is" if you're having problems identifying the correct form; if it fits, then use it's; if it doesn't, use its. (Its is usually followed by a noun.)

    Example:
    It's foolish to judge a book by its cover.

29. **Lay, Lie**—Both are verbs. **Lay** is a transitive verb, which must always be followed by a direct object (either a noun or a pronoun). Although it appears archaically in poetry and in song, it is *incorrect* to say, "I'm going to lay down to rest." **Lie** is an intransitive verb; it is not followed by an object.

    Hint:
    You always *lay* something down, as a hen does an egg. Then it *lies* there.

    Examples:
    He lay the baby in the crib before going to lie down.

    Contrast:
    He had *lain* on the ground for twenty minutes before someone noticed him. (*lain* is the past participle of *lie*)

    Kim Campbell *laid* to rest the notion that a woman couldn't be Prime Minister. (*laid* is the past participle of *lay*)

30. **Led, Lead**—**Led** and **lead** are forms of the irregular verb **to lead** (long ē); the present tense is also **lead**. However, the past tense and the past participle are **led** (short ĕ). Writers may become confused by the noun "lead," the metal, which looks like "to lead," but is pronounced like "led." Therefore, when they come to write the past tense "led," they may wrongly substitute the noun "lead," rather than the verb.

    Hint:
    Don't be led astray by thinking there is an "a" in "led."

    Example:
    Although she led in the polls by a 2:1 margin three months ago, today she leads by only a slight margin.

31. **Loose, Lose**—**Loose** is the adjective meaning "not tight"; **lose** is a verb meaning "not to be able to find," or "to be defeated."

    Hint:
    When you lose something, it is lost. "Lost" is spelled with one "o."

    Example:
    If you don't tighten that loose button, you're going to lose it.

32. **More Than, Over**

33. **On, Upon**

34. **Onset, Outset**—Both are nouns that mean a "beginning." **Outset** means "setting out," for example, on a journey or to do something; you can also use the phrase "at the outset" to refer to the early events of a narrative or play. **Onset** refers to a force or condition that comes upon one.

    Example:
    At the outset of my fourth decade, I experienced the onset of mild osteoarthritis.

35. **Passed, Past**

36. **Principal, Principle**

37. **Raise, Rise**

38. **Recur, Reoccur**

39. **So, Very**

40. **Than, Then**—**Than** is a conjunction used in comparisons (He's happier than he knows). **Then** is an adverb with temporal connotations meaning "consequently," "at that time," "after that," etc.

    Hint:
    If you're comparing one thing to *an*other, use "th*an*." "Then 'tells when'."

    Example:
    Warren said he was better at darts than Mark, and then he challenged him to a game to prove it.

41. **That, Which**—See Part Seven, Section 5.1. #3.

42. **Their, There, They're**—**Their** is a possessive adjective meaning "belonging to them"; **there** is an adverb meaning "in that place"; **they're** is the contraction of "they are," the apostrophe indicating that the letter "a" is left out.

Hint:

If you're uncertain about "they're," substitute "they are"; "there" (meaning "in that place") is spelled the same as here ("in this place") with the letter "t" added.

Example:

There is no excuse for the rowdy behavior in there; they're supposed to be in their rooms.

43. **Through, Thru**

44. **Till, Until**

45. **To, Too—To** is a preposition indicating "direction towards"; **too** is an adverb meaning "also."

Hint:

"To" will usually be followed by a noun or pronoun as part of a prepositional phrase; substitute "also" for "too."

Example:

The next time you go to the store, may I come along, too?

46. **Usage, Use—**Many writers overuse **usage,** which refers to "a customary or habitual pattern or practise." It applies to conventions of groups of people, such as "language usage of the English." Usage shouldn't be used simply to characterize a repeated action.

Incorrect:

The usage of fax machines and e-mail has allowed businesses to increase their efficiency.

Example:

I have no use for people who are always correcting my usage of "whom."

47. **Weather, Whether**

48. **Were, We're, Where**

49. **Who's, Whose—Who's** is the contraction of "who is," the apostrophe indicating the omission of the letter "i." **Whose** is the possessive adjective meaning "belonging to whom?"

Hint:

Try substituting "who is." If it fits, then "who's" is the correct form.

Example:

Whose turn is it to do the dishes?

Who's going to do the dishes tonight?

50. **You're, Your—You're** is the contraction of "you are"; **your** is a possessive adjective that means "belonging to you."

Hint:

Try substituting "you are." If it fits, then "you're" is the correct form.

Example:

You're going to be sorry if you don't take your turn and do the dishes tonight.

APPENDIX A

Tense Encounters with Verbs: A Summary

"Tense" refers to time when the action or condition expressed by the verb took place (or is taking place, or will take place). Each *tense* can take one of four *forms*: **simple, progressive, perfect, and perfect progressive**. These forms further describe the aspect of the verb, as to when its action began, and its duration or completion.

The auxiliary (helping) verb for most forms determines the complete form of the verb. The auxiliary verb for the progressive tenses is "to be" (is, was, will be); for the perfect tenses, it is "to have" (has, had, will have).

1. Present Tenses

Simple Present (action or situation exists now or exists on a regular basis):

I call	We call
You call	You call
He/she/it calls	They call

I usually call for the pizza; you call for it this time.

Present Progressive (action is in progress):

I am sending	We are sending
You are sending	You are sending
He/she/it is sending	They are sending

Mr. Kahn is sending the package to you by courier.

Present Perfect (action began in the past and is completed in the present):

I have eaten	We have eaten
You have eaten	You have eaten
He/she/it has eaten	They have eaten

I have eaten the apple you gave me.

Present Perfect Progressive (action began in the past, continues in the present, and may continue into the future):

I have been hoping	We have been hoping
You have been hoping	Your have been hoping
He/she/it has been hoping	They have been hoping

We have been hoping to receive news from the Philippines.

2. Past Tenses

Simple Past (action or situation was completed in the past):

I saw	We saw
You saw	You saw
He/she/it saw	They saw

Garfield saw the moon rise last night over his burrow.

Past Progressive (action was in progress in the past):

I was talking	We were talking
You were talking	You were talking
He/she/it was talking	They were talking

James and Beth were talking about storms when the hurricane warning flashed onto their computer screen.

Past Perfect (action was completed in the past prior to another action in the past):

I had finished	We had finished
Your had finished	You had finished
He/she/it had finished	They had finished

Alex had finished the second assignment when the storm knocked out power to his computer.

Past Perfect Progressive (action in progress in the past):

I had been practicing	We had been practicing
You had been practicing	You had been practicing
He/she/it had been practicing	They had been practicing

The golf team sophomores had been practicing for the tournament all summer, but when school started their coach announced his resignation.

3. Future Tenses

Simple Future (action will occur in the future):

I will see	We will see
You will see	You will see
He/she/it will see	They will see

I will see the Rocky Mountains on my way to Vancouver.

Future Progressive (action will be continuous in the future).

I will be walking	We will be walking
You will be walking	You will be walking
He/she/it will be walking	They will be walking

Norm and Martee will be walking in the Marathon of Hope next Saturday morning.

Future Perfect (action in the future will be completed):

I will have gone	We will have gone
You will have gone	You will have gone
He/she/it will have gone	They will have gone

Sally will have gone around the moon several times before the ship leaves its lunar orbit.

Future Perfect Progressive (actions are ongoing up to a specific future time):

I will have been studying	We will have been studying
You will have been studying	You will have been studying
He/she/it will have been studying	They will have been studying

With the completion of this assignment they will have been studying verbs for 13 years.

Remember that verbs can reflect mood (conditional, subjunctive) and voice (active, passive), and auxiliary verbs can be used to indicate **conditions**, such as necessity (I should go), obligation (you must go), possibility (he may go).

Exercise

In the following passages, some of the verb forms are correct, but others need to be changed. All verbs are underlined; correct those that are incorrect.

A.

Nature was a precious gift. It provide energies that affect society today. Although it is a gift, nature needs our attention and care because it is fragile and easily destroyed. I never paid much attention to nature because I thought humanity's impact on the natural world was not important. A few years ago, an encounter with a squirrel has changed my view. I walk home one day, and I saw a gray squirrel picking up loose pine cones in the garden. I am watching the squirrel hopping joyfully around the yard. Suddenly, it starts to run across the street. But before it reached the other side of the street, a car hit it and killed it. I am devastated that the driver didn't even slow down, as if the life of a squirrel is worthless.

We should always respect what nature has offered us. The natural world is an important factor in maintaining a healthy life cycle. If this life cycle is not protected, the balance in the life cycle is destroyed, which will bring serious consequences to the lives of all human beings.

B.

I remember a camping trip that I was going on with a few of my friends. We were very unprepared and run into a few mishaps along the way. The trip occurred during the rainy season, and we have not brought any firewood. We have a hard time getting the fire to start, even after we borrowed wood and an axe from the campers next door. Of course, we forgot to bring a can opener, so we had to try stabbing at the tins with a Swiss army knife to get them open. We spend the night around our Coleman stove, trying to keep warm.

That night made us realize how much we took nature for granted. In our homes everyday we had many household appliances that made our lives easier for us. It is easy to forget that some people live in the world without these conveniences and relied on nature from dawn to dusk. This camping trip occurred a long time ago when I am much younger.
But the memory of that long night in the nature stays with me ever since.

APPENDIX B

The Journalistic Essay

You may be most familiar with the hard news story that appears under terse headlines in the front section of your daily newspaper along with dramatic photographs and eye-grabbing graphics. On the other hand, you may automatically turn to the "soft" feature pages that comprise part of lifestyle, arts and entertainment, or business supplements to weekend editions. Even the more specialized features are intended to have broad appeal; like the other forms of mass media, newspapers and magazines depend for their revenue on advertisers, and advertisers will invest in the places their ads can be assured maximum exposure. Along with reader demographics, which are used to profile the *kind* of reader likely to frequent any particular section of a newspaper, *size* of readership is the most important factor in decisions to invest advertising dollars.

Age-old formulas for concrete, direct writing are still drilled into journalism students and practised by professional journalists. Hard news stories use the inverted pyramid style of story construction with the vital questions (the "5 W's"—who, what, when, where, and why—and the one "H"—how) answered in the first paragraph, if possible. Older or less important information is put in the last paragraphs, where it can be easily cut if space is needed.

The nearly encyclopedic breadth of many dailies today is explained, in part, by competition from non-print media that offer a visual kaleidoscope envied by newspapers and magazines that they may try to emulate but can never quite match. Although print media cannot attract, entertain, divert, or stimulate their audience in the way that audio-visual media can, they *are* able to provide a wealth and depth of information succinctly to large groups of people—not just through news items, sports reports, stock market summaries, and the like, but through longer features that research and address the complexities of issues people encounter daily. Newspapers carry articles on timely and significant issues in the fields of science, technology, education, justice, culture, and politics.

Investigative journalism strives to shed light on contemporary issues of importance, which may have been under-reported in other media, or not covered at all. Like other forms of journalism, investigative reporting seeks a wide audience and uses many of the strategies of routine journalistic writing. These kinds of essays, along with feature and editorial-page writing in general, differ in two ways from essays in the academic disciplines:

1. Because they inevitably appear soon after being written, they can focus on issues that many readers relate to, understand, and are concerned about.
2. Because they anticipate a wide readership, they are usually informal in language and style, accommodating their readership for easy access to information and rapid assimilation at an average reading speed.

Of course, investigative essays are not the only kinds of journalistic writing that have these qualities. In most kinds of journalistic writing, currency and accessibility are essential attributes. The products of print media are designed for reading ease and speed so you can pick them up and put them down, or read them while you are on your way somewhere or otherwise putting in time.

However, longer, more analytical journalistic pieces, such as investigative essays, also share some important features with academic essays:

1. Many are lengthy, provide considerable detail, and rely heavily on external sources.
2. They are well-researched.
3. Though investigative journalism purports to deal with factual information—and can therefore be considered an example of expository writing—it contains an implied argument.

Some Features of Journalistic Writing

Style

- Language is simple, direct, and informal; colloquialisms—even slang—may abound, and contractions are almost always acceptable.
- Compressed constructions that are common in formal writing, such as appositives, are even more frequent in journalistic writing.
- Paragraphs are usually short, sometimes as short as one sentence, though four- to six-sentence paragraphs are not uncommon in longer journalistic works.
- References to the first-person are frequent in feature writing of all kinds—the writer may speak in the first-person "observer" voice, or as a first-person "participant" in works of creative non-fiction or literary journalism. The first-person participant is very common in the more formulaic kinds of journalism, such as travel and lifestyle features.

Content and Structure

- Because most journalistic prose presumes a wide readership, there is usually a greater stress on strategies to attract and keep the reader's interest—the "hook," for example, which refers to a catchy way to begin a journalistic piece of writing. Therefore, journalistic features, even investigative ones, are far less likely to use the logical approach to creating interest and are more likely to use a dramatic or emotional appeal at or near the beginning of the piece.
- Description and narration are much more common than in academic writing.
- Writers will briefly summarize complex or detailed material before moving on to the next point; in such instances, clarity and reading ease will supplant space considerations. Writers of scholarly articles will assume the reader's specialized knowledge of the topic—and will accordingly confine summaries to the beginning and ending of the article under the heading "abstract" or "conclusion."
- Facts and figures may be used extensively, but writers will try to make them accessible through analogies, similes, metaphors, and comparisons to familiar, everyday objects—another strategy to stimulate reader interest and help the reader understand the content.
- Writers of journalistic essays may refer to previous studies and other written documentation, but are likely to make greater use of contemporary authorities whose comments are reported orally through direct quotation or paraphrase.
- Interesting but not directly relevant issues or topics may be dispensed with altogether or written as mini-essays with a separate heading and used as *sidebars* accompanying the main story; a sidebar may also focus intensively on one particular aspect of the main story.

A Special Case:
On-line Learning and Writing

Increasingly, students and teachers alike are discovering the advantages of using computers for more than word-processing. A few years ago, only the most adventurous teachers were creating Web pages; now, students can take full courses on-line and many courses include on-line components. Although "on-line" is equated with "innovative," it is becoming more likely that you will encounter some kind of Internet classroom during your post-secondary education.

Many students are hesitant to take Web-based courses, thinking that sophisticated computer skills might be required. However, if you can use a word-processing program to create text documents and if you can manage e-mail, you already possess the basic skills for any on-line learning situation. Although systems of course delivery vary, they are designed to be used by people who are not computer specialists, and they all include support networks for those who encounter difficulties. In addition to the "help" links that every system includes, however, is another resource: most institutions have on-line "help desks" that students can access via the Internet or by telephone. If your keyboard freezes or your system crashes, someone is nearby to talk you through each step of the recovery process. Each encounter with such resources has an additional benefit: one learns a bit more about using servers and/or software, which increases self-confidence.

On-line curriculum delivery offers considerable flexibility and independence, but places more responsibility on the student than classroom learning does. You need disciplined work habits and awareness of your own writing strengths, for example. No one will remind you to complete your readings or your assignments, and computer-related problems are considered poor excuses for late essays. If you have questions about course materials, you need to take the initiative and contact your instructor directly. For students who tend to let more talkative peers speak up in class, this setting will not help you to change your habits and you may find yourself disadvantaged.

On the other hand, many introverted students find it much easier to communicate with their teachers via e-mail, enjoying the freedom of anonymity. Many students are attracted to on-line learning because of its unusual freedom and adaptability: like more traditional forms of distance education, students frequently have the option of creating their own work schedules, by deciding on when they "attend" class, for instance. However, unlike traditional distance education courses, on-line courses usually offer greater student-teacher and student-student interaction.

Most on-line courses feature some kind of "discussion" forum in which students and their teachers communicate by posting messages (like e-mail messages) organized into specific topic areas. Such "message boards" allow you to "speak" publicly—in much the same way that you would in a classroom—and receive comments or feedback from others in the course. These discussion forums allow private communication, too: instead of e-mailing a classmate or your teacher through your regular server, course e-mail/discussions are restricted to people registered in your course.

The amount and frequency of contact within a class can vary widely, as do the kinds of assignments. Many students prefer to post their thoughts at least weekly; they feel less isolated, and the familiarity allows them to ask questions with less self-consciousness. In on-line writing courses, regular participation is extremely helpful, because you are writing constantly. Most student writers in such courses discover that their writing skills improve even more dramatically than in more conventional settings, because the more they write, the easier it becomes.

The kinds of assignments you will encounter in an on-line writing course will be roughly equivalent to those you would find in any university writing course. There may be group projects and presentations, "timed" essays and quizzes, as well as chat rooms for "real time" discussions. Usually, the syllabus for the course will look like any you would receive in person, although course descriptions may include more detail. The same is true of the course notes: teachers generally try to anticipate questions or difficulties more overtly than they would in the classroom and the amount of work will be about the same.

A Sample On-line Discussion

What follows is an excerpt from an on-line discussion of the short story "The Demon Lover," by Anglo-Irish writer Elizabeth Bowen. The story is set during the London Blitz of 1941, the most infamous of the WW II bombings of England. As the protagonist, Mrs. Drover, searches in her London house for items to take back to her temporary home in the country, she finds a mysterious letter apparently written by her lover, a soldier to whom she had made a rash vow 25 years before. Gradually, she becomes convinced that the lover, presumed dead, is in the house with her and expects her to meet him at the "prearranged hour." The discussion topic below addresses the nature of the story as either a supernatural tale or a story of psychological breakdown.

Author : AMANDA CAMPBELL
Date: Monday, February 21, 2005 11:55am
    Could it be that Mrs. Drover herself might be dead? Could it be that she is coming back to this house which seems to be rundown and where the caretaker no longer works? As Mrs. Drover passed, "no human eye watched her." This might imply that she does not exist and therefore no one can see her. She is a supernatural body that has come back to the place where she once lived. Maybe she does not know herself that she is dead and that she believes that she is alive. Words used early in the story, such as "dead," "shuttered," "dark," and "dead air," led me to believe that there was some supernatural element. The letter from her lost love might have been sitting on the table for years waiting for her to come home to. But maybe it could all be just a dream. The screams that come from Mrs. Drover at the end of the story may indicate her waking up from a horrible dream.

Author: ERIKA JOHNSON
Date: Monday, February 21, 2005 1:05pm
    My initial thoughts were aligned with Amanda's in that it appears as though Mrs. Drover has died. In the first few paragraphs, Bowen describes a scene that is dark and gloomy, and repeatedly uses "dead" to affirm the lifeless, cold atmosphere of the house. Also, if Mrs. Drover had a caretaker for the house and he was off that particular week, there is no way a house could accumulate so much dirt, dust, and film in such a short time. After reading the story over again, it would be my guess that Mrs. Drover is in fact having a sort of mental breakdown where all her past thoughts and emotions are rushing up, possibly because of the letter. Although she may be dreaming, the letter is a sort of catalyst to confront and deal with her past experiences (involving her presumably dead fiancé). Through her dream she is able to walk through the vacant house and experience the life that she once had. The letter symbolizes lost love and gives her a chance to remember and reflect on a life that could have been.

Author: ALSTON ACHARYA

Date: Monday, February 21, 2005 2:40pm

   One of the reasons I feel the story is psychological is the strict focus on the main character. If there were other characters, someone to witness a ghost or something of that sort, then it could be more easily considered supernatural. But since there is only one major character, all focus is on her and her perception. If it's a psychological story of how she loses her mind and is dealing with her own guilt, then no witness is necessary.

Author: MARIE PERRY

Date: Monday, February 21, 2005 2:59pm

   I think "The Demon Lover" is a supernatural tale showing the horrors of war. The setting focuses on bombs and bombing, and Mrs. Drover thinks of the bombs. Mrs. Drover is haunted by this sinister lover who seems to be war itself. Women's lovers left for war, and they made promises to wait for each other, just as Mrs. Drover did to the faceless man. When he dies she is upset and eventually tries to start life anew. The letter from the lover brings back memories of this horrid war and inspires panic and anxiety from her. When she meets him in the taxi, it is as though she has come face to face with one of the most terrifying things in the world, something that shouldn't have a face. Mrs. Drover meets a supernatural devil who takes her to hell, and that devil is war. What person in his or her right mind wouldn't scream?

Author: OLIVER LECLAIR

Date: Monday, February 21, 2005 8:26pm

   Before reading Amanda's response, the possibility of Mrs. Drover being dead did not register. Having reread the story with the idea of her being dead, I can see that the letter itself supports it. The letter was delivered to a "shuttered" house, and only the absent caretaker had access to the house. The letter was not addressed and lay on undisturbed dust, which implies that a person did not place it there. The possibility of Mrs. Drover's death is implied within the letter itself when the writer "K" states that "nothing has changed." Death is perpetual. Finally, the "arranged" hour that Mrs. Drover so desperately tries to avoid and the fact that the letter applies to whatever day she reads it convey the sense of her trying to escape either a death that has already arrived or that she knows is inevitable and near.

Author: LIAM BRIDGER

Date: Monday, February 21, 2005 11:51pm

   I see this story as being a dream or, I suppose, a nightmare. The idea of Mrs. Drover not being watched by any human eye can be thought of as no one else around, simply because no one needs to be around in a dream. The feelings of paranoia are consistent with the common dream of being chased where you sense something is after you but have no clue where it may be. Certainly the ending where the victim meets the horrible face mere inches apart strikes me as supernatural, almost a cliché movie ending. However, it could also lean towards the psychological, as the dreams and nightmares of people, though perhaps including supernatural entities, are still conjured up by disturbed minds.

APPENDIX D

Peer Edit Forms

Peer Edit Form: Formal Outline

The essay outline provides the structure on which the essay itself will be built. Therefore, as an editor, you should pay special attention to the relation among the parts (Introduction, body paragraphs, Conclusion), to the order of arguments (weakest to strongest? strongest to weakest? some other logical order?), as well as to the strength and effectiveness of each main point. Are they adequately developed? Is the claim supported?

Instructions

Use the check boxes below to record the fact that you have considered and evaluated the criteria. Use the space following to add suggestions, comments, questions, and advice.

Introduction

❏ Does it attract your interest?

❏ Does it announce the topic?

❏ Does it contain a two-part direct thesis statement announcing the topic and showing the reader what the writer contends *about* the topic?

❏ Is the claim one of fact, value, or policy?

❏ Is the thesis statement interesting, specific and manageable?

    ❏ interesting

    ❏ specific

    ❏ manageable

Body Paragraphs

❏ Does each paragraph contain at least one main idea that can be easily identified as such? If not, which paragraph(s) don't do this?

❏ Does each paragraph contain at least two sub-points that help develop the main point? If not, which paragraph(s) don't?

❏ Has the writer been able to provide support for his/her argument? If not, suggest ways that he/she could use kinds of evidence to do this (e.g., examples, facts/statistics, personal experience, outside sources, etc.)

❏ Do the paragraphs appear to be organized using any of the rhetorical patterns discussed in Part Three, Section 1.1. e.g., definition, cause/effect, problem-solution, compare and contrast? If not, what method seems appropriate for any of the paragraphs? If one or more of the paragraphs are organized in any of these ways, does the method seem appropriate to the main idea/topic?

❏ Are the main points ordered in a logical and persuasive way? If not, what could you suggest as an alternate arrangement?

❏ Are there at least two levels represented in the outline (main points and sub-points)? Are the elements of co-ordination and subordination applied correctly? Is parallel structure applied to main points and the levels of sub-points?

Conclusion

❏ Does it successfully summarize or restate the argument without sounding repetitious?

❏ Does it go beyond the introduction by enlarging on the implications of the thesis, by urging a change in thought or call to action, or by making an ethical or emotional appeal?

Final Comments or Suggestions?

Writer's Name: _____

Editor's Name: _____

Peer Edit Form: Argumentative Essay First Draft

Your first draft is the stage at which you make the transition from large-scale structural concerns to those focusing on your developing argument—in your final draft, you will work further on these areas, along with clear expression, grammatically sound prose, etc., responding to editorial suggestions as well as your clearer conception of your argument as a result of having written the draft.

Instructions

Use the check boxes below to record the fact that you have considered and evaluated the criteria. Use the space following to add suggestions, comments, questions, and advice. In addition, *underline places in the essay where you would like to draw the writer's attention to possible grammatical problems* (such as fragments, comma splices, apostrophe problems, lack of parallelism, misplaced or dangling modifiers, pronoun agreement, case, and/or consistency), *or stylistic problems* (such as passive constructions or other instances where the writing could be made more concise, direct, or forceful—you should also note possible spelling errors along with errors in mechanics and presentation).

Introduction

❑ Does the Introduction function successfully?
  ❑ interesting?
  ❑ announces subject and contains thesis statement; is the claim arguable?
  ❑ suggests the main way the argument will be organized? (e.g., definition, cause/effect, time order, division, compare and contrast, question/answer, etc.)
  ❑ does the writer establish him/herself as credible and trustworthy? How?

Body Paragraphs

❑ Does the argument seem complete, and does the order of the paragraphs appear logical?
❑ Look at paragraphs individually. Are any too short? Too long?
❑ Is each paragraph unified (relates to one main idea)? If not, which one(s) aren't?
❑ Is each paragraph coherent? If not, which one(s) aren't?
❑ Do paragraphs contain topic sentences?
❑ Is the order of the sentences natural?
❑ Are there appropriate transitions between sentences, enabling you to see the relationship between consecutive sentences?
❑ Does the writer successfully use repetition, rephrasing, synonyms or other devices to achieve coherence?
❑ Does each paragraph seem developed adequately?
❑ Are there different organizational methods used to develop the argument? Which ones? Are they effective?
❑ What kinds of evidence are produced? Are they used effectively? You don't have to refer to specific paragraphs—only note if they appear to be present to help support the thesis:
  ❑ examples, illustrations?
  ❑ personal experience?
  ❑ analogies
  ❑ precedents?
  ❑ outside authorities/secondary sources?
  ❑ other?
❑ Are there points where the argument seems strained, weak, incomplete, and/or illogical? Are there any fallacies (e.g., cause/effect fallacies, fallacies of irrelevance, emotional/ethical fallacies)?

Conclusion

❑ Does the conclusion function as a satisfying ending? Does it summarize and/or generalize?

Other Criteria

❑ Has the arguer presented him/herself credibly?

❑ Conveyed knowledge?

❑ Seems trustworthy and reliable?

❑ Appears to be fair?

❑ Is the opposing view acknowledged?

❑ Is the writer's voice impartial and objective?

❑ Are there any examples of slanted language?

❑ Is the opposing view successfully refuted (as in the point-by-point method)?

❑ Has the writer used any elements of style to assist in the argument (e.g., imagery, analogies—figurative language, distinctive voice or tone, particular choice of words, sentence variety, etc.)? Can you suggest any additional stylistic features that might help?

❑ Are there any places in the draft where the language seemed unclear or where a point was unclear due to the way it was expressed?

❑ If the writer used sources, are they integrated smoothly and grammatically? Are all direct quotations, summaries, paraphrases, ideas acknowledged?

Final Comments or Suggestions?

Writer's Name: _____

Editor's Name: _____

Peer Edit Form: Expository Essay First Draft

Your first draft is the stage at which you make the transition from large-scale structural concerns to those focusing on integrating your research with your own ideas to create a synthesis—in your final draft, you will work further on these areas, along with the attempt to achieve conciseness, clear expression, grammatically sound prose, etc.

Instructions: Use the check boxes below to record the fact that you have considered and evaluated the criteria. Use the space following to add suggestions, comments, questions, and advice. In addition, *underline places in the essay where you would like to draw the writer's attention to possible grammatical problems* (such as fragments, comma splices, apostrophes, lack of parallelism, misplaced or dangling modifiers, pronoun agreement and/or consistency), *or stylistic problems* (such as passive constructions or other instances where the writing could be made more concise, direct, or forceful—you should also note possible spelling errors along with errors in mechanics and presentation).

Introduction

❑ Is the Introduction successful?
   ❑ interesting?
   ❑ announces subject and contains thesis statement with a *claim of fact*, a hypothesis to be tested, or a question to be answered?
   ❑ suggests the main way the argument will be organized?
❑ Does the writer establish him/herself as credible and trustworthy? How?

Body Paragraphs

❑ Does the essay seem complete, and does the order of the paragraphs appear logical?
❑ Look at paragraphs individually. Are any too short? Too long?
❑ Is each paragraph unified (relates to one main idea)? If not, which one(s) aren't?
❑ Is each paragraph coherent? If not, which one(s) aren't?
❑ Do paragraphs contain topic sentences?
❑ Is the order of the sentences natural?
❑ Are there appropriate transitions between sentences, enabling you to see the relationship between consecutive sentences?
❑ Does the writer successfully use repetition, rephrasing, synonyms or other devices to achieve coherence?
❑ Does each paragraph seem developed adequately?
❑ Has the writer used secondary sources effectively? Note any exceptions.
❑ Do all the sources seem reliable?
❑ Does the writer use a sufficient number of sources? Is there an over-reliance on one source? Which one?
❑ Does the writer show familiarity with the sources used?
❑ Do the secondary sources appear to be relevant to the points discussed?
❑ Is each reference integrated smoothly into the essay?
   ❑ stylistically?
   ❑ grammatically?
❑ Has the context been made sufficiently clear in each instance?
❑ Do brackets and ellipses appear to have been used correctly?
❑ Are any other kinds of evidence produced in addition to secondary sources (for example, analogies, personal experience, illustrations, or examples)?
❑ Does the essay appear to be fundamentally focused on exposition (explaining) rather than argumentation (persuasion)?

Conclusion

❏ Does the conclusion function as a satisfying ending? Does it summarize and/or generalize?

Other Criteria

❏ Has the writer presented him/herself credibly?

❏ Conveyed knowledge?

❏ Seems trustworthy and reliable?

❏ Appears to be fair?

❏ Is the writer's voice impartial and objective?

❏ Has the writer used any elements of style to assist in the argument (e.g., imagery, analogies—figurative language, distinctive voice or tone, particular choice of words, sentence variety, etc.)? Can you suggest any additional stylistic features that might help?

❏ Are there any places in the draft where the language seemed unclear or where a point was unclear due to the way it was expressed?

Final Comments or Suggestions?

Writer's Name: _____

Editor's Name: _____

Peer Edit Form: Literary Essay First Draft

Your first draft is the stage at which you make the transition from large-scale structural concerns to your developing argument—in your final draft, you will refine your argument and polish it with clear expression, grammatical prose, perfect punctuation, and your own finishing touches.

Intructions

1. Check the item when you have considered and evaluated the criterion.
2. Use the space following to add suggestions, comments, questions, and advice.
3. Underline places in the essay where you notice possible grammatical problems (such as sentence fragments, comma splices, apostrophe, lack of parallelism, misplaced or dangling modifiers, pronoun disagreement and/or inconsistency), or stylistic problems (such as passive constructions or other instances where the writing could be made more concise, direct, or forceful). Note spelling errors and errors in mechanics and presentation.

Introduction

❏ Is the Introduction successful?

    ❏ interesting?

    ❏ announces subject and contains thesis statement with a *claim of interpretation*? suggests the writer's purpose: Book review? Text-centred analysis? Context-centred analysis?

    ❏ states the work(s) being discussed and the organizational method, if appropriate (e.g., compare and contrast)

    ❏ suggests most important focus (character, point of view, setting, mood, tone, analysis of technique)?

    ❏ gives appropriate background, if needed (may be important in context-centred analysis)?

❏ Does the writer establish him/herself as credible and trustworthy? How?

Body Paragraphs

❏ Does the reading/analysis seem complete, and does the order of the paragraphs appear logical?

❏ Look at paragraphs individually. Are any too short? Too long?

❏ Is each paragraph unified (relates to one main idea)? If not, which one(s) aren't?

❏ Is each paragraph coherent? If not, which one(s) aren't?

❏ Do paragraphs contain topic sentences?

❏ Is the order of the sentences natural?

❏ Are there appropriate transitions between sentences, enabling you to see the relationship between consecutive sentences?

❏ Does the writer successfully use repetition, rephrasing, synonyms or other devices to achieve coherence?

❏ Does each paragraph seem developed adequately?

❏ What kinds of evidence are produced? You don't have to refer to specific paragraphs—only note if they appear to be present to help support the thesis:

    ❏ examples from the text(s)?

        ❏ representative and relevant?

        ❏ are there a sufficient number?

        ❏ textual references cited appropriately (according to the conventions for citing poetry, fiction, and drama)?

        ❏ has the context been made sufficiently clear in each instance?

        ❏ do brackets and ellipses appear to have been used correctly?

❑ If secondary sources have been used, are they integrated smoothly and grammatically? Are all direct quotations, summaries, paraphrases, ideas acknowledged?

   ❑ secondary sources used effectively (to introduce or provide general information; support, explain, or expand; disagree or qualify)?

   ❑ other kinds of evidence used?

❑ Are there points where the reading seems strained, weak, incomplete, and/or illogical?

Conclusion

❑ Does the conclusion function as a satisfying ending? Does it summarize and/or generalize?

Other Criteria

❑ Has the writer presented him/herself credibly?

   ❑ conveyed knowledge?

   ❑ seems trustworthy and reliable?

   ❑ appears to be fair?

❑ Has the writer used any elements of style to assist in the argument (e.g., imagery, analogies—figurative language, distinctive voice or tone, particular choice of words, sentence variety, etc.). Can you suggest any additional stylistic features that might help?

❑ Are there any places in the draft where the language seemed unclear or where a point was unclear due to the way it was expressed?

Final Comments or Suggestions?

Writer's Name: _____

Editor's Name: _____

Index

abstract, 10, 12, 171–2
accept, 421
acknowledgement: rebuttal and, 113–14
addresses: commas and, 331
ad hominem, 118
adjectives, 311–13; co-ordinate/non-co-ordinate, 331; redundant use of, 397
adverbs, 311–12; commas and, 330; conjunctive, 311–12, 336–7; redundant use of, 396–7; sentence, 328
affect, 421
Agar, Nicholas, 137–49
agreement, 349–56; pronoun-antecedent, 354–6; subject-verb, 349–54
allegory, 253, 294–5
alliteration, 253, 295
allot, 422
all right, 422
allude, 422
allusion, 422
allusions, 253, 295
a lot, 422
alright, 422
American Psychological Association (APA) style, 155, 182–3, 184–92; samples of, 127–32, 137–49, 180, 219–22, 230–8; in-text citations, 184–8; non-textual sources, 188, 192; References Section, 188–92
among, 423
amount, 423
analogy, 78, 79, 92, 109
analogy: organization using, 78
analysis: cost-benefit, 77–8; critical, 242; literary, 241, 242; textual, 247–51; types of, 71–9
anapest, 298
anaphora, 252, 295
anecdotes, 92
antecedent-consequent: organization using, 76
antecedents: agreement and, 354–6; missing, 359–60

APA style; *see* American Psychological Association style
apostrophe(s): contractions and, 346–7; poetic, 253, 295; possession and, 345–6
appeals, 98–9, 100–1
appositives, 307–8, 330; case and, 366
archetypes, 253, 295
argument(s), 31–2; argumentative essays and, 99–100, 109–14; expository essays and, 152; kinds of, 98–9
argumentative essays, 81, 98–150; claims and, 101–9; classic model for, 124–5; evidence and, 105–9; faulty reasoning and, 117–23; outline for, 124–6; peer edit form for, 445–6; reasoning and, 109–12; rebuttal and, 112–14; samples of, 124–49
argument of the beard, 120
Aristotle, 98, 99, 266
articles: as part of speech, 306; magazine, *see* journals
assimilation: expository essay and, 153–4
assonance, 253, 295
audience, 15–21; claims and, 103–4; explicit, 18; general, 17; implicit, 17–18; orientation of, 19–20; profile for, 20–1; rebuttal and, 112–13
authorities, 107, 156–7
authority worship, 118
authors: APA style and, 186–7, 189–90; Chicago style and, 204–5, 207–8; MLA style and, 194–5, 197–9

Bacon, Francis, 380–1
bandwagon, 118
begging the question, 117–18
beside/besides, 423
between, 423
bias/biased, 423–4
bibliographies: annotated, 173; Chicago style, 207–10; research and, 161; working, 161–2

bildungsroman, 262
BioMed Central, 170
"black hole constructions," 403–4
blank verse, 298
block method: compare and contrast essays and, 84–5
Bloom, Allan, 417
books: research and, 166
Boolean operators, 169
brackets: mixed citation and, 181
brainstorming, 21–3
Business Source Elite, 170

caesura, 252
canon: literary, 255; traditional (Western), 255
CANSISM, 170
case: objective, 365; pronouns and, 364–7, 368–9; subjective, 365
case studies, 92, 108; example of, 115–16
cause-effect: organization using, 75–6
CBE (Council of Biology Editors) style, 182
certain consequences, 119
Channing, Edward T., 99
character: fiction and, 259, 263
chiasmus, 252, 296
Chicago Manual of Style, The, 202
Chicago (Note) style, 155, 182–3, 202–10; Bibliography, 207–10; in-text citations, 202–4; non-textual sources and, 206–7, 210; sample of, 228–30
chronology: organization using, 72
citations, 175; APA style, 184–92; Chicago style, 202–10; journal, 167; literary essays and, 271; mixed, 178–9; MLA style, 193–201; necessary versus unnecessary, 183–4; parenthetical, 183; styles of, 182–210
cite, 424

claims: arguable, 102; evidence and, 105–9, 111–12; fact, 152; "holding back," 124; interesting, 103–4; interpretation, 91; kinds of, 90–1; logic and, 109–12; manageable, 104–5; policy, 91, 104–5; specific, 102–3; staking, 101–5; value, 91

clarity, 394–414; revising and, 30

classification: organization using, 75

clauses, 321–2; dependent, 317–18, 319, 321–3, 329; independent, 317–18, 319, 321–3, 327–9, 335–7, 339; as fragments, 317–18; non-restrictive, 330; restrictive, 330

clichés, 413–14

climax, inverted, 55

"Cloning and Identity," 137–50

clustering, 21, 25

coherence, 59–61

Coleridge, Samuel Taylor, 240

Collins, George R., 73

colons, 338–9

comedy, 267–8; high, 267; low, 267

comma(s), 326–32, 344–5; addresses and, 331; adjectives and, 331; adverbs and, 330; dates and, 332; dependent clauses and, 329; independent clauses and, 327–9; introductory word and, 328; "no-comma" rules, 344–5; numbers and, 332; other punctuation and, 332; parenthetical information and, 329–31; quotation marks and, 332; serial, 327; titles and, 330

comma fault, 323–4

commands, 315

"comma sense," 331–2

comma splice, 323–4, 344

common ground, 113

common knowledge, 119

compare and contrast essays, 78–9, 83–90, 155–6; sample of, 87–9

comparisons, 366–7; parallelism and, 386–7

composing, 21; see also writing

compounds: parallelism and, 384–5

conceit, 296

conciseness, 395–400

conclusions, 65–8; circular, 66; spiral, 66

conflict: fiction and, 262

conjunctions, 321–2; co-ordinating, 312–13, 319, 321–2, 324, 384–5; correlative, 312–13, 385–6; subordinate, 312–13, 318, 319, 321–2

connotations, 6

Conrad, Joseph, 264

consonance, 296

construction(s): balanced, 380–1; "black hole," 403–4; elliptical, 367; passive, 400–2; sentence, 372–87; weak, 400–6

contractions, 346–7

conventions: language, 302–3; poetic, 254

co-ordinate elements, 58, 380–7

co-ordination: outlines and, 26

cost-benefit: organization using, 77–8

Council of Biology Editors (CBE), 182

Council of Science Editors, 182

credibility, 91, 93–4; experts', 157; introductions and, 46

criticism, literary, 242; "3 C's" of, 243–4

cross-referencing, 163

currency: sources and, 157, 270–1

dactyl, 298

dashes, 339–40

databases, 166, 167–71; aggregator, 167; popular, 169–70

date, publication, 157, 270–1

definition, 103; method using, 71–2; essay, 81–3

degrees: commas and, 332

denotations, 6

description, 31, 32–3, 109; organization using, 73

desk-thumping, 120

Dickinson, Emily, 240

diction, 253, 296

dictionaries, 408–10

division: organization using, 75

documentation, 155; see also citations

dogmatism, 120

Doniger, Wendy, and Kelly Bulkley, 7, 8

doubling up, 396–7

doubtful causes, 118–19

drafts: discovery, 3–4; final, 2 29–31; first, 21, 29; peer edit form for, 445–8; process-reflective, 5

drama, 266–8

dramatic approach: introductions and, 45

dramatic monologue, 254

"easily obtainable information": plagiarism and, 17

EBSCOhost, 167–9

editing, 31

effect, 421

e.g., 424

either/or, 119

ellipses: mixed citation and, 180; poetic, 253, 296

elude, 422

emotion: arguments based o 98–9, 100–1

emotional approach: introductions and, 46

emphasis, 414–18; outlines and, 55

endnotes: Chicago style, 204–7; MLA style, 202

ends justify the means, 120

end-stopped, 252

enjambment, 252

ERIC (Educational Resourc Information Centre), 17

errors: punctuation, 320, 344–5; sentence construction, 372–87

essays: basics of, 44–68; definition 81–3; design c 90–4; expressive, 33; five–paragraph, 2; in-clas 36–41; journalistic, 436– kinds of, 31–9; models o 93–4; paragraphs and, 57 70–96; personal, 33–6, 74–5; presentation of, 420–1; sample, 33–5, 39–41, 82–3, 85–6, 126– 218–30; stages in writing 21–31; three-part, 152–5 two-part model for, 90– see also argumentative essays; compare and contrast essays; examinat essays; expository essays; literary essays

euphemisms, 405–6
evaluation, 242
evidence, 91–2, 105–9, 111–12; contradictory, 164; hard, 105–6, 107; kinds of, 92; soft, 105–6, 107
examination essays, 36–41; discernment and adaptability and, 38–9; instructions for, 37–8; organization and time management and, 37–8; recall and, 36–7
examples, 92, 107; organization using, 76–7
except, 421
expanders, search, 169
experts, 107, 156–7
exposition, 31–2, 152
expository essays, 102, 152–238; literary essay as, 240; organization of, 154; outlines for, 173–5; peer edit form for, 447–8; synthesis and, 152, 153–4

facts, 106; claims of, 90
fairness, 93
fallacies, 93, 110, 117–23
false analogy, 119, 120–1
false authority, 120
false cause, 119
false dilemma, 119
Fee, Margery, and Janice McAlpine, 303
fewer, 425
fiction: approach to, 262–6; forms of, 256–7; plot and, 262–3; *see also* drama; novels; poetry; short story
figures of speech, 253, 296
filling the void, 120
fine-tuning: revising and, 31
finite categories, 120
Finn, Adam, Nicola Simpson, Stuart McFadyen, and Colin Hoskins, 228–30
fixed forms, poetic, 254
footnotes: Chicago style, 204–7; MLA style, 202
formalist method, 252
formality: levels of, 303–4, 408–11
fortune-telling, 120
fragments, sentence, 316–18; add-on, 316–17; dependent clause, 317–18; "-ing," 317
free verse, 254

freewriting, 21, 23–5; directed, 4
Frost, Robert, 247
fuzzy categories, 120

"general knowledge": plagiarism and, 175
genres, literary, 251–68
gerunds, 367–8
Gom, Leona, 256–7
good, 425–6
Gottlieb, Anthony, 417–18
Grady, Wayne, 265
grammar, 302–91; choice-based, 304; concept-based, 305; definition, 302; parts of speech, 306–13; reading and writing and, 305; sentence, 313–18
guilt by association, 118

hasty generalization, 119, 121
Hawking, Stephen, 16
Hawthorne, Nathaniel, 265
Health Source Nursing/ Academic Edition, 170
holding back the claim, 124
hyperbole, 253
hypotheses, 108

iamb, 297
iambic pentameter, 298
idealism, 261
i.e., 424
IEL (IEEE/IEE Electronic Library), 170
illusion, 422
illustrations, 92, 107–8; organization using, 76–7
imagery, 253, 296
imagism, 255
incompletion: errors of, 316–18
inflection, 364
InfoTrac, 170
Ingenta, 169
integration: expository essays and, 154; secondary sources and, 175–81
intensives, hackneyed, 399–400
interjections, 306
Internet: APA style and, 187–8, 191–2; Chicago style and, 206, 209; literary essays and, 270; MLA style and, 196, 200–1; research using, 157–8, 164–5, 167–70

interpretation: claims, of, 92
interviewing: research and, 171
introductions, 44–50; first sentence of, 48–9; functions of, 44–7; length of, 47–50; reader interest and, 44–6
inventing, 3; *see also* pre-writing
irony, 253, 264, 296–7; dramatic, 297; situational, 297; tragic, 297; verbal, 296–7
it does not follow, 119
it's/its, 426

Jackson, Marni, 213
James, Henry, 263
jargon, 12
Johnson, Wendell, 394
journals: APA style and, 186, 190–1; Chicago style and, 205–6, 210; citations of, 167; literary essays and, 270–1; locating, 166–7; MLA style and, 194–5, 199–201; on-line, 270–1; peer-reviewed, 166
juxtaposition, 252

key words: research and, 163, 167–9
Kimball, Meredith M., 86–9
knowledge: credibility and, 93

language: figurative, 256, 296, 417–18; slanted or loaded, 122–3
lay, 426
lead, 426
Lear, Edward, 343
learning, on-line, 440–2
led, 426
less, 425
Lexis-Nexis Academic Universe, 169
library: research and, 161, 164–5, 170–1; on-line catalogues of, 166–7
lie, 426
limiters: search, 169
lists: parallelism and, 382–4; punctuating, 327, 337, 339
literary essays, 240–99; context-centred approach to, 242–3; evaluating, 243–4; kinds of, 241–2; peer edit form for, 440–50; research essay, 268–72; revising,

271–2; rough draft of, 244–6; samples, 256–8, 272–7; text-centred approach to, 242–3; topic and, 244–5

literary movements, 255

literary present, 246–7

literary terms, 294–9

literature: as unique encounter, 240–1; writing about, 246–7; *see also* literary essays

logic; *see* reasoning

logical approach: introductions and, 44–5

Longevity, 118

looping, 23

loose/lose, 427

McMaster, Lindsey, 278–93

MacNeice, Louis, 411–12

mapping, 21, 25

meaning: literature and, 241

metaphors, 253, 297; dead, 413–14

metonymy, 253, 297

metre, 252, 297–8

middle ground fallacy, 119

MLA style; *see* Modern Language Association style

Modern Language Association (MLA) style, 155, 182–3, 193–202; samples of, 133–6, 179, 223–7; footnotes, 202; in-text citations, 193–200; non-textual sources, 196, 201; Works Cited Section, 196–200

modifiers: adverbial, 311–12, 374; dangling, 376–8; misplaced, 373–8; one-word, 375–6

mood: poetry and, 253, 298

morality: arguments based on, 98–9, 100–1

motif, 298

Munro, Alice, 7

name-calling, 118

name-dropping, 118

narration, 31, 32–3; organization using, 73

narrators: types of, 264

naturalism, 265

Newspaper Source, 170

Noah's Ark Syndrome, 396–7

nominals, 405

non-sequitur, 119

note-taking, 12, 162–3

nouns, 307–8; attributive, 330; collective, 352; plural, 346; possessive, 345–6; predicate, 307–8; singular, 345–6; weak, 397, 404–5

novelette, 260

novella, 259, 260, 261

novels, 259, 260–3; epistolary, 261; Gothic, 261; modernist, 262; picaresque, 261; social-problem, 262; Victorian, 261–2

number, 423

numbers: commas and, 332

object: direct, 307–8; prepositions and, 307–8

only, 375–6

onomatopoeia, 253

onset, 427

open forms, poetic, 254

order: climax, 55; dramatic, 55; logical sentence, 60

organization, 21, 26–8, 70–9; antecedent-consequent method, 76; coherence and, 60, 62–3; primary methods of, 79, 81–90; outline, 55; secondary methods of, 79; spatial method of, 73

outlines, 3–4, 5–6; argumentative essays and, 124–6; developing, 56–7; formal, 26–7; graphic, 27–8; guidelines for, 55; implied, 55; literary essays and, 245–6; organization of, 55; peer edit form for, 444; research and, 163–4; research essays and, 173–5; scratch, 26; sentence, 27; sketch, 26; topic, 27; types of, 26–8; value of, 54–5

outset, 427

overview: revising and, 29–30

oxymoron, 253

paradox, 253, 298

paragraphs: basics of, 44–68; coherence and, 59–64; development of, 62–5, 70–80; introductory, 44–50; length of, 59; unity of, 58–9, 61, 62

parallelism, 252, 380–7, 417; two-stage approach to fixing, 381–2

paraphrase, 173, 175, 176, 177, 178; APA style, 184; Chicago style, 203–4; MLA style, 194

parentheses, 339–40

participles, 367–8; dangling, 376–8

parts of speech, 306–13

peer edit forms, 444–50

Pendergrast, Mark, 73

pentameter, 298

periodicals, 166; *see also* journals

personal: organization using, 74–5

personal communications: APA style and, 185; Chicago style and, 204; MLA style and, 194

personal experience, 92, 109

personification, 253, 298

persuasion, 99–100

phrases, 319–20; absolute, 416; adjectival, 320; adverbial, 320; infinitive, 416; non-restrictive, 330; noun, 320; opening, 416; participial, 416; phoney, 397–8; prepositional, 320, 416; restrictive, 330; signal, 179–80, 213; transitional, 336–7; verb, 320

plagiarism, 175–6

plot, 259, 262–3; comic 267; tragic, 268

Poe, Edgar Allan, 260

poetry, 251–8; biographical context of, 254; context-centred approach to, 253–; cultural, racial, gender base context of, 255; historical, cultural context of, 254–5; intuitive approach to, 252; narrative, 254; sample analysis of, 247–51; text-centred approach to, 252–; types of, 254

point-by-point method: compare and contrast essa and, 84–5

point-by-point rebuttal, 114

point of view, narrative, 259, 264

policy: claims of, 92

possession: apostrophes and, 345–6

post hoc, 119

postmodernism, 265–6

precedents, 92, 108, 120
précis, 171, 212–16; samples of, 214–16
precision, 408–11
predicate, 314–15; compound, 322
predication, faulty, 410–11
premises, 110–11
prepositions, 312
pre-reading, 10–12
pre-writing, 21–5
problem-solution: organization using, 77
process: organization using, 74
process-oriented writing, 3–4, 6
process-reflective writing, 4–6
Project Muse, 169
pronouns, 307–9; agreement and, 353, 354–6; case of, 364–7, 368–9; consistency of, 371–2; demonstrative, 309; forms of, 364–7; gender-neutral, 355; indefinite, 309; intensive, 309; interrogative, 308–9, 369; kinds of, 308–9; personal, 308, 364–7; possessive, 367–8; reciprocal, 309; reference and, 358–62; reflexive, 309; relative, 308, 368–9
proofreading, 31, 418–20
proposals; *see* research proposals
ProQuest, 169
PsycINFO, 170
publication date, 157, 270–1
punctuation, 326–45; errors in, 320, 344–5; *see also* apostrophes; commas; colons; dashes; quotation marks
Purdy, Al, 63

qualifiers, hackneyed, 399
question(s): active reading and, 10–14; audience and, 18, 19–20; organization using, 76; topic and, 21–3; writing purpose and, 14–15
quotation(s): APA style, 185; block format, 177; Chicago style, 202–3; direct, 177, 178–9, 181; literary essays and, 271; MLA style, 193; plagiarism and, 175; punctuating, 332, 338; unnecessary, 177–8

quotation marks, 177, 179; commas and, 332

reader-based prose, 17
reader interest, 44–6
reading: "active," 8, 10–15; close, 9; diffuse, 9; first, 12–13; focused, 9; literary, 243–4; one-way, 6–7; "passive," 6–7; pre-, 10–12; second, 13–14; selective, 9; thinking and reading and, 6–14; 3-D (Dimensional), 8; three-way, 8; two-way, 8
Readings: "Cloning and Identity," 137–50; "The Urban Working Girl in Turn-of-the-Century Canadian Fiction," 278–93
realism, 260, 264–5
reasoning: arguments based on, 98–9, 100–1; circular, 117; claims and, 109–12; coherence and, 60, 63–4; deductive, 110–12; faulty, 117–23; inductive, 109–10; precision and, 410–11; scientific, 109–10; testing, 111–12
rebuttal, 112–14
red herring, 118
redundancy, 396–7
reference, academic; *see* citations
reference, grammatical: ambiguous, 360–1; broad, 361–2; pronoun, 358–62; remote, 360; squinting, 360–1; vague, 361–2
References Section, APA style, 188–92
refutation, 112–14
reliability: credibility and, 93
repetition, 60, 64, 417
research, 21, 25, 155–6; expository essays and, 152, 153; first stage of, 161–2, 165–6; note-taking for, 162–3; sources for, 164–71; strategies for, 163–4
research proposal, 153, 158–61; format of, 158–9; purpose of, 158–9; samples of, 159–61
response (literary essay), 241
revising, 21, 29–31
rhetoric, 99
rhetorical devices, 253

rhetorical function of parts, 124–6
rhetorical modes of discourse, 31–3
rhetorical patterns, 70–9; *see also* organization
rhetorical stance: précis and, 213
rhyme, 253, 298–9
rhythm, 252, 299, 417; truncated, 298
roman, 261
romance, 260–1, 265; historical, 261
Rutland, R.A., 65

satire, 267
scanning, 9
Scientific Style and Format: the CBE Manual for Authors, Editors, and Publishers, 182
searches, Internet, 167–70
semicolons, 335–8, 345
sentences: complex, 321–2; compound, 321–2; compound-complex, 322; concluding, 58; cumulative, 416–17; definition of, 313–15; errors of incompletion and, 316–18; errors of combining, 323–4; errors of construction, 316–18, 323–4, 371–87; fused, 323–4; imperative, 315; length of, 414–15; periodic, 416–17; run-on, 323–4; topic 57–8, 59; variety in, 414–15
series: parallelism and, 382–4; punctuating, 327, 337, 339
setting, 259, 263–4
Shakespeare, William, 266
short story, 259–60
Showalter, Elaine, 59
sic, 181
sight, 424
signal phrases: mixed citation and, 179–80; précis and, 213
signal verbs: mixed citation and, 179
silencing, 121–2
Sillitoe, Alan, 13
similes, 253, 299
single effect, 260
site, 424
slippery slope, 119
software programs: research and, 162, 163

solution: organization using, 77
sonnet, 254
sources, research, 92, 164–71;
    alternative, 171; literary
    essays and, 268–72; primary
    and secondary, 92, 165,
    268; reliable, 106, 270;
    secondary, 165–6, 172–3,
    175–81, 269–71; third-
    party, 92, 185, 204, 194,
    199; see also citations;
    research
specificity, 411–14
speech: conventions of, 302–3
stanzas, 252, 299
statement, thesis; see thesis
    statement
statistics, 92, 106
straw man, 118
structures: balanced, 60;
    inverted pyramid, 44–5, 66;
    macrocosmic, 57–8; micro-
    cosmic, 58; parallel, 60, 64;
    plot, 262–3; poetry, 252;
    solidifying, 30–1
style, documentation:
    choosing, 182–4; see also
    American Psychological
    Association (APA) style;
    Chicago style; Modern
    Language Association
    (MLA) style
subject (grammatical), 307–8,
    314–15; complete, 315;
    compound, 322, 351–4;
    delayed, 416–17; finding,
    349–51; "invisible," 315;
    lacking, 316; simple, 315
subjective complement,
    307–8, 311
subjective completion, 307–8
subordination, 26, 55, 58
substantives, 307–8
summaries, 175, 176, 212–16;
    secondary sources and,
    172–3; three-step method
    for, 214
support, 90, 91–4; indirect,
    107–9
surrealism, 255
Swift, Jonathan, 51
syllogism, 111
symbols, 253, 299

synecdoche, 299
synonyms: coherence and,
    60, 64
syntax, 253, 299, 364
synthesis, 152, 153–4

tense: future, 433–4; literary
    present, 246–7; past, 432–3;
    present, 432
tetrameter, 298
"text": primary and secondary
    versus books, 9
than, 427
that's the way we've always
    done it, 120
their, 427–8
theme: comic, 268; literature
    and, 241, 259; tragic, 268
then, 427
there, 427–8
thesaurus, 409
thesis, 3
thesis statement, 44, 46, 48,
    50–4; literary essays and,
    240, 248; effective, 51;
    expanded, 50, 102; indirect,
    51; outlines and, 56–7;
    simple, 50
they're, 427–8
thinking: writing and, 2–14
time-order relationships, 76
titles: commas and, 330, 332;
    literary essays and, 271–2
to/too, 428
tone: poetry and, 253, 299
topics: arguable, 102; literary
    essays and, 244–5; organiza-
    tion and, 70–1; rebuttal
    and, 112
topoi, 99
Tradition, 120, 121
traditional linear model, 3, 6
tragedy, 268
transitions, 5, 60–1
treadmill logic, 117
trimeter, 298
trochee, 298
trustworthiness: credibility
    and, 93
two wrongs make a right, 118

understatement, 253
unity, 58–9, 61, 62

Universal Resource Locator
    (URL), 158; see also Internet
"Urban Working Girl in Turn-
    of-the-Century Canadian
    Fiction, The," 278–93
usage, 428
usage: grammar and, 303–4
use, 428

value: claims of, 91
variety, 414–18; sentence,
    414–15; structural, 416–18
verbs, 309–11; auxiliary,
    309–10; helping, 309–10;
    intransitive, 309–11, 366;
    linking, 309–11; modal,
    310; passive, 400–2; precise,
    412–13; signal, 179; tense
    of, 246–7, 432–4; transitive
    309–11; weak, 396–7,
    404–5

warrant, 111–12
Web; see Internet
well, 425–6
Wharton, Edith, 395
who's/whose, 428–9
"willing suspension of
    disbelief," 240
Woolf, Virginia, 214–16
word choice, 408–11
words: confusing, 421–9;
    omitting, 398–9
Works Cited, MLA style,
    196–200
WorldCat, 170
wraps, 58
writer-based prose, 17
writer-reader relationship,
    16–17, 18–19
writer's block, 23
writing, 14–21; conventions
    302–3; direct, 400–6;
    formal, 408–11; first draft
    21, 29; free, 4, 21, 23–5;
    models of, 3–6; on-line,
    440–2; process of, 2–6;
    purpose of, 14–15; stages
    of, 21–31

you're/your, 429